DICTIONARY
OF
ECCLESIASTICAL LATIN

DICTIONARY of ECCLESIASTICAL LATIN

*With an appendix of Latin expressions
defined and clarified*

LEO F. STELTEN

Dictionary of Ecclesiastical Latin
Copyright © 1995 by Hendrickson Publishers, Inc.
P. O. Box 3473
Peabody, Massachusetts 01961-3473
All rights reserved
Printed in the United States of America

ISBN-13: 978-1-56563-131-1
ISBN-10: 1-56563-131-5

Seventh printing — August 2006

Library of Congress Cataloging-in-Publication Data

Dictionary of ecclesiastical Latin: with an Appendix of Latin expressions
　　defined and clarified　/　edited by Leo F. Stelten.
　　　p. cm.
　　ISBN-13: 978-1-56563-131-1
　　ISBN-10: 1-56563-131-5
　　　1. Latin language—Church Latin—Dictionaries.　2. Latin language,
Medieval and modern—Dictionaries.　3. Latin language, Postclassical—
Dictionaries.　4. Liturgical language—Latin—Dictionaries.　5. Catholic
Church—Liturgy—Dictionaries.　6. Bible—Dictionaries.　I. Stelten,
Leo F., 1925–　.
PA2891.D53　　1995
477—dc20　　　　　　　　　　　　　　　　　　　　　95-4249
　　　　　　　　　　　　　　　　　　　　　　　　　　　　　CIP

Discipulis Meis

Praeteritis

Praesentibus

Futuris

Table of Contents

Preface

This dictionary is being prepared with the hope that it will be a handy and practical manual for seminary students once they have completed introductory courses in the Latin language. It may also prove useful to the laypeople, employed so frequently these days in chancery offices, who might be totally unfamiliar with Latin or whose knowledge of it goes back to high-school days. This book is not intended to be a research dictionary, nor is it intended for advanced and critical scholarship. An attempt has been made to prepare as inclusive a listing as possible of words from Sacred Scripture, from the Code of Canon Law, from the liturgy, and from the documents of Vatican II. A limited number of other words that have philosophical or theological connections have been included. Some of the Latin words are so similar to the English—in fact, at times they are simply transliterations from the English into Latin rather than vice versa—that it may seem unnecessary to include them. They are included, however, since, in some cases at least, the meanings are not quite so obvious and therefore need to be mentioned. It is not the purpose of this work to give the exact meaning of a particular word in a particular case. Such meanings and uses are to be found in commentaries and individual articles on the specific word or subject matter. An *Appendix* is also included, in which can be found the definitions and/or explanations of some legal and theological terms and other information that will be useful for those working in chancery offices. For words of a more technical nature and for more complete definitions one should consult a commentary or a more specific dictionary. This is especially true regarding words used in philosophy and theology. A partial list of such books can be found following the *Appendix.* Reverend Blase J. Cupich, rector/president of the Pontifical College Josephinum, granted me sabbatical leave in 1991 to begin this project.

I am indebted first of all to my students, who over the years have made me aware of the need for such a book, and to a number of people who assisted me in this project: Leo Worner, Peggy Worner, and John C. Thompson. Special thanks are due to my professional colleagues at the Pontifical College Josephinum: Monsignor Gerald F. Durst, Reverend Arthur J.

Espelage, OFM, Reverend D. William Lynn, SJ, and Mr. Peter G. Veracka. Monsignor Raymond L. Burke of the Office of the Signatura in Rome very kindly gave me permission to use, and supplied me with a copy of, the *Vocabularium Canonicum Latino-Anglicum*, which he edited for private use with the assistance of Reverend Ronald W. Gainer of the Diocese of Allentown and Reverend Michael J. Gorman of the Diocese of La Crosse. Mr. John R. Page, executive secretary of the International Commission on English in the liturgy, was very kind in sending me a copy of the yet unpublished "A Lexicon of Terms in the *Missale Romanum*," which was prepared for the Commission by the late Thomas C. O'Brien. Chorbishop John D. Faris, chancellor of the Diocese of Saint Maron, Reverend Kevin W. Vann of the Diocese of Springfield, Illinois, and Reverend Ignatius Harrington of the Byzantine Melkite Diocese of Newton, Massachusetts, were extremely helpful in the preparation of the *Appendix*. Thanks must also be expressed to those bishops and their respondents from the various dioceses throughout the United States for their time and effort in supplying me with words and phrases in answer to my letters of request. They helped me, and I hope that this work will be of some value to them and to their staffs. Special thanks for much-needed technical assistance must be given to Mr. Anthony E. Cutcher, a senior at the Josephinum. This project could not have reached its final form without the capable assistance of the very patient and ever pleasant Ms. Marie Mudd, a secretary at the Josephinum. Time and time again she reworked pages of the manuscript on the computer as corrections and changes were constantly being made. I am truly grateful to her. If any errors remain, they are my responsibility.

On Using This Book

I have tried to list the English meanings of the words according to Church or Church-related usage but other meanings are also included. Words with the same general meaning, but with slight variation of Latin form, are usually listed on the same line; if the variation is extreme, separate entries are given. Latin words which have variations only in spelling have the alternate spelling in parentheses.

Main entries for nouns are in the nominative case and appear in bold face, with the genitive and gender in regular type. If variations other than spelling occur (e.g., declension and gender, etc.) these forms appear in bold face in the nominative case without any parentheses. Only the first principal parts of verbs appears in bold face and the conjugation is shown by a number in parentheses after the principal parts. Principal parts are abbreviated except where changes in spelling occur. Deponent and semi-deponent verbs are indicated by name as well as by the participial ending in *-us*. Some verbs have both regular and deponent forms; in these cases one of the forms is given in parentheses without the principal parts. Gerund and gerundive forms which show obligation generally are not included. The same is true for present active and perfect passive participles, since the forms and meanings of these words can be determined from the regular principal parts. Some adjectives have First-Second (*us-a-um*) forms as well as Third declensional forms; both are given with the alternate form in parentheses. The comparative and superlative of frequently used adjectives is included in many instances. Most adverbs are listed in bold face under the adjective from which they are derived along with the designation *adv.,* but some are listed separately. The letters *i* and *j* are listed separately, following the practice of *Harper's Latin Dictionary.* A list of the books used in the preparation of this dictionary, as well as some other very useful reference works, can be found following the *Appendix.*

Leo F. Stelten
Pontifical College Josephinum
Columbus, Ohio
Feast of the Chair of St. Peter, 1994

Abbreviations

(1)	First Declension
(2)	Second Declension
(3)	Third Declension
(4)	Fourth Declension
abbrev.	abbreviation
abla.	ablative
acc.	accusative
adj.	adjective
adv.	adverb
B.V.M.	Blessed Virgin Mary
c.	common
comp.	comparative
conj.	conjunction
dat.	dative
defect.	defective
dep.	deponent
e.g.	exempli gratia, for example
etc.	et cetera, and so on
f.	feminine
gen.	genitive
imperat.	imperative.
imperf.	imperfect
impers.	impersonal
indecl.	indeclinable
indef.	indefinite
inf.	infinitive
interj.	interjection
interr.	interrogative
irreg.	irregular
m.	masculine
n.	neuter/nominative
N.T.	New Testament

O.T.	Old Testament
part.	participle
pass.	passive
perf.	perfect
pl.	plural
prep.	preposition
pres.	present
pron.	pronoun
semidep.	semideponent
subj.	subjunctive
superl.	superlative
voc.	vocative
w.	with

A

a: *interj.;* ah

a, ab, abs: *prep. w. abla.;* by, from

Áaron -ónis, *or indecl.:* m.; Aaron, brother of Moses

ábacus -i: m.; small table for cruets, credence, shelf in wall near altar

abaliéno -áre: (1); alienate, go away, depart, separate, remove, legally transfer

abámita -ae: f.; female ancestor, sister (of the following word)

ábavus -i: m.; great-great-grandfather, ancestor, forefather

Ábba: *indecl.; Aramaic;* Father

ábbas -abbátis: m.; abbot; *see Appendix*

abbátia -ae: f.; abbey, abbacy

abbatiális -is -e: pertaining to an abbot or abbey

abbátia nullíus: abbey exempt from ecclesiastical jurisdiction

abbatíssa -ae: f.; abbess

abbreviátor -óris: m.; one who makes abstracts from papal bulls

abbrévio -áre: (1); shorten, cut off, abbreviate

Abdías -ae: m.; Obadiah, a minor prophet; a book of the O.T.

abdicátio -ónis: f.; a renouncing, disowning

ábdico -áre: (1); renounce, abandon, give up

abdíco -ere -dixi -dictum: (3); disapprove of

ábditum -i: n.; hidden place, lair, secret

ábditus -a -um: concealed, hidden

ábdo -ere -didi -ditum: (3); hide, conceal, secrete

abdúco -ere -dúxi -dúctum: (3); lead away, carry away, seduce

abecedárium -ii: n.; the alphabet

abecetuórium -ii: n.; the act of tracing Greek and Latin alphabets on the floor while consecrating a church

Ábel: -élis, *or indecl.,* **Abélus** -i: m.; Abel

ábeo -íre -ívi -itum: (4); go away

aberrátio -ónis: f.; relief from anything irksome, diversion

abérro -áre: (1); go astray, wander

ab extrínseco: from the outside, externally

ab hómine: by or from a man; ecclesiastical penalty inflicted by a judge

abhórreo -horrére -hórrui: (2); shrink back or away from

Abías -ae: m.; Abia

abício: *see* **abjício**

abiégnus -a -um: of fir

ábiens -eúntis: *pres. part. of* **ábeo**

ábies -etis: f.; fir tree

abietárius -ii: m.; carpenter

ábigo -ere - égi -áctum: (3); banish, drive away

ab inítio: from the beginning

ab intrínseco: from the inside, internally

ab ipso (ípsa) convénto(-ta): *see Appendix*

Ábiron: *indecl.;* Abiram, a conspirator against Moses and Aaron

ábitus -us: m.; departure

abjécte: cowardly

abjéctio -ónis: f.; outcast; casting out

abjício (abício) -ere -jéci -jéctum: (3); refuse, throw away, cast off, debase, degrade, abandon abjúdico -áre: (1); take away by judgment, deny an oath

abjúngo -ere -júnxi -júnctum: (3); unlock, unloose

abjurátio -ónis: f.; abjuration, foreswearing, denial under oath, perjury; see Appendix

abjúro -áre: (1); deny an oath, perjure

ablácto -áre: (1); wean

ablátor -óris: m.; one who takes away

ablátus -a -um: perf. pass. part. of aúfero

ablegátio -ónis: f.; a sending away

ablégo -áre: (1); send off or away, remove

ábluo -ere -lui -lútum: (3); wash, cleanse

ablútio -ónis: f.; washing, ablution, pouring on, mixture of water and wine in the liturgy

abnegátio -ónis: f.; denial

abnegatívus -a -um: negative

abnegátor -óris: m.; a denier

ábnego -áre: (1); deny, refuse, be unwilling

abnórmis -is -e: unconventional, abnormal, irregular

ábnuo -ere -ui -úitum: (3); deny, refuse by nod of the head, reject

abnúto -áre: (1); deny repeatedly, refuse often by nod of the head

abóleo -ére -évi -itum: (2); destroy, abolish, terminate

abolésco -ere -évi: (3); decay little by little, vanish, cease

abolítio -ónis: f.; a removing, abolition, annulling, withdrawal

abólla -ae: f.; thick woolen cloak

abominábilis -is -e: detestable, hateful, worthy of destruction

abominátio -ónis: f.; detestation, aversion, loathing

abóminor -ári: dep. (1); abhor, hate, detest, loath

abórior -íri -órtus: dep. (4); disappear, pass away, set, miscarry, fail

abortívus -a -um: untimely, prematurely born, abortive

abórtus -us: m., abortívum -i: n.; abortion, miscarriage

ábra -ae: f.; maid

abrádo -rádere -rási -rásum: (3); rub off, take away, erase

Abrahámus -i, indecl. in the Psalms: m.; Abraham

abrenunciátio -ónis: f.; repudiation, renouncing

abrenúntio -áre: (1); renounce

abrípio -ere -rípui -réptum: (3); drag or tear away

abrogátio -ónis: f.; revocation, formal repeal; see Appendix

ábrogo -áre: (1); revoke, abrogate, annul

abrúmpo -ere -rúpi -rúptum: (3); loosen, separate, break

abrúptio -ónis: f.; a tearing away, a rending asunder, a divorce

abrúptus -a -um: steep, precipitous, broken off from, separated

abs: prep. w. abla.; by, from

Ábsalom: indecl.; Absalom, son of David and Maacah

abscédo -ere -céssi -céssum: (3); retire, depart

abscéssio -ónis: f.; separation, a going away

abscéssus -us: m.; death

abscído -ere -cídi -císsum: (3); cut off

abscíndo -ere -cidi -scíssum: (3); tear away, cut off

abscónditum -i: n.; a hidden place or thing; in abscóndito: in secret

abscónditus -a -um: hidden, concealed, secret, unknown, obscure, out of sight; abscóndite: adv.

abscóndo -ere -didi -ditum: (3); hide, conceal

abscónsio -ónis: f.; a shelter

abscónsus -a -um: hidden, secret, concealed, unknown

ábsens -éntis: absent; *pres. part. of* ábsum

abséntia -ae: f.; absence

absída -ae: f.; apse, apsis

absidátus -a -um: vaulted, arched

absidiále -is: n., absidióla -ae: f.; a smaller apse flanking a larger one

absílio -íre: (4); leap up, jump up; fly away

absímilis -is -e: unlike, dissimilar

absínthium -ii: n., absínthius -ii: m.; see absýnthium

ábsis -ídis: f.; apse

absísto -ere -stiti: (3); be exiled, cease, depart, withdraw

ábsit: God forbid, far be it

absolútio -ónis: f.; absolution, forgiveness, sacramental remission of sin; *see Appendix*

absolutórius -a -um: of or relating to absolution or acquittal

absolútus -a -um: perfect, complete, absolute; absolúte: *adv.*

absólvo -ere -sólvi -solútum: (3); absolve, pardon, release, forgive

absónus -a -um: unsuitable, incongruous; discordant

absórbeo -ére -ui -órptum: (2); swallow, gulp, absorb

ábsque: *prep. w. abla.;* without, apart from

abstémius -a -um: temperate, abstemious, abstaining

abstérgeo -ére -térsi -térsum: (2); blot out, wipe away

abstérreo -ére: (2); frighten away, deter, remove

ábstinens -éntis: temperate, abstinent

abstinéntia -ae: f.; abstinence, moderation, not eating certain foods

abstíneo -ére -ui -téntum: (2); abstain, hold back, refrain

abstráctio -ónis: f.; detachment, removal

ábstraho -ere -tráxi -tráctum: (3); bring forth, drag or draw away

abstrúdo -ere -úsi -úsum: (3); hide, conceal

ábsum -esse, áfui, afutúrum: be absent, be away

absúmo -ere -súmpsi -súmptum: (3); take away, lessen, destroy; consume

absúrde: absurdly, irrationally, discordantly

absúrditas -átis: f.; incongruity, absurdity

absýnthium -ii: n.; wormwood, absynth

Ábula -ae: f.; Avila

abúndans -ántis: rich, abundant, overflowing, abounding in, copious; abundánter, abúnde: *adv.;* abundántius: *comp. adv.*

abundántia -ae: f.; abundance, plenty, prosperity, richness

abúndo -áre: (1); abound, overflow, be rich, have abundance of

abúsio -ónis: f.; scorn, contempt

abúsor -óris: m.; abuser

abúsus -us: m.; wasting, using up, consuming, abuse, misuse

abútor -úti -úsum: *dep.* (3); abuse, misuse, destroy

abýssus -i: f.; abyss, the depths, the sea; place of the dead

a capélla: in chapel style, without musical accompaniment

ac: and, as

académia -ae: f.; academy, college

académicus -a -um: academic

Accaronítae -árum: m. pl.; people of Accaron or Ekron

acathólicus -a -um: non-Catholic; acathólice: *adv.*

accédit -ere: (3); *impers.;* it is added

accédo -ere -céssi -céssum: (3); approach, come near, accede, approve, assent to

accelerátio -ónis: f.; hastening

accélero -áre: (1); hurry, hasten

accéndo -ere -di -cénsum: (3); inflame, kindle, set fire to

accénseo -ére -ui -cénsum: (2); add, reckon in addition, count, number

accensíbilis -is -e: burning

accéntus -us: m.; accent; parts sung by celebrant in the liturgy

acceptábilis -is -e: acceptable, pleasing

accéptio (acceptátio) -ónis: f.; respect, acceptance, agreeing; favoritism; distinction; see Appendix

accépto -áre: (1); accept, receive

accéptus -a -um: acceptable, worthy, agreeable, welcome; as a n. noun: receipt

accérso (arcésso) -ere -sívi -sítum: (3); summon, call, arraign

accéssio -ónis: f.; entrance, admission, addition, accession

accessórius -a -um: accessory, adjunct; accessórie: adv.

accéssus -us: m.; approach, access; increase; inspection, examination

áccidens -éntis: n.; accident

accidéntia -órum: n. pl.; appearances, accidents

áccido -ere -cidi: (3); happen, take place, occur, come to pass; arrive, fall down upon

accíngo -ere -cínxi -cínctum: (3); gird, equip

áccio -íre -ívi(-ii) -ítum: (4); summon, call to, procure, take

accípio -ere -cépi -céptum: (3); accept, receive, take

accípiter -tris: m.; hawk

acclamátio -ónis: f.; exclamation, ceremonial greeting, a shout (usually, but not always) of approval

acclámo -áre: (1); cry out at, shout, exclaim

acclínis -is -e: bowing, leaning

acclíno -áre: (1); lean on or against

acclívis -is -e: inclined upward, ascending, steep

áccola -ae: c.; sojourner

áccolo -ere -ui -cúltum: (3); dwell by or near

accommodátio: -ónis: f.; adjusting, compliance, indulgence

accómmodo -áre: (1); adjust, incline, accommodate, put on, fit

accrédo -ere -crédidi -créditum: (3); believe

accrésco -ere -crévi -crétum: (3); grow, increase

accrétio -ónis: f.; increment, increase

accúbitus -us: m.; prostration, repose, reclining at table; seat, couch

áccubo áre: (1); lie down, recline

accúmbo -ere -cúbui -cúbitum: (3); sit at table, recline

accumulátio -ónis: f.; a heaping up, accumulation

accúmulo -áre: (1); heap up, augment, accumulate

accurátio -ónis: f.; carefulness, accuracy

accurátus -a -um: accurate, exact, careful; accuráte: adv.

accúrro -ere -cúrri(-cucúrri) -cúrsum: (3); occur, run to meet

accusátio -ónis: f.; accusation

accusátor -óris: m.; accuser

accusatórius -a -um: accusatory, of an accusation

accúso -áre: (1); accuse, blame, call to account publicly

acédior -ári: dep. (1); be pained, be wearied, be morose

acéphalus -a -um: without a head, unattached, without an ecclesiastical superior

ácer, ácris, ácre: ardent, bitter, sharp, keen; ácriter: adv.

acérbitas -tátis: f.; bitterness, evil, sinfulness

acérbus -a -um: bitter, sour, sharp, harsh; acérbe: *adv.*

acérra -ae: f.; casket or boat or container for incense

acérvo -áre: (1); heap up, amass

acérvus -i: m.; heap, pile, multitude of similar objects

acescéntia -ae: f.; acidity, sourness

acésco -ere, ácui: (3); become or turn sour

acetábulum -i: n.; dish, bowl

acétum -i: n.; vinegar, acid

achátes -ae: m.; agate

Achaz: *see* Ahaz

Achímelech: *see* Ahímelech

acícula -ae: f.; pin

ácidus -a -um: sour, tart; harsh; sharp; ácide: *adv.*

ácies -éi: f.; sharpness, acuity, keenness, edge; eye, pupil of eye; line of battle

ácinum -i: n., ácinus -i: m.; grape, stone of a grape, berry

acistárium -ii: n.; monastery

aclouthía -ae: f.; liturgical rite, Divine Office, in Eastern rite Churches

acolythátus -us: m.; acolyte or order of acolyte

acólythus -i: m.; acolyte

acquiésco -ere -quiévi -quiétum: (3); be satisfied with, follow, agree

acquíro -ere -quisívi -quisítum: (3); procure, acquire

acquisítio -ónis: f.; purchase, acquisition

acquisítus -a -um: acquired

ácra -órum: n., ácra -ae: f.; promontory, headland

ácriter: keenly, sharply, violently

acroáticus -a -um: designed for hearing only; esoteric

Act.: *abbrev. of* Ácta Apostólorum; the Acts of the Apostles

ácta -órum: n. pl.; things done, acts, accomplishments, decisions, records of

a process, register of public acts; *see* *Appendix*

Ácta Apostólicae Sédis: the Acts of the Apostolic See, official Vatican publication

Ácta Mártyrum: the Acts of the Martyrs

Ácta Sánctae Sédis: the Acts of the Holy See, now Ácta Apostólicae Sédis

Ácta Sanctórum: the Acts of the Saints

actinósus -a -um: glorious, full of rays

áctio -ónis: f.; action, deed, process, suit

áctio gratíarum: thanksgiving

Áctio sacrífica: Eucharistic Sacrifice

actívitas (actuósitas) -átis: f.; activity, movement, action

actívus (actuósus) -a -um: active, practical; actíve: *adv.*

áctor -óris: m., áctrix -ícis: f.; doer, petitioner, plaintiff, actor, agent

actuális -is -e, actuósus -a -um: actual, practical, active; actuóse: *adv.*

actuálitas -tátis: f.; reality, existence

actuárius -ii: m.; clerk, register, secretary, actuary

áctuo -áre: (1); implement, actuate

actuósitas -átis: f.; activity

actuósus: *see* actívus *or* actuális

áctu: actually

áctus -a -um: *perf. pass. part. of* ágo

áctus -us: m.; deed, act, work, office, the doing of an action; *see Appendix*

áctus nóxius: sin

acúitas -átis: f.; insight, sharpness, perception

acúleus -i: m.; sharp point, sting

acúmen -inis: n.; keenness, sharp point

acúo -ere -ui -útum: (3); sharpen, exercise

acupictúra -ae: f.; embroidery

ácus -us: f.; needle, pin

acutále: somewhat sharply

acútus -a -um: sharp, sharpened, keen, pointed, acute; **bis acútus:** two-edged

acystérium -ii: n.; monastery

ad: *prep. w. acc.;* to, toward, at, against, near, unto

ad amússim: exactly, accurately

ad beneplácitum nóstrum: at our good pleasure

ad cautélam: for caution or safety

ad díem: on the day

ad éxtra: external, outward

ad extrémum: finally

ad hoc: for this purpose, moreover, besides

ad hóminem arguméntum: an argument based on principles admitted by an opponent

ad hunc módum: in this way

ad id quod: beside that

ad intentiónem dántis: according to the intention of the donor

ad ínterim: in the meantime

ad ínvicem: one with another, among themselves, with each other

ad líbitum: at one's pleasure; refers to the choice of a prayer in the Office or Mass

ad lícite agéndum: for acting licitly

ad límina Apostolórum: to the threshold of the Apostles, to Rome; refers to each bishop's official visit to the Pope; *see Appendix*

Ad Majórem Déi Glóriam (A.M.D.G.): for the greater glory of God

ad méntem: according to the mind of

ad múltos ánnos: to many more years, a good-luck expression

ad nútum: at the nod of, at the will or approval of

ad nútum épiscopi: at the nod or pleasure of the bishop

ad nútum Sánctae Sédis: at the nod or pleasure of the Holy See

ad ómnia: withal, to crown all

ad postrémum: lastly

ad praésens: now, for the moment

ad quem: toward which, for which purpose or goal

ad rem: toward the matter, to the point, appropriate

ad súmmum: on the whole, in general

ad témpus: at the time, in time

ad última: to the last degree

ad vérbum: word for word, literally

adáctus -a -um: *perf. pass. part. of* ádigo

adaéquo -áre: (1); equalize, make adequate, level with

adaequátus -a -um: adequate, equal; adaequáte (adaéque): *adv.*

Ádam, Ádae, Adámus -i: m.; Adam

adamantínus -a -um: unconquered, adamantine, unable to be broken

ádamas -ántis: m.; a diamond, steel; something very hard

Adamíti -órum: m.; Adamites

ádamo -áre: (1); love greatly, fall in love

adamússim: accurately, exactly, according to rule

adapério -íre -pérui -pértum: (4); open

adapértio -ónis: f.; opening, explanation, disclosure

adaptátio -ónis: f.; adaptation, adjustment

adápto -áre: (1); adapt, adjust, fit

adáquo -áre: (1); water, give a drink to

adaúctus -us: m.; growth, increase, increment

adaúgeo -ére -aúxi -aúctum: (2); increase

áddecet -ére: (2); *impers.;* it is fit, it behooves, it becomes

addécimo -áre: (1); levy, tithe, tax

addéndus -a -um: to be added or joined

addíco -ere -díxi -díctum: (3); agree with; dedicate; surrender; give over

addictíssimus -a -um: most devotedly

addísco -ere -dídici: (3); learn in addition, be informed, hear addítio -ónis: f.; addition

additítius -a -um, additionális -is -e: additional

áddo -ere -didi -ditum: (3); add, add to, augment, join

addúco -ere -dúxi -dúctum: (3); bring, lead in, escort, prevail upon

adémptio -ónis: f.; seizure, taking away, expropriation

ádeo: even, so much, to that point, inasmuch as

ádeo: -íre -ívi(-ii) -ítum: (4); go to, approach, undertake

ádeps -ipis: c.; marrow, fat, the best part of the meat or animal; richness, the best, finest

adéptus -a -um: perf. pass. part. of adipíscor

adf- see also aff-

ádfero (áffero) -férre, attuli, allátum: irreg.; bring together, carry

adflúo -ere: (3); flow, overflow, hurry

adhaéreo -ére -haési -haésum: (2); cling to, adhere, cleve to

adhaésio -ónis: f.; adhesion, adhering

adhíbeo -ére -ui -itum: (2); add to, apply, make use of

adhortátio -ónis: f.; exhortation, encouragement; see Appendix

adhórtor -ári: dep. (1); encourage, exhort

ádhuc: still, yet, now, as, thus far, besides

adício: see adjício

ádigo -ere -égi -áctum: (3); impel, drive, drive to

ádimo -ere -émi -émptum: (3); remove, take away, deprive of

adimpleméntum -i: n., adimplétio -ónis: f.; completion, fulfillment, realization

adímpleo -ére -plévi -plétum: (2); fill, fulfill

adínflo -fláre: (1); swell up

adinvénio -íre -véni -véntum: (4); find, come upon

adinvéntio -ónis: f.; work, device, invention, plan, deed

adínvicem: adv.; strengthened form of ínvicem

adipíscor -písci, adéptus: dep. (3); obtain, acquire, gain, achieve, reach

áditus -a -um: approached, undertaken; perf. pass. part. of ádeo

áditus -us: m.; approach, entry, access, gate

adjáceo -ére: (2); lie near, be adjacent or contiguous to

adjício (adício) -ere -jéci -jéctum: (3); add, increase, direct one's thoughts toward, apply to; grant, throw toward

adjúdico -áre: (1); judge, sentence

adjuméntum -i: n.; help, assistance, aid

adjúnctio -ónis: f.; restriction, limitation, union, addition

adjúnctum -i: n.; addition, accessory circumstance

adjúngo -ere -júnxi -júnctum: (3); join, attach, annex, yoke

adjuraméntum -i: n.; oath, adjuration

adjúro -áre: (1); adjure, swear

adjútor -óris: m., adjútrix -ícis: f.; helper, assistant, coadjutor

adjutórium -ii: n.; help, assistance

ádjuvo -áre -júvi -jútum: (1); help, assist, support

adl- see also all-

adlabóro -áre: (1); work, labor, toil

adléctus -i: m.; one elected into a collegium

ádlego -ere -légi -léctum: (3); choose, elect

adminiculatívus -a -um: supporting, suitable or fit for support

adminículum -i: n.; support, prop, assistance

adminíster -tri: m.; assistant, attendant, one near to help

administrátio -ónis: f.; governing, administration, control, administering administratívus -a -um: administrative, directing

administrátor -óris: m.; one who administers or conducts, one appointed to administer a vacant parish or diocese, administrator

administratórius -a -um: ministering

administro -áre: (1); administer, manage, minister

admirábilis -is -e: wonderful, admirable, worthy of admiration

admirátio -ónis: f.; surprise, bewilderment

admíror -ári: dep. (1); admire, wonder at

admísceo -ére -míscui -míxtum: (2); to mix

admíssio -ónis, admissúra -ae: f.; admission, entrance, audience, entrance upon an inheritance; see Appendix

admíssor -óris: m.; perpetrator

admítto -ere -mísi -míssum: (3); admit, join, allow

admíxtio -ónis: f.; mixture, mixing

ádmodum: very, exceedingly, quite, up to the mark, completely; níhil or núllus ádmodum: nothing or no one at all

admóneo -ére -ui -itum: (2); warn, admonish

admonítio -ónis: f.; admonition, warning

admónitus -a -um: admonished, warned

admóveo -ére -móvi -mótum: (2); move, move near, bring

adn- see also ann-

adnávigo -áre: (1); sail to

adnécto -ere -néxui -néxum: (3); tie, bind, connect, annex

adnítor -níti -nísus or -níxus: dep. (3); strive

adnotátio -ónis: f.; comment, annotation

adnóto -áre: (1); note in writing

adnúmero -áre: (1); number, count again, enumerate

adóleo -ére -ui -últum: (2): burn, consume; honor, incense, worship; emit an odor, smell

adoléscens -éntis: m.; youth, young man

adolescéntia -ae: f.; youth, adolescence

adolescéntior -óris: m.; young man; as an adj.: younger

adolescéntula -ae: f.; very young maiden

adolescéntulus -i: m.; very young man

adolésco -ere -évi, adúltum: (3); grow up, come to maturity

Adonái: indecl: m.; Hebrew; Lord, God

adóptio -ónis: f.; adoption

adoptionísmus -i: m.; heresy of adoptionism

adoptívus -a -um: adopted

adópto -áre: (1); choose, select, adopt

ádor -óris: n.; grain, spelt

adorábilis -is -e: adorable, worthy of adoration

adorándus -a -um: adorable

adorátio -ónis: f.; adoration

adorátor -óris: m.; worshiper, adorer

adórior -oríri -órtus: dep. (4); rise up, undertake

Adórna thálamum: a Candlemas Day antiphon

adórno -áre: (1); provide, furnish, prepare, adorn

adóro -áre: (1); adore, worship, reverence, honor

Adóro Te: I adore You; a hymn in honor of the Eucharist composed by St. Thomas

adp- see also app-

adpertíneo -ére -ui -téntum: (2); appertain to

ádprecor -ári: dep. (1); worship, pray to

ads- see also ass-

adscísco -ere -scívi -scítum: (3); receive, admit, approve

adscríbo -ere -scrípsi -scríptum: (3); write, ascribe to, enroll, approve

adscríptio -ónis: f.; incardination, enrollment, formal membership, inscription, approval

adséntior -íri -sénsus: *dep.* (4); assent, approve

adsídeo -ére -sédi -séssum: (2); sit by or near

adsído -ere -sédi -séssum: (3); sit down

adsígno -áre: (1); assign, appoint, allot, ascribe

adspectábilis -is -e: visible, worthy of being seen

adspérgo -ere -spérsi -spérsum: (3); scatter, bespatter, sprinkle

adspersórium (asp-) -ii: n.; holy water sprinkler

adspício -ere -spéxi -spéctum: (3); look at or on

adspirátio -ónis: f.; blowing, breathing, exhalation

adspíro -áre: (1); inspire, breathe upon; aspire, desire to attain or reach

adstípulor -ári: *dep.* (1): agree to, strengthen

ádsto -áre -stiti: (1); stand by, assist, be present, attend

adstríngo -ere -strínxi -stríctum: (3); put under obligation, bind, fetter, draw close

ádsum -esse, ádfui (áffui): be present, attend, be mindful

adt- *see* att-

adulátio -ónis: f.; flattery

aduléscens -éntis: m.; youth

adúlter -i: m.; adulterer

adúltera -ae: f.; adultress

adulterínus -a -um: not genuine, bastard, adulterous

adultérium -ii: n.; adultery

adúltero -áre: (1); commit adultery; pollute; counterfeit

adúlterus -a -um: adulterous

adúltus -i: m.; an adult; in 1983 Code one who has completed the 18th birthday, in 1917 Code one who has completed the 21st

adúltus -a -um: adult, grown

adumbrátio -ónis: f.; sketch, outline, shadow, semblance, shade

adúmbro -áre: (1); shade, overshadow, represent imperfectly

adúno -áre: (1); unite, gather together

adúro -ere -rússi -rústum: (3); burn, burn up, set on fire, kindle

ádvena -ae: c.; temporary resident, alien, foreigner, stranger

advénio -íre -véni -véntum: (4); come, happen

adventícius -a -um: foreign, strange, unusual, extraordinary

advénto -áre: (1); come

adventéntia -ae: f.; knowledge, warning

Advéntus -us: m.; season of Advent

advéntus -us: m.; arrival, advent, coming

advérsa -órum: n. pl.; adversity, adverse things

adversárius -a -um: facing toward, turned against, opposite, adversary; *as a c. noun:* adversary; *as a n. pl. noun:* daybook, journal, record book

advérsitas -átis: f.; adversity, calamity, harm

advérsor -ári: *dep.* (1); resist, oppose

advérsum (advérsus): *adv. & prep. w. acc.;* against, opposite

advérsum -i: n.; harm

advérsus -a -um: turned toward, opposite, facing

adverténtia -ae: f.; awareness, attending, noticing, knowledge

advérto -ere -vérti -vérsum: (3); advert to, notice, perceive, remark

advesperáscit -scere -ávit (3); *impers.;* be toward evening

advígilo -áre: (1); keep guard, be watchful, be vigilant

advocáta -ae: f.; advocate

advocátio -ónis: f.; function of a patron, right of presentation to a vacant benefice

advocátus -i: m.; advocate, legal assistant, counsel, witness; *see Appendix*

Advocátus Diáboli: Devil's Advocate, slang name given to the Promoter of the Faith in the process of beatification or canonization

ádvoco -áre: (1); call, call to, summon

ádvolo -áre: (1); fly, fly to

advólvo -ere -vólvi -volútum: (3); to roll

ádytum -i: n.; sanctuary, holy of holies, inmost part

aédes -is: f.; dwelling, church, temple, palace, house

aedícula -ae: f.; little building, chapel, tabernacle, niche

aedíficans -ántis: m.; builder

aedificátio -ónis: f.; building; edification, good example, act of building up

aedificátor -óris: m.; repairer, builder

aedificatória -ae: f.; architecture, art of building

aedificátus -a -um: built, constructed

aedifícium -ii: n.; building

aedífico -áre: (1); build, construct; edify, instruct

aedítuus -i: m.; caretaker, warden, janitor, trustee

aéger -gra -grum, **aegrótus** -a -um: sick, ill

Aegídius -ii: m.; Giles

aégre: with difficulty, with regret, unwillingly

aegritúdo -inis, **aegrotátio** -ónis: f.; illness, sickness

aegróto -áre: (1); grow sick, be sick

aegrótus -a -um: sick, ill

Aegyptíacus (Aegýptius) -a -um: Egyptian

Aegýptii -órum: m.; Egyptians

Aegýptus -i: f.; Egypt

Aelamítae -árum: m.; Elamites

aémula -ae: f.; rival

aemulátio -ónis: f.; envy, emulation, striving after

aemulátor -óris: m.; zealous imitator

aémulor -ári: *dep.* (1); envy; emulate, endeavor to equal, rival

aémulus -a -um: emulating, rivaling

Aenéas -ae: m.; Aeneas, a paralytic healed by St. Peter

aéneus -a -um: of brozen, brazen

aenígma -atis: n.; riddle, difficult question, obscurity, enigma, mystery, allegory; **in aenígmate:** in a dark manner

Aénon: *indecl.;* Aenon, an unidentifiable place in the Jordan Valley

aequális -is -e: equal, even, uniform; **aequáliter:** *adv.*

aequálitas -átis: f.; equality

aequanímiter: calmly

aéque: equally, in like manner; **aéque ac:** as well as

aequilíbrium -ii: n.; level, horizontal position, equilibrium

aequinóctium -ii: n.; the equinox

aequíparo -áre: (1); compare, consider equal, liken

aequipóllens -éntis, **aequiválens** -éntis: equivalent, of equal value or significance; **equipollénter (equivalénter):** *adv.*

aéquitas -átis: f.; justice, equality, righteousness, equity, fairness; calmness, evenness of temper

aequiváleo -ére: (2); have equal power, be equivalent

aéquo -áre: (1); make level, equal

aéquor -óris: n.; the sea

aéquus -a -um: equal, right, level, favorable, just, fair, equitable; **aéquo ánimo:** cheerful in mind; **aéque:** *adv.*

áër, aëris: m.; the air

aeraméntum -i: n.; vessel or utensil of copper or bronze

aerárium -ii: n.; treasury

aéreus -a -um: of copper, bronze, or brass

aérius -a -um: airy, windy, raging, sky-colored, azure

aëronávigans -ántis: c.; airline personnel

aerugíno -áre: (1); to rust

aerúgo -inis: f.; rust, mildew, blight

aerúmna -ae: f.; affliction, hardship, trial, trouble

aerumnósus -a -um: sorrowing

aes, aéris: n.; copper, coin, money, pay; aes aliénum: debt

aesculánus -a -um: pertaining to copper or money

aéstas -átis: f.; summer

aesthética -ae: f.; esthetics

aestimábilis -is -e: valuable

aestimátio -ónis: f.; evaluation, count, appraisement

aestimátor -óris: m.; one who esteems or evaluates

aestimatórius -a -um: pertaining to the value of something

aéstimo -áre: (1); esteem, consider, appraise, judge

aestivális -is -e: pertaining to summer

aestívus -a -um: of summer

aéstuo -áre: (1); to be hot, scorch, kindle, rage

aéstus -us: m.; heat, rage, fire, vacillation

aétas -átis: f.; age; aetátem habére: be of age; see Appendix

aetérnitas -átis: f.; eternity

aetérnus -a -um, aeternális -is -e: eternal, without beginning or end; in aetérnum: forever

aéther -eris, acc. aéthera: m.; sky, upper air

aethérius -a -um: airy, of heaven, ethereal

Aethiópia -ae: f.; Ethiopia

Aéthiops -opis: m.; Ethiopian

aévum -i: n.; time, eternity, an age

Áfer -fra -frum: African

aff- see also adf-

affábilis -is -e: approachable, cheerful, courteous, affable

affábre: ingeniously, skillfully

affátim: earnestly, sufficiently, completely

affectátus -a -um: voluntary

afféctio -ónis: f.; disposition, feeling, frame of mind, will, volition, change of mind

affectívus -a -um: affective

affécto -áre: (1); pursue, strive after, imitate faultily

afféctus -us: m.; affection, love, devotion, desire, emotion

áffero -érre, áttuli, allátum: irreg.; bring to, bring forth, allege

affício -ere -féci -féctum: (3); attach to, affect, do something to, cause a change in, treat, exert influence

affígo -ere -fíxi -fíxum: (3); fasten, affix, impress on

affínis -is -e: allied, related, related by marriage

affínitas -átis: f.; affinity, relationship by marriage, union; see Appendix

affirmátio -ónis: f.; affirmation, declaration

affirmatívus -a -um: affirmative, affirming; affirmatíve: adv.

affírmo -áre: (1); affirm, prove, support, strengthen

affíxio -ónis: f.; nailing, fastening, joining

afflátus -us: m.; breath, spirit, a breathing upon, blowing, inspiration

afflictátio -ónis: f.; suffering, misery, punishment, chastisement

afflíctio -ónis: f.; affliction

afflígo -ere -flíxi -flíctum: (3); afflict, punish, chastise, mortify

áfflo -áre: (1); inspire, teach, breathe on
affluénter: generously, profusely
affluéntia -ae: f.; affluence, abundance, profusion, fullness
áffluo -ere -flúxi -flúxum: (3); flow, flow to; abound, be wealthy; hasten
áffor -ári: dep. (1); say, speak
affúlgeo -ére -fúlsi -fúlsum: (2); shine forth, glitter, appear
a fortióri: from the stronger positon; see Appendix
África -ae: f.; Africa
Africánus -a -um: of Africa, African
Áfricus -i: m.; southwest wind, south
ágape -es: f.; love, charity, love feast
Agaréni -órum: m. pl.; Agarites, Hagrites, descendants of Agar
agátur (agántur): let it (them) be treated, let it be a matter or question of
agénda -ae: f.; ritual; what must be done, agenda
ágens -éntis: m.; doer, agent, actor
áger -gri: m.; field, country, county, district
Aggaéus (Aggéus) -i: m.; Haggai, a minor prophet; a book of the O.T.
ágger, ággeris: m.; mound, heap, wall
aggéstus -us: m.; mound, heap
Aggéus -i: see Aggaéus
ággravo -áre: (1); make heavy, make worse, aggravate, burden
aggrédior -i -gréssus: dep. (3); go to, approach, undertake
aggregátio -ónis: f.; aggregation, a gathering together
ággrego -áre: (1); join with, add to
aggréssor -óris: m.; aggressor, one who attacks
Agiásmos -ou: m.; in the Greek rite, a book of solemn blessings
ágios -a -on: Greek; holy
ágito -áre: (1); shake, agitate, impel, disturb, excite
ágmen -inis: n.; throng, multitude, host

agnéllus -i: m.; little lamb
agnítio -ónis: f.; knowledge
ágnitor -óris: m.; one who knows or acknowledges
ágnitus -a -um: perf. pass. part. of agnósco
agnómen -inis: n.; surname
agnósco -ere -nóvi -nitum: (3); recognize, know, understand, perceive
agnosticísmus -i: m.; agnosticism
ágnus -i: m.; lamb
Ágnus Déi: Lamb of God, a part of the liturgy
ágo -ere, égi, áctum: (3); drive, do, express, put in motion, practice, discuss, treat, act; grátias ágere: to give thanks
ágon -ónis: m.; struggle, combat, contest, agony; in agóne: for the mastery
agónia -ae: f.; agony, death struggle
agonízo -áre: (1); struggle, suffer agony, die
agonósticus -a -um: pertaining to a contest or struggle
ágrapha -órum: n. pl.; things unwritten
agrárius -a -um: agrarian, of the field, farm, or land
agréstis -is -e: wild
agrícola -ae: m.; farmer, husbandman
agricultúra -ae: f.; agriculture
Áhaz: indecl.; Ahaz, king of Judah
Ahímelech (Achímelech): indecl.; Ahimelech, a friend of David
ain: 16th letter of the Hebrew alphabet
áit: defect. verb; he or she says; áiunt: they say
ála -ae: f.; wing, shelter
alabástrum -i: n.; alabaster, alabaster box
álacer (alácris) -cris -cre: active, quick, cheerful, eager, brisk, lively, nimble, ready; alácriter: adv.
alácritas -átis: eagerness, alacrity, cheerfulness, promptness

álapa -ae: f.; slap, blow, light blow on cheek, box on the ear

alátus -a -um: winged

álba -ae: f.; alb

albárius -a -um: white

álba Romána: surplice

álbeo -ére -ui: (2); become white

albésco -ere: (3); grow white, become bright

Albigénses -ium: m. pl.; Albigenses, heretical sect

álbor -óris: m.; whiteness

albúgo -inis: f.; film, white spot

álbum -i: n.; list, tablet, register

álbus -a -um: white; ripe

álea -ae: f.; game with dice, dice, chance, risk, venture

aleátor -óris: m.; gambler, dice player

aleatórius -a -um: pertaining to a gambler

áleph: first letter of the Hebrew alphabet

áles -itis: winged

Alexándria -ae: f.; Alexandria

Alexandríni -órum: m.; Alexandrinians

Alexandrínus -a -um: of Alexandria

álga -ae: f.; seaweed

algésco -ere, álsi: (3); become cold, catch cold

álgidus -a -um: cold

álias: elsewhere, at another time, at other times

álibi: elsewhere, otherwise, in other respects

alienátio -ónis: f.; alienation, transfer from one to another

alienígena -ae: m.; stranger, foreigner

aliéno -áre: (1); estrange, alienate

aliénus -a -um: strange, not one's own, foreign, alien

aliméntum -i: n.; nourishment, food

alimónia -ae: f.; support, food, nourishment

alimónium -ii: n.; nourishment, food

álio: elsewhere, to another person or place

alióqui, alióquin: otherwise, in other respects

aliquámdiu (aliquándiu): for a little while

aliquándo: at last, at times, at any time, heretofore, sometimes

aliquantísper: for a while

aliquántulum: a little, somewhat

aliquántum: somewhat, in some degree, considerably

aliqúatenus: to a certain degree or measure, somewhat, partly

áliqui -quae(-qua) -quod: some, any

áliquis -quis -quid: someone, something, anyone, anything

aliquómodo: in some manner, somehow

áliquot: some, several, a few

aliquóties: several times

áliter: otherwise; áliter átque: otherwise than

alitúrgicus -a -um: without liturgy

aliúnde: by another way, from another person or place

álius -a -ud: other, another

álius . . . álius: one . . . another

álii . . . álii: some . . . others

all- see also adl-

allabóro -áre: (1); work or labor hard

allátus -a -um: perf. pass. part. of áffero

allegátio -ónis: f.; allegation, dispatching, sending

allegátum -i: n.; account, something pledged

allégo -áre: (1); dispatch, commission; instigate; adduce; pledge

allegória -ae: f.; figure, allegory

allegórice: allegorically

allegóricus -a -um: allegoric

allelúia: Hebrew; alleluia (praise ye the Lord)

alleluiáticus -a -um: pertaining to the alleluia

témpus alleluiáticum: season in which the alleluia is said

vérsus alleluiáticus: verses containing the word "alleluia"

allevátio (alleviátio) -ónis: f.; elevation; alleviation

allévio (állevo) -áre: (1); lift up, raise up; lighten, alleviate, mitigate, relieve, comfort

allévo -áre: (1); make smooth

allício -ere -léxi -léctum: (3); allure, attract, charm

allído -ere -lísi -lísum: (3); dash upon, strike against, cast down

álligo -áre: (1); bind, tie

allocútio -ónis: f.; speech, address, discourse, encouragement; an address by the Pope to the cardinals

allóphylus -i: m.; foreigner, stranger

allóquium -ii: n.; exhortation, conversation

álloquor (ádloquor) -qui, allocútus: dep. (3); converse with, address, speak

almárium -ii: n.; sacristy

almúcia -ae: f.; amice

álmus -a -um: kind, gracious, dear, cherished, indulgent, forgiving, nourishing, bountiful, propitious

almútium -ii: n.; mozzetta

álo -ere, álui, áltum or álitum: (3); nourish, support, sustain

áloe -es: f.; aloes, bitterness

álogus -a -um: destitute of reason

álpha: alpha, first letter of the Greek alphabet

altarágium -ii: n.; altarage, stole fees, perquisites for baptism, marriage, etc.

altáre -is: n.; altar

altáre fíxum:; permanent altar

altáre máius: high altar

altáre mínus: side altar

altáre portábile: portable altar, altar stone

altáre privilegiátum: privileged altar

altáre viáticum: portable altar

altarísta -ae: m.; assistant priest

altárium -ii: n.; sanctuary; altar

álter -tera -terum: other of two, another

álter . . . álter: the one . . . the other

álter . . . ab áltero: one from the other

in áltero . . . in áltero: on the one hand . . . on the other hand

alterátio -ónis: f.; alteration, change

altércor -ári: dep. (1); to dispute

altérius: of one another

alternátim: alternately

altérno -áre: (1); change

altérnus -a -um: alternate, by turns, one after the other, interchangeable; altérnis: adv.

alterúter -tra -trum: one of two, either, one or the other; ad alterútrum: one to another

altília -árum: n. pl.; fatlings

áltilis -is -e: fatted, fattened

áltior -ior -ius: higher, deeper

Altíssimus -i: m.; the Most High

altitúdo -inis: f.; depth, height, high place

altrínsecus: on opposite sides

áltum -i: n.; the deep

áltus -a -um: exalted, high; deep; lofty, noble; álte: adv.; áltior -ior -ius: comp. adj.

alumnáticum -i: n.; annual tax for maintenance of a seminary

alúmnus -i: m., alúmna -ae: f.; student, pupil, one nourished and brought up, one who attended a school

alvéolus -i: m.; a bowl

álveus -i: m.; channel, bed of a river

álvus -i: f.; womb

áma -ae: f.; cruet

amábilis -is -e: loveable, amiable, lovely; amánter: adv.

Ámalek: indecl.; Amalekites, an early nomadic tribe in Palestine

amára -órum: n. pl.: bitterness

amarésco -ere: (3); become bitter
amarícor -ári: *dep.* (1); grow bitter
amaritúdo -inis: f.; bitterness, anguish
amárus -a -um: bitter, unkind, severe;
　amáre: *adv.*
amátor -óris: m., amátrix -ícis: f.; lover
amatórium -ii: n.; hymn of love
Ambiánum -i: n.; Amiens
ámbigo -ere: (3); to doubt
ámbio -íre -ívi(-ii) -ítum: (4): go
　around, canvas, strive for
ambítio -ónis: f.; ambition, strong
　desire, flattery, canvassing
ambitiósus -a -um: ambitious,
　encompassing, vainglorious
ámbitus -us: m.; cope; corridor, cloister;
　a walking about; environment,
　territory, scope, ambit, circle, area,
　extent
ámbo -ae -o: both
ámbo (ámbon) -ónis: m.; pulpit
ambolágium -ii: n.; amice
Ambrosiánus -a -um: of St. Ambrose,
　Ambrosian
Ambrósius -ii: m.; Ambrose
ámbulo -áre: (1); walk
ámen, ámen: *Hebrew;* so be it, verily
ámens -éntis: insane
améntia -ae: f.; madness, insanity,
　mental illness
América -ae: f.; America
amethýstus -i: f.; amethyst
amíca mórtis: things pertaining to death
amicábilis (amicális) -is -e: friendly,
　amicable
amício -íre -ícui(-íxi) -íctum: (4); wrap
　about, clothe
amicítia -ae: f.; friendship, league
amictórium -ii: n.; covering for the body
amíctus -a -um: clothed
amíctus -us: m.; vesture, garment, amice
amícus -a -um: friendly, kind, favorable;
　amíciter (amíce): *adv.*
amíssio -ónis: f.; loss

ámita -ae: f.; paternal aunt
amítto -ere -mísi -míssum: (3); send
　away, disperse, pardon
Ammonítes -is: m.; Ammonite
Ammonítidae -árum: f.; women of
　Ammon
ámo -áre: (1); to love
ámodo: henceforth, hereafter
amoénitas -átis: f.; pleasantness
amoénus -a -um: pleasant
ámor -óris: m.; love
Amorrhaéus -a -um: Amorrhite
amortizátio -ónis: f.; amortization,
　liquidation of a debt
Ámos: *indecl.;* Amos, a minor prophet; a
　book of the O.T.
amótio -ónis: f.; removal, removing
amóveo -ére -móvi -mótum: (2); put
　aside, remove, turn away
amovíbilis: -is -e: removable, movable
amovibílitas -átis: f.; removability
amphíbalus -i: m.; chasuble
amphitheátrum -i: n.; amphitheater
ámphora -ae: f.; pitcher, jug, bottle
ámple: richly, amply
ampléctor -plécti -pléxus: *dep.* (3),
　ampléxor -ári: *dep.* (1); embrace,
　encircle, hold fast, include;
　understand, love, esteem, welcome
ampléxus -us: m.; an embrace
amplificátio: -ónis: f.; amplification,
　increase, enlargement
amplificátor -óris: m.; one who extends
　or increases
amplífico -áre: (1); to increase
ámplio -áre: (1); make wider or larger,
　amplify, extend; delay a decision;
　ennoble, render glorious
amplitúdo -inis: f.; breadth, width,
　amplitude; distinction
ámplius: any more, yet more, besides,
　further, longer
ámplus -a -um: more, large, spacious,
　ample, great, strong, splendid,

distinguished, abundant; **ámple**
(**ámpliter**): *adv.;* **ámplior** -ior -ius:
comp. adj.

ampóla -ae: f.; cruet

ampolláta -ae: f.; cruet

ampúlla -ae: f.; phial, bottle, flask, vessel
for liquids, jar

ámputo -áre: (1); cut off, amputate, take
away, remove

ámula -ae: f.; small hook

amulétum -i: n.; amulet

ámulum -i: n.; starch

amússis -is: f.; a rule, a level; **ad
amússim:** exactly, accurately

amýgdala -ae: f.; almond

amydalínus -a -um: of almonds

amýgdalus -i: f.; almond tree

ámylum -i: n.; starch

an: or, whether

anabaptístae -arum: f. pl.; Anabaptists, a
Protestant sect

anabolárium (anabolágium) -ii: n.; veil,
covering, head covering, amice

anachoréta (anachoríta) -ae: m.; hermit,
anchorite

anachoréticus -a -um: eremitical,
anchoritic, of a hermit

anaglýphum -i: n.; sculpture in relief

anaglýptum -i: n.; image in relief

anagnósis -eos: f.; lectionary

anagnóstes -ae: m.; lector, reader

anagolaíum -i: n.; amice

analógia -ae: f.; harmony, analogy,
resemblance

analógium -ii: n.; lectern, pulpit,
reader's desk

análogus -a -um: suitable, appropriate

analphabetísmus -i: m.; illiteracy

análysis -is: f.; analysis

anamnésis -is: f.; *Greek;* commemoration

anáphora -ae: f.; Offertory in the Greek
Mass

anástasis -is: f.; the Resurrection

anáthema -atis: n., **anathematísmus** -i:
m.; anathema, curse, ban,
denunciation, thing given over to evil,
curse of excommunication

anáthema sit: let him/her be accursed

anathematízo -áre: (1); curse, denounce,
anathematize

ánceps -cípitis: two-edged, two-headed,
double; wavering, uncertain,
ambiguous, dangerous

ánchora (áncora) -ae: f.; anchor

ancílla -ae: f.; handmaid, maidservant

áncus -i: m.; group of musical notes

Andréas -ae: m.; Andrew

anéthum -i: n.; anise, dill

anfráctus -us: m.; winding, bending

angária -ae: f.; compulsory service for
public benefit; pl.: can refer to the
Ember Days

angário -áre: (1); to exact service,
compel, force, requisition

angélicus -a -um: angelic

ángelus -i: m.; angel, messenger

Ángli -órum: m.; the English

Ánglia -ae: f.; England

Anglicánus -a -um: Anglican

Ánglice: in or into English

Ánglicus -i: m.; Englishman

ángo -ere -xi -ctum (**ánxum**): (3); bind,
throttle, strangle, vex

ángor -óris: m.; distress

angório -áre: (1); compel, force

ánguis -is: c.; snake

anguláris -is -e: corner, angular

ángulus -i: m.; a corner, stay, bastion

angústa -ae: f.; narrow place

angústia -ae: want, anguish; **angústiae**
-árum: f.; tribulations, trials, difficulty,
necessities

angústio -áre: (1); make narrow,
straiten, hamper, distress

angústus -a -um: narrow, strait, close,
constricted, difficult; **angústa** -ae: f.,

angústum -i: n.; narrows, difficulty, danger; angúste: *adv.; see Appendix*

anhélo -áre: (1); desire, grasp, pant for

anílis -is -e: old womanish, of an old woman; aníliter: *adv.*

ánima -ae: f.; mind, soul, life, breath of life

animadvérsio -ónis: f.; perception, observation; reproach, censure, critical remark; punishment; *see Appendix*

animadvérto -ere -vérti -vérsum: (3); take notice of, observe, mark, regard, consider, discern, attend to

animaéquus -a -um: calm, undisturbed

ánimal -ális: n.; animal, beast, living being

animátio -ónis: f.; spirit, life, animation

ánimans -ántis: living, alive

ánimans -ántis: c.; living creature

ánimo -áre: (1); fill with breath, quicken, animate, endow

animósitas -átis: f.; high spirits, ardor, enthusiasm, ambition

ánimus -i: m.; soul, mind, heart, spirit, feeling, intellect

  ex ánimo: from the heart

  est éi in ánimo: he/she has in mind, intends

ann- *see also* adn-

annális -is: n.; annals, record

annáta média -ae: f.; annates, a tax on benefices in the 1917 Code

annécto (adn-) -ere, -néxui -néctum: (3); annex, tie, join, bind

annículus -a -um: one-year-old

annítor -níti -nísus: *dep.* (3); strive to, lean on, press against

anniversárium -ii: n.; anniversary

anniversárius -a -um: pertaining to an anniversary, annual

annóna -ae: f.; grain, crop, yearly produce, rations

annótinus -a -um, annuális -is -e: annual, year-old

ánnuens -éntis: *pres. part. of* ánnuo

annuláris (*more correctly* anu-) -is -e: pertaining to a ring

annúllo -áre: (1); annihilate, annul, destroy

ánnulus -i: m.; ring

Ánnulus Piscatóris: ring worn by the Pope on which is represented St. Peter casting a net

annumerábilis -is -e: able to be added to

annúmero -áre: (1); number

annunciátor (annuntiátor) -óris: m.; herald, one who announces

annuntiátio -ónis: f.; annunciation, declaration

annúntio -áre: (1); announce, relate, declare

ánnuo -ere -ui: (3); beckon, nod, wink, assent; *see Appendix*

ánnus -i: m.; year

ánnuus -a -um: yearly, annual, of a year's duration

anónymus -a -um: name unknown, without a name, anonymous

ánsa -ae: f.; opportunity, occasion, handle

ánstruo -ere -xi -ctum: (3); support

ánsula -ae: f.; loop, hook

Ansélmus -i: m.; Anselm

ánte: *adv. & prep. w. acc.;* before, in front of, forward

ántea: before, formerly, earlier

antéago -ere: (3); do before; anteáctus -a -um: past

antecédo -ere -céssi -céssum: (3); go ahead, surpass, go before

antecéllo -ere: (3); excel, surpass, rise

antecéssor -óris: m.; predecessor, forerunner

antéeo -íre -ívi(-ii) -ítum: (4); go before

ánte fáctum: before the fact

antelucánum -i: n.; dawn

antelucánus -a -um: before dawn, before daybreak

antemurále -is: n.; bulwark, outside wall

anténna -ae: f.; transverse beam of a cross; sailyard; antenna

antepéndium -ii: n.; a frontal, a hanging in front of the altar

antepóno -ere -pósui -pósitus: (3); place before, prefer

antepreparatórius -a -um: antepreparatory, pre-preparatory

ántequam: before, sooner than

antérior -óris: prior, previous, before, earlier, foremost

antésto -áre -steti: (1); stand before

antevérto -ere -vérti -vérsum: (3); precede, come before

Anthológion: a book in the Greek rite containing offices for feasts

anthropológicus -a -um: anthropological

antibráchium -ii: n.; forearm

antícipo -áre: (1); anticipate, prevent, forestall, act before

antídoron: blessed bread distributed after the liturgy in the Greek rite

antídotum -i: n., antídotus -i: m.; antidote, counterpoison, remedy

antiménsium -ii: n.; consecrated cloth used for an altar

antinómia -ae: f.; contradiction, conflict

Antiochéni -órum: m. pl.; Antiochians

Antiochénsis -is -e: of Antioch, Antiochian

Antiochénus -a -um: of Antioch, Antiochian

Antiochía -ae: f.; Antioch

ánti-páscha -átis: n.; Low Sunday in the Greek rite

antipéndium -ii: n.; see antepéndium

antíphona -ae: f.; antiphon

antiphonális -is -e: antiphonal

antiphonárium -ii: n.; book of antiphons, the Gradual

Antiphonárium Míssae: an early designation for the Gradual

Antiphonárium Offícii: a book containing antiphons for the Divine Office

antiphonárius -a -um: antiphonal

antiphonátim: antiphonally

Antíphones Maióres: the "O" antiphons of Vespers from Dec. 17 to 23 inclusive

antíphonus -a -um: antiphonal

antiquárius -ii: m.; antiquary, old scribe

antiquátus: see antíquus

antíquitas -átis: f.; antiquity, ancient times

antíquo -áre: (1); make old, keep in or restore to old condition

antíquus (antiquátus, antíquitus) -a -um: old, ancient, former, archaic, antique, outdated, from of old, long-standing

antisemitísmus -i: m.; anti-Semitism

antístes -itis: m.; bishop, presiding officer; in the O.T., a priest

antístes sacrórum: bishop

antístita -ae: f.; superioress

antísto -áre -stiti: (1); stand before

ántrum -i: n.; cave, den

Antvérpia -ae: f.; Antwerp

anuláris: see annuláris

ánulus -i: m.; ring

ánus -i: m.; hemorrhoids, disease of the anus, posterior part

ánus -us: f.; old woman

anxíetas -átis: f.; anxiety

ánxior -ári: dep. (1); be in anguish, be troubled

ánxius -a -um: afflicted, dejected, uneasy, anxious; ánxie: adv.

áper, ápri: m.; wild boar

apério -íre -pérui -pértum: (4); open, uncover, prove

aperítio -ónis: f.; opening, aperture

apérnor -ári: dep. (1); scorn

apérte: openly, plainly, sharply; apértius: more openly

ápex -icis: m.; point, summit, top

ápis -is: f.; bee

apíscor, apísci, áptus: *dep.* (3); seize, attack

Apocalýpsis -is: f.; book of Revelations, Apocalypse of St. John

apocalýpsis -is: f.; revelation, a disclosing

apocalýpticus -a -um: pertaining to the Apocalypse

apocatástasis -is: f.; restoration, re-establishment

apocrisiárius -ii: m.; envoy, nuncio, delegate

apócrypha -órum: n.; apocryphal writings (not included in the Bible)

apócryphus -a -um: apocryphal, not genuine, spurious

apógraphum (-graphon) -i: n.; transcript, copy

apologéticus -a -um: apologetic

apológia -ae: f.; apology, defense, justification, explanation

apoplécticus -a -um: apoplectic

apopléxia -ae: f.; apoplexy

apória -ae: f.; doubt, perplexity, embarrassment, disorder

apórior -ári: *dep.* (1); be in need, be perplexed, be pressed, waver, doubt, vacillate

apostásia -ae: f.; apostasy, repudiation of faith; *see Appendix*

apóstata -ae: m.; an apostate

apostáticus -a -um: apostate, rebel

apóstato -áre: (1); fall away, fall away from, apostatize

apostátrix -ícis: f.; an apostate

a posterióri: from the latter, reasoning from experience or observation, inductive

apóstola -ae: f.; female apostle

apostolátus -us: m., apostolícitas -átis: f.; apostleship, apostolicity, apostolate; *see Appendix*

Apostólicae Cúrae: a bull of Pope Leo XIII, 1896, in which Anglican orders were declared invalid

Apostólicae sédis grátia: by favor of the Apostolic See

apostolícitas -átis: *see* apostolátus

Apostólicum -i: n.; a book of Epistles

Apostólicus: a title applied to the Pope

apostólicus -a -um: apostolic; *see Appendix*

Apostólicus Rex: a title given to the kings of Hungary

Apostolórum commemorátio: a former feast in honor of all the apostles

apóstolus -i: m.; one who is sent, an apostle

apóstrapha -ae: f.; small mark or note, especially in music; apostrophe

apothéca -ae: f.; storeroom, cellar

app- *see also* adp-

appáreo -ére -ui -itum: (2); be evident, appear, shine forth

apparátus -us: m.; preparation, equipment, apparatus

apparítio -ónis: f.; apparition, appearance, manifestation

appáritor -óris: m.; servant, usher

ápparo -áre: (1); prepare, make ready, provide, furnish

appellátio -ónis: f.; appellation, appeal

appellátor -óris: m.; one who appeals, appellant

appellatórius -a -um: relating to an appellant

appéllo -áre: (1); call, appeal, name, address, entitle

appéllo -ere -puli -púlsum: (3); bring, drive to, direct, move

appéndo -ere -péndi -pénsum: (3); balance, weigh out, weigh

appensórius -a -um: with a handle

appetítio -ónis: f.; grasping for, inclination, appetite, desire

appetítor -óris: m.; coveter

appetítus -us: m.; appetite, hunger, passion

appetivítus -a -um: having an appetite for

áppeto -ere -ívi(-ii) -ítum: (3); pursue, fall upon, attack, reach to; wish for, hunger after, desire

Áppius -a -um: Appian

applicábilis -is -e: applicable

applicátio -ónis: f.; application, attachment, a joining

ápplico -áre -ávi(-ui) -átum(-itum): (1); add to, bring, apply, join, place, set to shore, connect with, touch at

appóno -ere -pósui -pósitum: (3); proceed, put to, add to, do unto, put near, set, place

appósitus -a -um: appropriate, suitable, fit; **appósite:** adv.

apprehéndo -ere -héndi -hénsum: (3); take hold of, seize, apprehend, press to, embrace, lay hands on

apprétio -áre: (1); value, prize, put a price on

appríme: exceedingly, above all, especially, first of all

ápprimo -ere -préssi -préssum: (3); press to

approbátio -ónis: f.; approval, approbation, sanction

ápprobo -áre: (1); assent, approve, favor, establish, confirm

appropínquo -áre: (1); draw near, approach

appróprio -áre: (1); appropriate, make one's own

appropriátio -ónis: f.; appropriation

appróximo -áre: (1); approach, draw near to

Aprílis -is: m.; month of April

a prióri: from the former, reasoning based on self-evident propositions, deductive

aptátio -ónis: f.; adaptation

aptitúdo -inis: f.; aptitude

ápto -áre: (1); prepare, adapt, fit, adjust

áptus -a -um: fitting, suitable, appropriate, right; **ápte:** adv.

ápud: prep. w. acc.; in presence of, at the home of, among, near, with, at, by

áqua -ae: f.; water

aquadúctus -us: m.; aqueduct, watercourse, conduit

aquamaníle -is: n.; basin for use at the Lavabo

aquamánus -us: m.; dish for washing hands

aquáticus (aquátus) -a -um: watery, moist, full of water; thin

áquila -ae: f.; eagle

Aquilánus -a -um: of Aquila

áquilo -ónis: m.; north wind

Aquínas -átis: of Aquin

Aquínus -i: m.; Aquinas

Aquisgranénsis -is -e: of Aachen

Aquitánia -ae: f.; Aquitaine

a quo: by whom, from where

ára -ae: f.

   ára viatória, ára lapídea: altar, altar stone

   ára itinerária, gestatória: portable altar

Árabes -um: m. pl.; Arabs, Arabians

Arábia -ae: f.; Arabia

Aragónia -ae: f.; Aragon

aránea -ae: f.; spider

aratiúncula -ae: f.; furrow

arátor -óris: m.; plowman

arátrum -i: n.; plow

árbiter -tri: m., **árbitra** -ae: f.; judge, arbitrator, umpire, witness

arbitrális -is -e: arbitrated, by arbitrators

arbitrárius -a -um: under arbitration, uncertain, arbitrary

arbitrátor -óris: m.; arbitrator, master, judge

arbitrátus -a -um: decided, judged, arbitrated

arbitrátus -us: m.; choice, decision, direction, inclination

arbítrium -ii: n.; free choice, free will, decision, opinion

árbitror -ári: *dep.* (1); think, decide, judge

árbor -oris: f.; tree

arbústa -órum: n. pl.; branches

arbústum -i: n.; orchard

árca -ae: f.; box, chest, ark

Arcádius -a -um: Arcadian

arcánum -i: n.; secret place, secret, mystery; arcána -órum: n. pl.; secrets, mysteries, hidden things

arcánus -a -um: secret, hidden

arcárius -ii: m.; treasurer

árceo -ére -ui -ctum (árcitum): (2); prevent, enclose, shut in

arcésso (accérso) -ere -ívi -ítum: (3); summon

arceuthínus -a -um: pertaining to a fir tree

arch- (archi-): a prefix denoting high rank

archaeológia -ae f.; archaeology

archaeológicus -a -um: pertaining to science of archaeology and antiquities, archaeological

archángelus -i: m.; archangel

archetýpus -a -um: original, archetype

archibasílica -ae: f.; archbasilica, cathedral church

archicántor -óris: m.; leader of a choir of cantors

archicapellánus -i: m.; almoner; chief chaplain

archiconfratérnitas -átis: f.; archconfraternity

archidiaconátus -us: m.; deanery, the office of archdeacon

archidiáconus -i: m.; archdeacon

archidiocésis -is: f.; archdiocese

archiepiscopális -is -e: archiepiscopal

archiepiscopátus -us: m.; archbishopric

archiepíscopus -i: m.; archbishop; *see* Appendix

archimandríta -ae: m.; archimandrite, abbot of a Russian or Oriental monastery

archimímus -i: m.; player, leading actor

archiparaphonísta -ae: f.; the fourth in rank in a schola cantorum

archipraésul -is: m.; archbishop

archiprésbyter -eri: m.; archpriest

archipresbyterátus -us: m.; archpresbyterate

archisodálitas -átis: f., archisodalítium -ii: n.; archsodality, archconfraternity

archistérium -ii: n.; monastery

archisynagógus -i: m.; ruler of a synagogue

architéctus -us: m.; architect

architriclínus -i: m.; chief steward

archívium -ii, archívum -i: n.; archives; *see* Appendix

arcosólium -ii: n.; arched recess as a burial place in the Catacombs

árcto -áre: (1); compress, contract

árctus -a -um: *see* ártus -a -um

árctus (árcus) -us: m.; rainbow, bow

árcula -ae: f.; small box or chest

árdens -éntis: flaming, burning, ardent; ardénter: *adv.*

árdeo -ére, ársi, ársum: (2); burn, glow, be on fire

ardésco -ere, ársi, ársum: (3); kindle, take fire

árdor -óris: m.; burning

árduus -a -um: difficult, steep, elevated, lofty, steadfast

área -ae: f.; floor, threshing floor, courtyard

área mártyrum: burial place

arefácio -ere -féci -fáctum: (3); parch

aréna (haréna) -ae: f.; arena, ground, sand, area in front of house

arenária -ae: f.; sandpit, catacomb

áreo -ére, árui: (2); dry up, be dry, wither

aréola (arióla) -ae: f.; small plot, garden

Areopagíta -ae: m.; Areopagite, member of the court of the Areopagus

arésco -ere, árui: (3); become dry, dry up, pine away

argénteus -a -um: silver; *as a m. noun:* piece of silver, money

Argentorátum -i: n.; Strasbourg

argumentátio -ónis: f., arguméntum -i: n.; argument, debate, proof, evidence; *see Appendix*

argumentósus -a -um: rich in material, rich in proof, busy

árguo -ere -ui -útum(-úitum): (3); make clear, expose, accuse, rebuke, convince

Ariáni -órum: m. pl.; Arians

Arianísmus -i: m.; heresy of Arianism; *see Appendix*

árida -ae: f.; dryness, dry land

áridus -a -um: dry, parched, arid, withered

Áriel: *Hebrew;* Ariel, Lion of God, God's altar, city of Jerusalem

áries -etis: m.; ram, battering ram; sea monster; beam for support

Arimathaéa -ae: f.; Arimathea

aríolus -i: m.; cunning person

árma -órum: n. pl. arms, weapons, armor, defense

Árma Chrísti: an emblem formed by instruments of the Passion

armaménta -árum: n. pl.; vessels or utensils for any purpose; tackle of a sailing vessel

armamentárium -ii: n.; armory

armaríolum -i: n.; small chest

armárium -ii: n.; locker, wardroom, vault, closet

armatúra -ae: f.; armor

armátus -a -um: armed

armellínum -i: n.; ermine

Arméni -órum: m. pl.; Armenians; *see Appendix*

arméntum -i: n.; herd, cattle

ármiger -gera -gerum: bearing arms or armor

armílla -ae: f.; bracelet

Armórum Chrísti: a feast formerly celebrated in honor of the instruments of the Passion

ármus -i: m.; shoulder

áro, aráre: (1); plough

aróma -atis: n.; aroma, spice, perfume, aromatic substance

aromatízans -ántis: aromatic, fragrant

aromatízo: -áre: (1); make aromatic, make sweet or fragrant

arreptítius -a -um: raving mad

árrha -ae: f., árrhabo -ónis: m.; wedding gift, pledge; earnest money; money paid down

arrídeo -ére -rísi -rísum: (2); laugh, smile

árrigo -ere -réxi -réctum: (3); rouse, excite, stir up

arrípio -ere -rípui -réptum: (3); seize, snatch, take, lay hold

arrogántia -ae: f.; presumption, arrogance

ars, ártis: f.; art, trade, scheme, skill, profession

ártemon (ártemo) -ónis: m.; topsail

arthrítis -idis: f.; gout, arthritis

articulátus -a -um: distinct

artículus -i: m.; finger, joint, member; point, moment of time; division, part, article; **artículo mórtis:** at the moment of death

ártifex -icis: m.; maker, author, artificer

artificiális -is -e: artificial

artifícium -ii: n.; craft, skill, handicraft

artophórion: n.; vessel in which the Blessed Sacrament is kept in Greek churches

ártus -a -um: fitted, close, strait, narrow, confined, short, strict, severe; *as a n. noun:* narrow place, passage; **árte:** *adv.*

ártus -us: m.; limb, joint

árula -ae: f.; small altar, base of the altar
arundinétum -i: n.; growth of reeds, thicket of rushes
arúndo -inis: f.; reed; staff for three candles formerly used on Holy Saturday
arúspex (harúspex) -icis: m.; soothsayer
arvína (arvínula) -ae: f.; fat
árvum -i: n.; field, sown field
arx, árcis: f.; throne, fortress, castle, refuge, stronghold
as, ássis: m.; copper coin, farthing
asc- *see also* **adsc-**
ascélla -ae: f.; pinion, wing; armpit
ascéndo -ere, ascéndi, ascénsum: (3); ascend, climb, go up
ascénsio -ónis: f.; ascension
ascénsor -óris: m.; rider, climber, one who mounts
ascénsus -us: m.; ascent, means of ascent; chariot
ascésis -is(-eos): f.; discipline, training
ascéta -ae: m.; hermit, ascetic; penitent
ascetérium -ii: n.; monastery
ascéticus -a -um: ascetical
ascétria -ae: f.; female ascetic, nun
áscia -ae: f.; hatchet, carpenter's ax
áscio -íre -ívi(-ii) -ítum: (4); get, take; admit
ascísco -ere -scívi -scítum: (3); receive, approve
ascopéra -ae: f.; satchel, wallet
ascríbo -ere -scrípsi -scríptus: (3); ascribe, apply, attribute
ascríptio -ónis: f.; addition in writing, enrollment; *see Appendix*
aséllus -i: m.; donkey, young ass
Aser: *indecl.;* Aser, Asher, son of Jacob and Zilpah; a tribe of Israel
Ásia -ae: f.; Asia
Asiánus -a -um: of Asia, Asian
ásina -ae: f.; she-ass
asinárius -a -um: pertaining to an ass; **móla asinária:** millstone

ásinus -i: m.; ass
asp- *see also* **adsp-**
aspéctus -us: m.; countenance, vision, sight, appearance, aspect, look
ásper -a -um: sharp, rough, difficult
aspergíllum -i: n.; sprinkler
aspérgo -ere -spérsi -spérsum: (3); to sprinkle
aspérgo -inis: f.; a sprinkling
aspéritas -átis: f.; roughness, sharpness, harshness, severity, unevenness
aspernátor -óris: m.; contemner
aspérnor -ári: *dep.* (1); despise
áspero -are: (1); make rough
aspérsio -ónis: f.; sprinkling, aspersion
aspersórium -ii: n.; sprinkler
aspérsus -a -um: sprinkled, spattered
aspício -ere -spéxi -spéctum: (3); look at, regard, behold
aspíro -áre: (1); assist, aspire to, be favorable to, breathe
áspis -idis: f.; asp, adder
aspórto -áre: (1); bring
ass- *see also* **ads-**
assécla -ae: m.; follower
assecurátio -ónis: f.; insurance
assecútio -ónis: f.; perception, comprehension, knowledge
assénsus -us: m.; assent, agreement, approval
asséntior (asséntio) -íri -sénsus: *dep.* (4); agree, assent, approve, consent
ássequor -qui -secútus: *dep.* (3); follow, observe, obtain
ásser -eris: m.; plank, board, lath
ássero -ere -sérui -sértum: (3); assert, remark, claim
assértio -ónis: f.; assertion
assértor -óris: m.; defender, champion
asservátio -ónis: f.; keeping, reservation
assérvo -áre: (1); protect, guard, preserve, watch over, reserve
assésio -ónis: f.; sitting as an assessor, act of assessing

asséssor -óris: m., asséstrix (assís-) -ícis: f.; assessor, aid, assistant

asseveránter: absolutely, emphatically

asseverátio -ónis: f.; strong affirmation, assertion, statement

assídeo -ére -sédi -séssum: (2); sit, be seated

assidúitas -átis: f.; custom

assíduus -a -um: continual, unceasing, constant; assídue: adv.

assignátio -ónis: f.; marking, showing, assignment, allotment

assígno -áre: (1); assign, designate

assímilis -is -e: similar, like

assímilo -áre: (1); compare, make like to, imitate, simulate

assímilor -ári: dep. (1); to be compared, become like

Assísinas -átis: of Assisi

Assísium -ii: n.; Assisi

assisténtia -ae: f.; assistance, help, attendance

assísto -ere ástiti: (3); stand near, assist, defend

assístrix -ícis: f.; attendant, assistant

associátio -ónis: f.; association, accompaniment, escort

assócio -áre: (1); escort, come over, associate, work with

assóleo -ére: (2); be usual, be accustomed to; ut ássolet (ádsolet): as is wont to happen, as usual

assuésco (assulésco) -ere: (3); become accustomed to

assuméntum -i: n.; a patch

assúmo -ere -súmpsi -súmptum: (3); assume, receive, take, raise

assúmptio -ónis: f.; assumption, act of being taken up

Ássur: Assyria

ássus -a -um: roasted, broiled

Assýrii -órum: m. pl.; Assyrians

ast: but, and, on the other hand

asteríscus -i: m.; asterisk; small metalic cover set over Host at outdoor Mass

ásto (ádsto) -áre, ástiti: (1); stand by or near

astríngo -ere -strínxi -stríctum: (3); tighten, contract, draw or bind together, fetter; se astríngere: be guilty of

astrológia -ae: f.; astrology, study of the stars

ástrum -i: n.; star

ástruo -ere -strúxi -strúctum; (3); establish, support, form, build, teach

ástus -us: m.; cleverness, cunning

astútia -ae: f.; subtlety, craftiness

astútus -a -um: wise, prudent, astute

asýlum -i: n.; refuge, place of sanctuary, asylum

at: but, instead, on the contrary, on the other hand

áter -tra -trum: black, dark

atheísmus -i: m.; atheism

átheus -i: m.; atheist

Athénae -árum: f. pl.; Athens

athenaéum -i: n.; school, atheneum, place of study

athenaéum máius: university

Atheniénsis -is -e: Athenian, of Athens

athléta -ae: m.; athlete, wrestler, champion, master

átomus -a -um: uncut, undivided; momentary

átque: and, and in addition, and also, and even; áliter átque: otherwise than

átqui: however, but, nevertheless

atraméntarium -ii: n.; inkwell

atraméntum -i: n.; ink

átrium -ii: n.; hall, court, vestibule

atróphia -ae: f.; consumption, wasting away

átrox -ócis: fierce, horrible, terrible, atrocious

áttamen: nevertheless, nonetheless, but yet, but also

attemperátio -ónis: f.; adjusting, accomodation, fitting

atténdo -ere -téndi -téntum: (3); attend, hearken, consider, mind, look to, listen to; take heed, beware

attentátio -ónis: f.; attempt, effort, trying

attentátum -i: n.; prohibited innovation during a process

atténto -áre: (1); attempt, try, attack

atténtus -a -um: attentive; **atténte:** *adv.;* **atténtius:** *comp. adv.*

attenuátus -a -um: feeble, weak; destitute

atténuo -áre: (1); weaken, diminish

áttero -ere -trívi -trítum: (3); bruise, destroy, rub away, ruin

attestátio -ónis: f.; evidence, proof, testimony; attestation, act of attesting

attéxo -ere -téxui -téctum: (3); weave, plait, add

attíneo -ére -tínui -téntum: (2); pertain to, belong to

attíngo -ere -tigi -táctum: (3); draw on, manage, attain, arrive at

attóllo -ere: (3); support, lift up

attónitus -a -um: stunned, astonished

áttraho -ere -tráxi -tráctum: (3); draw to, draw in, drag, force, attract

attrécto -áre: (1); lay hands on, feel, touch, grope for, seek to find

attríbuo -ere -ui -útum: (3); bestow, grant, attribute, allot to, assign

attribútio -ónis: f.; a giving

attribútum -i: n.; attribute, predicate

attrítus -a -um: hard

átvero: however

aúctor -óris: m.; author, founder, creator, originator

auctóritas -átis: f.; authority

auctoritatíve: with authority, authoritatively

aúctrix -ícis: f.; authoress; mother

aúctus -a -um: *perf. pass. part. of* **aúgeo**

aúctus -us: m.; growth, increase, augment, abundance

audácia -ae: f.; boldness, bravery, courage, valor

audácter (audénter): boldly

aúdeo -ére, aúsus: *semidep.* (2); to dare, venture

Audiéntes -ium: m. pl.; hearers, public penitents in the early Church

audiéntia -ae: f.; hearing, attention, audience

aúdio -íre: (4); hear, listen to

audítio -ónis: f.; hearing, report, audition

audítor -óris: m.; hearer, listener, disciple; account examiner; *see Appendix*

auditórium -ii: n.; hearing, examination; lecture room, hall

audítus -us: m.; a hearing

aúfero -férre, ábstuli, ablátum: *irreg.;* take away, remove

aufúgio -ere -fúgi: (3); flee

aúgeo -ére, aúxi, aúctum: (2); enlarge, increase

augésco -ere, aúxi: (3); to increase

auguméntum -i: n., **augmentátio** -ónis: f.; increase, augment, advancement

aúgur -úris: c.; soothsayer

augurátrix -ícis: f.; sorceress

aúguror -ári: *dep.* (1); prophesy

augustális -is -e: of Augustus, imperial; *as a m. noun:* member of imperial military or religious group

Augustianísmus -i: m.; Augustinism, the teaching of St. Augustine

Augustínus -i: m.; Augustine

augústus -a -um: majestic, august, venerable, sacred, worthy of honor; **augúste:** *adv.;* **Augústus** -i: m.; Augustus, month of August

aúla -ae: f.; dwelling, hall, court, temple; **aúla transvérsa:** transept

aulaéum -i: n.; hanging, canopy, curtain

aúra -ae: f.; breath, air, breeze

auratúra -ae: f.; gilding

Aureliánus -i: m.; Aurelian
auréola -ae: f.; halo, nimbus, auriole
aúreus -a -um: golden, of gold; aúreus
-i: m.; piece of gold
aurichálcum -i: n.; brass
aurícula -ae: f.; ear
auriculáris -is -e: auricular, pertaining
to the ear
auriculárius -ii: m.; secret adviser,
listener
aurifrisiátus -a -um: embroidered with
gold
aurifrísius -a -um: gold-embroidered
auríga -ae: c.; charioteer
aurilégulus -i: m.; gold collector
auriphrygiátus (auriphrýgius) -a -um:
embroidered with gold
aúris -is: f.; ear
aúro -áre: (1); overlay with gold
auróra -ae: f.; dawn, morning, daybreak
aurúgo -inis: f.; jaundice, paleness,
mildew
aúrum -i: n.; gold
ausculátor -óris: m.; listener
auscúlto -áre: (1); listen
auspicátus -a -um: auspicious, happy
auspícium -ii: n.; omen, divination;
idolatry, heathen worship
aúspico -áre: (1); foretell
aúspicor -ári: dep. (1); begin
aúster -tri: m.; south, south wind
austéritas -átis: f.; austerity, rigor,
severity
austérus -a -um: austere
Austrália -ae: f.; Australia
austrális -is -e: south, southern
aut: or, or rather; aut . . . aut: either . . .
or
aútem: however, whereupon, but, and,
and also
cóntra aútem: but on the other hand
íllud quídem . . . sed aútem: to be sure
. . . but still

authentícitas -átis: f.; genuineness,
authenticity
authéntico -áre: (1); authenticate, verify
authénticum -i: n.; document certifying
the genuineness of a relic
authénticus -a -um: genuine, authentic,
original; authéntice: adv.
autobiográphia -ae: f.; autobiography
autóchthonus -a -um: indigenous,
native, innate
autógraphum -i: n.; autograph copy,
original written document
automátio -ónis: f.; automation
autonómia -ae: f.; autonomy
autónomus -a -um: autonomous
autumnális -is -e: autumn, autumnal;
withered
autúmnus -i: m.; autumn
aútumo -áre: (1); affirm, say yes, assert,
aver; feel, think
auxiliárius -a -um, auxiliáris -is -e:
auxiliary, helping; see Appendix
auxiliátor -óris: m., auxiliátrix -ícis: f.;
helper
auxílior (auxílio) -ári: dep. (1); help,
aid, assist, support
auxílium -ii: n.; aid, help, support
avarítia -ae: f.; avarice, covetousness
avárus -a -um: covetous, avaricious
áve: hail, hello, greetings
avéllo -ere -vélli(-vúlsi) -vúlsum: (3);
separate, tear away, withdraw
Áve María: Hail Mary
Avénio -ónis: f.; Avignon
áveo -ére: (2); crave, pant after
avérnus -i: m.; the infernal regions
aversátor -óris: m., aversátrix -ícis: f.;
one who rebels or oppresses, apostate
avérsio -ónis: f.; aversion, turning away,
apostasy
avérsor -ári: dep. (1); turn away from,
avoid, repel, hate
avérto -ere -vérti -vérsum: (3); turn
away, ward off, avert, divert, pervert

ávia (áva) -ae: f.; grandmother
ávidus -a -um: eager, desirous, greedy;
  ávide: adv.; avídius: comp. adv.
ávis -is: f.; bird
avítus -a -um: ancestral, of a grandparent
avocátio -ónis: f.; diversion, interruption
ávoco -áre: (1); withdraw, call away,
  remove, recall, divert, revoke, distract
ávolo -áre: (1); fly away, fly
avúlsus -a -um: perf. pass. part. of avéllo
avúnculus -i: m.; uncle
ávus -i: m.; grandfather
axílla -ae: f.; side, armpit

áxis -is: m.; axle, axis; wheel; heavens,
  pole
Azarías -ae: m. pl.; Azarias
Azótii -órum: m. pl.; Azotians
Azótus -i: f.; city of Azotus
Ázrael: Aramaic; Azrael, the angel of
  death
azýma -órum: n. pl.; unleavened bread
Azýmes: Azyme, the feast of the
  unleavened bread
azymíta -ae: m.; one who uses
  unleavened bread for the Eucharist
azýmus -a -um: unleavened,
  unfermented

B

Báal: *indecl.;* Baal, a Syrian diety
Bábel: *indecl.;* Babel
Babélicus -a -um: of Babel
Bábylon -ónis: f.; Babylon
Babylónii -órum: m. pl.; Babylonians
báca (bácca) -ae: f.; berry, fruit of the olive
baccalaúreus (bacalárius) -i: m.; bachelor (academic)
bácchor -ári - átus: *dep.* (1); revel, rant, be raving wild
bácile -is: n.; basin
bácilis -is -e: low, base
bacíllum -i: n.; staff, rod
Báctri -órum: m. pl.; Bactrians
báculum -i: n., báculus -i: m.; rod, staff, stick, crook
báculus pastorális: crozier
bájulo -áre: (1); carry, bear
balbútio -íre: (4); babble, stammer, stutter
baldachínum -i: n., baldachínus -i: m.; canopy
bálo -áre: (1); bleat, talk foolishly
bálneum -i: n.; bath
bálsamum -i: n.; balm, balsum
bálteus -i: m.; belt
Baltimorénsis -is -e: of Baltimore
bancále -is: n.; cushion
bánnum -i: n.; a ban; pl.: banns (publication) of marriage
baptísma -atis: n.; baptism
baptismális -is -e: baptismal
baptísmus -i: m., baptísmum -i: n.; baptism; washing, sprinkling
Baptísta -ae: m.; John the Baptist
baptistérium -ii: n.; baptistry

baptizátor -óris: m.; minister of baptism
baptízo -áre: (1); baptize
Barábbas -ae: m.; Barabbas
Barachías -ae: m.; Barachias
baráthrum -i: n.; lower world, bottomless pit, abyss
bárba -ae: f.; beard
Bárbari -órum: m. pl.; natives of Barbary
Barbariánus a -um.: of Barbary
barbáricus -a -um: foreign, barbarian
barbáries -éi: f.; foreign land, barbarism, rudeness
bárbarus -a -um: foreign, strange, barbarian
barbátus -a -um: bearded
bárbitos -i: m., bárbiton -i: n.; lute, lyre
barbitónsor -óris: m.; barber
bárdus -a -um: stupid, dull
baríle -is: n.; cask
Barjésus -i: m.; Bar-jesus, Elymas
Bárnabas -ae: m.; Barnabas
báro -ónis: m.; baron
Barsábas -ae: m.; Barsabas
Bartholoméus -i: m.; Bartholomew
Bartimaéus -i: m.; Bartimaeus
Báruch: *indecl.;* Baruch; a book of the O.T.
Básan (Báshan): *indecl.;* Bashan, a region east of the Jordan
basílica -ae: f.; basilica, church; originally the form of a church
basílicus -a -um: kingly, royal, splendid
basilíscus -i: m.; basilisk, lizard, venemous serpent
Basílius -ii: m.; Basil
básis -is: f.; foundation, base, pedestal; báses -ium: f. pl.; feet

bássus -a -um: low, bass

batállum -i: n.; clapper (of a bell)

Bathshéba (Bethsába, Bethsábee): *indecl.;* Bathsheba

batíllum -i: n., **batíllus** -i: m.; fire shovel, chafing dish, incense pan

bátuo (báttuo) -ere -ui: (3); beat, strike, hit

bátus -i: m.; liquid measure

bdéllium -ii: n., **bdélla** -ae: f.; bdellium, a costly gum; a term of endearment

beatificátio -ónis: f.; beatification, act of beatifying

beatífico -áre: (1); beatify, make happy

beatitúdo -inis, **beátitas** -átis: f.; happiness, bliss, beatitude, blessedness

beátus -a -um: blessed, happy; a title given to saints in heaven and to some whose veneration is approved by the Holy See

Béda -ae: m.; Bede

Beélzebub: *indecl.,* **Beélzubul** -úlis: m.; Beelzebub

béhmoth: *Hebrew;* some large animal

Behtlaéus (Behtleémicus): *see* **Bethlehemítis**

békah: *Hebrew;* half a shekel

Bélgae -árum: m. pl.; Belgians

Bélgium -ii: n.; Belgium

bellátor -óris: m.; warrior

bellicósus -a -um: warlike, of war

béllicus -a -um: warlike; **vása béllica:** n. pl.; arms

belligerátor -óris: m.; warrior

bellígero -áre: (1); wage war, war

béllo (béllor) -áre: (1); wage war, fight, war, battle

béllua -ae: f.; savage beast

béllulus (béllus) -a -um: pretty, elegant, beautiful, fine, neat, handsome, costly; **béllule (bélle):** *adv.*

béllum -i: n.; war, battle

béma -tis: n.; sanctuary; bishop's chair; pulpit

béne: well

Benedicámus Dómino: Let us bless the Lord

Benedícite: Bless you, Praise God, a monastic greeting

benedíco -ere -díxi -díctum: (3); bless, praise

benedíctio -ónis: f.; benediction, blessing, formula for a blessing

benedictionále -is: n.; book with formulas of blessings

Benedíctus: the Canticle of Zechariah; *see Appendix*

Benedíctus -i: m.; Benedict

benefácio -ere -féci -fáctum: (3); do well, do good to

benefáctor -óris: m.; benefactor

benefáctum -i: n.; favor, good deed, benefit

beneficéntia -ae: f.; liberality, kindness, beneficence

beneficiális -is -e: beneficial

beneficiárius -a -um: pertaining to a favor or benefice

beneficiárius -ii: m.; holder of a benefice, a prebendary

beneficiátus -i: m.; holder of a benefice, a prebendary

benefícium -ii: n.; benefit, favor, benefice; *see Appendix*

benéficus -a -um: beneficent

beneplácens -éntis: acceptable

benepláceo -ére -ui -plácitum: (2); to be pleasing to

beneplácitum -i: n.; approval, favor, pleasure, good will

beneplácitus -a -um: acceptable, agreeable, well-pleasing

benesónans -ántis: melodious, sweet-sounding, loud

Benevéntum -i: n.; Benevento

benevólens -éntis: well-wishing, obliging

benevoléntia -ae: f.; good-will, benevolence

benévolus (benívolus) -a -um: kind,
benevolent; benévole: *adv.*
benígnitas -átis: f.; goodness, benignity,
kindness
benígnus -a -um: merciful, loving, good,
gracious, benign, kindly, favorable;
benígne: *adv.*
benívolus: *see* benévolus
Bénjamin: *indecl.;* Benjamin, son of
Jacob and Rachel; tribe of Israel
béo -áre: (1); bless
Bernárdus -i: m.; Bernard
berýllus -i: m.; beryl, precious stone
béstia -ae: f.; beast
bestiálitas -átis: f.; bestiality
beth: second letter of the Hebrew alphabet
Bethánia -ae: f.; Bethany
Béthlehem (Béthleem, Béthlem):
indecl.; Hebrew, Bethlehémum -i: n.;
Bethlehem
Bethlehemítis -is -e, Behtlaéus
(Behtleémicus, Bethlemíticus) -a
-um: of or pertaining to Bethlehem
Bethphánia -ae: f.; a former name for
Epiphany
Bethsába (Bethsábee): *see* Bathshéba
Bethséda (Bethsaída, Bethsátha):
Hebrew; a pool in Jerusalem
biárchus -i: m.; commissary,
superintendent of provisions
Bíblia -ae: f.; the Bible
Bíblia Paúperum: a picture book for
religious instruction in the 15th
century
bíblicus -a -um: biblical
bibliothéca -ae: f.; library
bibliothecárius -i: m.; librarian
bíbo -ere, bíbi, bíbitum: (3); drink
bíceps -cípitis: two-edged, two-handed,
two-headed
bícolor -óris: of two colors
bídens -éntis: f.; animal for sacrifice;
having two teeth or two rows of teeth;
sheep; hoe or mattock

biduánus -a -um: for a period of two
days
bíduum -i: n.; space of two days
bíduus -a -um: for a period of two days
biénnium -ii: n.; space of two years
bifaciátus -a -um, bífrons -fróntis:
two-faced, two-sided
bigámia -ae: f.; bigamy
bígamus -i: m.; bigamist
bilaterális -is -e: bilateral, mutual
bilíbris -is -e: weighing two pounds
bilínguis -is -e: double-tongued,
treacherous, bilingual
bílis -is: f.; hypochondria, bile; anger;
melancholy
bilocátio -ónis: f.; bilocation (being in
two places at once)
bimátus -us: m.; two years of age
biméstris -is -e: of two months;
biméstre: *adv.*
binátio -ónis: f.; duplication, bination
bíni -ae -a: two, two of a kind, in pairs,
two by two
bíno -áre: (1); duplicate, binate (offer
two Masses in one day)
biológicus -a -um: biological
bipertítus (bipartítus) -a -um: double,
with two parts
birétum (birrétum) -i: n.; biretta
bis: twice
biscéntum: *indecl.;* two hundred
bisómus -a -um: for two bodies
bisséxtilis (bisex-) (bisséxtus) ánnus:
leap year (in a leap year there are two
"sixth" days before the calends of
March)
bístropha -ae: f.; two musical notes of
the same pitch
bithalássus -a -um: between two seas
bitúmen -inis: n.; pitch, slime, cement
bivírga -ae: f.; two square and tailed
musical notes
blánde: softly, tenderly, caressingly

blandiméntum -i: n.; allurement, flattery, fawning

blándior -íri -ítus: *dep.* (4); coax, caress, flatter

blándior -ior -ius: softer, more soothing, smoother

blandítia -ae: f.; flattery

blándus -a -um: soothing, soft, smooth, fondling

Blásius -ii: m.; Blaise

blasphemábilis -is -e: deserving of reproach, censurable

blasphémia -ae: f.; blasphemy, reviling, contumelious language toward God

blasphémo -áre: (1); blaspheme

blasphémus -i: m.; blasphemer

blátio -íre: (4); babble, utter foolish things

Boanérges: Sons of Thunder, James and John, sons of Zebedee

Bohémi -órum: m. pl.; Bohemians

Bolesláus -i: m.; Boleslav

bólis -idis: f.; sounding lead

bólus -i: m.; a throw or cast

bombácium -ii: n.; cotton

bómbyx -ycis: m.; silkworm; silk; cotton, wadding

Bonipórtus -us: m.; Good Havens

bónitas -átis: f.; goodness, kindness

bónum -i: n.; good, advantage; *see* Appendix

　bóna -órum: n. pl.; goods, possessions

　bónum commúne: common good

bónus -a -um: good; in bónum: for good

boreália -órum: n. pl.; northern parts

boreális -is -e: northern

bórith: *Hebrew;* soap, cleanser, soapwort

bos, bóvis: c.; ox, cow, bullock

bótrus -i: m.; bunch, cluster of grapes

bráca -ae: f.; coat; brácae -árum: f. pl.; breeches

bracátus -a -um: wearing trousers or breeches

brácchium (bráchium) -ii: n.; arm

brachiále -is: n.; bracelet

bractéola -ae: f.; golden spangle

bránchia -ae: f.; gill of a fish

brándeum -i: n.; handkerchief; sheet; silk or cloth covering for relics

brávium -ii: n.; prize

bréve -is: n.; list, brief, summary

breviárium -ii: n.; abridgment, summary, condensed copy; Breviary, a book containing the Divine Office

Breviárum Piánum: the Breviary prescribed by Pope Pius V

Breviárum Sánctae Crúcis: Breviary of the Holy Cross, compiled by Cardinal Quinonez about 1535

brévio -áre: (1); shorten, abridge, condense

bréviculus -a -um: somewhat short; in bréviculo: after a little while

brévis -is -e: short, brief; in brévi: in a short space or brief time; brévi (bréviter): *adv.;* brévior -ior -ius: *comp. adj.; see Appendix*

brévitas -átis: f.; shortness

Británni -órum: m. pl.; Britons, British

Británnia -ae: f.; England

Britónes -um: m. pl.; Britons, British

brúchus -i: m.; locust, grasshopper

brúma -ae: f.; winter

brumális -is -e: wintry, of winter

brútus -a -um: brute, irrational

búbalus -i: m.; buffalo, ox, African stag, gazelle; búbalus -i: f.; cow, wild cow

búbulus (búbalus) -a -um: pertaining to cattle or oxen

bucále -is: n.; water jug, pitcher

búcca -ae: f.; cheek

búccino -áre: (1); sound a trumpet

bucélla -ae: f.; fragment, morsel, small mouthful, sop

búcina -ae: f.; trumpet

Buddhísmus -i: m.; Buddhism

búfo -ónis: m.; toad

búgia -ae: f.; hand candlestick

búlbus -i: m.; onion

Bulgári -órum: m. pl.; Bulgarians

búlla -ae: f.; papal document, bull, seal of a papal document; *see Appendix*

bullárium -ii: n.; collection of papal bulls; *see Appendix*

búllio -íre: (4), **búllo** -áre: (1); bubble, boil; fly in a passion, rage

búrdo -ónis: f.; mule, beast of burden, burden

búrsa -ae: f.; burse, case

búrsula -ae: f.; small burse or case

bútyrum -i: n.; butter, cheese

Byblos (Gébal): *indecl.;* Byblos, a city in Phoenicia

býssinus -a -um: of linen or silk

býssus -i: m.; fine linen, silk

Byzantínus (Byzántius) -a -um: Byzantine; *see Appendix*

Byzántium -ii: n.; Byzantium or Constantinople

C

cábus -i: m.; kettle, corn measure

cácabus -i: m.; earthen pot

cacúmen -inis: n.; tip, summit, peak, highest point

cadáver -eris: n.; corpse, dead body, carcass

Cádes: *Hebrew;* Cades, Kadesh, a city in Edom south of Palestine

cádo -ere, cécidi, cásum: (3); fall, fall prostrate, fall into sin

caducárius -a -um: epileptic

cadúcitas -átis: f.; weakness, perishableness, frailty

cadúcus -a -um: perishable, weak, frail, transitory

cádus -i: m.; jug, large vessel, cask, barrel

cae- *see also* coe-

caecátus -a -um: blinded

caécitas -átis: f.; blindness, darkness, spiritual blindness

caécus -a -um: blind; *as a noun:* blind person

caecútio -íre -ívi: (4); see badly, be blind

caédes -is: f.; slaughter, massacre

caédo -ere, cecídi, caésum: (3); cut, cut down, hew, strike, beat, kill

caélebs -ibis: angelic, heavenly, unmarried, celibate

caéles -itis: heavenly

caeléstis -is -e: heavenly, divine, celestial; caeléstia -ium: n. pl.; heavenly things, high places

caéli -órum: m. pl.; the heavens

caelibátus (coel-) -us: m.; celibacy

caelícola -ae: c.; inhabitant of heaven

caélitus: divinely, by divine inspiration

Caélius -a -um: Caelian

caélum (coélum) -i: n., caeli -orum: m. pl. heaven, sky

caementárius -ii: m.; mason

caeménto -áre: (1); cement, fasten with mortar

caeméntum -i: n.; cement, mortar

caénum -i: n.; dirt, filth, mud, mire

caereiále -is: n.; book of ceremonies

caeremónia (caeri-) -ae: f.; ceremony, sacred rite

Caeremoniále Episcopórum: Ceremonial of Bishops

Caeremoniále Románum: Roman Ceremonial

caeremoniális -is -e: ceremonial

caeremoniárius -ii: m.; master of ceremonies

caerimónia -ae: *see* caeremónia

caerimónior -ári: *dep* (1); worship, treat with due ceremony

caerúleus -a -um: light blue, blue

Caésar -aris: m.; Caesar, Roman emperor; caésar -aris: m.; emperor

Caesaraéa -ae: f.; Caesarea, a seaport town of Palestine

Caesaraéa Philíppi: Caesarea Philippi, a town in the north of Palestine

Caesaraugústa -ae: f.; Saragossa

Caesariénsis (Caesareénsis) -is -e: pertaining to Caesarea

caesáries -éi: f.; head of hair

caéspes -itis: m.; turf, sod

caétus (coétus) -us: m.; assemblage

Caínus -i: m.; Cain

Cajetánus -i: m.; Cajetan

calámitas -átis: f.; calamity, distress, misfortune

calamitósus -a -um: calamitous

cálamus -i: m.; reed, pen, fishing rod

cálathus -i: m.; a flat basket

calcábilis -is -e: able to be trod upon

calcáneum -ei: n.; heel

cálcar -áris: n.; spur

calcátor -óris: m.; treader of grapes, one who treads on something

calceaméntum -i: n.; shoe

calceátus -a -um: shod, with shoes on

calcedónius -ii: m.; precious stone, chalcedony

cálceo -áre: (1); put shoes on

cálcitro -áre: (1); kick

cálco -áre: trample on, tread on

cálculum -i: n.; calculation, computation

cálculo -áre: (1); compute, reckon, count

cálculus -i: m.; pebble, stone; coal; counter

caldária -ae: f.; cauldron; warm bath

calefácio -ere -féci -fáctum: (3); to warm

calefáctio -ónis: f.; heat, heating

calefácto -áre: (1); heat, make warm

calefío -fíeri -fáctus: (3); pass. of calefácio, grow warm

caléndae -árum: f. pl.; calends, first day of the month

calendárium -ii: n.; caleandar, register of accounts

cáleo -ére -ui -itúrum: (2); glow, become warm, be inflamed, be roused

cálidus -a -um: hot

cáliga -ae: f.; sandal, boot, buskin, stocking worn by bishop, half boot

caliginósus -a -um: dark, misty, cloudy

calígo -áre: be in darkness, waste away, be misty

calígo -inis: f.; darkness, cloud, mist, dark cloud, thick atmosphere

cálipha -ae: f.; caliph

cálix -icis: m.; chalice, goblet, cup

cálleo -ére -ui: (2); be hardened, know by experience, understand

callíditas -átis: f.; craftiness

cállidus -a -um: crafty, subtle; **cállide:** adv.

cállis -is: c.; footpath, narrow way

cállus -i: m.; hard skin

cálor -óris: m.; heat

calóta -ae: f.; skullcap

calúmnia -ae: f.; calumny, oppression, false accusation

calumniátor -óris: m.; calumniator, oppressor

calúmnior -ári: dep. (1); calumniate, oppress, accuse falsely, slander

calumniósus -a -um: calumnious, false, deceitful

Calvária -ae: f.; Calvary

calvária -ae: f.; skull

Calviniánus -a -um: of Calvin

Calvinísta -ae: m.; Calvinist

cálveo -ére: (2); be bald

cálvus -a -um: bald

calx -cis: f.; heel, foot; goal, end of page, limit; small stone, counter; lime; **víva cálce:** in quicklime

calybíta -ae: f.; hermit, cabin dweller

Camaldulénsis -is -e: Camaldolese, of Camaldoli

camaúra -ae: f.; close-fitting cap

Cámbria -ae: f.; Wales

cambúta -ae: f.; crosier

camelaúcium -ii: n.; red velvet hood sometimes worn by the Pope

camelopárdus -i: m.; giraffe

camelóttum -i: n.; a kind of cloth

camélus -i: m.; camel

cámera -ae: f.; chamber, room, vault, small room, camera; see Appendix

camerális -is -e: pertaining to a small room or chamber

camerárius -ii: m.; chamberlain

camínus -i: m.; furnace, forge, fire

camísia -ae: f.; alb

camísium -ii: n.; alb

campágus -i: m.; sandal, slipper

campána -ae: f.; bell

campanárium -ii: n.; belfry

campanárius -ii: m.; bell ringer

campaníle -is: n.; belfry

campánula -ae: m.; little boy

campéster -tris -tre: flat, pertaining to a plain

cámpus -i: m.; field, plain, campus

cámus -i: m.; bit for a horse, curb, muzzle

Cána -ae: f.; Cana of Galilee

Cánaan: *indecl.;* Canaan, a biblical land and people

cancellária -ae: f.; chancery; *see Appendix*

cancellárius -ii: m.; chancellor

cancellátio -ónis: f.; a folding; crossing out; fixing, measuring

cancellátus -a -um: crossed, cancelled, crossed out

cancéllo -áre: (1); fold; cross out

cancéllus -i: m.; grating, lattice, enclosure, partition between nave and sanctuary

cáncer, cáncri: m.; malignant tumor, cancer, crab

candéla -ae: f.; candle, lamp

candelábrum -i: n.; candlestick, chandelier for lamps

candélula -ae: f.; small taper

cándens -éntis: red-hot, glowing hot, burning

cándeo -ére -ui: (2); shine, glitter

candésco -ere, cándui: (3); become glittering white, shine, glow

candidátio -ónis: f.; whiteness

candidátus -a -um: white-robed; *as a noun:* candidate

cándido -are: (1); make glittering or white

cándidus -a -um: white

candífico -áre: (1); make white

cándor -óris: m.; brightness, radiance, candor, frankness, openness

cáneo -ére -ui: be white, gray, hoary

cánis -is: c.; dog

canístrum -i: n.; basket

caníties: *no gen. and dat.;* f.; old age, gray hair

cánna -ae: f.; reed, cane, flute, windpipe, ell

cánnabis -is: f.; linen

cáno -ere, cécini, cántum: (3); sing, celebrate in song, prophesy

cánon -ónis: m.; canon, norm, rule; part of the Mass; catalog, list; model; ecclesiatical title; **cánon Sanctórum:** canon of the saints, the official list of canonized saints

canónia -ae: f.; prebend of a canon

canonicális -is -e, **canónicus** -a -um: of a canon, canonical; *see Appendix*

canonicátus -us: m.; office of a canon

canónicus -a -um: canonical; **canónice:** *adv.; as a noun:* a canon; *see Appendix*

canonisátio (-zátio) -ónis: f.; canonization

canoníssa -ae: f.; canoness

canonísta -ae: m.; one learned in Canon Law, canonist

canonízo -áre: (1); canonize

cánor -óris: m.; song

canórus -a -um: melodious, harmonious

cantábilis -is -e: worthy of song

Cantabrígia -ae: f.; Cambridge

cantátio -ónis: f.; song

cantátor -óris: m., **cantátrix** -ícis: f.; singer, musician

cantatórium -ii: n.; old name for Gradual book

cantátrix -ícis: musical, singing

cántharus -i: m.; large pitcher, holy-water vessel; well

cánthus -i: m.; rim or tire of wheel

Cántica Gráduum: Gradual Psalms

cantículum -i: n.; brief song

cánticum -i: n.; song, canticle

cantiléna -ae: f.; music, song

cantíllo -áre: (1); warble, chirp

cántio -ónis: f.; song

cánto -áre: (1); sing, play, crow

cántor -óris: m., cántrix -ícis: f; cantor, singer

Cantuária -ae: f.; Canterbury

cántus -us: m.; song, chant, crowing

Cántus Gregoriánus: Gregorian chant, plainchant

cánus -a -um: gray, hoary

capácitas -átis: f.; capacity, capability

cápax -ácis: fit for, capable, apt, suitable; spacious

capélla (cappélla) -ae: f.; chapel, choir; a capélla: unaccompanied

capéllae magíster: choirmaster

capellánus (cappellánus) -i: m.; chaplain

capéllus -i: m.; hat

capésso -ere -ívi(-íi) -ítum: (3); seize, lay hold of, gain, undertake, execute

Caph: 11th letter of the Hebrew alphabet

Caphárnaum: indecl.; Capharnaum

capillaméntum -i: n.; hair, wig

capillatúra -ae: f.; hair dressing or adornment

capíllus -i: m.; hair, beard

cápio -ere, cépi, cáptum: (3); capture, take, catch; hold, contain; receive, obtain; understand

Capistránum -i: n.; Capistrano

capitális -is -e: capital, chief, first; relating to life; mortal

capitáneus -ei: m.; captain, leader

capitéllum -i: n.; head of a column; short lesson, little chapter

capitilávium -ii: n.; washing of the head

capítium -ii: n.; collar, hood

Capitolínus -a -um: Capitoline

Capituláre -is: n.; a list of initial and concluding words of Epistles and Gospels of the Missal; a book containing Orations

capituláris -is -e: pertaining to a chapter

capítulum -i: n.; little chapter, cathedral chapter, chapter of the Bible, prominent part

cáppa -ae: f.; large cloak

Cáppadox -ócis: c.; a Cappadocian

cápparis -is: f.; caper tree

cappélla -ae: f.; chapel

cappellánia -ae: f.; chaplaincy

cappellánus -i: m.; chaplain

cáprea -ae: f.; wild she-goat, roe

caprínus -a -um: pertaining to a goat

cápsa -ae: f.; small case for relics, repository, box

capsélla -ae: f.; little box, coffer

cápsula -ae: f.; vessel for Benediction Host, small container

cáptio -ónis: f.; trap, net, prey, booty, act of taking

captiósus -a -um: fallacious, deceitful

captívitas -átis: f.; captivity, bondage

captívo -áre: (1); take captive

captívus -a -um: captured, captive; as a noun: prisoner

cápto -áre: (1); seek after, desire

captúra -ae: f.; catch of fish

cáptus -a -um: perf. pass. part. of cápio

cáptus -us: m.; catching, capacity, comprehension, mental grasp

Capuccínus -a -um: Capuchin

capulátus -a -um: hooded

cáput -itis: n.; head, chapter, principal division, heading; cáput nullitátis: reason for nullity; cáput súper pédibus in amóre: head over heels in love; see Appendix

capútium -ii: n.; hood

carbasínus -a -um: green

cárbo -ónis: m.; coal

carboárius -ii: m.; collier, coal burner

carbúnculus -i: m.; carbuncle; small piece of coal; disease

cárcer -eris: m.; prison

carcerális -is -e: pertaining to prison

Carchedónius -a -um: Carthaginian

cardinálátus -us: m.; cardinalate

cardinális -is: m.; cardinal, chief, principal; see Appendix cardinalítius -a -um: pertaining to a cardinalship

cárdo -inis: m.; hinge, door, pole of the earth

cárduus -i: m.; thistle

caréctum -i: n.; sedgebush, rushes

caréna -ae: f.; fast of forty days

caréntia -ae: f.; lack

cáreo -ére -ui -itum: (2); lack, be wanting in, be devoid of

cárica -ae: f.; dried fig

carína -ae: f.; ship, keel

cáritas -átis: f.; charity, love, esteem, affection; *see Appendix*

caritatívus -a -um: charitable

Carmelítae -árum: c. pl.; Carmelites

Carmélus -i: m.; Carmel, Mount Carmel

cármen -inis: n.; song, canticle, lay

carnális -is -e: bodily, carnal, sensual, fleshy

carnálitas -átis: f.; sensuality

carnáliter: sensually

cárneus -a -um: carnal, of flesh .

cárnifex -icis: m.; executioner

carníficus -a -um: corporal, of the flesh

cárniger -era - erum: bearing flesh

cáro, cárnis: f.; flesh, meat; the lower appetites or passions

Cárolus -i: m.; Charles

carpentárius -ii: m.; carpenter

cárpo -ere -psi -ptum: (3); seize, pluck

carrúca -ae: f.; carriage, coach

cárta *see* chárta

cartállus -i: m.; basket

Carthágo -inis: f.; Carthage

Carthusiáni -órum: m. pl.; Carthusians, charterhouse monks

cárus -a -um: dear, beloved

cáseum -i: n.; cheese

cásia (cássia) -ae: f.; cassia, wild cinnamon, aromatic tree

cassídile -is: n.; wallet, satchel

Cassínas -átis, Cassinénsis -is -e: of Monte Cassino

Cassínum -i: n.; Monte Cassino

cássis -ídis: f.; helmet

cásso -áre: (1); annul, make void, destroy

cássus -a -um: useless, vain, empty

castéllum -i: n.; town, walled town, village

castífico -áre: (1); cleanse, render chaste, purify

castigátio -ónis: f.; chastisement, punishment, correction

castígo -áre: (1); reprove, punish, chastise, correct

cástitas -átis, castimónia -ae: f.; chastity, purity

cástra -órum: n. pl.; camp, military camp

castraméntor -ári: *dep.* (1); pitch camp, encamp

castrátio -ónis: f.; castration

castrénsis -is -e: of or pertaining to camp

cástro -áre: (1); castrate

cástrum -i: n.; camp, fort, castle, fortification

cástrum dolóris: catafalque

cástus -a -um: chaste, pure, unpolluted, guiltless, spotless; *see Appendix*

cásula -ae: f.; chasuble; cottage, hut, small house

cásus -us: m.; case, peril, chance, misfortune, happening, accident, emergency

catábulum -i: n.; stable, menagerie

cataclýsmus -i: m.; deluge, flood

catacúmba -ae: f.; underground room, catacomb

catálogus -i: m.; catalogue, list, enumeration

Cátana (Cátina) -ae: f.; Catania, a town at the foot of Mt. Aetna

catarácta -ae: f.; cataract, waterfall, rushing waters; floodgate, drawbridge, grating catarráctes -ae: m.; waterfall; floodgate

catásta -ae: f.; platform, scaffold, the rack

catástropha -ae: f.; turning point, catastrophe, disaster

catechésis -is(-eos): f.; catechetical instruction, interrogation, catachesis

catechéta -ae: *see* catechísta

catechéticus -a -um: catechetical

catechisátio -ónis: f.; questioning, catechizing

catechísmus -i: m.; catechism

catechísta (catechéta) -ae: c.; catechist, one who teaches catechism

catechísticus -a -um: of the catechism

catechízo -áre: (1); teach, instruct, teach by question and answer

catechumátus (catechumenátus) -us: m.; catechumenate, the time of instruction before baptism; *see Appendix*

catechúmenus -i: m., catechúmena -ae: f.; catechumen

categória -ae: f.; category, predicament, accusation

catéllus -i: m.; little dog, whelp

caténa -ae: f.; chain, bond

caténula -ae: f.; small chain

catérva -ae: f.; crowd, throng, congregation

catervátim: in troops, in groups

Cathartárium -ii: n.; *see* purgatórium

cathárticum -i: n.; purification

cáthedra (cathédra) -ae : f.; chair, seat; pulpit; professorship; episcopal office, bishop's throne; ex cáthedra: from the chair; *see Appendix*

cathedrális -is -e: pertaining to an official see or cathedral

Cathedrális Ecclésia: cathedral

cathedráticum -i: n.; cathedraticum, an annual tax paid to a bishop; *see Appendix*

catholícitas -átis: f.; catholicity

cathólicus -a -um: universal, Catholic; Cathólice: *adv.; see Appendix*

cathúrnus -i: m.; pride, majesty, haughtiness

catínum -i: n., catínus -i: m.; vessel, dish

cátulus -i: m.; cub, whelp

caúcus -i: m.; cruet

caúda -ae: f.; tail, trail or edge or train of a garment

caudatárius -ii: m.; trainbearer

caúdex: *see* códex

caúla -ae: f.; fold, sheepfold

caúma -átis: n.; heat

Caúrus -i; *see* Córus

caúsa: *prep. w. gen.:* on account of, for the sake of

caúsa -ae: f.; cause, case; means; reason, motive; judicial process, suit; síne caúsa: in vain, without cause; *see Appendix*

causális -is -e: of a cause, causal; causáliter: *adv.*

Caúsae Maióres: greater cases or causes

caúso -áre: (1); to cause

caúte (caúto): carefully, circumspectly, cautiously

caúterio -áre: (1); brand, burn, mark with a brand

caútio -ónis, cautéla -ae: f.; caution, warning, precaution, security, warranty, bond, bail, guarantee, surety

cautióne: with caution

caúto: *see* caúte

caútum -i: n.; concern; caútum ésse: provide, caution

cávea -ae: f.; cage

cáveat émptor: let the buyer beware

cáve cánem: beware of the dog

cáveo -ére, cávi, caútum: (2); beware, take care, take heed

cavérna -ae: f.; cave, cavern, hollow place

cavíllor -ári: dep. (1); to jest

-ce: *an inseparable, strengthening, demonstrative enclitic*

cédo -ere, céssi, céssum: (3); withdraw,
yield, allow, grant, move

cedrínus -a -um: of cedar

cédrus -i: f.; cedar tree

celatúra -ae: f.; canopy over altar

céleber -bris -bre: renowned, famous,
solemn

célebrans -ántis: m.; celebrant,
officiating minister

celebrátio -ónis: f.; celebration,
performance of a sacred function

célebret: he may celebrate; official
written statement that a priest may
celebrate Mass (that he is in good
standing); see Appendix

celébritas -átis: f.; feast, celebration

célebro -áre: (1); celebrate, perform,
practice; see Appendix

céler -eris -e: swift, quick, speedy, fast;
celériter: adv.

celéritas -átis: f.; speed, quickness,
swiftness

célero -áre: (1); hasten, hurry

celeúma -ae: see celúma

célla -ae: f.; cellar

cellárium -ii: n.; pantry, storeroom,
chamber

cellerárius (cellárius) -ii: m.; cellarer,
manager of supplies, steward

céllula -ae: f.; hut

célo -áre: (1); hide, conceal

celsitúdo -inis: f.; height, highness,
exaltation

célsus -a -um: high, sublime, noble

céltis -is: f.; chisel, tool

celúma (celeúma) -ae: f.; shout, song

ceméntum -i: n.; cement, bonding

céna (coéna) -ae: f.; meal, banquet,
dinner, supper

cenodóxia -ae: f.; vainglory

cenotáphium -ii: n.; cenotaph, catafalque

cénseo -ére -ui -sum: (2); think,
approve, estimate, call

cénsor -óris: m.; censor, examiner

censúra -ae: f.; blame; censure,
ecclesiastical punishment; censorship;
see Appendix

censurátus -a -um: censured, under
censure

cénsus -us: m.; cost, expense, census,
appraisal, tribute, rating

centenárius -a -um: hundredfold,
centenary

centéni -ae -a: a hundred each

centésimus -a -um: hundreth

centrális -is -e: central, in the middle

céntrum -i: n.; middle, center

céntum: indecl.; hundred

céntuplus -a -um: hundredfold; as a n.
noun: a hundredfold

centúrio -ónis: m.; centurion

cephálicus -i: m.; musical note in
Gregorian chant

Céphas: indecl.; Aramaic; rock; surname
of Simon Peter

céra -ae: f.; wax

cerástes -is(-ae): m.; horned serpent

cérebrum -i: n.; brain

ceremónia (cerimónia) -ae: f.; ceremony

ceremoniále (cerimoniále) -is: n.;
directory for ceremonies

ceréolus -i: m.; small candle

cereostátum -i: n.; candlestick,
candelabrum

céreus -a -um: made of wax

céreus -i: m.; taper, wax candle

cerevísia (cervísia) -ae: f.; beer

cerimónia -ae: see ceremónia

cerimoniále -is: see ceremoniále

cérno -ere, crévi, crétum: (3); discern,
see, understand

cérnuus -a -um: prostrate, with bowed
heads, falling down

ceroferárium -ii: n.; candlestick

ceroferárius -ii: m.; torchbearer

certámen -inis: n.; fight, struggle, strife,
contest

certátim: eagerly, earnestly

cértior fíeri: to be informed; *see* **fío**

certitúdo -inis: f.; certitude

cérto -áre: (1); fight, contend, struggle

cértus -a -um: fixed, certain, determined; **cérte (cérto):** *adv.*

cérva -ae: f.; doe, hind

cervícal -ális: n.; pillow

cervicátus -a -um: stiff-necked

cervísia -ae: *see* **cerevísia**

cérvix -ícis: f.; neck

cérvus -i: m.; stag, hart, deer

céspes: *see* **caéspes**

cessátio -ónis: f.; ceasing, cessation; **cessátio a divínis:** suspension of divine service

céssio -ónis: f.; surrendering, giving up

césso -áre: (1); cease, stop, delay, loiter

céte -ion: n. pl.; whale, dolphin

céterus -a -um: other, rest, remaining
    de cétero: finally
    ceteróqui (ceteróquin): otherwise, for the rest
    céteris páribus: other things being equal

cétus -i: m.; whale

ceu: as, like, as when, as it were, just as

Chalcedonénsis -is -e: of Chalcedon

chalcedónius -ii: m.; chalcedony

Cham: *indecl.:* m.; Ham, son of Noah

chamaéleon -ónis(-óntis): m.; chameleon, lizard

chameúnia -ae: f.; a place to sleep on the ground

Chánaan: *indecl.;* Canaan

Chananaéus -a -um: Canaanite

chancellárius -ii: m.; chancellor, diocesan official; *see Appendix*

cháos (cháus) -i, *often indecl.:* n.; empty space, the boundless, lower world, chaos, dark gulf

charácter -eris: n.; character, spiritual mark

charádrius -ii: m.; a bird, yellow in color

charísma -atis: n.; spiritual gift, charism

charismáticus -a -um: charismatic, pertaining to spiritual gift; *see Appendix*

cháritas -átis: f.; *see* **cáritas**

charitatívus -a -um: charitable

chárta -ae: f.; paper, writing, letter, map

chartáceus -a -um: of paper

chárta glóriae: altar card

chártula -ae: f.; small piece of paper

chartulárius -ii: m.; keeper of archives

chárus -a -um: *see* **cárus**

cháus -i: *see* **cháos**

chérub: *indecl.;* cherub; **chérubim:** m. pl.; cherubim, choir of angels

chiánter -tri: m.; choirboy

chirógraphum -i: n.; handwriting, bond

chirothéca -ae: f.; glove

chirúrgia -ae: f.; surgery

chirúrgicus -a -um: surgical

chirúrgus -i: m.; surgeon

chlámys -idis, **chlámyda** -ae: f.; cloak

Chlóe (Chlóes) -es: f.; Chloe

choerogríllus -i: m.; hare

chorális -is -e: choral

choraúlis -is: m.; young chorister

chórda -ae: f.; string, stringed instrument, cord, cincture

chórdula -ae: f.; tape, ribbon, cord

chórea -ae: f.; choir, dancing, dance

chorepíscopus -i: m.; auxiliary bishop

chóricus -a -um: of the choir, choral

chorísta -ae: m.; chorister, member of a choir

chórus -i: m.; choir, singing, sanctuary, those in the sanctuary

chrísma -atis: n.; chrism, sacred oils, unction, anointing

chrismále -is: n.; linen cloth, cerecloth, corporal, pall; pyx

chrismális -is -e: pertaining to chrism

chrismárium -ii: n.; vessel for chrism

chrismátio -ónis: f.; anointing with chrism; *see Appendix*

chrismatórium -ii: n.; see chrismále
Christiádes -um: c. pl.; Christians
Christiádum -i: n.; Christendom
Christiánitas -átis: f.; Christian religion,
Christianity
christianízo - áre: (1); profess
Christianity
Christiánus -a -um: Christian;
Christiáne: adv.
Christícola -ae: c.; worshipper of Christ
Chrístifer -fera -ferum: Christ-bearing
Christifidélis -is -e: follower of Christ,
faithful to Christ; as a noun: one of the
Christian faithful; see Appendix
chrístus -a -um: anointed
Chrístus -i: m.; Christ, the Anointed
One, Messiah
chrónicon -i: n.; chronicle
chronísta -ae: m.; chronicler, person
who chants narrative parts in the
Passion
chronológia -ae: f.; chronology
chronológicus -a -um: chronological
chrysólithus -i: m.; topaz, chrysolite
chrysoprásus -i: m.; chrysoprase
Chúsai: indecl.: m.; Chusai, Husai, a
friend of King David
chytrópus -i: m.; a pot with feet
cibária -órum: n. pl.; food, sustenance,
victuals
cíbo -áre: (1); feed, give to eat
cibórium -ii: n.; ciborium, vessel for
Sacred Hosts, tabernacle
cíbus -i: m.; food, meat, fuel
cicátrix -ícis: f.; wound, scar, mark,
bruise
cicindéle -is: n.; lamp made of glass
cicónia -ae: f.; crane, stork
cicúta -ae: f.; hemlock
cidáris -is: f.; Persian miter
cíeo, ciére, cívi, cítum: (2); invoke, call
by name, rouse, move
cilícinus -a -um: made of haircloth

cilícium -ii: n.; sackcloth, haircloth, hair
shirt
cimélium -ii: n.; treasure
cimitérium -ii: n.; cemetery
cinctículus -i: m.; apron
cinctórium -ii: n.; girdle
cinctúra -ae: f.; cincture, belt
cínctus -us: m.; girdle
cinematographéum -i: n.; cinema
cinematográphicus -i: m.; movie
scriptwriter
cíngo -ere, cínxi, cínctum: (3); gird
cíngulum -i: n., cíngulus -i: m.; girdle,
cincture, belt
cínifes -um: m. pl.; gnats, flies
cínis -eris: m.; ashes, cinders; díes (Féria
Quárta) Cínerum: Ash Wednesday
cinnamómum -i: n.; cinnamon
cinýra -ae: f.; lute, harp
círca, círciter: round about, all around
círca: prep. w. acc.; around, in respect to,
on sides of, about
circitórium -ii: n.; curtain, veil
circúeo (circúmeo) -íre -ívi(-íi) -itum:
(4); go about, encompass, canvass,
walk around, surround
circúitor -óris: m.; inspector
circúitus -us: m.; circuit, circle; in
circúitu: round about
círculus -i: m.; circle
circumamíctus -a -um: clothed about,
invested
circumcído -ere -cídi -císum: (3);
circumcise
circumcíngo -ere -cínxi -cínctum: (3);
gird about
circumcísio -ónis: f.; circumcision
circumcursátio -ónis: f.; attention
circumdátio -ónis: f.; wearing, putting
on
circúmdo -áre -dedi -datum: (1); go
around, encompass, put around
circúmdolo -áre: (1); hew around with
an axe

circumdúco -ere -dúxi -dúctum: (3);
lead about

circúmeo: *see* circúeo

circumérro -áre: (1); wander round,
stroll about

circúmfero -férre -túli -látum: *irreg.;*
carry about, divulge

circumfluéntia -ae: f.; superabundance

circumfódio -ere -fódi -fóssum: (3); dig
a ditch or trench around

circumfúlgeo -ére -fúlsi -fúlsum: (2);
shine round about

circumgésto -áre: (1); carry around

circuminséssio -ónis: f.; coexistence; *see*
Appendix

circúmligo -áre: (1); bind up or around

circúmlino -ere: (3), circumlínio -íre:
(4); smear all over

circumornátus -a -um: adorned round
about, decorated around

circumpédes -um: m. pl.; footgear,
sandals

circumpléctor -plécti -pléxus: *dep.* (3);
clasp around, encircle, surround

circumpóno -ere -pósui -pósitum: (3);
place or put upon

circumquáque: all around

circumscríbo -ere -scripsi -scriptum:
(3); circumscribe, outline boundaries

circumscríptio -ónis: f.;
circumscription, encircling, outlining
boundaries

circumsédeo -ére -sédi -séssum: (2); sit
around

circumsépio -íre -si -tum: (4); surround,
enclose

circumsísto -ere -stéti: (3); surround

circumspéctio -ónis: f.; foresight,
caution, circumspection

circumspéctor -óris: m.; one who sees
everything, spy, watchman

circumspício -ere -spéxi -spéctum: (3);
look around, seek for, observe

circumstántia -ae: f.; detail,
circumstance, condition, state,
attribute; circumstántia -ium: n. pl.;
details, circumstances

circúmsto -stáre -stéti: (1); be present,
stand around

circúmtego -ere -téxi -téctum: (3); cover
around

circumvénio -íre -véni -véntum: (4);
approach, circumvent, overreach,
surround, evade, beset

circumvéntio -ónis: f.; encirclement,
defrauding, deceit

circumventórius -a -um: deceitful,
fradulent

circúmvolo -áre: (1); fly about

Císson (Císon, Kíshon): Kishon, a river
in northern Palestine

Cisterciénsis -is -e: of Citeaux,
Cistercian

cistérna -ae: f.; pit, ditch, cistern

cit.: *abbrev. for* citátus -a -um, *perf. pass.*
part. of cíto; cited, named

citátio -ónis: f.; citation, calling; *see*
Appendix

citatórius -a -um: relating to a citation;
as a n. noun: summoning before a
tribunal

citátus -a -um: swift, rapid, hurried,
urged, driven

cíto: quickly, speedily, soon

cíto -áre: (1); call, cite, summon, testify,
name

cíter -tra -trum: hither, on this side;
citérior -ior -ius: *comp.;* nearer, closer,
on this side, sooner, earlier

cíthara -ae: f.; harp, cither

citharízo -áre: (1); play the harp

citharoédus -i: m.; harpist

cítra: *adv. & prep. w. acc.;* on this side,
aside from, except, apart from, within,
beyond

cítrinus (cítreus) -a -um: citrus

cívicus -a -um, civílis -is -e: civil, civic;
civíliter: *adv.*
civílitas -átis: f.; citizenship
civilizátio -ónis: f.; civilization
cívis -is: c.; citizen
cívitas -átis: f.; city, state, citizenship
Civitátes Foederátae Américae
Septentrionális, *gen.* Civitátum
Foederátarum A. S.: f. pl.; United
States of America
cládes -is: f.; defeat, disaster
clam: secretly, privately; *prep. w. acc. or
abla.:* without the knowledge of
clámito -áre: (1); shout loudly
clámo -áre: (1); proclaim, shout, call, cry
out
clámor -óris: m.; a shout, cry, clamor
clamorósus -a -um: loud, clamorous
clandestínitas -átis: f.; secrecy
clandestínus -a -um: secret
clángo -ere: (3); to clang, shout
clángor -óris: m.; noise, shout, clang
Claravallénsis -is -e: of Clairvaux
clarésco -ere, clárui: (3); shine forth,
become clear, be visible
clarificátio -ónis: f.; glorification
clarífico -áre: (1); extol, praise, glorify
cláritas -átis: f.; clarity, light, brightness,
glory, renown
clárus -a -um: clear, well-known,
manifest, brilliant, famous, bright,
shining, evident; cláre: *adv.;* clára
vóce: in a clear voice, distinctly
clássicus -a -um: classic
clássis -is: f.; rank, order, class; fleet, navy
cláthri (clátri) -órum: m. pl., clátra
-órum: n. pl.; grate, lattice, grating
claúdico -áre: (1); limp, be lame
claúdo -ere, claúsi, claúsum: (3); close,
shut
claúdus -a -um: lame
claúsa -ae: f.; cell
claustrális -is -e: of the cloister
claústrum -i: n.; cloister, monastery

claúsula -ae: f.; end, conclusion;
sentence, section, clause
clausúra -ae: f.; cloister, enclosure
cláva -ae: f.; cudgel, mace, maul, club
clavícula -ae: f.; small key, bolt
claviculárius -ii: m.; key bearer
cláviger -eri: m.; key or mace bearer
clávis -is: f.; key
clávus -i: m.; nail
clémens -éntis: merciful, loving,
clement; cleménter: *adv.*
cleméntia -ae: f.; clemency, mercy
Cléophas -ae: m.; Cleophas, Klopas
clericális -is -e: clerical, priestly
clericátus -us: m.; clerical state
cléricus -i: m.; cleric, clerk
clérus -i: m.; clergy; assignment by lot
clíbanus -i: m.; oven, furnace
clíens -éntis: c.; client
clímacus -i: m.; three musical notes in
descending scale
clínicus -i: m.; physician, patient
confined to bed
clínsa -ae: f.; small handbell
clípeum -i: n., clípeus -i: m.; shield,
buckler
clívis -is: f.; two musical notes, the
second of which is lower than the first
clivósus -a -um: hilly, ridged, steep
clívus -i: m.; hill
cloáca -ae: f.; sewer, drain
clócca -ae: f.; bell
cloccárium -ii: n.; belfry, clock tower
Clodovéus -i: m.; Clovis
clúeo (clúo) -ére: (2); be named, be
called
Cluniacénsis -is -e: of Cluny
Cluníacum -i: n.; Cluny
clúsor -óris: m.; smith
clýpeum (clýpeus): *see* clípeum
Cnídus (Gnídus) -i: f.; Cnidus
coacérvo -áre: (1); heap up, collect

coácte: by restraint, constraint, or compulsion

coáctio -ónis: f., **coáctus** -us: m.; compulsion, coercion

coactívus -a -um: coercive

coáctus -a -um: *perf. pass. part. of* **cógo**

coadjúto -áre: (1); urge, help, assist

coadjútor -óris: m.; helper, assistant, coadjutor; *see Appendix*

coadjutória -ae: f.; assistantship, office of assistant

coadjútus -a -um: assisted, aided, helped; *as a noun:* one who has an assistant

coadunátio -ónis: f.; summary, a uniting into one, gathering, meeting

coadúno -áre: (1); unite, join together, meet

coaedífico -áre: (1); build together

coaequális -is -e: coequal

coaéquo -áre: (1); make equal, fill up, rank with

coaetáneus -a -um: equal, equal in age, contemporary

coaetérnus -a -um: coeternal

coaévus -i: m.; one equal in age, contemporary

coágito -áre: (1); shake together

coagménto -áre: (1); join together

coagulátus -a -um: curdled

coágulo -áre: (1); curdle

coalésco -ere -álui -álitum: (3); grow together, unite

coangústo -áre: (1); hem in, straiten, afflict

coapóstolus -i: m.; fellow apostle

coápto -áre: (1); fit, join, adjust together

coárcto -áre: (1); abbreviate, force, constrain, confine

coassístens -éntis: m.; coassistant

coccíneus -a -um: scarlet

cóccinum (cóccum) -i: n.; scarlet

cóchlea -ae: f.; screw; spiral; snail

cóchlear -áris: n.; spoon

cóctilis -is -e: cooked, baked, burned

coctória -ae: f.; kiln

cócus -i: m.; a cook

códex (caúdex) -icis: m.; code, code of laws, book, document, scroll, ledger; *see Appendix*

codificátus -a -um: codified, arranged

codicíllus -i: m.; appendix to will, codicil, brief written note

coe- *see also* **cae-** *or* **ce-**

coeléctus -a -um: elected together

coéles -itis: m.; saint

coeléstis (cae-) -is -e: heavenly, divine, celestial

Coeléstis aúlae jánua: Gate of Heaven

coelibátus (cae-) -us: m.; celibacy

coelícola (cae-) -ae: c.; dweller in heaven

coélicus -a -um: heavenly, celestial

coélitus: from heaven

coélum -i: n.; heaven

coemetérium -ii: n.; cemetery

coémo -ere -émi -émptum: (3); buy, purchase together

coéna: *see* **céna**

coenáculum -i: n.; dining room, refectory

coéno -áre: (1); have supper, dine

coenobiárcha -ae: m.; abbot

coenobíta -ae: m.; monk

coenobíticus -a -um: pertaining to monastic life, monastic

coenóbium -ii: n.; monastery, convent

coenomyía -ae: f.; common fly

cóeo -íre -ívi -itum: (4); meet, come together, have sexual intercourse

coepíscopus -i: m.; fellow bishop

coépi -ísse, coéptum: (3); *defect.;* begin

coéptum -i: n.; beginning, undertaking

coépulor -ari: *dep.* (1); feast together

coérceo -ére -cui -citum: (2); check, restrain, prune, enclose

coёrcítio -ónis: f.; coercion, restraint, compulsion, check coercitívus -a -um: compelling, coercing

coétus (coítio, coítus) -us: m.; a joining or meeting together, assembly, group; sexual union

Coétus coélicus ómnis: entire heavenly host

coexténdo -ere -téndi -ténsum(-téntum): (3); have the same extension or expansion

cogitátio -ónis: f.; thought, plan, design

cogitátum -i: n.; care; thought, reflection, idea

cogitátus -us: m., cogitaméntum -i: n.; counsel, thought

cógito -áre: (1); think, cogitate; take counsel, propose, purpose; reflect; see Appendix

cognáta -ae: f.; cousin

cognátio -ónis: f.; kindred, relationship, progeny, descendant

cognátus -i: m.; kinsman

cognítio -ónis: f.; knowledge, idea, investigation, trial

cógnitor -óris: m.; witness, knower

cognoméntum -i, cognómen -inis: n.; surname, family name

cognómino -áre: (1); to name

cognóminor -ári: dep. (1); be surnamed

cognoscíbilis -is -e: knowable

cognoscibílitas -átis: f.; ability to be known or understood

cognoscibíliter: knowingly, recognizably

cognoscitívus -a -um: aware, cognizant

cognósco -ere -nóvi -nitum: (3); get acquainted with, learn, perceive, recognize, learn by inquiry; adjudicate

cógo -ere, coégi, coáctum: (3); compel, force, lead, constrain

cohabitátio -ónis: f.; cohabitation, living together

cohábito -áre: (1); live with

cohaerénter: continuously, uninterruptedly

cohaeréntia -ae, cohaésio -ónis: f.; coherence, connection, cohering, cohesion

cohaéreo -ére -haési -haésum: (2); cleave to, hold together, cling, be consistent, remain, agree

cohaéres (cohéres) -édis: m.; coheir

cohaésio -ónis: see cohaeréntia

cohíbeo -ére -ui -itum: (2); hold together, restrain, confine, contain, hinder

cohibítio -ónis: f.; restraint

cóhors -tis: f.; cohort, guard, band

cohortátio -ónis: f.; exhortation

cohórtor -ári: dep. (1); encourage, exhort

coincído -cídere -cídi -císum: (3); coincide

coinquinátio -ónis: f.; a polluting, pollution

coínquino (cónquino) -áre: (1); defile

cointélligo -ere: (3); understand, presume

coítio -ónis: f.; see coétus

coítus: see coétus

cóla -ae: f.; strainer

cólaphus -i: m.; cuff, blow, strike

colatórium -ii: n.; strainer

coll- see also conl-

collábor -i -lápsus: dep. (3); fall, collapse

collaborátio -ónis: f.; collaboration, working together; see Appendix

collabóro -áre: (1); work together with, cooperate

collactáneus -i: m.; foster brother

collaétor -laetári -laetátus: dep. (1); rejoice together

colláre -is: n.; collar

collárium -ii: n.; Roman collar

collaterális -is -e: collateral

collátio -ónis: f.; meeting, gathering, assembly, conference; collection; discussion

collátor -óris: m.; collector

collátus -a -um: *perf. pass. part. of*
cónfero
collátus -us: m.; a conferring, a bringing
together
collaudátio -ónis: f.; praise
collaudátor -óris: m.; one who praises
collaúdo -áre: (1); praise very much,
praise together
collécta -ae: f.; collection, money
contribution; Collect at Mass
collectáneum -i: n.; book of Collects
collectárium -ii: n.; book of Collects
colléctio -ónis: f.; collection, summary
collectivísticus (collectívus) -a -um:
collective
colléctor -óris: m.; fellow student
colléctus -a -um: contracted, narrow,
shut; *perf. pass. part. of* cólligo -ere
colléga -ae: c.; companion, fellow
collegiális -is -e: collegial, acting
together; collegiáliter: *adv.; see*
Appendix
collegiáta -ae: f.; institution, collegiate
church
collegiátus -a -um; collegiate, corporate,
of a group
collégium -ii: n.; college, body of clergy,
company, society, school; *see Appendix*
Collégium Sácrum: college of cardinals
collído -ere -lísi -lísum: (3); cast down,
strike together, bruise, crush, clash
colligátio -ónis: f.; band
cólligo -ere -légi -léctum: (3); take in,
gather up, collect, contract, bring
together
cólligo -áre: (1); bind, tie, fasten
together, connect, unite
collíneo -áre: (1); direct in a straight
line, aim
collineáte: skillfully, artistically
collínus -a -um: hilly, on a hill
colliquefácio -ere -féci -fáctum: (3);
melt, dissolve, liquefy
colliquésco -ere -liqui: (3); melt

cóllis -is: m.; hill
collocátio -ónis: f.; disposition,
arrangement, erecting
cólloco -áre: (1); place, set, put up,
station, arrange, employ
collocútio -ónis: *see* collóquium
collocútor -óris: m.; one who talks with
another
collocutórium -ii: n.; parlor, visiting
room
collóquium -ii: n., collocútio -ónis: f.;
conversation, conference, discourse
cólloquor -qui -cútus(-quétus): *dep.* (3);
converse together, negotiate with
colluctátio -ónis: f.; struggle, struggling,
wrestling
collúceo -ére -ui -itum: (2); burn, shine
on all sides, be illuminated
collúctor -óris: m.; interlocutor
cóllum -i: n.; neck
collumnéla -ae: *see* columella
collúsio -ónis: f.; collusion
collúsor -óris: m.; playmate, companion
collústro -áre: (1); illuminate
collybísta -ae: m.; money changer
collýrida -ae: f.; cake, roll, pastry
collýrium -ii: n.; salve, paste
cólo -áre: (1); refine
cólo -ere, cólui, cúltum: (3); celebrate,
worship, honor; cultivate, till
colóbium -ii: n.; cowl-like habit or tunic
colocýnthis -idis: f.; cucumber, wild
gourd
cólon (cólum) -i: n., cólus -i: m.; colon,
intestine
colónia -ae: f.; city, colony
Colónia Agrippína: Cologne
Coloniénsis -is -e: of Cologne
colónus -i: m.; inhabitant, dweller
cólor -óris: m.; color
colorátus -a -um: colored
cóloro -áre: (1); color, give tone to, gloss
over
Colóssae -árum: f. pl.; Colossae

Colossénses -ium: c.; Colossians
Colossénsis -is -e: of Colossae
cólum -i: n.; strainer; colon, intestine
colúmba -ae: f.; dove, pigeon;
dove-shaped vessel for the Eucharist in
the early Church
columélla (collumnéla) -ae: f.; pillar,
small column
cólumen -inis: n., colúmna -ae: f.;
column, pillar
Colúmnae Flagellátio: the Scourging at
the Pillar
columnáris -is -e: in form of a pillar
cólus -i: see colon
cóma -ae: f.; hair, lock of hair
cómam nutríre: to allow hair or beard
to grow freely
cóma fictília: wig
cómans -ántis, comátus -a -um: having
long hair
combíno -áre: (1); unite, combine,
associate with, be joined with
combúro -ere -ússi -ústum: (3); burn,
consume
combústio -ónis: f.; burning
combustúra -ae: f.; burning
cómedo -ere -édi -ésum(-éstum): (3);
eat, devour, consume entirely
cómes -itis: c.; companion, associate,
count, earl, official
comessátio -ónis: f.; banquet, feasting,
reveling
comessátor -óris: m.; banqueter
comestábilis -is -e: eatable
coméstio -ónis: f.; eating, consumption
coméstor -óris: m.; eater
cóminus: in close combat
cómitas -átis: f.; kindness, gentleness
comitátus -a -um: accompanied,
attended
comitátus -us: m.; company, escort;
imperial count
comítia -órum: n. pl.; assembly, elections
comitíssa -ae: f.; countess

comítium -ii: n.; meeting
comitíva -ae: f.; escort, retinue
cómitor (cómito) -ári: dep. (1);
accompany, be together, follow
commáculo -áre: (1); stain, pollute
commártyr -is: c.; fellow martyr
commáter -tris: f.; godmother, female
sponsor
commemorátio -ónis: f.; remembrance,
commemoration, mention
Commemorátio ómnium Fidélium
Defunctórum: feast of All Souls
commemoratórium -ii: n.; list, record,
memorandum
commémoro -áre: (1); commemorate,
remember
comménda -ae: f.; a temporal income
without spiritual obligation
commendatárius (commendatítius) -a
-um: commendatory
commendátio -ónis: f.; recommendation
comméndo -áre: (1); commemorate,
commend, recommend
commensális -is: m.; table companion
commensúro -áre: (1); measure or make
equal, correspond
commentariénsis -is: m.; court clerk
commentárium -ii: n., commmentárius
-ii: m.; commentary, record,
publication
commentátor -óris: m.; commentator,
reporter
comméntum -i: n.; fiction, falsehood,
invention
commércium -ii: n.; action, transaction,
dealing, business, commerce,
correspondence
cómmigro -áre: (1); travel, go, migrate
commílito -ónis: m.; fellow soldier
comminátio -ónis: f.; threat, menace
comminíscor -minísci -méntum: dep.
(3); invent, contrive
comminíster -tri: m.; fellow minister

cómminor -ári: *dep.* (1); threaten, rebuke, charge

commínuo -ere -ui -útum: (3); break into small pieces

commisariátus -us: m.; commissioner, office of commissioner

commisárius (commiss-) -ii: m.; commissioner, trustee

commísceo -ére -míscui -míxtum(-místum): (2); mingle, lie with

commíseror -ári: *dep.* (1); to pity

commísio (commíss-) -ónis: f.; commission, committee

commissárius -ii: *see* commisárius

commissórius -a -um: commissorial

commissúra -ae: f.; patch, piece, coupling, joint

commístio -ónis: f.; mixture

commítto -ere -mísi -míssum: (3); commit, engage in, begin, entrust, undertake

commíxtio -ónis: f.; mingling, mixture, intermingling

commóditas -átis: f.; fitness, convenience, due measure, ease

cómmodo -áre: (1); lend, oblige, adapt

cómmodum -i: n.; blessing, favor, convenience

cómmodus -a -um: convenient, fit, polite; cómmode: *adv.*

commonefácio -ere: (3); strongly remind, impress, admonish

commóneo -ére -ui -itum: (2); admonish, remind, impress upon

commonítio -ónis: f.; warning, reminder

commorátio -ónis: f.; dwelling, habitation, residence

commórior -móri -mórtuus: *dep.* (3); die together with

cómmoror -ári: *dep.* (1); tarry, delay, stay, abide, dwell, remain

commóstro -áre: (1); show or demonstrate clearly

commótio -ónis: f.; commotion, disturbance, movement, agitation

commóveo -ére -móvi -mótum: (2); move, stir up, excite

communicábilis -is -e: communicable

communicátio -ónis: f.; sharing, communication, notification; *see* Appendix

communicátor -óris: m.; partaker

commúniceps -ipis: m.; fellow townsman

commúnico -áre: (1); partake, communicate, receive, share

commúnio -íre -ívi (-ii) -ítum: (4); fortify, make very secure

commúnio -ónis: f.; communion; commúnio láica: the lay state; *see* Appendix

commúnis -is -e: common, ordinary, general, public, commonplace; commúne -is: n.; that which is common; commúniter: together, in common, jointly, generally; commúnius: *comp. adv.;* in commúne: for all, for common use, goal or advantage; *see* Appendix

communitárius -a -um: community, with others, communal

commúnitas -átis: f.; commonwealth, community

commutátio -ónis: f.; change, exchange, barter, sale

commúto -áre: (1); change, substitute

cómo -ere, cómpsi, cómptum: (3); comb, adorn the hair

compáctio -ónis: f.; a joining together, uniting, frame

compáctus -a -um: compacted; *perf. pass. part. of* compíngo

compáges -is, compágo -inis: f.; joint, bodily structure, framework, outline

compágino -áre: (1); join together

cómpar -aris: c.; companion

cómpar -aris: like, equal, similar

comparátio -ónis: f.; comparison, preparation

compárco -ere -pársi -pársum: (3); save up, scrape together

compáreo -ére -ui: (2); appear, be present, be at hand

cómparo -áre: (1); prepare, make ready, buy, compare

cómpars -ártis: c.; partner

compárticeps -cipis: sharing jointly

compáter -tris: m.; sponsor

compátiens -éntis: having compassion

compátior compáti, compássus: *dep.* (3); suffer with

compatrónus -i: m.; fellow patron

compedítus -i: m.; captive, prisoner

compéllo -ere -púli -púlsum: (3); restrain, compel, oblige, subdue, overcome

compéllo -áre: (1); accost

compéndio -áre: (1); shorten, abridge

compenetrátio -ónis: f.; compenetration, uniting equally

compensátio -ónis: f.; compensation

compénso -áre: (1); compensate, balance, equalize

compérco -ere -pérsi: (3); save

comperendíno -áre: (1); defer a cause to the third day following or later

compério -íre -péri -pértum: (4); find, obtain certain knowledge

cómpes -edis: f.; shackle, foot fetter

compésco -ere -péscui: (3); restrain, withhold, fasten together

compéstror -ári: *dep.* (1); clothe in an apron

cómpetens -éntis: suitable, authorized, fit; **competénter:** *adv.*

competéntia -ae: f.; official qualification, competence

cómpeto -ere -ívi (-ii) -ítum: (3); to be capable of, be fit for, agree with, meet

compíngo -ere -pégi -páctum: (3); construct, furnish with, join together

cómpitum -i: n.; crossroads

compláceo -ére -ui -itum: (2); be acceptable to, please

complacítior -ior -ius: more favorable

complácitus -a -um: favorable, pleased

compláno -áre: (1); level, plane

complánto -áre: (1); plant together

compléctor -plécti -pléxus: *dep.* (3); surround, comprehend, embrace, encircle

complénda -ae: f.; Post-Communion

cómpleo -ére -plévi -plétum: (2); accomplish, fill, fulfill, end, finish

complétor -óris: m.; one who fills up

Completórium -ii: n.; Compline

cómplex, cómplicis: participating in; *as a c. noun:* accomplice

compléxio -ónis, **compléxitas** -átis: f.; combination, connection, association; dilemma, complexity

compléxo (compléxor) -áre: (1); embrace, join, combine

complícitas -átis: f.; complicity

cómplico -áre: (1); fold together

complódo -ere -plósi -plósum: (3); strike or beat together

complúres -es -a(-ia): several

compóno -ere -pósui -pósitum: (3); compose, reconcile, arrange, put together

compórto -áre: (1); bring together, collect, bring, lay up

cómpos -otis: sharing in, possessed of, master of, having control of; **súi cómpos:** of sound mind

compóstio -ónis: f.; arrangement, composition

compósitus -a -um: comely, well-arranged, orderly, decked out, ready

composséssor -óris: m.; joint possessor

compotátor -óris: m.; drinking companion

comprehéndo -ere -héndi -hénsum: (3); understand, comprehend; apprehend, obtain

comprehénsio -ónis: f.; comprehension, understanding, seizing

cómprimo -ere -préssi -préssum: (3); restrain, suppress, squeeze, keep down, press together

cómprobo -áre: (1); prove, approve, establish

compromissárius -a -um: pertaining to an arbitrator; *as a noun:* one elected by compromise

compromíssum -i: n.; compromise, reciprocal agreement

compromítto -ere -mísi -míssum: (3); promise mutually

comprovinciális -is -e: born in the same province

compúnctio -ónis: f.; sorrow, compunction, remorse, sorrow for sin

compúnctus -a -um: remorseful, struck in conscience, sorrowful

compúngo -ere -púnxi -púnctum: (3); feel remorse, grieve for, wound, puncture, sting; be conscience-struck

cómputo -áre: (1); reckon, count, compute

cómputus -i: m.; reckoning, calculation

conátus -a -um: *perf. part. of* cónor

conátus -us: m., conámen -inis: n.; attempt

concalefáctio -ónis: f.; warning

concalésco -ere -cálui: (3); burn, glow, glow hot, become warm

concaptívus -i: m.; fellow captive

cóncavus -a -um: hollow, arched, concave, vaulted, bent, curved; cóncava -órum: n. pl.; hollows, a glen

concédo -ere -céssi -céssum: (3); grant, concede, submit to

concelebrátio -ónis: f.; celebration, concelebration

concélebro -áre: (1); celebrate together, concelebrate

concéntus -us: m.; harmony, concord, agreement

concéptio -ónis: f., concéptus -us: m.; conception, concept

Concéptio Chrísti: feast of the Annunciation

Concéptio Immaculáta: Immaculate Conception of the B.V.M.

concéptus -a -um: *perf. pass. part. of* concípio; concéptus -us: m.; concept, thought, purpose

concérto (concertor) -áre: (1); strive eagerly

concéssio -ónis: f.; concession, permission

cóncha -ae: f.; shell, holy-water fount

conchuéla -ae: f.; font, small shell

cóncido -ere -cidi: (3); fall down, be disheartened

conci- *see also* conti-

concído -ere -cídi -císum: (3); cut to pieces, kill, cut down, strike down

conciliábulum -i: n.; marketplace; unlawful council

Concília Mártyrum: n. pl.; a burial place for martyrs

conciliáris -is -e: conciliar, of a council; *see Appendix*

conciliarísmus -i: m.; theory of conciliarism

conciliátio -ónis: f.; reconciliation, union

conciliátor -óris: m., conciliátrix -ícis: f.; conciliator, arbitrator, ambassador

concílio -áre: (1); win over, unite, make friendly, procure

concílium -ii: n.; council, assembly; *see Appendix*

concínno -áre: (1); fit together carefully, frame, weave, forge, contrive, prepare, order

concínnus -a um: elegant, polished

cóncino -ere -cínui -céntum: (3); sing, celebrate in song

cóncio -ónis: f.; sermon; gathering, assembly

concionátor -óris: m.; preacher; haranguer

concionatórius -a -um: of a sermon; of a gathering of people

conciónor (conti-) -ári: *dep.* (1); preach, deliver an address; harangue

concípio -ere -cépi -céptum: (3); conceive; comprehend

cóncito -áre: (1); arouse, excite

conciúcula -ae: f.; short sermon, brief address

concívis -is: c.; fellow citizen

concláve -is: n.; room, room that may be locked, chamber

conclavísta -ae: m.; cardinal in a conclave

conclúdo -ere -clúsi -clúsum: (3); enclose, shut in, conclude

conclúsio -ónis: f.; ending, termination, closing, conclusion

concólor -óris: of the same color

concomitántia -ae: f.; association

concómitor -ári: *dep.* (1); attend, accompany

concordántia -ae: f.; concordance, agreement

concordátio -ónis: f.; reconciliation, agreement

concordátum -i: n.; concordat; **concordáta** -órum: n. pl.; things agreed upon; *see Appendix*

concórdia -ae: f.; union, peace, harmony, concord

concórdo -áre: (1); agree, be of one mind

concorporális -is -e: of the same body or company

concorporátus -a -um: united in one body

concorpóreus -a -um: of one body with

cóncors -córdis: harmonious, of one mind; **concórditer:** adv.

concreátus -a -um: created together

concrédo -ere -didi -itum: (3); entrust, consign, commit

cóncreo -áre: (1); create together

cóncremo -áre: (1); burn up, consume

cóncrepo -áre -pui -crépitum: (1); sound, resound, rattle

concrésco -ere -crévi -crétum: (3); grow together, unite; harden, stiffen, congeal, thicken, dry up; increase

concubína -ae: f., **concubínus** -i: m.; concubine

concubinárius -a -um: of or relating to concubines; *as a noun:* keeper of concubines

concubinátus -us: m.; adulterous intercourse, concubinage

concúbitor -óris: m.; bedfellow

concúbitus -us: m., **concubítio** -ónis: f.; cohabitation, coitus

concúlco -áre: (1); tread, trample

concúmbo -ere -cúbui -cúbitum: (3); to lie with

concupiscéntia -ae: f.; concupiscence, yearning of lower appetites, inordinate desire

concupiscíbilis -is -e: valuable, very desirable

concupiscitívus -a -um: passionately desiring

concupísco -ere -cupívi -pitum: (3); be desirous of, covet, long for

concúpitor -óris: m.; one who covets, coveter

concurréntia -ae: f.; concurrence, mutual participation

concúrro -ere, -cúrri, -cúrsum: (3); assemble, join, concur, collaborate; happen, meet, run together; compete

concúrsus -us: m., **concúrsio** -ónis: f.; concurrence, coinciding, assembly, combination; competitive exam; attack, competition

concútio -ere -cússi cússum: (3); strike, cause to tremble, alarm

condécoro -áre: (1); decorate

condeléctor -ári: *dep.* (1); be delighted with

condemnátio -ónis: f.; sentence, condemnation

condemnatórius -a -um: condemnatory

condémno -áre: (1); condemn

condénsum -i: n.; thicket; condénsa -órum: n. pl.; woods, leafy boughs

condénsus -a -um: leafy, thickly covered

condescéndo -ere -scéndi -scénsum: (3); condescend, descend

condício (condítio) -ónis: f.; condition, agreement, compact, stipulation, proposition, terms

condíco -ere -díxi díctum: (3); agree upon, talk over; arrange, appoint

condíctum -i: n.; arrangement, agreement

condígnus -a -um: worthy to be compared with, very deserving

condiméntum -i: n.; seasoning, spice

cóndio -íre -ívi -ítum: (4); preserve, season, embalm

condiscípulus -i: m.: fellow disciple

condísco -ere: (3); learn with, learn thoroughly

condítio -ónis: f.; condition, stipulation, a work, nature; *see also* condício

conditionátus -a -um: conditional, conditioned; conditióne: *adv.*

cónditor -óris: m.; founder, creator, author

conditórium -ii: n.; storeroom

cóndo -ere -didi -ditum: (3); found, establish, form, fashion, produce, preserve, bury

condóctor -óris: m.; fellow teacher

condolésco -ere -dólui: (3); have compassion; feel pain, suffer severely, ache

condóleo -ére -dólui: (2); suffer greatly, suffer with another, have compassion

condóminus -i: m.; co-owner, one who shares dominion

condonátio -ónis: f.; donation, gift

condonátus -i: m.; lay brother, oblate

condóno -áre: (1); pardon, condone, remit

condúco -ere -dúxi -dúctum: (3); hire, lead, conduct

condúctio -ónis: f.; bringing together, uniting, hiring

conductítius -a -um: hired, mercenary

condúctor -óris: m.; contractor, employer, conductor

condúctum -i: n.; rented house, dwelling place

Condúctus Páschae: Low Sunday

condúlco -áre: (1); sweeten

conécto -ere -xui(-xi) -xum: (3); join, connect

conéxio (conn-) -ónis: f.; connection, close union

confábulor -ári: *dep.* (1); talk

conféctio -ónis: f.; making, producing, confection

confércio -íre -férsi -fértum: (4); cram together

conferéntia -ae: f.; conference, meeting, gathering; *see Appendix*

cónfero -érre -tuli, collátum: *irreg.*; grant, confer, bring together, collect, compare; se conférre: take oneself toward

confessárius -ii: m.; confessor

conféssio -ónis: f.; confession, acknowledgment, profession of faith, sacrament of reconciliation; *see Appendix*

confessionále -is: n., confessionális -is: f.; confessional

confessionális -is -e: of confession

conféssor -óris: m.; confessor, martyr

conféstim: immediately, at once

confício -ere -féci -féctum: (3); complete, make thoroughly; destroy

confíctus -a -um: forged

confidélis -is: c.; fellow believer

confidénter: confidently

confidéntia -ae: f.; confidence

confído -ere -físus: *semidep.* (3); trust, confide, hope, be of good heart

confígo -ere -fíxi -fíxum: (3); nail, fasten, fix in

configurátus -a -um: made like, conformable, fashioned

configúro -áre: (1); fashion, form, shape; reflect

confíngo -ere -xi -fíctum: (3); invent, devise

confirmándus -i: m., confirmánda -ae: f.: candidate for confirmation

confirmátio -ónis: f.; confirmation, sacrament of confirmation

confírmo -áre: (1); strengthen, confirm, uphold

confíteor -éri -féssus: *dep.* (2); confess, praise, acknowledge

Confíteor: a prayer admitting guilt and seeking pardon

cónflans -ántis: refining, purifying

conflátilis -is -e: molten; *as a n. noun*: molton image

conflátor -óris: m.; metal caster

conflatórium -ii: n.; furnace, crucible

conflictátio -ónis: f.; dispute, conflict

conflícto -áre: (1); contend with, struggle with

conflíctus -us: m.; conflict, discussion

conflígo -ere -flíxi -flíctum: (3); strive, endeavor, conflict

cónflo -áre: (1); forge, melt, weld, refine, enflame, bring about

conflóreo -ére -ui: (2); bloom or flourish together

cónfluo -ere -flúxi: (3); flow together, resort

confódio -ere -fódi -fóssum: (3); stab, pierce

confoederátio -ónis: f.; union, confederation

confoédero -áre: (1); bind together, conform

conformátio -ónis: f.; formation, shaping, forming, fashioning

confórmis (conformális) -is -e: similar, like, agreeing with

confórmitas -átis: f.; conformity, agreement

confórmo -áre: (1); form, fashion, shape, conform, educate

confortátio -ónis: f.; comfort, consolation, solace

confórto -áre: (1); strengthen, encourage

confórtor -ári: *dep.* (1); wax strong, take courage

confóveo -ére -fóvi -fótum: (2); support, promote, care for

confráctio -ónis: f.; breaking, breach, gap

confractórium -ii: n.; prayer at end of Canon in Ambrosian rite

confráter -tris: m.; brother, confrere, guild brother

confratérnitas -átis: f.; sodality, confraternity, association

confrátria -ae: f.; sodality

confricátio -ónis: f.; rubbing together, friction

cónfrico -áre: (1); rub together

cónfrigo -ere -fríxi -fríctum: (3); burn up

confríngo -ere -frégi -fráctum: (3); break into pieces, shatter, burst

confrónto -áre: (1); confront

confúgio -ere -fúgi: (3); flee, take refuge

confúndo -ere -fúdi -fúsum: (3); put to shame, confound, confuse, disturb

confúsio -ónis: f., confusionísmus -i: m.; confusion, shame

confúsus -a -um: confused, disordered, shamed; confúse: *adv.*

confúto -áre: (1); confute, check, overthrow, silence

congaúdeo -ére -gavísus: *semidep.* (2); rejoice with

congelátus -a -um: frozen
congemísco -ere: (3); sigh deeply
cóngener -eris: kindred, of same race
cóngero -ere -géssi -géstum: (3); heap up, collect, construct
conglobátim: in heaps, in a mass
conglobátio -ónis: f.; heaping or crowding together
conglorífico -áre: (1); glorify with others
congloríficor -ári: dep. (1); be glorified with
conglútino (conglútinor) -áre: (1); bind together, cleave to
congrátulor -ári: dep. (1); rejoice with, congratulate
congregátio -ónis: f.; congregation, gathering, company, assembly, community bound by a common rule; see Appendix
cóngrego -áre: (1); gather together, assemble, congregate
congréssio -ónis: f., congréssus -us: m.; meeting, congress
cóngrua -ae: f.; salary of a pastor
cóngruens -éntis, cóngruus -a -um: proper, seasonable, suitable, apt, fitting, agreeable, becoming; cóngrue, congruénter: adv.; see Appendix
cóngruo -ere -ui: (3); agree with, run together, correspond with
congýro -áre: (1); surround
conjectúra -ae: f.; guess, conjecture
conjício -ere -jéci -jéctum: (3); conjecture, guess, interpret, conclude, infer
conjucúndor -ári: dep. (1); rejoice with or together
conjugális -is -e: conjugal, marital
conjugátus -a -um: married
conjugicídium -ii: n.; murder of one's spouse
conjúgium -ii: n.; union, connection, marriage, wedlock
cónjugo -áre: (1); unite in marriage

conjúnctim (conjúncte): jointly, together, in common, in unity
conjúnctio -ónis: f.; union, joining together, conjunction
conjúngo -ere -júnxi -júnctum: (3); join, bind together, unite, have affinity with
cónjunx -júgis: c.; spouse, husband, wife
conl- see also coll-
conlactáneus -i: m.; foster brother
conlísio (collísio) -ónis: f.; concussion, shock, striking together
conm- see comm-
connaturáliter: in a natural way
connécto -ere -néxui -néxum: (3); unite, fasten, join together
connéxio -ónis: f.; connection, relation; see also conexio
conníveo -ére -nívi (níxi): (2); wink, blink, become drowsy
connúbium (conu-) -ii: n.; matrimony
connúmero -áre: (1); number with, reckon among
conopaéum (conopéum) -i: n.; canopy
cónor -ári: dep. (1); try, endeavor, attempt
conp- see comp-
conquádro -áre: (1); to cut square
conquásso -áre: (1); crush, shake
cónqueror -eri -quéstum: dep. (3); complain, bewail
conquiésco -ere -quiévi -quiétum: (3); to rest
cónquino: see coínquino
conquíro -ere -quisívi -quisítum: (3); seek carefully
conquisítio -ónis: f.; discussion, dispute
conquisítor (conquístor) -óris: m.; disputer, debater
conr- see also corr-
conrégno -áre: (1); reign with
conresúscito -áre: (1); raise up together with
consalúto -áre: (1); salute one another

consanguíneus -a -um: related by blood; *as a m. noun:* cousin, male blood relative; *as a f. noun:* cousin, female blood relative; *as a pl. noun:* kindred, relations

consanguínitas -átis: f.; blood relationship, consanguinity; *see Appendix*

conscéndo -ere -scéndi -scénsum: (3); ascend, mount, climb

conscénsus -us: m.; an ascending, mounting

cónscia -ae: f., cónscius -i: m.; witness, participant, accomplice

consciéntia -ae: f.; conscience, consciousness, acknowledgment

conscíndo -ere -scídi -scíssum: (3); rend, tear, split

cónscius -a -um: conscious, knowing; cónscie: *adv.*

conscríbo -ere: (3); enroll, elect, transcribe, commit to writing, inscribe

consecrátio -ónis: f.; consecration

consecrátor -óris: m.; consecrator

consecratórius -a -um: consecratory

cónsecro -áre: (1); consecrate, hallow, sanctify

consectárius -a -um: following, consequent; *as a n. noun:* conclusion, inference, result

consecútio -ónis: f.; attainment, pursuit, consequence, effect

consédo -ere -sédi -séssum: (3); sit, sit with

consénior -óris: m.; fellow elder

consénsus -us: m., consénsio -ónis: f.; agreement, concord; *see Appendix*

consentáneus -a -um: fit, suitable

conséntio -íre -sénsi -sénsum: (4); consent, agree

consepélio -íre -sepelívi (-ii) -sepúltum: (4); bury with

consequénter: consequently, subsequently

cónsequor -i -secútus: *dep.* (3); obtain, follow, pursue

cónsero -ere -sévi -situm(-satum): (3); sow or plant with something

conservátio -ónis: f.; conservation, keeping, preserving

consérvo -áre: (1); preserve, keep, save, protect, keep untouched

consérvus -i: m., consérva -ae: f.; fellow servant

conséssus -us: m.; assembly, a sitting together

consideráte: considerately

considerátio -ónis: f.; consideration, contemplation, reflection

consídero -áre: (1); consider, look, regard, contemplate

consído -sídere -sídi -séssum: (3); sit down together, hold council

consignatórium -ii: n.; a room in which confirmation was administered

consígno -áre: (1); sign with, record, seal, certify

consiliárius -ii: m.; advisor, judge, counselor

consílior -ári: *dep.* (1); plan, take counsel, meditate, figure out, consult

consílium -ii: n.; counsel, plan, deliberation, advice, council, consultation

consímilis -is -e: like, similar

Consisténtes -ium: m. pl.; a class of penitents in the early Church

consísto -ere -stiti: (3); stand together, stand firmly, continue, become set

consistoriális -is -e: pertaining to a consistory

consistórium -ii: n.; consistory

consobrínus -i: m., consobrína -ae: f.; cousin

consociátio -ónis: f.; association

consócio -áre: (1); associate with, share

consolátio -ónis: f.; consolation, comfort

consolátor -óris: m.; comforter

consólido -áre: (1); strengthen

consólo -áre: (1); console

consólor -ári: *dep.* (1); comfort, console, encourage

cónsonus -a -um: harmonious, consonant

cónsors -sórtis: partaking, having a common lot, sharing

cónsors -sórtis: c.; sharer, partaker, consort

consórtium -ii: n., consórtio -ónis: f.; company, partnership, union, fellowship, community; *see Appendix*

conspársio: *see* conspérsio

conspéctor -óris: m.; spectator, inspector

conspéctus -us: m.; sight, survey, view, look, presence

conspérgo -ere -spérsi -spérsum: (3); strew, sprinkle, moisten, spatter

conspérsio (conspársio) -ónis: f.; sprinkling, dough, paste

conspicíllium -ii: n.; a place to look from, eyeglass

conspício -ere -spéxi -spéctum: (3); see, look at intently, consider, perceive

conspícuus -a -um: visible, conspicuous, striking, remarkable

conspirátio -ónis: f.: agreement, common opinion, a working together, conspiracy

conspíro -áre: (1); agree, unite, act in harmony, conspire

cónspuo -ere -spui -spútum: (3); spit at or upon

constabílio -íre: (4); make firm, confirm, establish

cónstans -ántis: steady, firm, constant; constánter: *adv.*

constántia -ae: f.; firmness, constancy

Constantiniánus -a -um: of Constantine

Constantinópolis -is: f.; Constantinople

Constantinopolitánus -a -um: of Constantinople

Constantínus -i: m.; Constantine

constellátio -ónis: f.; constellation

consternátus -a -um: in consternation

constítuo -ere -ui -útum: (3); set, determine, make, appoint, constitute, establish, arrange

constitútio -ónis: f.; constitution, establishment, foundation, structure, determination, order; *see Appendix*

constitutívus -a -um: determining, constituent, component

constitútus -a -um: placed, situated; *as a n. noun:* institution, law, agreement

cónsto -áre -stiti -státum: (1); exist, consist, stand firm, stand with; *see Appendix*

constríngo -ere -strínxi -stríctum: (3); bind fast, restrain

constrúctio -ónis: f.; an erecting, building, joining, construction

cónstruo -ere -strúxi -strúctum: (3); build, frame together

constúpro -áre: (1); to corrupt

consubstantiális -is -e, consubstantívus -a -um: being of one substance with, consubstantial

consúdo -áre: (1); sweat much

consuefácio -ere -féci: (3); make accustomed, to accustom

consuésco -ere -suévi -suétum: (3); to be accustomed, to be wont

consuetúdo -inis: f.; custom, interchange, intimacy; *see Appendix*

consuétus -a -um: accustomed, usual, customary

cónsul -ulis: m.; consul

cónsulo -ere -súlui -súltum: (3); consult, consider, ponder, reflect, weigh seriously, deliberate, take counsel

consultátio -ónis: f.; consultation

consúltius: more wisely

consultívus -a -um: consultative

consúlto -áre: (1); weigh, ponder, consider maturely, deliberate

consúltor -óris: m.; counselor, consultor, adviser

consúltum -i: n., consúltus -us: m.; resolution, decree

consummátio -ónis: f.; consummation, a perfecting, end of the world, summary

consummátor -óris: m.; finisher

Consummátum est: it is finished

consúmmo -áre: (1), **consúmo** -ere -súmpsi -súmptum: (3); consume, finish, end, complete, consummate, perfect

consúmptio -ónis: f.; complete destruction, consumption, wasting

cónsuo -ere -sui -sútum: (3); sew or stitch together

consúrgo -ere -surréxi -surréctum: (3); stand up, rise up, rise with

contabésco -ere -tábui: (3); pine or waste away

contáctus -a -um: *perf. pass. part. of* **contíngo**

contáctus -us: m.; touch, contact

contagiósus -a -um: contagious

contágium -ii: n., **contágio** -ónis: f.; contagion, negative influence; touch; temptation

contaminátio -ónis: f.; contamination

contámino -áre: (1); defile, contaminate

cóntego -ere -téxi -téctum: (3); cover, envelop

contémno -áre: (1); despise, disdain, defy, disregard

contémno -ere -témpsi -témptum: (3); despise, slight

contémpero -áre: (1); infuse, mix, conform, adopt

contemplátio -ónis: f.; contemplation

contemplatívus -a -um: contemplative

contemplátor -óris: m.; contemplator

contémplo -áre: (1); contemplate, ponder

contémplor -ári: *dep.* (1); consider carefully, regard

contemptíbilis -is -e: contemptible

contémptio -ónis: f.; contempt

contémptor -óris: m.; despiser

contémptus -a -um: despised, contemptible

contémptus -us: m.; contempt, scorn, disdain

conténdo -ere -téndi -téntum: (3); strive, strain, assert, maintain, try, contend

contenébro -áre: (1); darken, obscure

conténtio -ónis: f.; obstinacy, contention, strife, quarrel, wrangling

contentiósus -a -um: contentious, rebellious; **contentióse:** *adv.*

conténtus -a -um: content, satisfied; *perf. pass. part. of* **contíneo** *or* **conténdo**

contérnans -ántis: three years of age

cóntero -ere -trívi -trítum: (3); crush, break to pieces, grind, bruise

contérritus -a -um: frightened

contestátio -ónis: f.; an attesting, testimony; former name for Preface of the Mass; *see Appendix*

contéstis -is: c.; co-witness

contéstor -ári: *dep.* (1); testify, bear witness, initiate a lawsuit

contéxo -ere -xui -xtum: (3); weave, entwine, braid, join together

contéxtus -us: m.; context, connection, joining, coherence

conti- *see also* **conci-**

conticésco -ere -tícui: (3); be silent

contignátio -ónis: f.; woodwork

contíguus -a -um: near, contiguous

continátor (contionátor) -óris: *see* **concionátor**

cóntinens -éntis: adjacent, contiguous; continual, consecutive, uninterrupted; moderate; continent; **continénter:** *adv.*

cóntinens -éntis: n.; hinge, joint

continéntia -ae: f.; abstinence, restraint, self-denial

continéntia -iórum: n. pl.; adjoining places, neighborhood, continent

contíneo -ére -tínui -téntum: (2); keep or bind together, possess, contain, confine, hold in check, restrain

contíngo (contínguo) -ere -tigi -táctum: (3); touch, belong to, affect, happen, reach to, border upon

continnátus -a -um: continual

continuátio -ónis, continúitas -átis: f.; continuation, succession, connected series

contínuo -áre: (1); continue, last

contínuus -a -um: continual, infinite, joined; contínuo: adv.

cóntio -ónis: f.; sermon, gathering

contiónor: see conciónor

contituláris -is -e: titular

contórqueo -ére -tórsi -tórtum: (2); twist, wind about, contort, turn

cóntra: adv. & prep. w. acc.; against, before, opposite; see Appendix

cóntra aútem: but on the other hand

cóntra haec: in answer to this

cóntra jus, cóntra légem: against the law

e cóntra: on the contrary

haec cóntra: this in reply

contráctus -us: m.; bargain, contract, agreement

contradíco -ere -díxi -díctum: (3); contradict, contend with, oppose, resist, thwart, object to

contradíctio -ónis: f.; reply, contradiction, counterargument

contradíctor -óris: m.; opponent

contradictórium -ii: n; a speaking against, defense; see Appendix

contráeo -íre -ívi -itum: (4); go against

cóntraho -ere -tráxi -tráctum: (3); contract, commit, collect, draw in

contrapúncticus -a -um: pertaining to a counterpoint

contrapúnctum -i: n.; counterpoint

contraríetas -átis: f.; opposition, contrariety

contrárium -ii: n.; the reverse, the opposite

contrárius -a -um: opposite, contrary, lying over against; as a n. noun: the opposite or reverse; e contrário: on the contrary

contrécto -áre: (1); to handle

contremísco -ere -trémui: (3); tremble

cóntremo -ere -ui: (3); tremble

contribulátus -a -um: troubled

contríbulis -is: m.; tribesman

contríbulo -áre: (1); crush, shatter

contríbuo -ere -tríbui -bútum: (3); help, contribute, unite, add

contribútum -i: n.; contribution

contrísto -áre: (1); make sad

contrítio -ónis: f.; grief, sorrow, contrition

contrítus -a -um: contrite, sorrowful

controvérsia -ae: f.; controversy, contention, dispute

controvérsus -a -um: disputed, controverted

controvérto -ere -ti -sum: (3); deny, oppose, voice opposition

contubérnium -ii: n.; domicile, habitation; togetherness, intimacy, comradeship, tent-mate

contúeor -éri -túitus: dep. (2); look at attentively, consider

contúitus -us: m.; mental contemplation

contumácia -ae: f.; insolence, stubbornness, obstinacy, refusal to obey, contumacy

cóntumax -ácis: stubborn, obstinate; contumáciter: adv.

contumélia -ae: f.; outrage, insult, contumely

contumélio -áre: (1); abuse, insult

contumeliósus -a -um: contumelious

contúndo -ere -túdi -túsum: (3); beat, bruise, subdue

conturbátio -ónis: f.; trouble

contúrbo -áre: (1); disturb, trouble, disquiet, vex, confuse

contútor -ári: dep. (1); keep safe

conúbium -ii: n.; marriage

conúmero -áre: (1); number among

conváleo -ére -válui: (2); regain health, recover strength, get well

convalésco -ere -válui: (3); gain strength, convalesce

convalidátio -ónis: f.; convalidation; see Appendix

conválido -áre: (1); validate, make valid

convállis -is: f.; valley

convéllo -ere -vélli -vúlsum: (3); pluck, tear up

convéniens -éntis: agreeing, coming together, uniting

conveniénter: suitably, duly

conveniéntia -ae: f.; agreement

convénio -íre -véni -véntum: (4); agree, assemble, summon, combine, be convenient or suitable, unite

conventículum -i: n.; assembly, meeting, gathering

convéntio -ónis: f.; agreement, concord, compact, convention; assembly, meeting

conventionális -is -e: of an agreement or compact, conventional

Conventuális -is: c.; Conventual Franciscan

conventuális -is -e: conventual, pertaining to a convent or monastery

convéntus -a -um: perf. pass. part. of convénio

convéntus -i: m.; respondent

convéntus -us: m.; assembly, meeting, convention; religious community; convent; see Appendix

conversátio -ónis: f.; conversation; conduct, manner of living

convérsio -ónis: f.; moral change, conversion

convérso: to the contrary, on the other hand, in a contrary manner

convérso -áre: (1); turn around, turn, change

convérsor -ári: dep. (1); dwell, live, keep company with, abide

convérsus -i: m., convérsa -ae: f.; one who has changed, convert

convérto (convértor) -ere -vérti -vérsum: (3); change, convert, alter, refresh, turn

convéscor -vésci: dep. (3); eat with

convicánus -i: m.; fellow villager

convícior: see convítior

convícium -ii: n.; insult, reproach

convíctio -ónis: f.; proof, demonstration

convíctus -us: m.; living, manner of life, social life, living together, feast

convínco -ere -víci -víctum: (3); convict, convince, prove to

convítior (convícior) -ári: dep. (1); revile, reproach, insult

convivántes -ium: m. pl.; banqueters

convivéntia -ae: f.; living and working together, cooperation

convivífico -áre: (1); quicken together, restore to life

convívium -ii: n.; banquet

convívor (convívo) -ári: dep. (1); feast with, eat

convocátio -ónis: f.; assembly, convocation

cónvoco -áre: (1); call together

convólvo -ere -vólvi -volútum: (3); roll up

coodíbilis -is -e: exceedingly hateful

cooperátio -ónis: f.; cooperation, help for one another

cooperatívus -a -um: cooperative

cooperátor -óris: m., cooperátrix -ícis: f.; fellow helper, assistant, coworker

coopérior (coopério) -íre -pértus: dep. (4); clothe, cover, overwhelm

coóperor (coópero) -ári: dep. (1); work with, cooperate

coopertórium -ii: n.; a cover

cooptátio -ónis: f.; a joining, admission to a society or order

coópto -áre: (1); elect; make fit, form, join together, get ready

coordinátio -ónis: f.; coordination, arranging together

coórdino -áre: (1); coordinate, work together

cóphinus -i: m.; basket

cópia -ae: f.; plenty, abundance; supplies, wealth, resources, store, riches

copiátes -ae: m.; sexton, gravedigger

copiósitas -átis: f.; abundance

copiósus -a -um: copious, plentiful, in great numbers; copióse: abundantly, plentifully

Cópta -ae: m.; Copt, an Egyptian Christian

Cópticus -a -um: Coptic, of the Coptic rite

cópula -ae: f.; union, bond

cópulo -áre: (1); join together, bless in marriage, join in marriage

cópulor -ári: dep. (1); embrace, be united with

cóquo -ere, cóxi -cóctum: (3); cook, bake, boil

cor, cordis: n.; heart; innermost part, mind

córam: adv. & prep. w. abla.; in person, personally, openly, publicly, in the presence of, before, face to face; see Appendix

córam epíscopo: in the presence of the bishop

córam Sacratíssimo: in the presence of the Blessed Sacrament

corbán: Hebrew; corban, gift

corbóna (corbána) -ae: f.; treasury

cordíger -era -erum: wearing a cord

Córe: indecl.; Core, descendant of Levi

coriárius -ii: m.; a tanner

Corínthii -órum: m. pl.; Corinthians

Corínthus -i: m.; Corinth

córium -ii: n.; hide

córneus -a -um: made of horn

cornícula -ae: f.; little crow

corniculárius -ii: m.; trumpeter

córnix -ícis: f.; crow

córnu -us: n.; horn; mountain peak; side of altar; symbol of strength

cornucópia -ae: f.; emblem of abundance

cornucópium -ii: n.; bracket for holding candles, sconce

cornúpeta -ae: f.; act of goring with horns

cornútus -a -um: horned

corollárium -ii: n.; corollary

coróna -aé: f.; crown, wreath, rosary, tonsure, eternal reward

coronátio -ónis: f.; coronation

coronátor -óris: m.; crowner

corónis -idis: f.; cornice; line or flourish marking the end

coróno -áre: (1); to crown

corónula -ae.; f.; ornament on a miter; rim of a laver

corporále -is: n.; corporal

corporális -is -e, corpóreus (corpuléntus) -a -um: pertaining to the body, corporeal, physical, bodily; corporáliter: adv.

corpuléntia -ae: f.; density, corporeity, corpulence, grossness of body

córpus -oris: n.; body; see Appendix

Córpus Chrísti: feast in honor of the Body of Christ

Córpus Mýsticum: Mystical Body, the Church

córpus delícti: body of the crime, part or substance necessary to prove crime was committed

corpúsculum -i: n.; small body

corr- *see also* conr-

corréctio -ónis: f.; correction, chastisement, amendment

corréptio -ónis: f.; rebuke, reproach

correspóndeo -ére: (2); respond or answer strongly

córreus -i: m.; co-criminal, joint criminal

corrígia -ae: f.; latchet, shoe lace

córrigo -ere -réxi -réctum: (3); establish; correct, reform, amend

corrípio -ere -rípui -réptum: (3); reproach, reprove; seize, rob, plunder, usurp

corróboro -áre: (1); strengthen, back up

corrogátio -ónis: f.; contribution, assembly, gathering

corrósio -ónis: f.; gnawing

corrúmpo -ere -rúpi -rúptum: (3); corrupt, pervert, spoil, break to pieces

córruo -ere -rui: (3); fall to the ground, sink down, be ruined

corruptéla (-télla) -ae, corrúptio -ónis: f.; bribery, evil, seduction, corruption, seducer

corruptíbilis -is -e, corruptívus (corruptórius) -a -um: corruptible, perishable

corruptibílitas -átis: f.; corruptibility

Córsica -ae: f.; Corsica

cortína -ae: f.; curtain; caldron, kettle

córus -i: m.; measure, bushel

Córus (Caúrus) -i: m.; Corus, Caurus, the northwest wind

coruscámen -inis: n.; splendor

coruscátio -ónis: f.; lightning, flash

corúsco -áre: (1); shine, glitter

corúscus -i: m.; lightning

córvus -i: m.; raven

cósta -ae: f.; rib, side

cóstula -ae: f.; rib

cotidiánus -a -um: daily; cotídie (quotídie): *adv.;* daily

cótta -ae: f.; surplice

cotúrnix -ícis: f.; quail

coútor, coúti, coúsus: *dep.* (3); communicate or deal with

crápula -ae: f.; drunkenness

crapulátus -a -um: overindulged, inebriated, surfeited

cras: tomorrow

crassíties -éi: f.; thickness, fatness

crassitúdo -inis: f.; thickness, fatness, density, sediment, clod

crássus -a -um: thick, fat, dense, dull, stupid

crástinus -a -um: relating to tomorrow

crástina díe: tomorrow

díes crástina: the following day

in crástinum: on the next day

cráter -eris: m.; bowl

cratícula -ae: f.; grating, gridiron

crátis -is: f.; grating, gridiron, screen

creábilis -is -e: able to be created

creágra -ae: f.; fleshhook, hook, fork

creátio -ónis: f.; creation

creatívus -a -um: creative

creátor -óris: m., creátrix -ícis: f.; creator, maker, producer

creatúra -ae: f.; creature

créber -bra -brum: thick, close, pressed together, frequent, numerous, abundant, repeated; crébre, crébro: *adv.*

crebrésco -ere, crébui: (3); become frequent, grow strong, repeat often, increase, spread

crédens -éntis: c.; believer; pl.: the faithful

credéntia -ae: f.; credence, small table in sanctuary for vessels

credentárius -ii: m.; server

credíbilis -is -e: trustworthy

credibílitas -átis: f.; credibility

créditor -óris: m.; creditor

créditus -a -um: entrusted; *as a n. noun:* credit, loan

crédo -ere -didi -ditum: (3); believe, trust

Crédo: a prayer as a profession of faith; part of the Mass

credúlitas -átis: f.; belief, faith, credulity, gullibility

cremátio -ónis: f.; cremation

cremátor -óris: m.; burner, cremator

crémium -ii: n.; fuel, firewood, dry fuel, tinder

crémo -áre: (1); burn, cremate, consume by fire

créo -áre: (1); create, produce, bring forth

crepído -inis: f.; foot, base, foundation

crepitáculum -i: n.; clapper, rattle

crépito -áre: (1); crack, crackle, crash

crépitus -us: m.; explosion

crépo -áre -ui -itum: (1); crack, burst asunder, resound

crepúsculum -i: n.; twilight, dusk

crésco -ere, crévi, crétum: (3); grow, increase, spring up, thrive, flourish

créta -ae: f.; chalk

Créta -ae: f.; Crete

Creténses -ium, Crétes -um: m. pl.; Cretans

críbro -áre: (1); sift

crímen -inis: n.; sin, guilt, accusation, charge, offense; *see Appendix*

criminális -is -e: criminal

criminátor -óris: m., criminátrix -ícis: f.; slanderer, false witness, false accuser, detractor

críminor (crímino) -ári: *dep.* (1); accuse

criminósus -a -um: criminal, slanderous, calumnious, reproachful

crísis -is: f.; decision, crisis

critérium -ii: n.; criterion, criteria, standard, rule

críticus -a -um: critical, judicious, censorious

cróceus -a -um: scarlet, saffron, orange-colored

crócia (crócea) -ae: f.; crosier; long mantle with cape and sleeves

crócio -íre: (4); croak as a raven

crocodílus -i: m.; crocodile

crócum -i: n., crócus -i: m.; saffron

crotálum -i: n., crotálus -i: m.; clapper, used instead of a bell

cruciáta -ae: f.; crusade

cruciátio -ónis: f.; torment, punishment, torturing, torture

cruciátor -óris: m.; crusader; crucifier, torturer

cruciátus -us: m.; torment, torture

crúcifer -eri: m.; crossbearer

crucifígo -ere -fíxi -fíxum: (3); crucify

crucifíxus (-um) -i: m.(n.); crucifix

crúcio -áre: (1); torment, torture, crucify

crucisignátio -ónis: f.; signing with the sign of the cross

crudélis -is -e: cruel

crúditas -átis: f.; indigestion, overloading of stomach, crudity

crúdus -a -um: raw

cruénto -áre: (1); lash, torment, make bloody

cruentátus -a -um: bloody, bleeding

cruéntus -a -um: bloody, bleeding

crúor -óris: m.; gore, blood, flowing blood

crurifrágium -ii: n.; breaking of the legs of crucified felons

crus, crúris: n.; leg, shank

crústula -ae: f.; small cake

crux, crúcis: f.; cross, instrument of suffering

    crux commíssa: cross shaped like the letter T

    crux decussáta: cross shaped like the letter X

    crux immíssa: cross with a transverse arm

crýpta -ae: f.; catacomb, crypt, vault, basement

crystállum -i: n.; crystal

crystállus -i: m.; crystal, ice

cubiculárius -ii: m.; private chamberlain

cubículum -i: n.; bedroom, chamber, apartment

cubíle -is: n.; bed, couch; lair, den; pl.: fornication

cúbitum -i: n.; forearm, cubit

cúbo -áre -ui -itum: (1); recline, lie down

cucúlla -ae: f.; cowl, choir cloak

cucullátus -a -um: wearing a cowl

cucúllus -i: m.; cowl

cucumerárium -ii: n.; cucumber field

cúdo -ere, cúdi, cúsum: (3); beat, pound, stamp, coin

cuíque súum: to each his own

cúius est: whose it is, to whom it pertains

cuiuscémodi: of what kind soever

cuiúsmodi: of what kind

cúlcita (cúlcitra) -ae: f.; bed, bolster, pillow, cushion, couch, mattress

cúleus -i: m.; leather sack

cúlex -icis: m.; gnat

culína -ae: f.; kitchen; victuals

cúlmen -inis: n.; top, summit, height, culmination

cúlmus -i: m.; a stalk

cúlpa -ae: f.; guilt, fault, error, sin, blame

culpábilis -is -e, culpósus -a -um: blameworthy, culpable, full of guilt, guilty; culpabíliter: adv.

culpabílitas -átis: f.; culpability, guilt, guiltiness

cúlpo -áre: (1); blame, disapprove, find fault with

cúlte: elegantly

cultéllus -i: m.; small knife

cúlter -tri: m.; knife

cúltio -ónis: f.; veneration, reverence

cúltor -óris: m., cúltrix -ícis: f.; planter, cultivator, dresser, professor, worshiper, dweller

cultuális (culturális) -is -e: of worship or cult, liturgical

cultúra -ae: f.; care, culture, worship

culturális -is -e: cultural, of culture

cúltus -us: m.; worship, reverence, cult; cultivation, care; cúltus sociális: common public service

cum: prep. w. abla.; with; úna cum: together with; conj.: when, while, since, although, whereas

cúmi (kum): Aramaic; arise

cumínum -i: see cymínum

cumulátim: in heaps, abundantly, fully; cumulátius: more fully

cumulátio -ónis: f.; accumulation

cumulatívus -a -um: accruing, cumulative

cúmulo -áre: (1); increase, fill up, heap up, enlarge

cúmulus -i: m.; a pile, heap, mass

cunábula -ae: f.; a cradle, nest

cúnae -árum: f. pl.; cradle, nest; early childhood

cúnctans -ántis: slow, lingering, loitering

cúnctor -ári: dep. (1); tarry, delay

cúnctus -a -um: all, whole, entire; cúncta faústa: all things are favorable

cúneus -i: m.; wedge

cunículus -i: m.; a mine

cupíditas -átis: f.; eager desire, greed, avarice

cupído -inis: f.; desire, longing

cúpidus -a -um, cúpiens -éntis: desirous, wishful, eager, fond, passionate; cúpide, cupiénter: adv.

cúpio -íre -ívi (-ii) -ítum: (4); long for, wish for, desire

cupítor -óris: m.; one who desires

cúppa -ae: f.; the cup of a chalice

cur: why, to what purpose

cúra -ae: f.; care, solicitude, concern; see Appendix

curatéla -ae: f.; guardianship

curátio -ónis: f.; care, attention, healing, management, charge, administration

curátor -óris: m.; curate, curator, guardian, caretaker; *see Appendix*

curátus -i: m.; curate, assistant, associate

cúria -ae: f.; court, Curia; *see Appendix*
Cúria Romána: Papal Court or Curia; *see Appendix: cúria; Romána Cúria*
Cúria Triumphális: Church triumphant

curiósus -a -um: attentive, diligent, careful, thoughtful, devoted, curious

cúro -áre: (1); take care of, pay attention to, manage, administer, attend to; cure, heal

cúrrens -éntis: current

currículum -i: n.; course, curriculum, course offerings, career

currílis -is -e: of a chariot

cúrro -ere, cucúrri, cucúrsum: (3); run, run the course of life

cúrrus -i: m.; chariot, car

cúrsim: hastily, quickly

cúrsito -áre: (1); run up and down

cúrsor -óris: m.; runner, messenger, courier

cúrsus -us: m.; course, career, race; Divine Office or Breviary; passage of time; course of study; progress, direction; voyage, journey; **Cúrsus Mariánus:** Office of the B.V.M.

cúrto -áre: (1); lessen, abbreviate

cúrtus -a -um: shortened

curvatúra -ae: f.; curve, crook of a crosier

curvésco -ere: (3); bend over, make a curve, be crooked or curved

cúrvo -áre: (1); bend, bow, curve

cúrvus -a -um: bent, bowed, arched, curved, crooked

cúspis -idis: f.; sharp point, point of a nail or spear

cussínus -i: m.; cushion

custódia -ae: f.; guard, custody, protection, confinement; pyx; prison, cell; care

custódio -íre: (4); guard, watch, protect, preserve

custodítio -ónis: f.; observance, keeping, care, guardianship, custody

cústos -ódis: c.; attendant, guardian, watchman, overseer; **cústos mártyrum:** keeper of relics

cutícula -ae: f.; skin

cútis -is: f.; skin

cýathus -i: m.; cup, tumbler

cýclas -adis: f.; robe

cýclus -i: m.; cycle, circle

cycnéus -a -um: of a swan

cýcnus -i: m.; swan

cýmba -ae: f.; small boat

cýmbalum -i: m.; cymbal

cymínum (cumínum) -i: n.; cumin, parsley

cýnicus -i: m.; cynic

Cýnicus -a -um: of Cynic philosophy; *as a noun:* a Cynic

cypressínus -a -um: of cypress

cypréssus -i: f.; cypress tree

Cypriánus -a -um: Cyprian; *as a noun:* a Cyprian

Cýprus -i, **Cýpris** -idis: f.; Cyprus

cýprus -i: f.; henna or cypress tree

Cyrenaéus (Cyrenaícus) -a -um, **Cyrenénsis** -is -e: of Cyrene

Cyréne -es: f.; Cyrene

Cyríllus -i: m.; Cyril

D

Dan: *indecl.;* Dan, son of Jacob and Bilhah; tribe of Israel

Daciánus -i: m.; Dacian

daémon -ónis: m.; evil spirit, demon, devil

daemoníacus -i: m.; possessed person

daemoníacus -a -um: demoniacal

daemonícola -ae: m.; demon worshipper, heathen

daemónium -ii: n.; evil spirit, demon, devil

Daémon Mútus: Oculi Sunday, third Sunday of Lent

dáleth: fourth letter of the Hebrew alphabet

Dálmatae -árum: m. pl.; Dalmatians

dalmática -ae: f.; dalmatic, vestment of a deacon

Damascéni -órum: m. pl.; Damascenes

Damascénus -a -um: Damascene

Damáscus -i: m.; Damascus

Damiánus -i: m.; Damian

damiúrgus -i; *see* demiúrgus

damnábilis -is -e: worthy of condemnation or damnation

damnáta stirps: condemned human race

damnátio -ónis: f.; damnation, condemnation

damnífico -áre: (1); injure

dámno -áre: (1); to condemn

damnóse: ruinously

damnósus -a -um: harmful, mistaken

dámnum -i: n.; punishment, injury, damage, loss, evil

dámula -ae: f.; doe, gazelle

Dáni -órum: m. pl.; Danes

Dániel -élis: m.; the prophet Daniel; a book of the O.T.

Danúbius -ii: m.; Danube river

daps, dápis: f.; food, meal, banquet

dápsilis -is -e: plentiful

Datária -ae: f.; Dataria; *see Appendix*

Datárius -ii: m.; cardinal-president of the Dataria

Dáthan: *indecl.;* Dathan, a conspirator against Moses and Aaron

dátio -ónis: f.; act of giving, distributing, allotting, gift

dátis dándis: with all that must be supplied having been supplied

dátor -óris: m.; giver, distributor

dátus -a -um: *perf. pass. part. of* do

dátum -i: n.; gift

Dávid -idis, *or indecl.:* m.; David

Davídicus -a -um: Davidical, of King David

de: *prep. w. abla.;* from, down from, about, concerning, out of, out from, on account of; *see Appendix*

de cétero: as for the rest

de condígno: out of worthiness

de cóngruo: out of suitablity

de indústria: on purpose

múltis de caúsis: for many reasons

qua de caúsa: for which reason

de témpore: of the (Church) season

déa -ae: f.; goddess

dealbátus -a -um: white, bright, pure

deálbo -áre: (1); make white, purify, cleanse; plaster, whitewash

deambulácrum -i: n.; gallery, corridor

deambulátio -ónis: f.; a walking abroad, promenade

deámbulo -áre: (1); walk about, walk much, promenade, take a walk deargénto -áre: (1); plate with silver

deaurátus -a -um: gilded

deaúro -áre: (1); cover with gold, gild

de Beáta: Office or Mass of the B.V.M.

debellátor -óris: m.; conqueror

debéllo -áre: (1); wage war

débeo -ére -ui -itum: (2); owe, ought

débilis -is -e; maimed, feeble, weak, infirm

debílitas -átis: f.; weakness, infirmity, debility

debilitátio -ónis: f.; a weakening

debílito -áre: (1); weaken

débite: duly, appropriately, fittingly

débitor -óris: m., débitrix -ícis: f.; debtor

débitum -i: n.; debt, duty, sin

débitus -a -um: due, owed; débite: adv.

decachórdus -a -um: ten-stringed

decálogus -i: m.; Decalogue, Ten Commandments

decálvo -áre: (1); make bald, cut the hair

decanátus -us: m.; deanery, deanship

decantátio -ónis: f.; singing

decánto -áre: (1); sing, repeat often

decánus -i: m.; dean

décas -adis: f.; decade, set of ten

decédo -ere -céssi -céssum: (3); depart, resign, die

décem: ten

Decémber -bris: m.; December

decéndium -ii: n.; period of ten days

decénni -ae -a: of ten years

decénnis (decennális) -is -e: of ten years; decénnis: adv.

decénnium -ii: n.; period of ten years

décens -éntis: becoming, decent, suitable, proper, fitting, seemly; decénter: adv.

decéntia -ae: f.; decency, propriety

decéptio -ónis: f.; deception

decéptor -óris: m.; deceiver, enemy

decérno -ere -crévi -crétum: (3); determine, decide, intend; ordain, decree

decérpo -ere -cérpsi -cérptum: (3); pluck, take or pull away

decérto -áre: (1); strive

decéssio -ónis: f.; departure

decéssor -óris: m.; predecessor

décet -ére, décuit: (2); impers.; it fits, it is becoming, it is proper

décidens -éntis: fading, falling

décido -ere -cidi: (3); fall down, wither, die, perish, fail

decído -ere -cídi(-císi) -císum: (3); cut off; decide, settle, determine

décima -ae, decimátio -ónis: f.; tithe, tenth

décimo -áre: (1); levy a tithe

décimus -a -um: tenth

decípio -ere -cépi -céptum: (3); deceive, catch, snare, beguile

decípula -ae: f.; snare, trap

decísio -ónis: f.; settlement, agreement, decision; a lessening; see Appendix

decisórius -a -um, decisívus -a -um: decisive, deciding

declamátio (declarátio) -ónis: f.; declamation, declaration; see Appendix

declaratórius -a -um: declaratory

decláro -áre: (1); make clear, show, demonstrate, declare

declíno -áre: (1); incline, lean to one side, go or step aside, turn away

declívis -is -e: sloping, inclined

decóctus -a -um: ripened

decollátio -ónis: f.; beheading

decóllo -áre: (1); behead

decóloro -áre: (1); discolor

decóquo -ere -cóxi -cóctum: (3); boil, roast, cook, melt

décor -óris: m.; beauty, comeliness, elegance, grace

decorátio -ónis: f.; decoration, adornment

décoro -áre: (1); adorn, decorate, endow, honor

decórtico -áre: (1); strip bare, tear off the bark

decórus -a -um: beauteous, comely, fitting, seemly, suitable, proper

decrépitus -a -um: infirm

decrésco -ere -crévi -crétum: (3); decrease, wane, disappear

decreméntum (decrétum) -i: n.; decree, ordinance, principle

decretália -ium: n. pl.; decretals; *see Appendix*

decretális -is -e: of a decree

decretalísta -ae: m.; decretalist; *see Appendix*

decretísta -ae: m.; decretist; *see Appendix*

decretórius -a -um: imperative, peremptory, decisive, decreeing

decrétus -a -um: *perf. pass. part. of* **decérno** *and* **decrésco**

decrétum -i: n.; decree, ordinance, principle; *see Appendix*

decúmbo -ere -cúbui: (3); lie down, recline, lie ill, be sick

decúrio -ónis: m.; counselor; captain of ten

decúrro -ere -cucúrri(-cúrri) -cúrsum: (3); run through, trickle; have recourse to

decúrsus -us: m.; downward course, descent, watercourse, a running down, stream; passing of time

décus -oris: n.; beauty, grace, glory, honor, distinction

decússo -áre: (1); to cross

dédecens -éntis: unbecoming

dédecet -ére -décuit: (2); *impers.;* it is unseemly or unsuitable

dedecórus -a -um: shameful, vile

dédecus -oris: n.; shame, dishonor, disgrace, vice

dedicátio -ónis: f.; dedication

dédico -áre: (1); dedicate, consecrate

dedignátio -ónis: f.; scorn, indignation, refusal

dedígnor -ári: *dep.* (1); scorn, disdain, reject, refuse

dedítio -ónis: f.; surrender, giving up, capitulation

dédo -ere, dédidi, déditum: (3); give up, yield, surrender, consign, devote, dedicate

dedúco -ere -dúxi -dúctum: (3); conduct, lead, lead away, bring down, bring to trial

dedúctio -ónis: f.; deduction, observation, argument

dedúctor -óris: m.; deserter

de éa: the Office of a feria, as distinct from the Office of a feast

de fácto: actually, in reality, in fact, concerning the fact or facts, objectively

defaecátus -a -um: purified, refined, cleansed

defaéco (deféco, defíco) -áre: (1); cleanse, refine, purify

defatigátio -ónis: f.; wearying, weariness, fatigue, exhaustion

defatígo (defetígo) -áre: (1); exhaust, wear out, tire

deféco: *see* **defaéco**

deféctio -ónis: f., **deféctus** -us: m.; defect, failing, ceasing, sin, defection, revolt, lack; *see Appendix*

deféndo -ere -féndi -fénsum: (3), **defénso** -áre: (1); defend, repel, guard, protect

defénsio -ónis: f.; protection, defense

defénsor -óris: m.; defender; *see Appendix*

défero -férre -tuli -látum: (3); bring, bring down, submit, report

deférveo -ére: (2); subside, effervesce

defetígo: *see* **defatígo**

defetíscor, defetísci, deféssus: *dep.* (3); become weary or tired out

defício -ere -féci -féctum: (3); fail, faint,
be wanting, pine for, vanish
defíco: *see* defaéco
de Fíde: *see Appendix*
defígo -ere -fíxi -fíxum: (3); fix, fashion,
define
defínio -íre: (4); solve, define,
determine, limit; *see Appendix*
definítio -ónis: f.; definition,
determination, measure
definitívus -a -um: definitive, final;
definitíve: *adv.*
definítor -óris: m.; one who defines
defíxus -a -um: fixed, fashioned
deflagrátio -ónis: f.; a burning,
conflagration, consuming by fire
deflágro -áre: (1); be burnt down, be
consumed by fire
deflécto -ere -fléxi -fléctum: (3); turn
aside, deflect
défleo -ére -flévi -flétum: (2); weep over,
bewail, lament
défluo -ere -flúxi -flúxum: (3); pass
away, wither, fall, cease, disappear,
vanish, flow from, flow away
defóret: *another form of* deésset, *imperf.*
subj. of désum
déforis: from without, outside
deformátio -ónis, defórmitas -átis: f.;
blemish, deforming, defacing,
disfiguring, deformity, pattern
defórmis -is -e: deformed, misshapen
defórmo -áre: (1); disfigure, engrave,
delineate
defraúdo -áre: (1); cheat, defraud
defúgio -ere -fúgi: (3); flee, avoid, escape
defúnctio -ónis: f.; death
defúnctus -a -um: dead, deceased
defúndo -ere -fúdi -fúsum: (3); pour out
defúngor -fúngi -fúnctus: *dep.* (3); die,
depart, finish, complete; perform,
discharge
dégener -eris: ignoble, unworthy
degenerátio -ónis: f.; degeneration

deglútio -íre: (4); swallow up
dégo -ere, dégi: (3); live, spend time
degradátio -ónis: f.; degradation,
deprivation, rank reduction; *see*
Appendix
dégrado -áre: (1); reduce in rank,
deprive of office
degústo -áre: (1); taste, partake of
dehortátor -óris: m.; dissuader
déifer -era -erum: God-bearing
deífico -áre: (1): make a god
deíficus -a -um: rendering godlike, deific
deício: *see* dejício
déin: then, thereupon, thereafter,
afterwards
deínceps: henceforth, again, any longer,
any more, in order of succession, from
now on, after this
deínde: then, finally
deíntus: from within
Deípara -ae: f.; Mother of God,
God-bearer
Deípnon: n.; *Greek;* banquet, Mass
Deísmus -i: m.; theory of Deism, which
admits to a creating God but not a
providential God
Déitas -átis: f.; divinity, deity, Godhead
dejício -ere -jéci -jéctum: (3); cast down,
throw out, overthrow
de júre: by right or law
dejúro -áre: (1); swear solemnly
delábor -i -lápsus: *dep.* (3); fall down,
glide down, sink
delátio -ónis: f.; denunciation
delátor -óris: m.; bearer, crossbearer
delatúra -ae: f.; accusation
delectábilis -is -e: delightful
delectaméntum -i: n.; delight, source of
delight or pleasure, sweetness
delectátio -ónis: f.; delight, pleasure,
amusement
delécto -áre: (1); cause pleasure
deléctor -ári: *dep.* (1); rejoice, be
pleased, take delight in

deléctus -a -um: chosen, selected; *perf. pass. part. of* déligo

deléctus (dil-) -us: m.; choice, selection, levy

delegátio -ónis: f.; delegation, assignment, substitution; *see Appendix*

delegátus -us: m.; delegate; *see Appendix*

delégo -áre: (1); entrust, assign, send, transfer, delegate, dispatch; *see Appendix*

delénio -íre: (4); soften, soothe, charm

déleo -ére -évi -étum: (2); destroy, blot out, annihilate, abolish, end

delibátio -ónis: f.; first fruit

deliberátio -ónis: f.; deliberation, consultation

deliberatívus -a -um: deliberative

deliberátus -a -um: deliberate, positive, definite, certain, assured; deliberáte: *adv.*

delíbero -áre: (1); consider, consult, deliberate

delíbo -áre: (1); pluck, gather, cull, take away a little, sacrifice

delíbuo -ere -ui -útum: (3); destroy, wash away, blot out, besmear, anoint

delicátus -a -um: delightful

delícia -ae: f., delícium -ii: n.; delight

deliciósus -a -um: delicious, pleasant, voluptuous, fond of pleasure

delictórum reátus: sin, guilt of sin

delíctum -i: n.; crime, sin, fault, dishonor, offense

déligo -ere -légi -léctum (3); choose, resolve, wish, select

delimitátio -ónis: f.; a marking out, limitation

delíneo -áre: (1); outline; prophesy

delínquo -ere -líqui -líctum: (3); fail, sin, do wrong, offend

delíquium -ii: n.; fluidity, instability

deliraméntum -i: n.; nonsense, folly

delitésco -ere -tui: (3); lie hidden

delónge: from afar

delúbrum -i: n.; temple, shrine

delúdo -ere -lúdi -lúsum: (3); mock, delude, cheat

demándo -áre: (1); entrust, put in charge, commit

demélior -íri: *dep.* (4); consume, destroy, demolish, lay waste

deméntia -ae: f.; madness, insanity, foolishness

deménto -áre: (1); craze, deceive

deméreor -éri: *dep.* (2); deserve

demérgo -ere -mérsi -mérsum: (3); sink, drown, submerge, plunge, swallow

deméritum -i: n.; defect, demerit

demétior -íri -ménsus: *dep.* (4); measure or mete out

démeto -ere -méssui -méssum: (3); mow, harvest, reap, gather

Demétrias -ádis: m.; Demetrias

deminorátio -ónis, deminútio -ónis: f.; decrease, loss

demínuo -ere -ui -útum: (3); lessen, diminish

deminútio -ónis: *see* diminútio

demíror -ári: *dep.* (1); wonder at

demísse: humbly

demíssio -ónis: f.; lowliness

demíssus -a -um: lowly, humble

demítto -ere -mísi -míssum: (3); sink, settle, lie down, forgive

demiúrgus (damiúrgus) -i: m.; maker, supreme power

démo -ere, démpsi, démptum: (3); take away, subtract, remove

demográphicus -a -um: demographic

demólior -íri: *dep.* (4); consume, demolish, destroy, remove

demonstrátio -ónis: f.; description, demonstration, pointing out

demónstro -áre: (1); show, discover, demonstrate, point out

demorátio -ónis: f.; a lingering, remaining, abiding

demórior -móri -mórtuus: *dep.* (3); die

demóror -ári: *dep.* (1); dwell, abide, linger, delay, retard

demórtuus -a -um: dead

demóveo -ére -móvi -mótum: (2); remove, move, move away

demúlceo -ére -múlsi -múlsum(-múlctum): (2); persuade, soften

démum: at last, at length, finally, just, only, precisely

demúto -áre: (1); change

denárius -ii: m.; denarius, a Roman coin of small value; denárius Sáncti Pétri: Peter's pence

denegátio -ónis: f.; denial, rejection, refusal

dénego -áre: (1); deny, refuse, reject

déni -ae -a: by tens; ter dénis: thirtyfold

denígro -áre: (1); blacken

dénique: at length, lastly, finally, in short, accordingly

denotátio -ónis: f.; mark of disgrace

dénoto -áre: (1); denote, specify, mark out, point out

dens -tis: m.; tooth

dénsus -a -um: thick, dense

denticulátum -i: n.; lace

denticulátus -a -um: pointed

denúbo -ere -núpsi -núptum: (3); marry, be married

denudátio -ónis: f.; act of stripping

denúdo -áre: (1); lay bare, strip, uncover

denuntiátio (denunci-) -ónis: f.; denunciation, prohibition, announcement, publication

denúntio -áre: (1); announce, declare, proclaim, make an official announcement; threaten, denounce

dénuo: again, a second time, once more, anew

deordinátio -ónis: f.; disorder

deórsum: lower, downward, beneath

deósculor -ári: *dep.* (1); to kiss

Déo grátias: thanks be to God

Déo volénte: God willing

depásco -ere -pávi -pástum: (3); feed upon, consume

depéllo -ere -púli -púlsum: (3); drive away, dispel, keep from

dependéntia -ae: f.; dependence

depéndeo -ére -pepéndi: (2); hang down, depend, be subject to

deperdítio -ónis: f.; loss

depérdo -ere -didi -ditum: (3); destroy, ruin, lose

depéreo -íre: (4); perish, be lost

dépilo -áre: (1); peel, skin, pluck

depíngo -ere -pínxi -píctum: (3); depict, paint

deplóro -áre: (1); deplore, grieve over

depóno -ere -pósui -pósitum: (3); take, bring, or throw down; remove, separate; give evidence, make a deposition

depopulátio -ónis: f.; laying waste, plundering, pillaging, marauding

depópulor -ári: *dep.* (1); ravage

deportátio -ónis: f.; deportation, banishment

depórto -áre: (1); banish

depósco -ere -popósci: (3); demand, beseech, appoint

deposítio -ónis: f.; deposition, burial, laying aside, removal, putting away; degradation

Deposítio Sánctae Maríae Vírginis: Assumption of the B.V.M.

depósitum -i: n.; deposit, security

depósitus -a -um: divested, deposited, laid away, laid out dead

depraedátio -ónis: f.; plundering

depraédo -áre: (1); rob

depraédor -ári: *dep.* (1); plunder

depravátio -ónis: f.; depravity

deprávo -áre: (1); corrupt, pervert

deprecábilis -is -e: gracious, merciful

deprecátio -ónis: f.; prayer, supplication, entreaty

deprecátor -óris: m.; pleader, intercessor

deprecatórius -a -um: pertaining to prayer or a request

déprecor -ári: *dep.* (1); entreat, pray, supplicate

deprehéndo -ere -héndi -hénsum: (3); perceive, find; seize, take

déprimo -ere -préssi -préssum: (3); press or weigh down, afflict, oppress

De Profúndis: Psalm 129, a prayer for the dead

deprómo -ere -prómpsi -prómptum: (3); bring or pour out, produce, fetch

depudésco -ere: (3); become shameless

depúlsio -ónis: f.; driving off, defense

depúrgo -áre: (1); to wash

deputátio -ónis: f.; deputation, assignment, appointment

députo -áre: (1); depute, appoint, count, number, assign, prune, condemn

derelíctio -ónis: f.; an abandoning, disregarding, deserting, forsaking

derelínquo -ere -líqui -líctum: (3); abandon, leave, forsake, desert

derepénte: suddenly

derídeo -ére -rísi -rísum: (2); deride, mock, scoff at, laugh at

derípio -ere -rípui -réptum: (3); tear or snatch away

derísus -us: m.; scorn, mockery, derision

derívo -áre: (1); convey aboard, divert, distribute

derogátio -ónis: f.; revocation; *see* Appendix

derogatórius -a -um: restrictive, derogating

dérogo -áre: (1); detract from, repeal, restrict, modify

desaévio -íre -ii -ítum: (4); rage violently

descendéntes -ium: c. pl.; descendants

descéndo -ere -scéndi -scénsum: (3); descend, come or go down

descénsio -ónis: f., **descénsus** -us: m.; descent, a going down

descísco -ere -scívi -scítum: (3); withdraw, sever; be true to self

describo -ere -scrípsi -scríptum: (3); describe, enroll, copy, represent

descríptio -ónis: f.; decription, record, entry, census, enrolling

de seq.: *abbrev. for* **de sequénti fésto;** feast of the following day

désero -ere -sérui -sértum: (3); neglect, forsake, desert

desérsum: from above

desértio -ónis: f.; desertion, neglect, treason

desértor -óris: m.; deserter, rebel

desértum -i: n.; desert, wilderness

desértus -a -um: deserted, desolate, arid

desérvio -íre: (4); serve zealously, be devoted to

déses -idis: lazy, idle, slothful

desiderábilis -is -e: desirable

desideránter: with longing

desidérium -ii: n.; desire, lust, yearning for, pining for

desídero -áre: (1); desire, long for, earnestly wish for

desídia -ae: f.; sloth

designátio -ónis: f.; designation, disposition, arrangement

desígno -áre: (1); signify, appoint, designate, assign, define

desílio -íre -sílui -súltum: (4); leap

désino -ere -sívi(-sii) -sítum: (3); cease, leave off, close

desísto -ere -stiti -stitum: (3); desist, cease

desolátio -ónis: f.; desolation, grief, sorrow, ruin

desolatórius -a -um: destroying

desolatórius -ii: m.; destroyer

desolátus -a -um: desolate

desólo -áre: (1); lay waste, bring to desolation, leave alone, forsake

despéctio -ónis: f.; contempt; outcast

despéctus -a -um: despicable, contemptible

desperáte: desperately

desperátio -ónis: f.; desperation, despair

despéro -áre: (1); to despair

despicábilis -is -e: unworthy

despício -ere -spéxi -spéctum: (3); look away from, neglect, disdain, hate

despólio -áre: (1); strip, despoil

despóndeo -ére -spóndi -spónsum: (2); espouse, betroth

desponsátio -ónis: f.; betrothal

desponsátus -a -um: betrothed

despónso -áre: (1); betroth, espouse

despótice: despotically

déspuo -ere -spui -spútum: (3); spit

destérno -ere -strávi: (3); uncover, unsaddle

destinátio -ónis: f.; destination, goal, resolution, purpose

déstino -áre: (1); define, fix, consider, design, determine, bind

destítuo -ere -stítui -stitútum: (3); abandon, leave alone

destitútio -ónis: f.; putting away, abandoning

destrúctio -ónis: f.; destruction, pulling down; refutation

destrúctor -óris: m.; destroyer

déstruo -ere -strúxi -strúctum: (3); destroy, ruin

desuésco -ere -suévi -suétum: (3); put aside custom, disuse

desuetúdo -inis: f.; disuse

désum -ésse -fui: fail, be wanting, be absent

desúmo -ere -súmpsi -súmptum: (3); select, choose

désuper (desúrsum): from above

détego -ere -téxi -téctum: (3); disclose, uncover, detect

deténdo -ere -téndi -ténsum: (3); unstretch, relax

deténtio -ónis: f.; detention, detaining, keeping back

deténtor -óris: m.; detainer, one who holds back

deténtus -a -um: perf. pass. part. of detíneo

detérgeo -ére -térsi -térsum: (2); wipe away, cancel

detérior -ior -ius: inferior

determinátio -ónis: f.; determination

Determinísmus -i: m.; theory of determinism

detérmino -áre: (1); determine, limit, bound, fix, settle

detérreo -ére -ui -itum: (2); deter or prevent by fear

detérrimus -a -um: worst

detestátor -óris: m.; curser, one who detests

detéstor -ári: dep. (1); curse, detest

detíneo -ére -ui -téntum: (2); withhold, detain, engage

detórqueo -ére -tórsi -tórsum(-tórtum): (2); twist

detráctio -ónis: f.; detraction, slander, taking away

detrácto: see detrécto

détraho -ere -tráxi -tráctum: (3); slander, calumniate; take away; distort, misrepresent

detrectátio -ónis: f.; refusal

detrécto (detrácto) -áre: (1); speak against, disparage, speak evil of, depreciate, refuse, decline

detriméntum -i: n.; loss, detriment, damage

detrúdo -ere -trúsi -trúsum: (3); force away, thrust down

deturbátor -óris: m.; dispossessor, disturber of property

detúrpo -áre: (1); defile, disfigure

Déus -i: m.; God, the Deity

Deuteronómium -ii: n.; Deuteronomy, a book of the O.T.

devásto -áre: (1); devastate, lay waste

devénio -íre -véni -véntum: (4); arrive at, come from, reach

deversórium -ii: n.; lodging

devérto (devórto) -ere -ti -sum: (3); lodge, resort to, turn aside

devíncio -íre -vínxi -vínctum: (4); bind, fetter, obligate

devínco -ere -víci -víctum: (3); subdue, conquer

dévio -áre: (1); detour, depart

devíto -áre: (1); avoid, shun

dévius -a -um: devious, wandering from the way

dévoco -áre: (1); call away or down

devolutívus -a -um: devolving to

devólvo (devólvor) -ere -vólvi -volútum: (3); roll down, sink back, hand over, transfer, deprive

devorátio -ónis: f.; prey, devouring

devorátor -óris: m.; glutton, devourer

dévoro -áre: (1); devour, swallow, gulp down

devórto: see devérto

devotátio -ónis: f.; vow, imprecation (used in good & bad sense)

devótio -ónis: f.; devotion; vow, allegiance, imprecation, incantation (used in good and bad senses)

devótus -a -um: devoted, devout, pious, faithful; devóte: adv.

devóveo -ére -vóvi -vótum: (2); vow, devote, mark out

déxter -a -um (-tra -trum): right

déxtera (déxtra) -ae: f.; right hand; ad déxtram: at the right hand

dextéritas -átis: f.; dexterity, skill

dextrále -is: n.; armlet, bracelet

dextralíolum -i: n.; bracelet

diabólicus -a -um: diabolic, devilish, of the devil

diábolus -i: m.; devil, Satan

diaconális -is -e: of a deacon

diaconándus -i: m.; one to be made a deacon

diaconátus -us: m.; diaconate, the order of deaconship

diaconía -ae: f.; diaconate, service, ministry, hospice

Diacónicon: n.; Greek; a book for the use of deacons in the Greek rite

diacónicum -i: n.; sacristy

diaconíssa -ae: f.; deaconess

diaconissátus -us: m.; order of deaconess

diáconus -i: m., díacon -is: n.; deacon

diadéma -atis: n.; diadem, crown

diálogus -i: m.; dialogue, conversation

diamétros -i: f.; diameter; e diamétro: diametrically

Diána -ae: f.; the goddess Diana

diapáson: n.; Greek; a whole octave in music

diapénte: n.; Greek; an interval of a fifth in music; medicine with five ingredients

diárium -ii: n.; diary, daily record, journal, daily allowance

diárius -a -um: daily

diatéssaron: n.; Greek; an interval of a fourth in music; a harmony of the four Gospels

dicanícium -ii: n.; mace

dicastérium -ii: n.; office, bureau

dicátus -a -um: dedicated, hallowed

dício -ónis: f.; domination, power, control, jurisdiction

díco -áre: (1); dedicate, consecrate, devote, make known

díco -ere díxi díctum: (3); say, speak, mention, relate, affirm, declare

dictámen -inis: n.; order, prescrption, command, precept

dictatórius -a -um: of a dictator, dictatorial

díctio -ónis: f.; language

dícto -áre: (1); say repeatedly, order, dictate, prescribe

díctor -óris: m.; speaker, orator

díctu: *supine;* to say, in the saying

díctum -i: n.; word, saying, command

díctus -us: m.; word, saying, command

didácticus -a -um: teaching, didactic, intellectual

Didascália Apostolórum: a third-century treatise on the public life of the Church

didráchma -ae: f., didráchma -atis, didráchmon -i: n.; half shekel, double drachma

didúco -ere -dúxi -dúctum: (3); draw apart, divide, separate

Dídymus -i: m.; "twin"; the apostle Thomas

díes -éi: c.; day

ad díem: on the day

de díe in díem: from day to day

díes féstos ágere: spend holy days

díes natális: birthday

in díes: daily

Díes Domínica: Sunday, the Lord's Day

Díes Epiphaniórum, Díes lúminum: Epiphany

Díes Írae: Day of wrath, a 13th-century hymn formerly used at funerals

Díes pánis álbi: former name for Maundy Thursday

diétim: day by day, daily

diffamátio -ónis: f.; defamation

diffámo -áre: (1); accuse, slander; publish, spread abroad

dífferens -éntis: different

differéntia -ae: f.; difference

differéntior -ior -ius: more different

díffero -érre, dístuli, dilátum: *irreg.;* defer, differ, cast off, scatter; publish, divulge; delay

diffícilis -is -e: difficult; difficile (difficúlter): *adv.*

difficúltas -átis: f.; obstinacy, difficulty

diffidéntia -ae: f.; unbelief, want of faith; suspicion; disobedience

diffído -ere -físus: *semidep.* (3); mistrust

diffíndo -ere -fídi -físsum: (3); split, open, cleave

diffíteor -éri: *dep.* (2); disavow, deny

díffluo -ere -flúxi -flúxum: (3); flow freely, fall out, dissolve, melt

diffórmatas -átis: f.; lack of conformity, disagreement

diffúgio -ere -fúgi -fúgitum: (3); flee

diffúndo -ere -fúsi -fúsum: (3); pour forth, spread throughout

diffúsio -ónis: f.; spread, diffusion

diffúsus -a -um: wide, extensive, spread out

dígero -ere -géssi -géstum: (3); digest, arrange

digéstus -a -um: set in order

dígitus -i: m.; finger, toe

dignánter: worthily

dignátio -ónis: f.; condescension, graciousness

dígnitas -átis: f.; honor, worth, merit, dignity

dígnor -ári: *dep.* (1); grant, vouchsafe

dignósco -ere -nóvi: (3); discern, distinguish

dígnus -a -um: worthy, deserving, merited; dígne: *adv.*

digrédior -i -gréssus: *dep.* (3); depart, digress

dijúdico -áre: (1); judge, discern, examine, discriminate, decide

dikérium (dikérion): double candlestick used by Greek bishops

dilácero -áre: (1); tear to pieces

dilánio -áre: (1); tear asunder, slander

dilápido -áre: (1); squander

dilárgio (dilárgior) -íre: (4); give liberally

dilatátio -ónis: f.; an enlarging, expansion, spread

dilátio -ónis: f.; delay

diláto -áre: (1); extend, enlarge, make broad, open wide

dilatórius -a -um: dilatory, delaying

dilaúdo -áre: (1); praise highly, be grateful to

diléctio -ónis: f.; love

diléctus -a -um: beloved, lovely; *perf. pass. part. of* díligo

diléctus -us: *see* deléctus

dilículum -i: n.; dawn, daybreak

díligens -éntis: diligent, careful; diligénter: *adv.*

diligéntia -ae: f.; diligence, accuracy, carefulness, attentiveness

diligéntius: more diligently, more carefully

díligo -ere -léxi -léctum: (3); love, prize, esteem highly

dilínio -áre: (1); disturb, harass, torment mentally

dilucésco -ere -lúxi: (3); grow light, become day

dilúcidus -a -um: lucid, sane, clear, bright, evident, plain, distinct; dilúcide: *adv.*

dilúculo: early

dilúculum -i: n.; dawn

díluo -ere -ui -útum: (3); wash, efface

dilúvium -ii: n.; flood

dimáno -áre: (1); flow in different directions

diménsio -ónis: f.; reasoning, judgment

dimétior -íri -ménsus: *dep.* (4); mete out, measure

dímico -áre: (1); fight, struggle, contend

dimidiátus (dimídius) -a -um: half, divided in half

dimídio -áre: (1); divide in halves

dimídius -a -um: half; *as a n. noun:* half

dimínuo -ere -ui -útum: (3); lessen, diminish

diminútio (demin-) -ónis: f.; dimunition, lessening, decrease

dimíssio -ónis: f.; dismissal, discharge

dimissoriális -is -e, dimissórius -a -um : pertaining to a discharge, dismissal, or release, dimissorial

dimítto -ere -mísi -míssum: (3); send away, dismiss; forgive; allow, permit, leave

dinúmero -áre: (1); count, number

Diocletiánus -i: m.; Diocletian

dioecesánus -a -um: diocesan; *see Appendix*

dioecésis -is(-eos): f.; diocese; *see Appendix*

Dionýsius -ii: m.; Dionysius, Dennis

dióryz -igis: f.; canal, channel

díplois -ídis: f.; cloak, mantle, double cloak

diplóma -ae: f.; diploma, charter

dipóndium -ii: n.; two farthings

dipóndius -ii: m.; weight of two farthings

dípsas -adis: f.; a kind of serpent

díptychon -i: n.; diptych, a list for commemorations

diréctio -ónis: f.; direction, righteousness, uprightness

directívus -a -um: directive, helpful, positive

diréctor -óris: m.; director

directórium -ii: n.; directory, the Ordo; *see Appendix*

diréctum -i: n.; straight line

diréctus -a -um: direct, helpful, guiding, straight, proper

in dirécto: the right way

in diréctum: without modulations, plain

dirécte: *adv.*

dirémptio -ónis: f.; separation

diríbitor -óris: m.; distributor, sorter

dírigo -ere -réxi -réctum: (3); guide, set right, straighten, direct; *pass.:* prosper

dírimens -éntis: invalidating, diriment

dírimo -ere -émi -émptum: (3); nullify, disolve; separate, divide, interrupt; frustrate, destroy

dirípio -ere -rípui -réptum: (3); plunder, rob, despoil

dirúmpo -ere -rúpi -rúptum: (3); break asunder, cleave

díruo -ere -ui -útum: (3); destroy, demolish, overthrow

dírus -a -um: fearful, dreadful, horrible, cruel

dis- (di-); *inseparable particle usually indicating separation, but sometimes indicating negation or intensity*

dis, dítis: rich, wealthy, prosperous; dítior -ior -ius: *comp.*

discalceátus -a -um: barefoot, unshod, discalced

discántus -us: m.; descant, upper voice in part singing

discédo -ere -céssi -céssum: (3); depart, deviate, leave

discéptio (disceptátio) -ónis: f.; dispute, debate, discussion; judgment, judicial award

discépto -áre: (1); dispute, discuss, determine, judge

discérno -ere -crévi -crétum: (3); distinguish, discern, decide, separate, settle

discérpo -ere -cérpsi -cérptum: (3); rend, tear

discéssio -ónis: f.; a going away, departure, separation, revolt

discéssus -a -um: separated, divided; *perf. pass. part.* of discédo

discéssus -us: m.; removal, departure, separation

discídium -ii: n.; separation, disagreement, a tearing apart

disciplína -ae: f.; discipline, study; habit, instruction, systematic training; chastisement, punishment with a view to correction; knowledge, course of study

disciplína arcáni: discipline of the secret, knowledge kept from the catechumens in the early Church

disciplináris -is -e: disciplinary

discipulátus -us: m.; discipleship

discípulus -i: m., discípula -ae: f.; disciple

discíssus -a -um: rent, torn

dísco -ere, dídici: (3); learn

díscolor -óris: speckled, of different colors

díscolus -a -um: deformed

discoopério -íre: (4); expose, uncover, remove

discórdia -ae: f.; discord, disagreement, dissension

discórditer: disproportionally

discórdo -áre: (1); disagree

díscors -córdis: discordant, disagreeing, opposed

discrepántia -ae: f.; discrepancy, discordance, dissimilarity

díscrepo -áre: (1); differ, disagree, vary, sound differently

discréte: carefully, with delicacy and caution, quietly, wisely

discrétio -ónis: f.; separation; discretion, discrimination, power of distinguishing, discernment; *see* Appendix

discrétor -óris: m.; judge, discerner

discrímen -inis: n.; distinction, difference, decisive point, peril

discriminális -is -e: that which serves to divide; discriminále -is: n.; headdress, hairpin

discriminátio -ónis: f.; discrimination, wise judgment

discrímino -áre: (1); distinguish; braid, plait

discrúcio -áre: (1); to torture

discúbitus -us: m.; place at the table

discúmbens -éntis: m.; guest

discúmbo -ere -cúbui -cúbitum: (3); sit down, sit or recline at table

discúrro -ere -cucúrri(-cúrri) -cursum: (3); run to and fro

díscus -i: m.; dish, paten in the Greek rite

discússio -ónis: f.; discussion, pleading a case; revision

discútio -ere -cússi -cússum: (3); plead a case; disperse, scatter

discúto -ere: (3); examine, discuss, inquire into

disérte: eloquently, distinctly, expressly, clearly

disertitúdo -inis: f.; eloquence

disértus -a -um: eloquent, fluent

dísgrego -áre: (1); rend asunder

disídium -ii: see dissídium

disílio -íre: (4); leap from one place to another

disjício -ere -jéci -jéctum: (3); rend, scatter, disperse

disjunctíve: separately, disjunctively

disjúngo -ere -júnxi -júnctum: (3); put asunder

dismembrátio -ónis: f.; dismemberment, separation

dismembrátus -a -um: dismembered

dismémbro -áre: (1); distribute, break up, separate, dismember

díspar -is: unlike, unequal, different

dispáritas -átis: f.; discrepancy, difference, inequality; see Appendix

dísparo -áre: (1); to part, divide

dispéctor -óris: m.; searcher, examiner

dispéndium -ii: n.; expense, cost

dispéndo -ere -pénsus: semidep. (3); weigh out, dispense

dispensátio -ónis: f.; dispensation, relaxation of law; stewardship; see Appendix

dispensátor -óris: m.; steward, dispenser

dispensatórius -a -um: dispensing, administering

dispénso -áre: (1); distribute, dispense, disperse, regulate

dispérdo -ere -didi -ditum: (3); destroy, cut off

dispéreo -íre -ii: (4); perish, be entirely ruined

dispérgo -ere -spérsi -spérsum: (3); scatter, disperse, spread

dispérsio -ónis: f.; dispersal, dispersion, scattering

dispértio -íre: (4); distribute, separate, part, divide

dispício -ere -éxi -éctum: (3); distinguish, detect, discover

displíceo -ére -plícui -plícitum: (2); displease

dispóno -ere -pósui -pósitum: (3); order, dispose, arrange

dispositío -ónis: f.; disposition, providence, arrangement

dispositívus -a -um: arranging, disposing

dispósitor -óris: m.; disposer

disputátio -ónis: f.; argumentation, dispute, debate

dísputo -áre: (1); dispute, treat about, preach, argue

disquíro -ere: (3); inquire, carefully investigate

disquisítio -ónis: f.; inquiry, investigation

disrúmpo -ere -rúpi -rúptum: (3); break asunder, disrupt, sever

dísseco (díssico) -áre -sécui -séctum: (1); cut, dissect

dissémino -áre: (1); scatter, sow, disseminate, spread abroad

disténsio -ónis: f., disténsus -us: m.; quarrel, dissension

disténsus -a -um: different, differing

disséntio -íre -sénsi -sénsum: (4); dissent, disagree, protest, object, refuse to give assent, differ

díssero -ere -sérui -sértum: (3); discuss, dispute, explain, expound, examine, treat

díssico: see déssico

díssidens -éntis: dissenting, inimical, discordant, at variance

dissídeo -ere -sédi séssum: (2); disagree, differ

dissídium (disídium, discídium) -ii: n.; quarrel, separation, disagreement, discord

díssilo -áre: (1); be torn apart

dissímilis -is -e: unlike, dissimilar

dissimilitúdo -inis: f.; difference

dissímulo -áre: (1); conceal, dissemble, fake, feign, hide, keep secret

dissipátio -ónis: f.; scattering, dispersing, destruction, desolation

díssipo -áre: (1); lay waste, destroy, scatter, abolish, waste

díssitus -a -um: widely scattered

dissolútio -ónis: f.; destruction, breaking down, dissolution

dissolútus -a -um: feeble, loose

dissólvo -ere -sólvi -solútum: (3); dissolve, loose, destroy, scatter, free, release

dissonántia -órum: n. pl.; discord, differences

dissuádeo -ére -suási -suásum: (2); advise or speak against, dissuade

dissuásio -ónis: f.; dissuasion, advising to the contrary

distabésco -ere: (3); waste away

dístans -ántis: distant, separate

distántia -ae: f.; distance, difference, diversity

disténdo (disténno) -ere -téndi -téntum(-ténsum): (3); detract, stretch apart, rack, perplex

disténtio -ónis: f.; fullness, occupation

disténtus -a -um: filled up, full, distended, occupied, busy

distillátio -ónis: f.; bodily fluid

distíllo -áre: (1); drip, drop

distínctio -ónis: f.; distinction, difference, division

distínctus -a -um: adorned, decorated, separated, distinct, clear; distíncte: adv.

distíneo -ére -ui -téntum: (2); keep apart, separate, hold off

distínguo -ere -stínxi -stínctum: (3); divide, separate, discriminate, speak distinctly

dísto -áre: (1); be apart or distinct

distórtus -a -um: misshapen

distráho -ere: (3); forcibly divide, distract, frustrate, perplex

distríbuo -ere -ui -útum: (3); distribute, divide

distribútio -ónis: f.; distribution, allotment

distributívus -a -um: distributive

distribútor -óris: m.; distributor

distríctio -ónis: f.; strictness, severity

distríctus -a -um: strict, severe; distrícte (distríctim): adv.

distríctus -us: m.; district, division

distúrbo -áre: (1); drive apart, drive into confusion, disturb, upset

ditátor -óris: m.; an enricher

ditésco -ere: (3); grow rich

dithalássus -a -um: open to two seas

dítio -ónis: f.; power, sovereignty, dominion, authority

dityssimus -a -um: very rich, richest

dítius: more abundantly

díto -áre: (1): endow, enrich

dítto -áre: (1); repeat, declare

díu: long time, long, by day

   jam díu: for a long time

   quam díu: as long as

diurnále -is: n.; a book containing Lauds to Compline

diurnárius -ii: m.; journalist, diary keeper

diúrnum -i: n., diurnále -is: n.; Book of Hours

diúrnus -a -um: daily, per day, lasting for a day, of a day

díus -a -um: godlike, divine, noble

diútius: for a longer while, longer

diutúrnus -a -um: of long duration, lasting

divéllo -ere -vélli -vúlsum: (3); rend, tear asunder

divéndo -ere -véndidi -vénditum: (3); sell

diversífico -áre: (1); vary, be different, diversify

divérsitas -átis: f.; diversity, disagreement

diversórium (deversórium) -ii: n.; inn, lodging-place, lodging

divérsus -a -um: different, opposite, contrary; *perf. pass. part. of* divérto in divérsum: back; divérse: *adv.*

divérto (divórto) -ere -vérti -vérsum: (3); turn away or aside, differ, deviate, go opposite

díves, dívitis: m.; rich man, rich

divéxo -áre: (1); plunder, tear apart

dívido -ere -vísi -vísum: (3); divide, part, put asunder, separate

divinátio -ónis: f.; divination, foreseeing

divínitas -átis: f.; divinity

divínitus: by divine help, divinely, from heaven

divínus (dívus) -a -um: divine; *see Appendix*

divisíbilis -is -e: divisible

divísio -ónis: f.; part, division, portion

divítia -ae: f.; wealth; pl.: riches

divítior -ior -ius: wealthier, richer

divórtium -ii: n.; divorce, division

divórto: *see* divérto

divulgátio -ónis: f.; publishing, spreading abroad

divúlgo -áre: (1); spread around

dívus -a -um: divine, holy; *as a noun:* saint

do, dáre, dédi, dátum: (1); give

dóceo -ére, dócui, dóctum: (2); teach, instruct

docíbilis -is -e: teachable

dócilis -is -e: attentive, docile; docíliter: *adv.*

docílitas -átis: f.; docility

dóctor -óris: m.; dóctrix -ícis: f.; doctor, teacher; *see Appendix*

Dóctor Angélicus: Angelic Doctor, St. Thomas Aquinas

Dóctor Commúnis: Universal Doctor, St. Thomas Aquinas

Dóctor Ecstáticus: Exalted Doctor, Denis the Carthusian

Dóctor Eucharísticus: Eucharistic Doctor, St. John Chrysostom

Dóctor Exímius: Excellent Doctor, Francis Suarez

Dóctor Grátiae: Doctor of Grace, St. Augustine of Hippo

Dóctor Irrefragábilis: Unanswerable Doctor, Alexander of Hales

Dóctor Mariánus: Marian Doctor, St. Anselm of Canterbury

Dóctor Mellífluus: Honeysweet Doctor, St. Bernard of Clairvaux

Dóctor Mirábilis: Marvelous Doctor, Roger Bacon

Dóctor Seráphicus: Seraphic Doctor, St. Bonaventure

Dóctor Súbtilis: Subtle Doctor, John Duns Scotus

Dóctor Universális: Universal Doctor, St. Albert the Great

doctorális -is -e: doctoral, pertaining to the degree of doctor

doctrína -ae: f.; doctrine, instruction, teaching, learning

doctrinális -is -e: doctrinal, theoretical

dóctus -a -um: learned

documentális -is -e: documentary

documentátio -ónis: f.; documentation, proof, reminder

documéntum -i: n.; document, example, proof, warning, specimen dógma -atis: n.; dogma, edict, defined doctrine

dogmáticus -a -um: dogmatic, doctrinal, relating to doctrine or dogma; dogmátice: adv.

dolénter: painfully, with grief or sorrow

dóleo -ére -ui -itum: (2); grieve, suffer, be sorrowful, hurt

dolíolum -i: n.; cask, small keg

dólium -ii: n.; earthenware cask

dólo -áre: (1); hew with an axe

dólor -óris: m.; sorrow, pain, dolor

dolorósus -a -um: sorrowful, painful; dolénter: adv.

dolósitas -átis: f.; deceitfulness

dolósus -a -um: false, deceitful; dolóse: adv.

dólus -i: m.; fraud, deceit, guilt, craft, deception, subtlety

D.O.M.: abbrev. for Déo Óptimo Máximo, to God, the Best, the Greatest

dóma -atis: n.; roof, dwelling, house

domésticus -a -um: domestic

doméstici -órum: m. pl.; those of the household, domestics

domicelláris -is: m.; candidate for a prebend

domicílium -ii: n.; house, home, dwelling, abode, domicile; see Appendix

dómina -ae: f.; lady, mistress

dominátio -ónis: f.; domination, rule, sovereignty

dominatívus -a -um: ruling, governing, dominating; see Appendix

dominátor -óris: m.; ruler, lord

dominátus -us: m.; rule, command, mastery, tyranny

Dómine: voc.; Lord; dómine: sir

Domínica -ae: f.; Sunday

Domínica benedícta: Trinity Sunday

Domínica capitilávium: Palm Sunday

Domínica cárnis prívii: Sunday before Lent

Domínica Competéntium: Palm Sunday

Domínica daémon mútus: third Sunday of Lent

Domínica de pánibus: Laetare Sunday, the middle Sunday of Lent

Domínica Rósa (de Rósa): Rose Sunday, a name for Laetare Sunday

Domínica Exsúrge: Sexagesima Sunday (no longer exists)

Domínica flórum: Palm Sunday

Domínica Gaudéte: third Sunday of Advent

Domínica Hosánna: Palm Sunday

Domínica in álbis: Low Sunday, the first Sunday after Easter

Domínica indulgéntiae: Palm Sunday

Domínica májor: a Sunday of the first order (this classification no longer exists)

Domínica mediána: Laetare Sunday

Domínica nóva: Low Sunday

Domínica Pástor Bónus: Good Shepherd Sunday, the second Sunday after Easter

Domínica Quintána: first Sunday of Lent

Domínica Ramispálma: Palm Sunday

Domínica refectiónis: Laetare Sunday

Domínica répus: Passion Sunday

Domínica Resurrectiónis: Easter Sunday

Domínica Resurréxi: Easter Sunday

Domínica Rosárum: Sunday after the Ascension

Domínica Spíritus Dómini: Pentecost

Domínica vácans: second Sunday of Lent (formerly had no special Office)

Domínicae vágae: Sundays after the Epiphany (no longer exist)

dominicále -is: n.; small linen cloth in which the faithful received Holy Communion dominicális -is -e: pertaining to Sunday or to the Lord

Dominicánus -a -um: Dominican

Domínicum -i: n.; Holy Eucharist

domínicum -i: n.; a church together with all its possessions

Domínicus -i: m.; Dominic

domínicus -a -um: pertaining to the Lord, of a master

domínium: -ii: n.; mastery, power, control, rule; property

dóminor -ári: dep. (1); dominate, rule, prevail over, have dominion over

Dóminus -i: m.; voc. Dómine; Lord; dóminus -i: m.; lord, master

Dóminus vobíscum: may the Lord be with you

Domitiánus -i: m.; Domitian

domítius -a -um: pertaining to the house

dómne: voc.; sir

dómnus -i: m.; lord, master

dómo -áre -ui -itum: (1); tame, control, conquer

domúncula -ae: f.; small dwelling

dómus -us, dómus -i: f.; house; de dómo in dómum: from house to house

donárium -ii: n.; shrine, temple, place in temple for offerings

donátio -ónis: f.; gift, donation

Donatístae -árum: m. pl. Donatists

donátor -óris: m.; giver, donor

donátus -i: m.; an oblate

donátus -us: m.; gift, present

dónec: until, while, as long as

dóno -áre: (1); give, grant, forgive, remit a debt

dónum -i: n.; gift, present

dórmio -íre: (4); sleep, lie down to rest

dormitátio -ónis: f.; slumber

dormítio -ónis: f.; repose, sleep

Dormítio Beátae Maríae: Assumption; see Appendix

dormíto -áre: (1); sleep, be lazy

dorsuále -is: n.; back of a chair; curtain around back of altar

dórsum -i: n.; back

dos, dótis: f.; gift, dowry, endowment, talent, qualification

dotális -is -e: belonging to a dowry

dotátio -ónis: f.; endowment

dóto -áre: (1); endow

doxológia -ae: f.; doxology; see Appendix

dráchma -ae: f.; drachma, small Greek coin, often with an image of a ruler

dráco -ónis: m.; dragon, snake, demon

draconárius -ii: m.; flag bearer

dramáticus -a -um: dramatic

dromedárius -ii: m.; dromedary

dubíetas -átis, dubitátio -ónis: f.; doubt, uncertainty

dúbito -áre: (1); doubt, hesitate, waver; non dubitáre: firmly believe

dúbius -a -um: doubtful, doubting, uncertain; as a n. noun: doubt, hesitation; dúbie (dubitánter): adv.; see Appendix

ducátus -us: m.; guidance, rank, leadership

ducentésimus -a -um: two hundreth

ducénti -ae -a: two hundred

ducilóquus -a -um: sweetly speaking

ducíssa -ae: f.; duchess

dúco -ere -dúxi -dúctum: (3); lead, bring; consider, hold, reckon; dispose; dúcere in matrimónium: marry

dúctilis -is -e: drawn, beaten out, made of beaten metal

dúcto -áre: (1); lead

dúctor -óris: m.; leader, commander

dúctus -us: m.; leadership, direction, purpose; the swing of a censer

dúdum: just now, a little while ago, not long since; jam dúdum: long, a long time

duéllo -áre: (1); to duel

duéllum -i: n.; conflict, duel, single combat

dúlce: sweetly
dulcédo -inis: f.; sweetness, goodness
dulcésco -ere -céssi: (3); become sweet
dúlcis -is -e: sweet, kind, fresh
dúlcior -ior -ius: sweeter
dulcisónus -a -um: harmonious, sweet sounding
dúlciter: sweetly
dulcitúdo -inis: f., dúlcor -óris: m.; sweetness
dúlia -ae: f.; religious veneration given to a creature
dum: while, yet, until
dúmmodo: provided that, if only, as long as
dumtáxat: insofar as, only, to this extent
dúo, dúae, dúo: two
duódecim: twelve
duodécimus -a -um: twelfth
duodenárius -a -um: containing twelve
duodéni -ae -a: twelve each
duodevigésimus -a -um: eighteenth
duodevigínti: eighteen
dúplex -icis: twofold, double, insincere
duplicátus -a -um: double

duplícitas -átis: f.; deceit
dúplico -áre: (1); repeat, double
dúplo: doubly, in a double sense
dúplum -i: n.; a double
durátio -ónis: f.; duration
duricórdia -ae: f.; hard-heartedness
duríssimus -a -um: hardest, most difficult
durítia -ae, duríties -éi: f.; hardness
dúro -áre: (1); make hard; persevere, endure, remain, last
dúrus -a -um: hard, stiff, obstinate, tough, harsh; dúra -órum: n. pl.; hardships; dúre: adv.
dux, dúcis: c.; guide, leader, captain, duke, commander
dynámicus -a -um: dynamic, forceful, aggressive
dynamísmus -i: m.; dynamism, strong force or power
dysc- see also disc-
dýscolus -a -um: impudent, harsh, severe, peevish, irritable
dysentéria -ae: f.; dysentery

E

e *or* **ex:** *prep. w. abla.;* from, out of

eádem: by the same road

eátenus: so far, so long, hitherto

ébenus -i: m.; ebony

ébibo -ere -bibi -bíbitum: (3); drink in or up, drink in mentally

Ebionítae -árum: m. pl.; Ebionites

Eborácum -i: n.; York

eblándior -íri: *dep.* (4); obtain by flattery

ebóreus -a -um: of ivory

ebríetas -átis: f.; drunkenness, excess

ebriósus (ébrius) -i: m.; drunkard

ébrius -a -um: drunk, drunken

ebúllio -íre: (4); bubble, break forth, send out

ébur -óris: n.; ivory

eburnéolus (ebúrneus) -a -um: of ivory

écce: *interj.;* behold

ecclésia -ae: f.; assembly, gathering, church, the Church; *see Appendix*

ecclesiális -is -e: ecclesial

Ecclesiástes -is: m.; Ecclesiastes, a book of the O.T.

Ecclesiásticus -i: m.; Ecclesiasticus, a book of the O.T.

ecclesiásticus -a -um: ecclesiastical, pertaining to the Church; *see Appendix*

ecclesíola -ae: f.; a little church

ecóntra (econtrário): on the other hand, on the contrary

écstasis -is: f.; rapture, ecstacy, trance

ecstáticus -a -um: entranced, enraptured, ecstatic

ecténia -ae: f.; ectene, a prayer in the Greek liturgy

edíco -ere -díxi -díctum: (3); publish, decide, determine

edictális -is -e: by edict, according to edict

edíctum -i: n.; decree, edict

edísco -ere -dídici: (3); learn by heart, learn thoroughly

edíssero -sérere -sérui -sértum: (3); set forth, explain, relate, expound

editícius -a -um: proposed, put forth

edítio -ónis: f.; statement, publication, edition

éditor -óris: m.; exhibitor, editor, producer, publisher

éditus -a -um: lofty

édo -ere (ésse), édi, ésum: (3); eat, consume, devour, corrode

édo -ere, édidi, éditum: (3); promulgate, proclaim, publish; bring or set forth, give birth to, beget, produce, give out

edóceo -ére -ui -dóctum: (2); teach completely, instruct

édolo -áre: (1); plane, hew

Édom: *indecl.;* Edom, a name given to Esau, the elder son of Isaac

Edomítes -um: m. pl.; Edomites, descendants of Esau or Edom

édomo -áre: (1); tame thoroughly, subdue, vanquish, conquer

edórmio -íre: (4); sleep away

educátio -ónis: f.; training, bringing up, education

educatívus -a -um: educational

educátor -óris: m., **educátrix** -ícis: f.; tutor, teacher, educator

éduco -áre: (1); bring up, provide for, foster, nourish, sustain, train, educate

edúco -ere -dúxi -dúctum: (3); take away, bring out, produce, bring forth, lead out, lead forth edúlis -is -e: edible

edúlium -ii: n.; food

edúrus -a -um: very hard

éffatha: see éphphatha

effátu: supine; to say, to express

effátum -i: n.; announcement, axiom, prediction

effátus -a -um: pronounced, designated, determined, established, proclaimed

efféctio -ónis: f.; a doing, effecting, performing, practicing

effectívus -a -um: effective, productive; effectíve: adv.

efféctor -óris: m.; maker, doer

efféctus -a -um: perf. pass. part. of effício

efféctus -us: m.; effect, answer, result; reward; accomplishment, work

effeminátus -a -um: effeminate

efferátus -a -um: wild, raging

éffero -férre, éxtuli, elátum: irreg.; raise up, lift, exalt, elevate, publish

effervésco -ere -férbui(-férvi): (3); boil up, rage

éffetha: see éphphatha

efficácia -ae, efficácitas -átis: f.; accomplishment, efficacy, efficiency, power, influence

efficácior -ior -ius: more effective or efficient

éfficax -ácis: zealous, effectual, powerful; efficáciter: adv.

effício -ere -féci -féctum: (3); make, effect, become, perform

effígies -éi: f.; figure, image

effíngo -ere -fínxi -fíctum: (3); form, fashion, rub, express, portray, wipe out

efflágito -áre: (1); entreat

éfflo -áre: (1); give forth, breathe out

efflóreo -ére: (2), efflorésco -ere: (3); blossom forth, bloom, flourish

éffluo -ere -flúxi: (3); flow out, issue

efflúvium -ii: n.; a flowing out, outlet

effódio -ere -fódi -fóssum: (3); dig, break through, dig out, excavate

éffor -ári -fátus: dep. (1); utter, speak out

efformátio -ónis: f.; formation

effórmo -áre: (1); shape, form, fashion

effrenátus -a -um: unbridled, without rein, ungoverned, unruly

éffrons -óntis: shameless, insulting, bold, brazen

effugátio -ónis: f.; a driving away, putting to flight

effúgio -ere -fúgi -fúgitum: (3); avoid, escape from, shun

éffugo -áre: (1); drive away from

effúlgeo -ére -fúlsi -fúlsum: (2); shine upon

effúndo -ere -fúdi -fúsum: (3); pour out, pour forth, bring out, shed

effúsio -ónis: f.; a pouring forth, effusion, profusion, shedding

effúsus -a -um: excessive

effútio -íre: (4); babble, chatter

e.g.: abbrev. for exémpli grátia; for example

égens -éntis: needy

egénus -a -um: needy

égeo -ére -ui: (2); be in want, have need of, be destitute

egéstas -átis: f.; need, want, poverty

égo: I

egoísmus -i: m.; egoism

egoísticus -a -um: egotistical

égomet: emphatic for égo

egrédior -i -gréssus: dep. (3); come out, march forth, go out, go forth, depart

egrégius -a -um: illustrious, famous, distinguished, eminent, excellent; egrégie: adv.

egréssio -ónis: f., egréssus -us: m.; departure, going forth, egress, flight; digression

éheu: interj.; ah

éia (éja): interj.; quick! come then! well!

eíleton: n.; Greek; corporal in the Greek rite

ejéctio -ónis: f.; ejéctus -us: m.;
banishment, exile

ejício (eício) -ere -jéci -jéctum: (3); cast
out, drive out, expel, thrust out, exile

ejulátus -us: m.; lamentation, lamenting,
bemoaning, cry

éjulo -áre: (1); wail, lament

ejúro -áre: (1); deny, refuse, abandon

ejúsmodi: of this sort, of such kind; et
ejúsmodi: and the like

elábor, elábi, elápsus: dep. (3); slip away,
fall out

elaborátio -ónis: f.; elaboration,
persevering effort

eláboro -áre: (1); elaborate, work out,
take pains with

Elamítae -árum: m. pl.; Elamites

elánguens -éntis: growing weak

elanguésco -ere -lángui: (3); grow weak
or faint

elápsus -us: m.; lapse

elárgior -íri: dep. (4); give out,
distribute, bestow

eláta -ae: f.; spray

elátio -ónis: f.; elevation, raising up;
carrying out, burial; pride

elátus -a -um: elevated, raised, chosen,
lifted up, carried up, proud

eléctio -ónis: f.; election, choice,
selection, election to salvation

electívus -a -um: elective

eléctor -óris: m.; elector

eléctricus -a -um: electric

eléctrum -i: n.; electrum

eléctus -a -um: chosen, elect, bright,
beautiful, saved in eternity; elécta
-órum: n. pl.; chosen bits, dainties;
eléctus -i: m, elécta -ae: f.; candidate

eleemósyna -ae: f.; alms

élegans -ántis: elegant, choice, graceful,
beautiful, adorned

eléison: Greek; have mercy on us

elementáris -is -e, elementarius -a -um:
elementary, rudimentary

eleméntum -i: n.; element, first principle

elénchus -i: m.; list, review, refutation

elevátio -ónis: f.; lifting up, elevation

élevo -áre: (1); elevate, raise, lift up

Éli: Hebrew; my God

elício -ere -lícui -lícitum: (3); bring
forth, elicit, produce, allure, call out

elído -ere -lísi -lísum: (3); throw open,
cast or dash down

éligo -ere -légi -léctum: (3); elect,
choose, select, pick out

elimáte: clearly, exactly

eliminátor -óris: m.; purifier, cleanser

elímino -áre: (1); eradicate, eliminate

elíngo -ere: (3); lick up

Eliséus -i: m.; Eliseus

Elízabeth: indecl.; Elizabeth

elógium -ii: n.; eulogy, expression of
praise, maxim, statement

Éloi: Aramaic; my God

elóngo -áre: (1); be far off, go far off,
remove far off, elongate

eloquénter: eloquently

eloquéntia -ae: f.; eloquence, oratory

elóquium -ii: n.; word, speech

elóquor -i -locutus: dep. (3); clarify,
elucidate, speak out

elúceo -ére: (2); shine forth, stand out
clearly, be apparent

elucésco -ere: (3); begin to be light

elúcido -áre: (1); explain

elúcubro -áre: (1); compose by
lamplight, compose with great labor

éluo -ere -ui -útum: (3); wash clean,
purify, cleanse

emanátio -ónis: f.; emanation

emancipátus -a -um: emancipated,
declared free

emáno -áre: (1); flow out, spring,
emanate, become known

emárceo -ére: (2); decay, wither

embléma -atis: n.; emblem

emblemáticus -a -um: of emblems

embólium -ii: n.; episode, interlude

embolísmus -i: m.; insertion

emendátio -ónis: f.; correction, conversion, betterment

emendíco -áre: (1); beg, solicit

eméndo -áre: (1); amend, chastise

eméntior -íri: *dep.* (4); pretend, falsify

emérgo -ere -si -sum: (3); emerge, come forth, get clear

eméritus -a -um: deserving, veteran; **eméritus** -i: m., **emérita** -ae: f.; retired person; **eméritum** -i: n.; pension

émico -áre -mícui -micátum: (1); shine forth, pour forth

émigro -áre: (1); depart, wander forth, remove from a place, leave, emigrate

éminens -éntis: excellent; **eminénter:** *adv.*

eminéntia -ae: f.; excellence, a standing out; the title of a cardinal

eminentíssimus -a -um: most eminent

emíneo -ére -mínui: (2); stand out, be above, be plain, be visible, be apparent

éminus: at a distance

emissárius -ii: m.; emissary, scout, spy; attendant; scapegoat

emíssio -ónis: f.; emitting, making religious profession, sending out, letting go; **in emíssione:** in exile

emítto -ere -mísi -míssum: (3); send out, cast out, yield, release

Emmánuel: *Hebrew;* Emmanuel, God with us

émo -ere, émi, émptum: (3); buy

emóllio -íre: (4); soften

emoluméntum -i: n.; advantage, gain, profit

emóneo -ére: (2); warn, admonish

emortuális -is -e: pertaining to death; **campána emortuális:** passing bell, death knell

emóveo -ére -móvi -mótum: (2); move out

empháticus -a -um: emphatic

emphyteúsis -eos: f.; emphyteusis, lease on church goods

emphyteúta -ae: c.; lessee

emphyteúticus -a -um: pertaining to emphyteusis

empíricus -a -um: based on experience, experiential

empórium -ii: n.; market

émptio -ónis: f.; purchase, buying

émptor -óris: m.; buyer, purchaser

emunctórium -ii: n.; snuffer for trimming candles and lamps

emundátio -ónis: f.; glory, splendor, majesty; cleansing

emúndo -áre: (1); cleanse well

en: *interj.;* lo, behold

enarrátio -ónis: f.; conversation

enárro -áre: (1); relate, tell, publish, declare, show forth

enáscor -ci -nátus: *dep.* (3); spring up, be born

enávigo -áre: (1); sail away, swim

Encaénia -órum: n. pl.; feast of the Dedication of the Temple

encaénio -áre: (1); put on something new, consecrate

enchirídion -ii: n.; manual, handbook

encólpium -ii: n.; medal worn on neck

encýclicus -a -um; general, universal, circular; **encýclica epístula:** encyclical letter; *see Appendix*

Éndor: *indecl.;* Endor, a town southeast of Nazareth

Enéas -ae: m.; *see* **Aenéas**

energía -ae: f.; energy, efficiency

energúmenus -a -um: possessed by a devil

enérvis -is -e, **enérvus** -a -um: weak, nervelesss, enervated, effeminate, unnerved; **enérviter:** *adv.*

enígma: *see* **aenígma**

énim: for, indeed, in fact, because, truly

enimvéro: certainly, to be sure, truly

eníteo -ére: (2), enitésco -ere: (3); shine forth, gleam, brighten

eníor -i -níxus: *dep.* (3); exert, struggle, bring forth, bear, strive

eníxe: eagerly, earnestly, strenuously

enódo -áre: (1); make clear

enórmis -is -e: enormous, irregular, immoderate, immense, unusual; **enórmiter:** *adv.*

ens -éntis: n.; being

ens in quántum ens: being inasmuch as it is being

ens ratiónis: rational being, human being

énsis -is: m.; sword, sword blade

entitatívus -a -um: of the nature of a being

enúbilo -áre: (1); make clear

enucleáte: plainly, clearly

enúcleo -áre: (1); lay open, make clear, explain, clean out

enumerátio -ónis: f.; enumeration

enúmero -áre: (1); count, number, enumerate

enuntiátio -ónis: f.; declaration, proposition, enunciation

enúntio -áre: (1); declare, disclose, announce, tell, divulge

enútrio -íre: (4); nourish, sustain, preserve

éo: and for that reason, there, to that place

éo . . . quo: so much . . . by how much; to that extent . . . insofar as; *with comparatives:* the . . . the . . .

éo úsque: up to that time, until

éo, íre, íi (ívi), ítum: go, proceed

éous -a -um: from the east, pertaining to dawn, morning

eoúsque: to that point

epácta -ae: f.; epact

epárchia -ae: f.; diocese in the Eastern Church; *see Appendix*

ephébeum -i: n.; school, college

ephébia -ae: f.; school for youth

ephébia -órum: n. pl.; youth center

ephébus -i: m.; page, youth between 16 and 21 years old

ephémeris -ídis: f.; journal, diary, daybook

Ephésii -órum: m. pl.; Ephesians

Ephesínus -a -um: of Ephesus

éphi: *indecl.:* n.; ephah, a Hebrew measure

éphod: *indecl.;* ephod, a Jewish vestment, amice

éphphatha (éphpheta): *Hebrew;* be opened

Éphraem (Éphraim): *indecl.:* m.; Ephraem, Ephraim, son of Joseph; a tribe of Israel; **fílii Éphraem:** sons of Ephraim, Ephraimites

Éphrata (Éphrathah): *Hebrew;* another name for Bethlehem

epiclésis -is: f.; invocation, calling down, summoning

Epicuréi -orum: m. pl.; Epicureans

epigonátion -ii: n.; *Greek;* genuále -is: n.; an ornament on a bishop's cincture in the Greek rite

epilépticus -a -um: suffering from epilepsy

epimánikon -i: n.; *Greek;* maniple in the Greek rite

epinícion -ii: n.; feast celebrated after a victory

Epiphánia -ae: f.; Epiphany, feast of Kings, Twelfth Day

Epiphánia secúnda: so called to distinguish Jan. 6 from Christmas, which was the first Epiphany

epiphónus -i: m.; second of two musical notes and smaller than the first

episcopális -is -e: episcopal; *see Appendix*

episcopáliter: in episcopal fashion

episcopátus -us: m.; episcopate, bishopric, overseer, post of authority

episcópium -ii: n.; see, bishop's residence

epíscopus -i: m.; bishop, patriarch; *see* Appendix

epíscopus castrénsis: military bishop

epíscopus chóri: director of a choir

epíscopus tituláris: titular bishop; *see* Appendix

epísema -tis: n.; tail on note in music to show prolongation

epístola (epístula) -ae: f.; epistle, letter

Epistolárium -ii: n.; book of Epistles

epistoléIla -ae: f.; short epistle

epistólium -ii: n.; letter

epístula -ae: *see* epístola

epistýlium -ii: n.; architrave

epitáphium -ii: n.; epitaph, eulogy, funeral oration

epithalámium -ii: n.; marriage song

epitrachélion -ii: n.; stole

épulae -árum: f. pl.; feast, feasts

épulor -ári: *dep.* (1); feast, make merry, rejoice, banquet

éques -itis: m.; rider, horseman

equéster -tris -tre: equestrian

équidem: truly, indeed, certainly

equipollénter: *see* aequipóllens

equúleus -i: m.; rack, instrument of torture

équus -i: m.; horse

equivalénter: *see* aequipóllens

erádico -áre: (1); root up, eradicate

erádo -ere -rási -rásum: (3); destroy, strike, cut off

eréctio -ónis: f.; erection, lifting up; permit to travel

eréctus -a -um: attentive, erect

ereméticus -a -um: solitary, pertaining to a hermit

eremíta -ae: m.; hermit

éremus (erémus) -i: m.; wilderness, desert, solitude, waste; hermitage

érga: *prep. w. acc.;* to, toward, in respect to, over against, opposite

ergástulum -i: n.; prison, workhouse, house of detention for slaves

érgo: therefore, then, consequently

erícius -ii: m.; porcupine

érigo -ere -réxi -réctum: (3); erect, lift up, set up, raise up, place up

erípio -ere -rípui -réptum: (3); rescue, deliver from, snatch away

ermellinéus -a -um: of ermine

erogátio -ónis: f.; paying, distribution

érogo -áre: (1); distribute, disperse, pay out, bequeath

eróticus -a -um: erotic

errátum -i: n.; mistake, error

érro -áre: (1); make a mistake, err, go astray, wander, rove

érro -ónis: m.; wanderer, vagabond, night prowler, vagrant

erróneus -a -um: wrong, erroneous

érror -óris: m.; error, deception, mistake

erubésco -ere -rúbui: (3); be ashamed, blush, grow red

erúca -ae: f.; caterpillar, worm

erúcto -áre: (1); utter, declare; belch forth, overflow, bring forth; publish

erúdio -íre: (4); discipline, instruct, teach, educate

erudítio -ónis: f.; learning

erudítus -a -um: informed, instructed

erúmpo -ere -rúpi -rúptum: (3); crush, erupt, break up, break out

éruo -ere -ui -útum: (3); pluck out, tear away, deliver, rescue, save; destroy from the very foundation

érutor -óris: m.; rescuer

ésca -ae: f.; food, meat, eats, eating

eschatológia -ae: f.; eschatology, study of the final things, study of the end of the world

eschatológicus -a -um: eschatological, pertaining to the end

esculéntus -a -um: eatable

Ésdras: *indecl.;* Esdras; a name sometimes given to the book of the O.T. known as Ezra; also an apocryphal book of the O.T.

esotericísmus -i: m.; theory of
esotericism

ésse: *inf. of* sum

esséndi: of being; esséndo: in being

esséntia -ae: f.; essence

essentiális -is -e: essential; essentiáliter:
adv.

est: *with gen. & inf.*: it is up to (this
person to do this)

Ésther: *indecl.;* Esther, a book of the O.T.

esúriens -éntis: c.; hungry person

esúrio -íre: (4); be hungry, hunger for

ésus -us: m.; bread, food, eating

et: and, even, then, also
  et cétera, et céteri: and so forth, and
    the rest
  et ejúsmodi: and the like
  et . . . et: both . . . and

éthecae -árum: f. pl.; portico, gallery

éthice -es, éthica -ae: f.; moral
philosophy, ethics

éthicus -a -um: ethical, moral

éthnici -órum: m. pl.; heathens, pagans,
Gentiles

éthnicus -a -um: heathen, pagan, Gentile

ethnológia -ae: f.; ethnology

ethnologícus -a -um: ethnological, of
ethnology

étiam: also, and, too, yea, certainly; quin
étiam: yea indeed

etiámnum: still yet

etiámsi: even if, although

étsi: although, even if

eúcharis -is -e: gracious, agreeable

eucharístia -ae: f.; thanksgiving, the
Holy Eucharist

eucharistiále -is: n.; vessel for
preserving the Holy Eucharist

eucharistiális -is -e, eucharísticus -a
-um: pertaining to the Holy Eucharist

euchélaion -i: n.; *Greek;* holy oil and the
sacrament of anointing in the Greek
rite

euchológion -ii: n.; euchologion; *see
Appendix*

eúge: well done, good!

eulógia -ae: f.; a present, a name used
for the Holy Eucharist

eunúchus -i: m.; eunuch

euroaquílo -ónis: m.; northeast wind

Európa -ae: f.; Europe

eúrus -i: m.; east wind

euthanásia -ae: f.; euthanasia

Éva -ae: f.; Eve

evácuo -áre: (1); do away with, empty,
make void, put away, evacuate, cancel

evádo -ere -vási -vásum: (3); evade,
escape

evágino -áre: (1); unsheathe, draw out
of the scabbard

évagor -ári: *dep.* (1); wander, stray

evanésco -ere -vánui: (3); vanish, fade
out, become vapid or dissipated, die

evangeliárum -i: n.; book of Gospels

evangélicus -a -um: evangelical, of the
gospel; evangélice: *adv.*

evangelísta -ae: m.; evangelist, author of
a Gospel

evangelistárium -ii: n.; book of Gospels

evangélium -ii: n.; the gospel, a Gospel,
message, good tidings

evangelizátio -ónis: f.; evangelization,
preaching the gospel; *see Appendix*

evangelízo -áre: (1); evangelize, preach
the gospel, proclaim good tidings

evánuo -ere: (3); become vain or empty
or foolish

evásio -ónis: f.; escape, deliverance, a
going out

éveho -ere -véxi -véctum: (3); raise,
carry out

evéllo -ere -vélli -vúlsum: (3); pull,
pluck out, tear

evénio -íre -véni -véntum: (4); come
out, come forth, happen, befall

evéntum -i: n., evéntus -i: m.; issue,
event, outcome, occurence

evérro -ere -vérri -vérsum: (3); sweep out, clean out

evérsio -ónis: f.; overthrow, destruction, disruption, subverting

evérto -ere -vérti -vérsum: (3); overthrow, overturn, take away, make void, pervert, agitate, destroy

evíctus -a -um: *perf. pass. part. of* evínco

évidens -éntis: apparent, visible, manifest; evidénter: *adv.*

evidéntia -ae: f.; evidence

evigilátio -ónis: f.; awakening

evígilo -áre: (1); be vigilant, awake

evínco -ere -víci -víctum: (3); bring about, induce, prevail, vanquish

evíscero -áre: (1); gnaw, waste

evitándus -a -um: that which must be avoided

evíto -áre: (1); shun, avoid

evocátio -ónis: f.; evocation, calling forth

évoco -áre: (1); summon, call forth

evolútio -ónis: f.; evolution, development, unfolding

evolutívus -a -um: evolutionary

evólvo -ere -vólvi -volútum: (3); develop, roll away, unroll, unfold

evóvae: a meaningless word used in choral books to show some vowel sounds

evulgátio -ónis: f.; making known, publication

evúlgo -áre: (1); make known, publish, divulge

ex: *prep. w. abla.;* out of, from; *see Appendix*

ex advérso: opposite

ex aéquo: justly

ex cápite: from the head or from the chapter

ex Cáthedra: from the chair (of Peter); refers to infallibility of the Pope; *see Appendix*

ex éo quod: from the fact that, because

ex fíde: in good faith

ex íllo: since then, from that place or time

ex improvíso: suddenly

ex longínquo: from a distance

ex offício: officially, by virtue of office; *see Appendix*

ex ópere operáto: by the work having been performed, effective because the work was done; *see Appendix*

ex ópere operántis: by the work of the worker, effectiveness comes from disposition or capabilities of the worker; *see Appendix*

ex párte: in part

ex párte mulíeris: on the part of the woman

ex párte víri: on the part of the man

ex pártibus: from the parts or sides

ex profésso: avowedly, openly

ex tóto: wholly

ex úsu: expediently

ex utráque párte: from each side or part

exacerbátio -ónis: f.; exasperation, bitterness, irritation, provocation

exacérbo -áre: (1); provoke, embitter

exáctio -ónis: f.; levying of tribute, tax, demanding

exáctor -óris: m.; tax collector, one who makes a demand, oppressor

exáctus -a -um: precise, exact, accurate, sharp; exácte: *adv.*

exácuo -ere -ui -útum: (3); sharpen, whet, stimulate, encourage

exacútus -a -um: sharpened, stimulated

exaedífico -áre: (1); build

exaéquo -áre: (1); equal, make equal

exaéstuo -áre: (1); heat, boil, burn

exággero -áre: (1); grow worse, increase, exaggerate

exágito -áre: (1); attack, drive out, disturb, harass

exaltátio -ónis: f.; high praise, exaltation, raising up

exálto -áre: (1); extol, exalt, lift up,
glorify, elevate in rank or honor

exámen -inis: n.; test, examination,
agony, struggle

examinátor -óris: m.; examiner,
arbitrator

examinátus -a -um: careful, exact,
scrupulous

exámino -áre: (1); test, try, weigh, refine,
purify, ponder, consider

exántlo -áre: (1); exhaust, endure, bar,
suffer much from toil

exapério -íre: (4); disclose, explain,
disentangle

exarchía -ae: f.; exarchy; see Appendix

exárchus -i: m.; exarch, Primate; see
Appendix

exárdeo -ére -ársi -ársum: (2); kindle,
inflame, break out

exardésco -ere -ársi -ársum: (3); be
inflamed, take fire, be kindled

exarésco -ere -árui: (3); become dry,
wither, dry up

exármo -áre: (1); disarm

éxaro -áre: (1); write on wax, plough,
dig up, print, till

exasperátio -ónis: f.; bitterness,
exasperation

exasperátor -óris: m., exasperátrix -ícis:
f.; one who provokes

exáspero -áre: (1); provoke, embitter

exaudíbilis -is -e: worthy of being heard

exaúdio -íre: (4); hear favorably, hear
graciously, hearken to, answer

exaudítio -ónis: f.; favorable answer to a
prayer

exaudítor -óris: m.; one who listens
graciously to a prayer

excaéco -áre: (1); blind, mentally blind

excalceátus -a -um: barefooted,
discalced, unshod

excandésco -ere -cándui: (3); take fire,
burn with anger

excardinátio -ónis: f.; excardination; see
Appendix

excárdino -áre: (1); excardinate

excarnífico -áre: (1); tear to pieces

éxcavo -áre: (1); dig out

excédo -ere -céssi -céssum: (3); go
beyond, exceed, go out, go away,
depart, transgress, yield, retire

excéllens -éntis: distinguished, excellent;
excellénter: adv.

excelléntia -ae: f.; excellence

excéllo -ere -céllui -célsum: (3); be
eminent, excel, elevate

excélsa -órum: n. pl.; high places

excélsitas -átis: f.; preeminence,
loftiness, height

excélsum -i: n.; high position; excélsa
-órum: n. pl.; high places

in excélsis: in the highest

in excélso: on high

excélsus -a -um: lofty, high, sublime,
august, glorious

Excélsus -i: m.; the Most High

excéptio -ónis: f.; exception

exceptionális -a -um: exceptional

exceptórium -ii: n.; reservoir, receptacle

excéptus -a -um: only, excepted

excérebro -áre: (1); make senseless,
deprive of brains, to brain

excérpo -ere -si -tum: (3); pick out,
select

excéssus -us: m.; excess, departure,
transgression, going out, deviation,
loss of self-possession, death

excídium -ii: n.; annihilation

excído -ere -cídi -císum: (3); hew or cut
down

excípio -ere -cépi -céptum: (3); take out,
accept, make an exception for, exclude

excísus -us: m.; slip, cut, piece

éxcito -áre: (1); excite, stimulate, kindle,
appeal to, raise up

éxcitor -óris: m.; awakener

Éxcitor méntium: awakener of souls, Christ

exclámo -áre: (1); cry out, exclaim

exclaustrátio -ónis: f.; exclaustration; *see Appendix*

exclaustrátus -a -um: exclaustrated, outside the cloister

exclúdo -ere -clúsi -clúsum: (3); reject, exclude, drive away, keep out

exclúsio -ónis: f.; exclusion

exclusívus -a -um: exclusive; **exclusíve:** *adv.*

excogitátio -ónis: f.; invention, thinking out, contriving, devising

excógito -áre: (1); devise, invent

excólo -áre: (1); strain out

éxcolo -ere -cólui -cúltum: (3); cultivate, tend, work for; worship; ennoble, perfect

excommunicátio -ónis: f.; excommunication; *see Appendix*

excommúnico -áre: (1); excommunicate

excóquo -ere -cóxi -cóctum: (3); refine, boil down, burn out; destroy

excório -áre: (1); flay

éxcors -córdis: foolish, unlearned

excrésco -ere -crévi -crétum: (3); grow

excúbiae -árum: f. pl.; keeping watch

éxcubo -áre: (1); keep watch, guard

excúlco -áre: (1); tread or beat out

excúltus -a -um: *perf. pass. part. of* **éxcolo**

excúrsus -us: m.; running out, passage

excusátio -ónis: f.; excuse, justification, dispensation

excúso (excússo) -áre: (1); excuse, absolve, plead as an excuse; **ad excusándas excusatiónes:** to seek excuses

excússio -ónis: f.; act of shaking, a shaking down; interrogation, examination

excússus -a -um: cast out, thrown down or out

excútio -ere -cússi -cússum: (3); search, examine, interrogate; shake

exe- *see also* **exse-**

execrábilis -is -e: detestable

execraméntum -i: n.; abomination

execrátio -ónis: f.; curse, malediction, object of execration

éxecror -ári: *dep.* (1); curse, execrate

executoríus -ii: *see* **exsecutívus**

éxedra -ae: f.; hall, large room

exegésis -eos, **exegétice** -es: f.; exegesis, the art of interpretation

exegéta -ae: c.; exegete, interpreter of Scripture

exémplar -áris: n.; example, model, copy

exempláris -is -e: serving as an example or pattern, exemplary

exémplum -i: n.; example

exémptio -ónis: f.; exemption

exémptus -a -um: exempt

éxeo -íre -ívi (-ii) -itum: (4); go out, depart

exéquiae (exséquiae) -árum: f. pl.; funeral rites

exequiális (exsequiális) -is -e: of funeral rites

exércens -céntis: c.; operator, worker, doer, performer

exérceo -ére -cui -citum: (2); exercise, practice; meditate, pray; work at; occupy

exercitátio -ónis: f., **exercítium** -ii: n.; exercise, practice

exercítia spirituália: retreat, spiritual exercises

exército -áre: (1); exercise, employ, use, engage, occupy; *pass.:* ponder

exércitus -us: m.; host, army

exfornicátus -a -um: given to fornication

exhaúrio -íre, -haúsi, -haústus: (4); exhaust, empty out, end, remove

exhaústus -a -um: exhausted

exhíbeo -ére -ui -itum: (2); exhibit, show, display, present; return, deliver, offer; entertain; promise

exhibítio -ónis: f.; display, exhibition, example

exhílaro -áre: (1); make cheerful, gladden

exhonorátio -ónis: f.; shame

exhonóro -áre: (1); dishonor, disgrace

exhórreo -ére -hórrui: (2); shudder

exhortátio -ónis: f.; exhortation, encouragement, an encouraging

exhórto (exhórtor) -áre: (1); encourage, exhort

éxhumo -áre: (1); exhume

éxiens, exeúntis: pres. part. of éxeo

exigéntia -ae: f.; exigency, urgency, emergency

éxigo -ere -égi -áctum: (3); to demand

exigúitas -átis: f.; scarcity, smallness, shortness

exíguus -a -um: little, scanty, small, short, poor

exílitas -átis: f.; shrillness

exílium -ii: n.; exile, banishment

exímius -a -um: wonderful, priceless, extraordinary, select

éximo -ere -émi -émptum: (3); draw out, banish, deliver, release, take away

exinánio -íre: (4); empty, pour out, exhaust; raze, destroy utterly

exinanítio -ónis: f.; emptiness

exínde: henceforth, then, thenceforth, thereupon, therefrom

existéntia -ae: f.; existence

existentialísmus -i: m.; doctrine of existentialism

existimátio (exsistimátio) -ónis: f.; esteem, estimation, judgment

exístimo -áre: (1); think, reckon, judge, be of opinion, take account of

exísto (exsísto) -ere, éxstiti, éxstitum: (3); exist, be visible, emerge, appear

exitabíliter: ruinously, perniciously

exitiális -is -e: destructive

exítium -ii: n.; destruction, ruin, death, ending

éxitus -us: m.; death, end; departure, exit, going out; conclusion, result, outcome

éxitus -a -um: gone, left, departed; perf. pass. part. of éxeo

éxitus viárum: highways

Éxodus -us: m.; Exodus, a book of the O.T.

exomologésis -is: f.; confession of sin

exónero -áre: (1); free from a burden, unload, relieve, free

exópto -áre: (1); wish eagerly, hope for

exorábilis -is -e: placable, able to be entreated

exorátio -ónis: f.; petition, prayer, mercy

exorcísmus -i: m.; exorcism

exorcísta -ae: f., exorcístus -i: m.; exorcist

exorcistátus -us: m.; minor order of exorcist, which no longer exists

exorcízo -áre: (1); exorcise

exórdium -ii: n.; beginning, source, institution

exórior -íri -órtus: dep. (4) with some forms in (3); spring up, rise, appear

exornátus -a -um: embellished

exórno -áre: (1); adorn, provide with

exóro -áre: (1); pray, plead, beseech, supplicate, implore, entreat earnestly

exósculo -áre: (1); kiss

exósus -a -um: hated

exp- see also exsp-

expándo -ere -pánsi -pánsum or pássum: (3); stretch, spread out

expánsio -ónis: f.; spreading out, expansion

expavésco -ere -pávi: (3); tremble, be terrified

expectátio -ónis: f.; expectation

expécto -áre: (1); expect, await

expediéndus -a -um: settled, disentangled

expédio -íre: (4); deliver, detach, be expedient, expedite, hasten, free, prepare, arrange; *impers.:* it is advantageous, useful or expedient

expedíte: readily, promptly, without difficulty or impediment; see *Appendix*

expedítio -ónis: f.; act of dispatching, expedition

expedítus -a -um: well-appointed, light-armed

expéllo -ere -puli -púlsum: (3); drive out, expel, thrust forth

expéndo -ere -péndi -pénsum: (3); weigh

expénsa -ae: f.; expense

expénsio -ónis: f.; expenditure, expense

expénsum -i: n.; payment, money paid

expergefácio -ere -féci -fáctum: (3); arouse, wake up

expergíscor -sci -perréctus: *dep.* (3); awaken, wake up

experiéntia -ae: f., **experiméntum** -i: n.; experiment, test, trial, proof, experience

expérior -íri -pértus: *dep.* (4); try, endeavor, experience, test

éxpers -értis: lacking in, destitute

expértus -a -um: expert, experienced, proved, tested; **expértus** -i: m., **expérta** -ae: f.; expert, one who has experience

éxpeto -ere -ívi -ítum: (3); desire, seek eagerly

expiátio -ónis: f.; expiation, atonement

expiatórius -a -um: satisfactory, expiatory

éxpio -áre: (1); explain, expound; cleanse, purify; make amends for, propitiate, expiate, make atonement for

expíro: see **exspíro**

explanátio -ónis: f.; explanation

expláno -áre: (1); explain, expound

explánto -áre: (1); cast out

explaúdo: see **explódo**

éxpleo -ére -plévi -plétum: (2); fill, fulfill, finish, complete

explétio -ónis: f.; expiration

expletívus -a -um: serving to fill out, expletive

explicátio -ónis: f.; unfolding, expounding, explanation

explicatívus -a -um: explanatory

explícitus -a -um: explicit, plain, clear; **explícite:** *adv.*

éxplico -áre -ávi(-ui) -átum(-itum): (1); explain, extend, unfold, display, unroll, spread out, make clear, develop

explódo (explaúdo) -ere -plódi -plósum: (3); to hiss

explorátio -ónis: f.; examination, exploration

explóro -áre: (1); explore, investigate

expólio -íre: (4); polish, redecorate

expólitor -óris: m.; polisher

expóno -ere -pósui -pósitum: (3); set before, make manifest, set forth, expound, explain

expórrigo -ere -réxi -réctum: (3); expand, stretch out

expósco -ere -popósci: (3); plead, entreat earnestly, demand vehemently

expósitio -ónis: f.; exhibition, act of exposing, explanation, setting forth, narration, exposition

expostulátio -ónis: f.; expostulation, complaint

expóstulo -áre: (1); demand vehemently, require, dispute

exprésse: expressly, clearly, distinctly

expréssio -ónis: f.; expression, a pressing out

éxprimo -ere -préssi -préssum: (3); express, represent, describe

éxprobo -áre: (1); upbraid, reproach, reprove

exprobrábilis -is -e: worthy of reproach

exprómo -ere -prómpsi -prómptum: (3); draw out, exhibit, display, discover, state

expúgno -áre: (1); fight against, overthrow, afflict, oppress, blot out, cancel

éxpuo -ere -pui: (3); spit, spit upon

expurgátio -ónis: f.; vindication, justification

expurgátus -a -um: expurgated

expúrgo -áre: (1); purge, drive out, cleanse, purify

exquíro -ere -sívi -sítum: (3); seek, inquire diligently, seek after

exquisítio -ónis: f.; research, inquiry, investigation

exquisítor -óris: m.; searcher, investigator

exquisítus -a -um: exquisite, carefully sought out, excellent, made certain, properly considered

exsánguis -is -e: bloodless

exsaturátus -a -um: filled, having enough, satisfied

exsáturo -áre: (1); satisfy

exscíndo -ere -scídi -scíssum: (3); raze to the ground

exscríbo -ere: (3); write out, copy

exsecrábilis (execrábilis) -is -e: abhorrent, detestable, accursed

exsecrándus -a -um: detestable

exsecrátio -ónis: f.; abomination, curse, malediction; profanation, loss of consecration

éxsecror -ári: dep. (1); curse, execrate

exsecútio -ónis: f.; performance, execution, accomplishment; management; discussion; prosecution

exsecutívus (executórius) -a -um: executive

exsecútor -óris: m., exsecútrix -ícis: f.; performer, executor; see Appendix

exséquiae -árum: f. pl. funeral rites, funeral, burial

exsequiális -is -e: funereal, of a funeral

éxsequor -qui -cútus: dep. (3); follow, perform, secure, fulfill

éxsero -ere -sérui -sértum: (3); exert, put forth, reveal, show

exsícco -áre: (1); dry up, make dry

exsílio -íre -sílui -súltum: (4); leap, leap out, spring up, rise

exsílium (exílium) -ii: n.; exile, banishment

exsis- see also exis-

exsisténtia -ae: f.; existence

exsísto (exísto) -ere, éxstiti, éxstitum: (3); come forth, appear, emerge, proceed, arise, become

exsólvo -ere -sólvi -solútum: (3); pay back, restore, present; loose

éxsors -sórtis: deprived of, without

exspectátio -ónis: f.; expectation, hope, waiting, longing

exspécto -áre: (1); expect, look for, long for, wait for, trust, await, anticipate, hope for; dread

exspíro (expíro) -áre: (1); expire, die, exhale

exspólio -áre: (1); rob, despoil

éxspuo -ere -spui -spútum: (3); spit

exst- see also ext-

éxstasis (éxtasis) -is: f.; ecstasy, bewilderment, amazement

exstímulo -áre: (1); excite, stimulate, goad, instigate, prick

exstínctio (extínctio) -ónis: f.; dissolution, annihilation, slaughter, extinction

exstinctívus -a -um: exstinguishing, annihilating

exstínctor -óris: m.; destroyer, annihilator

exstínguo (extínguo) -ere -stínxi -stínctum: (3); extinguish, quench, put out, kill, destroy

exstírpo -áre: (1); tear to pieces, root out, eradicate

éxsto -áre -stiti: (1); stand out, stand forth, appear, come forth, exist

éxstruo (éxtruo) -ere -strúxi -strúctum: (3); build, raise, erect

exsuffátio -ónis: f.; act of blowing

exsúfflo -áre: (1); blow away

éxsul -sulis: banished; éxsul -sulis: c.; exile, refugee

éxsulo (éxulo) -áre: (1); live in exile, banish or be banished

exsultábilis -is -e: joyful

exsultátio -ónis: f.; delight, jubilation, joy, gladness, exultation

Exsúltet: the song at the lighting of the paschal candle on Holy Saturday

exsúlto -áre: (1); rejoice

exsúpero (exúpero) -áre: (1); excel, surpass

exsúrgo (exúrgo) -ere -surréxi -surréctum: (3); arise, awaken

exsúscito -áre: (1); arouse

ext- see also exst-

extális -is: m.; rectum, gut, entrails

éxtasis -is: see éxstasis

exténdo -ere -téndi -ténsum(-téntum): (3); stretch, extend

exténsio -ónis: f.; extension, addition

exsténsor -óris: m.; one who extends

exténuo -áre: (1); weaken, reduce, punish, chasten

éxter -tera -terum, extérnus (éxterus) -a -um: outward, external, foreign, on the outside, strange; extérior -ior -ius: comp.; extérius: adv.

extérgeo (extérgo) -ére -térsi -térsum: (2); wipe, wipe dry, wipe away

extérior -ior -ius: exterior, outward

extérmino -áre: (1); drive out, banish

exterminátor -óris: m.; exterminator, destroyer

extermínium -ii: n.; utter destruction, extermination

extérnus -a -um: belonging to another, external; extérne: adv.

extérreo -ére -térrui -térritum: (2); frighten

éxterus -a -um: foreign, outside; éxterus -i: m., éxtera -ae: f.; foreigner; extérior -ior -ius: outer, exterior, outward

extimésco -ere -tímui: (3); to fear

extínctio -ónis: f.; see exstínctio

extinctórium -ii: n.; extinguisher, candlesnuffer

extínguo: see exstínguo

extolléntia -ae: f.; insolence, haughtiness, pride

extóllo -ere -tuli: (3); lift up, raise up, exalt; in the pass.: be insolent

extórqueo -ére -tórsi -tórtum: (3); twist, extract, extort

extórris -is -e: exiled

éxtra: prep. w. acc.; except, beyond, out of, without, outside of, besides; adv.: outside; see Appendix

éxtra-sacramentális -is -e: extrasacramental

extradiocesánus -a -um: extradiocesan, outside a diocese

éxtraho -ere -tráxi -tráctum: (3); draw out, extract, withdraw

extrajudiciális -is -e: extrajudicial; extrajudiciáliter: adv.

extramuránus -a -um: without walls; beyond walls

extráneus -a -um: external, strange, foreign, unrelated

extráneus -i: m., extránea -ae: f.; stranger, foreigner

extraordinárius -a -um: extraordinary, from another source, from the outside

extrémus -a -um: extreme, last, final; as a n. noun: end, tip, farthest or outermost part

extríco -áre: (1); extricate, remove, disentangle

extrínsecus -a -um: outer, outside, extrinsic, inessential

extrínsecus: *adv.;* on the outside, from
  without
extrúdo -ere -trúsi -trúsum: (3); throw
  or thrust out
extúrbo -áre: (1); drive away
exu- *see also* **exsu-**
exúbero -áre: (1); abound, make full
exultátio -ónis: f.; exultation, rejoicing
exúndo -áre: (1); overflow, abound

éxuo -ere -ui -útum: (3); strip off, divest,
  deprive, despoil, take off, put off,
  deliver
exúro -ere -ússi -ústum: (3); consume,
  burn up
exúviae -árum: f. pl.; mortal remains
Ezéchiel -is: m.; the prophet Ezekiel; a
  book of the O.T.
Ézra -ae: m.; Ezra; a book of the O.T.

F

fáber -bri: m.; maker, artificer, carpenter, worker, fabricator

fáber -bra -brum: skillful, ingenious; **fábre:** *adv.*

fabrefácio -ere -féci -fáctum: (3); make, manufacture

fábrica -ae: f.; workshop, building, trade; fund

fabricátio -ónis: f.; structure, something made, act of making

fabricátor -óris: m.; maker, framer, artificer, worker, forger, builder

fábrico (fábricor) -áre: (1); make, work, fashion, build, forge

fabrílis -is -e: pertaining to a carpenter; **fabrília** -ium: n. pl.; carpenter's tools or work done by a carpenter

fabríliter: skillfully, in a workmanlike manner

fábula -ae: f.; byword, tale, story, narrative, common talk

fabulátio -ónis: f.; fable, idle talk, lie, gossip

fabulátor -óris: m.; storyteller, narrator

fábulo (fábulor) -áre: (1); talk, tell, narrate, converse

facésso -ere -céssi -ítum: (3); depart, do eagerly, cause, bring about; depart

fácies -éi: f.; face, appearance, form, countenance, aspect

a fácie: because of, from before

fácie ad fáciem: face to face

fácilis -is -e: easy, pleasant; **fácile, facíliter:** *adv.*

facílitas -átis: f.; facility, ease

facílius: more easily

fácinus -oris: n.; crime

fácio -ere -féci -fáctum: (3); make, cause, commit, grant, do

fáctio -ónis: f.; faction, party

factiósus -a -um: quarrelsome

factispécies -éi: f.; specific details, facts of a case

factitátor -óris: m.; maker, doer, perpetrator

factítius -a -um: artificial

fáctor -óris: m.; maker, doer, creator

fáctum -i: n.; deed, act, work

factúra -ae: f.; creation, work, deed, performance, handiwork

fácula -ae: f.; small torch, burning splinter

facúltas -átis: f.; authority, faculty, power; ability, means, resources; *see Appendix*

faeculéntus -a -um: worthless, thick, impure, filthy, pertaining to dregs

facultatívus -a -um: optional

fae- *see also* **foe-**

faenerátor -óris: m.; creditor, money lender, usurer

faénero -áre: (1); lend money at interest

faénum (foénum, fénum) -i: n.; grass, hay

faénus (foénus, fénus) -eris: n.; loan

faex, faécis: f.; mire, ooze, dregs, ground, sediment

fálcitas -átis: f.; falseness

fálda -ae: f.; garment of white silk worn by the Pope on solemn occasions

faldistórium -ii: n.; chair with armrests but no back, faldstool

fallácia -ae: f.; falsehood, deceit, deception

falláciter: falsely

fállax -ácis: deceitful, vain, unreliable, untrustworthy

fállo -ere, féfelli, fálsum: (3); deceive, make a slip, trick, cheat, disappoint, dupe, err, break one's word; *pass.:* be mistaken

falsárius -ii: m.; forger

fálsitas -átis: f.; error, falsehood

fálso -áre: (1); falsify

fálsus -a -um: false, lying, untrue, deceptive, spurious; *as a n. noun:* falsehood, lie; **fálso:** *adv.*

falx, fálcis: f.; sickle, pruning hook, scythe

fáma -ae: f.; report, fame, rumor, reputation

famélicus (famílicus) -a -um: hungry, famished

fámes -is: f.; hunger, famine

família -ae: f.; family, household; religious community

familiális -a -um: of or relating to a family

familiáris -is: c.; servant in a household; intimate friend, acquaintance

familiáris -is -e: friendly, familiar, intimate, of a family

familiáritas -átis: f.; intimacy, familiarity

familiáriter: in a familiar manner

famílicus: *see* famélicus

famósus -a -um: renowned, famous

fámula -ae: f.; servant, maidservant

famulátus -us: m.; service, obedience, slavery

fámulor -ári: *dep.* (1); serve

fámulus -i: m.; servant, attendant

fanále -is: n. torch, candle

fáno -ónis: m.; maniple, striped amice worn by the Pope

fáno -áre: (1); dedicate, consecrate

fánum -i: n.; temple, shrine

fánulum -i: n.; small temple, shrine

farciátura -ae: f.; insertion

fárcio -íre, fársi, fársum (fártum, fáretum): (4); stuff, insert, cram; fill in, insert between verses

farína -ae: f.; meal, flour

farínula -ae: f.; fine flour, small amount of flour

fársia -ae: f.; an insertion into parts of the Mass

fas: *indecl.:* n.; right, lawful, divine law, duty

fáscia (fáscea) -ae: f.; band, ribbon, bandage, fillet, sash

fascículus -i: m.; sheaf, bundle, bunch; issue, packet, fascicle

fascinátio -ónis: f.; fascination, bewitching

fascinátor -óris: m.; charmer, enchanter

fáscino -áre: (1); bewitch, enchant, charm

fascíola -ae: f.; bandage, ribbon

fas est: it is right to, has freedom to, it is lawful for

fastídio -íre: (4); scorn, shrink from, despise, spurn

fastidiósus -a -um: fastidious, disdainful

fastídium -ii: n.; weariness, monotony, aversion, loathing

fastígium -ii: n.; height, summit, gable

fastígo -áre: (1); exhaust, intoxicate

fástus -us: m.; pride, arrogance

fatália -ium: n. pl.; time limit, deadline; *see Appendix*

fáteor -éri, fássus: *dep.* (2); admit, confess, avow, allow, show

fatigátio -ónis: f.; toil

fatigátus -a -um: weary

fátigo -áre: (1); tire, weary

fatísco (fatíscor) -ere: (3); decrease, crack, crack open, fall apart

fátue: foolishly

fatúitas -átis: f.; folly

fátum -i: n.; prediction, fate

fátuus -a -um: foolish; fátuus -i: m., fátua -ae: f.; fool

faúces -ium: f. pl.; throat, jaws, palate,
taste

faúcitas -átis: f.; prosperity

faústus -a -um: fortunate, favorable,
happy, choice

faútor -óris: m.; patron, adviser,
protector, favorer

fáveo -ére, fávi, faútum: (2); help,
protect, favor, promote

favílla -ae: f.; ashes

fávor -óris: m.; favor, care, approval,
goodwill; see Appendix

favorábilis -is -e: favorable

fávus -i: m.; honeycomb, honey

fax, fácis: f.; torch, flame

fe- see also foe-, fae-

febrícito -áre: (1); have a fever

fébris -is: f.; fever

Februárius -ii: m.; February

fecundátio -ónis: f.; act of making
fertile, fruitful, or productive

fecúnditas -átis: f.; fruitfulness

fecúndo -áre: (1); replenish, fill, make
fruitful

fecúndus -a -um: fruitful, prolific, fertile

fel, féllis: n.; gall

felícitas -átis: f.; felicity

felíciter: happily, favorably, fruitfully,
successfully

félix -ícis: happy, blessed

féllico (féllito, féllo) -áre: (1); suck

fel. mem.: abbrev. for felícis memóriae;
of happy memory

fel. rec.: abbrev. for felícis recordatiónis;
of happy memory

fémina -ae: f.; woman, female person

feminália -ium, femorália -órum: n. pl.;
breeches

féminus -a -um: female

fémur -oris(-inis): n.; thigh, loins

fenestélla -ae: f.; niche, small window

fenéstra -ae: f.; window

fénum -i: see faénum

fénus -i: see faénus

fer.: abbrev. for féria; day of the week

ferális -is -e: of the dead, funereal,
deadly, fatal, dangerous

Ferália -ium: n. pl.; festival of the dead,
feast of All Souls

feráliter: in a savage manner

féra péssima -ae: f.; wild beast

férculum (ferículum) -i: n.; dish, tray,
food, bread, course at a banquet; bier,
litter

fére: almost, approximately

ferétrum -i: n.; bier, litter

féria -ae: f.; day of the week; pl.: feast
days, holidays

féria májor: feast of high rank

féria quárta: Wednesday

Féria Quárta Cínerum: Ash
Wednesday

féria quínta: Thursday

Féria Quínta in Coéna Dómini: Holy
or Maundy Thursday,
commemoration of the institution of
the Holy Eucharist

féria secúnda: Monday

féria séxta: Friday

Féria Séxta in Parascéve: Good Friday

féria tértia: Tuesday

feriális -is -e: ferial, pertaining to a feria,
weekday

feriátio -ónis: f.; feast, celebration of a
feast

feriátus -a -um: festive

fério -íre: (4); strike, slay, smite; make a
treaty

férior -ári: dep. (1); rest from work, keep
a holiday

féritas -átis: f.; savagery, fierceness

feraméntus -a -um: fermented

ferículum -i: see férculum

férme: almost

fermentáceus -i: m.; person who uses
unleavened bread

fermentátus -a -um: fermented, loose,
soft, spoiled, corrupted

ferménto -áre: (1); to leaven

ferméntum -i: n.; leaven, yeast

féro, férre, túli, látum: irreg.; carry, bring, produce, support, yield, suffer, pass, bear; *see Appendix*

ferócitas -átis: f.; untamed courage, fierceness

férox -ócis: fierce

ferraíola -ae: f.; short cape reaching halfway to the elbows

ferraméntum -i: n.; iron tool

ferrátus -a -um: ironclad, made of iron, pointed, sharp

férreus -a -um: made of iron, iron

férrum -i: n.; iron, sword

férrum characterátum: form for baking altar breads

férrum oblatórium: iron form for baking altar breads

fértilis -is -e: fertile, fruitful, prolific

feruefácio -ere: (3); inflame, excite

férula -ae: f.; wand, long staff

férus -a -um: untamed, wild; férus -i: m., féra -ae: f.; wild beast

férvens -éntis: hot, fervent; fervénter: *adv.;* fervéntius: *comp. adv.;* fervénte díe: in the heat of the day

férveo -ére -bui: (2); boil, glow

fervésco -ere: (3); grow warm or fervent, begin to boil

férvidus -a -um: glowing, hot, burning, fiery, vehement

férvor -óris: m.; fervor

féssus -a -um: weary

fésta -órum: n. pl.; festival, feast

festinánter (festináto): hastily, speedily, rapidly, in haste

festinátio -ónis: f.; haste, hurry, dispatch, speed

festíno -áre: (1); hasten, hurry; festína lénte: hurry slowly

festínus -a -um: hastening

festívitas -átis: f.; festivity, feast

festívus -a -um: festive, of a feast, pleasant, agreeable, lively

festúca -ae: f.; stalk, mote, splinter

féstum -i: n.; feast, festival

féstum chóri (féstum pro chóro): formerly a feast of obligation for those in choir service

Féstum Dómini: a feast of Our Lord

féstum festórum: greatest of feasts, Easter

féstum fóri: formerly a feast of obligation for all

Féstum Magórum: feast of the Magi or Wise Men, Epiphany

Féstum Régum: feast of the Kings, Epiphany

Féstum Stéllae: Epiphany

Féstum Theophániae: feast of the manifestation of the Lord, Epiphany

féstus -a -um: festal, sacred, of a feast, hallowed

féteo -ére: (2); have bad smell, stink

fétidus -a -um: stinking

féto (foéto) -áre: (1); bring forth, breed, hatch, impregnate, fructify

fétor -óris: m.; offensive smell, stench

fetósus (foetósus, fetuósus) -a -um: prolific, productive, fruitful

fétus (foétus) -a -um: pregnant, breeding, fruitful, productive, newly delivered, full, filled

fétus (foétus) -us: m.; fetus, bearing, bringing forth, dropping, hatching, young, offspring, progeny, brood, fruit, produce

fíala: *see* phíala

fíat: let it be done, so be it, amen; *subj. of* fío

fíbra -ae: f.; fiber, filament, vocal chord, voice

fíbula -ae: f.; clasp, brooch, buckle

fíbulo -áre: (1); bind, bind with clasps

ficárius -a -um: pertaining to figs

ficétum -i: n.; fig plantation

fícte: falsely

fíctilis -is -e: earthen, made of clay

fíctio -ónis: f.; guile, fiction, creation

fictítius -a -um: fictitious

fíctor -óris: m.; maker

fíctus -a -um: deceitful, feigned

ficúlnea -ae, fícus -i, ficus -us: f.; fig, fig tree

Fideísmus -i: m.; doctrine of fideism

fidejúbeo -ére: (2); be or give surety

fidejússio -ónis: f.; surety, giving surety, being surety

fidejússor -óris: m.; bondsman, surety

fidélis -is -e: faithful; Fidéles -ium: c. pl.; the faithful, the believers; see Appendix; fidéliter: adv.; fidélius: comp. adv.

fidélitas -átis: f.; faithfulness, fidelity, trustworthiness

fídens -éntis: faithful, sincere, true; fidénter: adv.

fídes -ei: f.; faith, faithfulness, the virtue of faith, Christian religion; see Appendix

   ex fíde: in good faith, as a matter of faith

   últra fídem: incredible

fídes -is: f.; usually pl.: fídes -ium: f.; lute, lyre, harp, stringed instrument

fidículus -i: m.; viola, musical instrument

fído -ere, fisus: semidep. (3); put confidence in, trust

fidúcia -ae: f.; boldness, trust, confidence; cum fidúcia: boldly

fiduciáliter: boldly, with confidence, trustingly, decisively

fiduciálius: more confidently

fiduciárius -a -um: of or relating to something thing held in trust; fiduciárie: adv.

fídus -a -um: faithful, reliable, trustworthy, dependable

figméntum -i: n.; creation, formation, production, anything made, picture, image, fancy

fígo -ere, fíxi, fíxum: (3); make firm, fix, fashion, pierce

fígulus -i: m.; potter

figúra -ae: f.; figure, fashion

figuráliter: figuratively

figurátio -ónis: f.; prefiguration, allegory

figurátus -a -um: symbolical, allegorical

figúro -áre: (1); symbolize, represent allegorically

fília -ae: f.; daughter

filiális -is -e: filial

filiátio -ónis: f. sonship, filiation; see Appendix

filíetas -átis: f.; sonship

fílii Ádam: descendants of Adam, people

filíolus -i: m.; little child

filióque: and from the Son; see Appendix

fílius -ii: m.; child, son, descendant

fílum -i: n.; thread, cord, string

fímbria -ae: f.; hem, fringe, edge, border

fímus -i: m.; dung

finális -is -e: final

finálitas -átis: f.; finality, last

fíndo -ere, fídi, físsum: (3); plow, split, cleave

fíngo -ere, fínxi, fíctum: (3); feign, pretend, imagine, mold, shape, form, fashion, make

fínio -íre: (4); finish, end, complete

fínis -is: m.; end, boundary, border, limit; see Appendix; fínes -ium: m. pl.; territory; síne fíne: without end, continually

finítimus -a -um: bordering on, neighboring; as pl. noun: neighbors

fío -eri, factus: pass. of fácio; be made, be done, become, happen, fulfill

   fáctum est: it came to pass, it happened

   fíat: so be it

   ut fit: as is commonly the case

firmále -is: n.; brooch for a cope

firmaméntum -i: n.; prop; sky, firmament; a making fast, pillar, anything that makes strong; workmanship

fírmitas -átis: f.; steadfastness

fírmo -áre: (1); make strong, make firm, establish, fix, keep

fírmus -a -um: firm, inflexible, steadfast; **fírmiter:** *adv.*

fiscélla -ae: f., **físcus** -i: m.; basket

fístula -ae: f.; pipe, whistle, flute, reed, sweet cane

fíxus -a -um: fixed, fast, immovable, constant; **fíxe:** *adv.*

fixtúra (fixúra) -ae: f.; imprint, print, opening, perforation

flabéllum -i: n.; fan

flábilis -is -e: moving, fleeting

flácceo -ére: (2); be flabby

fláccidus -a -um: weak, drooping, flabby, feeble, languid

flagellátio -ónis: f.; scourging

flagéllo -áre: (1); scourge, whip, lash, strike, beat

flagéllum -i: n.; whip, scourge

flagitiósus -a -um: disgraceful

flagítium -ii: n.; shameful crime

flágito -áre: (1); beseech, entreat, demand earnestly

flágrans -ántis: zealous, ardent, burning, flaming, eager, vehement; **flagránte delícto:** *see Appendix;* **flagránter:** *adv.*

flágro -áre: (1); burn, glow, blaze, be eager

flámen -inis: n.; wind, breath, spirit

Flámen Supérnum: divine breath, the Holy Spirit

flámma -ae: f.; flame

flámmans -ántis: flaming

flammésco -ere: (3); become inflamed

flámmeus -a -um: flaming, fiery

flámmifer -fera -ferum: flaming

flámmo -áre: (1); burn with passion or eagerness

flámmula -ae: f.; little flame

flátus -us: m.; breath, blowing, blast

flavésco -ere: (3); turn yellow or gold in color

flávor -óris: f.; brightness, glitter

flébilis -is -e: sad, sorrowing, weeping, wretched

flécto -ere, fléxi, fléxum: (3); bend, bow, curve; *see Appendix*

Fléntes -ium: c. pl.; weepers

fléo -ére, flévi, flétum: (3); lament, weep, cry

flétus -us: m.; weeping, bewailing

flexíbilis -is -e: flexible, supple

flexúra -ae: f.; a bend, turning, turn

fléxus -a -um: kneeling; **génu fléxo:** with knee bent

flo -áre: (1); to blow

flócculus (flóccus) -i: m.; tassel

flórens -éntis: flowering, in flower

Florentínus -a -um: of Florence

flóreo -ére -ui: (2); flower, bloom, flourish, prosper

florésco -ere: (3); begin to blossom or flourish

flóreus -a -um: flowery

flóridus -a -um: plentiful, flourishing; flowery

flos, flóris: m.; flower

flósculus -i: m.; tuft, little flower, tassel

fluctuátio -ónis: f.; insecurity, going to and fro, hesitation, fluctuation, vacillation

flúctuo (flúctuor) -áre: (1); toss about, fluctuate, vacillate, be restless, waver, hesitate, be driven or tossed about, be doubtful

flúctus -us: m.; wave, billow, storm, affliction

fluéntum -i, **flúmen** -inis: n.; river, stream, flood, flowing or running water

fluéntus -a -um: flowing
fluésco -ere: (3); melt, become fluid
flúmen -inis: *see* fluéntum
flúo -ere, flúxi, flúxum: (3); to flow
flúvius -ii: m.; river, stream
flúxus -a -um: transitory
flúxus -us: m.; issue, flux, flowing, tide, flow
focária -ae: f.; focárius -ii: m.; a cook
fóculus -i: m.; portable stove, chafing dish
fódio -ere, fódi, fóssum: (3); to dig
foe- *see also* fae-, fe-
foederátio -ónis: f.; federation
foederátus -a -um: united, allied, federated
foédero -áre: (1); establish by agreement, make a treaty
foéditas -átis: f.; filth
foédo -áre: (1); disfigure, pollute, defile, mar, deform, make foul
foédus -a -um: detestable, filthy, vile, ugly, abominable, horrible
foédus -eris: n.; covenant, treaty, agreement, compact, pact
foénum -i: *see* faénum
foénus -oris: n.; interest, profit
foet- *see* fet
foétans -ántis: f.; milch ewe
fólium -ii: n.; foliage, leaf, page
foméntum -i: n.; poultice
fómes -itis: m.; nourishment, stimulant, fire, fuel, tinder, incitement
fons, fóntis: m.; source, fountain, fount, well, baptistry
fons baptismális: baptismal font
fons lustrális: holy water font
fontális -is -e: of a fountain, fountainlike
forámen -inis: n.; cleft, hole, eye of a needle
foráneus -a -um: of the outside, away from, remote, forane; *as a f. noun:* deanery

fóras (fóris): out of doors, out, in public, forth, outside
fórceps -ipis: m.; forceps, tongs
fóre: *shorter form of* futúrus -a -um ésse
forénsis -is -e: legal, forensic, public, of the marketplace
fórent: *another form of* éssent, *the imperf. subj. of* sum
fóres -um: f. pl.; doors, gate entrance
fórfex -icis: f.; shears
forínsecus: from without
fóris: *see* fóras
fóris -is: f.; door
fórma -ae: f.; form, pattern, shape, formula; *see* Appendix
formábilis -is -e: able to be formed or fashioned, formable
formále -is, formálium -ii: n.; large brooch for a bishop's cope
formális -is -e: formal, having a set form; formáliter: *adv.*
formátio -ónis: f.; formation, training
formátrix -ícis: f.; one who forms
formátus -a -um: formed, fashioned
formélla -ae: f.; cake
formíca -ae: f.; ant
formíco -áre: (1); creep, crawl
formído -áre: (1); be afraid, be in awe, tremble
formído -inis: f.; terror, dread, fear
formidolósus -a -um: fearful
fórmo -áre: (1); form, fashion, train, guide
formósus -a -um: beautiful
fórmula -ae: f.; set of words, formula, form, rule
formulárium -ii: n.; formulary, list or set of formulae or rules
fórnax -ácis: f.; oven, furnace
fornicária -ae: f.; fornicatress
fornicátio -ónis: f.; fornication
fornicátor -óris: m.; fornicator
fórnico (fórnicor) -áre: (1); commit fornication, fornicate, be unfaithful

fors fórtis: f.; chance, luck; fórte: by chance, nísi fórte: unless by chance

fórsitan: perhaps, perchance, maybe

fortásse (fortássis): perhaps

fórtis -is -e: strong, valiant, brave, mighty, steadfast, grevious, courageous, powerful, vigorous, firm; fórtior -ior -ius: *comp.;* fortíssimus -a -um: *superl.;* a fortióri: with the greater force; fórtiter: *adv.*

fortitúdo -inis: f.; strength, power, might, fortitude

fortúito (fortúitu): by chance

fortúitus -a -um: casual, accidental, chance, fortuitous

fortúna -ae: f.; fortune, fate, chance, luck (good or bad)

fórum -i: n.; open space, marketplace, forum; court of law, tribunal; *see Appendix*

fórum cómpetens: the proper court

fóssa -ae: f.; ditch, trench, grave

fossárius -ii: m.; sexton

fóssor -óris: m.; grave digger, sexton

fóvea -ae: f.; ditch, pit, lair, hole, pitfall, trap

fóveo -ére, fóvi, fótum: (2); cherish, warm, foment, assist, favor, support, caress, encourage, sustain

fráctio -ónis: f.; breaking, fracture

fractúra -ae: f.; breaking, breach, fracture, crack

fráctus -a -um: *perf. pass. part. of* frángo

fraéno -áre: (1); restrain, bridle

frágilis -is -e: weak, poor, frail, fragile

fragílitas -átis: f.; frailty, weakness

frágmen -inis, fragméntum -i: n.; fragment, piece

frágor -óris: m.; crash, noise, din

fragrántia -ae: f.; fragrance

frágro -áre: (1); smell sweetly

frámea -ae: f.; sword

Franciscális -is -e, Francíscus -a -um: Franciscan

Fráncus -a -um: of the Franks

frángia -ae: f.; fringe

frángo -ere, frégi, fráctum: (3); break, break off, deal

fráter -tris: m.; brother, friar

fratérnitas -átis: m.; fraternity, brotherhood

fratérnus -a -um: fraternal, brotherly; fratérne: *adv.*

fraudátor -óris: m., fraudátrix -ícis: f.; cheat, deceiver

fraúdo -áre: (1); cheat, withhold, defraud, deprive

fraudulénter: falsely, fraudulently, deceitfully

fraduléntia -ae: f.; deceitfulness, disposition to defraud

fraus, fraúdis: f.; error, fraud, wile, deception

frémitus -us: m.; anger, fury, murmuring, shouting, clashing

frémo -ere -ui -itum: (3); rage, roar, clamor, shout

fréndo -ere -ui, fréssum (frésum): (3); gnash with teeth, bruise, grind

fréno -áre: (1); bridle

frénum -i: n.; curb, bridle

fréquens -éntis: frequent, repeated, common, crowded, filled

frequentátio -ónis: f.; frequentation, frequency, crowding together, companionship, dating

frequénter: frequently, often

frequéntia -ae: f.; frequency, multitude, crowd

frequénto -áre: (1); frequent, have recourse to, celebrate, visit often, collect in large numbers, date, keep company

frétum -i: n.; sea, strait, sound, a swelling or raging

frétus -a -um: trusting, relying on, strengthened

friábilis -is -e: easily broken, brittle

frigésco -ere, fríxi: (3); become cold
frígidus -a -um: cold, causing cold,
  inactive, not pious, uncooperative
frígium (phrý-) -ii: n.; mitre
frígus -oris: n.; cold, frost, cool
frisiátus -a -um: embroidered
frixórium -i: n.; frying pan
frondésco -ere -ui: (3); blossom, become
  leafy
fróndeo -ére: (2); be leafy, flourish
frondósus -a -um: leafy
frons, fróndis: f.; leaf, leafy branch,
  foliage
frons, fróntis: f.; forehead, front, van,
  brow
frontále -is: n.; frontal of an altar
frontispícium -ii: n.; front
frúctifer (frúgifer) -fera -ferum,
  fructuósus -a -um: fruitful,
  fruit-bearing, productive, fertile,
  profitable; fructuóse: adv.
fructificátio -ónis: f.; production of fruit
fructífico -áre: (1); be fruitful
fructuósus -a -um: beneficial, fruitful,
  profitable, advantageous, productive;
  fructuóse: adv.
frúctus -us: m.; fruit, produce, trees;
  reward, profit, benefit; posterity,
  offspring, children
frugálitas -átis: f.; simplicity, frugality
frúgifer -era -erum: fruit-bearing,
  fruitful, fertile
fruítio -ónis: f.; use, enjoyment,
  possession
fruméntum -i: n.; grain, corn, rye,
  wheat, barley, meal
frúor -i, frúctus: dep. (3): enjoy, obtain,
  delight in, use
frústra: in vain, without effect, to no
  purpose, uselessly
frústro -áre: (1); deceive, disappoint,
  trick, rob
frústror -ári: dep. (1); annul, make void,
  deceive, frustrate

frústulum -i: n.; little bit, small piece
frutétum (frutéctum) -i: n.; branch;
  copse, thicket
frútex -icis: m.; plant, shoot, shrub
frux, frúgis: f.; fruit
fúco -áre: (1); paint, disguise
fúcus -i: m.; red, purple, rouge; deceit,
  pretense
fúga -ae: f.; flight, refuge, escape,
  avoidance
fúgio -ere, fúgi, fúgitum: (3); flee
fugitavárius -ii: m.; one who catches
  and returns runaway slaves
fugitívus -a -um: fugitive, runaway
fúgo -áre: (1); put to flight, chase
fulciméntum -i: n.; prop
fúlcio -íre, fúlsi, fúltum: (4); prop up,
  support, stay, strengthen, make steady
Fuldénsis -is -e: of Fulda
fúlgeo -ére, fúlsi: (2); shine, glow, flash,
  be conspicuous
fúlgidus -a -um: shining
fúlgor -óris: m., fúlgur -uris: n.;
  brightness, lightning, thunderbolt
fulgúro -áre: (1); flash forth, shine,
  lighten, glitter, glisten
fúllo -ónis: m.; fuller
fúlmen -inis: n.; lightning, thunderbolt
fulmíneus -a -um: of lightning,
  splendid, brilliant, dangerous
fúltus -a -um: supported by, charged
  with, propped up
fúlvus -a -um: gold-colored
fumárium -ii: n.; chimney
fumigabúndus -a -um: smoking, smoky
fúmigo (fúmo) -áre: (1); to smoke
funále -is: n.; torch, candle, candlestick
fúnctio -ónis: f.; function
fúnctus -a -um: perf. pass. part. of fúngor
fúnda -ae: f.; sling
fundamentális -is -e: fundamental,
  basic; fundamentáliter: adv.

fundaméntum -i: n., fundátio -ónis: f.; foundation, base, establishment, founding

fundátor -óris: m.; founder

fundibulárius -ii: m.; slinger

fundíbulum -i: n.; sling

fúnditus: completely, utterly, totally, from the foundation

fúndo -áre: (1); found, establish, set in place, secure

fúndo -ere, fúsi, fúsum: (3); pour

fúndus -i: m.; base, foundation, estate, piece of land

funébris -is -e: funereal, of a funeral; as a n. pl. noun: funeral rites or services

funerális -is -e: deadly, woeful

funeráticus -a -um: of a funeral

fúnero -áre: (1); inter, bury with funeral rites

funéstus -a -um: filled with mourning, mournful, dismal, deadly, fatal, destructive; funéste: adv.

fungíbilis -is -e: fungible, interchangeable

fúngor -i, fúnctus: dep. (3); perform, exercise

funículus -i: m.; string, slender cord, measuring line; estate, portion, lot

fúnis -is: m.; rope, cord, band; fúnes -ium: m. pl.; fetters

fúnus -eris: n.; funeral, interment; fúnera -um: n. pl.; death, corpses

fur, fúris: c.; thief

fúria -ae: f.; fury, rage

furiósus -i: m., furiósa -ae: f.; mad or insane person

fúror -ári: dep. (1); steal

fúror -óris: m.; indignation, wrath, rage, fury, insanity

fúrtum -i: n.; theft, robbery, trick; fúrtum fácere: steal

fuscínula -ae: f.; fork, hook

fúse: at length, in great detail

fusória -ae: f.; foundry

fúsus -i: m.; spindle

físco -áre: (1); darken

fúscus -a -um: black

fúsio -ónis: f.; fusion, merger

fúsius: more fully

fusória -ae: f.; foundry

fústis -is: m.; club, staff, cudgel

fusúra -ae: f.; casting of metals

fúsus -a -um: perf. pass. part. of fúndo -ere

fúsus -i: m.; spindle

fúsus -us: m.; outpouring

fútilis (fúttilis) -is -e: vain, worthless, futile, idle, untrustworthy; fútile: adv.

futúrus -a -um: about to be, future; as a n. noun: the future

G

Gábbatha -ae: f.; Gabbatha, the tribunal of judgment in Jerusalem

Gábaon -ónis: f.; Gabaon, a city of Judea

Gábriel -élis: m.; the archangel Gabriel

Gad: *indecl.;* Gad, son of Jacob and Zilpah; a tribe of Israel

Gálaad: *indecl.; see* **Gílead**

Gálatae -árum: c.; Galatians

gálbanum -i: n.; galbanum, oriental gum

gálbanus -a -um: yellowish

gálea -ae: f.; helmet

galeátus -i: m.; man wearing a helmet

gáleo -ónis: m.; galleon

galerículum -i: n.; skullcap

galérus -i: m.; cardinal's hat

Galilaéa -ae: f.; Galilee

galilaéa -ae: f.; cloistered walk

Galilaéus -a -um: Galilean, of Galilee

Gállia -ae: f.; France

Gallicanísmus -i: m.; theory of Gallicanism, condemned by the Church

gallicántus -us: m., **gallicínium** -ii: n.; cock's crow; a signal announcing the fourth watch of the night

gallícula -ae: f.; small shoe

gallína -ae: f.; hen

gállus -i: m.; cock

Gamáliel -élis: m.; Gamaliel

garális -is: f.; lavabo basin

gárrio -íre -ívi (-ii) -ítum: (4); chatter, prate

gárrule: garrulously

gárrulus -a -um: talkative, chattering, babbling

gaúdeo -ére, gavísus: *semidep.* (2); rejoice, be glad

Gaudéte: third Sunday of Advent

gaudimónium -ii: n.; joy

gaudiósus -a -um: joyful

gaúdium -ii: n.; joy, gladness, delight; *see Appendix*

gáza -ae: f.; riches, treasure

gazophylácium -ii: n.; treasury, treasure, sacristy

Gébal: *see* **Býblos**

gehénna -ae: f.; *Hebrew;* hell, place of torment

gélda (geldónia) -ae: f.; guild

gélu -us: n.; frost, cold

gemebúndus -a -um: groaning

geméllio -ónis: f.; small cruet

geminátus -a -um: doubled, twofold

géminus líquor: blood and water

gémitus -us: m.; groan, moan, sigh, sorrow

gémma -ae: f.; jewel, gem, precious stone

gemmárius -ii: m.; jeweler

gemmátus -a -um: adorned with gems

gémmula -ae: f.; small gem

gémo -ere -ui -itum: (3); lament, sign, groan

géna -ae: f.; cheek

genealógia -ae: f.; genealogy

géner -eri: m.; son-in-law, brother-in-law

generális -is -e: general, generic; *as a m. noun:* a general; *see Appendix*

generálitas -átis: f.; generality

generáliter: in general, generally

generátim: by kinds or species or classes or divisions

generátio -ónis: f.; generation, period of time; birth, pedigree; fruit

generátor -óris: m.; first author, producer, generator

género -áre: (1); beget, produce, bring to life, create

generósitas -átis: f.; generosity, nobility, goodness

generósus -a -um: of noble birth, of superior quality, noble, excellent

Génesis -is: f.; the Book of Genesis

génesis -is: f.; generation, birth, creation

génetrix (génitrix) -ícis: f.; mother, Mother of God

geniális -is -e: pertaining to generation or birth; of or belonging to enjoyment, jovial

geniáliter: jovially, gaily

genículo (genículor) -áre: (1); kneel, genuflect

genículum -i: n.; knee

génimen -inis: n.; fruit, produce

genísta -ae: f.; broom

genitále -is: n.; womb

genitális -is -e: of birth

génitor -óris: m.; father, Creator

génitrix -ícis: see génetrix

génitus -a -um: newly born, begotten

géno -ere -ui -itum: (3); bear, beget

genocídium -ii: n.; genocide

gens, géntis: f.; nation, family, people, the chosen people

géntes -ium: m. pl.; Gentiles, heathen, all non-Jewish peoples

génticus -a -um: national, belonging to a nation

gentilícius: see gentilítius

gentílis -is -e: gentile, heathen; Gentíles -ium: m. pl.; Gentiles

gentílitas -átis: f.; heathendom, paganism

gentíliter: in heathen fashion, like the Gentiles

gentilítius (gentilícius) -a -um: pertaining to a race or family, tribal, national

génu -us: n.; knee

fléctere génua: kneel

génu fléxo: kneeling

genuále -is: see epigonátion

Genuflecténtes: public penitents in the early Church, kneelers

genuflécto -ere -fléxi -fléxum: (3); genuflect, bend the knee

genufléxio -ónis: f.; genuflection, bending of the knee

genuflexórium -ii: n.; kneeling bench

genuínitas (genuítas) -átis: f.; innateness, naturalness, genuinity, genuineness

genuínus -a -um: innate, native, genuine, authentic, natural, real; genuíne: adv.

génus -eris: n.; nation, race, kind, people, class, descent, species

ex génere: from my own nation

génus ferárum: wild beasts

génus reptántium: reptiles

in génere: in general

geográphicus -a -um: geographic, of geography

Geraséni -órum: m. pl.; Gerasenes or Gergesenes

germána -ae: f.; sister

Germánicus (Germánus) -a -um: German

germánitas -átis: f.; relationship between brothers and sisters

germánus -a -um: genuine, real, actual, true

germánus -i: m.; brother

gérmen -inis: n.; sprout, bud, sprig, fruit, produce

gérmino -áre: (1); bring forth, bud, blossom, spring up, sprout

géro -ere, géssi, géstum: (3); bear; celebrate, do, act, conduct oneself, reign; manage

gérulus -i: m., gérula -ae: f.; bearer, carrier; doer, worker gésta -órum: n. pl.; deeds, acts, proceedings, things accomplished

gestatórium -ii: n.; litter

gestatórius -a -um: portable

gestátus -us: m.; bearing

gestículor -ári: dep. (1); gesticulate, make gestures

géstio -íre: (4); long for, desire eagerly; exult, be joyful

géstio -ónis: f.; management, administration, performance

gésto -áre: (1); carry, wear, report

géstus -a -um: done, accomplished; res géstae: deeds, accomplishments

Gethsémani: indecl; Gethsemane

ghímel: third letter of the Hebrew alphabet

gígas -ántis: m.; giant, hero, strongman

gígno -ere, génui, génitum: (3); beget, bring forth

gílda (gélda, geldónia) -ae: f.; guild, group, association

Gílead (Gálaad): indecl.; Gilead, territory east of the Jordan river

gípsum -i: n.; gypsum, plaster of paris

glácies -ei: f.; ice

gládius -ii: m.; sword

glans, glándis: f.; acorn

glárea -ae: f.; gravel

glaúcus -a -um: bluish gray

gléba -ae: f.; clod, lump of earth

glébula -ae: f.; small lump or substance

glísco -ere: (3); blaze up, rage, swell

glóbulus -i: m.; button, bead, shot

glóbus -i: m.; ball

glória -ae: f.; glory, honor, majesty, reward of the saints

Glória: a song that is part of the Mass

gloriánter: boastingly, exultingly

gloriátio -ónis: f.; glory, boasting

glorificátio -ónis: f.; act of glorifying

glorífico -áre: (1); glorify, extol

gloríola -ae: f.; halo, nimbus

glórior -ári: dep. (1); glory in

Gloriósae Dóminae: the "Golden Bull" of Pope Benedict XIV, 1748

gloriósus -a -um: glorious, full of glory; glorióse: adv.

glóssa -ae: f., glosséma -atis: n.; gloss, an explanation of an obsolete or foreign word; see Appendix

glúten -inis: n.; glue, bond

glútino -áre: (1); bind, glue

glútinum -i: n.; glue, solder

glútio -íre: (4); swallow

gnárus -a -um: knowing

gnávus: see návus

Gnídus -i: see Cnídus

Gnosticísmus -i: m.; heresy of gnosticism; Gnóstici -órum: m. pl.; followers of gnosticism

Gólgatha -ae: f.; Golgatha, the Hebrew name for the place of the Crucifixion

Gomórrha -ae: f.; Gomorrah, a city north of the Dead Sea

gossípium (gossýpium) -ii: n.; cotton; gossípium cerátum: thin taper

Góthi -órum: m. pl.; Goths

grabátum -i: n., grabátus -i: m.; small bed, cot, mattress

grácilis -is -e: slender, graceful

gradále -is: see graduále

gradátim: gradually, by degrees, step by step

grádior -i, gréssus: dep. (3); walk, follow, conduct oneself, live, step

graduále (gradále) -is: n.; Gradual, a book containing words and music for liturgical chants

Graduále -is: n.; a brief verse that was part of the pre–Vatican II liturgy

graduális -is -e: pertaining to steps or stairs

grádus -us: m.; step, degree, place, position

Graécus -a -um: Greek; Graéce: in Greek

grámen -inis: n.; grass, turf

grammática -ae: f.; grammar
grammátice: grammatically
grandaévus -a -um: of great age
grandésco -ere: (3); become great, grow
grandíloquus -a -um: eloquent
grándinat -áre: (1); impers.; it hails, it
hails upon
grándis -is -e: great
grandísculus -a -um: a little older,
somewhat grown-up
gránditer: strongly, mightily
grándo -inis: f.; hail, hailstorm
gránulum -i: n.; seed, small grain; bead
of the rosary
gránum -i: n.; grain
grássor -ári: dep. (1); rage, be violent
gratánter: joyously, gladly
grátes -ium: f. pl.; thanks
grátia -ae: f.; grace, favor, mercy,
kindness, supernatural gift; grátia
with gen.: for the sake of, on account
of; grátiae -árum: f. pl.; thanks
grátias ágere: give thanks
in grátiam: in favor of, for the sake of,
toward
vérbi grátia, exémpli grátia: for
example
gratiárum áctio: thanksgiving
gratíficor (gratífico) -ári: dep. (1);
gratify, oblige
gratiósus -a -um: favored, beloved,
popular, agreeable, highly regarded;
gratióse: adv.
grátis: free, freely
gratitúdo -inis: f.; gratitude, thanks
gratúito: without payment or profit,
gratuitously
gratúitus -a -um: free, voluntary,
spontaneous
gratulabúndus -a -um: joyful
gratulátio -ónis: f.; rejoicing
gratulatórie: in a congratulatory manner
grátulor -ári: dep. (1); exult, rejoice,
manifest joy

grátus -a -um: pleasing, agreeable,
gracious, thankful, beloved, dear,
acceptable; gráte: adv.
gravámen -inis: n.; trouble, harm,
disadvantage
gravánter: with difficulty
gravátus -a -um: heavy, loaded down
gravédo -inis: f.; heaviness, pregnancy
grávida -ae: f.; pregnant woman
grávido: see grávo
grávidor -ári: dep. (1); grow heavy,
become pregnant
grávidus -a -um: heavy, laden, filled,
full, pregnant, in labor
grávis -is -e: heavy, grievous, serious,
burdensome, severe, violent; gráviter:
adv.
grávitas -átis: f.; weight
grávo (grávido) -áre: (1); burden,
oppress, be burdensome, weigh down;
grieve
gregátim: in flocks or crowds
grégo -áre: (1); collect into a group,
assemble
Gregoriánus -a -um: Gregorian
gremiále -is: n.; lap cloth for the bishop
at pontifical functions
grémium -ii: n.; lap
gréssus -us: m.; step, stride, going,
course of life, movement, advance
grex, grégis: m.; flock, herd, crowd,
people of Christ
grossitúdo -inis: f.; thickness
gróssus -i: m.; young or green fig
gróssus -a -um: thick, dull
gryps, grýphis: m.; griffin
gubernáculum (gubernium) -i: n.,
gubernátio -ónis: f.; helm, rudder;
government, management
gubernátor -óris: m.; helmsman, pilot,
governor
gubérno -áre: (1); guide, direct, conduct,
steer, govern, manage, rule
gúla -ae: f.; gullet, gluttony

Guliélmus -i: m.; William

gúrges -itis: m.; stream, eddy, whirlpool, raging abyss, waters

gurgústium -ii: n.; cabin, hovel, hut

gustátus -us: m.; taste

gústo -áre: (1); to taste

gústus -us: m.; a taste, flavor

gútta -ae: f.; drop, spot, speck, a little bit; oil of myrrh, aloes

gúttur -uris: n.; throat, palate, mouth, taste; gluttony

gynaecéum -i, **gynaecíum** -íi: n.; women's part of a house

gymnásium -ii: n.; gymnasium, high school, college

gypsátus -a -um: coated or covered with gypsum

gýpsum -i: n.; plaster of paris

gýrus -i: m.; circle, compass

H

Hábacuc: *indecl.; Hebrew;* Habakkuk, a minor prophet; a book of the O.T.

habéna -ae: f.; rein

hábeo -ére -ui -itum: (2); have, hold, consider; *see Appendix*
béne habére: be well, recover
mále habére: to be ill

habetúdo -inis: f.; dullness

hábilis -is -e: capable, supple, handy, easily managed

habílitas -átis: f.; ability, aptitude

habitábilis -is -e: habitable, fit for living, habitable; cívitas habitábilis: Jerusalem

habitáculum -i: n., habitátio -ónis: f.; dwelling, house, apartment, home, habitation

hábitans -ántis: c., habitátor -óris: m.; dweller, inhabitant

hábito -áre: (1); live, dwell, abide, inhabit

habituális -is -e: habitual; habituáliter: *adv.*

habitúdo -inis: f.; form, condition, appearance, state of being

hábitus -a -um: *perf. pass. part. of* hábeo

hábitus -us: m.; habit, garb, dress, garment, clothing; appearance, condition, disposition

hac: here, in this way, by this side; hac íllac: here and there

Hacéldama: *Aramaic;* Akeldama, the field of blood, the potter's field

hac íllac: here and there

háctenus: so far, up to this point, only this, only so much

Hadriánus -i: m.; Hadrian

haéccine: is this? are there?

haedínus (hoédinus) -a -um: of a young goat

haedúlea -ae: f., haédus (hoédus) -i: m.; young goat, kid

haemorrhoíssus (hemorrhoíssus) -a -um: having a flow of blood

haeréditas -átis: f.; inheritance, possession

haéreo -ére, haési, haésum: (2); stick fast, adhere, cling

haeresiárcha -ae: m.; archheretic, heresiarch

haéresis -is(-eos): f.; heresy; *see Appendix*

haeréticus -a -um: heretical; *as a noun:* heretic

haesitátio (hesitátio) -ónis: f.; hesitation

haésito (hésito) -áre: (1); hesitate, doubt, be perplexed, be at a loss, waver, stagger

hagiógraphus -a -um: of sacred or holy writings

hagiógraphus -i: m.; sacred writer

hágios: *see* ágios; *see Appendix*

halátio -ónis: f.; breathing, breath

hálito -áre: (1); breathe

hálitus -us: m.; breath, exhalation

hallelújah (allelúia): *indecl.; Hebrew;* praised be God

hálo -áre: (1); breathe, exhale

háma -ae: f.; bucket

Hamartigenía -ae: f.; Origin of Sin, a poem by Prudentius

hámula -ae: f.; small hook

hámus -i: m.; hook, fishhook

Hanc ígitur: This therefore, the first two words of a prayer in preparation for the Consecration in the pre–Vatican II liturgy

hánnapus -i: m.; incense boat
har- *see also* ar-
haréna -ae: f.; sand
haríolus -i: m.; soothsayer
harmónia -ae: f.; harmony
harmónicus -a -um: harmonious,
harmonic; **harmónice:** *adv.*
harundíneus -a -um: of reeds, like a reed
harúndo (arúndo) -inis: f.; reed, cane,
rod, shaft, twig
harúspex -icis: *see* arúspex
hásta -ae: f.; spear, pike, javelin
hastíle -is: n.; staff, shaft, staff of a
processional cross
hastílis -is -e: on a staff, supported by a
shaft or staff
haud (haudquáquam, haut): not at all,
by no means
haúrio -íre, haúsi, haúsum: (4); drink,
draw out, draw water, drain, swallow;
derive
haústus -us: m.; drink, draught, drawing
of water
haut: *see* haud
he- *see also* hae-
he: fifth letter of the Hebrew alphabet
hebdómada -ae, **hébdomas** -adis: f.;
period of seven days, week
Hebdómada albária: week before Low
Sunday
Hebdómada authéntica: Holy Week
Hébdomas indulgéntiae;: Holy Week
Hébdomas lamentatiónum: Holy
Week
Hébdomas luctósa: Holy Week
Hébdomas múta: Holy Week
Hébdomas nígra: Holy Week
Hébdomas última: Holy Week
hebdomadárius -a -um: lasting a week
hebdomadárius -ii: m.; choir official
serving for a week
hebénius -a -um: of ebony
hébes -étis(-ítis): dull, stupefied
hébeto -áre: (1); blunt, make dull

Hebraéus -a -um, **Hebráicis** -is -e:
Hebrew
Hebraéus -i: m., **Hebraéa** -ae: f.; a
Hebrew
Hebráice: in Hebrew
Hebráicus -a -um: pertaining to Hebrew
hédera -ae: f.; ivy
hedonísmus -i: m.; hedonism
Hégumen -menis: m.; superior of a
Basilian monastery
hei- *see also* ei-
hei: woe, alas
héjulor -ári: *dep.* (1); wail, lament
hélica -ae: f.; a winding
héluo -ónis: m.; glutton
Helvétii -órum: m. pl.; the Swiss
hemitónium (hermitónium) -ii: n.;
halftone in music
hemorrhoíssus -a -um: *see*
haemorrhoíssus
hemorrhoíssus -i: m., **hemorrhoíssa**
-ae: f.; one suffering from a
hemorrhage
heortológia -ae: f.; science of feasts
héptas -adis: f.; the number seven in
Greek
hérba -ae: f.; grass, blade of grass, herb,
plant, blade of wheat, corn
hérbidus -a -um: full of grass
hereditárius -a -um: original,
hereditary, pertaining to inheritance
heréditas -átis: f.; heredity, inheritance,
heirship
herédito -áre: (1); inherit, be an heir
héres -édis: c.; heir, heiress
héri: yesterday
herinácius -ii: m.; hedgehog, porcupine
hérma -ae: f.; metallic bust serving as a
reliquary
hermitónium -i: *see* hemitónium
herniósus -a -um: ruptured
Heródes -is: m.; Herod
Herodiáni -órum: m. pl.; Herodians

heródio -ónis: m., heródius -ii: m.;
heron, stork
heroícitas -átis: f.; heroism, heroicity
heróicus -a -um: heroic
hérus -i: m.; master, lord, owner,
proprietor
hesi- see haesi-
hespéria -ae: f.; land to the west, Italy,
Spain
hestérnus -a -um: of yesterday; díes
hestérna: yesterday
hetaeriárcha -ae: m.; official of a
confraternity
heterosexuális -is -e: heterosexual
heth: eighth letter of the Hebrew
alphabet
heu: alas, woe
Héva -ae: f.; Eve
héxas -adis: f.; the number six in Greek
hiacínthinus: see hyacínthinus
hibernális - is -e, hibérnus -a -um:
wintry
Hibérnia -ae: f.; Ireland
Hibérni -órum: m. pl.; the Irish
hibérno (híemo) -áre: (1); spend the
winter
hibérnus: see hibernális or hiemális
hic, haec, hoc: this, he, she, it
ab hac párte: on this side
ad hoc: besides, for this purpose
cóntra haec (haec cóntra): in answer
to this
hunc in módum (ad hunc módum): in
this way
hic: adv.; here, on this occasion
hiemális -is -e, hibérnus -a -um: wintry,
of winter
híemans -ántis: stormy, wintry, frozen,
cold, raging
híemo: see hibérno
híems -emis: f.; winter
hierárcha -ae: m.; member of hierarchy;
see Appendix

hierárchia -ae: f.; hierarchy, governing
body of the Church
hierárchicus -a -um: hierarchical
hieráticus -a -um: hieratic, pertaining to
sacred uses
Hieremías -ae: m.; Jeremiah; the
prophet Jeremiah; a book of the O.T.
Hierónymus -i: m.; Jerome
Hierosolimitánus -a -um: of Jerusalem
Hierosólyma -ae: f., -órum: n. pl.;
Jerusalem
hierothéca -ae: f.; reliquary
Hierúrgia -ae: f.; sacred rite, liturgy, the
Mass
Higgaíon: a word found in the Psalms, its
meaning doubtful; possibly "thought"
or some technical musical term
hilarésco -ere: (3); become joyful
hílaris -is -e: cheerful, joyful, smiling
hiláritas -átis: f.; cheerfulness, hilarity
hinc: hence, away from here, in this
direction, on this side; hinc et hinc:
one on each side
Hinduísmus -i: m.; Hinduism
hínnio -íre: (4); to neigh
hínnulus -i: m.; young hart, young mule
Híppo -ónis: m.; Hippo, a town in north
Africa
Hipponénsis -is -e: of Hippo
hírcus -i: m.; he-goat
hirúdo -inis: f.; leech
hirúndo -inis: f.; swallow
Hispánia -ae: f.; Spain
Hispánus -a -um: Spanish
híspidus -a -um: rough, coarse
história -ae: f.; history, narrative,
narration
historícitas -átis: f.; historicity
históricus -a -um: historic, historical
hístrio -ónis: m.; stage player, actor
hódie: today, this day, at the present time
hodiérnus -a -um: relating to today;
hodiérna díe: on this day
hoed- see haed-

Hollándia -ae: f.; Holland, Netherlands

holocaústum -i, holocautóma -atis: n.; holocaust, burnt offering

hológraphus -a -um: entirely written by one's own hand

holoséricum -i: n.; silk, velvet

hólus -eris: n.; herb, vegetable

homicída -ae: c.; murderer

homicídium -ii: n.; murder, homicide

homiléticus -a -um: of homilies or preaching; *as a n. pl. noun:* the art of preaching, homiletics

homília -ae: f.; homily

homiliárium -ii: n.; collection of homilies

hómo -inis: m.; human being, man, person, husband

homógium -ii: n.; homage

homoioúsius -a -um: of like substance, similar, resembling

homooúsius -a -um: of the same substance, consubstantial

homosexuális -is -e: pertaining to homosexuality; *as a c. noun:* homosexual person

homosexuálitas -átis: f.; homosexuality

Homuncionítae -árum: m. pl.; a Christian sect that considered Jesus as man only

honéstas -átis: f.; honor, riches, respectability, integrity, honesty

honésto -áre: (1); make honorable, dignify, adorn with honor

honéstor -ári: *dep.* (1); be earnest, be grave, be serious

honéstus -a -um: honest, decent, noble; honéste: *adv.*

hónor (hónos) -óris: m.; honor, distinction, esteem, reward, acknowledgment; honóris caúsa: for the sake of honor, an honorary degree

honorábilis -is -e, honorátus (honorificátus, honoríficus) -a -um: honorable, conferring honor

honorárium -ii: n.; stipend, reimbursement, honorarium

honorárius -a -um: honorary, of honor

honorátus: *see* honorábilis *or* honoríficus

honorificéntia -ae: f.; honor, glory

honorífico (honóro) -áre: (1); honor, glorify

honoríficus (honorátus, honorificátus) -a -um: honorable, honorary, respected, adorned; honorífice (honoráte): *adv.*

honóro -áre: (1); honor, respect, adorn

hónos -oris: *see* hónor

hóra-ae: f.; hour

horárius -a -um: pertaining to hours; horárium -ii: n.; daily schedule

hordeáceus -a -um: of barley

hórdeum -i: n.; barley

Hóreb: *indecl.;* Horeb, Sinai; the mountain of Moses and the burning bush

horológion -ii: n.; horologion; *see* Appendix

horológium -ii: n.; water clock, sundial, clock, watch

horréndus -a -um: dreadful, horrible, horrid, frightful

hórreo -ére -ui: (2); fear, abhor, shrink from, disdain, shudder

horrésco -ere, hórrui: (3); spurn

hórreum -i: n.; barn, storehouse, granary

horríbilis -is -e, hórridus -a -um: horrible, dreadful

horripilátio -ónis: f.; bristling of the hair

hórror -óris: m.; dread, horror

hortaméntum -i: n., exhortation, encouragement

hortátio -ónis: f.; encouragement, exhortation

hortátor -óris: m.; comforter, encourager

hortatórius -a -um: cheering, comforting, encouraging

hórtor -ári: *dep.* (1); exhort, encourage

hortulánus -i: m.; gardener

hórtus -i: m.; garden

Hosánna (Hosiánna, Osánna): *Aramaic;* Hosanna, God save, a Hebrew exclamation of praise

hóspes -itis: c.; host, guest, guest-friend, stranger

hospitále -is: n.; hospital, guesthouse, guestroom

hospitális -is -e: of a guest; hospitális dómus: guesthouse

hospitálitas -átis: f.; hospitality

hospítium -ii: n.; hospice, asylum, inn, hospitality

hóspitor -ári: *dep.* (1); lodge, be a guest

hóstia -ae: f.; host, victim, sacrifice, offering, gift

hóstia pacífica: peace offering

hóstia pro peccáto: sin or debt offering

hostiária -ae: f.; vessel for hosts

hósticus -a -um, hostílis -is -e: hostile, unfriendly, inimical

hostílitas -átis: f.; enmity, hostility

hóstis -is: c.; enemy, devil

huc: hither, to this place or end; huc et ílluc: to and fro

húccine: so far

hucúsque: hitherto, thereupon, thus far

hujúsmodi: of this kind, of such kind

hum- *see also* um-

humanísmus -i: m.; humanism

humanísticus -a -um: humanistic

humánitas -átis: f.; humanity, human nature, kindness, culture, good breeding, compassion, courtesy

humánus -a -um: human, humane; humániter (humáne): *adv.; see* Appendix

humécto -áre: (1); moisten

humerále -is: n.; humeral veil, shoulder veil used at Benediction, amice

humérulus -i: m.; side

húmerus -i: m.; shoulder

humicubátio -ónis: f.; lying on the ground as a form of penance

humíditas -átis: f.; moisture

húmidus -a -um: wet, moist

Humiliáti -orum: m. pl.; humble ones, members of a penitential association of the Middle Ages

humiliátio -ónis: f.; humiliation

humiliátus -a -um: humbled

humílio -áre: (1); humiliate, humble, bring low, level to the ground, debase

húmilis -is -e: humble, lowly; humíliter: adv.

humílitas -átis: f.; humility, lowness, misery, humiliation, wretchedness

húmo -áre: (1); bury, inter

húmor -óris: m.; fluid, moisture, desire

húmus -i: f.; earth, soil, land, ground; húmi: on the ground

Húnni -órum: m. pl.; Huns

hyacínthinus (hiac-, iac-) -a -um: color of hyacinth; *as a f. noun:* a dark-colored precious stone, an amethyst

hybernális: *see* hibernális

hýdria -ae: f.; water jar, pot

hydrópicus -a -um: afflicted with dropsy

hydrópisis -is: f., hýdrops -ópis: m.; dropsy

hygiénicus -a -um: hygienic

hylomorphísmus -i: m.; the theory of matter and form in Scholastic philosophy

hymnárium -ii: n.; collection of hymns

hýmnicus -a -um: of hymns

hymnízo -áre: (1); sing hymns, worship in song

hymnódia -ae: f.; singing of hymns

hymnológion: *Greek;* hymn book, in the Greek rite

hýmnus -i: m.; hymn, song of praise

Hýmnus Ambrosiánus: the "Te Deum"

Hýmnus Angélicus: the "Gloria in Excelsis"

hyperbólice: with exaggeration

hyperdúlia -ae: f.; superior veneration, veneration due the B.V.M.

hypermétricus -a -um: exceeding a meter

hypnotísmus -i: m.; hypnotism

hypócrisis -is: f.; hypocrisy, imitation

hypócrita (-crites) -ae: c.; hypocrite

hypodiáconus -i: m.; subdeacon

hypógeum -i: n.; crypt, vault, basement

hypostáticus -a -um: essential, substantial, hypostatic; see Appendix

hypótheca -ae: f.; pledge, security, mortgage

hýrax -ácis: m.; a rodent

hyssópus -i: m., hyssópum -i: n.; hyssop

I

i: *see also* letter J; words that begin with i as a consonant are found under J

iacínthinus: *see* **hyacínthinus**

iánthinus -a -um: violet

íbex -icis: m.; wild goat

íbi: there, in that place, in this

ibídem (íbid.): in the same place, in that very place

íbis -is *or* -idis: f.; ibis, a bird of Egypt

ícon -onis: f.; icon, image

iconástasis -eos: f.; iconostasis, a partition that separates the sanctuary from the body of a Greek church

Iconoclásta -ae: m.; iconoclast, one who opposes the veneration of images, image-breaker

Iconomáchi -órum: m. pl.; iconoclasts

íctus -us: m.; blow, stab, stroke, beat, thrust, stress, stream

id: n. *sing. of* **is**; on that account
   id aetátis, id témporis: at that age
   id est: that is

idcírco (ídeo): therefore, on that account, for that reason

ídea -ae: f.; idea, archetype

idealísmus -i: m.; theory of idealism

ídem, éadem, ídem: same; *with* **ípse:** selfsame

idénticus -a -um: identical

idéntidem: repeatedly, again and again

identífico -áre: (1); be identical with

idéntitas -átis: f.; identity, sameness

ídeo: for that reason, on that account, therefore

ideológia -ae: f.; ideology, body of ideas

idióma -atis: n.; idiom, peculiarity in language, language

idióta -ae: c.; ignorant person

idípsum: together, forthwith, completely, that very thing

Idíthum: *indecl.; Hebrew;* Idithun, a choir leader

idólium -ii: n.; temple for an idol

idolátra (-tres), idololátria (-tres) -ae: c.; idolater

idolátria (idololátria) -ae: f.; idolatry

idolóthytum -i: n.; food offered to idols

idólum -i: n.; idol, false god

idonéitas -átis: f.; fitness, meetness, usefulness

idóneus -a -um: suitable, fitting, appropriate, sufficient, satisfactory, proper, apt; **idónee:** *adv.*

Idumaéa -ae: f.; Edom, Mount Seir

Idumaéus -a -um: of Edom, Edomite

ídus, íduum: f. pl.; the ides; the 15th day in Mar., May, July, Oct.; the 13th in the other months

i.e.: *abbrev. for* **id est**; that is

ígitur: therefore, accordingly

ignárus -a -um: ignorant, inexperienced, unacquainted with

Ignátius -ii: m.; Ignatius

ignávia -ae: f.; idleness, laziness, sloth, cowardice, listlessness

ignáviter: lazily, slothfully, without spirit

ignávus -a -um: slothful, idle, listless, inactive

ignésco -ere: (3); burn, catch fire, glow with passion

ígneus -a -um: fiery, burning, flaming, glowing with heat

ígnis -is: m.; fire; lightning; pl. *can mean:* desires of the flesh

ignítus -a -um: fire-tried, burned,
 refined, purified
ignóbilis -is -e: base, obscure, unknown,
 ignoble, inglorious
ignobílitas -átis: f.; dishonor, obscurity
ignomínia -ae: f.; shame, ignominy,
 confusion, disgrace, dishonor
ignominiósus -a -um: disgraceful,
 ignominious, shameful
ignorábilis -is -e, ignótus -a -um:
 unknown
ignoránter: through ignorance
ignorántia -ae, ignorántio -ónis: f.;
 ignorance, lack of knowledge or
 acquaintance; see Appendix
ignóro -áre: (1); be ignorant of, not
 know, ignore
ignósco -ere -nóvi -nótum: (3); not
 notice, overlook, pardon, forgive,
 ignore
ignótus: see ignorábilis
I.H.S.: the first three letters of the name
 Jesus in Greek
ílex -icis: f.; holm oak
ílla: there, in that direction
illábor -i -lápsus: dep. (3); sink down,
 descend, fall, glide down, slip into a
 habit
illabóro -áre: (1); work at, work upon
íllac: there, at that place
illaésus -a -um: unharmed
illamentátus -a -um: unlamented
illápsus -a -um: flowing, outpouring
illátus -a -um: perf. pass. part. of inféro
ílle, ílla, íllud: that, he, she, it, the former
 íllum et íllum lócum: such and such a
  place
 íllud quídem . . . sed étiam: to be sure
  . . . but still
illécebra -ae: f.; allurement, enticement,
 charm, attraction, lure, inducement
 (in a good or bad sense)
illécto -áre: (1); allure, attract, invite

illéctus -a -um: unread, not read, not
 collected, not gathered
illéctus -a -um: perf. pass. part. of illício;
 seduced
illéctus -us: m.; allurement, seduction
illegítime: unlawfully, illegitimately
illegitímitas -átis: f.; illegitimacy
illegítimus -a -um: unlawful, not
 permitted, illegitimate
illibátus -a -um: unblemished,
 unimpaired, undiminished,
 uncurtailed
íllic: there
illício -ere -léxi -léctum: (3); entice,
 allure, seduce, decoy, inveigle
illícitus -a -um: forbidden, illicit, illegal;
 illícite: adv.
íllico: immediately, on the spot, in that
 very place
illído -ere -lísi -lísum: (3); strike, knock,
 beat, dash against
ílligo -áre: (1); fetter, bind, impede,
 entangle, encumber, attach to
illimitátus -a -um: unlimited
íllino -ere -lévi -lítum: (3); smear,
 bedaub, paint over, spread over, cover
illiterátus -a -um: unlettered, illiterate,
 uneducated
ílluc (íllo): thither, to that place or
 person or matter
illucésco -ere -lúxi: (3); shine upon,
 shine forth, give light, illuminate,
 enlighten
illúdo -ere -lúsi -lúsum: (3); mock,
 delude, deceive, laugh at, sport, play,
 ruin, disgrace, deride
illumináte: clearly, luminously
Illumináti -órum: m. pl.; Illuminati, a
 heretical sect
illuminátio -ónis: f.; light, illumination,
 an enlightening
illuminátor -óris: m.; enlightener
illuminatórium -ii: n.; baptistry

illúmino -áre: (1); enlighten, illuminate, make clear, adorn, cause to shine, set in clear light

illúsio -ónis: f.; illusion, mockery, irony

illúsor -óris: m.; mocker

illusórius -a -um: ironical, mocking

illustrátio -ónis: f.; brightness, illustration

illustrátor -óris: m.; illustrator, enlightener

illústris -is -e: glorious, full of light, illustrious, clear

illustríssimus -a -um: most illustrious

illústro -áre: (1); enlighten, adorn, illuminate, cause to shine, glorify, illustrate, elucidate, explain

íma -órum: n. pl.; lowest things, depths

imaginárius (imaginátus) -a -um: decorated with pictures or images, fancied, imagined

imaginátio -ónis: f.; imagination, mental image

imáginor -ári: dep. (1); imagine, picture to oneself

imágo -inis: f.; image, likeness, picture, form, appearance

imbecílitas -átis: f.; weakness, imbecility, feebleness

imbecíllus (imbecillósus) -a -um: feeble, weak

imbéllis -is -e: cowardly

ímber -bris: m.; rain, shower, storm

ímbibo -ere -bibi: (3); drink in, imbibe

ímbuo -ere -ui -útum: (3); fill, nourish, instruct, initiate

imitátio -ónis: f.; example, imitation

imitátor -óris: m.; follower, imitator

imitátrix -ícis: f.; female follower, imitator

ímitor (ímito) -ári: dep. (1); imitate, copy, represent

immaculábilis -is -e: unable to be stained

immaculátus -a -um: immaculate, spotless, undefiled, stainless, blameless

immáculo -áre: (1); stain, defile

immánis -is -e: brutal, savage; huge

immánitas -átis: f.; cruelty, fierceness

immániter: cruelly, frightfully, dreadfully, monstrously

immarcescíbilis -is -e: imperishable, unwithering

immateriális -is -e: immaterial

immatúrus -a -um: immature, unripe; **immatúre:** adv.

immediátus -a um: direct, immediate; **immediáte:** adv.

immedicábilis -is -e: incurable

ímmemor -oris: unmindful, forgetful

immemorábilis -is -e: immemorial, unexpressible, indescribable

immemorátio -ónis: f.; oblivion, forgetfulness

imménsitas -átis: f.; infinity

imménsus -a -um: immense, infinite, unmeasurable, all-pervading

immérgo -ere -mérsi -mérsum: (3); dip into, immerse, plunge, merge

immérito: unworthily, undeservedly

immérsio -ónis: f.; immersion

immígro -áre: (1); go into, remove

ímminens -éntis: imminent, threatening

immíneo -ére -ui -itum: (2); project over, hang down, threaten, be imminent or near, impend; aspire to

immínuo -ere -ui -útum: (3); abate, diminish, lessen

imminútio -ónis: f.; diminution, lessening

immísceo -ére -míscui -místum(-míxtum): (2); mix in, mingle with, join with, blend, become involved with

immiséricors -córdis: merciless, unmerciful

immíssio -ónis: f.; infusion, sending in, letting loose, setting forth

immítia -órum: n. pl.; harsh things, cruelties

immítis -is -e: harsh, cruel

immítto -ere -mísi -míssum: (3); send, insert, put into, encamp, cast , introduce

immíxtio -ónis: f.; mixture, blending, mix

ímmo (ímo): on the contrary; *can be either positive or negative:* yes indeed, by all means; no indeed, by no means; **ímmo máximo:** most certainly

immóbilis -is -e: immovable, immobile

immobílitas -átis: f.; immobility

immobíliter: steadfastly, immovably, unshakenly

immoderántia -ae: f.; excess

immoderátus (immódicus) -a -um: without measure, immoderate, excessive, intemperate; **immoderáte:** *adv.*

immodéste: unbecomingly

immolatícius -a -um: to or for sacrifice

immolátio -ónis: f.; offering, immolation; a name for the Preface

ímmolo -áre: (1); immolate, sacrifice, sprinkle meal on victim; render

immórior -i -mórtuus: *dep.* (3); die

ímmoror -ári: *dep.* (1); stay, remain, linger

immortális -is -e: immortal

immortálitas -átis: f.; immortality

immortáliter: immortally, imperishably

immótus -a -um: unmoved, unchanged, steadfast

immundítia -ae: f.; uncleanness, impurity

immúndus -a -um: unclean, impure, foul

immúnio -íre: (4); fortify

immúnis -is -e: immune, free from, preserved

immúnitas -átis: f.; immunity, freedom, exemption

immutatívum -i: n., **immutátio** -onis: f.; change, alteration, modification, interchange

immúnitus -a -um: unprotected

immutábilis -is -e: unchangeable, immutable

immutátio -ónis: f.; change, interchange, substitution

immúto (immútor) -áre: (1); change, alter

ímo: *see* **ímmo**

imp- *see also* **inp-**

impacíficus -a -um: not peaceful

impaénitens -éntis: not repenting, impenitent

ímpar -is: unequal, uneven, dissimilar

imparátus -a -um: unprepared

imparílitas -átis: f.; inequality

impártio -íre: (4); communicate, share, bestow, impart

impassíbilis -is -e: not susceptible to pain, passionless

impátiens -éntis: impatient, unable to endure

impatiéntia -ae: f.; impatience

impediméntum -i: n.; impediment, obstacle to certain actions; *see Appendix*

impédio -íre: (4); impede, lower, prostrate, entangle, prevent

impéditor -óris: m.; obstructer, hinderer

impéllo -ere -puli -púlsum: (3); push, thrust, impel, urge on, incite

impéndeo -ére: (2); threaten, overhang, be imminent

impéndium -ii: n.; charge, expense

impéndo -ere -péndi -pénsum: (3); lay out, expend, spend; use; ensure, extend; devote, apply

impénsus -a -um: ample, considerable, expensive, zealous, earnest; **impénse:** *adv.; as a f. noun:* cost, charge, expense

imperátor -óris: m.; emperor

imperátus -a -um: ordered, enjoined; *see* *Appendix*

imperféctio -ónis: f.; imperfection

imperféctus -a -um: unfinished, imperfect, incomplete

imperiósus -a -um: mighty, powerful, far-ruling, domineering

imperítia -ae: f.; ignorance, lack of skill or knowledge; inexperience

impérito (ímpero) -áre: (1); command, have power over, order, direct, rule

impérium -ii: n.; dominion, empire, reign, power, command, sovereignty

ímpero -áre: (1); rule, command, enjoin, order

imperscrutábilis -is -e: impenetrable

imperturbábilis -is -e: imperturbable

impértio (impértior) -íre -ívi (-ii) -ítum: (4); bestow, impart, share, grant, communicate

impertítio -ónis: f.; imparting, bestowing, granting

impérvius -a -um: impassible, impervious

impetígo -inis: f.; skin disease, dry scurf

ímpeto -ere: (3); attack, assail

impetrátio -ónis: f.; intercession, accomplishment, request obtained

impetrátor -óris: m.; one who obtains, obtainer, procurer

ímpetro -áre: (1); obtain, gain, effect, accomplish

ímpetus -us: m.; force, attack, violence, impulse, rush, vigor, rapid motion, assault, fury, ardor

impíetas -átis: f.; impiety, wickedness, sin, misdeed, transgression, lack of reverence

ímpiger -gra -grum: diligent, industrious, quick; **ímpigre:** *adv.*

impíngo -ere -pégi -páctum: (3); push back, put back, strike

impinguésco -ere -píngui: (3); become fat

impínguo -áre: (1); make or become fat

ímpius -a -um: wicked, ungodly, godless, irreverent; **ímpie:** *adv.*

impláno -áre: (1); lead astray

implantátio -ónis: f.; implementation, implanting, putting in

implánto -áre: (1); implant, put in, add, plant, establish

implécto -ere: (3); plait, twist, weave, wind, entwine

impleméntum -i: n.; implement, tool, instrument, means

ímpleo -ére -plévi -plétum: (2); fill, accomplish, celebrate, satiate

implétio -ónis: f.; fulfilment

impléxus -a -um: complex, complicated, involved

impléxus -us: m.; embrace, infolding, entwining

implicaméntum: -i: n.; entanglement

implicátio -ónis: f.; implication, involvement, suggestion

implícitus -a -um: implicit, involved, confused; **implícite:** *adv.*

ímplico -áre: (1); entangle, envelop, implicate

implóro -áre: (1); implore, beseech

impoénitens -éntis: impenitent, unrepentent

impollútus -a -um: undefiled, spotless, perfect

impóno -ere -pósui -pósitum: (3); lay upon, put upon, impose, set, set over

importábilis -is -e: insupportable, unbearable, heavy

impórto -áre: (1); bring in, import, introduce, convey

importúnitas -átis: f.; insolence, impoliteness

importúnus -a -um: unsuitable, unfavorable, troublesome, rude, ill-adapted, unjust, inconvenient; **importúne:** *adv.*

ímpos -otis: *w. gen.;* not master of, without control of

imposítio -ónis: f.; imposition, laying on, application

impossíbilis -is -e: impossible

impossibílitas -átis: f.; impossibility

impoténtia -ae: f.; impotence

impraesentiárum: here, now

imprecátio -ónis: f.; invoking of evil; prayer

ímprecor -ári: *dep.* (1); invoke good or evil upon a person, curse

impréssio -ónis: f.; impression, stamp

imprimátur: it may be printed; *see Appendix*

imprímis (in prímis): first of all, chiefly, especially

imprímo -ere -préssi -préssum: (3); print, press into, engrave

impróbitas -átis: f.; importunity, depravity, wickedness

ímprobo -áre: (1); blame, disapprove, reject, find fault with

ímprobus -a -um: evil, troublesome, wrong, bad; **ímprobe:** *adv.*

Impropéria: the Reproaches in the Office of Good Friday

impropérium -ii: n.; shame, reproach, disgrace

imprópero -áre: (1); reproach, taunt, upbraid

impróvidus -a -um: unexpected, unforeseen, sudden

improvíso: suddenly, unawares

improvísum -i: n.; emergency

imprúdens -éntis: foolish, imprudent; **imprudénter:** *adv.*

impúbes -eris, **impúbis** -is: youthful, beardless, under age, below the age of puberty

impudéntia -ae: f.; shamelessness

impudicítia -ae: f.; immodesty, impurity

impudícus -a -um: shameless, impudent

impugnátio -ónis: f.; assault, attack, challenge

impugnátor -óris: m.; enemy

impúgno -áre: (1); attack, assail, oppose, challenge

impúlsio -ónis: f.; external pressure, influence

impúlsus -a -um: *perf. pass. part. of* **impéllo**

impúlsus -us: m.; pressure, shock, impulse, excitement

impúritas -átis: f.; uncleanness, impurity, pollution

impúrus -a -um: impure

imputábilis -is -e: imputable

imputabílitas -átis: f.; imputability

imputátio -ónis: f.; charge, accusation

ímputo -áre: (1); reckon, account as a fault

ímus -a -um: deepest

in: *prep. w. acc.;* to, toward, into, for, against; *prep. w. abla.:* in, on, among, at; *see also Appendix*

    in abséntia: not being present

    in artículo mórtis: at the moment of death

    in cásu necessitátis: in case of necessity

    in coéna Dómini: at the Lord's Banquet, the Last Supper

    in díe: on the day

    in flagránte delícto: at the moment of the crime

    in génere: in general

    in glóbo: collected or lumped together

    in latitúdine: at liberty

    in língua vulgári: in the common language

    in lóco paréntis: in place of parent; as a guardian

    In Paradísum: Into Paradise, a hymn sung at a funeral liturgy

in péctore: in the heart or mind, not revealed publicly

in perículo mórtis: in danger of death

in perpétuum: forever

in persóna Chrísti: in the person of Christ

in pláno: on the level

in príma instántia: in the first instance

in prímis: see imprímis

in próximo: at hand

in úsu: at the moment of using

inadverténtia -ae: f.; inadvertence

inaccesíbilis -is -e, inaccéssus -a -um: inaccessible, unapproachable

inácuo -ere -ui -útum: (3); sharpen

inadaequátus -a -um: inadequate

inaequális -is -e: unequal, uneven, unlike

inaequálitas -átis: f.; inequality

inaequilíbrium -ii: n.; imbalance

inaestimábilis -is -e: priceless, inestimable

inalienábilis -is -e: inalienable

inálto -áre: (1); elevate, raise up, go up, heap up

inamárico -áre: (1); embitter

inámbulo -áre: (1); walk up and down, walk to and fro

inamissíbilis -is -e: unable to be lost

inamovíbilis -is -e: irremovable

inanlóquium -ii: n.; vain talk

inánime: inanimately

inánis -is -e: vain, empty, void

inániter: vainly, uselessly

inaquósus -a -um: without water, dry; inaquósum -i: n.; desert

inarátus -a -um: unplowed

inargentátus -a -um: plated with silver

inaugúro -áre: (1); take omens, practice augury, divine

inaurátio -ónis: f.; gilding

inaúrio -íre: (4); give hearing to, grant an answer to

inaúris -is: f.; earring

inaúro -áre: (1); gild, cover with gold

inauxiliátus -a -um: not supported

inb- see imb-

incálceo -ére -ui: (2); be warm

incalésco -ere -cálui: (3); grow warm

incanésco -ere -cánui: (3); be grayheaded

incantátor -óris: m.; wizard, enchanter

incánto -áre: (1); sing over, consecrate, charm, bewitch, enchant

incápax -ácis: incapable, indissoluble, indestructible

incapábilis -is -e: incomprehensible

incapabílitas -átis: f.; incomprehensibility

incapácitas -átis: f.; incapacity

incapácito -áre: (1); render incapable, make ineligible, disable

incarcerátio -ónis: f.; incarceration, imprisonment

incardinátio -ónis: f.; formal incorporation of a clergyman into diocese, incardination

incardíno -áre: (1); incardinate, become member of diocese

incarnátio -ónis: f.; incarnation, embodiment, union of divine and human in Christ

incarnátus -a -um: incarnate

incáro (incárno) -áre: (1); make incarnate, make flesh, clothe with flesh

incássum: in vain, uselessly, to no purpose

incastratúra -ae: f.; mortise, tenon

incaúte: unexpectedly, unawares

ince- see also incoe-

incédo -ere -céssi -céssum: (3); go, walk, enter in, go about, approach

incéndo -ere -céndi -cénsum: (3); burn, kindle, heat, set fire

incéndium -ii: n.; flame, fire, conflagration

incensárium (incensórium) -ii: n.; censer

incensátio -ónis: f.; incensing

incénso -áre: (1); to incense

incensórium -ii: see incensárium

incénsum -i: n.; incense; sacrifice
incénsum suavíssimum: most fragrant incense
incénsus -a -um: incensed
incentívum -i: n.; incentive
incéntor -óris: m.; promoter, provoker
incéptio -ónis: f., incéptus -us: m., incéptum -i: n.; endeavor, beginning, undertaking, initiative
incéptus -a -um: *perf. pass. part. of* incípio
incértus -a -um: uncertain, hidden, doubtful, dubious, vague, undecided, hesitating, irresolute; incértum -i: n.; uncertainty
incessábilis -is -e: unceasing, incessant; incessabíliter; *adv.*
incéssans -ántis: continual, unceasing; incessánter: *adv.*
incéstum -i: n.; incest
inchoátio -ónis: f.; beginning
inchoatíve: initially, in the beginning
ínchoo (íncoho) -áre: (1); begin, commence
íncidens -éntis: incidental; incidénter: *adv.*
íncido -ere -cidi -cásum: (3); fall into, happen upon, meet
incído -ere -cídi -císum: (3); cut into, carve, engrave, inscribe
incípio -ere -cépi -céptum: (3); begin, commence
incircumcísus -a -um: uncircumcised
incircumscríptus -a -um: incomprehensible, infinite, unlimited
incisúra -ae: f.; incision
incísus -a -um: cut
incitaméntum -i: n.; inducement, incentive, incitement
incitátor -óris: m.; inciter, investigator, instigator
íncito -áre: (1); cry out loudly, incite, provoke
inclinátio -ónis: f.; tendency, inclination

inclíno -áre: (1); bow, bend, lean, incline
inclúdo -ere -clúsi -clúsum: (3); include, enclose, obstruct
inclúsa -ae: f.; incluse, anchoress
inclusíve: inclusively
inclúsor -óris: m.; a smith
ínclytus -a -um: glorious, renowned
incoe- *see also* ince-
incoenátus -a -um: fasting, without supper
íncoho: *see* ínchoo
íncola -ae: c.; dweller, inhabitant, resident
incolátus -us: m.; residence, stay, dwelling in a place, sojourn
incólumis -is -e: safe, unharmed, uninjured
incolúmitas -átis: f.; safety, good condition, soundness
incombústus -a -um: not burnt, unconsumed
incommátio -ónis: f.; imperfect state
incómmodum -i: n.; discomfort, inconvenience, disadvantage, misfortune
incómmodus -a -um: inconvenient, unsuitable, disagreeable
incommunicábilis -is -e: incommunicable
incommutábilis -is -e: immutable, unchanging
incommutabílitas -átis: f.; unchangeableness, immutability
incommutabíliter: unchangeably, immutably
incomparábilis -is -e: incomparable; incomparabíliter: *adv.*
incompassíbilis -is -e: unable to suffer with or share another's pain
incompatíbilis -is -e: incompatible
incompellábilis -is -e: unable to be named or addressed
incómpetens -éntis: insufficient, incompetent

incompeténtia -ae: f.; incompetence, insufficiency

incompósitus -a -um: disordered

incomprehensíbilis -is -e: incomprehensible

inconcrétus -a -um: bodiless, incorporeal

inconcúbius -a -um: relating to the dead of night

inconcússe: firmly, resolutely

inconfusíbilis -is -e: unable to be confused or embarrassed

incóngruus -a -um: incongruous, unfitting, inconsistent, unsuitable; **incongruénter:** adv.

inconstabilítio -ónis: f.; not standing firmly

incónstans -ántis: unstable, inconstant

inconstántia -ae: f.; inconstancy, fickleness, changeableness, wandering

inconsuétus -a -um: unusual, unused, unaccustomed

inconsúltus -a -um: unadvised, not consulted, without asking advice, imprudent, inconsiderate, indiscreet; **inconsúlte:** adv.

inconsummátio -ónis: f.; nonconsummation, incompleteness

inconsummátus -a -um: undeveloped, imperfect, unfinished, incomplete, unconsummated

inconsútilis -is -e, **inconsútus** -a -um: without a seam, made in one piece

incontaminábilis -is -e: undefilable

incontaminátus -a -um: undefiled

incontemplábilis -a -um: unable to be contemplated or looked at

incontemptíbilis -is -e: not to be despised

incontíguus -a -um: unable to be touched

incóntinens -éntis: incontinent

incontinéntia -ae: f.; incontinence

incontradicábilis -is -e: undeniable

incontrítus -a -um: not contrite

inconveniénter: improperly

inconvertíbilis -is -e: unchangeable

inconvincíbilis -is -e: not to be convinced

incorporális -is -e: bodiless, incorporeal

incorporátio -ónis: f.; embodying, incorporating, incorporation

incorpóreus -a -um, **incorporábilis** -is -e: incorporeal, without a body

incórporor (incórporo) -ári: dep. (1); be incorporated, enter into a body, incorporate

incorrigíbilis -is -e: incorrigible

incorrigibílitas -átis: f.; incorrigibility

incorruptéla -ae: f.; incorruption, immortality

incorruptíbilis -is -e: incorruptible

incorruptibílitas -átis: f.; immunity from corruption, incorruption

incorruptibíliter: imperishably, incorruptibly

incorrúptio -ónis: f.; incorruptibility, imperishableness

incorrúptus -a -um: incorrupted

incrassátus -a -um: hardened

incrásso -áre: (1); grow fat, render gross

increátus -a -um: uncreated, not begotten

increbrésco -ere -crébui: (3); become frequent, increase, prevail

incredíbilis -is -e: incredible, unbelievable

incredúlitas -átis: f.; unbelief, incredulity

incrédulus -a -um: faithless, incredulous, unbelieving

increméntum -i: n.; increase, increment, growth, augmentation

increpátio -ónis: f.; rebuke, scolding, chiding, threat

increpatórius -a -um: rebuking, scolding, chiding

íncrepo -áre -crépui(-pávi) -itum(-pátum): (1); rebuke, reprove, blame, chide, scold, rattle

incrésco -ere -crévi: (3); increase, grow

incruéntus -a -um: bloodless; incruénte: adv.

íncubo -áre: (1); lie in, lie on

incúlco -áre: (1); trample in, mix in, impress upon, force upon

inculpábilis -is -e: blameless, innocent, guiltless

inculpándus -a -um: not blameworthy

incúltus -a -um: untilled

incúmbo -ere -cúbui -cúbitum: (3); recline, lean on, apply to

incunábula -órum: n. pl.; swaddling clothes, cradle; beginning, early days of

incunctánter: readily, without delay, unhesitatingly

incurábilis -is -e: incurable

incúria -ae: f.; neglect, carelessness, indifference

incúrro -ere -cúrri(-cucúrri) -cursum: (3); come upon, run against, charge, incur, commit a fault

incúrsio -ónis: f.; attack

incúrso -áre: (1); run or strike against

incúrsus -us: m.; attack, assault

incúrvo (incúrvor) -áre: (1); bend, curve, bow

incúrvus -a -um: bent, curved, crooked

incútio -ere -cússi -cússum: (3); strike, inflict

indágo -áre: (1); investigate, inquire

índe: thence, from there, from that time, thereafter, henceforth

indébitus -a -um: undue, not owed

indébito (indébite): unduly, without just cause

indeclinábilis -is -e: firm, unwavering

indecórus -a -um: unbecoming, shameful, indecorous

indeféctus -a -um: undiminished, unfailing, unexhausted, unweakened; indefectibíliter: adv.

indeféssus -a -um: unwearied, untired, tireless; indefésse: adv.

indefíciens -éntis: unfailing, continuous; indeficiénter: adv.

indefinítus -a -um: indefinite, unspecified; indefiníte: adv.

indelébilis -is -e: indelible, enduring, imperishable

indeliberáte: involuntarily

indemnátus -a -um: uncondemned

indémnis -is -e: protected, exempt from liability

indémnitas -átis: f.; indemnity, security for loss or damage

indepéndens -éntis: independent; independénter: adv.

independéntia -ae: f.; independence

indesinénter: unceasingly, continually

indeterminátus -a -um: undefined, indeterminate

indevolutívus -a -um: not transferred, indevolutive; see Appendix

índex -icis: m.; sign, index, list; indication, pointer, token, proof

Índia -ae: f.; India

Indiánus (Índus) -a -um: Indian, pertaining to India

indicátio -ónis: f.; direction, indication, reference

indicíbilis -is -e: unable to be told in words

indícium -ii: n.; evidence, proof, sign, mark, disclosure

índico -áre: (1); indicate, proclaim, tell, show, reveal, inform, declare, give evidence

indíco -ere -díxi -díctum: (3); publish, announce, appoint, impose, inflict, ordain, command, declare publicly

indíctio -ónis: f.; indiction

Índicus -a -um: Indian

indífferens -éntis: indifferent;
indifferénter: adv.
indifferentísmus -i: n.; indifferentism
indígena -ae: c.; native
índigens -éntis: needy, poor, in want;
índigens -éntis: c.; poor person
indígeo -ére -ui: (2); want, need, lack,
require
indigéstus -a -um: undigested
indígnans -ántis: angry, indignant
indignátio -ónis: f.; anger, indignation,
disdain
indígnitas -átis: f.; unworthiness,
baseness
indígnor -ári: dep. (1); be angry, be
indignant, be offended, consider
unworthy
indígnus -a -um: unworthy,
undeserving; indígne: adv.
índigus -a -um: needy
indiréctus -a -um: indirect; indirécte:
adv.
indisciplinátus (indisciplinósus) -a
-um: unskillful, undisciplined
indiscrétim: without distinction
indiscriminátus -a -um: indiscriminate;
indiscriminátim: adv.
indissolubílitas -átis: f.; indissolubility
indispensábilis -is -e: indispensable
indispertíbilis -is -e: indivisible
indisposítio -ónis: f.; indispostion
indissímilis -is -e: not unlike
indissociábilis -is -e: inseparable
indissolúbilis -is -e: imperishable,
indissoluble
indissolubílitas -átis: f.; indissolubility
indistíncte: without distinction
índitus -a -um: given, imposed
individuális -is -e, individualísticus -a
-um: individual; see Appendix
Individualísmus -i: m.; theory of
individualism
individúitas -átis: f.; indivisibility
indivíduum -i: n.; individual

indivíduus -a -um: indivisible,
inseparable
indivísus -a -um: undivided; indivíse:
adv.
índo -ere -didi -ditum: (3); put in, put
into, give to, introduce
indocíbilis -is -e: unteachable
indóctus -a -um: unlearned
índoles -is: f.; genius, talent, character,
nature
indomitábilis -is -e: not to be subdued
indórmio -íre: (4); sleep
indubitánter (indúbie): without doubt
indubitátus (indúbius) -a -um:
unwavering, certain, undoubted
indúbito -áre: (1); doubt
indúciae -árum: f. pl.; truce, extension
of time, armistice
indúco -ere -dúxi -dúctum: (3); lead in,
introduce, induct
indúctio -ónis: f.; induction
inductórius -a -um: misleading,
seducing
indulgéntia -ae: f.; indulgence, pardon,
forgiveness, remission; see Appendix
indúlgeo -ére -dúlsi -dúltum: (2); grant,
forgive, be indulgent, indulge, give,
bestow, gratify, be forbearing
indultárius -ii: m.; person possessing an
indult
indultívus -a -um: by indult or grant
indúltum -i: n.; indult, release from
obligation, concession; see Appendix
induméntum -i: n.; apparel
índuo -ere -ui -útum: (3); clothe, put
on, cover, engage in
indúro -áre: (1); dry up, harden
Índus -a -um: of India, Indian
indúsium -ii: n.; shirt
indústria -ae: f.; industry, purpose,
diligence; de indústria: on purpose
industriális -is -e: industrial
industrializátio -ónis: f.;
industrialization

indústrius -a -um: industrious, active, diligent, zealous

indútus -a -um: clothed

inébrio -áre: (1); soak, make drunk, intoxicate, inebriate, water

inédia -ae: f.; fasting, hunger, abstinence

inéditus -a -um: unpublished, not made known

ineffábilis -is -e: ineffable, unutterable, unspeakable

ineffabíliter: in an unspeakable manner, unutterably

inéfficax -ácis: ineffective, inefficient; inefficáciter: adv.

ineluíbilis -is -e: unable to be washed out, indelible

ineluctábilis -is -e: unavoidable, inevitable

inemigrábilis -is -e: not capable of removing

inenarrábilis -is -e: indescribable

íneo -íre -ii(-ívi) -itum: (4); enter, enter upon, undertake, begin; foédus iníre: form a pact

ineptitúdo -inis: f.; absurdity, foolishness

inéptus -a -um: stupid, inept, silly, unsuited, awkward

inérmis -is -e: unarmed, defenseless

inerrabíliter: indescribably

inérrans -antis: not wandering, fixed, immobile

íners -értis: simple, inactive, idle, lazy

inértia -ae: f.; inactivity, idleness, inertia, lack of skill

inerudítio -ónis: f.; ignorance

inésse -fui: see ínsum

inevitábilis -is -e: unavoidable, inevitable

inevulsíbilis -is -e: inseparable

inexcusábilis -is -e: inexcusable

inexhaústus -a -um: inexhausted

inexorábilis -is -e: inexorable, unable to be moved by asking

inexpectátus -a -um: unexpected

inexpértus -a -um: inexperienced, unaccustomed

inexplébilis -a -um: insatiable, extraordinary

inexplebíliter: insatiably

inexpugnális -is -e: invincible

inexquisítus -a -um: unsearchable

inextinguíbilis -is -e: unquenchable, inextinguishable

inextricábilis -is -e: inextricable

infallíbilis -is -e: infallible; infallibíliter: adv.

infallibílitas -átis: f.; infallibility

infámia -ae: f.; evil report, ill fame, infamy, disgrace

infámis -is -e: infamous, spoken of poorly, disreputable

infándus -a -um: unspeakable, unheard of

ínfans -ántis: c.; infant, child, babe; see Appendix

infántes expósiti et invénti: foundlings

infántia -ae: f.; infancy, childhood

infanticídium -ii: n.; infanticide

infantílis -is -e: infantile

infántula -ae: f., infántulus -i: m.; babe, infant

infatigabíliter: indefatigably

infatuátus -a -um: tasteless

infaústus -a -um: unfortunate, unpropitious

inféctus -a -um: undone, unfinished, impossible

inféctus -a -um: spoiled, infected; perf. pass. part. of infício

inféctus -us: m.; dyeing

infecúnditas -átis: f.; sterility, barrenness

infecúndus -a -um: sterile

infelícitas -átis: f.; unhappiness, wretchedness

infélix -ícis: unhappy, unlucky; infelíciter: adv.

infénsus -a -um: hostile, dangerous

inférior -ior -ius: lower, below

infermentátus -a -um: unleavened

inférnus -a -um: infernal, of hell; inférnus -i: m.; grave, underworld, nether world, hell, Sheol

ínfero -érre -tuli, illátum: irreg.; bring in, inflict, bear, wage

inferuésco -ere: (3); become enflamed

ínferus -a -um: pertaining to the grave or underworld or hell; ínferus -i: m.; underworld, hell, infernal regions, abode of the dead, Sheol; ínferi -órum: m. pl.; those in underworld, the dead

infestátio -ónis: f.; assault, attack, infestation, harassment

inrésto -áre: (1); attack, molest, disturb, harass

inféstus -a -um: hostile

inrício -ere -féci -féctum: (3); stain, pollute, infect, dip into

infidélis -is -e: unfaithful, unbelieving

infidélitas -átis: f.; faithlessness, infidelity

infidígraphus -a -um: writing without faith

in fíeri: in becoming, from potency to act

infígo -ere -fíxi -fíxum: (3); fasten in, thrust in, stick fast, infix

ínfimus -a -um: lowest, meanest, of the lower world

infinítus -a -um: infinite

infírmitas -átis: f.; infirmity, sickness, disease, weakness

infírmo -áre: (1); weaken, annul, refute, disapprove

infírmor -ári: dep. (1); be weak, be sick, be diseased

infírmus -a -um: weak, sick, infirm

inflammátio -ónis: f.; fire

inflámmo -áre: (1); inflame, kindle, burn, set on fire

inflátio -ónis: f.; pride, swelling, inflation

inflátus -a -um: swollen, puffed up, inflated

inflécto -ere -fléxi -fléctum: (3); bend, bow, curve

inflíctio -ónis: f.; infliction, adversity, affliction

inflígo -ere -íxi -íctum: (3); inflict, impose, strike against

ínflo -áre: (1); puff up, blow up

ínfluo -ere: (3); flow or run into

inflúxus -us: m.; inpouring, rush, influence, impact, influx

informátio -ónis: f.; information, outline, sketch, explanation, pattern, representation, draft

informatívus -a -um: informative

infórmitas -átis: f.; shapelessness, lack of form

infórmiter: formlessly

infórmo -áre: (1); fashion, form, mold, represent, shape, train

ínfra: prep. w. acc. & adv.; under, beneath, below

infrahumánus -a -um: subhuman

ínfremo -ere -frémui: (3); groan

infréno -áre: (1); bridle, curb, restrain, check, control

infríngo -ere -frégi -fráctum: (3); infringe upon, break

infructuósitas -átis: f.; barrenness, unproductivity

infructuósus -a -um: barren, unfruitful

infrunítus -a -um: bold, senseless, tasteless

ínfula -ae: f.; miter, band hanging from miter, chasuble

infulátus -a -um: mitered

infúndo -ere -fúdi -fúsum: (3); pour into, infuse, water, impart

infúsio -ónis: f.; infusion, pouring into, outpouring

infusórium -ii: n.; tube, pipe, container

infúsus -a -um: instilled

ingémino -áre: (1); repent

ingemísco (ingemésco) -ere -gémui: (3); wail, sigh, groan

ingéntus -a -um: unbegotten, innate

ingénium -ii: n.; natural character, nature, genius

íngens -éntis: huge, vast, great

ingénuus -a -um: native, indigenous, natural, inborn

íngero -ere -géssi -géstum: (3); infuse, pour into, execute

ingrátus -a -um: unpleasant, disagreeable, ungrateful, thankless

ingravésco -ere: (3); become serious

ingrávido -áre: (1); impregnate, weigh down, burden, oppress

íngravo -áre: (1); weigh down, molest, make severe, aggravate, harden

ingrédior -i -gréssus: dep. (3); enter, come in, advance, begin

ingréssus -us: m.; procession, going into, entering, entrance

íngruo -ere -ui: (3); assault

ínguen -inis: n., ínguina -ae: f.; groin

inhábilis -is -e: incapable, unfit, unable

inhabílitas -átis: f.; incapacity, disqualification

inhabílito -áre: (1); incapacitate, prevent from acting, disqualify; see Appendix

inhabitábilis -is -e: uninhabitable

inhabitátio -ónis: f.; indwelling

inhabitátor -óris: m.; inhabitant

inhábito -áre: (1); dwell, abide, live

inhaerédito: see inherédito

inhaeréntia -ae: f.; inherent quality

inhaéreo -ére -haési -haésum: (2); adhere to, inhere, cling

inhaesitánter: unhesitatingly

inherédito (inhaer-) -áre: (1); appoint an heir

inhiánter: greedily, eagerly, with open mouth

inhíbeo -ére: (2); prevent, check, hold back, restrain

inhibítio -ónis: f.; inhibition, restraining, backing up

ínhio -áre: (1); long for, gape after

inhonéstus -a -um: dishonorable, disgraceful; inhonéste: adv.

inhonorátio -ónis: f.; dishonor

inhonorátus -a -um: unrewarded, not honored

inhonóro -áre: (1); dishonor

inhumánitas -átis: f.; inhumanity

inhumánus -a -um: brutal, inhuman

inhumátus -a -um: unburied

ínibi: in that place, therein, in that matter, near at hand

início (injício) -ere: (3); throw in, inject, cause, inspire

inimicítia -ae: f.; enmity

inimíco -áre: (1); make enemies, set against

inimícus -a -um: hostile, unfriendly; as a noun: enemy, foe

ininterpretábilis -is -e: difficult to explain

iníquitas -átis: f.; iniquity, sin, injustice

iníquus -a -um: unjust, wicked, godless; as a noun: evildoer; iníque: adv.

initiális -is -e: initial, incipient, original, beginning

initiátio -ónis: f.; initiation, participation

initiatíva -ae: f.; initiative

inítio -áre: (1); initiate, admit to sacred rites, originate

inítium -ii: n.; commencement, beginning, start, top

ínitus -a -um: begun, entered upon

injício: see início

injúngo -ere -júnxi -júnctum: (3); impose, enjoin, inflict

injurátus -a -um: unsworn

injúria -ae: f.; injury, wrong, injustice

injuriósus -a -um: injurious, wrongful, unjust

injustítia -ae: f.; injustice, sin, iniquity

injústus -a -um: unjust, godless, unrighteous; injúste: adv.

inl- *see* ill-

inm- *see* imm-

innátus -a -um: inborn, innate

innécto -ere: (3); insert

innítor -i -níxus(-nísus): *dep.* (3); rely on, lean upon, rest on

ínnocens -éntis: innocent, pure, clean, guiltless, harmless, blameless; innocénter: *adv.*

innocéntia -ae: f.; innocence, integrity, uprightness

innócuus (innóxius) -a -um: blameless, innocent

innódo -áre: (1); fasten with a knot, be bound by, implicate

innominátus -a -um: unnamed

innotésco -ere -nótui: (3); become known, make known

innovátio -ónis: f.; innovation, renewing, alteration

ínnovo -áre: (1); renew, alter

innóxius: *see* innócuus

innumerábilis -is -e, innúmerus -a -um: countless, innumerable, numberless

ínnuo -ere -ui: (3); make a sign, signal to, hint, intimate, nod

innúptus -a -um: unmarried

innútrio -íre: (4); nourish, bring in

inoboédiens (inobé-) -éntis: disobedient

inoboediéntia (inobé-) -ae: f.; disobedience

inobservántia -ae: f.; nonobservance

inoffénsus -a -um: unhurt

inolésco -ere -évi -ítum: (3); grow in or on

inólitus -a -um: ingrown, inveterate, implanted, rooted

inópero (inóperor) -áre: (1); work in, produce, effect, operate

inopértus -a -um: uncovered, naked

inópia -ae: f.; want, need, poverty

inopináte: unexpectedly

inopinátus -a -um: unexpected

inopportúnus -a -um: unfitting, inopportune; inopportúne: *adv.*

ínops -opis: destitute, needy, indigent, afflicted, without means

inordinátus -a -um: disordered, irregular; inordináte: *adv.*

inordinátio -ónis: f.; disorder

inp- *see also* imp-

inpértio (inpértior) -íre -ívi (-ii) -ítum: (4); share with one another, communicate, bestow

inpértus -a -um: uncovered, naked

inputríbilis -is -e: incorruptible

ínquam: *defect. verb;* I say

inquiéto -áre: (1); disturb, disquiet

inquietúdo -inis: f.; restlessness

inquiétus -a -um: restless, unquiet, undefiled; inquiéte: *adv.*

inquinaméntum -i: n., inquinátio -ónis: f.; stain, soil, filth, pollution

inquinátus -a -um: defiled, polluted

ínquino -áre: (1); spoil, pollute, defile, contaminate

inquíro -ere -sívi -sítum: (3); seek, seek after, desire, search

inquisítio -ónis: f.; search, inquiry, investigation

Inquisítio -ónis: f.; Inquisition

inquisítor -óris: m.; inquisitor, officer of the Inquisition

ínquit: *defect. verb;* he or she says; ínquiunt: they say

inr- *see also* irr-

inréptio -ónis: f.; a creeping in

I.N.R.I.: *abbrev. of* Iésus Nazarénus Rex Iudaeórum; Jesus of Nazareth King of the Jews

insanábilis -is -e: incurable

insánia -ae: f.; insanity, madness, folly, frenzy

insánio -íre: (4); be mad or insane, rage

insánus -a -um: mad, insane, foolish; *as a noun:* insane or mad person

insatiábilis -is -e: insatiable, ambitious

inscítia -ae: f.; ignorance
ínscius -a -um: not knowing, ignorant, unaware
inscríbo -ere -scrípsi -scríptum: (3); write over, inscribe
inscríptio -ónis: f., inscríptum -i: n.; inscription, title
inscrutábilis -is -e: inscrutable, unsearchable
inscúlpo -ere -scúlpsi -scúlptum: (3); carve, engrave, brand
insecútor -óris: m.; pursuer, persecutor
inseducíbilis -is -e: not to be drawn away
insémino -áre: (1); sow, plant, implant, fertilize, impregnate
insensátus -a -um: foolish, senseless; as a noun: fool
insensíbilis -is -e: insensible
inseparabíliter: inseparably
inseparábilis -is -e: inseparable
insepúltus -a -um: unburied
ínsero -ere -ui -sértum: (3); introduce, enroll, insert, intrude
ínsero -ere -sévi -situm: (3); implant, ingraft, insert
insértio -ónis: f.; putting in, insertion, ingrafting, grafting
insértus -a -um: fixed, rooted
insérvio -íre: (4); serve, attend to
insídeo -ére -sédi -séssum: (2); rest upon
insídia -ae: f.; deceit; insídiae -árum: f. pl.; ambush, snare, plot, treachery
insidiátor -óris: m.; plotter, spy, traitor
insídio -áre: (1); lay snares
insídior -ári: dep. (1); lie in wait for, watch for, ambush, plot
insidiósus -a -um: cunning, artful, deceitful, dangerous
insígne -is: n.; badge, distinctive sign, insignia, uniform
insígnio -íre -ii(-ívi) -ítum: (4), insígno -áre: (1); adorn, honor, endow, distinguish, make known, sign, engrave
insígnior -ior -ius: more outstanding

insígnis -is -e: noted, notable, remarkable, eminent, prominent, extraordinary, special; insígniter: adv.
insígno: see insígnio
ínsimul: both, at the same time, at once, together
insimulátus -a -um: pretended, feigned, undisguised
insinuátor -óris: m.; introducer
insínuo -áre: (1); insinuate, convey, make known, teach
insípiens -éntis: foolish, unwise
insipiéntia -ae: f.; folly, foolishness
insísto -ere -stiti: (3); press on, pursue, persist, strive for
ínsitus -a -um: ingrafted
ínsolens -éntis: haughty, arrogant
insolénter: arrogantly
insoléntia -ae: f.; excess, extravagance, pride
insolésco -ere: (3); become insolvent, behave extravagantly
insólitus -a -um: unaccustomed, unusual
insolúbilis -is -e: insoluble, unable to be solved or unlocked
insolútus -a -um: unsolved
insómnis -is -e: sleepless
ínsono -áre -sónui -sónitum: (1); sound, resound, roar
ínsons -óntis: innocent
insordésco -ere -dui: (3); become dirty or stained
insperátus -a -um: unexpected, unhoped for
inspérgo -ere -spérsi -spérsum: (3); sprinkle
inspéctio -ónis: f.; inspection, examination
inspício -ere -spéxi -spéctum: (3); gaze upon, contemplate, examine, inspect
inspirátio -ónis: f.; inspiration, breath, power
inspirátor -óris: m.; inspirer
inspíro -áre: (1); breathe into

instábilis -is -e: unstable, inconstant, changeable, with no fixed abode; instabíliter: *adv.*

ínstans -ántis: present, instant; instánter: *adv.*

instántia -ae: f.; instance, stage of a trial, presence, perseverance, insistance; *see Appendix*

ínstar: *indecl.:* n.; image, likeness, resemblance, kind, appearance; *w. gen.:* like to, after the fashion of

instaurátio -ónis: f.; renewal

instaurátor -óris: m.; restorer

instaúro -áre: (1); renew, restore, comprise, repeat, strengthen

instígo -áre: (1); urge, stimulate, stir up, incite, rouse

instíllo -áre: (1); pour by drops, instil, inspire

instímulo -áre: (1); urge on, prick, stimulate

instínctus -us: m.; inspiration, instinct

ínstita -ae: f.; bandage, winding band

institia -ae: f.; goodness

ínstitor -óris: m.; merchant

instítuo -ere -ui -útum: (3); ordain, institute, cause, procure, establish, instruct

institútio -ónis: f.; institution, manner of life, religious order, arrangement, disposition, instruction, principles

institútor -óris: m.; founder, tutor, creator

institútrix -icis: f.; foundress

institútum -i: n.; precept, custom, regulation; purpose, plan; mode of life; institution, institute

ínsto -áre -stiti: (1); insist, persist, threaten, stand, press upon, wait, follow closely, approach, solicit

instrépero -ere: (3); utter, resound

instrúctio -ónis: f.; instruction, preparation, training; *see Appendix*

Instrúctio Clementína: regulations about the Forty Hours devotion issued by Pope Clement VIII in 1592

instrúctor -óris: m.; instructor, auditor, preparer of a case; *see Appendix*

instrúctus -a -um: drawn up, ordered, prepared, arranged, instructed

instruméntum -i: n.; instrument, tool; document, record; means; *see Appendix*

ínstruo -ere -strúxi -strúctum: (3); draw up, arrange; instruct, teach, prepare; regulate

insubsidiátus -a -um: unsupported

insubvertíbilis -is -e: not to be overturned

insúdo -áre: (1); sweat at

insuefáctus -a -um: accustomed to

insufíciens -éntis: insufficient

insufficiéntia -ae: f.; lack, insufficiency

insufflátio -ónis: f.; breathing upon

insúfflo -áre: (1); blow, blow upon, breathe upon, inflate

ínsula -ae: f.; island

insulánus -i: m., insulána -ae: f.; islander

insúlsus -a -um: tasteless, insipid; silly, absurd, awkward, bungling; insúlse: *adv.*

insúlto -áre: (1); scoff at, taunt, insult

insúltus -us: m.; a reviling, a scoffing, insult

ínsum, inésse, ínfui: be in or on, belong to

insúmo -ere -súmpsi -súmptum: (3); consume

ínsuo -ere -sui -sútum: (3); sew up

ínsuper: *adv. & prep. w. acc. & abla.;* in addition to, moreover, futhermore, besides, above, over, over and above, yea also

insuperábilis -is -e: insurmountable, unconquerable

insúrgo -ere -súrrexi -súrrectum: (3); rise up, revolt against

insuspicábilis -is -e: unsuspected

intáctus -a -um: inviolate, untouched, untried

intaminábilis -is -e: undefilable

intaminátus -a -um: unspotted

ínteger -gra -grum: whole, entire, correct, sound, fresh, vigorous, blameless, intact, perfect, unharmed; íntegre: adv.

integrális -is -e: integral

íntegrans -ántis: making up a whole

intégritas -átis: f.; integrity, wholeness, soundness, purity, virginity, uprightness, health

íntegro (intégro) -áre: (1); renew, make whole, restore, heal

intellectuális -is -e: of the intellect, intellectual

intelléctus -us: m.; sense, meaning, insight, understanding, intellect

intéllegens (intélli-) -éntis: intelligent, knowing, able to perceive; intellegénter: adv.

intellegéntia (intelli-) -ae: f.; knowledge, understanding, intelligence, discernment, judgment

intellegíbilis (intelli-) -is -e: intelligible, intellectual

intéllego (intélli-) -ere -léxi -léctum: (3); perceive, understand, feel, attend to, know, give heed to, grasp

intemerátus -a -um: spotless

intempestátus (intempestívus, intempéstus) -a -um: unseasonable, untimely, inopportune; intempésta nox: the dead of night

inténdo -ere -téndi -ténsum(-téntum): (3); regard, look at, hearken, mark, go toward, intend, direct, aim, stretch, tighten, consider mercifully, propose árcum inténdere: bend a bow, shoot inténdere ánimum: direct attention to

inténsitas -átis: f.; emphasis

inténsus: see inténtus

intentátor -óris: m.; one who does not tempt

inténtio -ónis: f.; intention, purpose

inténto -áre: (1); threaten, aim

inténtus (inténsus) -a -um: anxious, waiting eagerly for, attentive to, intent, intense

ínter: adv. & prep. w. acc.; between, among, during, within

intercédo -ere -céssi -céssum: (3); intercede, interpose on behalf of, intervene, involve

intercéssio -ónis: f.; intercession

intercído -ere -cídi -císum: (3); divide, separate, cleave, cut

intercípio -ere -cépi -céptum: (3); intercept, interrupt, rob

interclúdo -ere -clúsi -clúsum: (3); block, hinder, shut off

intercúrro -ere: (3); intervene, run or go between

interdependéntia -ae: f.; interdependence

interdíco -ere: (3); interpose, interdict, forbid, prohibit

interdíctum -i: n.; interdict, prohibition; see Appendix

interdiocesánus -a -um: interdiocesan

intérdiu: by day, in the daytime

intérdum: sometimes, occasionally, now and then

intérea: in the meantime, meanwhile, nevertheless, anyhow

intéreo -íre -ívi -itum: (4); die, perish

ínterest: impers.; it concerns, it makes a difference

interféctio -ónis: f.; killing

interféctor -óris: m.; killer, slayer

interfício -ere -féci -féctum: (3); kill, slay, destroy, murder

intér-hio -áre: (1); be open between

interíbilis -is -e: perishable, mortal

interício (interjício) -ere: (3); thrown in, interject, add

ínterim: meanwhile, in the meantime, for the moment, sometimes

intérimo -ere -émi -émptum: (3); kill,
slay, destroy, annihilate

intérior -ior -ius: inward, interior, inner;
interióra -órum: n. pl.; entrails;
intérius: more inwardly, interiorly,
within, closely, inside

interióritas -átis: f.; innermost depths

interítio -ónis: f.; destruction

intéritus -a -um: perished, destroyed;
perf. pass. part. of intéreo

intéritus -us: m.; death, destruction,
overthrow, annihilation

interjício: see interício

interlocutórius -a -um: interlocutory,
interrupting

intérloquor -i -locútus(-loquútus): dep.
(3); interrupt

intermédius -a -um: intermediate

interminátus -a -um: endless, infinite

intermíssio -ónis: f.; ceasing,
intermission, interruption

intermítto -ere -mísi -míssum: (3);
leave, let pass, interrupt, suspend,
pause, stop, leave a space between,
break off

intermutátus -a -um: interchanged

internationális -is -e: international

internécio -ónis: f., internécium -ii: n.;
carnage, massacre

internúntius -ii: m.; internuncio, one
serving several nations

intérnus -a -um: internal, inward, inner

íntero -ere -trívi -trítum: (3); rub,
crumble, break, bruise, pound into

interpellátio -ónis: f.; interruption,
hindrance; intercession; formal
questioning

interpéllo -áre: (1); interrupt, disturb,
obstruct, hinder; intercede; interrogate

interpolátio -ónis: f.; false alteration,
interpolation

intérpolo -áre: (1); falsify, corrupt;
polish, give a new form to, interpolate

interpóno -ere: (3); interpose, insert,
put between

interposítio -ónis: f.; introduction,
introducing, bringing forward;
insertion; interval

intérpres -pretis: c.; interpreter,
mediator, translator

interpretátio -ónis: f.; interpretation,
translation; see Appendix

intérpreto (intérpretor) -áre: (1);
interpret, translate

interrásilis -is -e: intergraven, in relief

interrogátio -ónis: f.; question,
interrogation, argument, pledge,
inquiry, examination

interrogatórium -ii: n.; questionnaire

intérrogo -áre: (1); inquire, request,
examine, test, try, demand

interrúmpo -ere -rúpi -rúptum: (3);
divide, break into, cleave, break apart

interrúptio -ónis: f.; interruption

interscríbo -ere -scrípsi -scríptum: (3);
write between, interscribe

intérsero -ere -sérui -sértum: (3); place
between, interpose, add

intérsero -ere -sévi -sítum: (3); sow or
plant between

intersíleo -ére: (2); be silent in the
meantime

intérstes, -stitis: standing between

interstítium -ii: n.; interruption,
interval, short time between

íntersum -ésse -fui: be present, attend,
be different, take part in, differ;
impers: it concerns, interests, or makes
a difference

intertrúdo -ere: (3); thrust between

intervállum -i: n.; space, interval,
intermission, break

intervénio -íre: (4); intervene, happen,
occur, interfer with

intervéntio -ónis: f., intervéntus us: m.;
intervention, intercession, intrusion,
occurence

intervéntor -óris: m.; intercessor

intervéntus -us: m.; coming between, intervention, appearance

intestínus -a -um: internal, inward; *as a n. noun:* entrails, bowels, innermost parts

inthronízo -áre: (1); enthrone

intimátio -ónis: f.; notice, announcement, communication

intímitas -átis: f.; intimacy, privacy

íntimo -áre: (1); intimate, announce, make known

íntimus -a -um: innermost, most secret, close, most profound; **íntima** -órum: n. pl.; bowels; **íntime:** *adv.;* **intímius:** *comp. adv.*

intíngo -ere -tínxi -tínctum: (3); dip into, steep

intitubábilis -is -e: firm, unwavering

intolerábilis -is -e: unbearable, overwhelming, intolerable; **intolerabíliter:** *adv.*

intolerántia -ae: f.; intolerance, impatience, insolence

intonátio -ónis: f.; intonation, act of intoning

íntono -áre -tónui -tonátum: (1); to thunder

intortícium -ii: n.; torch

íntra: *adv. & prep. w. acc.;* within, inside, during

íntra múros: within the walls, intramural

íntra nos: among us, between us

intricátio -ónis: f.; intricacy

intríco -áre: (1); entangle, perplex, embarrass

intrínsecus -a -um: inward, inner; **intrínsece (intrínsecus):** on the inside, within, internally, inwardly

íntro: within

íntro -áre: (1), **intróeo** -íre: (4); enter, go in, pierce

intródeo *see* intróeo

introdúco -ere: (3); introduce, bring in, lead in

introdúctio -ónis: f.; introduction, beginning, leading in

introductívus (introductórius)-a -um: introductive, introductory

intróeo (intródeo) -íre: (4); enter, go in

Intróitum: Introit, the opening prayer in the pre–Vatican II liturgy

intróitus -us: m.; entrance, act of entering, prelude, beginning

introgrédior -i -gréssus: *dep.* (3); go in, come in

intromítto -ere -mísi -míssum: (3); send into, cause to enter

introspício -ere -spéxi -spéctum: (3); look into

intúeor -éri -túitus: *dep.* (2); consider, look at, gaze upon, behold

intuítio -onis: f.; intuition

intuitívus -a -um: intuitive

intúitus -us: m.; mind, view, purpose, consideration

intumésco -ere -túmui: (3); swell up

íntus: within, inside, inwardly

inúltus -a -um: unavenged, unpunished

inundántia -ae, inundátio -ónis: f.; inundation, flood, multitude

inúndo -áre: (1); overflow, flood, inundate

inúnguo -ere -únxi -únctum: (3); smear with ointment, anoint

inútilis -is -e: useless, worthless, unprofitable, impractical, injurious; **inutíliter:** *adv.*

inutílitas -átis: f.; unprofitableness

in" vádo -ere -vási -vásum: (3); invade, enter, assault, swamp, attack, entrap

invalésco -ere -válui: (3); become strong, prevail, gather strength

invalíditas -átis: f.; invalidity

inválido -áre: (1); make invalid; *see ·* *Appendix*

inválidus -a -um: weak, invalid;
inválide: adv.

invásor -óris: m.; invader, usurper

ínveho -ere -véxi -véctum: (3); bear,
bear in, carry in, attack, introduce

invénio -íre -véni -véntum: (4); find,
discover, obtain, come upon, meet
with, invent

inventárium -ii: n.; inventory, list

invéntio -ónis: f.; finding, discovery

invéntor -óris: m.; inventor, discoverer

inverecúndia -ae: f.; impudence

invertibílitas -átis: f.; unchangeableness

invérto -ere -vérti -vérsum: (3); turn
about, turn over, invert

investigábilis -is -e: unsearchable,
inscrutable, unfathomable,
unaccountable, not to be traced

investigátio -ónis: f.; investigation,
inquiry

investigátor -óris: m.; examiner,
investigator

invéstigo -áre: (1); search out, seek after,
search into, trace

investitúra -ae: f.; investiture; see
Appendix

inveterásco -ere -ávi: (3); grow old

inveterátus -a -um: old, decrepit

invétero (invéteror) -áre: (1); abolish,
end; grow old, be enfeebled, fail in
strength

ínvicem: in turn, by turns, alternately,
each other, one another; ad ínvicem:
among themselves; see also vícis

invíctus -a -um: unconquerable,
invincible, unsubdued

invídeo -ére -vídi -vísum: (2); envy,
grudge, be jealous

invídia -ae: f.; envy, hatred, odium,
jealousy, ill-will

ínvidus (invidiósus) -a -um: envious; as
a noun: envious person

invigilántia -ae: f.; watchfulness,
vigilance

invígilo -áre: (1); watch over, pay
attention to

invincíbilis -is -e: invincible,
unconquerable

inviolábilis -is -e, inviolátus -a -um:
inviolable, imperishable, unassailable;
inviolabíliter: adv.

inviolabílitas -átis: f.; inviolability

invísco -ere: (3); fix deeply in mind

invisíbilis -is -e: invisible; invisibíliter:
adv.

invíso -ere -vísi -vísum: (3); visit,
inspect, look after

invitátio -ónis: f.; invitation, challenge,
incitement

invíto -áre: (1); invite, entertain,
summon, challenge

invítus -a -um: unwilling, against one's
will

ínvius -a -um: trackless, impassable,
without a way, pathless; ínvium -ii: n.;
wasteland, desert

invocátio -ónis: f.; invocation

invocatívus -a -um: imploring, invoking

ínvoco -áre: (1); call upon, invoke

involuméntum -i: n.; covering, envelope,
swaddling clothes

involuntárius -a -um: involuntary

involúntas -átis: f.; unwillingness

invólvo -ere -vólvi -volútum: (3); wrap
up, roll up, cover, envelop

ióta: indecl.: n.; iota, jot

i.p.i.: abbrev. for in pártibus infidélium;
in the lands of the infidels

ípse -a -um: intensive pron.: self
éo ípso: because of this very thing
id ípsum: that very thing
ípse díxit: he himself said
ípso fácto: by that very fact; by the fact
itself
ípso júre: by the law itself
Ipsum Esse: Being Itself, God
quod ípsum: which of itself alone

íra -ae: f.; anger, wrath, eternal punishment

iracúndia -ae: f.; wrath, anger

iráscor -i, irátus: *dep.* (3), íro -áre: (1); be angry or full of wrath

irátus (iracúndus) -a -um: angry

Irenaéus -i: m.; Irenaeus

irenísmus -i: m.; irenicism, peace movement

íri: *used with perf. pass. part. to form future pass. inf.;* to be going to be

íris -idis *or* -is: f.; rainbow

íro: *see* iráscor

irr- *see also* inr-

irrádio -áre: (1); illuminate, shine, cast rays of light

irrationábilis -is -e; irrational

irrationabíliter: senselessly

irrecogitátio (inr-) -ónis: f.; thoughtlessness

irrecuperábilis -is -e: irreparable, unalterable

irreductíbilis -is -e: unable to be reduced

irreformábilis -is -e: unalterable, unchangeable

irrefrenábilis -is -e: uncontrollable, unquenchable

irregressíbilis (inr-) -is -e: from which there is no return

irreguláris -is -e: irregular

irreguláritas -átis: f.; irregularity, impediment; *see Appendix*

irreligióse: impiously

irremissíbilis (inr-) -is -e: unpardonable

irreparábilis -is -e: irreparable, irrevocable

irrépo -ere -répsi -réptum: (3); creep into, sneak in

irreprehensíbilis -is -e: blameless, unspotted

irrétio -íre: (4); ensnare, trap, embarrass, punish

irréverens (inr-) -éntis: irreverent, disrespectful

irreveréntia -ae: f.; irreverence, disrespect

irrevocábilis -is -e: irrevocable; irrevocabíliter: *adv.*

irrídeo -ére -rísi -rísum: (2); mock, laugh at

irrigátio -ónis: f.; moistening, irrigation, watering

írrigo -áre: (1); water, irrigate

irríguus -a -um: watered, irrigated

irrisíbilis (inr-) -is -e: ridiculous, laughable

irrísio -ónis: f.; mockery, scoffing

irrísor -óris: m.; scoffer, derider, mocker, scorner

irritábilis -is -e: irritable, easily roused

irritátio -ónis: f.; annulment, provocation, irritation

irritátor -óris: m.; provoker

írrito -áre: (1); annul, make void, invalidate, nullify; *see Appendix*

irríto -áre: (1); provoke, annoy, excite to anger, stir up

írritus -a -um: void, invalid, undecided, without effect, vain

irrogátio -ónis: f.; imposition, infliction

írrogo -áre: (1); impose, inflict

irrúgio -íre: (4); roar out

irrúmpo -ere -rúpi -rúptum: (3); break in, intrude, interrupt, violate, burst forth

írruo -ere -ui: (3); rush, rush in, beset, press upon

is, éa, id: he, she, it, this, that

Isaácus -i, *or indecl.:* m.; Isaac

Isaías -ae: m.; the prophet Isaiah; a book of the O.T.

Iscarióta -ae: m., Iscariótes -is: m.; Iscariot

Islámicus -a -um: Islamic

Ismaelíta -ae: c.; Ishmaelite

Íssachar: *indecl.;* Issachar, son of Jacob and Leah; tribe of Israel

Ísrael -is, *or indecl.:* m.; Jacob; Israel

Israelíta -ae: c.; Israelite

Israelíticus -a -um: of Israel

íste, ísta, ístud: this, that, the latter, that very, that despicable

ístinc: hence, from the place

istiúsmodi (istíus módi, istímodi): of that kind, such

íta: thus, so, even, in this manner

Itália -ae: f.; Italy

ítaque: therefore, and so, and accordingly, and thus

ítem: likewise, just so, also, further

íter, itíneris: n.; journey, departure, way, road, route, method

iterátio -ónis: f.; renewal, repetition

ítero -áre: (1); repeat

íterum (iteráto): again, a second time, once more, once again

ítidem: in like manner

itínerans -ántis: c.; traveller

itinerárium -ii: n.; itinerary; prayers for a safe journey

itíneror -ári: *dep.* (1); travel

íto -áre: (1); go, move

Ituraéa -ae: f.; Iturea

J

jáceo -ére -ui -itum: (2); lie down, sleep, lie ill

jácio -ere, jéci, jáctum: (3), jácto -áre: (1); cast, hurl, throw

Jácob: *indecl.;* Jacob

Jacóbus -i: m.; James

jáctans -ántis: boastful, vainglorious

jactánter: boastfully

jactántia -ae: f.; vainglory

jactantículus -a -um: somewhat boasting

jactátio -ónis: f.; boasting, bragging

jactátor -óris: m.; boaster

jácto: *see* jácio

jactúra -ae: f.; loss, a throwing away

jáctus -us: m.; cast, throw

jáculum -i: n.; arrow, dart, javelin

jam: now, already, immediately, soon, just now; *w. negatives:* no more, no longer

jamdúdum (jamprídem): now, for a long time

jámjam: on the point of, at this very moment

jámvero: indeed

Janículum -i: n.; Janiculum, one of the hills in Rome

jánitor -óris: m.; porter, gatekeeper, doorkeeper, janitor

Jansenístae -árum: f.; Jansenists, followers of the heresy of Jansenism

jánua -ae: f.; gate, door

Januárius -ii: m.; month of January

Japónia -ae: f.; Japan

jáspis -idis: f.; jasper, green-colored precious stone

jécor -is (jecínoris): n.; liver

jejunátio -ónis: f.; fasting, abstinence

jejunátor -óris: m.; one who fasts

jejuniósus (jejúnus) -a -um: fasting, hungry

jejúnium -ii: n.; fast, fasting, abstinence

jejúno -áre: (1); fast, abstain

jejúnus: *see* jejuniósus

jentáculum -i: n.; breakfast

Jeremías -ae: m.; the prophet Jeremiah; a book of the O.T.

Jéricho: *indecl.:* f.; city of Jericho

Jerichontínus (Jerichún-) -a -um: of Jericho

Jerosólyma -ae: f., -órum: n. pl.; Jerusalem

Jerosólymi -órum: m. pl.; people of Jerusalem

Jerosolymitánus -a-um: of Jerusalem

Jerúsalem: *indecl.:* n.; Jerusalem; *also:* Hierosólyma -ae: f.; Hierosólyma -órum: n. pl.; Jerosólyma -ae: f.; Jerosólyma -órum: n. pl.

Jésus, Jésu: m.; *dat., abla., voc.* Jésu; *acc.* Jésum; Jesus

Joánnes (Johá-) -is: m.; John

Job -is, *or indecl.,* Jóbus -i: m.; Job

jócor -ári: *dep.* (1); jest, joke

jocóse: in jest, jokingly

jocósus -a -um: humorous, witty, merry, sportive

joculáris -is -e: laughable, jocular

jod: tenth letter of the Hebrew alphabet

Jóel -is: m.; Joel, a minor prophet; a book of the O.T.

Johánnes -is: *see* Joánnes

Jónas -ae: m.; Jonas, a minor prophet; a book of the O.T.

Jónathas -ae: m.; Jonathan

Jordánis -is: m.; Jordan river

Jóseph: *indecl.,* Joséphus -i: m.; Joseph

Jóshua -ae: m.; Joshua; a book of the O.T.

Jóvis -is: m.; Jove, Jupiter

júbar -is: n.; radiance, beaming light

júbe: *imperat. of* júbeo; be pleased, graciously grant, please

júbeo -ére, jússi, jússum: (2); order, request, ask, grant, pray

jubilaéum -i: n., jubilaéus -i: m.; jubilee, jubilee year

jubilaéum május: golden jubilee

jubilaéum mínus: silver jubilee

jubiláris -is -e: of a jubilee

jubilátio -ónis: f.; jubilation, rejoicing, gladness, retirement

jubilátus -a -um: retired

júbilo -áre: (1); rejoice, sing joyfully, exult, retire

júbilum -i: n.; joy, shout of joy, jubilee

júbilus -i: m.; joyful melody

jucúnde: merrily, pleasantly, agreeably, delightfully

jucúnditas -átis: f.; cheerfulness, pleasure, pleasantness

jucúndo -áre: (1); shout for joy

jucúndor -ári: *dep.* (1); be glad, be joyful, have joy

jucúndus -a -um: pleasing, acceptable, fortunate, happy

Júda (Júdas) -ae, Júda: *indecl.:* m.; Judah, son of Jacob and Leah; a tribe of Israel; Jude

Judaéa -ae: f.; Judea

Judaéus (Judáicus) -a -um: Jewish; *as a noun:* a Jew

Judáice: in Jewish fashion

Judaísmus -i: m.; Judaism

judaízo -áre: (1); judaize

Júdas -ae: m.; Jude, Judas

Júdas Iscariótes: Judas of Karioth, Judas Iscariot

júdex -icis: m.; judge; *see Appendix*

judicátio -ónis: f.; judgment, opinion

judicatórius -ii: m.; pertaining to a judge

judicátus -us: m.; office of judge

judiciális -is -e: judicial; judiciáliter: *adv.; see Appendix*

judiciárius -a -um: judiciary

judícium -ii: n.; judgment, trial, investigation, sentence, ecclesiastical trial; judícium ágere: dispense justice, settle a dispute, make a judgment

júdico -áre: (1); judge, adjudge, determine, decide, esteem, value, examine, declare, conclude

Júdith: *indecl.;* Judith; a book of the O.T.

jugális -is -e: of a yoke, connecting

júgerum -i: n.; acre

júgis -is -e: continual, perpetual; joined; júgiter: *adv.*

júglans, juglándis: f.; walnut

júgo -áre: (1); bind, connect, yoke

júgulo -áre: (1); cut the throat, slay

júgulum -i: n., júgulus -i: m.; throat

júgum -i: n.; yoke, fetter, bond, slavery

Július -ii: m.; month of July

juméntum -i: n.; beast of burden; pl.: cattle

júnctim: both together, successively

júnctio -ónis: f.; joining

junctúra -ae: f.; joint

júncus -i: m.; bulrush

júngo -ere, júnxi, júnctum: (3); join, bind, unite, connect

júnior -ior -ius: younger, rather young

juníperus -i: f.; juniper tree

Június -ii: m.; month of June

Júpiter (Júppiter), Jóvis: m.; Jupiter, Jove, Zeus

juraméntum -i: n.; oath

jurátus -a -um: bound by an oath

juráto: under oath

júre: justly, with justice; *see Appendix*

jureconsúltus: *see* jurisconsúltus

jureperítus: *see* jurisperítus

jurgátor -óris: m.; jurgátrix -ícis: f.; quarrelsome person

júrgium -ii: n.; quarrel, wrangling, dispute, contention

júrgo (júrgor) -áre: (1); quarrel

jurídicus -a -um: juridical, judiciary; **jurídice:** *adv.; see Appendix*

jurisconsúltus (jureconsúltus) -a -um: skilled in the law; *as a noun:* lawyer, judge

jurisdíctio -ónis: f.; jurisdiction; *see Appendix*

jurisdictionális -a -um: jurisdictional

jurisperítus (jureperítus) -a -um: skilled in the law; *as a noun:* lawyer, judge, legal expert

jurisprudéntia -ae: f.; law, jurisprudence; *see Appendix*

júro (júror) -áre: (1); swear, take an oath

jus, júris: n.; law, justice, judgment, right; *see Appendix*
    jus réddere: render justice
    jus dícere: judge

jus, júris: n.; broth, soup

jusjurándum, jurisjurándi: n.; oath

juspatronátus, jurispatronátus: m.; right of patronage

jússio -ónis: f., **jússum** -i: n.; command, order, law, prescription, consent

jússus -us: m.; *used only in the abla.:* **jússu:** by command or order or decree

justificátio -ónis: f.; justification, justice, ordinance, precept, law

justificátor -óris: m., **justificátrix** -ícis: f.; one who justifies

justífico -áre: (1); justify, account righteous, do justice, make righteous

Justiniánus (Justínus) -i: m.; Justinian

justítia -ae: f.; justice, innocence, righteousness, rectitude, moral integrity, fairness; pl.: precepts, judgments; *see Appendix*

jústus -a -um: just, right, righteous; **júste:** *adv.*

juvámen -inis: n.; help, assistance

juvénculus -a -um: young; *as a m. noun:* young man, young bullock; *as a f. noun:* young woman, maiden

juvéncus -a -um: young, *as a noun:* young animal

juvenésco -ere -vénui: (3); be young, reach the age of youth

juvenílis (juvenális) -is -e: young, youthful, suitable for youth, juvenile

júvenis -is -e: in the flower of age; *as a c. noun:* youth, young man or woman, teenager

juvénta -ae, **juvéntus** -útis: f.; age of youth, time of youth, teens

júvo -áre: (1); help, aid, assist, support; *impers.:* it pleases, it gratifies

júxta: *adv. & prep. w. acc.;* at hand, close or next to, near, according to, alike, immediately after

júxtim: near, close by

K

Kadésh: *indecl.;* Kadesh, a place in the desert between Egypt and Canaan

Kal.: *abbrev. for* **Kaléndae**

Kaléndae -árum: f. pl.; calends or first day of the Roman month

Kalendárius -ii: m.; calendar

Kédar: *indecl.;* Kedar, an Arabian tribe

Kíshon: *see* **Císson**

kum: *see* **cúmi**

Kyriále -is: n.; book containing some sung parts of the Mass

Kyrie: *voc.; Greek;* Lord

L

labárum -i: n.; a banner of the cross said
to have been used by the emperor
Constantine, a monogram made of the
Greek letters X and P

labásco -ere: (3); totter, yield, give way,
begin to fall

lábea (lábia) -ae: f.; lip

labécula -ae: f.; small spot or stain

labefácio -ere -féci -fáctum: (3); shake,
loose, weaken

lábes -is: f.; stain, blot, blemish, spot,
defect

lábia -ae: see lábea

lábilis -is -e: falling, tottering

lábium -ii, lábrum -i: n.; lip, edge of a
cup

lábor -óris: m.; labor, toil, effort; see
Appendix

lábor -i, lápsus: dep. (3), lábo -áre: (1);
slip, fall, waver, totter, be unstable,
stumble, glide down, escape

laboriósus -a -um: laborious, toilsome;
laborióse: adv.

labóro -áre: (1); labor, toil, bear up
under, be wearied

lábrum -i: n.; vessel, basin, vat; see
lábium

labrúsca -ae: f.; wild grape

labúrnum -i: n.; laburnum tree

lac, láctis: n.; milk

lácer -era -erum: ragged, torn, maimed

lacerátio -ónis: f.; tearing, mangling,
laceration

lácero -áre: (1); rend, tear, wound,
lacerate, mangle

lacésso -ere, lacessívi, lacessítum: (3);
provoke, excite, stimulate, irritate,
exasperate

lacínia -ae: f.; small tassel

lácrima (lácruma, lácryma) -ae: f.; tear

lacrimábilis -is -e, lacrimósus -a -um:
woeful, lamentable, worthy of tears,
tearful, pitiable, mournful, sorrowful

lacrimátio -ónis: f.; weeping

lácrimo (lácrimor) -áre: (1); weep, shed
tears, show sorrow

lacrimósus: see lacrimábilis

lácruma (lácryma) -ae: see lácrima

láctens -éntis: f.; suckling

lácteo -ére: (2); suck, be a suckling

lacticínium -ii: n.; food prepared from
milk

lácto -áre: (1); give suck; entice, allure

lactúca -ae: f.; lettuce

lacúna -ae: f.; cavern, cavity, hollow,
ditch, pit, chasm; void, gap, defect; see
Appendix

lácus -us, lácus -i: m.; den, cave, pit,
place of the dead, lake, tank, tub, vat,
reservoir, pitfall, trap

laédo -ere, laési, laésum: (3); injure,
harm, damage, wound

laésio -ónis: f.; harm, wound, injury,
lesion, attack

laesúra -ae: f.; lesion, injury

laetabúndus -a -um: full of joy

laéte: gladly, joyfully

laetífico -áre: (1); rejoice, cheer,
gladden, delight, give joy

laetítia -ae: f.; gladness, happiness,
delight

laéto -áre: (1); cause to rejoice, make
someone rejoice

laétor -ári: dep. (1); rejoice, be glad, be
joyful, take delight in

laétus -a -um: joyful, glad

laéva -ae: f.; the left, left hand; **ad laévam:** on the left hand or arm
laevigátus -a -um: polished, smooth
lagánum -i: n.; cake
lagéna (lagaé-) -ae: f.; bottle, flask, vessel, jug, pitcher
lagúncula -ae: f.; small bottle, flask, or vessel
laicális -is -e, **láicus** -a -um: lay, common, belonging to the lay state; *as a noun:* layperson; *see Appendix*
laicátus -us: m.; the lay state
laicíso -áre: (1); laicize, reduce to lay state
laicisátio -ónis: f.; laicization; *see Appendix*
lámbo -ere, lámbi: (3); lick
lámed: 12th letter of the Hebrew alphabet
lamentátio -ónis: f., **laméntum** -i: n.; lament, weeping, lamentation, wailing
Lamentátiones -um: f. pl.; Lamentations, a book of the O.T.
laménto (laméntor) -áre: (1); lament, weep, mourn, wail
lámia -ae: f.; wild beast; sea monster; owl
lámina -ae: f.; plate, metal plate
lámma: *Aramaic;* why
lámpada -ae: f.; lamp
lampadárium -ii: n., **lampadárius** -ii: m.; support for lamps, chandelier
lámpas -adis: f.; torch, lamp, flame
lána -ae: f.; wool
láncea -ae: f.; lance, spear
lanceárius -ii: m.; lancer
lanceátus -a -um: spear-shaped
lánceo -áre: (1); wield a lance
lancéola -ae: f.; small lance or spear
láncino -áre: (1); mangle
láncis -is: f.; event
láneus -a -um: woolen
lánguens -éntis: weak, faint, languid
lángueo -ére -ui: (2); faint, swoon, be feeble, listless, inactive, languid

languésco -ere, lángui: (3); become weak, faint, languid
lánguidus -a -um: infirm, sick, weak, faint, feeble, languid, listless; *as a noun:* invalid; **lánguide:** *adv.*
lánguor -óris: m.; languor, feebleness, sickness, ill health, infirmity
laniátus -us: m.; mangling
lánio -áre: (1); mangle
lantérna (latérna) -ae: f.; lantern
lantgrávius -ii: m.; landgrave, baron, count
lanx -cis: f.; shallow dish, pan
Laodicéa (Laodicía) -ae: f.; Laodicea
lapidárius -ii: m.; stonecutter, mason
lapídeus -a -um: of stone
lapidicína -ae: f.; stone quarry
lapidicínus -a -um: pertaining to sculpture
lápido -áre: (1); to stone
lapíllus -i: m.; gem
lápis -idis: m.; stone
láppa -ae: f.; burr
lápsus -a -um: fallen; *perf. pass. part. of* **lábor**
lápsus -us: m.; falling, slipping, lapse; moral lapse, apostasy; passage of time
Lapúrdum -i: n.; Lourdes
láquear -is: n.; rafter, ceiling, panel
laqueátus -a -um: with a paneled ceiling
láqueus -i: m.; snare, trap, halter, net, noose, bond
lárge: largely, abundantly, plentifully
lárgiens -éntis: bountiful
lárgior -íri: *dep.* (4); bestow, grant, donate
lárgior (largítor) -óris: m.; one who grants, giver, bestower
lárgitas -átis: f.; bountifulness, largess, bounty, liberality
largítio -ónis: f.; donation, generosity, bribery
largíto -ónis: m.; imperial treasury
largítor -óris: *see* **lárgior**

lárgius: more abundantly

lárgus -a -um: abundant, plentiful

láridum -i: n.; lard

lárus (láros) -i: m.; mew, seabird

lárva -ae: f.; ghost, mask, skeleton

larvátus -a -um: skeleton-like, masked, hidden, incipient

lascívus -a -um: lewd, lustful, licentious, impudent

lassitúdo -inis: f.; weariness, lassitude

lásso -áre: (1); make weary, tire, exhaust

lássus -a -um: faint, weary, tired, exhausted, languid

láte: broadly, extensively, widely

latébra -ae: f.; concealment, subterfuge

latebrósus -a -um: secret, obscure, retired, hidden, full of holes, porous

laténter: secretly

láteo -ére -ui: (2); be hidden, be concealed, remain in private

láter -eris: m.; brick

laterális -is -e: lateral, of the side

Laheránus: Lateranus, an old Roman family name

látere: at the side, on the flank

latérna (lantérna) -ae: f.; lantern

látex -icis: m.; liquid, water

latíbulum -i: n.; covert, hiding place

latifúndium -ii: n.; landed property, large estate, farm

Latína Pórta: the Latin Gate

Latíne: in Latin

latínitas -átis: f.; Latin style, Latin law, Latinity

latinízo (latíno) -áre: (1); translate into Latin

Latínus -a -um: Latin

látito -áre: (1); be concealed, lie hidden

latitúdo -inis: f.; breadth, width, extent; in latitúdine: at liberty

látor -óris: m.; bearer, proposer of a law

latreúticus -a -um: pertaining to the worship of God

látria -ae: f.; worship, adoration, cult due the Trinity

látro -ónis: m.; robber, thief

látro -áre: (1); bark

latrocínium -ii: n.; brigandage

latrúnculus -i: m.; robber, bandit, rover, highwayman

látus -a -um: wide, broad; láte: adv.; perf. pass. part. of féro

látus -eris: n.; side, flank

laudábilis -is -e: worthy of praise, laudable, glorious, valuable, excellent; laudabíliter: adv.

laudátio -ónis: f.; praise, commendation, testimony

laudátor -óris: m.; one who praises

Laúdes -um: f. pl.; office of Lauds

Laúdes Divínae: Divine Praises, a prayer used at Benediction

Laudétur Jésus Chrístus: May Jesus Christ be praised

laúdo -áre: (1); praise, glorify, commend

laúra -ae: f.; monastery, settlement of anchorites in Egypt

laúrea -ae: f.; laurel, triumph, victory, wreath; academic degree

lauréntius -a -um: crowned with laurel

laúrus -i: f.; laurel or bay tree

laus, laúdis: f.; praise

laútumus -i: m.; stonecutter

laútus -a -um: elegant, sumptuous, splendid, grand, washed

Lavábo: the ceremonial washing of hands in the liturgy

lavácrum -i: n.; bath, flood, water of baptism, washing

lávo -áre (lávere), lávi, laútum (lótum, lavátum): (1,3); wash, bathe, wash away

láxo -áre: (1); relax, let drop, widen, enlarge

laxísmus -i: m.; laxism

láxus -a -um: loose, lax, relaxed

Lázarus -i: m.; Lazarus

leaéna -ae: f.; lioness

lébes -étis: m.; kettle, basin, washbasin, metal vessel

lectíca -ae: f.; litter

lecticárius -ii: m.; litter bearer, coffin bearer, pallbearer

léctio -ónis: f.; lesson, reading, Epistle, lecture; class

Lectionárium -ii: n.; a book of lessons for the Divine Office

lectiúncula -ae: f.; short lesson

léctor -óris: m.; reader, lector, formerly one of the minor orders

lectorátus -us: m.; office of lector or reader

lectoríle -is, **lectórium** -ii: n.; lecturn, reader's stand

léctulus -i: m.; small bed, couch

léctum -i: n., **léctus** -i: m.; bed, couch

léctus -a -um: chosen, selected; eminent, choice, excellent; read, recited; *perf. pass. part. of* **légo**

lécythus -i: m.; flask

legális -is -e: legal, lawful; *see Appendix*

legátio -ónis: f.; legation, embassy, office of ambassador

legátum -i: n.; bequest, legacy

legátus -i: m.; legate, ambassador, envoy; *see Appendix*

legénda -órum: n. pl.; things to be read

Legendárius -ii: m.; book of Epistles

légifer -era -erum: lawgiving; *as a noun:* lawgiver

legíle -is: n.; lectern, bookstand

légio -ónis: f.; legion, band

legislátio -ónis: f.; making of a law, legislation

legislatívus -a -um: legislative

legislátor -óris: m.; legislator, lawgiver, lawmaker

legisperítus -i: m.; lawyer

legitimátio -ónis: f.; legitimation

legitimátus -a -um: legitimate

legitímitas -átis: f.; legitimacy

legítimo -áre: (1); make legitimate, legitimate

Legítimum -i: n.; a name for the Canon of the Mass

legítimum -i: n.; ordinance

legítimus -a -um: legal, legitimate; **legítime:** *adv.*

légo -áre: (1); commission, dispatch, entrust, will, delegate, bequeath, send on public mission

légo -ere, légi, léctum: (3); read, recite, gather, choose

legúmen -inis: n.; vegetable, bean, pulse

léma (lámma): *Aramaic;* why

lemníscus -i: m.; ribbon, cord (from which tassels are hung)

lénio -íre: (4); relieve, mitigate

lénis -is -e: smooth, mild, easy, soft; **léne, léniter:** *adv.*

lénitas -átis: f.; meekness, tenderness

léno -ónis: m.; pimp

lenocínium -ii: n.; pandering, pimping, traffic in vice, allurement

lentésco -ere: (3); relax

lentícula -ae: f.; vial, small flask, little bottle; lentil

léntus -a -um: pliant, tough, flexible, tenacious, sticky, slow, sluggish, lingering, indifferent, lasting; **lénte:** *adv.*

léo -ónis: m.; lion

leopárdus -i: m.; leopard

lépra -ae: f.; leprosy

leprósus -a -um: leprous; **hómo leprósus:** leper

lesbianísmus -i: m.; lesbianism

lésbius -a -um: lesbian

Lésbos (-us) -i: f.; Lesbos, island home of the poetess Sappho

lethális -is -e: lethal, fatal, mortal

lethárgia -ae: f., **lethárgus** -i: m.; coma, drowsiness, lethargy

lethárgus -a -um: drowsy, lethargic

leúnculus -i: m.; young lion

levámen -inis: n.; alleviation, rest,
mitigation, consolation

Lévi: *indecl;* Levi, son of Jacob and Leah;
tribe of Israel

levíathan: *indecl;* aquatic monster,
serpent, crocodile

levigátus -a -um: smooth, polished

lévigo -áre: (1); polish

lévis -is -e: light, slight, trivial, easy;
léviter: *adv.*

lévitas -átis: f.; lightness, fickleness,
levity, shallowness

Levítes (Levíta) -ae: m.; Levite, deacon

Levíticus -a -um: of a Levite, Levitical;
Leviticus, a book of the O.T.

lévo -áre: (1); raise, lift up, take away,
lighten

lex, légis: f.; law; légem fácere: keep the
law; *see Appendix*

libámen -inis: n., libaméntum -i: n.,
libátio -ónis: f.; libation, drink
offering, partaking

líbanus -i: m.; frankincense

Líbanus -i: m.; Mount Lebanon

libátio -ónis: f.; libation, partaking,
drink offering

libatórium -ii: n.; pouring vessel

libélla -ae: f.; cent, small sum of money

libéllus -i: m.; bill, petition for a
juridical case, written accusation,
complaint; small book, notebook,
magazine; *see Appendix*

líbens (lub-) -éntis: ready, willing,
cheerful, glad, with pleasure; libénter:
adv.

libéntia (lub-) -ae: f.; delight, pleasure,
joy, cheer

líber -era -erum: free, abandoned,
fearless; líber -eri: m.; freeman; líbera
-ae: f.; freewoman; líbere: freely,
openly, boldly, steadfastly; líberi
-órum: m. pl.; children; libérius:
comp. adv.

líber -bri: m.; book; *see Appendix*

liberális -is -e: of freedom, befitting a
freeman, noble, liberal, bountiful,
generous, abundant; liberáliter: *adv.*

liberalísmus -i: m.; liberalism

liberálitas -átis: f.; liberality, generosity

liberátio -ónis: f.; liberation, freedom,
setting free, ransom, acquittal,
discharge

liberátor -óris: m.; liberator, protector,
deliverer

liberátus -a -um: freed, liberated

líbero -áre: (1); liberate, free, acquit,
discharge

libértas -átis: f.; freedom, liberty

libertínus -a -um: of a freed person; *as a
noun:* freed man or woman

líbet (lúbet) -ére líbuit, líbitum est: (2);
impers.; it pleases, is agreeable

libído -inis: f.; lust, passion, sexual desire

líbitum -i: n.; pleasure, liking; pro
líbito: at pleasure

líbo -áre: (1); touch, taste, pour out,
sacrifice, consecrate

líbra -ae: f.; pound, balance, scale

libraméntum -i: n.; equilibrium, balance

librárius -ii: m.; copyist

líbro -áre: (1); weigh, balance, poise

líbum -i: n.; offering, cake offering

licéitas -átis: f.; liceity, something licit or
legal

licéntia -ae: f.; permission, license,
licentiate

licentiátus -a -um: having a licentiate

líceo -ére -cui -itum: (2); be valued or
esteemed, to cost, be for sale

lícet, -ére lícuit, lícitum est: (2); *impers.;*
it is allowed, lawful, or permitted, one
may

lícet: although

liciatórium -ii: n.; beam, weaver's beam

licitátio -ónis: f.; auction, bidding

lícitus -a -um: legitimate, licit, lawful;
lícite: *adv.; see Appendix*

lícium -ii: n.; lace, web

líctor -óris: m.; lictor, special attendant
ligámen -inis: n.; bond, previous bond;
see Appendix
ligaméntum -i: n.; bandage
ligatúra -ae: f.; bunch, cluster; band,
ligature
ligátus -a -um: bound
lígito -áre: (1); quarrel, strive
lígneus -i: m.; wooden
lígnum -i: n.; wood, tree, stick, staff, the
Cross
lígo -áre: (1); bind, tie, oblige
lígo -ónis: m.; spade, hoe
lígula -ae: f.; ribbon
ligúrius -ii: m.; ligure, a hard,
transparent gem
liliátus -a -um: lily-white, decorated
with lilies
lílium -ii: n.; lily
limátus -a -um: polished
límax -ácis: f.; snail, slug
límen -inis: n.; threshold; ad límina: to
the threshold of the apostles, to Rome;
see Appendix
límes -itis: m.; boundary, limit, path
limináre -is: n.; floor, threshold
limitátio -ónis: f.; limitation,
determination
límito -áre: (1); bound, limit
limitróphus -a -um, limitróphes -is -e:
neighboring
limpidíssimus -a -um: very smooth
límus -i: m.; slime, mud, mire, dirt
línea -ae: f.; linen, line, thread
lineaméntum -i: n.; feature, delineation,
lineament; pl: outline; see Appendix
líneus -a -um: linen, of flax
língo -ere, línxi, línctum: (3); lick
língua -ae: f.; tongue, language
linguátus (linguósus) -a -um:
loquacious, talkative, eloquent,
expressive
linguísticus -a -um: linguistic

línio -íre: (4); smear, bedaub, spread,
anoint
linítio -ónis: f.; glazing of a vestment
líno -ere, lívi (lévi), lítum: (3); spread
over
linóstimus -a -um: of linen
línquo -ere, líqui: (3); leave
linteámen -inis: n., línteum -i: n.; linen
cloth
lintéolum -i: n.; small piece of linen
línum -i: n.; flax, linen
lippésco -ere: (3); become bleary-eyed
lipsanothéca -ae: f.; storehouse for relics
liquábilis -is -e: able to be dissolved
liquefácio -ere -féci -fáctum, liquésco
-ere, lícui: (3); líquo -áre: (1); melt,
dissolve, liquify, make liquid
liquefactívus -a -um: melting
liquefáctus -a -um: melted
líqueo -ére, lícui (líqui): (2); be fluid or
liquid, be evident or clear
líquidus -a -um: liquid, flowing, fluid; as
a n. noun: liquid, water, clearness,
certainty; líquido: adv.
líquor -óris: m.; liquid
lis, lítis: f.; lawsuit, litigation, debate,
contention; líte pendénte: while
litigation is pending
litánia -ae: f.; litany; litániae -árum: f.
pl.; supplication
lite- see litte
literárius -a -um: literary
lithóstrotos -i: m.; Greek; pavement
litigátor -óris: m.; litigant, party in a
lawsuit
litigiósus -a -um: contested, claimed,
disputed, quarrelsome
lítigo -áre: (1); litigate, quarrel, wrangle,
sue, strive
líto -áre: (1); offer public sacrifice
líttera (lítera) -ae: f.; letter of the
alphabet; pl.: record, list, bill, letter,
literature, document, learning; see
Appendix

litterárius -a -um: literary, pertaining to learning

litterátio -ónis: f.; study of reading and writing, study of languages

litteratúra -ae: f.; writing, learning, literature, culture

líttus (lítus) -oris: n.; shore

litúra -ae: f.; daubing or covering with paint

litúrgia -ae: f.; liturgy, the Mass, public worship or service; see Appendix

litúrgicus -a -um: of the liturgy, liturgical

lítus -oris: see líttus

lívidus -a -um: spiteful, envious, malicious

lívor -óris: m.; bruise

locális -is -e: local, of a place; locáliter: adv.

locátio -ónis: f.; renting, contracting, leasing

lóco -áre: (1); place, hire out, locate, rent, lease

lóculus -i: m.; bier, coffin, casket; purse, small place

locumténens -tis: m.; substitute

lócuples -étis: rich

locupletátio -ónis: f.; wealth, riches

locupléto -áre: (1); enrich

lócus -i: m.; place, room, station, position; pl.: texts, passages, citations; lóca -órum: n. pl.; places

in lóco: in place of

lócus sigílli (L.S.): the place of the seal or signature

locústa (luc-) -ae: f.; locust

locútio -ónis: f.; word, expression, phrase

locútor -óris: m.; speaker

locútus -a -um: perf. part. of lóquor

lódix -ícis: f.; blanket, sheet

lógicus -a -um: logical, reasonable; lógice: adv.

longaévitas -átis: f.; longevity

longaévus -a -um: aged, old, long-lived

longánimis -is -e: long-suffering, patient

longanímitas -átis: f.; long-suffering

longanímiter: patiently

lónge: afar, far off, at a distance

a lónge: from afar

lónge latéque: far and wide

longínquus -a -um: far; de or ex longínquo: from afar; longínquum: adv.

longitúdo -inis: f.; length

longitúrnitas -átis: f.; long duration

longitúrnus -a -um: long-enduring

lóngus -a -um: long; lónge (lóngiter, lóngum): adv.; lóngior -ior -ius: longer; lóngius: comp. adv.

loquéla -ae: f.; speech, manner of speech, language

lóquor, lóqui, locútus: dep. (3); speak, talk, converse, tell, utter

loraméntum -i: n.; thong, fastener

loríca -ae: f.; breastplate

loricátus -a -um: clothed in mail or armor, protected

lórum -i: n.; whip, scourge, thong, leather strap

Lot: indecl.: m.; Lot

lótio -ónis: f.; washing

lótus -a -um: washed

L.S.: see lócus

lub- see also lib-

lúbitus -a -um: pleasing

lúbricum -i: n.; slipperiness

lúbricus -a -um: slippery, dangerous, impure

Lúcas (Lúca) -ae: m.; Luke

lúceo -ére, lúxi: (2); shine, glitter, give light

lucernárium -ii: n.; candlelighting time, candlelight, lamp

lucérna -ae: f.; candle, lamp, light

lucernáre -is: n.; a name for Vespers in the Eastern church

lucésco -ere, lúxi: (3); begin to shine, grow light, dawn

lúcidus -a -um: bright, lightsome, full of light, clear, lucid, irreproachable; lúcide: *adv.*

lúcifer -i: m.; morning star, daystar, bringer of light; used by the Fathers to refer to Satan, the fallen light-bearer

lúcifer -era -erum: light-bearing

lucísator -óris: m.; light-producer, author of light

lucratívus -a -um: lucrative, profitable

lucrifácio -ere: (3); win, gain, profit

lucrifío -fíeri -fáctum: (3); be won, be gained, be acquired

lúcror -ári: *dep.* (1); convert, gain, profit, win, acquire, persuade

lúcrum -i: n.; gain, profit, lucre, advantage

luctámen -inis: n., luctátio -ónis: f.; wrestling, struggling

luctuósus -a -um: sorrowful, sad, mournful

lúctus -us: m.; grief, mourning, lamentation

lucubrátio -ónis: f.; night work, nocturnal or laborious study

luculéntus -a -um: bright, splendid, full of light, excellent, distinguished, admirable; luculénte, luculénter: *adv.*

lúcus -i: m.; grove

lucústa -ae: *see* locústa

ludíbrium -ii: n.; scorn, mockery, derision, jest, laughingstock

ludíficor -áre: *dep.* (1); mock, delude, make sport of, frustrate

lúdo -ere -si -sum: (3); play, sport, frisk, frolic, mimic, mock

lúdus -i: m.; game, sport, pastime, fun, diversion, play

lúes -is: f.; disease, plague, calamity

Lugdúnum -i: n.; Lyons

lúgeo -ére, lúxi, lúctum: (2); lament, bewail, grieve, mourn over

lumbáre -is: n.; girdle

lúmbus -i: m.; loin

lúmen -inis: n.; light, brightness, splendor, luminary, light of glory; *see Appendix*

lumináre -is: n.; light

lúna -ae: f.; moon
díes Lúnae: Monday
lúna miélis: honeymoon

lunáticus -i: m.; epileptic, lunatic

lúnula -ae: f.; crescent-shaped container for the Blessed Sacrament

lúo -ere, lúi, lutúrus: (3); loose, atone for, wash away, set free, pay the penalty

lupánar -áris: n.; brothel

lupínus -a -um: wolfish

lúpus -i: m.; wolf

lúrco (lúrcor) -áre: (1); devour

lúscus -a -um: one-eyed

lusórium -ii: n.; place for shows, games, and spectacles

lustrális -is -e, lustrálus -a -um: purifying, cleansing, holy, blessed, cleansing from guilt, lustral

lústro -áre: (1); purify, cleanse; illuminate, consider, review

lústrum -i: n.; luster, purification, period of five years

lúsus -us: m.; game, sport, play

lúter -is: m.; washbasin

Lutétia -ae: f., Lutétia Parisiórum: Paris

lúteus -a -um: of clay

Lutheranísmus -i: m.; Lutheranism

Lútherus -i: m.; Luther

lúto -áre: (1); daub with mud, besmear

lútum -i: n.; clay, dirt, mire, mud

lux, lúcis: f.; light, dawn, light of a lamp, star, moon; lúcis ánte términum: before the end of daylight

lúxor (luxórior) -ári: *dep.* (1); revel, riot, live luxuriously

luxúria -ae: f.; luxury, dissipation

luxuriósus -a -um: wanton, luxurious, extravagant, wasteful, riotious; luxurióse: *adv.*

lúxus -us: m.; debauchery, luxury,
excess, extravagance, lust
Lycaónia -ae: f.; country of Lycaonia in
southeast central Asia Minor
Lycaónice: in the speech of the
Lycaonians
lycéum -i: n.; high school, college
lychnúchus -i: m.; support for lamps or
candles, chandelier
lýchnus -i: m.; lamp

lýmpha -ae: f.; water
lymphaéum -i: n.; large bowl or basin of
water
lyncúrius -ii: m., lyncúrium -ii: n.; see
ligúrius
lýra -ae: f.; lute, lyre; lýra tetrachórdis:
violin
Lýstra -ae: f., Lýstra -órum: n. pl.;
Lystra, a city in Lycaonia

M

Macedónia -ae: f.; Macedonia
macéllum -i: n.; market, meat market
macerátio -ónis: f.; mortification
macéria -ae: f.; wall, fence
mácero -áre: (1); mortify, afflict
Machabaéi -órum: m. pl.; Maccabees, a book of the O.T.
machaéra -ae: f.; knife, short sword
máchina -ae: f.; machine, device, fabric, frame, mechanism, structure
machinaméntum -i: n.; trick, device
machinátio -ónis: f.; mechanism, machinery, device
máchinor -ári: *dep.* (1); contrive, devise, plot, invent
Mahométus -i: m.; Mohammed
mácies -ei: f.; emaciation, thinness, poverty
maciléntus -a -um: thin, lean
macrésco -ere, mácrui: (3); become thin
mácte: bravo, well done
mácto -áre: (1); immolate, sacrifice, slaughter; reward, honor, glorify; augment, enrich, extol
mácula -ae: f.; stain, blemish, spot, blot
máculo -áre: (1); accuse, blame, spot
maculósus -a -um: spotted
mae- *see also* **moe-**
maestíficus -a -um: making sad
maésto (moést-) -áre: (1); make sad, grieve, affect
madefácio -ere: (3); moisten, make wet
mádeo -ére, mádui: (2); drink too much, be drunk
madésco -ere, mádui: (3); become wet
Mádian (Mídian): *indecl.;* Madian, a descendant of Abraham; a nomadic tribe

maéleth: *see* **mahéleth**
maéreo -ére: (2); grieve, mourn, be sad, be sorrowful
maéror -óris: m.; sadness, grief, mourning
maéstus -a -um: sad, dejected, sorrowful, cast down, melancholic
Mági -órum: m. pl.; Magi
mágia -ae: f.; magic, sorcery
mágicus -a -um: magical, of magic
mágis: rather, more, to a greater extent; **plus mágis:** far more
magíster -tri: m.; master, teacher, director
magistérium -ii: n.; office of teacher, teaching authority, magisterium; *see* **Appendix**
magístra -ae: f.; mistress, teacher, directress
magistrátus -us: m.; magistrate, high official, civil office
magnália -ium: n. pl.; wonders, wonderful works, great things
magnanímitas -átis: f.; greatness of soul, magnanimity
magnánimus -a -um: high-minded, magnanimous, high-spirited, courageous
mágnas -átis, **magnátus** -i: m.; nobleman, magnate
mágnes -étis: m.; magnet, lodestone
magnetophónicus -a -um: tape-recording
magnetophónium -ii: n.; tape recorder
Magníficat: *see* **Appendix**
magnífice: nobly, generously
magnificéntia -ae: f.; magnificence, majesty, splendor, glory

magnífico -áre: (1); magnify, exult, glorify, praise, enlarge

magníficus -a -um: glorious, sublime, rich

magníloquus -a -um: boastful, vaunting

magnipéndo -ere -péndi: (3); esteem highly

magnitúdo -inis: f.; greatness, power, majesty, size, magnitude

magnópere: greatly, very much, exceedingly

mágnus -a -um: great, mighty, large; mágna -órum: n. pl.; great things; mágna ex párte: in a great degree

mágus -i: m.; wise man, learned man, wizard, magician, sorcerer

mahéleth (maéleth): indecl.; Hebrew; harp, lute

maiéstas -átis: f.; majesty, dignity, grandeur

maiestáticus -a -um: majestic, sublime

máior -óris: c.; adult, one who has reached majority (21 by the 1917 Code, 18 by the 1983 Code)

máior -ior -ius: greater, larger, elder, major

maióres -um: m. pl.; elders, forefathers

maióritas -átis: f.; majority

Maíus (Május) -i: m.; month of May

maiúsculus -a -um: rather large

Malachías -ae: m.; Malachi, a minor prophet; a book of the O.T.

malágma -átis: n.; plaster, poultice

mále: badly, grievously, wrongly; mále habére: be ill

maledíco -ere -díxi -díctum: (3); curse, speak evil, revile, reproach, abuse, slander

maledíctio -ónis: f., maledíctum -i: n.; curse, cursing, railing, abusive talk

maledícus -a -um: cursed, accursed; as a noun: curser, railer

malédicus -a -um: foul-mouthed, abusive, slanderous; malédice:

slanderously, abusively; as a noun: curser, railer

malefácio -ere: (3); do evil, harm, injure

malefáctor -óris, maléficus -i: m.; malefactor, evildoer, magician

malefáctum -i: n.; injury, ill deed

maléfice: maliciously, mischievously

maléficus -a -um: evil-doing, criminal, vicious, magical

malévolus -a -um: malicious, envious, spiteful, malevolent

malígnans -ántis: wicked, malicious

malígne (malitióse): wickedly, malignantly, maliciously, enviously

malígnitas -átis, f.; evil, malice, ill nature, malignity, vice, wickedness, naughtiness

malígno (malígnor) -áre: (1); act badly or wickedly, malign

malígnus -a -um: malignant, evil, malicious, bad; as a noun: evildoer

malítia -ae: f.; malice, spite, ill will, cunning, evil

malitiósus -a -um: wicked, malicious; malitióse: adv.

málo, málle, málui: (irreg.) prefer, choose rather, desire

malleátor -óris: m.; hammerer

málleus -i: m.; hammer, mallet

Málleus Arianórum: "Hammer of the Arians," a title given to St. Hilary

mallúvium -ii: n.; dish for washing

máltha -ae: f.; mortar, putty

málum -i: n.; apple

málum médicum: lemon

málum púnicum (granátum): pomegranate

málus -a -um: bad, evil, wicked; as a n. noun: evil or bad thing

Mamertínus -a -um: Mamertine

mamílla (mámma) -ae: f.; breast, pap

mammóna (mammónas) -ae, mámmon -os: m.; wealth, riches, cupidity, mammon

Mammotréctus -i: m.; a book
containing strange words from the
Bible and the Breviary

mámzer -is: *see* mánzer

Manásses, Manásse: m.; *Hebrew;*
Manasseh, the eldest son of Joseph; a
tribe of Israel

mancípium (mancúpium) -ii: n.; taking
by the hand, legal purchase, right of
possession, ownership, property, slave

máncipo -áre: (1); deliver up, give title
to, transfer

máncus -a -um: lame, crippled,
incomplete, defective, infirm,
imperfect

mandatárius -ii: m.; agent, one
entrusted with a mandate

mandátum -i: n.; command, order,
mandate, credentials, ritual of washing
feet in Maundy Thursday liturgy

mándo -áre: (1); command, order, give
charge to, send word, enjoin, entrust,
commission, mandate

mándo -ere, mándi, mánsum: (3),
mandúco -áre: (1); eat, chew

mandórla -ae: f.; a nimbus framing a
figure

mandragóra (mandragóras) -ae: m.;
mandrake, herb, plant

manducátio -ónis: f.; eating

mandúco (mandúcor) -áre: (1); chew,
masticate, eat

máne: in the morning, early morning;
válde máne, súmmo máne, prímo
máne: very early in the morning

manéntia -áe: f.; permanence

máneo -ére, mánsi, mánsum: (2); wait,
remain, tarry, abide; *see Appendix*

mánibus exténsis: with hands extended

mánibus júnctis: with hands joined

mánicae -árum: f. pl.; manacles, bonds,
fetters, handcuffs, sleeves, grappling
irons

manicátus -a -um: fettered, tied,
furnished with sleeves

Manichaéi -órum: m. pl.; Manichaeans

mánico -áre: (1); come early in the
morning

manifestátio -ónis: f.; manifestation,
showing, display, revelation

manifésto -áre: (1); reveal, manifest,
make known, discover

maniféstus -a -um: manifest, clear,
open, visible, evident, plain; maniféste
(manifésto): *adv.*

maníle -is: n.; basin for washing hands

manípulus -i: m.; maniple; sheaf, small
bundle, handful

mánna -ae: f., mánna: *indecl.:* n.;
manna, food from heaven

máno -áre: (1); flow, run, drip, exude,
spread

mánsio -ónis: f.; dwelling, abode, home

mansionariátus -us: m.; office of
resident priest

mansionárius -ii: m.; sexton, sacristan,
custodian, holder of a small benefice

mansiúncula -ae: f.; little room or
dwelling, chamber, compartment

mansuéto -áre: (1); make tame, tame

mansuetúdo -inis: f.; meekness,
mildness, clemency, courtesy

mansuétus -a -um: meek, mild, humble,
gentle, soft

mansúrus -a -um: enduring

mantélla -ae: f., mantéllum (mantélum)
-i: n.; mantle, cloak

mantellétum -i: n.; cape covering the
surplice of a prelate

mantíle -is: n.; towel, napkin

mantíssa -ae: f.; addition, supplement,
an extra, dessert

mánto -áre: (1); remain, wait for

manuális -is -e: manual

manudúctio -ónis: f.; direction,
initiation, guidance

manudúctor -óris: m.; choir leader in
early Church, director

manufácio -ere: (3); make by hand

manufáctus -a -um: made by hand
manuleátus -a -um: with sleeves
mánus -us: f.; hand
manuscríptum -i: n.; manuscript
manutérgium -ii: n.; napkin, towel
mánzer (mámzer) -eris: illegitimate; *as a noun:* bastard
máppa -ae: f.; cloth, altar cloth
máppula -ae: f.; napkin, handkerchief
Maranátha: *Aramaic;* the Lord cometh
márceo -ére: (2); wither, droop, be faint, grow weak, become feeble
marcésco -ere: (3); fade away, decay
márchio -ónis: m.; marquis
márcidus -a -um: withered, delicate, exhausted, weak
Márcus -i: m.; Mark
Mardochaéus -i: m.; Mardochai
máre -is: n.; sea
Máre Rúbrum: Red Sea
margaríta -ae: f., margarítum -i: n.; pearl
márgo -ónis: f.; border
María -ae: f.; Mary
Mariális -is -e, Mariánus -a -um: pertaining to Mary
marínus -a -um: of the sea, marine
maritiális -is -e: marital, relating to marriage, of wedlock
marítimus -a -um: maritime, of the sea; marítima -órum: n. pl.; seacoast
maríto -áre: (1); marry, give in marriage
marítus -a -um: matrimonial, nuptial, conjugal, married; maríta -ae: f.; wife; marítus -i: m.; husband
mármor -óris: n.; marble
marmóreus -a -um: of marble
Mars, Mártis: m.; the god Mars, war, battle, the planet Mars
marsúpium -ii: n.; moneybag, purse
márte: with authority; próprio márte (márte suo): by one's own authority, on one's own initiative
Mártius -ii: m.; month of March

mártyr -is: m.; martyr
martyrárius -ii: m.; keeper of relics of martyrs
martýrium -ii: n.; martyrdom
martyrológium -ii: n.; martyrology, list of martyrs and saints
Martyrológium Hieronymiánum: a martyrology compiled about AD 600 and bearing the name of St. Jerome
Martyrológium Románum: Roman Martyrology
masculínus (másculus) -a -um: male, masculine
mássa -ae: f.; lump, mass, bulk, fund, aggregate
Mássa -ae: f.; Massa, Massah; a place in the desert
massális -is -e: belonging to a mass, all together
Massónicus -a -um: of the Masons
masturbátio -ónis: f.; masturbation, self-abuse
máter -tris, mátrix -ícis: f.; mother; *see Appendix*
materfamílias, matrisfamílias(-liae): f.; mistress of a home, matron
matéria -ae: f.; matter, subject, material; *see Appendix*
materiális -is -e: material; materiáliter: *adv.*
materialísmus -i: m.; materialism
matérnitas (matrícitas) -átis: f.; motherhood, maternity
matérnus -a -um: maternal
matértera -ae: f.; maternal aunt, mother's sister
mathemáticus -a -um: mathematical
matrícitas -átis: *see* matérnitas
matrícula -ae: f.; catalogue, list
matriculária -ae: f.; deaconess
matrimoniális -is -e: matrimonial; matrimoniáliter: *adv.*
matrimónium -ii: n.; marriage, matrimony; matrimónium míxtum: a

marriage of two of different faiths; *see Appendix*

matrína -ae: f.; godmother, female sponsor

mátrix -ícis: f.; mother; source, origin; public register, list, role

matróna -ae: f.; matron, woman of quality

matróneum -i: n.; part set off for women in the early churches

Matthaéus (Matthéus) -i: m.; Matthew

Matthías -ae: m.; Matthias, the disciple surnamed Justus

maturátio -ónis: f.; hastening, acceleration, growth, maturation

maturésco -ere -ui: (3); ripen, come to maturity

matúritas -átis: f.; fullness, ripeness, maturity, perfection; *see Appendix*

matúro -áre: (1); grow, mature, develop

matúrus -a -um: mature, developed, timely, ripe, fit, proper; **matúri** -órum: m. pl.; adults; **matúrior** -ior -ius: *comp. adj.;* **matúre:** *adv.*

matutínum -i: n.; night watch, Matins

matutínum tenebrárum: Tenebrae service of Holy Week

matutínus -a -um: early, morning, of morning

mausoléum -i: n.; splendid sepulcher

maxílla -ae: f.; cheek, jaw, cheekbone, jawbone

máxime: chiefly, especially, to the greatest extent, the highest degree; **quam máxime:** as much as possible

maximópere: exceedingly

maximus -a -um: very great, greatest, most grievous, maximum

mázza -ae: f.; mace

mazzérius -ii: m.; mace-bearer

measurábilis -is -e: measurable

meátus -us m.; passage, way

mechánicus -a -um: of machines, mechanical; **mechánice:** *adv.*

medéla -ae: f.; healing remedy, cure, healing

médeor -éri: *dep.* (2); heal, cure

Média Annáta -ae: f.; a tax on benefices in the 1917 Code

médians -ántis: halved, divided; *pres. part. of* **médio**

mediánte: by means of

mediáte: indirectly

mediátio -ónis: f.; mediation

mediátor -óris: m., **mediátrix** -ícis: f.; mediator, intermediary

médica -ae: f.; clover

medicámen -inis: n.; medicine

medicaméntum -i: n.; drug, remedy, medicine

medicátio -ónis, **medicína** -ae: f.; remedy, healing power, medicine

medicinális -is -e: healing, salutary, medicinal; *see Appendix*

médico -áre: (1); cure, heal

médicus -a -um: medical, healing; *as a noun:* physician

Médicus (Médus) -a -um: Persian, Assyrian, Median

medíetas -átis: f.; half, medium, middle course, midst

médio -áre: (1); be in the middle, mediate, halve, divide

mediócris -is -e: middling, moderate, indifferent, mediocre

mediócritas -átis: f.; mediocrity

meditabúndus -a -um: designing, planning, meditating

meditátio -ónis: f.; meditation, reflection, thought, contemplation

meditatórium -ii: n.; preparation, place of preparation

médito (méditor) -áre: (1); meditate, reflect, think, plan, devise, ponder

médium -ii: n.; middle, midst, medium, mean, half

médius -a -um: middle, mid, central; **médie:** *adv.*

medúlla -ae: f.; marrow, finest part

medullátus -a -um: full of marrow, fat, rich, abounding in richness

medúllitus: in the very marrow, in the innermost part, from the heart

Médus: *see* Médicus

meípsum: myself

mel, méllis: n.; honey

Melchísedech: *indecl.;* Melchisedech

mélior -ior -ius: better; in mélius: for the better; mélius: *adv.*

meliorátio -ónis: f.; improvement, melioration, bettering

melísma -átis: f.; modulation in chant

melismáticus -a -um: melodious

Mélita -ae: f.; Malta

mellífluus -a -um: dripping with sweetness

mélos -i: m. *or n.;* hymn, song, melody

melóta -ae, melóte -is: f.; sheepskin, coat or habit of sheepskin

mem: 13th letter of the Hebrew alphabet

membrána -ae: f.; membrane, parchment, skin

membrátim: from limb to limb

mémbrum -i: n.; limb; part, division; member

memént o, mementóte: *sing., pl. imperat.;* be mindful of, remember

Memént o: prayer of remembrance in the liturgy

mémini: *perf., defect. verb;* remember, be mindful of

mémor -óris: mindful of, calling to mind, remembering

memorábilis -is -e: memorable, remarkable, worthy of mention

Memoráre: a prayer in honor of the B.V.M. attributed to Bernard of Clairvaux

memorátus -us: m.; mention

memorátus -a -um: mentioned, above mentioned, remembered

memória -ae: f., memoriále -is: n.; remembrance, memory, memorial, commemoration, souvenir

Memoriále Rítuum Benedícti XIII: an old book of ceremonies for Ash Wednesday and Holy Week

memoriális -is -e: memorial

mémoro (mémoror) -áre: (1); remember, recall, relate

mendácium -ii: n., mendácitas -átis: f.; lie, untruth, lying, falsehood

méndax -ácis: false, deceitful, unreliable, prone to lying; *as a noun:* liar

mendicábulum -i: n.; beggar, mendicant

mendicátio -ónis: f.; begging

mendícitas -átis: f.; want, poverty

méndico (méndicor) -áre: (1); beg

méndicus -a -um: beggarly, in want, indigent, needy; *as a noun:* beggar

mendósitas -átis: f.; faultiness

mens, méntis: f.; mind, soul, spirit; ménte cáptus: mentally disturbed

ménsa -ae: f.; upper surface of altar, altar table; banquet; bank; table

ménsio -ónis: f.; measuring

ménsis -is: m.; month

ménsor -óris: m.; measurer, surveyor

menstruátus -a -um: menstruous

ménstruo -áre: (1); happen monthly, menstruate, pollute

ménstruus -a -um: monthly, happening monthly

mensúra -ae: f.; measure, size

mensurábilis -is -e: measurable, short

ménta (méntha) -ae: f.; mint

mentális -is -e: mental

mentálitas -átis: f.; mentality, mind, intention

méntha -ae: *see* ménta

méntio -ónis: f.; mention

méntio (méntior) -íre: (4); lie, tell lies

méntum -i: n.; chin, throat

merácus -a -um: pure, unmixed

mercatúra -ae: f., mercátus -i, mercátus -us: m.; trade, traffic, commerce

mercatúram fácere: to engage in trade

mercenárius -ii: m.; paid servant, hireling, mercenary

mercenárius -a -um: mercenary

mérces -édis: f.; reward, ransom, hire, wages, pay, salary, price, income

mércor -ári: dep. (1); buy

Mercúrius -ii: m.; Mercury

Mercúrius díes: Wednesday

mére: merely, purely, entirely

méreo (méreor) -ére -ui -itum: (2); merit, win, deserve, earn, be worthy of

méretrix -ícis: f.; harlot

mérgo -ere, mérsi, mérsum: (3); sink, immerse, plunge, overwhelm

mérgulus -i: m.; diving bird

Mériba -ae: f.; Meribah, Meriba, a place in the desert

meribíbula -ae: c.; wine bibber

meridiánus -a -um: southern, of the south, noonday; as a n. noun: south

merídies -éi: m.; midday, noon, south; per merídiem: at noon

meridionális -is -e: south, southern

merídior (merído) -ári: dep. (1); rest at midday

mérito -áre: (1); deserve, merit

mérito: deservedly, rightly, justly

meritório: meritoriously

meritórius -a -um: meritorious, deserving of merit

méritum -i: n.; merit, desert, good work

mérum -i: n.; wine

mérus -a -um: pure, unmixed with water, undiluted; mére: adv.

merx, mércis: f.; merchandise, wares, goods

Méshech: indecl.; Meshech, an area and a tribe overcome by Israel

Mesopotámia -ae: f.; Mesopotamia

Messiánicus -a -um: of the Messiah, Messianic

Messía (Messías) -ae: m.; Messiah, Christ, Anointed One

méssis -is, méssio -ónis: f.; crop, harvest

méssor -óris: m.; harvester, reaper

mestítius -a -um: mixed, half-breed

-met: intensive suffix; self

méta -ae: f.; goal, boundary, limit

metállum -i: n.; metal, mine

metáphora -ae: f.; metaphor

metaphrástes -ae: c. translator of a book

metaphýsica -ae: f.; metaphysics

metatúra -ae: f.; a measuring out, marking off

methódicus -a -um: methodical

Methodístae -árum: m. pl.; Methodist, a Protestant denomination founded by John Wesley

methodológicus -a -um: methodological

méthodus (méthados) -i: f.; method, mode of proceeding, way of teaching

métior -íri, ménsus: dep. (4); distribute by measure, measure out, measure

méto -ere, méssui, méssum: (3); mow, gather harvest, reap

metréta -ae: f.; Greek liquid measure

métricus -a -um: metrical

metropólicus (metropolíticus) -a -um: of a metropolitan or archiepiscopal see

metrópolis -is: f.; capital city

metropolitánus -a -um: metropolitan

metropolitánus -i, metropólitus -i: m., metropólita -ae: m.; archbishop, metropolitan bishop; see Appendix

metropolíticus: see metropólicus

métrum -i: n.; verse, meter, measure

métuo -ere -ui -útum: (3); fear, dread, be afraid

métus -us: m.; dread, fear

méus -a -um: my, mine

mi: voc. of méus; my

míca -ae: f.; crumb, morsel, grain

mícans -ántis: radiant, shining, glittering, sparkling

Michaéas -ae: m.; Micah, a minor prophet; a book of the O.T.

Micháel -élis: m.; Michael

míco -áre: (1); shine, glitter, gleam, sparkle

Micrológus -i: m.; the name for a medieval explanation of the liturgy

Mídian: *see* Mádian

mígma -átis: n.; mixture, cattle food

mígrans -ántis: c.; migrant

migrátio -ónis: f.; migration, removal from one place to another, departure

mígro -áre: (1); depart, travel, go abroad

míles -itis: c.; soldier

mília -ium: n. pl.; thousands

mílies: a thousand times

mílitans -ántis: militant; *as a c. noun:* soldier

militáris -is -e: military, martial

militarísticus -a -um: militaristic

milítia -ae: f.; military service, army, soldiers, employment at court

mílito -áre: (1); serve in army, fight, hold office in court, war

mílium -ii: n.; millet

mílle: pl. míllia; thousand

Millenarísmus -i: m.; theory of millenarianism

milléni -ae -a: a thousand each

millésimus -a -um: thousandth

milliárium -ii: n.; milestone

míllies: a thousand times

mílvus -i: m.; stork

mímus -i: m.; actor, mime, mimic

mína (mna) -ae: f.; coin, Greek coin

mináciter: by threats, threateningly

mínae -árum: f. pl.; threats, menaces

mínax -ácis: threatening

míngo -ere, mínxi, mínctum: (3); urinate

mínimus -a -um: least, smallest, very small; *as n. noun:* very small thing; mínime: *adv.;* mínime véro: by no means

ministéllus -i: m.; non-Catholic clergy

miníster -tri: m., minístra -ae: f.; minister, servant, attendant, helper at the altar, official, agent

ministérium -ii: n.; ministry, service, office, duty

ministrális (ministeriális) -is -e: of a minister

ministrátio -ónis: f.; service, ministry, administration

ministrátor -óris: m.; one who serves

minístro -áre: (1); serve, minister to, wait on

míno -áre: (1); to drive

mínor -ári: *dep.* (1); threaten, menace

mínor, mínor, mínus: smaller, less, rather little

mínor -óris: c.; a minor; *see* maíor; *see* Appendix

minorátio -ónis: f.; decrease, diminution, abasement

Minóres, Fratres: members of the Order of St. Francis

Minóres, Órdines: minor orders

minorísta -ae: m.; one in minor orders

minóritas -átis: f.; minority, being a minor

minóro -áre: (1); be in want, diminish, decrease, shorten

mínuo -ere -ui -útum: (3); diminish, abate, make less, reduce, make smaller

mínus: less, by no means, not at all

paúlo mínus: almost

plus minúsve: more or less

si quo mínus: if not

minúsculus -a -um: rather small

minútiae -árum: f.; trifles, details

minútum -i: n.; minute, mite

minútum secúndum: a second of time

minútus -a -um: small, unimportant

mirabília -ium: n. pl.; wonders, wonderful things, marvelous works

mirabiliárius -ii: m.; wonder-worker

mirábilis -is -e: wonderful, marvelous; mirabíliter: *adv.*

mirábile díctu: wonderful to say

mirábile vísu: wonderful to see

mirabílium -ii, **mírum** -i, **miráculum** -i: n.; wonder, miracle

mirándus (mírus) -a -um: strange, extraordinary, wonderful, astonishing

mirificéntia -ae: f.; wonder, admiration

mirífico -áre: (1); make wonderful, show forth wonderfully, exalt

miríficus (mírus) -a -um: wonderful, marvelous, extraordinary, singular, strange; **mirífice, míre:** adv.

míror (míro) -ári: dep. (1); to wonder

mírum -i: see **mirabílium**

mírus: see **mirándus** or **miríficus**

Mísael: indecl.; Misael, Meshach

mísceo -ére -cui, míxtum: (2); mingle, mix, blend

míser -era -erum: wretched, miserable, unhappy, pitiable, unfortunate

miserátio -ónis, **misericórdia** -ae: f.; mercy, kindness, compassion

miserátor -óris: m.; one who shows compassion

mísere: miserably, wretchedly

miséreor -éri, miséritus (misértus): dep. (2), **míseror** -ári: dep. (1); pity, have mercy on, have compassion for, lament, bewail

miséria -ae: f.; misery, trouble, wretchedness, misfortune

misericórdia -ae: f.; compassion, mercy

miséricors -córdis: merciful, kind; **misericórditer:** adv.

míseror: see **miséreor**

Míssa -ae: f.; the Mass; see Appendix

missále -is: n.; Missal

missális -is -e: of the Mass

míssio -ónis: f.; mission, sending forth, act of being sent; see Appendix

míssio canónica: ecclesiastical appointment

missiológia -ae: f.; missiology

missiológicus -a -um: missiological

missionális -is -e, **missionárius** -a -um: missionary; as a c. noun: a missionary, one working in the missions

missionárius apostólicus: missionary with faculties from the Holy See

míssus -us: m.; envoy

mistícius (mix-) -a -um: of mixed race

místio -ónis: see **míxtio**

místum (míxtum) -i: n., **mistúra** -ae: f.; mixture

mitésco -ere: (3); grow old, become mild, subside

mítigo -áre: (1); mitigate, subdue, diminish, weaken, give rest, soften

mítis -is -e: meek, mild, gentle, tender

mítra -ae: f.; miter, bonnet, headdress

mítra auriphrygiáta: special miter for Lent and Advent

mitrátus -a -um: mitered

mítto -ere, mísi, míssum: (3); send, put, lay, rest

mixtícius: see **mistícius**

míxtio (místio) -ónis: f.; mixture, confounding, confusing

míxtum (místum) -i: n., **mixtúra** -ae: f.; mixture

míxtus -a -um: mingled, mixed

mna -ae: see **mína**

Móab: indecl.; Moab, descendant of Lot; a territory east of the Dead Sea

Moabítes -ae: m., **Moabítis** -idis: f.; inhabitant of Moab

móbilis -is -e: movable, mobile

mobílitas -átis: f.; fickleness, inconstancy, changeability, mobility

modális -is -e: modal

moderámen -inis: n.; management, direction, government

moderáte: moderately

moderátio -ónis: f.; moderation

moderátor -óris: m.; moderator, guide, director, adviser, confessor, superior; see Appendix moderátrix -ícis: f.; superioress, directress

Modernísmus -i:m.; doctrine of Modernism

modérnus -a -um: modern

móderor -ári: *dep.* (1); govern, guide, regulate, direct, advise

modéstia -ae: f.; modesty

modéstus -a -um: moderate, temperate, mild, modest, brief, calm, sober; modéste: *adv.*

módicum -i: n.; short while, a little bit

módicum quid: a little something

módicus -a -um: little, small, of moderate size, temperate

módius -ii: m.; bushel, peck, measure

módo: just now, now, presently, even now, only, merely, provided that; non módo: not only

modulátio -ónis: f.; melody, singing, chanting

modulátor -óris: m.; musician

módulor -ári: *dep.* (1): temper, regulate, mitigate, measure

módulus -i: m.; melody, rhythm, measure, small measure

módus -i: m.; measure, way, manner, fashion, mode, method, tone

quem ad módum: how, as

súpra módum: above measure

moécha -ae: f.; adulteress

moéchia -ae: f.; adultery

moéchor -ári: *dep.* (1); commit adultery

moéchus -i: m.; adulterer

moénia -ium(-órum): n. pl.; ramparts, walls, fortifications, bulwarks

moéror (maé-) -óris: m., moéstia (maé-) -ae: f., moestitúdo (maé-) -inis: f.; sadness, sorrow, grief, dejection, melancholy

moésto: *see* maésto

moéstus (maé-) -a -um: sorrowful, sad, afflicted, dejected, grieved

móla -ae: f.; millstone, mill

móla asinária: millstone

moláris -is: m.; molar, cheek tooth

molendínum -i: n.; mill

móles -is: f.; mass, bulk; trouble

moléstia -ae: f.; trouble, harm

moléstor -ári: *dep.* (1); molest

moléstus -a -um: troublesome, burdensome, annoying, grievous

molímen -inis: n.; effort, work

molínus -a -um: belonging to a mill

mólior -íri: *dep.* (4); plot, undertake, devise, practice

molítio -ónis: f.; demolition

móllio -íre: (4); soften, make smooth

móllis -is -e: soft, yielding, flexible; *as a n. noun:* soft garment

mólliter: gently

mólo -ere: (3); grind

momentáneus -a -um: momentary, short

moméntum -i: n.; importance, moment

monachísmus -i: m.; monasticism, monastic life

mónachus -i: m.; monk; mónacha -ae: f.; nun

monastérium -ii: n.; monastery; *see Appendix*

monásticus -a -um, monasteriális -is -e: monastic

móneo -ére -ui -itum: (2); admonish, warn

monetárius -a -um: of the mint or money

moniális -is: f.; nun

moníle -is: n.; necklace, jewel, collar

monítio -ónis: f., mónitum -i: n., mónitus -us: m.; admonition, warning, reminder

mónitor -óris: m.; admonisher, adviser, overseer, prayer leader, superintendent, prompter, monitor

monógama (monogámia) -ae: f.; monogyny, monogamy

monogénesis -is(-eos): f.; monogenesis, origin from one pair

Monophysítae -árum: f.; the heresy of Monophysitism; *see Appendix*

Monophysítes -um: m. pl.; followers of Monophysitism

monopólium -ii: n.; monopoly

Monotheísmus -i: m.; monotheism

Monothelítae -árum: f. pl.; the heresy of Monothelitism

Monothelítes -um: m. pl.; followers of Monothelitism

mons, móntis: m.; mountain, mount, hill

monstrántia -ae: f.; monstrance

mónstro -áre: (1); show, point out

mónstrum -i: n.; monstrosity

montána -órum: n. pl.; hill country

Montanísmus -i: m.; Montanism, a second-century schism

montánus -a -um: mountainous, of the hill country or mountains

monuméntum -i: n.; monument, grave, sepulcher, record

móra -ae: f.; delay, hindrance, pause, rest, space of time

morális -is -e: moral; **moráliter:** *adv.; see Appendix*

morálitas -átis: f.; morality

mórbidus -a -um: depraved, diseased

mórbus -i: m., **mórbum** -i: n.; disease, sickness, illness, fault

mórdax -ácis: stinging, piercing

mórdeo -ére, momórdi, mórsum: (2); bite, take hold upon

moribúndus -a -um: dying

morígerus -a -um: compliant, accommodating

mórior -i, mórtuus: *dep.* (3); die

móror -ári: *dep.* (1); delay, abide, dwell, tarry, linger

mors, mórtis: f.; death

mórsus -us: m.; bite, morsel, biting

mortális -is -e: mortal; **mortáliter:** *adv.*

mortaríolum -i: n.; small mortar, vessel, container

morticínum -i: n.; corpse, carcass

mórtifer -era -erum, **mortíficus** -a -um: deadly, fatal

mortificátio -ónis: f.; mortification

mortífico -áre: (1); mortify, kill

mortíficus: *see* **mórtifer**

mórtis íctus: stroke of death, mortal sin

mortuális -is -e: of death; *as a n. noun:* funeral, funeral liturgy

mórtuus -a -um: dead; *as a noun:* the dead

mórula -ae: f.; interval, brief delay

mórus -i: f.; mulberry tree

mos, móris: m.; custom, manner, action; **súpra mórem:** more than usual

Mosáicus -a -um: of Moses

Móses -is: *see* **Móyses**

motábilis -is -e: moving, changeable, fickle, capable of action

motéttum -i: n.; short song, motet

mótio -ónis: f., **mótus** -us: m.; motion, movement, action, tumult, tempest, emotion, moving

motívum -i: n.; motive, reason; *see Appendix*

mótor -óris: m.; mover, motor, impulse

mótu próprio: by one's own accord; *see Appendix*

mótus -us: m.; motion, movement, activity, impulse, initiative

móveo -ére, móvi, mótum: (2); move, stir, influence, effect, quake

mox: soon, afterwards, presently, at a later time

Móyses (Móses) -is *or* i: m.; *dat.* Móysi; *acc.* Móysen; Moses

mozétta (mozzétta) -ae: f.; short cape

múcro -ónis: m.; point, sharp edge

múgio -íre -ívi(-íi) -ítum: (4); rumble, groan, bellow, low

múla -ae: f., **múlus** -i: m.; mule

múlceo -ére, múlsi, múlsum (múlctum): (2); charm, soothe, appease, delight

múlcta -ae: f.; fine, monetary penalty

múlcto -áre: (1); fine, punish by fining

múlgeo -ére, múlsi, múlsum (múlctum): (2); milk, pour out as milk

muliébris -is -e: feminine

múlier -eris: f.; woman, wife

muliércula -ae: f.; disgraceful woman, common woman, woman

mulíeris -is -e: womanly

múlsum -i: n.; sweet wine

multifáriam: at sundry times, on many sides, in many places

multifórmis -is -e, multifárius -a -um: manifold, various, diverse, multiform

multifórmitas -átis: f.; multiformity

multifórmiter: in many or different ways

multígenus (multigénerus) -a -um: prolific, numerous, of many kinds, various

multilóquium -ii: n.; much speaking

multímodus -a -um: various, manifold

múltiplex -icis: manifold, many, far more, many times more

multiplícitas -átis: f., multiplicátio -ónis: f.; multiplicity, multiplication

multiplíciter: in many ways, in various ways, greatly

multíplico -áre: (1); multiply, enrich

multísonus -a -um: loud

multitúdo -inis: f.; multitude

multívolus -a -um: having many desires, longing for many or much

multivoráncia -ae: f.; gluttony

múlto: by much, much, a great deal

múltum: much, long, to a great degree, very, greatly

múltus -a -um: many, much, bountiful
  múlta nócte: late at night
  múltis de caúsis: for many reasons
  múltis post ánnis: after many years

múlus -i: see múla

mundánus -a -um: mundane, of the world

mundátio -ónis: f.; cleansing, purification

mundiális -is -e: worldly, mundane;
  mundiáliter: adv.

múndicors -dis: clean of heart

mundítia -ae: f.; cleanliness

mundípotens -éntis: world ruling

múndo -áre: (1); cleanse, clean, purify

múndus -i: m.; world, universe, earth, heavens

múndus -a -um: clean, pure, elegant, flawless, neat, nice

múnera: pl. of múnus

múnero (múneror) -áre: (1); bestow a gift, honor or reward with a gift, present, give

múnia -ium(-órum): n. pl.; gifts, services, duties, functions

múniceps -cipis: c.; citizen

municipátio -ónis: f.; citizenship

muníficens -éntis, muníficus -a -um: munificent, bountiful, generous, liberal

munificéntia -ae: f.; bountifulness

munímen -inis: n.; protection, rampart, defense, enclosure

múnio -íre: (4); defend, preserve, fortify, strengthen, protect, guard

munísculum -i: n.; snare

munítio -ónis: f.; fort, entrenchment

munitiúncula -ae: f.; small fortress

munítus -a -um: secure, defended, fortified

múnus -eris: n.; gift, bounty, present, offering; duty, office, employment, responsibility, service; bribe

munúsculum -i: n.; little gift

murénula -ae: f.; necklace

múrmur -uris: n.; murmuring

murmurátio -ónis: f.; murmur

murmurátor -óris: m.; murmurer

múrmuro -áre: (1); murmur, grumble, complain

múrra (múrrha, mýrrha) -ae: f.; myrrh, myrrh tree

murrátus (myrrhátus) -a -um: spiced, mingled with myrrh

múrreus (mýrrheus) -a -um: like myrrh,
   perfumed with myrrh
múrus -i: m.; wall
mus, múris: c.; mouse
músca -ae: f.; fly
muscárium -ii: n.; fan
música -ae: f.; instrumental music, music
musicális -is -e, músicus -a -um:
   musical, of music; as a noun: musician
musívum -i: n.; mosaic
musívus -a -um: artistic
Muslímus -a -um: Muslim
mussitátor -óris: m.; murmurer,
   grumbler
Musulmánus -a -um: Muslim
mústum -i: n.; new wine
mutábilis -is -e: changeable
mutabílitas -átis, mutátio -ónis: f.;
   change
mutátis mutándis: with the things
   changed that must be changed
mutatórium -ii: n.; place of change,
   sacristy; change of raiment
mutatórius -a -um: belonging to or
   pertaining to change
mutilátio -ónis: f.; mutilation, maiming
mútilo -áre: (1); mutilate, maim
múto -áre: (1); change, move
mútuo: mutually, to one another, in
   return, reciprocally

mútuor (mútuo) -ári: dep. (1); borrow
mútus -a -um: dumb, unable to speak; as
   a noun: mute person
mútuus -a -um: mutual, borrowed, lent;
   as a n. noun: a loan
mýrias -ados(-adis): myriad, the
   number ten thousand
myríca -ae: f.; tamaric, tamarisk
mýrrha -ae: see múrra
myrrhátus: see murrátus
mýrrheus: see múrreus
myrtétum (mystétum) -i: n.; myrtle
   bush or tree
mýrum -i: n.; ointment; Myron, see
   Appendix
mysteriále -is: n.; a vessel for holding
   the Blessed Sacrament
mysteriáliter: mysteriously
mystérium (mystérion) -ii: n.; mystery,
   secret knowledge
mystérius -a -um: of a mystery,
   mysterious
mystétum -i: see myrtétum
mýsticus -a -um: mystical, of deep
   meaning; as a noun: a mystic; mýstice:
   adv.; see Appendix
mythológia-ae: f.; mythology
mýthus (mýthos) -i: m.; myth, fable

N

N: *inserted in text stands for* **nómen**
náblium (náblum) -i: n.; harp
Náhum: *indecl.;* Nahum, a minor
prophet; a book of the O.T.
Naín: *indecl.;* Nain
nam (námque): *conj.;* for
nancíscor -i, nánctus (náctus): *dep.* (3);
obtain, get, reach; meet with
Náphtali: *see* **Néphtali**
narcíssus -i: m.; narcissus, daffodil
nárdus -i: f., **nárdum** -i: n.; nard oil;
nárdum spicátum: spikenard
náres -ium: f. pl.; nostrils, nose
narrátio -ónis: f.; narration, story,
narrative
narrátor -óris: m.; narrator, relater
nárro -áre: (1); say, tell, speak, relate,
narrate, record
nárthex -ícis: f.; interior vestibule of a
church, narthex, portico
náscor -i, nátus: *dep.* (3); be born
nássa -ae: f.; trap, snare, net
natális -is -e, **natalítius (-cius)** -a -um:
natal, of a birthday, of a saint's feast
day; *as a m. pl. noun:* birth, origin,
descent
natális -is, **natalítium** -ii: n.; birthday,
anniversary of a saint
Natális cálicis: Feast of the Chalice,
early name for Holy Thursday
Natális Eucharístiae: Birthday of the
Eucharist, Holy Thursday
natalítium -ii: *see* **natális** -is
natalítius -a -um: *see* **natális** -is -e
natatória -ae: f., **natatórium** -ii: n.;
pool, place for swimming
Náthan: *indecl.;* Nathan
Nathániel -is, *or indecl.:* m.; Nathaniel

nátio -ónis: f.; nation, people; pl.:
heathen, gentiles
nationális -is -e: national, of a nation
nationalísmus -i: m.; nationalism
natívitas -átis: f.; nativity, birth
natívus -a -um: inborn, innate, native
náto (nátito) -áre: (1); swim
natúra -ae: f.; nature
naturális -is -e: natural, illegitimate;
naturáliter: *adv.*
naturalísmus -i: m.; naturalism
nátus -a -um: born; *perf. pass. part. of*
náscor
nátus -us: m.; birth; **majóres nátu:**
elders, ancients
nátus -i: m.; son, offspring; pl.: children,
race, posterity
nauclérus -i: m., **nauclérius** -ii: m.;
captain of a ship
naufrágium -i: n.; shipwreck
naúfragus -a -um: shipwrecked
naúfrago -áre: (1); suffer shipwreck
naúlum (naúlon) -i: n.; passage money,
fare
naúsea -ae: f.; nausea, squeamishness
naúseo -áre: (1); vomit, be seasick
naúta -ae: m.; sailor
naúticus -a -um: nautical, of a ship
naútici -órum: m. pl.; sailors
navicélla -ae: f.; incense boat
navícula -ae: f.; little boat
naviculárius -a -um: of small boats
navigátio -ónis: f.; voyage
navígium -ii: n.; ship, boat, vessel
návigo -áre: (1): sail, navigate
návis -is: f.; ship, vessel; nave of a church

návitas -átis: f.; energy, zeal, promptness, enthusiasm

návo -áre: (1); act or do or perform something with zeal or diligence

návus (gnávus) -a -um: busy, diligent, active, zealous, prompt, assiduous; náviter: adv.

Názara -ae: f., Názareth: indecl.; Nazareth

Nazaráeus -i: m.; Nazarite, one set apart for service of God

Nazarénus (Nazarethánus, Nazaréus, Názarus) -a -um: of Nazareth, Nazarene

Názareth: see Názara

ne: not, lest, that not
　ne plus últra: than which there is nothing more
　ne . . . quídem: not even

-ne: enclitic interr. particle; whether, not

nébula -ae: f.; cloud, mist, fog, that which is soft and transparent

nec: not, and not, also not; nec . . . nec: neither . . . nor
　nécdum: not yet
　nécne: or not
　nécnon: and also, nor less, and yet, likewise, as well as

necessárius -a -um: necessary, unavoidable, necessário: adv.

necésse: indecl. n. adj.; necessary

necéssitas -átis: f.; want, need, poverty, necessity, distress; see Appendix

necessitúdo -inis: f.; necessity, inevitableness

nécne, nécnon: see nec

néco -áre: (1); kill, slay

necrológium -ii: n.; list of deceased, necrology, obituary note

necromantía -ae: f.; necromancy

néctar -áris: n.; nectar

nécto -ere, néxui (néxi), néxum: (3); weave, twine, connect

nédum: to say nothing of, much less, still less, by no means

nefándus -a -um: unspeakable, heinous, impious; nefánde: adv.

nefárius -a -um: impious, wicked, evil; nefárie: adv.

néfas: indecl.: n.; wrong, crime, sin, wickedness, something contrary to divine law

negátio -ónis: f.; denial, negation

negatívus -a -um: negative; negatíve: adv.

négito -áre: (1); deny frequently

negléctus -us: m.; neglect

neglegéntia -ae: f.; negligence, neglect, carelessness

néglego (négligo) -ere -léxi -léctum: (3); neglect, despise

négligens -éntis: negligent, careless; negligénter: adv.

negligéntia -ae: f.; negligence

négligo: see néglego

négo -áre: (1); deny, say no, refuse

negotiátio (negótio) -ónis: f., negótium -ii: n.; business, affair, matter, occupation, merchandise, traffic

negotiátor -óris: m.; businessman, merchant

negótior -ári: dep. (1); trade, make a profit, do business

negótium -ii: see negotiátio

Nehemías -ae: m.; Nehemiah; a book of the O.T.

némo -inis: n.; no one, nobody; see Appendix

nemorális -is -e: sylvan, of the woods

nemorénsis -is -e: of a wood or grove

némpe: truly, to be sure, namely, certainly

némus -óris: n.; forest, wood, grove, place of solitude

néo nére, névi, nétum: (2); spin

neoménia -ae: f.; new moon

neóphytus -a -um: newly converted; as a noun: neophyte, convert, novice

neoprésbyter -eri: m.; newly ordained priest

neotéricus -a -um: new, recent, modern; **neotérice:** *adv.*

népa -ae:f.; scorpion, crab

Néphtali (Náphtali, Néphthali): *indecl.; Hebrew;* Naphtali, son of Jacob and Bilhah; a tribe of Israel

népos -ótis: c.; nephew, niece, grandchild, descendant

néptis -is: f.; granddaughter

néquam: *indecl.;* wicked, evil, worthless

nequándo: lest, lest at any time

nequáquam: no, not, by no means, in no way

néque: and not, also not; **néque . . . néque:** neither . . . nor

néqueo -íre -ívi(-íi) -ítum: (4); be unable; *see Appendix*

néquior -ior -ius: more wicked

nequíssimus -a -um: very or most wicked; *as a noun:* very wicked person

nequítia -ae: f.; malice, evil, wickedness, iniquity

nervíceus -a -um: made of nerves or sinews

nérvus -i: m.; nerve, sinew, tendon, string of musical instrument

nescéntia -ae: f.; ignorance

néscio -íre -ívi -ítum: (4); be ignorant of, not know; **néscio quis:** some sort of, some one or other, certain

néscius -a -um: unknowing, unaware, ignorant

Nestorianísmus -i: m.; the heresy of Nestorianism; *see Appendix*

Nestórius -ii: m.; Nestorius, Nestor

neumatízo -áre: (1); chant protractedly on one syllable

neurósis -is(-eos): f.; neurosis

neúter -tra -trum: neither, neuter

néve: and not, nor, and lest

nex, nécis: f.; violent death

néxum -i: n.; legal obligation, being bound, restraint

néxus -a -um: joined, connected

néxus -us: m.; connection, joining, fastening, clasping

ni: if not, unless, that not

Nicaénus -a -um: Nicene, of Nicaea

níctus -us: m.; winking of an eye

nidífico -áre: (1); build a nest

nídus -i: m.; nest, brood

Níger: surname of Simeon of Antioch

níger -gra -grum: black

nigrédo -inis: f.; blackness

negrésco -ere: (3); become black, grow dark

nigríta -ae: c.; Negro

nigríticus -a -um: of Negroes

níhil (nil): *indecl.:* n.; nothing, not at all

níhil ádmodum: nothing at all

níhil áliud: nothing else

níhil est quod: there is no reason why

níhildum: nothing as yet

níhil innovétur: let nothing be altered; *see Appendix*

níhil óbstat: nothing stands in the way; *see Appendix*

nihilóminus: yet, nevertheless, notwithstanding

nihilanísmus -i: m.; nihilism

níhilum -i: n.; nothing

nil: *see* níhil

Nil síne Númine: nothing without God

Nílus -i: m.; Nile River

nimbátus -a -um: in a cloud or mist

nímbus -i: m.; cloud, storm, shower, halo, auriole

nímie (nímis, nímio): very much, extremely, exceedingly, greatly, beyond measure, too much, overmuch, very

nimíetas -átis: f.; excess, superfluity

nimírum: truly, certainly, undoubtedly

nímius -a -um: excessive, too great, too much, beyond measure; *as a n. noun:* excess, superabundance

níngo (nínguo) -ere, nínxi: (3); snow

Nínive -es: f.; Nineveh, Ninive; the ancient capital of Assyria

Ninivítae -árum: c.; Ninivites

nísi: unless, except, if not, but, in case that

    non nísi: only

    nísi véro: unless indeed

    nísi fórte: unless, to be sure

nísus -us: m.; effort, strength, endeavor, striving

nítens sídus: sun, daystar, Christ

níteo -ére -ui: (2); glitter, shine, glisten, be bright

nitésco -ere: (3); begin to shine

nítidus -a -um: smooth, clean, bright

nítor -óris: m.; splendor, brightness, brilliance, shining light

nítor, níti, nísus (níxus): *dep.* (3); endeavor, strive, lean upon, rest, be grounded on

nítrum -i: n.; niter, natural soda

níveus -a -um: snow-white

nix, nívis: f.; snow

níxor -ári: *dep.* (1); lean upon, rest upon, strive, strain

Nóah (Nóe): *indecl.,* **Nóa** -ae: m.; Noah

nóbilis -is -e: noble, high-born, of distinguished ancestry

nobílitas -átis: f.; nobility, noble birth, excellence, worth

nobíliter: nobly, excellently

nobílito -áre: (1); make known, make illustrious

nóceo -ére, -ui -itum: (2); harm, hurt, injure

nocívus -a -um: harmful, hurtful, injurious

nóctu (nócte, noctánter): at night, by night, in the night

nóctua -ae: f.; owl

Nocturnála -is: n.; Matins choir book

nocturnális -is -e, **noctúrnus** -a -um: of the night, nocturnal, nightly

nocuméntum -i: n.; harm, damage

nócuus (nodósus) -a -um: injurious, hurtful, harmful

nodósitas -átis: f.; intricacy, knottiness

nódus -i: m.; knot

Nóe: *see* **Nóah**

nólo, nólle, nólui: be unwilling, refuse, not want

nómas -ádis: c.; nomad

nómen -inis: n.; name

nominátim: by name, expressly, namely

nominátio -ónis: f.; naming, nomination, appointment; *see Appendix*

nominátor -óris: m.; nominator

nominátus -a -um: renowned, famed, nominated

nómino -áre: (1); name, nominate

nomocánon -ónis: m.; nomocanon; *see Appendix*

non: not, no

    non cónstat: it does not stand or agree; *see Appendix*

    nóndum: not yet

    non jam: no longer

    non módo (non sólum): not only

    non módo . . . sed étiam: not only . . . but also

    nónne: *interr. used when an affirmative answer is expected*

    nonníhil: n.; not nothing, something

    non nísi: only, only if, not unless

    nonnúllus -a -um: some, several; *often used as a noun*

    nonnúmquam (nonnúnquam): sometimes

    non obstánte: notwithstanding

    non plácet: it is not pleasing, not permitted, not granted

    non séquitur: it does not follow, it is not related

    non súi cómpos: not of right or sane mind; *see Appendix*

Nóna -ae: f.; hour of None

Nónae -árum: f. pl.; nones, the seventh day in March, May, July, Oct., the fifth day in the other months

nonagenárius -a -um: ninety years of age

nonagésimus -a -um: ninetieth

nonagintanóvem: ninety-nine

nóndum: *see* non

nónna -ae: f.; nun

nónne, nonníhil, nonnúllus, nonnúmquam (nonnúnquam): *see* non

nónnus -i: m.; monk

nónus -a -um: ninth

nonúsus -i: m.; disuse

nórma -ae: f.; norm, rule, standard, gauge, way of life; *see Appendix*

nos: we, us

noscíbilis -is -e: knowable

nósco -ere, nóvi, nótum: (3); know how, be acquainted with, recognize

nosocómium -ii: n.; hospital, infirmary

nósse: *short for* novísse

nóster -tra -trum: our, ours; *see Appendix*

nóta -ae: f.; note, sign, mark, notice; nóta fácere: show

notábilis -is -e: notable, remarkable, distinguished; notabíliter: *adv.*

notámen -inis: n.; token, sign

notárius -ii: m.; scribe, notary, clerk, amanuensis, secretary; *see Appendix*

notátim: notably, especially, in a marked way

notátio -ónis: f.; mental impression, observation, noting, marking, designation, characterizing

notificátio -ónis: f.; notification, communication; *see Appendix*

notificátor -óris: m., notificátrix -ícis: f.; communicator, public-relations person

notífico -áre: (1); notify, communicate, make known

nótio -ónis: f.; notion, idea, conception, examination

notítia -ae: f.; knowledge, news, fame, acquaintance with someone

nóto -áre: (1); mark, denote, prepare, designate, signify

notoríetas -átis: f.; notoriety

notórius -a -um: notorious, widely known; notórie: *adv.*

nótula -ae: f.; little mark

nótus -a -um: known; *as a n. noun:* friend, acquaintance

novácula -ae: f.; sharp knife, razor

novále -is: n.; new land, fallow land

Novatiáni -órum: m.; followers of Novatius; a Christian sect

nóve: recently, lately, newly, in an unusual manner

novélla -ae: f.; newly planted vine, shoot

novéllus -a -um: young, new; *as a n. pl. noun:* young shoots

nóvem: nine

Novémber -bris: m.; month of November

novéna -ae: f.; novena, period of nine days, devotion lasting nine days

novendiális -is -e: lasting nine days

novénnis -is -e: at the age of nine

novénnium -ii: n.; nine-year period, nine years

novensílis -is -e: new

novénus -a -um: nine, nine each

nóvies: nine times

novilúnium -ii: n.; new moon

novíssimus -a -um: last, latest, newest; *as a n. noun:* last state, end, bottom; novíssime: at last, latest, last of all

nóvitas -átis: f.; newness, conversion, new work or condition, freshness

novitiátus -us: m.; novitiate

novítius -a -um: of a novice; *as a noun:* novice

nóvo -áre: (1); make new, renew, refresh, change

nóvus -a -um: new, fresh, young;
    nóviter: *adv.; see Appendix*
nox, nóctis: f.; night
    in múltam nóctem: far into the night
    nox saéculi: spiritual darkness, sin
    per nóctes: every night
    séra nócte, múlta nócte: late at night
nóxa (nóxia) -ae: f.; injury, offense,
    crime, punishment, fault, sin,
    offender, criminal, sinner
noxiális -is -e, nóxius -a -um: evil,
    harmful, baneful, injurious, sinful,
    guilty, hurtful; *as a noun:* one who
    harms, injures, or sins; nóxie: *adv.*
núbes -is: f.; cloud
núbilum -i: n.; cloudy sky; pl.: clouds
núbo -ere, núpsi, núptum: (3); marry
núcleus -i: m.; kernel
nudátus (núdus) -a -um: naked, bare
núdipes -pedis: barefooted
núditas -átis: f.; nakedness, nudity,
    bareness, want
nudiusquártus: four days ago
nudiustértius: three days ago or day
    before yesterday
núdo -áre: (1); uncover
núdus: *see* nudátus
núgae -árum: f. pl.; trifles, nonsense, idle
    talk, jests
nugácitas (núgitas) -átis: f.; playfulness,
    frivolity, vanity, trifling
nugális -is -e, núgax -ácis: foolish,
    worthless, frivolous, empty, silly
nugátor -óris: m.; jester, joker, babbler,
    silly person, braggart, debauchee
núgitax -ácis: *see* nugácitas
nullátenus: not at all, by no means, in
    no way
núllibi: in no part, nowhere
nullificámen -inis: n.; contempt, a
    despising
núllitas -átis: f.; nullity
núllus -a -um: none, null
    núlla ex párte: in no way

nullusádmodum: none at all
núllus álter: no other
nullúsdum: none as yet
núllus únus: no one
num (númquid): *interr. used when a
    negative answer is expected;* if, whether
numárius: *see* nummárius
numélla -ae: f.; torture rack
númen -inis: n.; divine power, divine
    will or plan, divinity
numerátio -ónis: f.; enumeration
numerátor -óris: m.; counter, numberer
Númeri -órum: m. pl.; Numbers; a book
    of the O.T.
número -áre: (1); number, count,
    reckon, enumerate
numerósior -ior -ius: more or rather
    numerous
numerósitas -átis: f.; number, numbers,
    multitude
numerósus -a -um: numerous, manifold
númerus -i: m.; number
numísma -átis: n.; coin, medal, money
nummárius (numárius) -a -um: of
    money, venal, mercenary
nummulárius -ii: m.; money changer,
    banker
númmulus -i: m.; small coin
númmus -i: m.; coin
númqum (núnquam): never, at no time
númquid: *see* num
nun: 14th letter of the Hebrew alphabet
nunc: now, at present, at this moment;
    nunc . . . nunc: at one time . . . at
    another
Nunc dimíttis: *see Appendix*
núncio: *see* núntio
núncius -ii: *see* núntius
nuncupátio -ónis: f.; public offering,
    pronouncing of a vow
nuncupatíve: nominally, in a name
núncupo -áre: (1).; call, name
núndina -ae: f.; ninth day, market day;
    pl.: market place, fairs, bazaars

nundítio -ónis: f.; spiritual cleansing

núnquam: never

nuntiátio -ónis: f.; announcement, declaration, denunciation

nuntiátor -óris: m.; reporter, announcer, informer

núntio (nunc-) -áre: (1); announce, proclaim, declare, tell, denounce

núntium -ii: n.; news, message, announcement

núntius -a -um: informing, announcing, signifying

núntius -ii: m., núntia -ae: f.; messenger, herald, angel Gabriel, nuncio, ambassador of the Holy See, reporter; see Appendix

núper: recently, newly, lately; núper ádmodum: very recently

núpta -ae: f.; bride, spouse, wife

núptiae -árum: f. pl.; marriage, marriage celebration, wedding

nuptiális -is -e: nuptial, wedding, of a wedding

núpto -áre: (1); marry

nuptúriens -éntis: one going to be wed, one preparing for marriage

nuptúrio -íre: (4); desire to marry

núptus -i: m.; husband, spouse

núptus -us: m.; marriage, wedlock

núrus -us: f.; young married woman, daughter-in-law

núsquam: on no occasion, nowhere, at no time, never

nútans -ántis: feeble, inconstant

núto -áre: (1); nod, command by sign; wander, fail, waiver, totter, be unstable; be unresolved, be unsettled

nutrícius -ii: m., nutrícia -ae: f.; guardian, foster father or mother

nutriméntum -i: n.; food

nútrio (nútrior) -íre: (4); feed, foster, rear, suckle, nourish, support, maintain

nutrítor -óris: m.; patron, fosterer

nutritórius -a -um: pertaining to bringing up

nútrix -ícis: f.; nurse

nútus -us: m.; nod, command, beck, invitation, will, wish

nux, núcis: f.; nut

nycticórax -ácis: m.; night hawk

nyphaéum -i: n.; basin used for ablutions in early churches

Nyssénus -a -um: of Nyssa

O

o: oh

ob: *prep. w. acc. or abla.;* on account of, for, because of, in consideration of, toward, to, in return for, instead of, by reason of

obaerátus -a -um: in debt; *as a pl. noun:* debtors

obarmátus -a -um: armed

obármo -áre: (1); to arm

obaúdio -íre: (4); cause to be heard, obey

obc- *see also* **occ-**

obcaecátio -ónis: f.; blindness

obcaéco -áre: (1); to blind

obcrésco -ere: (3); increase, grow larger

obdórmio -íre: (4); sleep

obdormísco -ere: (3); fall asleep

obdúco -ere: (3); produce

obdúctio -ónis: f.; doubt, cloudiness, covering

obdúlco -áre: (1); sweeten

obdulésco -ere: (3); become sweet

obdurátio -ónis: f.; stubborness

obdúro -áre: (1); harden, make insensible

obe- *see also* **oboe-**

Óbed: *indecl.;* Obed, son of Ruth

obediénter: obediently

obediéntia -ae, **obedítio** -ónis: f.; obedience, compliance, submission to authority

obédio -íre: (4); obey, submit to, yield to

óbeo -íre: (4); die, fulfill, perform

obérro -áre: (1); wander about

obésus -a -um: fat, stout, obese

óbex -icis: c.; hindrance, obstacle

obf- *see also* **off-**

obfúsco -áre: (1); darken, blacken, obscure, vilify, degrade

óbiter: by the way, in passing, incidently

óbitus -us: m.; death

objéctio -ónis: f.; contempt, upbraiding, reproach, objection, throwing before, putting before

objectívus -a -um: objective; **objectíve:** *adv.*

objécto -áre: (1); put in the way, set against

objéctum -i: n.; object, thing

objéctus -us: m.; obstacle, appearance, sight, spectacle

objício -ere -jéci -jéctum: (3); drive away, charge against

objurgátio -ónis: f.; injury, blaming, reproving, rebuke, reprehension

objurgátor -óris: m.; blamer, reprover, scolder, chider

Oblátae -árum: f. pl.; Oblates

oblátio -ónis: f.; offering, oblation, religious sacrifice

oblátor -óris: m.; offerer, one who offers

oblatória -ae: f.; cruet

oblatrátor -óris: m.; railer, one who barks or shouts at

oblátus -a -um: offered; *perf. pass. part. of* **óffero;** *as a n. pl. noun:* the oblata, bread and wine offered at Mass

oblectaméntum -i: n., **oblectátio** -ónis: f.; pleasure, amusement, allurement

oblécto -áre: (1); delight, please, amuse

obligátio -ónis: f.; obligation, ensnaring, entangling, bond

obligatórius -a -um: obligatory

óbligo -áre: (1); entangle, involve, obligate, oblige

oblíquus -a -um: different, sidelong, oblique, slanting away, indirect; **in oblíquo:** indirectly

oblítero -áre: (1); blot out

oblitterátor -óris: m.; obliterator

oblívio -ónis: f., **oblívium** -ii: n.; oblivion, forgetfulness, being forgotten

obliviósus -a -um: forgetful

oblivíscor -i -lítus: *dep.* (3); forget

oblívium -ii: *see* **oblívio**

oblóngus -a -um: long

oblóquor -i -locútus: *dep.* (3); revile, slander, detract, speak against

obluctátio -ónis: f.; vehement opposition

obmúrmuro -áre: (1); murmur against

obmússito (obmússo) -áre: (1); whisper or mutter against

obmutésco -ere -mútui: (3); be dumb, be mute, be speechless, be silent

obnéxus -us: m.; connection

obnítor -ári: *dep.* (1); strive, struggle, push, press, lean

obníxe: earnestly, with all one's might

obnóxius -a -um: subject to, submissive, complying, liable, obedient to, exposed

obnúbilo -áre: (1); overcloud, darken, obscure, dim

obnúbo -ere -núpsi -núptum: (3); cover

oboe- *see also* **obe-**

oboediénter: obediently

oboediéntia -ae, **oboedítio** -ónis: f.; obedience

oboédio -íre: (4); obey, heed

óbolus (óbulus) -i: m.; obol, a small Greek coin

Óbolus S. Pétri: Peter's pence

obórior, oboríri -órtus: *dep.* (4); arise, appear

obrépo -ere -répsi -réptum: (3); take by surprise, creep upon, crawl to, steal upon

obréptio -ónis: f.; statement of falsehood; suprise attack, suprise or sudden temptation, a sneaking up; *see* *Appendix*

obrigésco -ere -rígui: (3); become stiff or frozen

obrízus (obrýsus) -a -um: fine, refined, finest; *as a n. noun:* fine gold

obrogátio -ónis: f.; obrogation; *see* *Appendix*

óbrogo -áre: (1); abrogate, evade, invalidate, supersede, modify

óbruo -ere -rui -rúptum: (3); bury, overwhelm, cover over

obrýsus: *see* **obrízus**

obscoénus (obscénus) -a -um: foul, filthy, offensive, obscene

obscúritas -átis: f.; obscurity, spiritual darkness

obscúro -áre: (1); darken, obscure

obscúrus -a -um: obscure, dark, secret; **in obscúrum:** into the darkenss; **obscúre:** *adv.*

obsecrátio -ónis: f.; prayer, entreaty, supplication, public prayer

óbsecro -áre: (1); beseech, implore, entreat

obsecúndo -áre: (1); comply or fall in with, be subservient to

óbsequens -éntis: dutiful, obedient, yielding

obséquiae -árum: f. pl.; funeral services

obséquium -ii: n.; homage, service, worship, deference, respect; *see* *Appendix*

óbsequor -i -secútus: *dep.* (3); obey, pay homage to, respect

óbsero -áre: (1); bolt, bar, fasten

óbsero -ere -sévi -sítum: (3); sow, plant

observábilis -is -e: remarkable, observable

Obsérvans -ántis: m.; Observant

observánter (observáte): carefully, observantly, sedulously

observántia -ae: f., **observátio** -ónis: f.; observance, abstinence, practice,

observation, reverence, respect; *see*
Appendix

observátor -óris: m.; observer

obsérvo -áre: (1); observe, watch, mark,
note, regard

óbses -idis: c.; hostage

obséssus -i: m.; one posessed by the devil

obsídeo -ere -sédi -séssum: (2); enclose,
beset, remain

obsídio -ónis: f.; siege

obsignátio -ónis: f.; sealing, sealing up

obsígno -áre: (1); seal, sign and seal

obsísto -ere -stiti: (3); resist, oppose,
withstand, hinder

obsolésco -ere -évi -étum: (3); grow old,
wear out, decay

obsolétus -a -um: obsolete, worn out,
cast off

obsónium -ii: n.; relish, sweetmeats

obstáculum -i: n.; hindrance, obstacle

obstetríco -áre: (1); be a midwife

obstétrix -ícis: f.; midwife

obstinátus -a -um: obstinate, stubborn,
resolute, determined; **obstináte:** *adv.*

obstipátio -ónis: f.; close pressure

obstipésco: *see* **obstupésco**

óbsto -áre -stiti -státum: (1); stop,
check, stand in front of, hinder,
oppose, stand against, obstruct,
impede; **non obstánte:**
notwithstanding

obstreptáculum -i: n.; outcry, clamor
against

obstríngo -ere -strínxi -stríctum: (3);
oblige, bind

óbstruo -ere -strúxi -strúctum: (3);
close, stop up, hinder, build against

obstrúsus -a -um: covered, concealed

obstupefácio -ere: (3); astonish,
astound, amaze

obstupésco (obsti-) -ere
-stípui(-stúpui): (3); be astonished,
amazed, astounded, or frightened

óbsum -esse, óbfui (óffui): be against, be
prejudicial to, hinder, injure

obsurdátus -a -um: made deaf

obsurdésco -ere: (3); become deaf

obtéctus -a -um: covered over

óbtego -ere -téxi -téctum: (3); cover,
protect

obtemperátor -óris: m.; one who obeys

obtémpero -áre: (1); obey, comply with,
submit to, attend to

obténdo -ere -téndi -téntum: (3); hide,
cover, stretch before, spread before

obtenebrátio -ónis: f.; darkness

obténebro -áre: (1); darken

obténebror -ári: *dep.* (1); be obscured

obténtus -us: m.; excuse, pleading

óbtero -ere -trívi -trítum: (3); crush,
trample

obtéstor -ári: *dep.* (1); entreat, implore;
adjure, call to witness

obtíneo -ére -tínui -téntum: (2); obtain,
secure, lay hold of, prevail, maintain,
occupy, hold

obtíngo -ere -tigi: (3); fall to the lot of,
happen, occur, touch, strike

obtrectátio -ónis: f.; detraction, envious
disparagement

obtrécto -áre: (1); disparage, decry

obtúndo -ere -túdi -túsum: (3); dull,
make blunt, weaken, make weary

obturátio -ónis: f.; stopping up of the
ears

obtúro -áre: (1); close, stop up, refuse to
listen

obtúsus (optúnsus, optúsus) -a -um:
blunt, dull, obtuse

óbulus -i: *see* **óbolus**

obumbrátio -ónis: f.; shadow,
overshadowing, darkening

obúmbro -áre: (1); overshadow, shadow,
darken, shade

obveniéntia -ae: f.; accident, chance

obvénio -íre: (4); meet, fall to, be
allotted to

obventiónes -um: f. pl.; income, revenue

obvérsor (obvérso) -ári: *dep.* (1); oppose, withstand, resist

óbviam: on the way, toward, against

óbviam íre: go to meet

óbviam veníre: meet

óbvio -áre: (1); meet, go forth to meet

óbvius -a -um: in or on the way, meeting, easy of access, affable, courteous, at hand, obvious

obvólvo -ere -vólvi -volútum: (3); wrap up, cover all around, muffle

occ- *see also* obc-

occásio -ónis: f.; occasion, opportunity, fit time; occasiónem náctus: having found the occasion

occásus -us: m.; setting, falling, setting of the sun

óccidens -éntis: m.; west, evening

occidentális -is -e: western

óccido -ere -cidi -cásum: (3); set, go down, fall, perish, die

occído -ere -cídi -císum: (3); kill, slay, knock down, beat

occísio -ónis: f.; slaughter, murder

occísor -óris: m.; murderer, killer

occisórius -a -um: for slaughter or killing

occipítium -ii: n.; back of head

occlúsus -a -um: closed up, restrained

occúbitus -us: m.; going down, setting; death

occúlco -áre: (1); tread, trample on

ócculo -ere -cúlui -cúltum: (3); hide, conceal

occúlto -áre: (1); hide, conceal

occultátio -ónis: f.; concealment, hiding

occúltis -is -e, occúltus -a -um: secret, concealed, private; occúltum -i: n.; secret or hidden sin, something hidden; occúlte, in occúlto: *adv.*

occúmbo -ere -cúbui -cúbitum: (3); fall, fall down, go down

occupátio -ónis: f.; occupation

occupátus -a -um: occupied, busy, engaged

óccupo -áre: (1); occupy, seize, take, invest, loan, lend

occúrrens -éntis: current, of the day

occurréntia -ae: f.; occurrence; meeting of two feasts on one day

occúrro -ere -cúrri -cúrsum: (3), occúrso -áre: (1); go to meet, meet, come to, occur

occúrsus -us: m.; meeting, course, occurrence, falling in with

océanus -i: m.; ocean, sea

océllus -i: m.; little eye

ócius: rapidly, speedily, more quickly

ócrea -ae: f.; metal greave

octáva -ae: f.; octave, a period of eight days, the eighth day after a feast

Octáva infántium: Low Sunday

Octáva mediána: Passion Sunday

Octavárium -ii: n.; a book containing readings for an octave

octávus -a -um: eighth

octíduum -i: n.; eight days

ócto: eight

Octóber -bris: m.; month of October

octogenárius -ii: m.; octogenarian

octogínta: eighty

oculáris -is -e: ocular

oculátus -a -um: sharp-eyed, seeing, conspicuous, visible

óculo -áre: (1); make or cause to see, make visible; enlighten

óculus -i: m.; eye

odíbilis -is -e: hateful

ódi, odísse: *defect. verb, perf. with pres. meaning;* hate, detest

ódium -ii: n.; hatred

ódor, odóris: m., odoraméntum -i: n., odorátus -us: m.; odor, smell

odóro (odóror) -áre: (1); to smell

oeconómia -ae: f.; economy, temporalities of an institution

oecónomus -i: m., oecónoma -ae: f.;
business manager, bursar

oeconómicus (oeconomísticus) -a -um:
economical, pertaining to temporalities

oecuménicus -a -um: ecumenical,
universal

oecumenísmus -i: m.; ecumenism

oenópola -ae: m.; dealer in wines

off- see also obf-

offendículum -i: n.; stumbling block

offéndo -ere -féndi -fénsum: (3); err,
offend, stumble, strike, knock against

offensíbilis -is -e: liable to stumble

offénsio -ónis, offénsa -ae: f.; offense,
aversion, disgust, hatred, dislike

offénsor -óris: m.; offender

ófferens principális: principal celebrant

offeréntia -ae: f.; offering

óffero, offérre, óbtuli, oblátum: irreg.;
offer, permit, allow, present, bring,
consecrate to God

offertória -ae: f.; cruet

offertórium -ii: n.; offertory; linen cloth
with which subdeacon held the paten

officiális -is -e: official; as a noun:
officer, official, member of diocesan
curia; see Appendix

offícians -ántis, officiátor -óris: m.;
celebrant

officiatúra -ae: f.; term of office

officína -ae: f.; workshop

offício -ere -féci -féctum: (3); impede,
hinder, oppose, hurt

offícium -ii: n.; office, service, duty,
courtesy, kindness, responsibility,
favor, liturgy of the Hours; see also
Appendix

Offícium Divínum: Divine Office, an
official service of prayer

Offícium Párvum B.V.M.: Little Office
of the Blessed Virgin Mary

Offícium Sánctae Maríae in Sábbato:
Office of the B.V.M. for Saturday

Offícium Tenebrárium: Matins and
Lauds of the last three days of Holy
Week

offúndo -ere -fúdi -fúsum: (3); pour out

offúsco -áre: (1); darken, obscure;
degrade

offúsus -a -um: concealing, spread
around

Og: indecl.; Og, king of Basan

ógdoas -adis: f.; the number eight

ólea -ae: f.; olive tree

ólea sáncta, oleórum sanctórum: n. pl.;
holy oils; see Appendix

oleárius -a -um: of olive oil

oleáster -tri: m.; wild olive tree

oleátus -a -um: moistened with oil

ólens -éntis: sweet-smelling

ólera -ae: f.; herb

óleum -i: n.; oil

Óleum catechumenórum: holy oil used
at baptism

Óleum infirmórum: oil for anointing
the sick

Óleum sanctórum: holy oil (chrism)
used for baptism, confirmation, holy
orders, and special consecrations

olfactoriólum -i: n.; smelling flask, scent
or perfume bottle

olfáctus -us: m.; smelling, smell, sense of
smell

olfácio -ere -féci -fáctum: (3); smell

olíbanum -i: n.; frankincense

ólim: formerly, once, once upon a time,
at times, long ago, for a long while

olíva -ae: f.; olive tree, olive

olivétum -i: n.; olive grove

Olivétum -i: n.; Mount Olivet

olívum -i: n.; olive oil

ólla -ae: f.; pot, earthenware jar, caldron;
óllae cárnium: fleshpots

ólor -óris: m.; swan

ólus -eris: n.; herb

oméga: last letter of the the Greek
alphabet

omíssio -ónis: f.; omission

omítto -ere: (3); omit, leave undone

ómnia -ium: n. pl.; all things; *see Appendix*

omnícreans -ántis: all-creating

omnígenus -a -um: all-begetting

omnímodus -a -um: complete, entire, of all sorts and kinds

omníno: altogether, entirely, totally, utterly

omnípater -tris: m.; father of all

omnipóllens -éntis: all-powerful, almighty

omnípotens -éntis: almighty, omnipotent, all-powerful, holding all

omnipoténtia -ae: f.; might

ómnis -is -e: all, every; **nóstrum ómnes:** all of us

omníscius -a -um: omniscient

omophágia -ae: f.; flesh-eater, cannibal

omophórion -ii: n.; *Greek;* the pallium of a bishop

ónager (onágrus) -i: m.; wild ass

ónero -áre: (1); burden, load down, overwhelm, oppress

ónerus (onerósus) -a -um: burdensome, heavy

onocentaúrus -i: m.; ass-centaur; impure person

onocrótalus -i: m.; pelican

onomásticus -a -um: pertaining to names

ontológia -ae: f.; ontology

ontológicus -a -um: ontological

ónus -eris: n.; burden, load, cargo, obligation

onustátus (onústus) -a -um: burdened, laden

onýchinus -a -um: of onyx

opácus -a -um: dark, obscure

ópera -ae: f.; work, labor, care, attention, aid, assistance, service, pains; **óperam dáre:** work hard at, devote oneself to

óperans -ántis: m.; worker, agent

operárius -a -um: working; *as a noun:* laborer, worker

operátio -ónis: f.; operation, work, toil, trade, business, virtue, action

operatívus -a -um: creative, formative

operátor -óris: m., **operátrix** -ícis: f.; worker, framer, maker, creator

operatótius -a -um: conducive to action

operculátus -a -um: with a lid or cover

opérculum -i: n.; lid, cover

operiméntum -i: n.; a covering

opério -íre: (4); clothe, cover, cover over

operistítium -ii: n. strike, work stoppage

óperor -ári: *dep.* (1); work, labor, be occupied with, cause, produce

operósus -a -um: hard, laborious, active, busy, productive

operósitas -átis: f.; elaborate workmanship, extra effort

operósus -a -um: active, busy, industrious, painstaking, efficacious, toilsome, laborious; **operóse:** *adv.*

opertórium -ii: n.; cover, vesture, mantle

ópes -ópum: f. pl.; riches, wealth, resources, property, substance

Óphir: *indecl.;* Ophir, a gold-producing country

ópifex -icis: c.; worker

opifícium -ii: n.; aid

opílio -ónis: m.; shepherd

opímus -a -um: rich, fruitful, fat, abundant

opinábilis -is -e: conjectural, open to opinions

opínio -ónis: f.; rumor, fame, opinion

opínor -ári: *dep.* (1); think, suppose, imagine

opitulátio -ónis: f.; help, assistance

opítulo (opítulor) -áre: (1); help, aid, assist

opórtet -tére opórtuit: (2); *impers.;* it is needful, necessary, fit, or proper

oppándo -ere: (3); spread or stretch out

oppánsum -i: n.; covering, envelope

óppeto -ere -ívi (-ii) -ítum: (3);
encounter, meet, meet with
oppidánus -a -um: of a town; *as a noun:*
citizen, townsperson
oppídulum -i: n.; small town, village
óppidum -i: n.; town
oppignerátor -óris: m.; one who pledges
or takes a pledge
oppígnero -áre: (1); pledge
oppílo -áre: (1); close up, shut up, stop
óppleo -ére -plévi -plétum: (2); fill, fill
up
oppóno -ere -pósui -pósitum: (3); set or
place against, oppose, expose, lay bare,
abandon; oppósitus -a -um: opposed
to, opposite
oppósitus -us: m.; an opposing,
interposition, intervention,
opposition, citation against
opportúnitas -átis: f.; want, need, due
time, suitable time, opportunity
opportúnus -a -um: fit, opportune,
seasonable; opportúne: *adv.;*
opportúnius: *comp. adv.*
oppositío -ónis: f.; opposition
oppósitor -óris: m.; one who opposes
oppréssio -ónis: f.; slavery, trouble,
oppression
oppréssor -óris: m.; suppressor
ópprimo -ere -préssi -préssum: (3);
oppress, overwhelm, crush, press down
oppróbrium -ii: n.; reproach, taunt,
derision, scorn, mockery, disgrace
oppúgno -áre: (1); attack, storm, besiege
ops, ópis: f.; help, aid, assistance, solace,
power, ability, support; ópe: with help
Ops, Ópis: f.; Ops, goddess of plenty,
riches, and power
optábilis -is -e: desired, desirable
optátio -ónis: f., optátum -i: n.; wish,
desire
óptimas -átis: m.; chief, aristocrat, most
important person

óptimus -a -um: best, perfect, very good;
óptime: *adv.*
óptio -ónis: f.; choice, option
ópto -áre: (1); wish, desire, choose,
select; *see Appendix*
optúnsus (optúsus): *see* obtúsus
opuléntia -ae: f.; opulence, wealth,
riches, resources, power
opuléntus -a -um: opulent, rich,
wealthy; opulénter: *adv.*
ópus -eris: n.; deed, work, wages, labor,
book
ex ópere operáto: by its own power
ópus citándum (op. cit.): the work
that must be cited
opus citatum (op. cit.): the work cited
ópus est: there is need, it is necessary
ópus habére: to have need
quánto ópere: how greatly, how much
súmmo ópere: in the highest degree
opúsculum -i: n.; small work
Ópus Déi: work of God; Divine Office
óra -ae: f.; border, edge, rim, extremity
oráculum -i: n.; oracle, revelation,
utterance, oratory, shrine
orális -is -e: oral
órans -ántis: praying; *pres. part. of* óro
orárium -ii: n.; stole
orátio -ónis: f.; prayer, supplication,
beseeching, oration, discourse
orationále -is: n.; book containing
Orations said at Mass
orátio reális: real or effective prayer
oratiúncula -ae: f.; short prayer
orátor -óris: m., orátrix -ícis: f.; speaker,
one who prays, petitioner
oratórium -ii: n.; oratory, local chapel;
see Appendix
orátus -us: m.; request, entreaty
orbátus -a -um: bereaved
órbis -is: m.; world, earth, circle, ring,
orbit
órbis terrárum: earth
orchéstra -ae: f.; orchestra

órcus -i: m.; infernal regions

Ordinále -is: n.; former name for the Ritual

ordinándus -i: m.; ordinand, candidate for holy orders

Ordinárium -ii: n.; a book containing a ritual

Ordinárium Divíni Offícii: Ordinary of the Divine Office, containing the parts that do not change

ordinárius -a -um: ordinary, regular, usual, in order; *as a m. noun:* an ecclesiastic who has ordinary (not delegated) jurisdiction, an ordinary; **ordinárie:** *adv.; see Appendix*

ordinátim: in order, in succession, successively

ordinátio -ónis: f.; ordination; ordinance, decree, system, regulation, curriculum; establishment

ordinátor -óris: m., **ordinátrix** -ícis: f.; one who ordains, arranger, regulator

ordinatórius -a -um: procedural

órdino -áre: (1); ordain, arrange, order, establish, appoint

órdior -íri, órsus: *dep.* (4); begin, commence

órdo -inis: m.; order, rite, manner, authority, ascendancy; *see Appendix*

Óreb: *indecl.; Hebrew;* Oreb, prince of Midian

orémus pro ínvicem: let us pray for one another

orétenus: orally

órfanus: *see* **órphanus**

orgánicus -a -um: organic, mechanical, of a musical instrument, musical; *as a noun:* musician; **orgánice:** *adv.*

organísmus -i: m.; organism

organíso -áre: (1); play the organ

organísta -ae: c.; organist

organizátio -ónis: f.; organization

organizátus -a -um: organized, arranged

órgano -áre: (1); sing harmonized chant

órganum -i: n.; musical instrument, organ, organ of the body

orichálcum -i: n.; brass

óriens -éntis: m.; orient, east, dawn, rising sun; **Óriens:** the Messias

orientális -is -e: oriental, eastern

Orientális -is: c.; a Catholic of the Eastern rites; *see Appendix*

orientátio -ónis: f.; orientation, guidelines, directives

originális -is -e, **originárius** -a -um; original, of origin; **origináliter:** *adv.*

orígo -inis: f.; origin, beginning, source

órior -íri, órtus: *dep.* (4); arise, come forth, appear

ornaméntum -i: n.; ornament, furniture, decoration, vestment

ornátus -us: m.; adornment, dress, decoration, equipment, furniture

órno -áre: (1); adorn, trim, garnish, decorate, equip

óro -áre: (1); pray, supplicate, offer petitions to, plead; *see Appendix*

orphanatróphium -ii: n.; orphanage

órphanus (órfanus) -a -um: without parents; *as a noun:* orphan

orthodóxus -a -um: orthodox

órtus -a -um: sprung, born, descended from; **órtus** -us: m.; east, rising of the sun, origin, birth; **órto máne:** early morning

ortygométra -ae: f. quail

óryx -gis: m.; wild goat

O Salutáris Hóstia: O Saving Victim; a Benediction hymn

os, óris: n.; mouth, face, countenance

os, óssis: n.; bone; **óssa:** *can be figurative in the pl.:* innermost part, soul

Osánna: *see* **Hosánna**

óscito -áre: (1); gape

osculatórium -ii: n.; crucifix with which kiss of peace was given

ósculor -ári: *dep.* (1); kiss, caress

ósculum -i: n.; kiss

Ósee: *indecl.,* **Ósea** -ae: m.; Hosea, a
minor prophet

ósor -óris: m.; one who hates

óssa: *see* **os**

ossuárium (ossárium) -ii: n.; bone urn,
vase for bones

osténdo -ere -téndi -ténsum(-téntum):
(3); show, display, expose

osténsio (ostentátio) -ónis: f.; showing,
display, evidence, revealing

ostensórium -ii: n.; monstrance,
ostensorium, vessel for Blessed
Sacrament at Benediction

osténto -áre: (1); show, exhibit, show off,
present, hold as an example, point out,
reveal, disclose

osténtum -i: n.; prodigy, unusual form
of a fetus

osténtus -us: m.; display, spectacle

ostiariátus -us: m.; former minor order
of porter

ostiárius -a -um: of the gate or door; *as
a noun:* porter, portress

ostiátim: from door to door

Óstia Tiberína -órum: m. pl.; Ostia

Ostiénsis -is -e: of Ostia

ostíolum -i: n.; small door

óstium -ii: n.; door, gate, entrance

óstrea -ae: f.; oyster

otiósus -a -um: idle, at leasure, with no
occupation, empty, useless; **otióse:** *adv.*

ótium -ii: n.; leisure, free time,
inactivity, idleness, rest, repose, quiet,
sloth

ovíle -is: n.; sheepfold

ovínus -a -um: of sheep

óvis -is: f.; sheep

óvo -áre: (1); rejoice

óvum -i: n.; egg

Oxónium -ii: n.; Oxford

P

pábulum -i: n.; food, fodder,
nourishment
pacális -is -e: peaceful, relating to peace
pacátrix -ícis: f.; peacemaker
pacátus (pacíficus) -a -um: pacified,
peaceful, peaceable, serene, quiet, calm
pácem: *see Appendix*
pácifer -a -um: peace-bringing
pacificále -is: n.; metal disk with image
of crucifix once used for the pax at
Mass
pacificátio -ónis: f.; pacification,
establishment of peace
pacificátor -óris: m.; peacemaker
pacífico (páco, pacíficor) -áre: (1);
pacify, grant peace, make peace
pacíficum -i: n.; peace offering
pacíficus -a -um: peaceful, quiet, at rest;
pacífice: *adv.*
pacíscor, pacísci, páctus: *dep.* (3); make
a bargain, agreement, or covenant
páco: *see* **pacífico**
pácta -ae: f.; betrothed spouse
páctio -ónis: f., **páctum** -i: n.; bargain,
contract, agreement, covenant
páctus -a -um: agreed upon, settled,
appointed, promised
pae- *see also* **pe-, poe-**
paéan -is: m.; hymn, paean, song of
triumph
paedagógia -ae: f.; instruction, teaching,
education
paedagógicus -a -um: pedagogical,
educational
paedagógus -i: m.; instructor,
pedagogue, custodian
paedíco -áre: (1); practice unnatural vice
paédor -óris: m.; filth, dirt

paelicátus -us: *see* **pelicátus**
paéne: almost, well-nigh
paénitens -éntis: c.; penitent
paeniténtia -ae: f.; penitence,
repentance, penance, sacrament of
reconciliation
paenitentiális -is -e: penitential
Paenitentiária -ae: f.; Sacred
Penitentiary, a tribunal of the Holy See
for matters of the internal form
Paenitentiárius -ii: m.; president of the
Paenitentiária
paeníteo (paeníteor) -ére -ui: (2); *often
impers.;* cause to repent, repent, be
sorry, be displeased, repent, be sorry,
rue, grieve
paénula -ae: f.; chasuble, cloak
Paganísmus -i: m.; paganism
pagánus -a -um: heathen, not a Jew or
Christian, pagan; peasant, rustic,
villager; *as a noun:* pagan, heathen
pagélla -ae: f.; altar card, card
pagína -ae: f.; page, leaf, paper
págus -i: m.; village
paidophília -ae: f.; pedophilia
paidophiliátor -óris: m.; pedophile
Palaestína -ae, **Palaestíne** -es: f.;
Palestine
Palaestíni -órum: m. pl.; inhabitants of
Palestine, Philistines
palaéstra -ae: f.; gymnasium, school
pálam: openly, publicly, without
concealment, apparently, evidently
palátha -ae: f.; dried fig
palatínus -i: m; palace official
palátium -ii: n.; palace, imperial court
palátum -i: n.; palate, taste
pálea -ae: f.; straw, chaff

paliúrus -i: m.; thorny shrub

pálla -ae: f.; pall, altar cloth, curtain, cover for chalice, cover for coffin

pállens -éntis: pale in color, pallid

pálleo -ére -ui: (2); fade, be pale

pallésco -ere, pállui: (3); grow pale, turn pale, lose color

pállidus -a -um: pale, pallid, wan

pállio -áre: (1); soften, relieve, cover, cloak

pallíolum -i: n.; small cloak

pállium -ii: n.; cloth, garment, cover for altar, cloak; pallium; *see Appendix*

pállor -óris: m.; paleness, pallor

pálma -ae: f.; palm, hand; palm tree, palm branch, sign of victory, hymn of victory

　Domínica in rámis palmárum: Palm Sunday

　Palmárum áltera díes: feast of the Ascension

palmatória -ae: f.; hand candlestick

pálmes -itis: m.; branch, shoot of a vine, vine

pálmus -i: m.; palm of the hand, hand; *as a measure:* span, twelve digits

pálor -ári: *dep.* (1); wander or stray about

palpátio -ónis: f.; trembling, terror

palpébra -ae: f.; eyelid

pálpito -áre: (1); blink, tremble, beat, throb

pálpo -áre: (1); handle, feel, touch

pálus -údis: f.; swamp

pálus -i: m.; a post, stake

palúster -tris, -tre: marshy

Pamphýlia -ae: f.; Pamphylia

pampínus -i: c.; vine leaf

panárium -ii: n.; breadbasket

Pandéctae -árum: f. pl.; Pandects, a collection of Roman laws

pándo -ere, pándi, pássum (pánsum): (3); open, lay bare, stretch out, expand, announce, tell, publish, speak out

pándus -a -um: bent, curved, crooked

pángo -ere, pánxi (pégi, pepígi), pánctum (páctum): (3); make, sing, compose, record, fix, fasten, ratify, agree, drive in, promise, pledge

panhágia -ae: f.; "all holy"; a pectoral cross worn by Greek bishops

panífica -ae: f.; cook, baker

pánis -is: m.; bread, loaf, food

　Pánis Angélicus: scriptural allusion to the manna in the desert; name of a hymn in honor the Blessed Sacrament

　Pánis coélicus: another name for the manna in the desert

paniséllus -i: m.; linen cloth formerly attached to the crosier

pannículus -i: m.; small cloth

pánnus -i: m.; cloth; pl.: swaddling clothes

panthéra -ae: f.; panther

Pantheísmus -i: m.; pantheism

Pápa -ae: m.; Pope

papális -is -e: papal; *see Appendix*

papátus -us: m.; papacy

Páphos (Páphus) -i: f.; Paphos, a city in Cyprus

papílio -ónis: m.; tent, pavilion, moth, butterfly

papílla -ae: f.; nipple, teat, breast

pápula -ae: f.; blister, pimple

papýrio -ónis: f.; place filled with reeds, papyrus marsh

papýrum -i: n., **papýrus** -i: m.; papyrus, reed used to make papyrus or writing material

par, páris: like, equal; *as a m. or f. noun:* companion, comrade, spouse; *as a n. noun:* pair, couple; **pári módo:** in like manner

parábilis -is -e: procurable

parábola -ae: f.; parable, similitude, illustration, comparison

parabolánus -i: m., parabolána -ae: f.; person who visited the sick in Eastern churches

parabólicus -a -um: parabolic

Parácletus (Paráclitus) -i: m.; Paraclete, Holy Spirit, advocate

paradígma -atis: n.; model, example

Paradísus -i: m.; Paradise

paradísus -i: m.; vestibule of a church; park, orchard

parágraphus -i: m.; paragraph

Paralipómenon: indecl., Paralipómena -órum: n.; Paralipomenon, two books of the O.T., also called Chronicles

parallélus -a -um: parallel, similar

parallelísmus -i: m.; parallelism

paralýticus -a -um: paralyzed, palsied; as a noun: one stricken with palsy

paramánus -us: f.; cuff, edge of sleeve

paraméntum -i: n.; sacred vestment, ornament

paramonárius -ii: m.; sexton, sacristan, prebendary

Páran: see Pháran

paranýmpha -ae: f.; bridesmaid

paranýmphus -i: m.; groomsman

paraphonísta -ae: c.; leader of a section of a choir

Parascéve -es: f.; day of preparation, day before Sabbath, Good Friday

parátio -ónis: f.; striving after, preparation

paratúra -ae: f.; preparation, furniture, furnishings

parátus -a -um: ready, prepared; perf. pass. part. of páro

párce: sparingly, moderately

parcimónia -ae: f.; self-denial

párcitas -átis: f.; frugality, temperance, moderation, sparingness

párco -ere, pepérci (pársi, párcui), pársum (párcitum): (3); spare, keep, preserve, forbear, abstain, desist

párcus -a -um: sparing, stingy

párcus -i: m.; park, enclosure

párdus -i: m.; leopard

parecclésia -ae: f.; oratory, chapel

paregorízo -áre: (1); soothe, alleviate

párens -éntis: c.; parent

parentális -is -e: parental, of parents

páreo -ére -ui: (2); appear, become visible, be evident; obey, comply with, yield to

páries, paríetis: m.; wall, wall of a house

pariétinae -árum: f., pl.; fallen walls, ruins

párilis -is -e: similar, like, equal

pário -ere, péperi, pártum: (3); bear, bring forth, be deliverd of a child, give birth

Parisiénsis -is -e: of Paris

Parísii -órum: m. pl.; Paris

Parisíacus -a -um: of Paris; as a noun: citizen of Paris, Parisian

páritas -átis: f.; equality, parity

páriter: at the same time, with one accord, together, similarly, equally

páro -áre: (1); prepare, provide, make ready, furnish, establish

paróchia (paroécia) -ae: f.; parish; see Appendix

Parochiále -is: n.; a book of instructions for pastoral duties

parochiális (paroeciális) -is -e: of a parish, parochial; see Appendix

parochiánus (paroeciánus) -i: m.; parishoner

párochus -i: m.; parish priest, pastor, benefice

paroec-: see paroch-

parópsis -idis: f.; dish

párra -ae: f.; owl, woodpecker, bird of ill omen

parricída -ae: c.; murderer, parricide

parrúcca -ae: f.; wig

pars, pártis: f.; part, portion, lot, share, allotted possession; pl.: party, faction, side, quarters; *see Appendix*

ab hac párte: on this side

áliqua ex párte: in some respect

ex párte: in part

mágna ex párte: in a great degree

núlla ex párte: in no way

parsimónia -ae: f.; frugality, thrift, parsimony

partiális -is -e: partial; partiáliter: *adv.*

párticeps -ipis: sharing, partaking, participating; *as a c. noun:* partaker, sharer, participant, fellow, partner

partícipans -ántis: m., participátio -ónis: f.; participation, sharing, taking part

particípium -ii: n.; participle

partícipo -áre: (1); share, participate, impart, acquaint

partícula -ae: f.; part, particle, small part or bit, small host, phrase

particuláris -is -e: particular, partial; particuláriter: adv.

particularísmus -i: m., particuláritas -átis: f.; particularism, exclusiveness

pártim: partly, in part

pártior -íri: *dep.* (4); divide, part, distribute, share

partítio -ónis: f.; division, partition, sharing

partúrio -íre: (4); be in travail, desire to bring forth, bring forth; intend, imagine, brood over, meditate

parturítio -ónis: f., pártus -us: m.; travail, bringing forth, parturition, childbirth, labor, birth

párum: little, less, too little, not enough

parúra -ae: f.; ornament, embroidered work

parvipéndo -ere -pepéndi -pénsum: (3); esteem lightly

párvitas -átis: f.; small quantity, littleness, parvity

párvulus -a -um: small, little, youthful, young; *as a noun:* little child

párvus -a -um: small, little

Páscha -átis: n., Páscha -ae: f.; Pasch, Passover, Easter

Páscha annotínum: anniversary of a baptism

Páscha claúsum: Low Sunday

Páscha competéntium: Palm Sunday

Páscha flóridum: Palm Sunday

Páscha médium: Wednesday after Easter

Páscha rosárum: Pentecost Sunday

Paschále Praecónium: an ancient song of praise chanted on Holy Saturday

paschális -is -e: paschal, pertaining to the Pasch

pásco -ere, pávi, pástum: (3); feed, nourish, shepherd

páscor -ári: *dep.* (1); feed oneself, eat

páscua -ae: f., páscuum -i: n.; pasture, food

pascuális -is -e, páscuus -a -um: of a pasture, grazing

pásser -is: m.; sparrow

passíbilis -is -e: capable of suffering, susceptible to pain

pássim: here and there, far and wide, up and down, everywhere

pássio -ónis: f.; suffering, passion

Passionále -is: n.; a book containing the Acts of the Martyrs

Passionárium -ii: n.; a book of the lessons for the second nocturn

passívus -a -um: passive, capable of feeling; passíve: *adv.*

pássus -a -um: *perf. part. of* pátior

pássus -us: m.; pace, step; mília pássuum: thousand paces (about a mile)

pastophórium -ii: n.; room adjoining the temple, sacristy, place for sacred vessels

pástor -óris: m.; pastor, shepherd; *see Appendix*

pastorále -is: n.; book of instructions for pastors; staff or crosier

pastorális -is -e: pastoral, watchful; *see Appendix*

pastorális báculus: crosier

pastorálitas -átis: f.; office of pastor

pástus -us: m.; food, sustenance, pasture

patefácio -ere: (3); open, lay open, expose

patélla -ae: f.; plate, dish

pátena -ae *see* **pátina**

pátens -éntis: open, wide, manifest, clear; **paténter:** *adv.*

páteo -ére -ui: (2); be extended or open, lie or stand open, be visible, be accessible, be receptive

páter -tris: m.; father; *see Appendix*

patéra -ae: f.; shallow bowl

paterfamílias, patrisfamílias(-liae): m.; master or head of a house

Patérna cláritas: Christ

patérnitas -átis: m.; paternity

patérnus -a -um: paternal, fatherly; **patérne:** *adv.*

patésco -ere -ui: (3); lie open or extended

pathológia -ae: f.; disorder, illness, pathology

pathológicus -a -um: pathological, sick, disordered

patíbulum -i: n.; yoke, gibbet, ignominy

pátiens -éntis: patient, long-suffering; **patiénter:** *adv.*

patiéntia -ae: f.; patience

pátina (pátena) -ae: f.; broad, shallow dish; paten

pátior (pátio) -i, pássus: *dep.* (3); endure, suffer, bear with, allow, undergo

Pátmos (-us) -i: f.; Patmos

Pátrae -árum: f. pl.; Patras

patrátor -óris: m.; worker

patrátus -a -um: performed, accomplished; *perf. pass. part.* of **pátro**

pátria -ae: f.; fatherland, country, native land

patriárcha (patriárches) -ae: m.; patriarch; *see Appendix*

patriarchális -is -e: patriarchal

patriarchátus -us: m.; district under jurisdiction of a patriarch

patriárches -ae: *see* **partiárcha**

patrícius -ii: m.; patrician, distinguished citizen

patrimoniális -is -e: patrimonial, of patrimony

patrimónium -ii: n.; patrimony, inheritance

patrínus -i: m.; sponsor, godfather

pátrius -a -um: of a father, paternal, ancestral, native

pátro -áre: (1); perform, achieve, accomplish, work, effect

patrocínium -ii: n.; patronage, protection, legal assistance

patrocínor -ári: *dep.* (1); defend, protect

patróna -ae: f., **patrónus** -i: m.; patron, advocate, protector

patronátus -us: m.; patronage

patruélis -is: c.; cousin

pátruus -i: m.; uncle

pátulus -a -um: extended, open

paúci -ae -a: few; **paúcis:** in a few words

paúcitas -átis: f.; fewness, scarcity, paucity

paúcus -a -um: few, little

paulátim: gradually, little by little, by degree, few at a time

paulínus -a -um: Pauline; *as a m. noun:* Paulinus

paulísper: for a little while

paúlo: by a little

paúlo mínis: almost, nearly

paúlulum: a short or little time, a little
paúlulus -a -um: very little; *as a n. noun:*
trifle, bit
Paúlus -i: m.; Paul
paúper -eris: poor, needy, helpless,
destitute, indigent, impoverished; *as a
c. noun:* poor person
paupérculus -a -um: poor
paupéries -éi, paupértas -átis: f.;
poverty, misery, abandonment
paúsa -ae: f.; pause, stop, end, rest,
cessation
pausátio -ónis: f.; repose, rest, halting,
pausing
pauxíllum -i: n.; a little, small amount
páveo -ére, pávi: (2), pávito -áre: (1);
fear, tremble with fear, quake
pavésco -ere, pávi: (3); become afraid
pávidus -a -um: terrified, fearful,
trembling
paviméntum -i: n.; floor, pavement,
ground, earth, dust
pávio -íre: (4); beat down
pávito: *see* páveo
pávor -óris: m.; fear, dread, terror
pax, pácis: f.; peace, blessing, prosperity;
see Appendix
paxíllus -i: m.; stick, peg, pin
pe- *see also* pae-
peccátor -óris: m., peccátrix -ícis: f.;
sinner, transgressor
peccátrix -ícis: sinful
peccátum -i: n.; sin
pécco -áre: (1); sin, transgress
pécten -inis: n.; comb
pectoróle -is: n.; brooch for fastening a
cope
pectorális -is -e: pectoral, of the chest
péctus -oris: n.; chest, breast; heart, soul,
mind, seat of affections
peculiáris -is -e: peculiar, unique,
special; peculiáriter: *adv.*
peculiáritas -átis: f.; peculiarity,
distinctiveness, singularity

pecúlium -ii: n.; property, private
property
pecúnia -ae: f.; money
pecuniárius -a -um: relating to money,
pecuniary
pecuniósus -a -um: rich, wealthy
pécus -oris: n.; sheep, cattle, herd
pécus -udis: f.; single head of cattle,
beast, brute, animal
péda -ae: f.; footstep
pedális -is -e: belonging to the foot; *as a
f. noun:* a measure the size of a foot, a
measure
pedáneus -a -um: relating to feet;
lígnum pedáneum: altar step
pédes -itis: m.; foot soldier
pedéster -tris -tre: on foot, pedestrian
pédes viátor: pilgrim
pédica -ae: f.; snare, trap, fetter
pediséquus -i: m.; follower, attendant
pedophilátor -óris: n.; pedophile,
pederast
pedophília -ae: f.; pedophilia, pederasty
pédum -i: n.; shepherd's crook, crosier
péior -ior -ius: worse
Pelagiáni -órum: m.; Pelagians
Pelagianísmus -i: m.; the heresy of
Pelagianism
pélagus -i: n.; sea, ocean, the deep
pelicátus (pelli-, paeli-) -us: m.;
concubinage
péllax -ácis: seductive, deceitful
pellicánus -i: m.; pelican
pellicátus -us: *see* pelicátus
pellícea -ae: f.; cassock
pellíceus (pellicius) -a -um: made of
skins, leather
pellício -ere -léxi -léctum: (3), pellíceo
-ére: (2); seduce, entice, allure, decoy
pellícula -ae: f.; little skin
péllis -is: f.; hide, skin, tent, tent cloth
péllo -ere, pépuli, púlsum: (3); cast out,
banish, drive away
pellúvium -ii: n.; basin for washing feet

pélta -ae: f.; shield

pelvícula -ae: f.; small basin or dish

pélvis -is: f.; basin, dish

péndeo -ére, pepéndi: (2); hang, hover, depend, be pending

péndo -ere, pepéndi, pénsum: (3); cause to hang down, suspend, weigh, ponder, estimate, consider, esteem, deliberate

péndulus -a -um: hanging

péne (paéne): almost, well-nigh

pénes: *prep. w. acc;* with, before, in the possession or power of, in the presence of, belonging to

penetrábilis -is -e: sharp, piercing, able to be penetrated

penetrália -ium: n. pl.; inmost parts or recesses, inmost chambers, closets, inmost self, spirit, life of the soul

pénetro -áre: (1); penetrate, enter

pénis -is: m.; tail, penis

pénitus -a -um: inward, interior, deep; **pénitus (pénite):** *adv.*

pénna (pínna) -ae: f.; feather

pennátus -a -um: feathered, winged

pénnula -ae: f.; small wing

pénsa -ae: f.; rations or provisions for a day

pensátio -ónis: f.; weighing out, compensation, recompense

pensátor (pénsor) -óris: m.; weigher, examiner

pénsio -ónis: f.; payment, pension

pensionárius -ii: m., **pensionária** -ae: f.; person on a pension

pensitátio -ónis: f.; payment, expense; valuables

pénsito (pénso) -áre: (1); pay, weigh, counterbalance, repay, compensate, make good, consider, ponder

pénsor -óris: m.; examiner, one who weighs or considers

pénsus -a -um: valued, prized, weighty, esteemed

pentacontárchus -i: m.; commander of fifty men

pentápolis -is: f.; district of five towns near the Dead Sea

Péntateúchus -i: m., **Pentatéuchum** -i: n.; Pentateuch, the first five books of the O.T.

pentecostális -is -e: Pentecostal

Pentecóste -es: f.; Pentecost, Whitsunday, fifty days after Easter

Pentecóstes Domínica: Pentecost

Pentecóstes média díes: Wednesday in Ember Week after Pentecost

penúria -ae: f.; want, need, penury, scarcity

pépo -ónis: m.; melon, pumpkin

per: *prep. w. acc.;* through, by

per áccidens: through its appearance or accidents, not of its very nature

per álium: through another

per módum áctus: *see Appendix*

per ómnia sáecula saeculórum: through all ages of ages (forever)

per se: in and of itself, by its very nature

péra -ae: f.; wallet, bag

perabúndans -ántis: extravagant, very numerous

peraéque: quite equally, quite evenly

perágens -éntis: c.; one who goes through to the end

pérago -ere -égi -áctum: (3); finish, accomplish, complete, go or pierce through, transfix, celebrate, attain

perágro -áre: (1); visit, travel, pass through

peramánter: very lovingly

perámbulo -áre: (1); walk about, go about, traverse, pass through

perantíquus -a -um: very ancient

peratténte: very attentively

percéllo -ere -cúli -cúlsum: (3); repel, shatter, ruin, strike down, overturn, daunt percéptio -ónis: f.; partaking, perception, comprehension, reception, collecting

percéptor -óris: m.; receiver, imbiber

percípio -ere -cépi -céptum: (3); take, partake, seize, attain, receive, hearken, perceive, learn; aúribus percípere: listen

pércitus -a -um: aroused, driven

pércolo -ere -cólui -cúltum: (3); reverence, honor, adorn, decorate

percóntans -ántis: inquiring

percontátio -ónis: f.; inquiry, interrogation

percóntor -ári: dep. (1); inquire

percrebésco (percrebr-) -ere: (3); become prevalent, be spread abroad, become well known

percrésco -ere crévi -crétum: (3); increase greatly

percúlsus -a -um: struck, smitten

percúpidus -a -um: very desirous

percúrro -ere -cucúrri(-cúrri) -cúrsum: (3); run through, hasten to, persevere to the end, travel, look over

percúsio -ónis: f.; rapid reflection

percússio -ónis: f.; striking, beating, beating time, rhythm, stroke

percússor -óris: m.; striker, assassin, executioner, bandit

percússus -a -um: struck down, killed, wounded, smitten, blighted

percútio -ere -cússi -cússum: (3); strike down, kill, wound

perdifficilis -is -e: very difficult

perdísco -ere -dídici: (3); learn thoroughly

perdítio -ónis: f.; perdition, ruin

pérditor -óris: m.; pérditrix -ícis: f.; destroyer, ruiner

pérdix -ícis: c.; partridge

pérdo -ere -didi -ditum: (3); lose, ruin, destroy

pérdolens -éntis: sorrowing, very sorrowful

perdúco -ere: (3); lead to, bring to, guide, conduct, lead through

perdúro -áre: (1); endure, last a long time, perdure, abide

perédo -ere: (3); eat up, consume

peréfficax -ácis: very efficient or efficacious

peréffluo -ere: (3); forget, drift away, flow through

péregre: abroad, in a strange land

peregrínans -ántis: c.; traveler, pilgrim

peregrinátio -ónis: f.; travel, pilgrimage

peregrínor (peregríno) -ári: dep. (1); travel, sojourn abroad, live in foreign lands

peregrínus -a -um: foreign, strange, exotic, from another land; as a noun: stranger, wanderer, pilgrim, traveler, foreigner; see Appendix

perémptio -ónis: f.; abatement; destroying

perémptor -óris: m.; destroyer, slayer

peremptórius -a -um: decisive, final,; peremptórie: adv.

perémptus -a -um: perf. pass. part. of périmo

perénnis -is -e: everlasting, lasting, eternal, perennial, perpetual; perénniter: adv.

perénnitas -átis: f.; eternity

perénno -áre: (1); last many years

péreo -íre -ii(-ívi) -itum: (4); perish, be lost, pass away, vanish, disappear, be wasted, die

perexsiccátus -a -um: very dried up

perféctio -ónis: f.; perfection, finishing, completing

perféctor -óris: m.; perfecter, one who completes, finisher

perféctus a -um: perfect, complete, finished, righteous, excellent; perfécte: adv.; see Appendix pérfero -férre -tuli -látum: irreg.; bear, bring, carry, carry through, report, complete

perfício -ere -féci -féctum: (3); make perfect, finish, perform, accomplish, work, effect, consummate, complete, do

pérfide: treacherously

perfídia -ae: f.; faithlessness

perfidiósus (pérfidus) -a -um: faithless, treacherous

perflámen -inis: n.; blast, breath, blowing through

pérfluo -ere -flúxi -flúctum: (3); flow, stream through

perfódio -ere -fódi -fóssum: (3); dig through, break open

perforátus -a -um: pierced

pérforo -áre: (1); pierce, bore through, perforate

perfricátio -ónis: f.; rubbing

perfríngo -ere -frégi -fráctum: (3); shatter, finish, break through

perfrúctio (perfruítio) -ónis: f.; complete enjoyment or fruition

pérfruor -frui -frúctus: dep. (3); enjoy thoroughly

pérfuga -ae: c.; deserter, fugitive

perfúgio -ere -fúgi -fúgitum: (3); flee, take refuge

perfúgium -ii: n.; refuge

perfúnctio -ónis: f.; performance, discharge

perfúndo -ere -fúdi -fúsum: (3); overwhelm, pour forth, pour over; fill with apprehension; moisten, anoint

perfúngor -fúngi -fúnctus: dep. (3); fulfil, perform, discharge

pergaméntum -i: n.; parchment

pérgamum -i: n.; pulpit

pérgo -ere, perréxi, perréctum: (3); proceed, continue

pérgula -ae: f.; beam for tapers or candles above an altar

perhíbeo -ére -ui -itum: (2); report, bear witness, propose, produce, attribute, ascribe, bestow, grant

períbolus -i: m.; circuit, enclosure

perichorésis -is(-eos): m.; see circuminséssio

períclitor -ári: dep. (1); be in danger, risk, jeopardize, try

perícope -es: f.; section of a book

periculósus -a -um: dangerous, perilous; periculóse: adv.

perículum -i: n.; danger, trial, peril, attempt, experiment; see Appendix

perículum mórtis: danger of death

perillústris -is -e: shining

périmo -ere -émi -émptum(-émtum): (3); destroy, slay, ruin, annihilate, remove completely

perínde: in like manner, just as

perindígeo -ére: (2); need greatly

perinsígnis -is -e: very remarkable, very conspicuous

periódicus -a -um: periodical, at regular intervals; as a n. noun: periodical (literature)

períodus -i: f.; complete sentence, period, legend, story, stage

peripséma -atis: n.; refuse, offscouring, filth

perirátus -a -um: angry, very angry

períscelis -idis: f.; anklet, leg band, garter

peristérium -ii: n.; dove-shaped container

peristróma -atis: n.; tapestry

perítia -ae: f.; skill, expertise, scientific knowledge

peritúrus -a -um: perishable

perítus -a -um, peritális -is -e: skilled, very learned; as a noun: expert, adviser; períte: adv.; see Appendix

perizóma -atis: n.; apron, girdle

perjúrium -ii: n.; false oath, perjury

perjúrius -ii: m., perjúria -ae: f.; perjurer

perjúro -áre: (1); swear falsely

perjúrus -a -um: oath-breaking, false, lying

perlábor -lábi -lápsus: *dep.* (3); glide along, slide through, slip through

pérlego -ere -légi -léctum: (3); examine accurately, read through

perliminária -órum: n. pl.; lintels

perlíno -ere -lívi(-lévi) -lítum: (3); besmear, anoint

perlúcidus -a -um: transparent

perlústro -áre: (1); traverse, pass over

permagníficus -a -um: very magnificent

pérmanens -éntis: permanent, enduring; permanénter: *adv.*

permáneo -ére -mánsi -mánsum: (2); remain, continue, endure, abide, persevere

permánsio -ónis: f.; a remaining, abiding in a place, persisting

pérmeo -áre: (1); go through, pass, cross, traverse

permísceo -scére -scui -stum (-xtum): (2); mix, commingle

permíssio -ónis: f., permíssus -us: m.; permission, leave

permíssus -a -um: permitted; permissíve: *adv.*

permítto -ere: (3); permit, suffer, allow, give leave, cede

permíxtio (permístio) -ónis: f.; mixture, mixing, confusion

permíxtus -a -um: intermingled, mixed, disordered, confused

permódicus -a -um: very small or moderate

permóveo -ére -móvi -mótum: (2); agitate, arouse

permúltus -a -um: very many, very much

permúndo -áre: (1); thoroughly cleanse or purify

permutátio -ónis: f.; exchange, change, alteration

permúto -áre: (1); change completely

pernecésse: *indecl. n. adj.;* very necessary, indispensable

pernícies -éi: f.; disaster, destruction

pernitiósus (perniciósus) -a -um: destructive, ruinous

pernócto -áre: (1); spend the night

peróro -áre: (1); pray, bring prayer to an end

perósus -a -um: hating

perpaúcus -a -um: very little; pl.: very few

perpéllo -ere -puli -púlsum: (3); urge, drive, compel, constrain, prevail on

perpéndo -ere -péndi -pénsum: (3); examine, weigh, consider, investigate

perpénsus -a -um: carefully examined

pérperam: perversely, wrongly, falsely

pérperus -a -um: perverse

pérpes -etis: perpetual, continuous, never-ending

perpéssio -ónis: f.; endurance, suffering

perpétior, pérpeti, perpéssus: *dep.* (3); endure, undergo, suffer

pérpetim: continually, unceasingly

pérpetro -áre: (1); do, perform, accomplish

perpetúitas -átis: f.; perpetuity, continuance, eternity

perpétuo -áre: (1); continue, make perpetual

perpétuus -a -um: everlasting, perpetual, continuous, unfailing, permanent; perpétuo (perpétue): *adv.*

perpláceo -ére -ui -itum: (2); please exceedingly

perplúres -ium: very many

perpólio -íre: (4); polish well

perpúlcher -chra -chrum: very beautiful

pérquam: as much as possible, extremely, exceedingly

perquíro -ere -quisívi -quisítum: (3); seek, examine carefully

perquisítio -ónis: f.; diligent search, careful examination

perrúmpo -ere -rúpi -rúptum: (3);
subdue, overpower, break through

Pérsa -ae: *see* Pérsis

Pérsae -árum: *see* Pérsi

perscríbo -ere -scrípsi -scríptum: (3);
write down, notify, relate in writing,
register

perscrutátio -ónis: f.; scrutiny

perscrútor (perscrúto) -ári: *dep.* (1);
search through, investigate

persecútio -ónis: f.; persecution

persecútor -óris: m.; persecutor

persecútus -a -um: *perf. part. of*
pérsequor

perséntio -íre: (4); perceive plainly, feel
deeply

pérsequor -qui -secútus: *dep.* (3);
pursue, follow perseveringly, persecute

perseverábilis -is -e: enduring,
persevering

perseverántia -ae: f.; perseverance

persevéro -áre: (1); persevere, persist,
continue, remain constant;
perseveránter: *adv.*

Pérsi -órum, Pérsae -árum: m. pl.;
Persians

Pérsis -idis, Pérsia -ae: f.; Persia

persísto -ere -stiti: (3); persist, remain

persitátio -ónis: f.; gift, payment

persolútio -ónis: f.; discharge,
performance, carrying out

persólvo -ere -sólvi -solútum: (3);
perform, discharge a duty, recite,
explain, offer, solve, pay, unloose

persóna -ae: f.; person, character, mask;
see Appendix

personális -is -e: personal, of a person;
personáliter: *adv.*

personálitas -átis: f.; personality,
character

personalizátio -ónis: f.; personal
relationship, personalization

personátus -a -um: masked, disguised

pérsono -áre -sónui -sónitum: (1);
shout, proclaim, sound, resound

perspéctor -óris: m.; one who
understands, a discerner

perspício -ere -spéxi -spéctum: (3); look
into, have regard for, examine

perspicúitas -átis: f.; clearness

perspícuus -a -um: evident, visible,
plain: perspícue: *adv.*

perstíllo -áre: (1); drip, leak

perstríngo -ere -strínxi -stríctum: (3);
lay hold upon, graze against, touch

persuádeo -ére -suási -suásum: (2);
persuade

persuasíbilis -is -e: convincing,
persuasive, eloquent

persuásio -ónis: f., persuásum -i: n.;
conviction, doctrine, belief, opinion,
persuasion

pertaésus -a -um: thoroughly weary

perténto -áre: (1); put to the test, try,
prove

perterrefácio -fácere -féci -fáctum: (3);
terrify thoroughly, scare the life out of

pertérreo -ére: (2); terrify greatly,
intimidate, frighten

pertimésco -ere -tímui: (3), pertímeo
-ére: (2); fear greatly

pertinácia -ae: f.; obstinacy, pertinacity,
constancy, firmness

pértinax -ácis: obstinate, persistent,
firm, pertinacious, tenacious,
constant; pertináciter: *adv.*

pertíneo -ére -tínui: (2); reach to,
stretch out for, belong to, pertain to,
relate to

pertíngo -ere: (3); extend to, come to,
reach, reach out for; attain

pertráctio -ónis: f.; a handling,
application

pertrácto (pertrécto) -áre: (1); handle,
treat, busy one's self with, investigate,
feel, scan, touch

pertránseo -íre: (4); go through, pass by,
traverse, pierce, go

perturbátio -ónis: f.; disturbance, confusion, disorder, trouble

pertúrbo -áre: (1); disturb, perturb

pertúsus -a -um: with holes, perforated

perúngo -ere -únxi -únctum: (3); anoint

perúrgeo -ére -úrsi: (2); urge ahead

perúro -ere -ússi -ústum: (3); parch, burn up, burn through

perútilis -is -e: very useful

pervádo -ere -vási -vásum: (3); come or go through

pérvago (pérvagor) -áre: (1); wander through, rove about

pervénio -íre -véni -véntum: (4); come, arrive, come to, attain to, reach

pervéntio -ónis: f.; arrival, coming

pervéntor -óris: m.; one who arrives

pervérsio -ónis: f.; perversion

pervérsitas -átis: f.; perversity, perverse inclination

pervérsus -a -um: perverse, evil; pervérse (pervórse): adv.

pervérto -ere -vérti -vérsum: (3); turn around, turn about

pervestigátio -ónis: f.; thorough search, investigation

pervestígo -áre: (1); search thoroughly, examine closely

pervetústus (pérvetus) -a -um: very old

pervicácia -ae: f.; stubbornness

pérvicax -ácis: f.; stubborn, obstinate, willful

pervígil -ilis: very or ever watchful

pervigílium -ii: n.; watch, vigil, eve, all-night watch

pervígilo -áre: (1); keep close watch, keep vigil

pervínco -ere -víci -víctum: (3); conquer, overcome

pervórse: see pervérsus

pérvius -a -um: passable, accessible, having a road through

pervulgátus (pervol-) -a -um: well-known

pervúlgo -áre: (1); make publicly known, publish

pes, pédis: m.; foot

péssimo -áre: (1); oppress, inflict harm on; make bad, spoil completely

péssimus -a -um: worst, most wicked, very evil, very serious, very grevious

péssulus -i: m.; bolt for a door

pessúmdo (pessúndo) -áre: (1); sink, ruin, destroy, undo, end

péstifer -a -um, péstilens -éntis: pestilential, destructive, noxious

pestiléntia -ae, péstis -is: f.; plague, pestilence

pétala -ae: f.; antipendium

pétens -éntis: c.; petitioner

petíbilis -is -e: able to be demanded

petítio -ónis: f.; petition, request, desire, prayer

petítor -óris: m., petítrix -ícis: f.; claimant, plaintiff, seeker

petitórium -ii: n.; complaint or declaration in a lawsuit

petitórius -a -um: petitory, of a petition

petítrix -ícis: see petítor

petítum -i: n., petítus -us: m.; a desire, request

péto -ere -ívi (-ii) -ítum: (3); ask, beg, beseech, entreat, request, seek, sue for, claim

pétra -ae: f.; rock

Pétra Ecclésiae: St. Peter

pétrinus (petrósus) -a -um: of stone

Pétrus -i: m.; Peter; Petrinus -a -um: pertaining to Peter

pétulans -ántis: wanton, lustful, freakish, capricious

petulánter: wantonly, boldly

phaenomenísmus -i: m.; phenomenalism

phaenómenon -i: n.; phenomenon

phalánga -ae: f.; band, group, host

phálero -áre: (1); adorn, decorate

phanerósis -is: f.; manifestation, revelation

phantásia -ae: f.; delusion, fancy, illusion, image, representation

phantásma -atis: n.; phantom, apparition, vision, appearance

phantásticus -a -um: imaginary, fantastic

Pháran (Páran): indecl.; Pharan, desert near the Dead Sea

Phárao -ónis: m.; Pharaoh

pharétra -ae: f. quiver

Pharisaéus -i: m.; Pharisee

pharisáicus -a -um: relating to the Pharisees, hypocritical

phármacum -i: n.; remedy, medicine

pharocántharus -i: m.; large chandelier

phárus -i: m.; candlestick

pháse -es: f.; rite, phase

Pháse: indecl.; Passover

phe: 17th letter of the Hebrew alphabet

phíala -ae: f.; censer, phial, small flask, vial, shallow bowl

Phílemon -ónis: m.; Philemon

Philippénses -ium: c. pl.; Philippians

Philippénsis -is -e: of Philippi

Philíppus -i: m.; Philip

Philistaéa -ae: f.; Philistia

Philisthaéus -i: m.; Philistine

Philisthíni -órum: m. pl.; Philistines

philocália -ae: f.; love of the beautiful

philósopha -ae: see philósophus

philosopháster -tri: m.; bad philosopher

philosóphia -ae: f.; philosophy

philosóphicus -a -um: philosophical

philósophus -i: m., philósopha -ae: f.; philosopher

philósophor -ári: dep. (1); philosophize

Phínees (Phínehas): indecl.; Phinees

Phoeníce -is(-es): f.; Phoenicia

photográphicus -a -um: photographic; photográphice: adv.

photostáticus -a -um: photostatic, photocopied; photostátice: adv.

phrásis is: f.; phrase, sentence

phrenésis -is: f.; madness, delirium, insanity, frenzy

phrenéticus -a -um: frantic, frenetic

phrýgium -ii: see frígium

phthísicus -a -um: consumptive

Phur: Purim, Jewish feast of Lots

phylactérium -ii: n.; phylactery, a frontlet worn by devout Jews

physharmónium -ii: n.; reed organ

phýsicus -a -um: physical, of physics, of nature, natural; phýsice: adv.

piaculáris -is -e: cleansing, expiatory, atoning

piáculum -i: n.; sin offering, propitiatory sacrifice, remedy, punishment, something requiring expiation, sin, crime, wicked deed, guilt

Piánus -a -um: pertaining to Pius

Piánus-Benedictínus -a -um: pertaining to Pius and Benedict

píctor -óris: m.; painter

pictúra -ae: f.; picture

píe: piously, mercifully

pientíssimus -a -um: most dutiful

píetas -átis: f.; piety, love of devotion, goodness, kindness, godliness, mercy, love and duty toward God, sense of duty

píger -gra -grum: lazy, slothful

píget -ére píguit, pígitum est: (2); impers.; it irks, troubles, disgusts, grieves

pígnero -áre: (1); pledge, bind one's self

pígnus -oris(-eris): n.; pledge, security

pigrédo -inis, pígritas -átis, pigrítia -ae, pigríties -éi: f.; slothfulness, indolence, sluggishness, laziness, weakness

pígreo -ére: (2); be slow or reluctant

pigrésco -ere: (3); become slow

pígritas -átis, pigrítia -ae, pigríties -éi: see pigrédo

pígritor (pígror) -ári: *dep.* (1); be slow,
  sluggish, tardy, dilatory, slack
pígro -áre: (1); be slow, indolent
pígror -óris: m.; indolence, sloth
píla -ae: f.; ball; pillar
Pilátus -i: m.; Pilate
pileátus -a -um: wearing a felt cap
piléolus -i: m.; small skullcap, zucchetto
pilósus -a -um: hairy
pílus -i: m.; hair
pincérna -ae: m.; cupbearer, butler
píneum -i: n.; pine cone
píngo -ere, pínxi, píctum: (3); paint,
  adorn, embellish
pinguédo -inis: f.; richness, fat,
  abundance, fatness
pinguésco -ere: (3); grow fat, become
  fertile
pínguia -órum: n. pl.; fat meats
pínguis -is -e: fat, strong, mighty
pínna (pénna) -ae: f.; feather, wing,
  edge, pinnacle, point
pinnáculum -i: n.; pinnacle
pínnula -ae: f.; little fin, little wing,
  plume
pípio -áre: (1); chirp
piráta -ae: m.; pirate
piscátor -óris: m.; fisherman, angler
piscículus -i: m.; little fish
piscína -ae: f.; pool, pond; sacrarium,
  baptismal font; fish market
píscis -is: m.; fish
píscor -ári: *dep.* (1); fish
písticus -a -um: true, genuine, pure, of
  best quality
pístor -óris: m.; baker
píus -a -um: holy, pius, just, merciful,
  loving, devoted, virtuous,
  conscientious; píe: *adv.*
Píus -i: m.; Pius
pix, pícis: f.; pitch
placábilis -is -e: easily appeased, placable
placátio -ónis: f.; appeasing, pacifying,
  soothing, propitiation, ransom

placénta -ae: f.; cake
pláceo -ére -ui -itum: (2); please, be
  pleasing, be acceptable
plácet: *impers.;* it is pleasing, it pleases;
  see Appendix
plácidus -a -um: favorable, quiet, still,
  placid, calm, gentle, mild, peaceful,
  soft; plácide: *adv.*
plácitum -i: n.; that which is pleasing or
  agreeable, agreement, resolution,
  purpose, decision, pledge
plácitus -a -um: acceptable
plácor -óris: m.; contentment
pláco -áre: (1); pacify, appease, placate,
  make atonement
plága -ae: f.; scourge, plague, blow,
  affliction, chastisement, wound
plága -ae: f.; flat surface, tract of land,
  district, zone, plain, desert
plagátus -a -um: sore, wounded
plagiárius -ii: m.; kidnapper, robber
plágo -áre: (1); wound, afflict, scourge
plágula -ae: f.; embroidered ornament
  on vestments, curtain
planatárium -ii: n.; branch, shoot
plánctum -i: n., plánctus -us: m.;
  lamentation, mourning
pláne: plainly, surely, simply
planéta -ae: f.; chasuble
planetárius -ii: m.; astrologer
plangimónium -ii: n.; lamentation
plángo -ere, plánxi, plánctum: (3);
  lament, bewail; beat
planificátio -ónis: f.; plan, foresight
planíties -éi: f., plánum -i: n.; plain,
  level surface
pláno -áre: (1); make plain, level, or even
plánta -ae: f.; twig, shoot, cutting, graft;
  sole, sole the foot
plantárium -ii: n.; nursery garden,
  ground, sole of the foot
plantátio -ónis: f.; planting, setting,
  transplanting

plánto -áre: (1); plant, set in place, make, form, create

plánum -i: *see* planíties

plánus -a -um: plain, level, flat, even, straight; pláne: *adv.*

plásma -atis: n.; something formed or molded, image, figure

plasmátor -óris: m.; maker, shaper, molder

plásmo -áre: (1); shape, mold, fashion, make, form

plástes -ae(-is): m.; maker, shaper

plátanus -i: f.; plane tree

plátea -ae: f.; street, highway

Pláto (Pláton) -ónis: m.; Plato

plaúdo -ere, plaúsi, plaúsum: (3); clap, strike, applaud

plaústrum -i: n.; cart, wagon

plaúsus -us: m.; applause

plebéius -a -um: plebian, relating to the people

plebs -is: f.; people, chosen people; pl.: congregations

plécta -ae: f.; border, ledge

plécto (pléctor) -ere: (3); beat, punish; cápite plécti: be beheaded

plécto -ere, pléxi (pléxui), pléxum: (3); plait, braid, weave

Plenárium -ii: n.; book of Epistles and Gospels for Mass

plenárius -a -um: plenary, full, plentiful; plenárie: *adv.; see Appendix*

plenilúnium -ii: n.; full moon

plenitúdo -inis: f.; fullness, plenitude

plénus -a -um: full, filled, plentiful, supplied, complete, entire; pléne (pléniter): *adv.;* plénius: *comp. adv.*

pleríque -aéque -aque: very many, the majority

plerúmque (plúrimum): mostly, commonly, for the most part

plíco -áre: (1); fold

plínthus -i: c.; plinth

plorátus -us: m.; lamentation, weeping, wailing

plóro -áre: (1); lament, weep, bewail, mourn

plumárius -ii: m.; embroiderer

plumbáta -ae: f.; leaden ball

plumbátum -i: n.; whip weighted with lead

plúmbum -i: n.; lead

plumésco -ere: (3); grow feathers

plúo -ere, plúi (plúvi): (3); rain

pluralísmus -i: m.; pluralism

pluralísticus -a -um: pluralistic

plurálitas -átis: f.; plurality

pluráliter: in the plural

plúres -es -a: more, several, rather many, quite a few

plúreus -i: m.; desk

plúries: often, frequently, several times

plúrimum (plerúmque): mostly, commonly, for the most part

plúrimus -a -um: most, very many, very great; quam plúrimi: as many as possible

plus, plúris: more, several; plus minúsve: more or less

plúsculus -a -um: many

plútor -óris: m.; one who sends rain

plúvia -ae: f.; rain

pluviále -is: n.; cope

plúvius -a -um: rainy

pneúma -tis: n.; spirit, breath

poculéntum -i: n.; drink

póculum -i: n.; goblet, cup

podátus -i: m.; two musical notes, the second being higher than the first

podéres (podéris) -is: m.; priestly garment reaching to the ankle

pódium -ii: n.; stage, platform

poe- *see also* pae-

poéna -ae: f.; pain, fine, punishment, expiation, penalty; *see Appendix*

poenális -is -e: penal, punishing, culpable, sinful, worthy of punishment

poenáliter: in a manner deserving of punishment

poénitens -éntis: penitent

poeniténtia -ae: f.; repentance, penitence, penance

poenitentiális -is -e: of penitence; *as a c. noun:* confessor

Poenitentiária -ae: f.; an ecclesiastical tribunal in Rome

poenitentiárius -ii: m.; priest authorized to absolve from reserved sins

poeníteo -ére -ui: (2); repent, regret, be sorry, cause to repent; **poénitet:** *impers.;* it makes (one) repent, it displeases

poésis -is(-eos): f.; poetry

poéta -ae: c.; poet

poéticus -a -um: poetic

polémice: polemically

polénta -ae: f.; barley

pólio -íre: (4); polish, make smooth, embellish, refine

políticus -a -um: political

polítus -a -um: *perf. pass. part. of* **pólio; políte:** *adv.*

pólleo -ére: (2); be strong, able, powerful, or mighty

pollíceor, pollicéri, pollícitus: *dep.* (2); promise, offer, proffer

pollicitátio -ónis: f.; promise, offer, pledge

pollínctor -óris: m.; one who prepares corpses for burial, mortician

pólluo -ere -ui -útum: (3); defile, befoul, pollute, profane, render ceremonially unclean

pollútio -ónis, **polónia** -ae: f.; defilement, pollution

Polónia -ae: f.; Poland

Polónus -a -um: Polish

pólus -i: m.; sky, heaven, pole of the earth

polyándria -ae: f.; polyandry, having more than one husband at the same time

polyándrion -ii: n.; graveyard, cemetery

polycandélium -ii: n.; frame for holding candles

Polycárpus -i: m.; Polycarp

polygámia -ae: f.; polygamy

polygénesis -is(-eos): m.; polygenesis, the descent of the human race from more than one set of parents

polyglóttus -a -um: polyglot, many-tongued

polymitárius -a -um: highly finished of damask; *as a noun:* embroiderer, weaver

polýmitus -a -um: of diverse threads or colors; *as a n. noun:* art of weaving

polyphonía -ae: f.; polyphony, musical compositon of several different melodies, harmony

polyphónicus (polýphonus) -a -um: polyphonic

polytheísmus -i: m.; worship of several gods, polytheism

pomárium -ii: n.; orchard

poméllum -i: n.; knob, node of a chalice

pómifer -a -um: fruit-bearing

pómpa -ae: f.; pomp, procession, parade

pompátice: with pomp

pómum -i: n.; apple, fruit

pómus -i: f.; fruit tree

ponderátor -óris: m.; weigher

póndero -áre: (1); weigh, consider, reflect on, ponder

póndus -eris: n.; load, weight, burden

póne: *prep. w. acc. & adv.;* behind, at the back of, after

pónens -éntis: m.; reporter, referee, relator; *see Appendix*

póno -ere, pósui, pósitum: (3); place, put, set aside, appoint

pons, póntis: m.; bridge

Pónticus -a -um: Pontic; máre
Pónticum: Black Sea

póntifex -icis: m.; pontiff, high priest,
bishop (especially the bishop of Rome,
the Pope); póntifex máximus: the
Pope

pontificále -is: n.; pontifical, a book of
rites performed by a bishop

pontificális -is -e, pontíficus
(pontifícius) -a -um: of the Pope,
pontifical, papal; pontificália -órum:
n. pl.; things pertaining to pontifical
ceremonies; pontificáliter: adv.

pontificátus -us: m.; pontificate, reign
of a pontiff

pontifícium -ii: n.; pontifical power,
papacy

póntus -i: m.; sea, ocean, the deep

popína -ae: f.; food, fare

póples -itis: m.; knee

populáres -ium: m. pl., pópulus -i: m.;
the people, populace

populáris -is -e: relating to or
proceeding from or designed for the
people, popular, democratic,
all-embracing

populátio -ónis: f.; population

pópulus -i: m.; populace, people,
multitide, crowd, host; in pópulis:
among the nations; see Appendix

porcínus (porcárius) -a -um: relating to
swine

pórcus -i: m.; swine, pig

porósus -a -um: porous

porphýrio -ónis: m.; waterfowl

porréctus -a -um: stretched out

pórrigo -ere -réxi -réctum: (3); extend,
stretch out, hold out, reach out, spread
out, present

porrígo -inis: f.; dandruff, itch, lice

pórro: farther on, afterwards, next,
furthermore, forward, then

pórta -ae: f.; door

portábilis -is -e: portable

portárius -ii: m.; porter, doorkeeper

porténdo -ere -téndi -téntum: (3);
predict, foretell, portend, indicate

porténtum -i: n.; portent, wonder,
prodigy, omen, sign, token

portícula -ae: f.; small door

pórticus -us: f.; porch, vestibule

pórtio -ónis: f.; portion, lot, share

portionárius -ii: m.; prebendary

pórtitor -óris: m.; carrier, bearer, porter

portiúncula -ae: f.; portion, small piece

Portiúncula -ae: f.; Portiuncula
Indulgence

pórto -áre: (1); carry, bear, bring,
uphold, sustain

Portugállia -ae: f.; Portugal

pórtus -us: m.; harbor, haven, port,
refuge, entrance

pósco -ere, popósci: (3); ask, demand,
beg earnestly, request

posítio -ónis: f.; position, act of placing

positívus -a -um: positive, settled,
agreed on; positíve: adv.

pósitor -óris: m.; founder

pósitus -a -um: perf. pass. part. of póno

posséssio -ónis: f.; possession, property,
substance

posséssor -óris: m.; possessor

possessórius -a -um; possesssory,
relating to possession; as a n. noun:
possessory suit

possíbilis -is -e: possible

possibílitas -átis: f.; possibility, power

possídeo -ére -sédi -séssum: (2); possess,
acquire, occupy, get possession of,
have, hold

póssum, pósse, pótui: be able, have
power, can

post: prep. w. acc. & adv.; after, behind,
later; múltis post ánnis: after many
years

postcommúnio -ónis: f.;
Postcommunion Oration

póstea: afterward, hereafter

posteáquam: after

postergále -is: n.; back of a seat

pósteri -órum: m. pl.; posterity, descendants

postérior -ior -ius: later, posterior, behind, latter, next, following; posterióra -um: n. pl.; back parts

postéritas -átis: f.; progeny, future, offspring

pósterus -a -um: following, coming after, subsequent, next; *as a pl. noun:* coming generations, descendants, posterity; **in pósterum:** in the future

posthábeo -ére: (2); esteem less, ignore, omit, postpone, neglect

pósthac: after this time, hereafter, henceforth, afterwards

pósthumus: *see* **póstumus**

postícum -i: n.; back door

postílla -ae: f.; popular commentary on liturgical scriptural readings

póstis -is: m.; doorpost, sidepost

postliminíum -ii: n.; return home

póstmodum: after, afterward

postpóno -ere -pósui -pósitum: (3); place or put after or later

póstquam: after, as soon as, when

postrémus -a -um: latest, last; **postrémo, ad postrémum:** lastly, finally, at last

postrídie: on the next day

póstulans -ántis: c.; one who petitions

postulátio -ónis: f.; petition, request, postulation, entreaty; *see Appendix*

postulátor -óris: m., **postulátrix** -ícis: f.; one who demands or requests, postulator, claimant

postulatórius -a -um: postulatory

postulátus -us: m.; postulancy, postulate, postulantship

póstulo -áre: (1); ask, request, entreat, demand, accuse

póstumus (pósthumus) -a -um: last, hindmost, rear

potábilis -is -e: fit to drink, potable

potáculum -i: n., **potátio** -ónis: f.; drinking bout, act of drinking

potátor -óris: m.; drinker, tippler

pótens -éntis: powerful, mighty, strong; **poténter:** *adv.*

potentátor -óris: m.; ruler, potentate

potentátus -us: m.; might, strength, power

poténter: powerfully, efficaciously

poténtia -ae: f.; power, strength, might, rule, ability, potency

potentiáliter: in might, in power

potéstas -átis: f.; power, authority, jurisdiction, strength, might, ability, control

pótio -ónis: f.; drinking, potion

potióno -áre, *no perf.,* -átum: (1); give to drink

pótior -ior -ius: better, greater, preferable, more important

pótior -íri, potítus: *dep.* (4); obtain, get possession of, become partaker of, be master of

potíssimum: chiefly, especially, most preferable, above all

pótius: *comp. adv.;* rather, more, preferably, above all

póto -áre: (1); drink, give or make a drink

pótrix -ícis: f.; female tippler

pótus -us: m.; drink, draught, drinking

práctica -ae: f.; practice

prácticus -a -um: practical, active; **práctice:** *adv.*

prae- *see also* **pre-, proe-**

prae: *adv. & prep. w. abla.;* before, in front, in preference

praeámbulus -a -um: going before

praebénda -ae: f.; benefice, prebend, allowance, subsidy

praebendárius -ii: m.; beneficiary, prebendary

praebendátus -i: m.; choral prebendary

praebéndo -áre: (1); give a prebend

praébeo -ére -bui -bitum: (2); grant, furnish, offer, hold out, exhibit, yield, show; se praebére: show oneself, behave

praebítio -ónis: f.; a furnishing, giving, supplying, providing

praécano -ere: (3), praecánto -áre: (1); foretell, predict, enchant

praecántor -óris: m.; enchanter

praecárius -a -um: precarious, uncertain, unfounded

praecatechizátus -a -um: previously instructed

praecatechumenátus -us: m.; precatechumenate

praecavéntia -ae: f.; insurance

praecáveo -ére -cávi -caútum: (2); be careful, be on guard, take precaution, provide for the future, beware

praecedéntia -ae: f.; precedence

praecédo -ere -céssi -céssum: (3); go before, precede, prepare

praecellénter: exceedingly, excellently

praecelléntia -ae: f.; excellence

praecéllo -ere: (3); excel, surpass, exceed

praecélsus -a -um: very high or lofty, sublime

praecéntor -óris: m.; capitular dignity, leader in chant

praéceps -ípitis: n.; precipice, steep place, cliff

praecéptio -ónis: f.; precept, injunction, rule

praeceptívus -a -um: preceptive, imperative, didactic

praecéptor -óris: m.; instructor, master, teacher

praecéptrix -ícis: f.; female teacher

praecéptum -i: n.; precept, command, law, ordinance, decree, statute; see Appendix

praecéptus -a -um: perf. pass. part. of praecípio

praecéssor -óris: m.; leader, superior, predecessor

praecído -ere -cídi -císum: (3); cut, cut off or down, cut in front, cut to pieces

praecinctórium -ii: n.; ornamental maniple worn by the Pope

praecíngo -ere -cínxi -cínctum: (3); gird, encircle with a girdle or belt

praécino -ere -cécini(-cínui) -céntum: (3); sing or play before

praecípio -ere -cépi -céptum: (3); instruct, teach, command, advise, warn, charge, prescribe, preach, anticipate

praecipitátio -ónis: f.; ruin, destruction

praecipítium -ii: n.; precipice

praecípito -áre: (1); cast headlong, fall headlong

praecípuus -a -um: special, extraordinary; praecípue: adv.

praecísio -ónis: f.; destruction, cutting off, down, or away

praecisíve: precisely

praeclárus -a -um: very clear, honorable, remarkable, splendid, famous, eminent; as n. pl. noun: valuables; praecláre: adv.

praecláritas -átis: f.; distinction, renown

praeclúdo -ere -clúsi -clúsum: (3); close, shut, shut up, close in front

praéco -ónis: m.; herald, crier, publisher, one who praises

praecógito -áre: (1); think beforehand

praecógnitus -a -um: known beforehand

praecognósco -ere -nóvi -nitum: (3); learn beforehand

praécolo -ere -cólui -cúltum: (3); cultivate before, revere, honor highly

praeconátio -ónis: f.; proclamation, singing of the Gospel

praeconisátio -ónis: f.; ratification of a bishop's appointment

praecónium -ii: n.; praise, commendation, publishing, making known

praeconsecrátus -a -um: previously consecrated

praecóquus -a -um: premature

praecórdia -órum: n. pl.; heart, hearts

praecúrro -ere -cúrri (-cucúrri) -cúrsum: (3); run before, take precedence over

praecúrsio -ónis: f.; a going before

praecúrsor -óris: m.; precursor, one who goes or runs before

praecútio -ere -cússi -cússum: (3); brandish, shake before

praéda -ae: f.; booty, plunder, prey

praedámno -áre: (1); condemn beforehand

praedátio -ónis: f.; robbery, plundering, taking spoils

praedátor -óris: m.; robber, plunderer, hunter, greedy person

praedecéssor -óris: m.; predecessor

praedélla -ae: f.; altar platform

praedestinátio -ónis: f.; determining beforehand, predestination

praedestinátus -a -um: predestined

praedéstino -áre: (1); ordain, appoint, ordain beforehand

praedicábilis -is -e: praiseworthy

praedicaméntum -i: n.; that which is predicted or predicated

praédicans -ántis, **praedicátor** -óris: m.; preacher

praedicátio -ónis: f.; preaching, making known publicly, praise, commendation, sermon, foretelling

praedicátor -óris: m.; preacher, proclaimer, eulogist

praédico -áre: (1); preach

praedíco -ere: (3); foretell, predict, prophesy

praedíctio -ónis: f.; predicting, prophesying

praedíctus -a -um: aforesaid, predicted

praediléctio -ónis: f.; loving interest or concern, predilection

praediléctus -a -um: beloved, chosen

praéditus -a -um: endowed, provided with, furnished, gifted

praédium -ii: n.; estate, farm, plot of land

praédo -ónis: m.; robber, plunderer

praedóceo -ére -dócui -dóctum: (2); teach or instruct beforehand

praédor -ári: *dep.* (1); rob, plunder, despoil

praedúlcis -is -e: very sweet

praeéligo -ere -légi -léctum: (3); choose beforehand

praeeminéntia -ae: f.; distinction, superior eminence

praeemíneo -ére: (2); excel, be remarkable

praéeo -íre -ívi (-ii) -itum: (4); go before, precede

praeexsísto -sístere -stiti -stitum: (3); preexist

praefátio -ónis: f.; preface, formula, form of words

praefátus -a -um: aforesaid, above-mentioned

praefectúra -ae: f.; prefecture

praeféctus -i: m.; prefect, overseer, governor, head, president

praéfero -érre -tuli -látum: *irreg.;* bear or carry in front, manifest, display, prefer, give preference to, carry by

praéferox -ócis: very cruel

praefício -ere -féci -féctum: (3); set over, place in charge or command

praefídens -éntis: overconfident, very confident

praefidénter: too confidently

praefígo -ere: (3); fashion in front, tip, point, block, prefix

praefigúro -áre: (1); prefigure

praefínio -íre: (4); appoint, predetermine, prescribe, limit

praefinítio -ónis: f.; purpose, predetermination

praefinítus -a -um: predetermined, prescribed, preappointed

praefóco -áre: (1); choke, strangle, drown, suffocate

praefúlgeo -ére -fúlsi: (2); shine forth

praégnans -ántis, **praégnas** -átis: pregnant, with child

praegnátio -ónis: f., **praegnátus** -us: m.; pregnancy

praegrándis -is -e: intense, exceeding, very great

praégravo -áre: (1); oppress, weigh down or upon, press heavily

praegrédior -i -gréssus: *dep.* (3); go before, precede

praegréssio -ónis: f.; precedence, going before

praegustátor -óris: m.; taster, foretaster

praegústo -áre: (1); taste beforehand

praehíbeo -ére: (2); give, offer, supply, furnish

praéiens -eúntis: going before, leading; *as a c. noun:* one who goes before or leads

praeintonátio -ónis: f.; intoning beforehand, intoning an antiphon

praejudicális -is -e: prejudicial, by a prior judgment

praejudícium -ii: n.; previous judgment, precedent, preliminary examination, prejudice, damage, disadvantage, example, objection

praejúdico -áre: (1); decide beforehand, prejudge

praelátio -ónis: f.; dignity, preference, guidance, bearing

praelatítius -a -um: preferential, relating to a prelate

praelatúra -ae: f.; governing position, prelateship, prelature

praelátus -i: m.; prelate, superior; *see Appendix*

praeléctio -ónis: f.; lecture

praelégo -áre: (1); bequeath beforehand

praélego -ere -légi -léctum: (3); read to others, select, choose, sail by or along

praeliátor -óris: m.; warrior

praelibátio -ónis: f.; oblation

praéligo -ere -légi -léctum: (3); bind in front, bind beforehand

praélio (praélior) -áre: (1); fight

praélium -ii: n.; battle, war, fight

praéloquor -i -locútus: *dep.* (3); announce beforehand

praelúceo -ére -lúxi: (2); surpass, outshine, shine before

praelúdium -ii: n.; prelude, eve, vigil

praelúdo -ere -lúsi -lúsum: (3); play beforehand, rehearse, prepare, premise, preface

praélum -i: *see* **prélum**

praematúrus -a -um: eager, premature, too early

praemedicátus -a -um: protected by medicines or charms

praemeditátio -ónis: f.; premeditation, considering beforehand

praemédito (praeméditor) -áre: (1); meditate before

praemeditatórium -ii: n.; place for preparation

praemiális -is -e: used as a reward

praémior -ári: *dep.* (1); reward, indicate for a reward

praemítto -ere -mísi -míssum: (3); set before, set forth a premise, to preface, dispatch

praémium -ii: n.; reward, prize, recompense

praemóneo -ére: (2); advise before, forewarn

praemonítio -ónis: f.; premonition, warning

praemónstro -áre: (1); indicate, point out

praenóbilis -is -e: distinguished

praenósco -ere -nóvi -nótum: (3); know beforehand

praénoto -áre: (1); mark, indicate before, designate, predict

praenuntiátor -óris: m.; foreteller

praenúntio -áre: (1); show before, announce, report, foretell

praenúntius -ii: m.; forerunner

praeóccupo -áre: (1); take by surprise, come before, overtake, anticipate, prejudice, preoccupy

praeópto -áre: (1); choose beforehand, pre-opt, prefer, desire

praeórdino -áre: (1); preordain

praeosténsus -a -um: foreshown

praeparátio -ónis: f.; preparation

praeparatórius -a -um: preparatory

praéparo -áre: (1); prepare, make ready, provide

praepédio -íre: (4); shackle, fetter, obstruct, impede, hinder

praepedítio -ónis: f.; hindrance, impediment

praepéndeo -ére -pepéndi: (2); hang before, hang in front

praepínguis -is -e: very rich

praepóllens -éntis: very powerful

praepóno -ere -pósui -pósitum: (3); place before, prefer, entrust with

praepositúra -ae: f.; archdeaconry, prelacy, priory, provostship

praepósitus -i: m.; dean, prior, provost, ecclesiastical superior

praepósterus -a -um: absurd, inverted, preposterous

praépotens -éntis: mighty

praepróperus -a -um: overhasty, sudden, too quick

praeputiátus -a -um: uncircumcised

praepútium -ii: n.; foreskin, prepuce; noncircumcision

praerequisítum -i: n.; prerequisite

praerípio -ere -rípui -réptum: (3); carry off before, take prematurely

praerogatíva -ae: f.; prerogative, privilege, special right

praeságio -íre: (4); presage, forebode, foretell

praeságus -a -um: predicting

praesanctificátus -a -um: previously sanctified

praesciéntia -ae: f.; foreknowledge

praescíndo -ere -scídi -scíssum: (3); prescind

praéscio -íre -scívi -scítum: (4), **praescísco** -ere -scívi: (3); find out or learn beforehand

praéscius -a -um: foreboding, foreknowing

praescríbo -ere -scrípsi -scríptum: (3); order, prescribe

praescríptio -ónis: f.; prescription; *see Appendix*

praescriptíve: *adv.;* with an exception

praescríptum -i: n., **praescríptus** -us: m.; precept, order, copy, task, lesson

praescríptus -a -um: written, prescribed, commanded, directed

praeséfero (prae se féro) -férre -túli -látum: *irreg.;* display, entail, take on, bear before oneself, bear with oneself

praésens -éntis: present, at hand, immediate, in person

praesentátio -ónis: f.; presentation, offering; **Praesentátio Dómini:** Candlemas Day; *see Appendix*

praeséntia -ae: f.; presence

praeséntio -íre -sénsi -sénsum: (4); feel beforehand, have a presentiment

praesénto -áre: (1); to present, show

praesépe -is, **praesépium** -ii: n.; manger, stall, crib

praesértim: especially, particularly

praeservátio -onis: f.; preservation, preserving, act of saving

praesérvo -áre: (1); preserve

praéses -idis: c.; president, chairperson, presider

praesidátus -us: m.; governorship

praesídeo -ére -sédi -séssum: (3); preside over, guard, govern, direct, give audience to

praesídium -ii: n.; presidency, protection, defense, guard, aid

praesignífico -áre: (1); signify, announce beforehand

praesígnis -is -e: distinguished

praesígno -áre: (1); represent, foreshadow, prefigure

praésono -áre: (1); resound, sound out

prae-spéro -áre: (1); hope beforehand

praestábilis -is -e: powerful, remarkable, preeminent

praéstans -ántis: gracious, eminent, distinguished, excellent

praestántia -ae: f.; excellence, superiority, preeminence

praestátio -ónis: f.; offering, presentation, payment, guaranty

praestigiátor -óris: m.; deceiver

praestítuo -ere -stítui -stitútum: (3); prescribe, appoint before, predetermine

praésto: here, at hand, ready, present

praésto -áre -stiti -stitum: (1); furnish, grant, guarantee, excel, stand before, serve, stand out

praestólor -ári: _dep._ (1); expect, wait for, perform

praestríngo -ere -strínxi -stríctum: (3); bind up

praestrúctio -ónis: f.; preparation

praéstruo -ere -strúxi -strúctum: (3); build in front, make ready

praésul -is: c.; patron, protector; _m. can mean:_ bishop, prelate

praésulor -ári: _dep._ (1); be a superintendent

praesúlto -áre: (1); leap, spring before

praésum -ésse -fui: rule, govern, be before, be placed over, preside over

praesúmo -ere -súmpsi -súmptum: (3); presume, take for granted, take before, anticipate

praesúmptio -ónis: f.; presumption, boldness, arrogance; _see Appendix_

praesúmptus (praesumptuósus) -a -um: taken for granted, presumed

praesuppóno -ere -pósui -pósitum: (3); presuppose

praeténdo -ere -téndi -téntum: (3); extend, stretch out before, present to, place before, pretend

praeténto -áre: (1); feel, try beforehand, try, test

praéter: _adv. & prep. w. acc.;_ besides, except, beyond, above, more than, past, before, in front of, by, along

praéter intentiónem: beyond the intention

praéter jus: beyond the law; _see Appendix_

praetérea: furthermore, besides, henceforth, hereafter, and

praetéreo -íre -ívi (-ii) -itum: (4); pass by or away, come to an end, cease, omit, skip, neglect, surpass, go beyond

praetergrédior -i -gréssus: _dep._ (3); go beyond, transgress, walk past, pass by, excel

praeterítio -ónis: f.; omission, oversight

praetéritus -a -um: gone by, past and gone, departed; _as a n. pl. noun:_ the past, bygone times or things

praeterlábor -bi -psus: _dep._ (3); slip away, glide by, pass by

praetermítto -ere: (3); let pass, omit, neglect, leave undone, overlook, wink at

praéterquam: besides, except, beyond, other than

praetervéhor -i -véctus: _dep._ (3); be carried past, sail past

praetéxtus -us: m.; pretext, excuse

praétor -óris: m.; praetor, magistrate, Roman official

praetoríolum -i: n.; cabin

praetórium -ii: n.; palace, governor's hall, courtroom, judgment hall, official residence, praetorium

praetórius -a -um: pretorian

praeváleo -ére -ui: (2); master, prevail against, be strong or powerful, override

praeválidus -a -um: very strong, very powerful, too productive

praevaricátio -ónis: f.; prevarication, transgression, violation of duty

praevaricátor -óris: m.; transgressor, sinner, apostate

praevárico (praváricor) -áre: (1); sin, transgress, rebel, break the law, be guilty of collusion, play a double part

praevénio -íre -véni -véntum: (4); prevent, come before, anticipate, come ahead, precede, look forward to, guide

praevéntio -ónis: f.; anticipation

praevéntus -us: m.; prevention

praevérto (praevértor) (-vórto, -vórtor) -ere -vérti -vérsum: (3); go before, anticipate, surpass, outstrip, outrun

práe-vians -ántis: going before

praeviátor -óris: m.; precursor

praevidéntia -ae: f.; security, foresight, pension

praevídeo -ére -vídi -vísum: (2); foresee, know beforehand

praévius -a -um: preceding, leading; praévie: adv.

praévius -ii: m.; forerunner

praevórto (praevórtor): see praevérto

prándeo -ére, prándi, pránsum: (2); eat

prándium -ii: n.; breakfast, meal, luncheon

prátum -i: n.; meadow

pravicórdius -a -um: having a depraved heart

právitas -átis: f.; wickedness, guilt, evil, irregularity

právus -a -um: evil, perverse, crooked, deformed; práve: adv.

práxis -is: m.; exercise, practice, proof; see Appendix

pre- see also prae-

prebénda -ae: f.; benefice

precárius -a -um: uncertain, precarious; precário: by request

precátio -ónis: f., precátus -us: m.; prayer, entreaty, supplication

precátor -óris: m.; one who prays

precatórius -a -um: intercessory, prayerful

precátus: see precátio

préces -um: f. pl.; prayers, requests

précor -ári: dep. (1); pray, beseech, beg, invoke, entreat, supplicate

predélla -ae: f.; platform directly in front of the altar

predicátor -óris: m.; preacher

pragmatísmus -a -um: pragmatic, practical; as a m. noun: pragmatism

prehéndo (préndo) -ere -di -sum: (3), prehénso -áre: (1); seize, catch, lay hold of

prélum (prae-) -i: n.; press, winepress, grape press; the press or news media

prémo -ere, préssi, préssum: (3); oppose, press upon, press

préndo: see prehéndo

prénso -áre: (1); grasp mentally

présbyter -eri: m.; priest, elder

presbyterális -is -e: priestly; see Appendix

presbyterátus -us: m.; priesthood

presbytérium -ii: n.; presbytery, assembly of clergy

presentátio -ónis: f.; presentation

préssio -ónis, pressúra -ae: f.; pressing down, pressure, distress, oppression, anguish, affliction, persecution

présso -áre: (1); distress, press

pressoríola -ae: f.; repository

pressúra -ae: f.; affliction, distress, oppression

préssus -a -um: subdued, suppressed, moderate, precise; **présse:** *adv.;* **préssius:** more distinctly, precisely, or accurately

pretiósus -a -um: precious, of great price

prétium -ii: n.; money, price, ransom money, value, worth

prex, précis: f.; prayer, request

prídem: long ago, long since, formerly

prídie: yesterday, on the day before

príma -ae: f., **prímas** -átis: n., **prímus** -i: m.; Primate, chief, one of the first

Príma -ae: f.; the hour of Prime

primaévus -a -um: youthful

primárius -a -um: first, principal, primary; **primário:** *adv.*

prímas -átis: m.; Primate, a title of honor; *see Appendix*

primatiális -is -e: primatial, relating to a Primate

primátus -us: m.; primacy

primicérius -ii: m.; dean of an official class or group

primigénius (primígenus) -a -um: first of its kind, original

primissárius -ii: m.; prebendary obliged to say an early Mass

primítiae -árum: f. pl.; first, firstborn, first fruits

primitívus (primogénitus) -a -um: first, firstborn

prímo (prímum, prímitus): first, first of all, in the first place, at first, for the first time; **prímo íctu óculi:** at first glance

primogénitum -i: n.; first birthright

primogenitúra -ae: f.; primogeniture

primogénitus -a -um: firstborn

primordiális -is -e: first, first of all, original, primordial

primórdium -ii: n.; origin, beginning

prímus -a -um: first, foremost, first part; **in prímis (inprímis, imprímis):** in the first place; **prímum (prímo):** *adv.; see Appendix*

prímus -i: *see* **príma**

prínceps -ipis: first, foremost, chief, principal; *as a m. noun:* sovereign, leader, prince, ruler; **príncipes sacerdótum:** chief priests

principális -is -e: first, original, perfect, free

principálitas -átis: f.; principality

principáliter: in the first palce, from the beginning, chiefly, principally

principátus -us: m.; public office, rule, dominion, sovereignty

principíssa -ae: f.; princess

princípium -ii: n.; beginning, source, foundation, principality, sovereignty, origin, principle

príncipor -ári: *dep.* (1); rule, begin

prínus -i: f.; holm tree

príor -íor -íus: first, former, prior, previous, preferable

priorátus -us: m.; priory, priorship; priority, preference

prioríssa -ae: f.; prioress

prióritas -tátis: f.; priority

príscus -a -um: original, ancient, antique, venerable

prístinus -a -um: former, previous, earlier, original, pristine

príus: previously, before, sooner, earlier

priúsquam: before, before that

privátio -ónis: f.; privation, deprivation, taking away; *see Appendix*

privatívus -a -um: lacking, deprived, negative; **privatíve:** *adv.*

privátus -a -um: private; **privátim:** *adv.; as a noun:* private person, private citizen

privilegiárius -a -um: enjoying a privilege, privileged

privilégio -áre: (1); grant a privilege

privilégium -ii: n.; privilege, private law, law for one person, special right; see *Appendix*

prívo -áre: (1); withhold, deprive, free from

pro: *adv. & prep. w. abla.;* for, on behalf of, before, according to, instead of, in front of, in favor of, in place of

pro alíquibus lócis: for some places

Pro Ecclésia et Pontífice: For the Church and Pope

pro hac více: for this one time

pro líbito: at pleasure

pro pópulo: for the people, Mass of obligation required of pastors of parishes

pro ráta: according to calculation or count, proportionately

pro re grávi: for a serious matter or reason

pro sémper: forever

pro témpore: for a time

pro-ávia -ae: f.; great-grandmother

pró-avus -i: m.; great-grandfather

probábilis -is -e: probable, credible, pausible; probabíliter: *adv.;* probabílius: *comp. adv.*

probabilísmus -i: m.; probabilism

probáticus -a -um: relating to sheep

probátio -ónis: f.; test, trial, probation, proof, approval

probatívus -a -um: probative, of proof

probátor -óris: m.; tester, examiner

probatórius -a -um: serving to prove, furnishing proof

próbitas -átis: f.; integrity, goodness

probléma -atis: n.; problem, enigma, riddle, puzzle

próbo -áre: (1); try, test, prove, examine, learn, find out, know, probe, investigate

próbrus -a -um: shameful, disgraceful, reproachful; *as a n. noun:* disgrace,

shame, abuse, reproach, vileness, indecency

próbus -a -um: good, fine, upright, excellent, fit; próbe: *adv.*

prócax -ácis: impudent, insolent

procédo -ere -céssi -céssum: (3); go or come forth, proceed from; procédere in diébus múltis: be far advanced in years

procedúra -ae: f.; procedure

procélla -ae: f. storm, tempest, gale

procellósus -a -um: stormy, wild

prócer -eris: m.; noble, prince, illustrious person

procérus -a -um: high, tall, long, extended; procére: *adv.*

processículum -i: n.; form (as a freedom-to-marry form)

processículus -i: m.; processiculus, a juridical report

procéssio -ónis: f.; procession, advance, parade, source, origin

processionále -is: n.; ritual book for processions

processionális -is -e: processional; processionáliter: *adv.*

processuális -is -e: relating to a juridical form

procéssus -us: m.; process, legal process, course

prócido -ere -cidi: (3); fall down, fall forward, prostrate

procínctus -us: m.; preparation for departure

proclámo -áre: (1); proclaim, cry out

proclívis -is -e, proclívus -a -um: sloping, going downwards, steep, downhill

procónsul -ulis: m.; proconsul, municipal officer

proconsuláris -is -e: proconsular

procreátio -ónis: f.; procreation, generation, begetting

prócreo -áre: (1); beget

prócul: afar off, far, far away, at a distance

procúlco -áre: (1); tread, trample upon

proculdúbio: without doubt

procúmbo -ere -cúbui -cúbitum: (3); lean or bend forward, sink down, bow

procurátio -ónis: f.; administration, management, taking care of, procuring, obtaining

procurátor -óris: m.; steward, agent, manager, administrator, proxy, procurator; see Appendix

procúro -áre: (1); administer, govern, take care of, tend, manage, look after

procúrro -ere -cúrri(-cucúrri) -cúrsum: (3); rush or run forward

prócus -i: m.; suitor, wooer

pródeo -íre: (4); come or go forth, come out

prodigiósus -a -um: miraculous, marvelous

prodígium -ii: n.; wonder, prodigy, marvel, miracle

pródigo -ere -égi -áctum: (3); drive forth

pródigus -a -um: prodigal, profuse, extravagant

proditío -ónis: f.; betraying, betrayal, treason, treachery

próditor -óris: m.; betrayer, traitor

pródo -ere -didi -ditum: (3); betray, bring forth, become profitable, report, produce, record, disclose

prodóceo -ére -ui -tum: (2); teach, inculcate

prodúco -ere -dúxi -dúctum: (3); produce, beget, bring forth

prodúctilis -is -e: drawn out, beaten

prodúctio -ónis: f.; production, prolonging, creation

productívitas -átis: f.; productivity

pródux -ducis: m.; twig, shoot, layer

proeliáris -is -e, proélians -ántis: relating to battle

proélior (prae-) -ári: dep. (1); fight, engage in battle

proélium (praé-) -ii: n.; battle, war

profanátio -ónis: f.; profanation, defilement, desecration

profánitas -átis: f.; profanity

profáno -áre: (1); desecrate, profane, defile

profánus -a -um: profane, unholy, ordinary, common

proféctio -ónis: f.; journey, departure

profécto (proféctum): really, certainly, truly, in fact, without doubt, in truth, verily

proféctus -a -um: perf. pass. part. of profício; perf. part. of proficíscor

proféctus -us: m.; source, growth, increase, progress

prófero -érre -tuli -látum: irreg.; bring forth, display, lay before, produce, offer, reveal, cite; vérbum proférre: speak

proféssio -ónis: f.; profession, declaration, acknowledgment

professionális -is -e: professional

proféssor -óris: m.; professor, teacher

proféssus -a -um: professed; ex profésso: openly

profício -ere -féci -féctum: (3); help, assist, advance, increase, prevail, effect, contribute, make progress

proficíscor -i -féctum: dep. (3); set out, go, proceed, travel

profícuus -a -um: profitable

profíteor -éri -féssus: dep. (2); profess, admit, acknowledge

proflígo -áre: (1); abolish, overthrow, scatter

próflo -áre: (1); blow or breathe forth

prófluens -éntis: f.; flowing river, running water

prófluo -ere -flúxi -flúctum: (3); flow forth, flow, run, issue

proflúvium -ii: n.; flood, flowing

prófor -fári: *dep.* (1); speak out, speak on behalf of, tell, relate, predict, foretell, propose, suggest

profúgio -ere -fúgi -fúgitum: (3); flee away

prófugus -a -um: fleeing, wandering, unsettled; *as a noun:* fugitive, refugee

profúndo -ere -fúdi -fúsum: (3); pour out or forth, cause to flow, rush out

profúndus -a -um: deep, profound, vast, bottomless, boundless; *as a n. noun:* depth, profoundness; **profúnde:** *adv.;* **profúndius:** *comp. adv.*

profúsio -ónis: f.; profusion, pouring out

profutúrus -a -um: profitable

progenerátor -óris: m.; ancestor, progenitor

progénies -éi: f.; offspring, progeny, generation, race, descent, descendant

in progéniem et progéniem: for all times

a progénie in progénies: from generation to generation, forever

progénitor -óris: m.; ancestor, founder of a family

progrédior -i -gréssus: *dep.* (3); go further, advance, go ahead

progréssio -ónis: f., **progréssus** -us: m.; progression, growth, progress, increase, advancement, going forward

progressívus -a -um: progressive

proh: *interj.;* oh! ah!

prohíbeo -ére -ui -itum: (2); forbid, restrain, hinder, hold in check

prohibítio -ónis: f.; prohibition

proínde: hence, accordingly, just as, as is, in like manner, in the same manner

projício -ere -jéci -jéctum: (3); cast down or away, cast upon, thrown into

prolábor -i -lápsus: *dep.* (3); fall away, lapse, fail, fall down

prolátio -ónis: f.; pronouncement

prolátus -a -um: *perf. pass. part. of* prófero

prolátus -us: m.; a bringing forward, advancement

prolegómena -órum: n. pl.; introduction, preface

próles -is: f.; offspring, child

prolíxitas -átis: f.; fullness

prolíxus -a -um: long drawn out, long, stretched, extended, favorable

prolíxe: freely, abundantly, copiously, earnestly; **prolíxius:** the longer, more earnestly

prólogus -i: m.; **prológium** -ii: n.; prologue, introduction

prolongátus -a -um: long

prolóngo -áre: (1); prolong, lengthen

próloquor -qui -locútus: *dep.* (3); declare, speak out

prolúdo -ere -lúsi -lúsum: (3); practice beforehand

próluo -ere -ui -útum: (3); wash off or out

prolúsio -ónis: f.; prelude

prólyta -ae: c.; student of law

prománo -áre: (1); flow or drip from, derive from, emanate

proméreo (proméreor) -ére -ui -itum: (2); merit, deserve, obtain, acquire

prómico -áre: (1); shine forth

promíscuus (promíscus) -a -um: promiscuous, indiscriminate

promíssio -ónis: f., **promíssum** -i: n.; promise

promíssor -óris: m.; promiser

promissórius -a -um: promissory, of a promise

promíssum -i: *see* promíssio

promítto -ere -mísi -míssum: (3); send ahead or forward, say beforehand, forbode, predict, promise, assure

prómo -ere, prómpsi, prómptum: (3); utter, bring forth, send forth, reveal, produce, express

promóneo -ére -ui -itum: (2); warn

promótio -ónis: f.; promotion, preferment, advancement

promótor -óris: m.; encourager, promoter, champion, prosecutor; *see* *Appendix*

promóveo -ére -móvi -mótum: (2); advance, promote, extend

promptitúdo -inis: f.; promptitude

promptuárium -ii: n.; storehouse, pantry

prómptus -a -um: prompt, willing, visible, quick; **prómpte:** *adv.;* **prómptius:** *comp. adv.*

prómptus -us: m.; visibility, readiness **in prómptu ésse:** be prepared **in prómptu:** manifest

promulgátio -ónis: f.; promulgation, publishing, making public; *see* *Appendix*

promúlgo -áre: (1); publish, make known, promulgate

pronáus (pronáos) -i: m.; vestibule of a church

pronuntiátio -ónis: f.; publication, judgment, pronouncement

pronúntio -áre: (1); declare, speak, pronounce, announce

Pro-Núntius (-Núncius) -ii: pro-nuncio; *see Appendix*

prónus -a -um: prone, flat, inclined, bent forward

prooémium -ii: n.; introduction, preface, prelude

Propagánda -ae: f.; *short for* de propagánda fíde; office of the Propagation of the Faith

propagátio -ónis: f.; spreading, extension, propagation

propagátor -óris: m.; propagator

propágo -áre: (1); spread, extend, enlarge, propagate

propágo -ínis: f.; branch, shoot, generation

própalo -áre: (1); make manifest or known, divulge

própe: *adv. & prep. w. acc.;* near, nigh, at hand, not far off, hard by, nearby

propéllo -ere -puli -púlsum: (3); drive out or away or before, propel

propémodum: almost, nearly, in like manner

propéndeo -ére -péndi -pénsum: (2); hang down, be inclined

propénsio -ónis: f.; inclination, propensity

propénsus -a -um: hanging down, inclined toward, approaching, heavy, important, disposed toward, favorable; **propénse:** *adv.*

properátim (properáto): hastily, speedily, quickly

própero -áre: (1); hasten, hurry

prophéta -ae, **prophétes** -is: m.; prophet

prophetía -ae: f.; prophecy

prophéticus -a -um, **prophetális** -is -e: prophetic, prophetical, of a prophet; **prophétice:** *adv.*

prophétis -idis, **prophetíssa** -ae: f.; prophetess

prophéto (prophetízo) -áre: (1); foretell, prophesy, predict

prophylácticum -i: m.; condom

propíno -áre: (1); drink to, pledge, offer a drink to, set before

propínquitas -átis: f.; relationship, nearness

propínquo -áre: (1); approach, attain

propínquus -a um: near, approaching, neighboring, near of kin; *as a noun:* neighbor, kin, relative

própior -ior -ius: nearer

propitiábilis -is -e: propitious, forgiving, forgivable, capable of atoning

propitiátio -ónis: f.; clemency, mercy, forgiveness, propitiation

propitiátor -óris: m.; propitiator, one who atones

propitiatórium -ii: n.; mercy seat, propitiatory, special seat in temple

propitiátus (propítius): mercifully, kindly, favorably

propítio (propítior) -áre: (1); be merciful, favorable, or kind

propítius -a -um: merciful, favorable, kind, propitious, forgiving, gracious

propóno -ere -pósui -pósitum: (3); set before, propose, prefer, determine, expose, offer, display, resolve

propórtio -ónis: f.; proportion, comparative relation

proportionálitas -átis: f.; proportion, proportionality

proportionátus -a -um: proportionate; proportiónate: adv.

propositio -ónis: f.; proposition, text, proposal, statement

propósitum -i: n.; design, purpose, plan, proposition, resolution

propósitus -a -um: proposed, intended

pro-praeféctus -i: m.; proprefect, vice-prefect

pro-praéses -idis: m.; propresider, proruler, vice-president

proprietárius -a -um: of the owner or proprietor

propríetas -átis: f.; ownership, property, peculiarity, quality

Próprium (Offícium): the part of the Missal or Breviary that has offices for special days

Próprium de Témpore: the Proper of the Season in the Breviary

Próprium Sanctórum: the Proper of the Saints in the Breviary

próprius -a -um: belonging to one, personal, particular, one's own, proper, special, peculiar, characteristic; as a n. noun: possession, property; próprie: adv.

própter: adv. & prep. w. acc.; because of, on account of, by reason of, near, near at hand

proptérea: therefore, for that cause, on that account

propugnáculum -i: n.; bulwark, rampart

propugnátor -óris: m.; defender

propúgno -áre: (1); fight for, defend, go forth to fight

propúlso -áre: (1); repel

propúrgo -áre: (1); cleanse beforehand

prorípio -ere -rípui -réptum: (3); escape, rush forth

prorogátio -ónis: f.; extension, postponement, continuance

prórogo -áre: (1); defer, put off, prolong, continue, protract

prórsus (prórsum): wholly, absolutely, straight on, forwards, directly, precisely, by all means, truly, certainly

prorúmpo -ere -rúpi -rúptum: (3); send forth, thrust forth, break forth

prósa -ae: f.; Sequence at Mass

prósator -óris: m.; ancestor

proscríbo -ere -scrípsi -scríptum: (3); publish, make known publicly, proscribe, outlaw

próseco (prósecro) -áre: (1); sacrifice; cut off or away

prosecútio -ónis: f.; prosecution, pursuit, continuation

prosélytus -a: um; foreign, strange; as a noun: sojourner, proselyte, convert

prósequor -qui -secútus: dep. (3); follow, accompany, regard, pursue, pay attention to, persecute

prosílio -íre -ui: (4); spring, leap up

prospectívus -a -um: prospective, looking ahead

prospécto -áre: (1); look forward, look forth upon, look for

prospéctor -óris: m.; guardian, provider, prospector

prospéctus -a -um: foreseen, provided for

própser (prósperus) -a -um: prosperous, favorable; as a n. pl. noun:

good fortune; prosperity; **próspere:** prosperously, agreeable to one's wishes

prospérgo -ere -spérsi -spársum: (3); sprinkle

prospéritas -átis: f.; prosperity

próspero (prósperor) -áre: (1); succeed, prosper

prospício -ere -spéxi -spéctum: (3); look, foresee, look into the distance, provide for

prostérno -ere -strávi -strátum: (3); spread over, overthrow, cast to the ground, prostrate, fall down, strew

prostíbulum -i: n.; brothel

prostítuo -ere -ui -útum: (3); to prostitute, place before, expose for prostitution, dishonor, sully

prostitúta -ae: f.; prostitute, harlot

prostitútio -ónis: f.; prostitution, fornication

prostitútor -óris: m.; prostitutor, panderer, violator

prósto -áre -stiti: (1); project, stand before, out, or forward

prostrátus -a -um: humble, prostrate

prósum, prodésse, prófui: be profitable, be advantageous, be useful, profit

pro-synodális -is -e: prosynodal

protéctio -ónis: f.; protection, covering

protéctor -óris: m.; protector

protéctrix -ícis: f.; protectress

prótego -ere -téxi -téctum: (3); cover, protect, defend, shelter

protélo -áre: (1); prolong

proténdo -ere -téndi -téntum(-ténsum): (3); hold up, stretch forward, extend, lengthen

prótenus (prótinus): constantly, immediately, straightway, forward, further

prótero -ere -trívi -trítum: (3); tread down, trample under foot

protérvio -ire: (4); be bold or shameless

protérvus -a -um: stubborn, insolent

Protestántes -ium: c. pl.; Protestants

protestátio -ónis: f.; protestation, declaration

protéstor (protésto) -ári: *dep.* (1); bear witness to, proclaim, protest

Prothonotárius -ii: *see* **Protonotárius**

prótinus: *see* **prótenus**

pro-tituláris -is -e: protitular

protocóllum -i: n.; record of a transaction

proto-diáconus -i: m.; protodeacon

protomártyr -is: m.; protomartyr

protonotariátus -i: m.; dignity or honor belonging to a protonotary

Protonotárius (Prothonotárius) -ii: m.; protonotary; *see Appendix*

protopárens -éntis: c.; first parent

protoplástus -i: m.; first man, Adam

protoprésbyter -eri: m.; protopresbyter; *see Appendix*

protosyncéllus -i: m.; protosyncellus: *see Appendix*

prótraho (prótrahor) -ere -tráxi -tráctum: (3); draw out, reveal, extend

protúrbo -áre: (1); disturb

prout (próuti): *conj.;* according to, in proportion to, just as, as, insofar as

provéctio -ónis: f.; progress, advancement

provéctus -us: m.; advancement, promotion, glorification

próveho -ere -véxi -véctum: (3); lead on, carry forward, advance

provénio -íre: (4); come forth, appear, originate, arise, succeed, result

provéntus -us: m.; result, issue, birth, revenue, crop, coming forth, increase

provérbium -ii: n.; proverb, adage

pro-vicárius -ii: m.; provicar, vice-vicar

providéntia -ae: f.; providence

providentiális -is -e: providential, with foresight

provídeo -ére -vídi -vísum: (2); see, behold, set, provide for, make preparation for, foresee, look ahead

próvidus -a -um: foreseeing, provident, cautious, prudent, circumspect, careful; próvide: *adv.; see Appendix*

província -ae: f.; province; *see Appendix*

provinciális -is -e: provincial, of a province; *see Appendix*

provísio -ónis: f.; foresight, provision, forethought; *see Appendix*

províso: *adv.;* with foresight

províso -ere: (3); store, stock, look out for

provísor -óris: m.; provider

provisórius -a -um: provisory, provisional, foreseeing

provísus -us: m.; provision, looking ahead or before, precaution

provocátio -ónis: f.; stimulation, challenge, appeal, recourse, provocation, encouragement

próvoco -áre: (1); provoke, arouse, stir up, excite, appeal

provolútus -a -um: lying prostrate

provólvo -ere -vólvi -volútum: (3); throw oneself down

próximus -a -um: near, nearest, next, neighboring; *as a noun:* neighbor, relative; in próximo: near at hand, very near, next, nearest; próxime: *adv.; see Appendix*

prúdens -éntis: wise, prudent, foreseeing, skilled, versed; prudéntior -ior -ius: *comp.;* prudénter: *adv.*

prudéntia -ae: f.; prudence, wisdom, understanding, discretion, knowledge

pruína -ae: f.; hoarfrost

prúna -ae: f.; live coal

prúriens -éntis: itching

prúrio -íre: (4); itch, long for, be eager for

psállo -ere, psálli: (3); chant, sing, chant the psalms, sing or give praise, sing to a stringed instrument

Psálmi poenitentiáles: the Penitential Psalms: 8, 31, 37, 50, 101, 129, and 142

psalmísta -ae: m.; psalmist

psalmódia -ae: f.; psalmody, chanting of psalms

psálmum -i: n., psálmus -i: m.; psalm

Psálmus Athanasiánus: Athanasian Creed

psalteriális -is -e: relating to psalms

psaltérium -ii: n.; psaltery (the 150 psalms of David), harp, stringed instrument

Psaltérium -ii: n.; the Psalter, part of the Divine Office

pseúdo-apóstolus -i: m.; false apostle

pseúdo-Chrístus -i: m.; false Christ

pseúdo-póntifex -icis: m.; antipope

pseúdo-prophéta -ae: m.; false prophet

psychiáter -tri, psychiátra -ae: c.; psychiatrist

psychiátria -ae: f.; psychiatry

psychiátricus -a -um: psychiatric

psýchicus (psychológicus) -a -um: of the mind, psychological

psychológia -ae: f.; psychology; psychológia in profúndum: depth psychology

psychólogus -i: m.; psychóloga -ae: f.; psychologist

Psychomáchia -ae: f.; Contest of the Soul, poem by Prudentius

psychopáthia -ae: f.; psychopathy

psychopathológia -ae: f.; psychopathology

psychopathológicus -a -um: psychopathological

psychóphthoros -i: m.; soul destroyer

psychósis -is(-eos): f.; psychosis

ptísana -ae: f.; barley

Ptolemaéus -i: m.; Ptolemee or Ptolemaïs, a seaport town near Tyre

pubértas -átis: f.; puberty

púbes (púber, púbis), púberis:
  grown-up, adult, pubescent, having
  reached the age of puberty
púbes (púbis) -is: f.; offspring, youth
publicánus -i: m.; publican, tax
  collector, sinner
publicátio -ónis: f.; publication;
  publicatiónes matrimoniáles:
  marriage banns
público -áre: (1); publish, make public;
  seize, lay waste
públicus -a -um: public, common, of the
  state or community; as a noun: public
  official; as a n. noun: public property,
  treasury, revenue; públice: adv.; see
  Appendix
pudénda -órum: n. pl.; private parts
púdens -éntis:, pudorátus -a -um:
  shamefaced, bashful, modest;
  pudénter: adv.
púdeo -ére -ui -itum: (2); be ashamed;
  most often impers.: cause shame
pudicítia -ae: f.; purity, chastity
pudícus -a -um: chaste, virtuous,
  modest, pure; pudíce: adv.
púdor -óris: m.; purity, modesty,
  decency, shame, disgrace
pudorátus: see púdens
puélla -ae: f.; girl, maiden
puéllus -i: m.; child, small boy
púer -i: m.; boy, child, servant
puerílis -is -e: childish
puerínus -i: m.; diminutive of púer
puerítia -ae: f.; childhood, boyhood,
  girlhood
puérpera -ae: f.; mother, child bearer
puérperus -a -um: childbearing
pugilláres -ium: m. pl.; writing tablet
pugíllus -i: m.; handful
púgio -ónis: f.; sword, dagger
púgna -ae: f.; fight, battle
pugnátor -óris: m.; fighter, combatant,
  warrior
púgnax -ácis: contentious, fighting

púgno -áre: (1); fight, do battle
púgnus -i: m.; fist
púlcher (púlcer) -chra -chrum:
  beautiful, fair, handsome, noble, fine,
  excellent; as a n. noun: beauty; púlchre
  (púlcre): adv.
pulchritúdo -inis: f.; beauty, majesty,
  splendor
púllulo -áre: (1); sprout, shoot up
púllus -i: m.; chicken, young fowl, young
  animal, colt
pulmentárium -ii: n.; meat, food,
  anything to eat
pulméntum -i: n.; savory meat, pottage
púlpitum -i: n.; lectern, pulpit,
  bookstand
pulsátor -óris: m.; clapper, striker,
  knocker, ringer
púlso -áre: (1); knock, strike, beat on,
  ring
púlsus -us: m.; stroke, beating, blow,
  pushing
pulvíllum (pulvínum) -i: n.; small
  cushion
pulvínar -áris: n.; pillow
pulvínus -i: m.; cushion
púlvus -eris: m.; dust, ashes
púmico -áre: (1); rub smooth, polish
punctátor -óris: m.; censor, punctator,
  recorder
púnctio -ónis: f.; pricking
púnctum -i: n.; period, moment, very
  small space, point, small hole, mark;
  púncto témporis: in an instant
púngo -ere, púpugi, púnctum: (3); stab,
  puncture, pierce, prick, sting, annoy
puníceus -a -um: of pumice stone,
  reddish color
Púnicus -a -um: Carthaginian, Punic
púnio -íre: (4); punish, chastise
punítio -ónis: f.; punishment,
  chastisement
pupílla -ae: f.; orphan girl, ward, small
  girl, pupil of the eye

pupilláris -is -e: relating to an orphan or ward

pupillátus -us: m.; orphanage

pupíllus -i: m.; orphan boy, ward, small boy

pupíllus -a -um: very small

púppis -is: f.; stern of a ship, ship

purgámen -inis: n.; means of purification, baptism

purgaméntum -i: n.; refuse

purgátio -ónis: f.; purification, purgation, expiation

purgatórium -ii: n.; purgatory

purgatórius -a -um: purifying, cleansing, purgative

purgátus -a -um: cleansed, purged

púrgo (purífico, púrgito) -áre: (1); purify, cleanse

purificátio -ónis: f.; purification

purificatórium -ii: n.; purificator, purifier

purífico -áre: (1); purify, cleanse

Púrim: _Hebrew;_ Jewish feast, Feast of Lots

púritas -átis: f.; purity, cleanness

púrpura -ae: f.; purple, purple cloth; **régis púrpura:** royal purple

purpurária -ae: f.; seller of purple

purpurátus -a -um: clad in purple

purpúreus -a -um: purple

púrus -a -um: pure, clean, undefiled; **púriter (púre):** _adv._

pusillánimis (puss-) -is -e: timid, fainthearted

pusillanímitas -átis: f.; timidity, cowardice, faintheartedness

pusíllitas -átis: f.; insignificance, smallness

pusíllus -a -um: little, small, tiny, puny; _as a n. noun.:_ little or insignificant matter

pussilánimis: _see_ **pusillánimis**

púta: for example, suppose

putátio -ónis: f.; pruning

putatívus -a -um: putative, reputed, supposed; **putatíve:** _adv._

púteus -i: m.; pit, well, trench, grave

púto -áre: (1); think, suppose, deem

putrédo -inis: f.; corruption, rottenness, putridness

putrefáctus (pútridus) -a -um: rotten, corrupt, putrid

putrefácio -ere -féci -fáctum: (3); make rotten, putrefy

putrefío -fíeri -fáctus: (3); become rotten

putrésco -ere -ui: (3); become rotten, putrified, disgusting

pútridus: _see_ **putrefáctus**

pútris -is -e: rotten, mortifying

pygárgus -i: m.; a kind of antelope, a fish hawk

pýra -ae: f.; pyre, large fire

pýramis -idis: f.; pyramid

pýrus -i: f.; pear tree

pýtho -ónis: c.; soothsayer, diviner

pythónicus -a -um: relating to divination

pythoníssa -ae: f.; witch

pýxis -idis: f.; ciborium, pyx, a vessel of gold or silver in which the Blessed Sacrament is preserved or carried

pyxómelum -i: n.; pyx, ciborium

Q

qoph: 19th letter of the Hebrew alphabet

qua: *adv.;* on which side, at which place, where, insofar as, as, in what manner, to what degree; qua . . . qua: partly . . . partly

quacúmque: *adv.;* whatsoever, wherever, in every manner

quadragéna -ae: f.; period of forty days

quadragenárius -a -um: of forty days

quadragéni -ae -a: forty each

Quadragésima -ae: f.; Lent

quadragesimális -is -e: relating to Lent, Lenten

Quadragésimo Ánno: *see Appendix*

quadragésimus -a -um: fortieth

quadragínta: *indecl. adj.;* forty

Quadragínta Horárum Orátio: Forty Hours' Adoration

quadrangulátus -a -um: quadrangular

quádrans -ántis: m.; fourth part, farthing

quadrátus -a -um: square

quadrátus -i: m.; quadrátum -i: n.; square, squareness

quadriduánus (quatri-) -a -um: of four days

quadriénnium -ii: n.; period of four years

quadrífluus -a -um: having four streams, flowing in four parts

quadrifórmis -is -e: quadriform, fourfold

quádrifrons -tis: four-faced

quadríga -ae: f.; chariot

quadrígamus -a -um: four times married

quadriméstre -is: n.; period of four months

quadringénti -ae -a: four hundred

quádro -áre: (1); correspond with, agree, fit exactly

quádrupes -edis: c.; four-footed animal

quádruplum -i: n.; fourfold

quádrus -a -um: square

quaérito -áre: (1); collect, beg, solicit arms, seek earnestly

quaéro -ere -sívi(-sii) -sítum: (3); require, reason, seek, ask for, interrogate, desire, examine

quaerulósus -a -um: complaining, querulous

quaésco (quaéso) -ere -ívi (-ii) -ítum: (3); beseech, beg, entreat, pray

quaesítor -óris: m.; investigator

quaesítum -i: n.; question; pl.: earnings, acquisitions, gains

quaesítus -a -um: select, uncommon, extraordinary

quaéstio -ónis: f.; inquiry, question, asking for indulgences for giving alms

quaéstor -óris: m.; quaestor, pardoner

quaestuárius -ii: m.; collector of alms

quaestuátio -ónis: f.; begging, collecting alms

quaéstuo -áre: (1); collect, solicit alms, beg

quaestuósus -a -um: profitable

quaéstus -us: m.; gain, advantage, profit, income

qualificátio -ónis: f.; qualification

qualificátus -a -um: qualified

quális -is -e: *interr. adj.;* what manner, what kind, what sort, as, such as

qualiscúmque -iscúmque -ecúmque: *rel. & indef. adj.;* of whatever kind or sort, any whatever

quálitas -átis: f.; quality, nature, property

quáliter: *adv.;* how, as, just as, in what
manner

quam: *adv.;* how, how much, how great;
tam . . . quam: both . . . and; *in
comparisons:* as, than; *with superlative:*
as . . . as possible
quam celériter: as quickly as possible
quam máxime: as much as possible
quam prímum: as soon as possible

quámdiu (quándiu): *adv.;* while, as long
as, until, how long, in that, inasmuch as

quámobrem (quam-ob-rem): *adv.;*
wherefore, for which reason, why

quamplúrimi -ae -a: as many as possible

quamprímum: *adv.;* as soon as possible

quámquam (quánquam): *conj.;*
although, though, and yet, nevertheless

quámvis: *adv.;* even, as you will, although

quándiu: *see* quámdiu

quándo: *adv.;* when, at what time, some
time, how long; *conj.;* when, since,
because

quandocúmque: *adv.;* at what time
soever; *conj.:* whenever, as often as, no
matter when

quandó-libet: *adv.;* at some time or
other, in due time

quándonam: *interr. adv.;* when

quandóque: *adv.;* at some time; *conj.:*
whenever, as often as, since

quandóquidem: *conj.;* seeing that,
because, since

quánquam: *see* quámquam

quánti: *gen. of price from* quántus -a
-um; at what price, of what value

quantíllus (quantúllus) -a -um: how
little, how small

quántitas -átis: f.; quantity

quánto: *adv.;* by how much, the more

quantócius: *comp. adv.;* sooner, more
quickly, as soon as possible

quantópere: *interr. & rel. adv.;* how
much, to what extent, with what care

quantúllus (quantíllus) -a -um: how
little, how small

quántum: *adv.;* as much as, so much as,
how much
quántum ad: so far as concerns
quántum fíeri pótest: as much as is
able to be done

quantumcúmque: *adv.;* however much,
of whatever size, as much as

quantúmvis: *adv.;* as great as you please,
howsoever much

quántus -a -um: how great, how much,
how many, of what size, as much as;
quánto . . . tánto: the more . . . the
more

quantúslibet -álibet -úmlibet: however
great

quaprópter (qua-própter): *interr. & rel.
adv.;* wherefore, on which account, why

quáqua: *adv.;* by whatever way,
whithersoever

quaquavérsum: *adv.;* every way, to all
sides

quáre: *interr. & rel. adv.;* why, for what
cause, by which means, wherefore

quartánus -a -um: belonging to the
fourth day

quártus -a -um: fourth;
quártusdécimus: fourteenth

quási: *adv.;* as it were, so to speak, about,
nearly, almost; *conj.;* as if, just as if, as
though
quási-domicílium -ii: n.; quasi
domicile
quási-párochus -i: m.; quasi pastor
quási-paroécia -ae: f.; quasi parish
quási-posséssio -ónis: f.; quasi
possession

Quasimódo géniti: Low Sunday, the first
Sunday after Easter

quassátio -ónis: f.; scourge, plague,
shaking

quásso -áre: (1); shake, shatter, break

quátenus (quátinus): *interr. & rel. adv.;* that, so that, insofar as, how far, until where, to what point or extent, as far as

quáter: *adv.;* four times

quatérnio -ónis: m.; company of four, body of four soldiers

quátinus: *see* **quátenus**

quátio -ere, quássi, quássum: (3); beat, shake, strike

quatriduánus -a -um: of four days

quatríduum -i: n.; space of four days

quátuor (quáttuor): *indecl.;* four

quatuórdecim: *indecl.;* fourteen

quátuor témpora: Ember Days

-que: *enclitic;* and

quemádmodum: *adv.;* in what manner, how; *conj.:* as, just as

quéo (quiéo) -íre -ívi (-ii) -ítum: (4); be able, can

quércus -i: f.; oak tree

queréla (querréla, querimónia) -ae: f., **quéstus** -us: m.; complaint, action, accusation

querellósus -a -um: full of complaints

quéror -i, quéstus: *dep.* (3); complain, lament

querréla -ae: *see* **queréla**

quéstus -us: *see* **queréla**

qui: *interr. & rel. adv.;* how, why, in what manner

qui, quae, quod: *rel. pron.;* who, which, what, that; *interr. adj.:* which, what, what kind of; *indef. adj.:* any; *indef. pron.:* anyone, anything

quía: *conj.;* for, because, that

quicúmque, quaecúmque, quodcúmque: *rel. pron.;* whoever, whatever, whichever, everyone who, each, any whatsoever

quid: *interr. pron.;* what, why

quid dícis: what do you say

quid pútas: what do you think

ut quid: to what purpose, why

quídam, quaédam, quóddam: *indef. pron.;* certain person or thing,

someone, something; *indef. adj.:* a certain, a kind of

quídditas -átis: f.; essence, whatness

quídem: *adv.;* indeed, to be sure, at least, too, also, for instance

íllud quídem . . . sed aútem: to be sure . . . but still

ne quídem: not even

quídlibet: *indef. n. pron.; see* **quílibet;** anything whatsoever

quídnam: *interr. n. pron.; see* **quísnam;** what then

quídpiam: *indef. n. pron.; see* **quíspiam;** anything

quídquid: *rel. pron.; see* **quísquis;** whatever

quídquid recípitur: whatever is received

quíes -étis: f.; rest, quiet, repose from work or cares

quiéscens -éntis: relating to rest

quiescéntia -ae: f.; quietness, quiescence

quiésco -ere -évi -étum: (3); cease, rest, be still, be at peace, be quiet

quietátio -ónis: f.; quiet, restfulness

quietísmus -i: m.; erroneous teaching of quietism

quiétus -a -um: peaceful, quiet, restful

quílibet, quaélibet, quódlibet: *indef. pron.;* any, anyone who will, anything whatsoever; *indef. adj.:* any, any at all, any you wish

quilísma -atis: n.; serrated note in music

quin: *formed from* **qui** *&* **ne;** *conj.; interr. & rel. particle;* that not, except that, unless, why not, who or which not, so that not, lest

quin étiam: yea indeed

quin ímmo: yea rather

quínam, quaénam, quódnam: *interr. pron.;* which, what

quíndecim: *indecl.;* fifteen

quingéni (quingenténi) -ae -a: five hundred each

quingentésimus -a -um: five hundredth

quingénti -ae -a: five hundred

quíni -ae -a: five each

quínimo (quinímmo): yea rather

quinquagenárius -a -um: fifty in number

Quinquagésima -ae: f.; Quinquagesima Sunday, the Sunday before Ash Wednesday

Quinquagésima paschális: paschal season

quinquagínta: *indecl.;* fifty

quínque: *indecl.;* five

quinquennális -is -e: happening every five years

quinquénnium -ii: n.; period of five years

quínquies: *adv.;* five times

quintílis -is: m.; month of July, the fifth month counting from March as the first month in the early Roman calendar; changed about 150 BC

quíntus -a -um: fifth

quípiam: *see* **quíspiam**

quíppe: *conj.;* for, certainly, indeed, to be sure, by all means, since; **quíppe qui:** since he, inasmuch as he

quíppini (quíppeni): certainly, by all means, why not

quis, quis, quid: *interr. pron.;* who, which, what; **néscio quis:** some sort of, certain, someone, I know not who; *after* **si, nísi, num, ne, ut, cum:** anyone, anything, someone, something

quísnam, quísnam, quídnam: *interr. pron.;* who then, which then, what then

quíspiam (quípiam), quaépiam, quódpiam: *indef. adj.;* any

quíspiam, quíspiam, quídpiam: *indef. pron.;* anyone, anything

quísquam, quaéquam, quídquam: *indef. pron.;* anyone, anything

quísque: *often used for* **quísquis** *or* **quicúmque**

quísque, quaéque, quódque: *indef. pron. & adj.;* whoever, whatever, each, every

quísquis, quaéquae, quídquid: *rel. pron.;* whoever, whosoever, whatever, whatsoever, each, every

quívis, quaévis, quídvis: *indef. pron.;* whosoever you will, whatever you will, anyone at all, anything at all

quívis, quaévis, quódvis: *indef. adj.;* any, any you please, any at all

quo: *adv.;* where, whither, wherefore, for which reason, why; *with conj.;* so that, in order that, to the end that

quóad: *adv.;* how far, how long; *conj.:* as far as, as long as; *prep. w. acc.:* with respect to, regarding

quoadúsque (quoad-úsque, quóad úsque): *conj.;* until, until that

quocírca: *conj.;* on that account, therefore

quocúmque: *adv.;* to whatever place, whithersoever

quod: *conj.;* that, which, what, because, although

   ad id quod: besides that

   éo quod: to the extent that

   ex éo quod: from the fact that

   níhil est quod: there is no reason why

   quod cóntra: whereas on the other hand

   quod ípsum: which of itself alone

   quod scíam: as far as I know

   quod si: but if

   quod vídi (q.v.): which I have seen

   súpra quod: besides

quodámmodo (quódam módo): *adv.;* in a certain way or measure, as it were

quodcúmque: *rel. n. pron.; see* **quicúmque;** whatsoever

quólibet: *adv.;* whithersoever you please

quóminus: *conj.;* so as not, that not; *after verbs of hindering:* from

quómodo: *adv.;* how, in what manner, in what way, as, just as

quomodocúmque (quoquomódo): *adv.;* in any way, in any way whatsoever, in whatever way, however

quóndam: *adv.;* once, formerly, at a certain time

quóniam: *conj.;* for, because, since, that, seeing that, whereas, inasmuch as

quóquam: *adv.;* whithersoever, to any place

quóque: *adv.;* also, too

quoquomódo: *see* **quomodocúmque**

quot: *indecl. adj.;* how many; **quótquot:** however many, no matter how many, as many as

quotánnis: *adv.;* yearly, annually

quoténnis -is -e: *interr. adj.,* of how many years

quotidiánus -a -um: daily; **quotídie:** *adv.*

quóties (quótiens): *adv.;* how often, how many times as, as often as

quotiescúmque (quotienscúmque): *adv.;* however often, as often as

quótquot: *see* **quot**

quoúsque: *adv.;* how long, how far, until when or where, to what extent

quuum (cum): *conj.;* since, when, as often as

qúo vádis: where are you going?

R

rábbi (rabbóni): *indecl.:* m.; *Hebrew;*
master, teacher, rabbi

rábide: madly, savagely, fiercely

rábidus -a -um: mad

rábies -éi: f.; madness, fury, rage,
fierceness

ráca (rácha): *indecl.; Aramaic;* silly
person, fool, worthless fellow, term of
abuse

racémus -i: m.; cluster

raciális -is -e: racial

radiátus -a -um: provided with rays

radicális -is -e: rooted, having roots,
essential

radícitus: by the roots, radically,
completely, utterly

rádico -áre: (1); take root

rádio (rádior) -áre (1): radiate, emit rays

radiophónia -ae: f.; radio

radiophónicus -a -um: broadcast by
radio, radiophonic

radiósus -a -um: radiant, beaming

rádius -ii: m.; ray, beam of light

rádix -ícis: f.; root; pl.: base, foundation;
in radícibus: at the foot

rádo -ere, rási, rásum: (3); scratch,
scrape away, erase, shave

Ráhab: *indecl.;* Rahab, the harlot

raméntum -i: n.; reed, thin stick

ramificátus -a -um: making branches,
branching out

rámus -i: m.; branch, bough, twig

ramúsculus -ii: m.; small branch

rána -ae: f.; frog

rápax -ácis: ravening, rapacious, greedy;
as a noun: extortioner

rápidus -a -um: rapid, swift, quick,
hurried, seizing, tearing

rápiens -éntis: ravening, rapacious

rapína -ae: f.; robbery, plundering,
pillage

rápio -ere -ui, ráptum: (3); catch, seize,
carry off, take away, take by force,
hurry away, ravish, strive for

ráptio -ónis: f.; abduction, rape

rápto -áre: (1); drag away

ráptor -óris: m.; robber, plunderer,
extortioner

ráptus -us: m.; abduction, robbery

ráro: rarely, seldom, far apart

rárus -a -um: rare, strange

rástrum -i: n.; rake

ráta -ae: f.; rate; fixed amount; **pro ráta:**
proportionately, in proportion

ratihabítio -ónis: f.; ratification,
approval

rátio -ónis: f.; reckoning, reasoning, way,
account, record, rule, plan, order,
reason, retribution; *see Appendix*

ratiocínium -ii: n., **ratiocinátio** -ónis: f.;
reasoning, reckoning, calculation,
syllogism

ratiócinor -ári: *dep.* (1); reckon,
compute, calculate

rationábilis (rationális) -is -e: endowed
with reason, reasonable, rational,
syllogistic; **rationabíliter
(rationáliter):** *adv.*

rationále -is: n.; oracular breastplate of
Jewish high priest, morse, medieval
episcopal insignia

rationálitas -átis: f.; reasonableness,
rationality

rátis -is: f.; raft, float

rátus -a -um: valid, settled, ratified,
fixed, reckoned, calculated

rátum et non consummátum: *see Appendix*

rátum habére: ratify, approve

raucésco -ere: (3); become hoarse

raúcitas -átis: f.; harshness, hoarseness

raúcus -a -um: hoarse

re-: *a prefix sometimes used for emphasis or repetition*

reaedífico -áre: (1); rebuild

reáctio -ónis: f.; reaction

reális -is -e: real, true; reáliter: *adv.*

reálitas -átis: f.; reality

reampléctor -i -pléxus: *dep.* (3); embrace again

reápse: in truth, indeed

reassúmo -ere: (3); take up, take up again

reátus -a -um: accused

reátus -us: m.; guilt, fault, crime, condition of an accused person; *see Appendix*

rebaptízo -áre: (1); rebaptize

rebellátor -óris: m., rebellátrix -ícis: f.; rebel, one who rebels

rebéllio -ónis: f.; rebellion

rebéllis -is -e: rebellious, insurgent

rebéllo -áre: (1); rebel, renew a war

recálcitro -áre: (1); kick, kick back

recálvus -a -um: bald in front, bald

recapitulátio -ónis: f.; summing up, recapitulation, repetition

recapítulo -áre: (1); recapitulate, go over again, summarize

recédo -ere -céssi -céssum: (3); fall away, stray, depart, leave, forsake, recede, retire, withdraw, turn aside

récens -éntis: recent, fresh, young; recénter: *adv.*

recénseo -ére -ui -cénsum(-cénsitum): (2); recall, review, examine, celebrate; enumerate, count

recénsio -ónis: f.; reviewing, mustering, enumeration, recension

receptáculum -i: n.; vessel, receptacle, reservoir, storehouse, magazine

receptíbilis -is -e: acceptable, recoverable

recéptio (receptátio) -ónis: f.; reception, receiving, accepting

recépto -áre: (1); receive, draw back, retire

recéptor -óris: m.; receiver

receptórium -ii: n.; parlor, sacristy

recéssus -us: m.; retirement, withdrawal, going back, secret, mystery

recidívus -a -um: recurring, repeating, falling into the same sin

récido -ere, réccidi (récidi), recásum: (3); fall back, return, turn out, relapse, result

recído -ere -cídi -císum: (3); cut away, cut back, abridge

reciperátio (recup-) -ónis: f.; recovery, regaining

recípero (recúp-) -áre: (1); restore, recover, revive

recípio -ere -cépi -céptum: (3); recover, receive, take back

recíprocus -a -um: returning, receding, alternating, reciprocal

recitátio -ónis: f.; recitation

recitátor -óris: m.; reader, reciter

récito -áre: (1); recite

reclámo -áre: (1); cry out against, contradict loudly

reclinatórium -ii: n.; back of a couch

reclíno -áre: (1); lay back, bend back, recline, cause to lean back

reclúsa -ae: f.; anchoress, female recluse

reclusérium -ii: n.; cell

reclúsus -i: m.; anchorite, recluse

recógito -áre: (1); think again, consider, reflect

recognítio -ónis: f.; recognition, recollection, examination, review, approval

recógnito -áre: (1); reflect, consider, think again, weigh, ponder, review

recognósco -ere -nóvi -itum: (3); review, inspect, examine, recognize, consider, approve, certify, authorize

recolléctio -ónis: f.; recalling, recollecting, recollection

récolo -ere -cólui -cúltum: (3); contemplate, recollect, reflect on, repair, renew, cultivate again

reconciliátio -ónis: f.; reconciliation, forgiveness

reconciliátor -óris: m., **reconciliátrix** -ícis: f.; intermediary, reconciler, restorer

reconciliátus -a -um: reconciled

reconcílio -áre: (1); reconcile, absolve, reunite, bring together again

recóndo -ere -didi -ditum: (3); hide, lay aside, lay up, conceal

reconvénio -veníre -véni -ventum: (4); make a counterclaim

reconvéntio -ónis: f.; counterclaim, countersuit

reconventiális -is -e: pertaining to a countersuit

recordátio -ónis: f.; record, memory, remembrance, receiving

recordátus -a -um: mindful

recórdo (recórdor) -áre: (1); recall, remember, record, call to mind, be mindful of

recreatórium -ii: n.; recreation place

récreo -áre: (1); refresh, treat, remake, renew, restore, quicken

récrepo -áre: (1); to echo

recrudésco -ere -crúdui: (3); break open again, become raw again, refuse, decline

rectitúdo -inis: f.; rectitude, righteousness

réctor -óris: m.; rector, ruler

réctus -a -um: right, correct, upright, straight, just, steadfast, stable, direct, proper; **in récto:** directly; *as a n. noun:* that which is right, straight, direct, pure, clean, steady; **récte:** *adv.*

recúbitus -us: m.; seat at table

récubo -áre: (1); recline

recúmbo -ere -cúbui: (3); lean, sit down, recline at table, eat with, dine with, sup

recuperátio -ónis: *see* **reciperátio**

recúpero -áre: (1); recover, recuperate

recúrro -ere -cúrri -cúrsum: (3); run back, occur, come or hasten back, return, recur

recúrsus -us: m.; recourse, appeal; *see Appendix*

recusátio -ónis: f.; refusal, rejection, objection

recúso -áre: (1); refuse, decline

recútio -ere -cússi -cússum: (3); strike back, cause to rebound

réda: *see* **rhéda**

redaccéndo -ere: (3); rekindle

redáctus -a -um: *perf. pass. part. of* **rédigo**

redáctus -us: m.; proceeds, produce

rédamo -áre: (1); love again, return love for love

redánimo -áre: (1); restore to life, quicken

redárguo -ere -gui -gútum: (3); confute, disprove, refute, contradict, admonish, urge to penance

redargútio -ónis: f.; retort, reproof, rejoinder, reply, refutation

reddítio -ónis: f., **rédditus** -us: m.; return, restoration, result, pay, profit, reward

rédditor -óris: m.; one who pays, payer

réddo -ere -didi -ditum: (3); restore, pay, render, return, give back, give what is due, reward; **certiórem réddere:** inform

redémptio -ónis: f.; redemption, deliverance, ransoming, release from sin and its penalties

redemptívus -a -um: redemptive

redémpto -áre: (1); redeem, ransom

redémptor -óris: m.; redeemer, rescuer, savior; see Appendix

rédeo -íre -ívi (-ii) -itum: (4); return, go or come back

redíco -ere: (3); respond

rédigo -ere -égi -áctum: (3); bring down, reject, despise, abhor, treat contemptuously, reduce, drive back

redimículum -i: m., redimícula -ae: f.; necklace, chaplet

redímo -ere -émi -émptum: (3); redeem, set free, ransom, deliver

redintegrátio -ónis: f.; restoration

redíntegro -áre: (1); restore, raise up

réditus -us: m.; return, coming or going back, revenue, returns, proceeds, funds

redivívus -a -um; renewed, living again

redóleo -ére -ui: (2); smell, emit a scent, be redolent of

redóno -áre: (1); give back

redúco -ere -dúxi -dúctum: (3); bring or lead back

redúctio -ónis: f.; bringing back, restoring, restoration

redúndo -áre: (1); overflow

redúplico -áre: (1); redouble, reduplicate

rédux -úcis: returned

refáctor -óris: m.; re-maker

reféctio -ónis: f.; refectory, guestchamber, refreshment; restoration, repairing

reféllo -ere -félli: (3); disprove, refute, rebut, show to be false, repel

réfero -érre, rétuli (réttuli), -látum: irreg.; yield, refer, relate, tell, bring back

refértus -a -um: crowded

refício -ere -féci -féctum: (3); mend, repair, refresh, restore, make over

refígo -ere -fíxi -fíctum: (3); tear, loose, unfasten, pull apart

reflécto -ere -fléxi -fléxum: (3); turn back, divert, reflect

refléxus -us: m.; reflex, bending back, recess, return

refléxus -a -um: crooked, bent back, reflected

reflóreo -ére -ui: (2), reflorésco -ere -rui: (3); bloom, bloom again, flower, be refreshed or revived, flourish

réfluus -a -um: flowing back

refocíllo -áre: (1); revivify, revive; relieve

refódio -ere -fódi -fóssum: (3); dig up or out

reformátio -ónis: f.; reformation

reformátor -óris: m.; restorer, reformer, transformer

refórmo -áre: (1); renew, reform, remake

refórmido -áre: (1); dread

refóveo -ére -fóvi -fótum: (3); revive, refresh, supply, cherish

refractárius -a -um: stubborn, contentious, refractory

refraéno (refréno) -áre: (1); bridle, check, restrain, curb, hold back

refrágium -ii: n.; resistance, opposition

refrágor (refrágo) -ári: dep. (1); oppose, resist, contest, object

refréno -áre: (2); check, restrain, hold back, refrain

refrigérium -ii: n.; cooling, consolation, refreshment, recreation

refrígero -áre: (1); refresh, cool, relieve, comfort, assist

refrigésco -ere -fríxi: (3); grow cold, abate, lose interest, grow stale, fail

refríngo -ere -frégi -fráctum: (3); break up or open

réfuga -ae: f.; fugitive, deserter, forsaker

refúgio -ere -fúgi -fúgitum: (3); flee, escape, take flight

refúgium -ii: n.; refuge, asylum

refúlgeo -ére -fúlsi: (2); shine brightly, glitter, illuminate

refúndo -ere -fúdi -fúsum: (3); pour out, pour back, restore

refuscátus -a -um: darkened, obscured

refúto -áre (1); resist, oppose, refute, repress

regália -ium: n. pl.; rights and privileges

regális -is -e: regal, royal

regáliter: regally, royally

regenerátio -ónis: f.; regeneration, renewal, rebirth

regenerátor -óris: m.; regenerator

regénero -áre: (1); bring forth again, regenerate spiritually

régens -éntis: m.; director

régero -ere -géssi -géstum: (3); bring or carry back, return, retort

regéstum (regístrum) -i: n.; record, register, bookmark, list

régimen -inis: n.; direction, guidance, government

regína -ae: f.; queen

régio -ónis: f.; region, country, land, section, territory

regionális -is -e: regional

regionárius -ii: m.; deacon of a region

regístrum -i: see regéstum

régius -a -um: royal, relating to king

regnátor -óris: m.; ruler, governor

regnícola -ae: c.; dweller in a kingdom

régno -áre: (1), régo -ere, réxi, réctum: (3); reign, rule, direct, govern, guide

régnum -i: n.; kingdom, reign

régrado -áre: (1); go down in rank

regrédior -i -gréssus: dep. (3); go back, return

regréssus -us: m., regréssio -ónis: f.; return, regress, retreat

régula -ae: f.; standard, rule, guide, pattern, model, example

reguláris -is -e: regular, of rule; reguláriter, regulátim: adv.

régulo -áre: (1); rule, govern, regulate, control

regulus -i: m.; petty king, prince, lord, chieftain; a kind of serpent

reiéctio (rejéctio) -ónis: f.; rejection

reício -ere, rejício -ere, -jéci -jéctum: (3); throw back, reject, repel, cast away

reincidéntia -ae: f.; reoccurence, reincidence

reinvénio -íre: (4); find again

reinvíto -áre: (1); invite again, invite in return

reípse -a -um: the very (re- shows emphasis)

rejéctio -ónis: f.; rejection

rejício: see reício

relábor -lábi -lápsus: dep. (3); slide back, relapse, return

reláte: in relation to

relátio -ónis: f.; report, relation; relátio annuális: annual report

relatívus -a -um: relative, relating to; relatíve: adv.

relátor -óris: m.; reporter, recorder, pónens

relátus -a -um: perf. pass. part. of réfero

relátus -us: m.; recital, narrative

reláxatio -ónis: f.; relaxation, ease, relief

reláxo -áre: (1); loose, forgive, mitigate, soften, widen, alleviate

relegátio -ónis: f.; banishment

relégo -áre: (1); banish, remove

rélego -ere -légi -léctum: (3); collect, gather again, travel or cross again, read over again

rélevo -áre: (1); raise, lighten, relieve, alleviate

relíctus -a -um: abandoned; perf. pass. part. of relínquo

relíctus -us: m.; a forsaking or abandoning

relígio -ónis: f.; religion, devotion, reverence, worshiping, conscientiousness, religious community

religiósitas -átis: f.; religiousness

religiósus -a -um: religious, pious, God-fearing, conscientious, of a religious community; religióse: adv.;

as a noun: a member of a religious community; *see Appendix*

réligo -áre: (1); bind, fasten

relínquo -ere -líqui -líctum: (3); forsake, abandon, relinquish, leave

relíquia -ae: f.; relic; pl.: remains, relics, the rest, the remainder, remnant

reliquiárium -ii: n.; reliquary, container for relics

réliquus -a -um: remaining; **et réliqua:** and so forth, and the rest

reluctátio -ónis: f.; assistance

relúctor -ári: *dep.* (1); contend, strive, struggle against, be hesitant

remándo -áre: (1); send back word, repeat a command

remáneo -ére -mánsi -mánsum: (2); be left, remain, abide

remeábilis -is -e: goes or comes back

remédio -áre: (1); heal, cure

remédium -ii: n.; remedy

rememorátio -ónis: f.; memory, remembrance

remémoror -ári: *dep.* (1); remember

rémeo -áre: (1); go or come back, return

remérgo -ere: (3); immerse again

remétior -íri -ménsus: *dep.* (4); measure again

rémex -igis: m.; rower

rémigo -áre: (1); row

remígro -áre: (1); wander back, come back, return

reminíscor -i: *dep.* (3); remember, call to mind, recollect, be mindful of

remíssio -ónis, **remíssa** -ae: f.; remission, forgiveness, absolution, pardon

remíssor -óris: m.; one who forgives

remissoriális -is -e: remitting

remítto -ere -mísi -míssum: (3); remit, pardon, forgive, relax, send back, refer to

remonstrántia -ae: f.; monstrance

remótio -ónis: f.; removal

remótus -a -um: remote, far off, distant

remóveo -ére -móvi -mótum: (2); take away, remove, set aside, put away

remunerátio -ónis: f.; reward, payment

remunerátor -óris: m.; rewarder

remúnero (remúneror) -áre: (1); pay, reward, remunerate

renascibílitas -átis: f.; rebirth

renáscor -násci -nátus: *dep.* (3); be born again, be regenerated, be born again spiritually

rénes -um(-ium): m. pl.; kidneys, loins, interior parts, intimate feeling of soul or mind

renídeo (reníteo) -ére: (2); shine

renítor -i -nísus (-níxus): *dep.* (3); struggle against, withstand, oppose

réno -áre: (1); swim back

renovátio -ónis: f.; renovation, renewal

rénovo -áre: (1); renew, build anew, restore

renuntiátio -ónis: f.; renunciation, resignation; *see Appendix*

renúntio -áre: (1); renounce, give up, relate, report, declare, appoint

rénuo -ere -ui: (3); refuse, deny by motion of the head, reject, decline

réor, réri, rátus: *dep.* (2); suppose, think, esteem

reósculor -ári: *dep.* (1); kiss again

repágula -ae: f.; enclosure, fence

repágulum -i: n.; restraint, barrier

repándus -a -um: bent backward, turned up

reparátio -ónis: f.; reparation, regeneration, healing

reparátor -óris: m., **reparátrix** -ícis: f.; restorer

réparo -áre: (1); restore, repair; **ánno reparátae salútis:** in the year of Redemption

repastíno -áre: (1); dig again, delve anew

repéllo -ere -púli -púlsum: (3);
overcome, cast off, repel, reject, drive
away or back

repéndo -ere -péndi -pénsum: (3); repay,
return, reward, requite

repénso -áre: weigh again,
counterbalance

repénte: suddenly

repentínus -a -um: sudden

repercússio -ónis: f., repercússus -us:
m.; rebounding, repercussion,
reflection

repercútio -ere -cússi -cússum: (3);
strike or push back, cause to rebound,
reverberate, re-echo, resound

repério -íre -péri -pértum: (4); find,
reveal, discover, obtain

repértor -óris: m.; discoverer, inventor,
author

repertórium -ii: n.; list, index, inventory

repetítio -ónis: f.; repetition

répeto -ere -ívi (-ii) -ítum: (3); repeat,
exact of, demand, ask back,
recommence, fetch, attack again, renew

repígnero (repígnoro) -áre: (1); redeem
a pledge

répleo -ére -plévi -plétum: (2); fill,
satisfy, refill, complete, replenish

réplico -áre: (1); reply, unfold again,
bend back, unroll

répo -ere -si -tum: (3); crawl, creep

repóno -ere -pósui -pósitum: (3); keep,
preserve, place, set back; see Appendix

repórto -áre: (1); bring back, receive

reportórium -ii: n.; inventory

repósco -ere: (3); claim, ask back again,
demand back

reposítio -ónis: f.; reposition, act of
replacing

repositórium -ii: n.; repository

repósitus -a -um: laid up, reposed

repraesentátio -ónis: f.; a showing,
exhibiting, manifestation,
representation

repraesénto -áre: (1); show, represent,
make manifest, exhibit

reprehéndo -ere -héndi -hénsum: (3); to
censure

reprehensíbilis -is -e: deserving of
rebuke or censure, reprehensible

reprehénsio -ónis: f.; censure, rebuke

réprimo -ere -préssi -préssum: (3);
repress, curb

reprobátio -ónis: f.; condemnation,
rejection

réprobo -áre: (1); reject, disapprove,
refuse, condemn

réprobus -a -um: false, spurious,
reprehensible, good-for-nothing

réprobus -i: m.; castaway

repromíssio -ónis: f.; promise

repromíssor -óris: m.; one who
promises, surety, bail

repromítto -ere -mísi -míssum: (3);
promise again, promise in return, bind
oneself

repropítio -áre: (1); propitiate again,
make propitiation for

réptile -is: n.; reptile

répto -áre: (1); crawl, creep

repubésco -ere: (3); grow young again

repudiátio -ónis: f.; rejection,
repudiation

repúdio -áre: (1); reject, repudiate

repúdium -ii: n.; divorce

repúgno -áre: (1); resist, disagree with,
fight against, deny

repúlso -áre: (1); drive back, repel

réputo -áre: (1); esteem, repute, account,
reckon, think over

Réquiem: Mass for the dead

réquies -éi(-étis): f.; rest, repose

requiéscant (-cat): may they (he, she)
rest in peace

requiésco -ere -évi -étum: (3); be at rest

requiétio (requítio) -ónis: f.; rest, repose

requiétus -a -um: rested, refreshed

requíro -ere -sívi -sítum: (3); need, require, seek, ask after, demand, search for

requisítio -ónis: f.; requisition

requisítum -i: n.; want, need; pl.: requisites, requirements

requítio -ónis: *see* requiétio

Rérum Novárum: *see Appendix*

res: 20th letter of the Hebrew alphabet

res, réi: f.; thing, matter, object, circumstance, affair; *see also Appendix*
  res géstae: deeds
  res familiáris: inheritance
  res pública: republic, state, government, politics, country

resárcio -íre, resártum: (4); restore, repair, compensate

rescindíbilis -is -e: revocable, rescindable

rescíndo -ere -scídi -scíssum: (3); annul, repeal

rescísco -ere -scívi(-scii) -scítum: (3); learn, find out, ascertain

rescíssio -ónis: f.; rescission, revocation, recall, annulment

rescissórius -a -um: rescinding, revoking, rescissory

rescríbo -ere -scrípsi -scríptum: (3); write again, write back

rescríptum -i: n.; rescript, written reply, copy; *see Appendix*

réseco -áre -sécui -séctum: (1); cut out, root out, curtail, check, stop

reserátus -a -um: open, unlocked

résero -áre: (1); reveal, open, make clear, unlock

reservátio -ónis: f.; reservation

resérvo -áre: (1); save, preserve, keep or hold back

residéntia -ae: f.; residence

residentiális -is -e: residential

resídeo -ére -sédi -séssum: (3); sit up, remain, reside

resíduus -a -um: remaining, left behind; *as a n. noun:* remainder, residue

resignátio -ónis: f.; resignation

resígno -áre: (1); resign, open, unseal, annul, cancel, invalidate

resína -ae: f.; balm

resipiscéntia -ae: f.; repentance, reformation, change of mind

resipísco -ere -sípui(-sipívi): (3); repent, come to one's right mind, recover, have a change of heart

resisténtia -ae: f.; resistance

resísto -ere -stiti: (3); withstand, resist, oppose

resolúbilis -is -e: able to be dissolved

resolútio -ónis: f.; dissolution, cancellation, loosening; escape, release

resolútus -a -um: careless, relaxed, unfastened, free

resólvo -ere -sólvi -solútum: (3); loosen, unbind, release, open, relax, separate, resolve

résono -áre: (1); resound, re-echo, express, convey

respéctio -ónis: f.; esteem, regard, visitation; judgment, survey, review

respectívus -a -um: respective, particular; respectíve: *adv.*

respéctus -us: m.; respect, care, regard, concern, consideration

respérgo -ere -spérsi -spérsum: (3); scatter, stain, sprinkle, shed

respício -ere -spéxi -spéctum: (3); look at, behold, consider, look back, respect, observe

respiraméntum -i: n.; relief, breathing space

respíro -áre: (1); breathe, find relief, sigh with longing

respléndeo -ére -ui: (2); shine, show forth, be bright

respóndeo -ére -spóndi -spónsum: (2); reply, answer, respond

responsábilis -is -e: responsible

responsabílitas -átis: f.; responsibility

responsális -is -e: relating to an answer or response

respónsio -ónis, responsúra -ae: f., respónsum -i: n.; reply, answer, response

Responsoriále -is: n.; a book containing the responses of the Office

responsórium -ii: n.; responsory

Responsórium Graduále: a book containing parts chanted at Mass

respónsum -i, responsúra -ae: see respónsio

respública, reipúblicae: f.; republic, commonwealth

réspuo -ere -ui: (3); spit upon, despise, reject

restaúro -áre: (1), restítuo -ere -ui -útum: (3); restore

restícula -ae, réstis -is: f.; line, cord

restínguo -ere -stínxi -stínctum: (3); extinguish, quench

restítuo -ere -ui -útum: (3); replace, return, reestablish

restitútio -ónis: f.; restitution, restoration, reinstatement; see Appendix

restitútor -óris: m.; restorer

résto -áre -stiti: (1); stop behind, remain, stand still, stand firm

restríctio -ónis: f.; restraint, restriction

restríngo -ere -ínxi -íctum: (3); restrain, restore, check

resúlto -áre: (1); resound, rebound, spring or leap back

resúmo -ere -súmpsi -súmptum: (3); take back, take again, recover, resume, restore one's courage

resúrgens -éntis: c.; a risen one

resúrgo -ere -surréxi -surréctum: (3); rise again, rise, rise from the dead

resurréctio -ónis: f.; resurrection

resúscito -áre: (1); rise up again, revive, restore, stir up, resuscitate

retárdo -áre: (1); check, stop, hold back, retard

réte -is: n.; net

reténdo -ere -di -tum(-sum): (3); slacken, unbend, relax

reténtio -ónis: f.; retention, keeping, maintenance

reténto -áre: (1); hold back, hold fast

reténtus -a -um: perf. pass. part. of retíneo and reténdo

retéxo -ere -téxui -téctum: (3); repeat, relate again, unweave, unravel, break up, cancel, annul

retiáculum -i: n.; snare, network

reticénda -órum: n. pl.; things to be kept secret

reticéntia -ae: f.; reticence, silence

retíceo -ére -ui -itum: (2); be silent, keep secret, conceal

retículum -i: n.; lace, network

retíneo -ére -tínui -téntum: (2); restrain, hold back, retain

retíolum (retináculum) -i: n.; little net

retórqueo -ére -tórsi -tórtum: (2); turn back, cast back, twist

retractátio -ónis: f.; revision, review, reconsideration, withdrawal, retraction

retrácto -áre: (1); reconsider, revise, review, withdraw, retract, refuse, decline

rétraho -ere -tráxi -tráctum: (3); withdraw, restrain

retríbuo -ere -ui -útum: (3); repay, bring, render, reward, requite

retribútio -ónis: f.; retribution, repayment, recompense

retribútio -ónis: f.; retribution, recompense, reward, benefit, repayment

retritúro -áre: (1); thresh again

rétro: back, behind, backward, after

retroáctus -a -um: past, inverted

retrofrotále -is: n.; reredos

retrográdior -i -gréssus: *dep.* (3); go backward

retrográdus -a -um: going backward

retrórsum: backward, back, retroactively

retrotábula -ae: f.; retable

retrotráctio -ónis: f.; retroaction, retroactivity

retrotráho -ere -áxi -áctum: (3); make retroactive, project into the past

retrúdo -ere: (3); thrust back, remove

retúndo -ere -túdi -túsum: (3); blunt, dull, deaden, weaken

Reuben: *indecl.;* Reuben, eldest son of Jacob and Leah; a tribe of Israel

réus -i: m.; accused, guilty one, criminal, culprit, defendant

revelátio -ónis: f.; revelation

revélo -áre: (1); reveal, disclose, make known, uncover

revéra: in truth, truly, indeed

revérbero -áre: (1); reproach, turn back, strike back, cause to rebound

reveréndus -a -um: reverend, revered

reverénter: reverently

reveréntia -ae: f.; reverence

reverentiális -is -e: reverent

revéreor -éri: *dep.* (2); stand in awe of, revere, respect; be ashamed, fear

revértor (revérto) -i -vérsus: *dep.* (3); turn back, return, turn about, revert

revídeo -ére -vídi -vísum: (2); review, reexamine, see again

revigésco -ere -vígui: (3); flourish again, start again

revincíbilis -is -e: able to be disproved

revíncio -íre -vínxi -vínctum: (4); bind, tie, tie back, bind in back

revínco -ere -víci -víctum: (3); subdue again, conquer, convict, refute

revirésco -ere -vírui: (3); become green again

reviscerátio -ónis: f.; the restoring of flesh

revísio -ónis: f.; examination, review, revision

revísor -óris: m.; examiner

revivésco: *see* revivísco

revivificátus -a -um: restored to life

reviviscéntia -ae: f.; act of reviving

revivísco (revivésco) -ere -víxi: (3); revive, come to life again, recover

revívo -ere -víxi -víctum: (3); revive

revocabíliter: revocably, revokingly

revocátio -ónis: f.; recall, revocation; *see Appendix*

révoco -áre: (1); recall, call away

revólvo -ere -vólvi -volútum: (3); roll back, unroll, unwind, revolve

rex, régis: m.; king

rhámnus -i: m.; bramble, thorny shrub

rhéda -ae: f.; carriage with four wheels, chariot

rhetórica -ae: f.; rhetoric

rhetóricus -i: m.; rhetorician

rhomphaéa (rúmpia) -ae: f.; long javelin, sword

rhýthmus -i: m.; rhythm

ríctus -a -um: open-mouthed, with expanded jaws

rídeo -ére, rísi, rísum: (2); laugh, laugh at, smile, mock, ridicule

rigátus -us: m.; a watering

rígens -éntis: rigid, unbending

rigésco -ere, rígui: (3); grow stiff or rigid, become numb

rígidus -a -um: rigid, stiff, unbending; rígide: *adv.*

rígo -áre: (1); water, wash, sprinkle, moisten, wet, irrigate

rígor -óris: m.; rigor, stiffness, inflexibility, numbness, firmness, sternness

rigoróse: rigorously, strongly

rímula -ae: f.; small crack, fissure, chink

rípa -ae: f.; bank, shore

rísus -us: m.; laughter

ríte: rightly, fitly, properly, with suitable
  ceremony
rituális -is -e: relating to rites; *see*
  Appendix
rituálitas -átis: f.; ritual
rítus -us: m.; rite, ceremony; *see*
  Appendix
rívulus -i: m.; brook, stream, rivulet
rívus -i: m.; river
ríxa -ae: f.; quarrel, strife, dispute
ríxor -ári: *dep.* (1); to quarrel
robígo (rub-) -inis: f.; rust
róbor (róbur) -óris: n. strength, oak,
  force, effect; róbor habére: take effect
roborátor -óris: m.; one who strengthens
róboro -áre: (1); strengthen, make
  strong, prevail
róbur -óris: *see* róbor
robústus -a -um: strong, mighty, firm,
  hard, powerful, stout, robust; robúste:
  adv.
róccua -ae: f.; alb
rochétta -ae: f., rochéttum -i: n.; rochet,
  a surplice with narrow sleeves
ródo -ere, rósi, rósum: (3); gnaw, nibble
  at, consume, corrode
rogátio -ónis: f., rogátus -us: m.;
  request, petition, rogation
rogátus -us: m.; request, petition
rógito -áre: (1); ask eagerly, inquire
  frequently
rógo -áre: (1); ask, pray, entreat, beseech,
  solicit
rógus -i: m.; funeral pyre, bonfire
Róma -ae: f.; Rome; *see Appendix*
Románi -órum: m. pl.; Romans
Románus -a -um: Roman
romphaéa -ae: *see* rhomphaéa
róridus -a -um: covered with dew
róro -áre: (1); bedew, cause dew to form
ros, róris: m.; dew
rósa -ae: f.; rose
rosáceus -a -um: rose-colored, pink
rosárium -ii, rosétum -i: n.; rosary

róseus -a -um: roseate
róstrum -i: n.; speaker's platform,
  pulpit, stage; prow; beak, snout, muzzle
róta -ae: f.; wheel, disk
Róta: Rota, a tribunal of the Curia; *see*
  Appendix: Romána Róta
Rotális -is -e: of the Roman Rota
róto -áre: (1); revolve, turn, cause to
  turn, roll around, whirl round
rotúndo -áre: (1); make round, round
  off; elaborate
rúbeo -ére -ui -itum: (2); blush, redden,
  be ruddy
rúber -bra -brum, rubicúndus (rúbeus,
  rubínus, rúbrus) -a -um: red, ruddy,
  ruby-colored
rubésco -ere -bui: (3); become red
rubéta -órum: n. pl.; thorns
rúbeus, rubicúndus: *see* rúber
rubígo -inis: f.; rust, mildew
rubínus: *see* rúber
rúbor -óris: m.; shame
rubríca -ae: f.; rubric, liturgical directive
rubricális -is -e: rubrical, of rubrics
rubricátus -a -um: dyed red, reddened
rubricísta -ae: m.; writer on rubrics,
  rubricist
rubríco -áre: (1); color red
rúbrus: *see* rúber
rúbus -i: m.; bush, bramble
rúdens -éntis: m.; rope, cord
rudiméntum -i: n.; rudiment,
  beginning, principle, commencement
rúdis -is -e: rough, ignorant, unused,
  raw, wild, unfinished, unpolished,
  awkward, uncultured
rúdis -is: f.; slender stick, stirring rod,
  foil, wooden sword
rúfus -a -um: red, ruddy
rúga -ae: f.; wrinkle
rúgio -íre: (4); call aloud, roar
rugítus -us: m.; roaring
rúgo -áre: (1); fold

ruína -ae: f.; ruin, destruction, invasion, breach, fall, debris

ruinósa -órum: n. pl.; ruins

rúmino -áre: (1); eat, feed upon

rúmor -óris: m.; fame, report, rumor, hearsay, popular opinion

rúmpia -ae: *see* rhomphaéa

rúmpo -ere, rúpi, rúptum: (3); break, break asunder, interrupt

runcína -ae: f.; carpenter's plane

rúnco -áre: (1); weed out, mow, pluck

rúo -ere, rúi, rútum: (3); hurry, rush, hasten, fall down, be ruined

rúpes -is: f.; rock, cliff, stony hill

rúptio -ónis, ruptúra -ae: f.; breaking open, rupture, injuring, fracture, damage

rúptor -óris: m.; violator

rurális -is -e: rural, rustic, of the country

rurícola -ae: c.; peasant, tiller, husbandman, rustic

rúrsum (rúrsus): anew, again, turned back, on the contrary, back

rus, rúris: n.; country, farm, lands, estate, rural place

rusticátio -ónis: f.; husbandry, agriculture, farming

rústice: like a rustic, awkwardly, boorishly

rústicus -a -um: relating to the farm or country, rural, rustic, simple; *as a m. noun:* farmer, husbandman

rúta (rútula) -ae: f.; rue, bitter herb

Ruth: *indecl.;* Ruth, a book of the O.T.

rútilo -áre: (1); glow, glitter, shine

rutíllus -a -um: yellow, auburn, golden

S

Sába: *indecl.;* Saba, Sheba, a people, city, and country of Arabia, famous for incense, myrrh, spices, and gold

sabacthíni: *Aramaic;* Thou hast forsaken me

Sabaéus -a -um: Sabaean

Sábaoth (Sább-): *indecl.:* pl.; *Hebrew;* heavenly hosts, armies, an appellation of the Lord as ruler over all

sabbáticus (sabbatínus) -a -um: pertaining to the Sabbath

sabbatísmus -i: m.; Sabbath rest, day of rest, keeping the Sabbath

sabbatízo -áre: (1); to rest on the Sabbath

Sábbatum -i: n.; Sabbath, Saturday, seventh day of the week, Jewish day of rest (under Christian law the day of rest was changed to Sunday in honor of the Resurrection); **sábbata** -orum: n. pl.; Sabbath; **úna sabbatórum:** the first day of the week

sabulósus -a -um: sandy, gravelly

sábulum -i: n.; sand, gravel

saccárius -a -um: pertaining to sacks

saccellárius (sacellárius) -ii: m.; chaplain

saccéllus (sácculus) -i: m.; small sack, pouch, purse

saccínus -a -um: made of sackcloth

sacculárius -ii: m.; almoner

sácculus -i: *see* **saccéllus**

sáccus -i: m.; sackcloth, bag, garb for times of penance, cassock worn by some confraternities

sacellánus -i: m.; sacristan, chaplain

sacellárius -ii: *see* **saccellárius**

sacéllum -i: n.; chapel, little sanctuary

sácer -cra -crum: sacred, consecrated, holy; *as a n.* pl. *noun:* sacred orders, sacraments, worship, oil; *see Appendix*

sacérdos -ótis: m.; priest

sacerdotále -is: n.; ritual

sacerdotális -is -e: sacerdotal, relating to a priest or the priesthood, priestly; *see Appendix*

sacerdótium -ii: n.; priesthood, priestly function

Sácrae Órdines: holy orders; *see Appendix*

Sacramentále -is: n.; a book of instructions for the administration of the sacraments; **sacramentále** -is: n.; a sacramental

sacraméntalis -is -e: sacramental; **sacramentáliter:** *adv.*

sacramentárium -ii: n.; sacramentary, book containing prayers of Mass for different feasts

Sacramentárium Gelasiánium: Missal ascribed to Pope Gelasius I

Sacramentárium Gregoriánum: Missal ascribed to Pope St. Gregory

Sacramentárium Leoniánum: Missal ascribed to Pope St. Leo I

sacraméntum -i: n.; symbol, rite, mystery, secret, sacrament (one of seven in the Roman Catholic Church), sacramental grace, the Eucharist, instrument of grace; *see Appendix*

Sácra Poenitentiária: Sacred Penitentiary; *see Appendix*

sacrárium -ii: n.; depository or basin for holy things, holy place; sacristy

sacrárius -ii: m.; sacristan

Sácra Romána Róta: Sacred Roman Rota, tribunal of appeal for the Holy See; *see Appendix: Romána Róta*

Sácrae Románae Rótae Decisiónes: decisions of the Rota

sacratórium -ii: n.; sacristy

sacrátus -a -um: sacred, holy, hallowed, consecrated; **sacráte:** *adv.*

sacrificális -is -e: of sacrifices, sacrificial

sacrificátio -ónis: f.; act of sacrificing

sacrificátor -óris: m.; sacrificer

sacrifícium -ii: n.; sacrifice, offering, oblation

sacrífico -áre: (1); sacrifice, offer up, make an offering

sacrilégium -ii: n.; sacrilege

sacrílegus -a -um: sacrilegious; *as a noun:* one who commits a sacrilege, church or temple violator

sacrísta -ae: c., **sacristánus** -i: m.; sacristan, vestryman

sacristía -ae: f.; sacristy, vestry

sácro -áre: (1); consecrate, make holy

sacrosánctus -a -um: sacred, most holy, inviolable, sacrosanct; *see Appendix*

sácrum -i: n.; holy thing, sacrifice of the Mass, sacred rites

Sácrum septenárium: sevenfold gifts

sáde: 18th letter of the Hebrew alphabet

Sadducaéi -órum: m. pl.; Sadducees, sect of Jews who denied the Resurrection

Sádoc: *Hebrew;* Sadoc, son of Azor and father of Achim

sae- *see also* **se-**

saéclum -i: *see* **saéculum**

saeculária -ium: n. pl.; celebration, secular feast

saeculáris -is -e: of the world, secular, temporal, worldly

saeculáritas -átis: f.; secularity, secular nature

saecularizátio -ónis: f.; secularization, release from a vow

saéculum (saéclum) -i: n.; time, period, age, lifetime, indefinite period of time, century, world, worldliness

a saéculo: from the beginning

a saéculo in saéculum: from beginning to end, forever, from eternity to eternity

in saécula: forever

in saécula saeculórum: world without end, forever, to ages of ages

in saéculum saéculi: forever

in (per) ómnia saécula: forever

saépe (saepenúmero): often, oftentimes, frequently, many times, repeatedly

saépio -íre, saépsi, saéptum: (4); hedge or enclose in

saéptum (séptum) -i: n., **saépes (sépes)** -is: f.; fence, wall, enclosure, hedge

saéviens -éntis, **saévus** -a -um: fierce, cruel, wild, savage, violent, raging

saévio -íre: (4); rage, be fierce, be furious, be cruel, be violent

saevítia -ae, **saévitas** -átis: f.; fury, ferocity, harshness, cruelty, fierceness, severity

sága -ae: f.; witch

sagácitas -átis: f.; sagacity, mental acuteness, keenness, shrewdness

sagáciter: keenley, sharply, acutely, sagaciously, quickly, accurately

ságax -ácis: having keen sense, of quick perception, sagacious

sagéna -ae: f.; net, dragnet, seine, snare

sagína -ae: f.; food, fodder, nourishment, fattening, stuffing, corpulence

saginátus -a -um: fatted, fattened, fat

sagíno -áre: (1); feed, fatten, cram full, nourish

ságio -íre: (4); feel keenly, perceive quickly

sagítta -ae: f.; arrow

sagittárius -ii: m.; archer

sagítto -áre: (1); shoot with arrows

ságma -atis: n.; saddle

ságum -i: n.; military cloak, mantle, blanket

sal, sális: m. & f.; salt

salárium -ii: n.; salary

salárius -a -um: relating to salt

saltátus -us: m.; religious dance

Sálem: *indecl.; Hebrew;* Salem, Jerusalem

Salérnum -i: n.; Salerno

Salesiáni -órum: m. pl.; Salesians, communities founded by Don Bosco

Salesiánus -a -um: of the Salesians

Salésium -ii: n.; Sales

Sálim: *indecl.;* Salim, an unidentified place in the Jordan valley

salínae -árum: f. pl.; salt pits, saltworks

sálio (sall-) -íre, *no perf.,* -ítum: (4); salt, season

sálio -íre, sálui, sáltum: (4); leap, spring, bound, jump

saliúnca -ae: f.; shrub, wild nard

salíva -ae: f.; spittle, saliva

sálix -icis: f.; a tree akin to the willow, willow branch, osier

sállio: *see* sálio

sállo: *see* sálo

Salmána: *see* Zalmúnna

Salmántica -ae: f.; Salamanca

Sálmon -ónis: m.; *Hebrew;* Salmon, father of Boaz

sálo (sállo) -ere, *no perf.,* sálsum: (3); salt, season

Sálomon -ónis: m.; King Salomon

salsíssimus -a -um: very salty

salsiúsculus -a -um: rather salty

salsúgo -inis: f.; saltiness, salty waste, desert, wilderness

saltátio -ónis: f.; dance, dancing

saltátrix -ícis: f.; dancing girl

saltátus -us: m.; religious dance

sáltem (sáltim): at least, at all events, anyhow; ne sáltem, néque sáltem, non sáltem: not even

sálto -áre: (1); dance

sáltus -us: m.; wasteland, marsh, forest, glade, pasture; leap, bound, jump

salúber (salúbris) -bris -bre: strong, wholesome, useful, good, healthful, salutary; salúbriter: *adv.*

salúbritas -átis: f.; health

sálus -útis: f.; salvation, health, deliverance, safety, help, greeting; *see Appendix*

salutáre -is: n.; savior, salvation

salutáris -is -e, salútifer (-ferus) -era -erum: salutary, saving, wholesome, helping, beneficial, health-giving

salutátio -ónis: f.; salutation, greeting

salutatórium -ii: n.; reception room for the bishop in the early churches

salutíferus (salútifer) -a -um: health-bringing, salubrious

salúto -áre: (1); salute, greet, keep safe, preserve

salutórius -a -um: theatrical

sálva reveréntia: with due reverence being preserved

salvátio -ónis: f. salvation, act of saving

salvátor -óris: m.; savior

sálve (salvéte, salvéto): *sing. (pl.) imperat. of* sálveo; hail, hello

sálveo -ére: (2); be well

Sálve Regína: Hail Queen, a hymn in honor of the B.V.M.

salvéte, salvéto: *see* sálve

salvífico -áre: (1); save, keep, rescue, preserve, deliver

salvíficus -a -um: saving, salvific, pertaining to salvation

sálvo -áre: (1); save, keep, rescue, preserve, deliver

sálvo melióre judício: with the better judgment being preserved

sálvus -a -um: safe, whole, saved, well, sound; sálvum me fac: save me

samárdacus -i: m.; juggler

Samaría -ae: f.; Samaria

Samaritánus -a -um: Samaritan

sambúca -ae: f.; sackbut, a kind of stringed musical instrument or harp; crosier, pastoral staff; seige machine for storming walls

sambúcus -i: f.; elder tree; **sambúcum** -i: n.; elderberry

sámech: 15th letter of the Hebrew alphabet

sámio -áre: (1); polish, furbish

Sámuel -élis: m.; Samuel; a book of the O.T.

sanábilis -is -e: remediable, curable

sanátio -ónis: f.; healing, sanation (a special form of validation); *see Appendix*

sáncio -íre, sánxi (sáncii, sancívi), sánctum (sancítum): (4); make sacred or inviolable, appoint, ordain, sanction, dedicate, ratify, forbid

sáncitus -a -um: sanctified, consecrated, sanctioned

Sáncta Sédes, Sánctae Sédis: f.; Holy See

sanctíficans -ántis: sanctifying

sanctificátio -ónis: f.; blessing, holiness, sanctification, sanctuary, shrine, holy place, sacred mystery, making holy

sanctificátor -óris: m.; sanctifier

sanctifícium -ii: n.; sanctuary, temple, shrine

sanctífico -áre: (1); sanctify, make holy or inviolable

sanctíloquus -a -um: speaking holily

sanctimónia -ae: f.; holiness, piety

sanctimoniális -is -e: pious, holy; *as a noun:* monk, nun, religious

sánctio -ónis: f.; rule, sanction, restriction, penalty

Sanctíssimum -i: n.; Blessed Sacrament

sanctitúdo -inis, **sánctitas** -átis: f.; holiness, piety, sanctity

Sanctoréle -is: n.; the part of the Breviary with offices of feasts of saints

sanctuárium -ii: n.; sanctuary, shrine, holy place

sánctus -a -um: holy, saintly, godly; *as a noun:* canonized saint; **Sánctus:** *can mean* the Sanctus of the Mass; **sánctior** -ior -ius: *comp.;* **sáncte:** *adv.*

sandálium -ii: n.; sandal, slipper

sáne: soberly, sensibly, rationally, truly; **sáne quam:** enormously

sanguíneus (sanguinárius) -a -um, **sanguináris** -is -e: of blood, bloody

sánguis -inis: m.; blood

sanguisúga -ae: f.; leech

sánies -éi: f.; matter, pus

sanitárius -a -um: of or pertaining to health, sanitary

sánitas -átis: f.; soundness, health, sanity, common sense

sáno -áre: (1); heal, cure, restore to health

sánus -a -um: healthy, whole, sane

saphírus -i: *see* **sapphírus**

sápidus -a -um: savory, relishing

sápiens -éntis: wise, discreet, sensible; **sapiéntior** -ior -ius: *comp.;* **sapiénter:** *adv.*

sapiéntia -ae: f.; wisdom, common sense, discretion, prudence

Sapiéntia -ae: f.; Book of Wisdom

sapientiális -is -e: pertaining to wisdom

sápio -ere -ii: (3); understand, be wise, perceive, taste, savor of, know; **idípsum sápere:** to be of one mind

sápor -óris: m.; taste, delicacy, flavor

sapórus -a -um: savory

sapphirínus -a -um: of sapphire

sapphírus (saph-) -i: m.; sapphire

sarabára -órum: n. pl.; wide trousers

Saracéni -órum: m. pl.; Saracens

sárcina -ae: f.; burden, pack

sárcio -íre, sársi, sártum: (4); repair, restore, patch, mend, make good, correct

sarcóphagum -i: n., **sarcóphagus** -i:m; sarcophagus, stone coffin

sárculum -i: n.; spade, hoe

Sardicénsis -is -e, Sardiánus -a -um: of
Sardis

Sardínia -ae: f.; Sardinia

sárdius (sardínus, sardónychus,
sardónichus) -a -um: of Sardian
stone, of carnelian, of precious stone

sárdius -ii, sárdo -inis: m., sárdonyx
-ychis: c.; carnelian, precious stone

Sárdus -a -um: Sardinian

sário: see sárrio

Sárion (Sírion): indecl.; Mount Hermon

sarméntum -i: n.; brushwood, faggot,
twigs

sárrio (sário) -íre -ui(-ívi) -ítum: (4);
sow or weed, cultivate

sartágo -inis: f.; pan for cooking

sartatécta -órum: n. pl.; repairs

sártus -a -um: repaired

sat: enough

satágito -áre: (1), sátago -ere -egi -áctum:
(3); be very busy, have enough to do,
be diligent, be troubled, satisfy, pay

Sátan: indecl., Sátanas -ae: m.; voc.
Sátana; Satan, the devil, an adversary

satánicus -a -um: satanic, devilish

satélles -itis: c.; guard, servant,
companion, officer of law

satellítium -ii: n.; support, escort, guard

sátio -áre: (1); satisfy, nourish, fill,
satiate, feed

sátio -ónis: f.; sowing

sátis: enough, greatly, exceedingly,
sufficiently; as an indecl. adj.: enough,
sufficient, satisfactory, adequate; sátis
supérque: enough and more than
enough

satisfácio -ere -féci -fáctum: (3); give
satisfaction, satisfy

satisfáctio -ónis: f.; satisfaction, amends,
reparation; satisfáctio pro poéna:
remission by satisfaction

satisfactionális -is -e: apologetic

satispássio -ónis: f.; punishment to be
undergone

sátor -óris: m.; sower, begetter, source

sátrapes (sátraps) -is, sátrapa -ae: m.;
governor, viceroy, satrap

sátum -i: n.; dry measure, standing corn;
pl.: crops

sátur -úra -úrum: full, sated

saturátio -ónis, satúritas -átis: f.; filling,
fullness, satisfaction, abundance,
satiety, repletion

satúro -áre: (1); fill, satisfy, sate

sátus -i, sátus -us: m.; measure, sowing,
planting, begetting, seed, stock

saúcio -áre: (1); wound, hurt, injure

saúcius -a -um: wounded, hurt, injured

Saúlus -i, Saul -úlis, or indecl.; Saul, the
king of Israel; the original name of
Paul

sáxeus -a -um: stony

saxiperérium -ii: n.; bag for slingshot
stones

sáxum -i: n.; stone, rock

scabéllum (-billium) -i: n.; stool,
footstool, low seat, altar step;
scabéllum pédum: ark of the covenant

scáber -bra -brum: rough, scabby, itchy,
mangy, scurfy

scabitúdo -inis: f.; irritation, itch

scábo -ere, scábi: (3); scratch, scrape

scaéna -ae: f.; stage, scene, appearance,
parade

scaénicus -a -um: of the stage, dramatic,
theatrical

scaéptrum -i: see scéptrum

scáevus -a -um: left; awkward, unfavorable

scála -ae: f.; ladder

scaláris -is -e: of steps or ladders

scálprum (scalpéllum) -i: n., scalpéllus
-i: m.; chisel, scalpel, lancet, knife,
pruning knife

scámma -atis: n.; wrestling place or
contest

scámnum -i: n.; seat, bench, stool, throne

scandalízo -áre: (1); scandalize, give
scandal, cause to fall or stumble

scándalum -i: n.; scandal, stumbling block, trap, obstacle

scándo -ere, scándi, scánsum: (3); climb, rise, ascend, mount, get up

scápha -ae: f.; boat, skiff

scápulae -árum: f. pl.; shoulders, back, wings, shoulder blades

scapuláre -is: n.; scapular, covering for the shoulders

scátebra -ae, scatúrigo -inis: f.; bubbling water, springwater, spring, source

scáteo -ére: (2), scatúrio -íre: (4); gush, swarm, abound, flow, bubble

scélero -áre: (1); defile, pollute, desecrate, contaminate

scelerátus -a -um: defiled, polluted, defamed, profaned

sceléstus -a -um: wicked, abominable, shameless, infamous, accursed

scélus -eris: n.; crime, wickedness, evil deed, sin, vice, fault

scenofactórius -a -um: pertaining to tentmaking

Scenopégia -orum: n. pl.; the Feast of Tabernacles

Scéptici -órum: m. pl.; Skeptics

scéptriger -a -um: scepter-bearing

scéptrum (scaéptrum) -i: n.; scepter, royal staff, symbol of authority

Scéva -ae: m.; Sceva, a Jewish priest

schéda (scída) -ae: f.; paper, sheet of paper, card

schédula (scídula) -ae: f.; small leaf or sheet of paper, ballot

schéma -atis: n.; form, outline, figure, draft, arrangement, schema

schínus -i: f.; mastic tree

schísma -atis: n.; split, schism, separation, disunion, breaking away; see Appendix

schismáticus -a -um: pertaining to schism, schismatic; as a noun: one who has broken away, a schismatic

schístus -a -um, schístos -a -on: split, cleft, divided; as a m. noun: schist, red oxide of iron

schóla (scóla) -ae: f.; school, class, lecture, dissertation, debate, leisure time for learning, sect, group, students

schóla cantórum: choir, group of singers

scholáris -is -e: of a school or group

scholásticus -a -um: belonging to a school, scholastic, name usually applied to the philosophy of St. Thomas Aquinas; scholásticus -i: m.; teacher, lecturer, rhetorician; scholástica -órum: n. pl.; school exercises

scída -ae: see schéda

scídula -ae: see schédula

scíens -éntis: knowing, expert, wise, skillful; scíenter: adv.

sciéntia -ae: f.; knowledge, science, skill, expertness

scientíficus -a -um: scientific; scientífice: adv.

scílicet: actually, naturally, of course, to be sure, certainly, namely, that is to say, to wit, evidently

scíndo -ere, scídi, scíssum: (3); cut, rend, tear asunder, divide, separate, part; scíndere médium: to cut into two pieces

scíniphes -ium: m. pl.; gnats, stinging insects

scintílla -ae: f.; a spark

scintíllo -áre: (1); sparkle, glitter

scío, scíre, scívi, scítum: (4); know, know how, understand, perceive, realize; quod scíam: as far as I know

scírpeus (sírpeus) -a -um: made of rushes

scírpus (sírpus) -i: m.; bulrush, rush

scíscitor -ári: dep. (1); inform one's self, inquire, investigate, examine, interrogate, question, ask, consult

scísco -ere, scívi, scítum: (4); inquire,
seek to know, find out, accept after
inquiry, approve, assent to

scissúra -ae, scíssio -ónis: f.; division,
splitting, rending, parting

scíssus -a -um: *perf. pass. part. of* scíndo

scítus (scíus) -a -um: knowing,
experienced, skilled, fit, suitable;
scítum -i: n.; statute, decree,
ordinance; scíte: skillfully, cleverly,
tastefully

scóla -ae: *see* schóla

scópa -ae: f.; broom, thin twig; scópis
mundátus: swept clean

scópo -áre: (1); sweep

scópo -ere: (3): investigate, search, test,
search thoroughly

scópulus -i: m.; rock, cliff, crag

scópus (scópos) -i: m.; aim, objective,
target, goal, scope

scória -ae: f.; dross

scórpio -ónis: m., scórpius -ii: m.;
scorpion; instrument of torture, whip

scórtor -ári: *dep.* (1); associate with or
employ harlots

scórtum -i: n.; immorality, harlot,
concubine, mistress

Scóti -órum: m. pl.; Scots

Scótia -ae: f.; Scotland

Scotísta -ae: m.; Scotist, follower of
Duns Scotus

scríba -ae: c.; scribe, writer, secretary,
clerk; Scríba -ae: m.; a member of the
scribes, a Jewish sect

scríbo -ere, scrípsi, scríptum: (3); write,
record

scrínium -ii: n.; chest, case, closet,
archives, bookcase, letter box, file

scríptio -ónis: f.; writing, composition

scríptor -óris: m.; writer, composer,
narrator

scríptum -i: n.; publication, writing,
document

Scriptúra -ae: f.; Holy Scripture

scríptus -a -um: written, recorded;
scrípte: *adv.*

scríta -órum: n. pl.; trifles

scrupulósus -a -um: exact, anxious,
precise, scrupulous

scrúpulus -i: m., scrúpulum -i: n.;
scruple, anxiety

scrutátio -ónis: f., scrutínium -ii: n.;
discerning, search, investigation,
inquiry, examining, scrutiny, ballot,
vote

scrutátor -óris: m., scrutátrix -ícis: f.;
searcher, examiner, investigator

scrútor (scrúto) -ári: *dep.* (1); search,
examine, investigate, scrutinize

scúlpo -ere, scúlpsi, scúlptum: (3); carve,
hew, chisel

scúlptile -is: n., sculptúra -ae: f.; idol,
graven image, sculpture

scúlptilis -is -e: carved, hewn, cut

scúlptus -a -um: graven, sculpted

scurrílitas -átis: f.; scurrility, buffoonery

scutárius -ii: m.; shieldbearer

scútra -ae: f.; shovel

scutulátus -a -um: checkered

scútulum -i: n.; escutcheon

scútum -i: n.; shield, buckler

scýphus -i: m.; cup, goblet

se: *3rd per. refl. pron., acc. & abla.;*
himself, herself, itself, themselves

sebáceus -a -um: of tallow

secédo -ere -céssi -céssum: (3); go away,
withdraw, depart, retire, secede,
separate

secérno -ere -crévi -crétum: (3);
separate, set apart, hide, sunder, sever,
distinguish, discern

secéssus -us: m.; retreat, withdrawal,
place of retirement

seclúdo -ere -clúsi -clúsum: (3); exclude,
shut away, seclude, shut off

séco -áre, sécui, séctum: (1); cut, cut off,
cut up

sécare médium: cut in two, destroy, upset

térra non sécta: untilled earth

secólligo -ere: (3); become part of

secréta -ae: f.; former Secret prayer of the Mass

secretális -is -e: hidden, secret

secretária -ae: f., **secretariátus** -us: m.; secretariate, secretary's office

secretárium -ii: n.; secret place, private chapel, place of retirement

secretárius -ii: m., **secretária** -ae: f.; secretary

Secrétum Míssae: Canon of the Mass

secrétus -a -um: secret, separate, separated, remote, retired, solitary, in private; **secréto:** *adv.; as a n. noun:* secret, something hidden, mystery, solitude, retreat

sécta -ae: f.; sect, faction, party, mode of life

sectátor -óris: m.; follower, pursuer, member of a sect

séctio -ónis: f.; section, division

séctor -ári: *dep.* (1); follow, follow eagerly or continually, pursue, strive after

sectúra -ae: f.; cutting

sécubo -áre: (1); live alone

secumféro -érre: irreg.; take along, carry with oneself, involve

secundárius -a -um: secondary, inferior, middling, second-rate

secundicérius -ii: m.; subdean

secúndo: a second time, secondly

secúndo -áre: (1); favor, bless, assist

secúndum: *prep. w. acc. & adv.;* in accordance with, according to, to the advantage of, afterwards; **secúndum quid:** according to which, relatively

secúndus -a -um: second, next, following, favorable

secúris -is: f.; ax, ax head, hatchet

secúritas -átis: f.; security, safety

secúrus -a -um: secure, safe, steadfast, quiet; **secúre:** *adv.*

sécus: otherwise, not so, differently, later; *rarely as prep. w. acc.:* by, beside, at, along, near

sécus quam *or* **átque:** otherwise than, differently from

non (haud) sécus: just so

non (haud) sécus quam *or* **átque:** otherwise than one would wish, wrongly, badly

secútus -a -um: *perf. part. of* **séquor**

sed: but, however, yet, and indeed

non sólum (módo) . . . sed étiam (quóque): not only . . . but also

sed énim: but in fact

sed et: as also

íllud quídem . . . sed aútem: to be sure . . . but still

sedátus -a -um: quiet, tranquil, composed, sedate

sédecim: sixteen

sédeo -ére, sédi, séssum: (2); sit

sédes -is: f.; seat, throne, See, headquarters, habitation

Sédes Apostólica: Apostolic See

sédes confessionális: confessional

séde impedíta: see being obstructed, no bishop administering; *see Appendix*

séde vacánte: see being vacant, no bishop reigning; *see Appendix*

sedíle -is: n., (**sedília** -ium: pl.); seat, station, bench, stool

sedítio -ónis: f.; sedition

seditiósus -a -um: seditious, factious, mutinous, turbulent; *as a noun:* conspirator

sédo -áre: (1); soothe, calm, appease, allay, still, assuage

sedúco -ere -dúxi -dúctum: (3); lead astray, seduce, deceive

sedúctilis -is -e: seducible, able to be led astray or seduced sedúctio -ónis: f.; drawing aside, misleading, seduction

sedúctor -óris: m., sedúctrix -ícis: f.; seducer, deceiver

seductórius -a -um: seductive

sédule (sédulo): diligently, zealously, designedly, industriously, busily

sedúlitas -átis: f.; watchfulness

sédulus -a -um: earnest, diligent, careful, zealous, mindful, solicitous, busy, industrious; sédulo: adv.

séges -etis: f.; corn, harvest, crop, produce

segméntum -i: n.; piece, segment, part, shaving

ségnis -is -e: slow, slothful, sluggish

segnítia -ae, segníties -éi: f.; slowness, tardiness, sluggishness

Segóvia -ae: f.; Segovia

segregátio -ónis: f.; separation, segregation

ségrego -áre: (1); separate, set aside, segregate

Séhon: see Síhon

seípse -ípsa -ípsum: he himself, she herself, it itself

seismógraphon -i: n.; seismograph

sejúnctim: separately, disjunctly

sejúngo -ere -júnxi -júnctum: (3); disjoin, sever, separate

Séla: indecl.; Hebrew; "rock"; Sela, a town in Palestine

seléctio -ónis: f.; selection

Seleúcia -ae: f.; Seleucia, a city of Syria

séligo -ere -légi -léctum: (3); select, choose

sélla -ae: f.; chair, stool

Sélmon: Hebrew; see Zálmon

Sem: indecl.; Sem, son of Noah

semánimis: see semiánimis

semántron -i: n.; sounding board

sémel: once, single time, at some or any time; sémel et bís: repeatedly

sémen -inis: n.; seed, semen, offspring, descendant

seméntis -is: f.; sowing, seeds

seménto -áre: (1); to bear seeds

seméstris -is -e: of six months, half-yearly, semiannual; as a n. noun: semester, six-month period

semetípse -ípsa -ípsum: more emphatic form of seípse

sémi-: prefix; half; thin, light

semiánimis (semánimis) -is -e, semiánimus -a -um: half-dead, half-alive

semicínctium -ii: n.; narrow girdle or apron

semi-dúplex -icis: semidouble

semifáctus -a -um: half-finished

semijejúnium -ii: n.; half fast

semimórtuus -a -um: half-dead

seminariáta -ae: m.; seminarian, student in a seminary

seminarísticum -i: n.; tax for maintenance of a seminary

seminárium -ii: n.; seminary, school for training clergy

seminátio -ónis: f.; planting of seed; intercourse

seminátor -óris: m.; sower

seminivérbius -a -um: word-scattering, babbling; as a noun: sower, babbler

sémino -áre: (1); sow, produce, beget

semiplenitúdo -inis: f.; semifulfilment

semi-plénus -a -um: half-full

semi-públicus -a -um: semipublic

semi-púnctum -i: n.; an inflection in chant

sémis, semíssis, sometimes indecl.: m.; half, half-unit, semi-unit

semisaúcius -a -um: half-wounded

sémita -ae: f.; path, way, lane, narrow way, footpath

semiústus -a -um: half-burnt

semivívus -a -um: half-dead, half-alive

semóveo -ére -móvi -mótum: (2); separate, remove, put aside, renounce

sémper: always, ever, at all times, forever

sémper et ubíque: always and everywhere

sémel et sémper: once and forever

sempitérnus -a -um: everlasting, eternal; **in sempitérnum:** forever

senátor -óris: m.; senator

senatórius -a -um: senatorial, of the senate; *as a m. noun:* senator; *as a n. noun:* reserved section

senátus -us: m.; senate, parliament, college, council

senéctus -a -um: old, aged; *as a noun:* old person

senéctus -tútis: f.; old age, senility

séneo -ére: (2); to be old or weak

senésco -ere -ui: (3); grow old, become aged, become weak, waste away

sénex -is: old, ancient; *as a c. noun:* old man or woman, aged person

senílis -is -e: old, aged, senile, pertaining to the elderly

sénior -óris: m.; older person, elder

sénior -ior -ius: older, elder, more mature, senior

sénium -ii: n.; feebleness of age, decline, senility

sénsa -órum: n. pl.; thoughts, notions

sensátus -a -um: wise; **sensáte:** *adv.*

sensíbilis -is -e: perceptible, apprehensible, sensible

sensibíliter: sensibly, in a way such as to effect the senses

sensífico -áre: (1); endow with sensation, make sensible

sénsim: slowly, softly, gradually

sensuális -is -e: endowed with feeling, sensitive, sensual

sénsus -us: m.; mind, feeling, sense, purpose, perception, understanding, meaning, idea, notion; *see Appendix*

senténtia -ae: f.; opinion, thought, sentiment, meaning, idea, purpose; sentence, judgment, maxim, aphorism, decision, vote; *see Appendix*

sentína -ae: f.; hold of a ship, bilgewater, refuse; lowest of the people, rabble

séntio -íre, sénsi, sénsum: (4); feel, experience, perceive, think, judge, observe, learn, notice, remark

seórsum (seórsim): aside, apart, especially, particularly, individually, privately

separátim: separately, apart

separátio -ónis: f.; separation, severance

séparo -áre: (1); separate, sunder

sepélio -íre -ívi (-ii), sepúltum: (4); bury

sépes -is: f.; hedge, fence

sepiméntum -i: n.; enclosure, chancel

sépio -íre, sépsi, séptum: (4); fence in, guard

sepóno -ere -pósui -pósitum: (3); put aside, put apart, exclude

sépta -órum: n. pl.; enclosure, wall

séptem: seven

Septémber -bris -bre: of September; *as a m. noun:* month of September

septemplíciter: sevenfold

Séptem Psálmi Paenitentiáles: the seven Penitential Psalms

septenárius -a -um: septenary, of seven

septénnium -ii: n.; period of seven years

septentrionális -is -e: north

sépties (séptiens): sevenfold, seven times

septifórmis -is -e, **séptuplus** -a -um: sevenfold

septimána -ae: f.; week

Septimána máior (sáncta): Holy Week

septimanárius -ii: m.; choir official serving for a week

séptimus -a -um: seventh

Septuagésimus -a -um: seventieth; **Septuagésima** -ae: f.; Septuagesima, the seventieth day, formerly the third Sunday before Lent

Septuagínta -ae: f.; Septuagint, the principal Greek text of the O.T.

septuagínta: seventy

séptum -i: *see* **saéptum**

séptuplus: *see* septifórmis

sepúlchrum (sepúlcrum) -i: n.; tomb, sepulcher, grave

sepulcrétum -i: n.; cemetery, crypt, burial vault

sepúlto -áre: (1); bury

sepultúra -ae: f.; burial, burial place, grave, interment

sepúltus -a -um: buried

séquax -ácis: following after

sequéla (sequélla) -ae: c.; follower, following

sequéntia -ae: f.; sequence, continuance, Sequence, continuation of the Gradual song

sequentiále -is: n.; book containing the various Sequences for the liturgy

seqúester -tris: m.; trustee, person with custody of property

sequestrátio -ónis: f.; sequestration

sequéstro -áre: (1); deposit for safekeeping, separate, put aside

séquor, séqui, secutus: *dep.* (3); seek to attain, follow, pursue, strive for

séquior -ior -ius: worse, lesser

séra -ae: f.; a bolt, bar

séraph: *indecl.; Hebrew;* seraph; séraphim: pl.; seraphim, the highest choir of angels

seráphicus -a -um: seraphic

séraphin (séraphim): *indecl.:* pl.; *Hebrew;* seraphim

seréne: calmly

sereníssimus -a -um: most serene or calm, sovereign

serénitas -átis: f.; sereneness, clearness, fair weather

serénus -a -um: bright, serene, clear, fair

séria -ae: f.; earthenware jar

seríceus (séricus) -a -um: silken

séricum -i: n.; silk

séries: *no gen. and dat.;* f.; series, row, succession

sérius -a -um: grave, earnest, serious; sério: *adv.;* sérius: *comp. adv.*

sérmo -ónis: m.; speech, discourse, sermon, saying, homily, word

sermocinátio -ónis: f.; discussion

sermocinátor -óris: m.; preacher

sermócino -áre: (1); preach a sermon, lead a discussion, dispute

sermócinor -ári: *dep.* (1); converse, talk, commune

sermúnculus -i: m.; little discourse, rumor, tittle-tattle, report

Sermólogus -i: m.; a book containing the discourses of the Fathers of the Church

séro: in the late evening

séro -ere, sévi, sátum: (3); to sow

serótinus (sérus) -a -um: late

sérpens -éntis: c.; creeping thing, serpent, snake

serpentínus -a -um: serpentlike

sérpo -ere, sérpsi, sérptum: (3); creep, crawl

sérra -ae: f.; saw

sérrans -ántis: like a saw

serrátus -a -um: saw-toothed

sérro -áre: (1); saw up

sérta -ae: f.; wreath, garland

sérus -a -um: late; séra nócte: late at night

sérva -ae: f.; female servant

Servátor -óris: m.; Savior

Sérvi -órum: m. pl.; Servites

servílis -is -e: servile, slavish

sérvio -íre: (4); serve, be in bondage, wait upon, do service to, obey

servítium -ii: n., sérvitus -útis: f.; service, servitude, subjection, slavery

sérvo -áre: (1); watch, observe, keep, preserve, reserve, save; *see Appendix*

sérvulus -i: m.; servant boy, young slave

sérvus -a -um: serving, slavish, servile, subject; *as a noun:* slave, servant, bondman

Sérvus Servórum Déi: Servant of the servants of God, a title of the Pope first used by St. Gregory the Great

sése: *variant form of* **se**

sésqui (sésque): one-half more, more by a half

séssio -ónis: f.; sitting, act of sitting, sitting down

séssor -óris: m.; rider

Seth: *indecl.;* son of Adam and Eve

seu: *see* **síve**

sevére: seriously, gravely, severely, austerely

sevéritas -átis: f.; severity, sternness, gravity, seriousness

sevérus -a -um: severe, sharp

sévoco -áre: (1); call away

sex: *indecl.;* six

sexagésimus -a -um: sixtieth; **Sexagésima** -ae: f.; Sexagesima, the sixtieth day, formerly the second Sunday before Lent

sexagínta: sixty

sexcentésimus -a -um: six hundredth

sexcénti -ae -a: six hundred

séxdecim (sédecim): sixteen

sexennális (sexénnis) -is -e: of six years

sexénnium -ii: n.; a period of six years

séxies (séxiens, séxto): six times

séxtus -a -um: sixth; **séxtum:** for the sixth time

sextusdécimus -a -um: sixteenth

séxta -ae: f.; Sext, a canonical prayer to be recited at the sixth hour as part of the Divine Office

Sextílis -is: m.; month of August

sexuális -is -e: sexual, pertaining to sex

sexuálitas -átis: f.; sexuality

séxus -us: m.; sex, gender

si: if

   si ópus est: if there is need

   si tu es cápax: if you are able *or* capable

síbi: *refl. pron. dat.;* to *or* for himself, herself, itself, themselves

síbimet (sibimetípsi): *emphatic and intensive forms of* **síbi**

síbilo -áre: (1); to hiss, whistle

síbilus -i: m.; hissing

Sibÿlla (Sibúlla) -ae; f.; Sibyl, a prophetess

sic: so, thus, in this way, likewise

síca -ae: f.; dagger, curved dagger

sicárius -ii: m.; assassin, murderer

siccátio -ónis: f.; a drying up

síccitas -átis: f.; drought, dryness

sícco -áre: (1); dry up, make dry

síccus -a -um: dry, thirsty, sober; **síccum** -i: n., **sícca** -órum: n. pl., **sícca** -ae: f.; desert, dry land

sícera -ae: f.; cider, strong drink

Síchima -ae: f., **Síchem:** *indecl.;* Shechem, Sichem, Samaritan town

Sicília -ae: f.; Sicily

síclus -i: m.; shekel, Hebrew coin

sícubi: in anywhere, wheresoever, if in any place

Sículus -a -um: Sicilian

sícut (sícuti): as, even as, just as, so as, since, like

sidéreum -i: n.; star, heavenly body

sidéreus -a -um: starry, of the stars, bright, brilliant; *as a n. noun:* star, heavenly body

sído -ere, sídi (sédi), séssum: (3); sit down, settle down

Sídon -ónis, **Sidónia** -ae: f.; Sidon

Sidóni -órum: m. pl.; Sidonians

Sidónius -a -um: of Sidon

sídus -eris: n.; star, constellation

sigillátim: *see* **singillátim**

sigillatívus -a -um: pertaining to a seal

sigillátus -a -um: adorned with small images or figures

sigíllum -i: n.; seal, signet; **sigílla** -órum: n. pl.; small figures or images sígla -órum: n. pl.; *contraction of* sigílla; signs of abbreviations, abbreviations

signáculum -i: n.; sign, mark, little seal, signet, mark of circumcision

signánter: carefully, significantly

signátor -óris: m.; witness

Signatúra -ae: f.; Signatura; *see Appendix*

sígnifer -i: m.; standard bearer, the leader of a procession

significánter: plainly, clearly, distinctly

significátio -ónis: f.; sign, banner, warning, standard, expression, indication, mark, meaning, significance

signífico (signíficor) -áre: (1); warn, give a sign, express, publish, signify, point out, indicate

sígno -áre: (1); mark, sign, seal, imprint, signify, stamp, make the sign of the cross

sígnum -i: n.; sign, token, signet, miracle, banner, signal

Síhon: *Hebrew;* Sihon, an Amorite king

siléntium -ii: n.; silence; siléntio: in silence, secretly

síleo -ére -ui: (2); be silent, hold one's peace

sílex -icis: m.; flint, rock, stone

silíqua -ae: f.; husk, pod

Sílo: *Hebrew;* Shiloh, a city in Ephraim

Síloam: *Hebrew;* Siloam, a pool near Jerusalem

sílva -ae: f.; woods, forest, grove

silvésco -ere: (3); grow wild

silvéster (silvéstris) -tris -tre: wild, woodland, belonging to a forest

Símeon -ónis: m.; Simeon; a son of Jacob; a tribe of Israel

Simeónis Féstum: Candlemas

símila -ae, similágo -inis: f.; fine flour, wheat flour, fine meal

similagéneus -a -um: of fine flour

símilis -is -e: like, similar, resembling; simíliter: *adv.*

similitúdo -inis: f.; similitude, likeness, parable, resemblance

símilo -áre: (1); compare, liken, make similar

Símon -ónis: m.; Simon

simónia -ae: f.; simony; *see Appendix*

simoníacus -a -um: simoniacal; simoníace: *adv.*

símplex -icis, símplius -a -um: pure, honest, frank, upright, unmixed, simple; simplíciter: *adv.*

simplícitas -átis: f.; simplicity

simplificátus -a -um: simplified

simplífico -áre: (1); simplify

símplius: *see* símplex

símul: at the same time, at once, together; símul ac: as soon as

simulácrum -i: n.; idol, likeness, image

simulátio -ónis: f.; dissimulation, pretense, bluffing

simulátor -óris: m.; copier, imitator, feigner, pretender, hypocrite

símulo -áre: (1); make like, copy, imitate, represent, feign

simúltas -átis: f.; enmity, jealousy, dissension, animosity, grudge, rivalry

sin: 21st letter of the Hebrew alphabet

sin: but if, if however, on the contrary, if not

Sína (Sínai, Sínas) -ae, *or indecl.:* f.; Mount Sinai; a desert and mountainous area

Sínae -árum: f. pl.; China

Sinaíta -ae: c.; dweller on Mount Sinai

sinápi (sinápe): *indecl.,* sinápis -is: f.; mustard, mustard seed

sincerásco -áre: (1); grow clear

sincéritas -átis: f.; sincerity, uprightness

sincérus -a -um: sincere, genuine, faithful, real; sincére (sincériter): *adv.*

sincínium -ii: n.; a solo

síndon -ónis: f.; fine linen, linen, muslin

síne: *prep. w. abla.;* without; **síne qua non:** without which there is nothing, an essential

singillátim (singúlatim, sigillátim, singuláre): separately, singly, one by one, individually

singuláris -is -e: remarkable, unique, excellent, solitary, single, singular, individual, eminent, solitary

singuláritas -átis: f.; oneness, singularity

singuláriter: alone, singularly, in oneness of mind or purpose

singulátim: *see* **singillátim**

síngulus -a -um: each, each one, each separately, every one, separate, individual, one by one, one at a time, apiece

per síngula: particularly

per síngulos díes: daily, every day

singúltus -us: m.; weeping, sobbing

siníster -tra -trum: left

sinístra -ae: f.; left hand

síno -ere, sívi, sítum: (3); allow, let be, permit, let alone

sinópis -idis: f.; red ocher, vermillion color

sínuo -áre: (1); bend, wind, curve, bow, swell

sínus -us: m.; breast, bosom; bay

Síon -iónis, or *indecl.:* m. or n.; city of Zion or Jerusalem

siquándo: if ever

síquidem: if, indeed, for, because of, since, inasmuch as

Sírion: *see* **Sárion**

sirp- *see* **scirp-**

Sísara -ae: m.; Sisera, Sisara, a commander for King Jabin

sísto -ere, stíti (stéti), státum: (3); stand, cause to stand, become, be, exist; **se sístere:** present oneself, appear

sístrum -i: n.; cornet

sitárcia -ae: f., **sitárcium** -ii: n.; bag for carrying food, vessel, container

sítiens -éntis: thirsty

Sitiéntes: day before Passion Sunday

sitiénter: thirstily, eagerly, greedily

sítio -íre: (4); thirst

sítis -is: f.; thirst, drought

situátio -ónis: f.; situation, circumstance

sítula -ae: f.; small pail

sítus -a -um: placed, lying, situated, founded

sítus -us: m.; place, site, region, situation

síve (seu): or, or if; **síve . . . síve;** either . . . or, whether . . . or

Slávi -órum: m. pl.; Slavs

Slavónicus (Slávicus) -a -um: Slavic

smarágdina -ae: f., **smarágdus** -i: c.; emerald

smarágdinus -a -um: of an emerald

smégma (smígma, zmégma) -atis: n.; detergent, soap, cleansing ointment or medicine

Smýrna -ae: f.; Smyrna

Smyrnaéi -órum: m. pl.; Smyrnians

sóboles -is: f.; offspring

sobríetas -átis: f.; sobriety, moderation, temperance

sobrínus -i, m., **sobrína** -ae: f.; cousin

socialísmus -i: m.; socialism

sóbrius -a -um: sober, temperate, prudent, thoughtful, recollected, moderate, sensible; **sóbrie:** *adv.*

sóccus -i: m.; slipper, sock

sócer -eri: m.; father-in-law; pl.: parents-in-law

sócia -ae: f.; female companion

sociábilis (sociális) -is -e: sociable, social, friendly, allied, of companionship; **sociáliter:** *adv.*

socializátio -ónis: f.; socialization

socíetas -átis: f.; society, company, fellowship, union, association

sócio -áre: (1); share in, combine, unite, associate, join

sociológia -ae: f.; sociology

sociológicus -a -um: sociological

sociopáthia -ae: f.; sociopathy, a personality disorder

sócius -a -um: allied, together, united; *as a noun:* companion, ally, comrade, partaker, sharer

socórdia -ae: f.; indolence, folly, stupidity, sloth

sócors -córdis: silly, foolish, weak-minded

sócrus -us: f.; mother-in-law; **sócrus** -us: m.: father-in-law

sodális -is: c.; companion, comrade, associate, member

sodálitas -átis: f., **sodalítium** -ii: n.; sodality, brotherhood, confraternity, guild, club, close association

sodalítius -a -um: of a sodality

sódes: if you please, please

Sódoma -ae: f., **Sódoma** -órum: n. pl.; Sodom, home of Lot

Sódami -órum: m. pl.; people of Sodom

sodomía -ae: f.; sodomy

Sodomíta -ae: c.; Sodomite

sol -is: m.; sun

sol- *see also* **soll-**

solácium (solátium) -ii: n.; comfort, support, solace, relief, consolation

solámen -inis: n.; comfort, relief, consolation, solace

soláris -is -e: solar, of the sun

solárium -ii: n.; top of a house, sunporch, sunroom, terrace, balcony, sundial

solátium -ii: *see* **solácium**

sólea -ae: f.; entrance to a sanctuary, sill; shoe, sandal

solémnis (solénnis) -is -e: solemn, festive; **solémniter:** *adv.*

solémnitas -átis: f., **solémne** -is: n.; solemnity, festival, feast day

sóleo -ére, solitus: *semidep.* (2); be accustomed to, be wont

sólers (sóll-) -értis: skillful, watchful, adroit, clever, inventive, ingenious; **solérter:** *adv.*

solidális: *see* **sólidus**

solidaméntum -i: n.; solid foundation

solidaríetas -átis: f.; solidarity, togetherness, unity

solíditas -átis: f.; solidity, firmness, steadfastness

sólido -áre: (1): establish, found, strengthen, make firm

sólidum -i: n.; entire sum, total, whole; **in sólidum:** as a body, jointly, altogether

sólidus -a -um, **solidális** -is -e: solid, firm, dense, real, substantial, joined; **sólide:** *adv.*

solilóquium -ii: n.; soliloquy, talking to one's self

solitárius -a -um: solitary, lonely, alone; *as a noun:* anchorite, person living alone

solitúdo -inis: f.; solitude, loneliness, wilderness

sólitus -a -um: usual, customary

sólium -ii: n.; throne, seat, chair of state, rule, flue

sollémnis (sollénnis) -is -e: solemn; **sollémne** -is: n.; solemnity, rite, ceremony; pl.: sacred festivals or observances; **sollémniter:** *adv.*

sollémnitas (sollé-) -átis: f.; festival, solemnity

sóllers (sólers) -tis: skilled, clever

sollértia -ae: f.; cleverness, ingenuity, skill

sollicitátio -ónis: f.; solicitation, seduction

sollícito (sol-) -áre: (1); solicit, tempt, seduce; *pass.:* be solicitous, be conscientious

sollícitudo (sol-) -inis: f.; solicitude, care, carefulness, anxiety, concern

sollícitus (sol-) -a -um: solicitous,
anxious, careful, concerned, diligent;
sollícite: adv.

sólor -ári: dep. (1); console

sólum -i: n.; ground, earth, floor, land,
soil

sólum (solúmmodo): alone, only,
merely, barely

non sólum: not only

non sólum . . . sed étiam: not only . . .
but also

únus solúsque: the sole and only one

sólus -a -um: only, alone, sole, single; see
Appendix

solútio -ónis: f.; dissolution, freedom,
loosening, payment

sólvo -ere, sólvi, solútum: (3); undo, set
free, loose, release, liberate, solve (in
the sense of explain), pay back, fulfill,
break, destroy

Sólymae -árum: f., Sólyma -órum: n.,
Sólymi -órum: m.; Jerusalem

Sólymus -a -um: of Jerusalem, of Jews

somniáliter: in a dream

somniátor -óris: m.; dreamer

sómnio -áre: (1); dream

sómnium -ii: n.; dream

somnoléntia (somnúlentia) -ae: f.;
somnolence, sleepiness, drowsiness

somnólentus (somnúlentus) -a -um:
drowsy, sleepy

sómnus -i: m.; sleep

sónans -ántis: sounding, resounding

sónitus -us, sónus -i: m.; noise, din,
sound, crash

sóno -áre, sónui, sónitum: (1); roar,
sound, resound, make a tumult or
noise

sonórus -a -um: resonant, sonorous,
sounding

sons, sóntis: guilty; as a c. noun:
offender, malefactor, criminal, guilty
person; as a n. noun: sin, crime

sónus -i, sónus -us: m.; sound, noise,
tone

sóphia (sophía) -ae: f.; wisdom

sophísticus -a -um: sophistic;
sophístice: adv.

Sophonías: see Zephanías

sópio -íre -ívi(-íi) -ítum: (4); lull to sleep

sópor -óris: m.; sleep, heavy sleep,
lethargy

sopóro -áre: (1); put to sleep

sopóror -ári: dep. (1); go to sleep

sórbeo -ére -ui: (2); suck up, swallow,
absorb

sorbitiúncula -ae: f.; small draught,
mess, dish

sórdeo -ére -ui: (2); be dirty or foul or
filthy

sórdes -is: f.; dirt, filth, defilement

sórdido -áre: (1); dirty, defile, pollute,
soil, or stain

sórdidus -a -um: unclean, defiled,
polluted; sórdide: sordidly

sóror -óris: f.; sister

sors, sórtis: f.; chance, lot, fate, destiny,
part, share, portion, dowry, divine
ordinance

sors hereditária: inheritance

sórtem míttere: cast lots

sortilégium -ii: n.; fortune-telling

sórtior (sórtio) -íri -ítus: dep. (4); cast
lots, decide by lot, choose, distribute,
select, obtain, get

sortítus -a -um: obtained by lot,
assigned, selected

sortítio -ónis: f.; lot

sóspes -itis: safe, saved, uninjured; as a c.
noun: savior, deliverer

sospitális -is -e: salutary

sóspitas -átis: f.; safety, health, welfare

sóspito -áre: (1); save, preserve, protect

sóter -éris: m.; savior

spádo -ónis: m.; eunuch

spárgo -ere, spársi, spársum: (3); sow,
fling, scatter, strew, sprinkle

spársim: scattered here and there

Spartiáni -órum: m. pl.; Spartans

spathárius -ii: m.; sword-bearer

spátior -ári: *dep.* (1); walk about, promenade

spatiósus -a -um: spacious, widespread, broad, long, large

spátium -ii: n.; space, extent, size, division of time, distance

spátula -ae: f.; branch, twig; scraper

spéca -ae: *see* spíca

speciális -is -e: special, one's own, individual, particular

speciáliter (speciátim): especially, in particular

specializátio -ónis: f.; specialization

spécies -éi: f.; species, kind, form, shape, appearance, view, comeliness, beauty, mien, likeness, reputation; *see* Appendix

specíficus -a -um: specific; specífice: *adv.*

spécimen -inis: n.; mark, sign, token, sample, specimen

speciósitas -átis: f.; beauty, good looks, handsomeness, comeliness

speciósus -a -um: fair, beautiful, comely, handsome, attractive, splendid

spectábilis -is -e: visible

spectáculum (spectáclum) -i: n.; show, spectacle, sight

spectatívus -a -um: speculative, contemplative

spectátor -óris: m., spectátrix -ícis: f.; observer, onlooker, watcher, spectator

spécto -áre: (1); observe, behold, contemplate, watch, look at, envision, tend toward, pertain to

speculátio -ónis: f.; observation, spying out, exploration

speculatívus -a -um: speculative

speculátor -óris: m.; eyewitness, spy, scout, explorer, examiner, investigator, watchman

spéculor -ári: *dep.* (1); spy, examine, watch carefully, investigate

spéculum -i: n.; mirror, glass

spécus -us: m., f., and n.; cave, hollow, den, cavity, pit, chasm, ditch, canal

spelúnca -ae: f.; cave, den, lair

spéro -áre: (1); hope, trust, expect, look forward to

spérma -atis: n.; seed, semen, sperm

spérno -ere, sprévi, sprétum: (3); reject, scorn, spurn, despise

spes -éi: f.; hope

sphaéra -ae: f.; circle, sphere, globe, ball

sphaérula -ae: f.; spherical bowl

spíca (spéca) -ae: f.; ear of grain, spike, point

spicátus -a -um: with thorns, spiked

spiculátor -óris: m.; executioner

spículum -i: n.; arrow, dart, ray

spína -ae: f.; thorn

spinétum -i: n.; thornbush

spíneus -a -um: of thorns

spínula -ae: f.; pin, small thorn

spiráculum -i: n., spirátio -ónis: f.; breath, spiration

spirámen -inis: n.; breathing, inspiration, blowing; airhole, vent

spírans -ántis: m.; that which breathes

spirital- *see* spiritual-

spirátio -ónis: f.; spiration; *see* Appendix

spiratívus -a -um: breathing

spirituális (spiritális) -is -e: belonging to the spirit, spiritual; *as a n. pl. noun:* spirits

spirituálitas (spiritálitas) -átis: f.; spirituality

spirituáliter (spiritáliter): in a spiritual sense, spiritually

spíritus -us: m.; breath, blowing, wind; spirit, ghost; life, soul, character, courage, morale

Spíritus Sánctus: Holy Spirit

spíro -áre: (1); breathe, blow gently, exhale

spléndeo -ére: (2); shine, glitter, be bright, glisten

splendésco -ere -ui: (3); become or grow bright

spléndidus -a -um: bright, shining, glittering, brilliant, splendid, magnificent; spléndide: brightly, with distinction, sumptuously

spléndor -óris: m.; splendor, brightness, lustre, sumptuousness

spoliátio -ónis: f.; robbing, stripping, plundering

spólio -áre: (1); strip, rob, plunder

spólium -ii: n.; booty, plunder; spólia -órum: n. pl.; spoils

spóndeo -ére, spopóndi, spónsum: (2); promise solemnly, bind, vow, pledge

spóngia -ae: f.; sponge

spons, spóntis: f.; free will, will spónte: voluntarily, willingly, freely súa spónte: of one's own accord, without aid of others

spónsa -ae: f.; bride

sponsális -is -e: pertaining to betrothal or espousal; as a n. pl. noun: betrothal, engagement, betrothal gift or feast

sponsalítius -a -um: spousal

spónsio -ónis: f.; promise, guarantee, security, agreement, engagement, bet

spónsor -óris: c.; sponsor, godparent, surety, bondsperson

spónsus -a -um: perf. pass. part. of spóndeo

spónsus -i: m.; bridegroom, spouse; pl.: engaged couple

spónsus -us: m., spónsum -i: n.; covenant, engagement; bail, surety

spontáneus -a -um: voluntary, spontaneous, willing

spónte (spontánee, súa spónte): willingly, voluntarily, spontaneously, of one's own accord

spórta -ae: f.; basket, hamper

sportívus -a -um: sportive, athletic

spórtula -ae: f.; little basket; gift

sprétus -a -um: perf. pass. part. of spérno

spúma -ae: f.; foam

spúmo -áre: (1); froth or foam

spumósus -a -um: foaming, full of foam

spúo: see spúto

spurcítia -ae: f.; filthiness

spúrius -a -um: illegitimate, baseborn, false; as a noun: bastard

spúto -áre: (1), spúo -ere: (3); spit

spútum -i: n.; spittle

squálidus -a -um: rough, unpolished, stiff, squalid, bad-looking, foul; squálide: without ornament, rudely

squálor -óris: m.; roughness, squalor, filthiness, foulness, neglect

squáma -ae: f.; scale of a fish

squamátus -a -um: with scales

squílla -ae: f.; small hand bell

Stábat Máter: The mother was standing; a Lenten hymn from the 14th century

stabílio -íre: (4); make firm, fix, establish

stábilis -is -e: firm, steadfast, steady; stabíliter: adv.

stabílitas -átis: f.; stability, firmness, durability, steadfastness

stabulárius -ii: m.; innkeeper, host

stábulum -i: n.; stable, shelter for cattle, stall, abode, dwelling, inn

stácta -ae, stácte -es: f.; myrrh, oil of myrrh

stádium -ii: n.; furlong, racecourse, stade, stadium, distance of 125 paces; stage, step

stágno -áre: (1); overflow, inundate

stágnum -i: n.; pool, lake, pond, swamp

stállum -i: n.; choir stall, stall

stándum est: it must be depended on, must rest with, must be upheld, must be observed, must be followed

stánneus -a -um: made of tin

stánnum -i: n.; tin

stantáreum -i: n.; large chandelier

státer -eris: m.; shekel, a Jewish coin

statéra -ae: f.; scales, balance, value of an object

statículum -i: n.; little statue, image

státicus -a -um: stationary, static, standing, stable

státio -ónis: f.; station, place, post, abode

státim: immediately, at once, presently; státim ac: as soon as

státio -ónis: f.; station, anchorage, post, garrison, abode, residence, dwelling

stationális -is -e: of a station

státua -ae: f.; image, statue

statuárius -ii: m.; sculptor

státuo -ere -ui -útum: (3); set, place, establish, appoint, resolve, cause to stand, erect, determine, decide

statúra -ae: f.; form, height, size, stature

státus -a -um: *perf. pass. part. of* sto *and* sísto

státus -us: m.; position, state, condition, posture, status, situation, appearance, rank

Státus Animárum: *see Appendix*

Státus Foederáti Américae Septentrionális, Státuum Foederatórum Américae Septentrionális: m. pl.; United States of America

statútus -a -um: appointed; statútum -i: n.; law, statute, regulation; *see Appendix*

stearína -ae: f.; stearin, stearic acid

stélla -ae: f.; star

stéllans -ántis, stellátus (stéllifer) -a -um: starry

stéllula -ae: f.; little star, asterisk

stémma -atis: n.; genealogical tree *or* table, pedigree, wreath, garland, coat-of-arms

Stéphanus -i: m.; Stephen

stércus -oris: n.; dung, dunghill, muck

stérilis -is -e: sterile, barren, unfruitful

sterílitas -átis: f.; barrenness, unfruitfulness, sterility

stérno -ere, strávi, strátum: (3); furnish, spread, strew, scatter, pave, stretch out, flatten, smooth

sterquilínium -ii: n.; dunghill, dung pit

stérto -ere -ui: (3); snore

stíbinus -a -um: of antimony

stíbium -ii, stíbi (stímmi) -is: n.; a sulpheret of antimony, antinomic stone, eyelash and eyebrow coloring

stígma -matis: n.; stigma, mark, reproduction of the Savior's wounds

stígmo -áre: (1); to mark or brand

stílla -ae: f.; drop, drip, tiny portion of time, moment

stíllo -áre: (1); to drip

stillicídium -ii: n.; raindrop

stílus (stýlus) -i: m.; writing tool, stylus, pen; manner of writing, style

stímmi -is: *see* stíbium

stímulo -áre: (1); prick, goad, stimulate, urge, spur on

stímulus -i: m.; sting, spur, goad, prod, lower end of a crosier

stípa -ae: *see* stúppa

stipéndium -ii: n.; recompense, stipend, offering, wage

stípes -itis: m., stips, stípis: m.; stem, family or common ancestor; branch, stock, trunk of a tree, log, post; *see Appendix*

stípo -áre: (1); pack, surround, compass about, crowd upon

stips, stípis: f.; alms, gift, donation, stipend, contribution; stips, stípis: m.: *see* stípes

stípula -ae: f.; stubble, straw, stalk

stipulátio -ónis: f.; agreement, bargain, stipulation, covenant, obligation, promise

stípulo -áre: (1); bargain, exact, stipulate

stírpitus: utterly, by the roots

stirps -is: f.; stock, branch, stem; lineage; stirps damnáta: fallen human race

stíva -ae: f.; plow handle

sto, stáre, stéti, státum: (1); stand, remain

Stóicus -a -um: Stoic, of Stoic philosophy; *as a noun:* a Stoic; Stóice: *adv.*

stóla -ae: f.; robe, garment, stole, a long narrow vestment worn around the neck indicative of priestly power

stomachánter: irritably

stómachor -ári: *dep.* (1); be irritated, fume, fuss, fret

stómachus -i: m.; stomach

stórax (stýrax) -ácis: f.; storax, resinous gum

stráges -is: f.; slaughter, massacre

stragulátus -a -um: pertaining to a coverlet or tapestry

strágulus (strágus) -a -um: pertaining to a covering, bedspread, blanket, rug, carpet, or cover; strágula -ae: f.; pall, covering for a corpse; strágulum -i: n.; bedspread, cover, rug, blanket, mattress

strámen -inis, straméntum -i: n.; straw, litter, covering, bundles of straw, bed of straw, bedclothes

strángulo -áre: (1): strangle

strátor -óris: m.; one who throws down

stratórium -ii, strátum -i: n.; couch; stratória -órum: n. pl.; bedding

strénuus -a -um: steadfast, vigorous, brisk, active, strenuous, prompt, resolute; strénue: *adv.*

strépitus -us: m.; din, loud noise, rumbling, creaking

strépo -ere -ui: (3); make loud noise, rattle, clash, clatter, rumble, roar

striátus -a -um: striped, grooved, fluted

strictúra -ae: f.; pressure, suffering

stríctus -a -um: close, tight, strict, brief, concise, drawn tight, slight, severe; strícte (stríctim): *adv.*

strídeo -ére -di: (2), strído -ere -di: (3); gnash, hiss, grind

strídor -óris: m.; gnashing, hissing, grinding, grating

stríngo -ere, strínxi, stríctum: (3); hold tight, bind, tie, touch, unsheathe

strópha -ae: f.; line of a poem or hymn, strophe

stróphicus -i: m.; group of musical notes of the same pitch

stróphium -ii: n.; garment, girdle; chaplet, headband

strúctilis -is -e: related to building

strúctor -óris: m.; builder

structúra -ae: f.; building, structure, construction

strúes -is: f.; heap, pile

strúo -ere, strúxi, strúctum: (3); pile up, arrange, devise, construct, erect

strúthio -ónis: m.; ostrich

stúdeo -ére -ui: (2); strive, study, be zealous, try

studiósus -a -um: eager, zealous, diligent, studious, anxious, assiduous, fond; studióse: *adv.*

stúdium -ii: n.; deed, practice, zeal, diligence, striving, endeavor, study, eagerness, assiduity, exertion, effort

stultilóquium -ii: n.; foolish talk

stultítia -ae: f.; foolishness, folly, stupidity

stúltus -a -um: silly, stupid; *as a noun:* fool; stúlte: stupidly

stúpa -ae: *see* stúppa

stupefácio -ere -féci -fáctum: (3); numb, stupify, deaden, stun, amaze

stupefáctus -a -um: stupified, stunned

stupéndus -a -um: wonderful

stúpeo -ére -ui: (2); be astonished, struck, amazed, or stunned

stupésco -ere: (3); grow astonished, become amazed

stúpidus -a -um: amazed, confounded

stúpor -óris: m.; numbness, stupor, insensibility, astonishment, stupidity

stúppa (stípa, stúpa) -ae: f.; coarse part of flax, tow, cotton stúprum -i: n.; violation, dishonor, disgrace, debauchery, lewdness, immorality, defilement

stýlus -i: *see* stílus; *see Appendix: stýlus Curiae*

stýrax -ácis: *see* stórax

Styx, Stýgis: f.; river Styx, hell

suádeo -ére, suási, suásum: (2); persuade, exhort, advise, urge, suggest, recommend, propose

suadíbilis -is -e: easy to persuade, persuadable

suápte natúra: by its very nature

suásio -ónis: f., suásus -us: m.; persuasion, advice, support, exhortation, counselling, backing, recommendation

suásor -óris: m.; adviser

suaveoléntia -ae: f.; fragrance, sweet odor

suavídicus -a -um: sweet-spoken, soft

suavífico -áre: (1); make dear or acceptable

suavifragrántia -ae: f.; fragrance

suavilóquium -ii: n.; speaking pleasant things

suávis -is -e: kind, good, sweet, gracious, pleasant, suave, agreeable; suáve: *adv.*

suávitas -átis: f.; sweetness, goodness, pleasantness, suavity

suáviter: sweetly, agreeably, delightfully, pleasantly

sub: *prep. w. acc. & abla.;* under, at the foot of, beneath, below, near, before; sub-: *a prefix often modifying or slightly altering the meaning of a word*

sub conditióne: conditionally

sub secréto: secretly

subadúno -áre: (1); unite

subaláres -ium: n. pl.; feathers under the wing

subárrho -áre: (1); pledge, espouse, give earnest money

subaúdio -íre: (4); hear, heed

subcinctórium -ii, subcíngulum -i: n.; an ornamental maniple worn by the Pope

subcinerícius -a -um: baked in ashes; subcinerícius pánis: hearth cake

subconféssio -onis: f.; the tomb of a martyr beneath a high altar

súbcrepo -áre: (1); crackle beneath

subdecánus -i: m.; subdean

subdelegátio -ónis: f.; subdelegation

subdélego -áre: (1); subdelegate

subdiácon -ónis, subdiáconus -i: m.; subdeacon

subdiaconális -is -e: of a subdeacon, subdiaconal

subdiaconátus -us: m.; subdeaconship, subdiaconate

subdiáconus -i: *see* subdiácon

sub dío (dívo), súbdiu: in the open air

súbditus -i: m.; servant, subject, layman

súbdo -ere -didi -itum: (3); subdue, subject, put under, supply

subdóceo -ére: (2); assist in teaching

súbdolus -a -um: sly, cunning, crafty, deceitful, subtle

subdúco -ere: (3); draw from under, pull up, take away, purge, calculate, evacuate, take by stealth

subelevátio -ónis: *see* sublátio

subéligo -ere: (3); choose further

súbeo -íre -ívi (-ii) -itum: (4); go up, go under, approach, draw near, follow, undergo, enter

subiáceo: *see* subjáceo

subício: *see* subjício

súbigo -ere -égi -áctum: (3); bring under, get under, dig up, cultivate, tame, break, subjugate, train, force

subínde: immediately

subíndico -áre: (1); indicate, point out, hint

subínfero -férre -tuli -illátum: irreg.; add, subjoin, say

subintélligo -ere -lexi -léctum: (3); understand a little

subíntro -áre: (1); enter into, enter stealthily, insinuate

subintrodúco -ere: (3); introduce secretly

subintróeo -íre -ívi (-ii) -itum: (4); go in, enter

subitáneus -a -um: sudden

subitátio -ónis: f.; suddenness

súbito: suddenly, unexpectedly

súbito -áre: (1); apply, supply

súbitus -a -um: sudden, unexpected

subjáceo (subiáceo) -ére -ui: (2); lie under, be subject to, belong to

Subjácum -i: n.; Subiaco

subjectíbilis -is -e: obedient, subject

subjéctio -ónis: f., **subjéctum** -i: n.; subjection

subjectívus -a -um: subordinate, subjective

subjéctum -i: n.; subject

subjício (subício) -ere -jéci -jéctum: (3); set, place under, subject to, submit to

subjugális -is: c.; one used to the yoke, an ass

súbjugo -áre: (1); bring under the yoke, subject, subjugate

subjúngo -ere -júnxi -júnctum: (3); add, add to, unite to, say again

sublátio (subelevátio) -ónis: f.; elevation, lifting or raising; removal

sublátus -a -um: *perf. pass. part. of* **tóllo** *and* **súffero**

súblevo -áre: (1); exalt, lift or raise up, support, sustain, console

súbligo -áre: (1); bind or tie below

sublímis -is -e, **sublímus** -a -um: lofty, sublime, high, on high, exalted

sublímina -órum: n. pl.; lofty things

sublímitas -átis: f., **sublíme** -is: n.; height, high station, loftiness

sublímiter (sublíme): aloft, sublimely, in a lofty manner

sublímo -áre: (1); exalt; elevate

sublímus: *see* **sublímis**

sublúceo -ére -lúxi: (2); gleam forth, glimmer

súbluo -ere -lui -lútum: (3); flow beneath, wash from below

subm- *see also* **summ-**

submérgo -ere -mérsi -mérsum: (3); sink, submerge, dip, plunge, drown

subministrátio -ónis: f.; supply, aid, ministration, service

subminístro -áre: (1); minister, supply, furnish

submíssio -ónis: f.; submission, lowering, dropping, sinking

submitrále -is: n.; bishop's skullcap

submítto -ere -mísi -missum: (3); let down, lower, set below, reduce, substitute, submit, dispatch

submóveo -ére -móvi -mótum: (2); move away, put away, dispel

submúrmuro -áre: (1); murmur a little

subnávigo -áre: (1); sail on the lee side

subnérvo -áre: (1); hamstring, weaken

súbniger -gra -grum: somewhat black

subnítor -níti -níxus(-nísus): *dep.* (3); rest upon, rely upon, be supported by

subnotátio -ónis: f.; subscription, undersigning

subobscúrus -a -um: somewhat obscure or dark; **subobscúre:** somewhat obscurely

súboles -is: c.; offshoot, offspring, progeny

subórdino -áre: (1); subordinate, place under

subórior -oríri -órtus: *dep.* (4); arise, proceed

subornátio -ónis: f.; subornation, bribery

subórno -áre: (1); instigate secretly, bribe, equip, provide

subp- *see also* **supp-**

sub-promótor -óris: m.; subpromotor in causes of saints

subr- see also surr-

subrelínquo -ere: (3); leave

subrépo -ere -répsi -réptum: (3); creep in, crawl under, approach secretly

subréptio -ónis: f.; deceit, concealment of truth, subreption

subrídeo -ére -rísi -rísum: (3); smile

subrogátio -ónis: f.; subrogation; see Appendix

súbrogo -áre: (1); substitute, put in another's place

subrúbeus -a -um: somewhat reddish

súbruo -ere -rui -rútum: (3); destroy, overthrow

subrútilo -áre: (1); glimmer forth

subsannátio -ónis: f.; derision, scorn, mockery, sneer, object of scorn

subsannátor -óris: m.; mocker, scoffer

subsánno -áre: (1); deride, mock, make fun of, laugh at

subscríbo -ere: (3); subscribe, sign, agree, prosecute

subscríptio -ónis: f.; subscription, signature, a note below

subscríptor -óris: m.; signer, approver

subsédeo -ére -sédi -séssum: (2); rest against, sit under, rest under

subséllium -ii: n.; seat, bench, pew

súbsequens -éntis, subsícuus -a -um: succeeding, subsequent, following

subséquium -ii: n.; sequel

súbsequor -qui -secútus: dep. (3); follow, follow after

subsérvio -íre: (4); be subject to, serve, comply with

subsícuus: see súbsequens

subsidárius (subsidiárius) -a -um: subsidiary, reserve, bringing support

subsidaríetas -átis: f.; subsidiarity, reserve help or aid

subsídium -ii: n.; help, aid, support, relief, assistance, provision

subsído -ere -sédi(-sídi) -séssum: (3); sit, sink, settle down, crouch, squat

subsígno -áre: (1); subscribe, sign below, undersign, pledge

subsílio -íre -sílui (-sílii) -súltum: (4); leap up, skip

subsisténtia -ae: f.; substance, reality, source or means of subsisting

subsísto -ere -stiti: (3); withstand, stand, exist, be, endure, remain, halt

substántia -ae: f.; substance, nature, essence; being, existence, property

substantiális -is -e: substantial

substantiáliter (substantíve): substantially, actually, in substance

substérno -ere -strávi -strátum: (3); spread out, strew, scatter, put under

substítuo -ere -ui -útum: (3); put or place under, substitute

substitútio -ónis: f.; substitution, appointing an alternate

substómachor -ári: dep. (1); become somewhat vexed

substráti -órum: m. pl.; those who kneel or prostrate themselves

substratórium -ii: n.; altar cloth

súbsum -ésse -fui: be under, among, at hand, near, close, or behind, underlie

subsútum -i: n.; lining of a garment

súbta -ae: f.; rochet

subtána (subtánna, subtánea) -ae: f.; soutane, cassock

súbtego -ere: (3): spread underneath

súbter (súbtus): beneath, below, underneath

subterfúgio -ere -fúgi: (3); evade, shun, spare, flee secretly, escape

subterfúgium -ii: n.; subterfuge

subterpósitus -a -um: placed under

subtéxo -ere -téxui -téxtum: (3); add, join to, fasten, annex, append

súbtile -is: n.; tunic of a subdeacon

subtílis -is -e: fine, thin, slender, minute, plain, simple, unadorned, exact, keen,

subtile; **subtília** -árum: n. pl.; fine
goods; **subtíliter:** *adv.*

subtílitas -átis: f.; subtlety, acuteness

subtráctio -ónis: f.; subtraction, taking
away, drawing back

súbtraho -ere -tráxi -tráctum: (3);
remove or take by stealth, escape

súbtus: below, underneath, beneath

subúcula -ae: f.; undergarment, shirt,
tunic

suburbánum (subúrbium) -i: n.;
suburb, suburban estate

suburbicárius (suburbánus) -a -um:
near the city, suburban

súbveho -ere -véxi -véctum: (3); bring
up from below

subvénio -íre -véni -véntum: (4); come
in, come up to, relieve, assist, come to
the aid of

subvéntio -ónis: f.; subsidy, subvention,
assistance

subvérsio -ónis: f.; ruin, destruction

subversívus -a -um: subversive,
undermining, plotting

subvérsor -óris: m.; destroyer,
overthrower, subverter

subvérto (subvórto) -ere -vérti -vérsum:
(3); upset, pervert, destroy, overthrow,
overturn, subvert

succédo -ere -céssi -céssum: (3); go
under or from, submit, follow, succeed

succéndo -ere -céndi -cénsum: (3); set
on fire, burn, kindle

succénseo (susc-) -ére -cénsui -cénsum:
(2); be enraged or be inflamed with
anger, be irritated

succéntor -óris: m.; accompanier, the
deacon who chants the part of the
Synagogue in the Passion

succéssio -ónis: f., **succéssus** -us: m.;
succession, advance, progress, issue

successívus -a -um: following,
successive; **successíve:** *adv.*

succéssor -óris: m.; successor, follower

succéssus -us: m.; success, succession,
happy issue, continuation; **succéssu
témporis:** in the course of time

succído -ere -cídi -císum: (3); cut off or
down, cut from below

súccido -ere -cidi: (3); fall, sink

succinctórium -ii: n.; apron

succinerícius -a -um: prepared under
ashes

súccinum -i: n.; amber, electrum

succlámo -áre: (1); shout at, cry out

Súccoth: *indecl.;* Succoth, a place east of
the Jordan river

succrésco -ere -crévi -crétum: (3); grow
or increase

súccubo -áre: (1); lie under

succúmbo -cúmbere -cúbui -cúbitum:
(3); fall dow, sink down, be overcome,
surrender, succumb, yield, submit

succúrro -ere -cúrri -cúrsum: (3); aid,
help, succor, run to the aid of, support

succúrsus -us: m.; help, assistance

súccus -i: m.; sap, juice

succúto -ere: (3); shake lightly, pluck

sucophánta -ae: *see* **sycophánta**

sucósus -a -um: juicy, succulent

sudaríolum (sudárium) -i: n.; cloth to
wipe off sweat, napkin, handkerchief,
maniple

súdes (súdis) -is: f.; stake, stick

súdor -óris: m.; sweat, perspiration

Suécia -ae: f.; Sweden

suésco -ere, suévi, suétum: (3); become
accustomed to, train, habituate, be
wont or used to

sufferéntia -ae: f.; patience, toleration,
endurance, suffering

súffero -érre, sústuli, sublátum: *irreg.;*
suffer, bear

suffíciens, -éntis: enough, sufficient;
sufficiénter: *adv.*

sufficiéntia -ae: f.; sufficiency,
contentment

suffício -ere -féci -féctum: (3); be
enough, suffice, imbue, tinge, afford,
avail, substitute, furnish

suffitórium -ii: n.; censer

sufflatórium -ii: n.; bellows

suffóco -áre: (1); choke, throttle, strangle

suffódio -ere -fódi -fóssum: (3); dig
below, undermine, dig up

suffóssio -ónis: f.; a digging under,
undermining

suffragáneus -a -um: suffragan; *as a m.*
noun: suffragan, a bishop in relation to
his metropolitan; *see Appendix*

suffrágans -ántis: favorable, helping

suffragátio -ónis: f.; prayer, choice, vote

suffrágium -ii: n.; suffrage, vote,
approval, support, opinion,
intercession, voice, judgment,
mediation

suffrágor (suffrágo) -ári: *dep.* (1); vote
for, approve, support, aid,
recommend, favor

suffúlcio -íre -fúlsi -fúltum: (4); support
under, prop up

suffúsio -ónis: f.; a pouring over, a
spreading, inflammation

suffusórium -ii: n.; pitcher, spout

súggero -ere -géssi -géstum: (3); add,
bring to mind, annex, subjoin, suggest,
promote, advise

suggéstio -ónis: f.; suggestion

suggéstum -i: n., suggéstus -us: m.;
platform, stage, podium, gallery

sugíllo (suggíllo) -áre: (1); annoy, taunt,
beat black-and-blue, insult, revile,
scoff at

súgo -ere, súxi, súctum: (3); suck

suicídium -ii: n.; suicide

súi júris: of one's own right; *see Appendix*

súlco -áre: (1); plough

súlcus -i: m.; furrow

súllaba -ae: *see* sýllaba

súlphur -uris: n.; brimstone, sulphur

sum, ésse, fúi, futúrum: be, exist, belong
to, pertain to

summ- *see also* subm-

súmma -ae: f.; summit, perfection, sum,
summary, whole; *see Appendix*

summárium -ii: n.; summary, abstract,
epitome

summárius -a -um: summary;
summárie: *adv.*

summátim: in short, briefly, summarily,
generally

súmme: highly, in the highest degree,
extremely, very

súmmitas -átis: f.; top, summit, point

summítto -ere -mísi -missum: (3); let
down, put below, substitute, send off

summópere: exceedingly

súmmus -a -um: highest, chief, main,
uppermost, supreme

súmma -ae: f.; the main thing, the
important matter, height,
completion, summit, sum, summary;
súmmum -i: n.; top, summit, end,
brim

súmmo ópere: in the highest degree

Súmmum Bónum: greatest good, God

ad súmmum: on the whole, in general,
at the most

in súmma: on the whole

Súmmus magíster: the Pope as teacher
of the Church

súmo -ere, súmpsi, súmptum: (3); take,
take up, lay hold of, assume, obtain,
reckon, consume

súmptio -ónis: f.; reception, taking up,
assumption

sumptuósitas -átis: f.; great expense,
costliness

súmptus -us: m.; cost, charges, expense

sumptuóse: sumptuously, expensively

Sunamítis -idis: c.; Sunamite

supéllex, supelléctilis, supelléctilis -is:
f.; furniture, household goods,
apparatus, ornament

súper: *adv. & prep. w. acc.*; above, over, on top of, toward, upon, beyond, in addition, moreover, besides, during; **sátis supérque:** enough and more than enough

superabundánter: more abundantly

superabundántia -ae: f.; much abundance

superabúndo -áre: (1); abound

superáddo -ere: (3); add over and above

superadúltus -a -um: grown up, fully mature

superaedífico -áre: (1); build upon

superámbulo -áre: (1); walk over or on

superátor -óris: m.; conqueror

supérbia -ae: f.; pride, insolence

supérbio -íre: (4); be proud, haughty, insolent; **supérbe:** *adv.*

supérbus -a -um: arrogant, proud, insolent, haughty

supércado -ere -cécidi: (3); fall upon

supercaeléstis -is -e: supercelestial, above the heavens, more than heavenly

supercértor (supercérto) -ári: *dep.* (1); contend, fight over

supercílium -ii: n.; eyebrow; pride, arrogance

supercrésco -ere: (3); increase

supercúrro -ere -cucúrri -cúrsum: (3); run beyond, surpass

superéffluens -éntis: overflowing

superéffluo -ere -flúxi: (3); overflow, run over; be superfluous; be exalted

superélevo -áre: (1); raise above

superéminens -éntis: surpassing, unsurpassable

superemíneo -ére: (2); overtop, excel

superérogo -áre: (1); ask, spend, or pay over and above

superexálto -áre: (1); exalt greatly, exalt above all others

superexténdo -ere -téndi -ténsum(-tum): (3); cover, stretch over, stretch

superextóllo -ere: (3); exalt above

superexúlto -áre: (1); boast

supérfero -férre -tuli -látum: *irreg.*; carry or bear over, excel

superfícies -éi: f.; surface, face, top, external appearance

superflúitas -átis: f.; excess

supérfluus -a -um: superfluous, overflowing, unnecessary

superfrontále -is: n.; reredos

superfúndo -ere -fúdi -fúsum: (3); pour over or out, extend

supergaúdeo -ére -gavísus: *semidep.* (2); rejoice over

supergloriósus -a -um: very glorious, exceedingly famous

supergrédior -i -gréssus: *dep.* (3); surpass, go over, exceed, overstep

superhumerále (superumerále) -is: n.; amice, ephod, a Jewish priestly garment

superimpéndo -ere: (3); spend, exhaust, use up

superímpleo -ére -plévi -plétum: (2); fill to overflowing

superimpóno -ere -pósui -pósitum: (3); place over or upon

superindúco -ere: (3); cover over; bring upon; mention later

superínduo -ere -ui -útum: (3); put on over, clothe with

superinspício -ere: (3); oversee

superinténdo -ere: (3); oversee

supérior -ior -ius: upper, higher, former; **supérius:** *adv.*

supérior -óris: c.; superior, person in charge

superioríssa -ae: f.; superioress

superlátio -ónis: f.; hyperbole, exaggeration

superlaudábilis -is -e: highly praised, very praiseworthy

superlimin   áre -is: n.; lintel

superliminária -ium: n. pl.; upper doorposts

superlúcror -ári: *dep.* (1); gain more, gain over and above

supérnae -árum: f. pl.; heaven

supernaturális -is -e: supernatural

supernaturálitas -átis: f.; supernaturality, supernaturalness

supernumerárius -a -um: supernumerary

supérnus -a -um: celestial, heavenly, above; **supérne:** upward, from above

súpero -áre: (1); overcome, conquer

superórdino -áre: (1); appoint in addition, add something to

superpellíceum -i: n.; surplice

superplénus -a -um: brimful

superpólluo -ere: (3); cover with pollution

superpóno -ere -pósui -pósitum: (3); lay or put or set over

súper ráto: *see Appendix*

superscríbo -ere -scrípsi -scríptum: (3); write over or upon

superscríptio -ónis: f.; superscription

supersédeo -ére -sédi -séssum: (2); sit upon or above, leave off, omit, refrain

supersémino -áre: (1); oversow, sow over other seeds

superspéro -áre: (1); hope greatly

supérstes -stitis: present, surviving, outliving; *as a c. noun:* survivor

superstítio -ónis: f.; superstition, fear, fanaticism

superstitiósus -a -um: superstitious, fanatical

supersubstantiális -is -e: necessary for sustenance

supérsum -ésse -fui: be over and above, remain, be left, be superfluous, survive, be adequate, suffice

superumerále -is: *see* **superhumerále**

súperus -a -um: upper, higher, divine, supreme; **súperus** -i: m.; angel;

supérior -ior -ius: higher, former, stronger; **supérrimus (suprémus)** -a -um: highest, last, latest; **supréma** -órum: n. pl.; last moments, death; **suprémum, suprémo:** for the last time

supervacáneus -a -um: superfluous

supervácue: without cause, wantonly, uselessly, superfluously

supervacúitas -atis: f.; vainglory

superváleo -ére: (2); surpass greatly

supervénio -íre -véni -véntum: (4); come in, upon, over or up, overtake, surprise

superventúrus -a -um: approaching, arriving, coming

supervéstio -íre: (4); clothe

supervívo -ere: (3); outlive

supínus -a -um: bent or inclined backward, lying on the back, supine, lazy, indifferent, careless

supp- *see also* **subp-**

súpparo -áre: (1); fit, adjust

suppedále -is: n.; platform

suppedáneum -i: n.; platform or upper step of altar; footstool

suppédito -áre: (1); give abundantly, furnish

súppeto -ere -ii(-ívi) -ítum: (3); be present, be enough, be available, be equal to, correspond to, demand secretly

supplantátio -ónis: f.; treachery, hypocritical deceit, act of tripping

supplánto -áre: (1); overthrow, trip, supplant

suppleméntum -i: n.; supply, supplement, fulfilling

súppleo -ére -plévi -plétum: (2); use, supply, make full or whole, complete

suppletórius -a -um: completing, supplying, supplementary

súpplex -icis: suppliant, low, humble, submissive, beseeching, asking on bended knee; *as a c. noun:* humble petitioner, suppliant

supplicátio -ónis: f.; prayer,
supplication, religious act

suppliciter: suppliantly, humbly

supplícium -ii: n.; a kneeling down
either in entreaty or to receive
punishment

súpplico -áre: (1); entreat, implore,
beseech, beg

suppóno -ere -pósui -pósitum: (3); put
under, substitute, falsify, forge,
suppose, presuppose

suppórto -áre: (1); bear, convey, bear
with, carry, support

suppositícius -a -um: substituted; false,
not genuine

suppréssio -ónis: f.; suppression,
pressing down, keeping back,
retaining, embezzlement

suppréssus -a -um: held back, kept in,
suppressed, checked, restrained, held;
supprésse: in a subdued voice

súpprimo -ere -préssi -préssum: (3);
detain, hold down, sink, check, stop,
keep secret

supputárius (supputatórius) -a -um: of
computing or reckoning

supputátio -ónis: f.; computation,
reckoning

supputátor -óris: m.; one who reckons
or computes

súpputo -áre: (1); count, compute, cut
off below, prune, trim

súpra: adv. & prep. w. acc.; on top, on
the upper side, above, before, over,
earlier, beyond

súpra mórem: more than usual

súpra quod: besides

supradíctus -a -um: aforesaid,
above-mentioned, aforementioned

supradioecesánus -a -um:
transdiocesan, of more than one
diocese

suprános -a -um: high, soprano

supraparoeciális -is -e: transparochial,
of more than one parish

suprascríptio -ónis: f.; suprascription

suprémus -a -um: latest, highest,
greatest, supreme, extreme; see also
súperus

súrculus -i: m.; twig, sprout, young
shoot, branch

súrditas -átis: f.; deafness

súrdus -a -um: deaf; as a noun: deaf
person

súrgo -ere, surréxi, surréctum: (3); rise
up, awake, arise, stand by

Súria -ae: see Sýria

surréctio -ónis: f.; rising again,
resurrection

surrípio -ere -rípui -réptum: (3); take by
stealth, steal away

súrrogo: see súbrogo

súrsum: above, upward; súrsum córda:
lift up (your) hearts, hearts upward

sus, súis: c.; pig, hog

suscénseo: see succénseo

suscéptio -ónis: f.; protection, defense,
reception, undertaking

suscéptor -óris: m.; receiver, protector,
defender, helper

suscípio -ere -cépi -céptum: (3); take,
receive, accept, uphold, undertake,
protect, guard, support, lift up

súscito -áre: (1); awaken, raise up, stir
up, erect, encourage

suspéndium -ii: n.; hanging, suspense of
judgment

suspéndo -ere -péndi -pénsum: (3);
hang up, suspend, hold off, hang,
interrupt

suspénsio -ónis: f.; withholding,
suspending, interruption, suspension;
see Appendix

suspensívus -a -um: suspending

suspénsus -a -um: suspended, hanging,
wavering, uncertain, hesitating;
suspénse: adv.

suspício -ónis: f.; suspicion, reproach

suspício -ere -spéxi -spéctum: (3);
regard, contemplate, look up or at,
admire; suspect, mistrust

suspiciósus (suspiti-) -a -um:
mistrustful, ready to suspect,
suspicious; suspicióse: in a suspicious
manner

súspicor -ári: *dep.* (1); suspect, dread,
form an opinion about, look at
enviously, conjecture, mistrust

suspírium -ii: n.; sigh, desire

suspíro -áre: (1); sigh, draw a deep
breath, desire, long for

suspitiósus: *see* suspiciósus

sustentátio -ónis: f.; support,
maintenance, sustenance, forbearance,
delay, suspension, deferring

sustentátor -óris: m.; supporter

sustentáculum -i: n.; nourishment,
sustenance, support, prop

susténto -áre: (1); maintain, support,
hold up, sustain

sustinéntia -ae: f.; patience, endurance

sustíneo -ére -ui -téntum: (2); endure,
sustain, undergo, wait upon, bear
with, support, maintain

sustóllo -ere: (3); raise, elevate, lift up,
build, erect, take away, remove

susurrátio -ónis: f.; a whispering

susúrro -áre: (1); whisper, murmur,
mutter, hum

susúrrus -a -um: whispering,
murmuring; *as a noun:* whisperer,
murmurer

súus -a -um: *refl. and possessive adj. for
the 3rd per. sing. and* pl.; his, her, its,
their, one's own

Sybillínus -a -um: Sibylline

sycómorus -i: f.; sycamore tree

sycophánta (suco-) -ae: f.; flatterer,
sycophant

sycophántia -ae: f.; craft, deception

sýllaba (súl-) -ae: f.; syllable; syllabátim:
syllable by syllable

sýllabus -i: m.; syllabus, register

sýlloge -es: f.; list, roll

syllogísmus (syllogísmos) -i: m.;
syllogism

syllogísticus -a -um: of a syllogism

symbolísmus -i: m.; symbolism

sýmbolum -i: n., sýmbolus -i: m.; creed,
symbol, profession of faith

sympathía -ae: f.; sympathy

symphónia -ae: f.; music, symphony,
concert, band, orchestra

symphoniácus -a -um: harmonized, of
concerts or musical groups; *as a noun:*
musician

sympsálma -átis: n.; playing of music
together

sýmptoma -atis: n.; symptom

synagóga -ae: f.; synagogue, assembly,
congregation

synallagmáticus -a -um: bilateral

synáxis -is: f.; gathering, Mass, Holy
Communion; *see Appendix*

syncéllus -ii: syncellus; *see Appendix:
protosyncéllus*

sýncope -es, sýncopa -ae: f.; faint,
swoon

syncretísmus -i: m.; syncretism, union,
reconciliation

syndicális -is -e: of or pertaining to a
labor union

synedrísta -ae: f.; Sanhedrin

sýngrapha -ae: f.; promissory note, bond

synníchium -ii: n.; umbrella

synódicus -a -um, synodális -is -e:
synodal; synódice: in accordance with
a synod's decrees

sýnodus -i: f.; synod, council; *see
Appendix*

synónymus -a -um: synonymous

synópsis -is: f.; list, synopsis, general
view

Synóptici -orum: m.; Synoptic Gospel
writers; Matthew, Mark, Luke

sýnthema -atis: n.; token or sign agreed
on, passport

sýnthesis -is: f.; mixture, compound, a
joining together

Sýntyche -es: f.; Syntyche

Sýri -órum: m. pl.; Syrians

Sýria (Súr-) -ae: f.; Syria

Syríacus (Sýrus) -a -um: Syrian;
Syríace: in the Syrian tongue

sýrtis -is: f.; sandbank

systéma -atis: n.; system

systemáticus -a -um: systematic, of a
system or coherent body of thought,
according to method; systemátice: adv.

T

tabélla -ae: f.; small table, tablet, or flat board

tabélla secretárum: altar card

tabellárius -ii: m.; courier, postman, mailman

tabéllio -ónis: c.; notary

tabérna -ae: f.; shop, inn, tavern, cottage

tabernáculum -i: n.; tent, tabernacle, pavillion, hut, Jewish tabernacle

tábes -is: f.; melting or wasting away, pestilence

tabésco -ere, tábui: (3); melt, languish, waste away, faint, be slowly consumed

tábidus -a -um: decaying, melting, consuming, dissolving, pining, wasting

tabífico -áre: (1); consume

Tabítha -ae: f.; Tabitha, a Christian woman from Joppa

tabitúdo -inis: f.; wasting away

tábula -ae: f.; tablet, table, writing table or board, a wooden instrument used instead of a bell in Holy Week; tábulae -árum: f. pl.; terms, stipulations; tábulae fundatiónis: founding charter

tabulárium -ii: n.; archives, registry office

tabulárius -ii: m.; archivist

tabulátio -ónis: f.; boarding, flooring

tabulátum -i: n.; board, floor of a building, platform

tábum -i: n.; pestilence, plague, clotted blood, moisture

táceo -ére -ui -itum: (2); be silent, be dumb, not speak

tacitúrnitas -átis: f.; silence

tácitus -a -um: silent; tácite: silently

táctus -us: m.; touch, handling, operation, influence, effect, blemish

taéda (téda) -ae: f.; torch, pine tree, board of pine

taédet -ére, taéduit: (2); impers.; it disgusts, it wearies

taédifer -fera -ferum: torch-bearing; as a noun: torchbearer

taédium -ii: n.; weariness, heaviness, loathing, irksomeness, tediousness

taeníola -ae: f.; small band or ribbon

taláris -is -e: reaching to the ankles; túnica taláris: outside coat

taléntum -i: n.; talent, weight, sum of money

tálio -ónis: f.; retaliation

tális -is -e: such, such kind, of such a kind; qua tále: of any sort

táliter: thus, so, in such manner

talítha: Aramaic; maiden

tálus -i: m.; ankle, foot, heel; die (as in playing dice)

tam: so, to such a degree, as, so much; tam . . . quam: both . . . and, whether . . . or, the . . . the, as much . . . as

támdiu (tándiu): so long, so very long; támdiu . . . quámdiu: till such time as, until

támen: nevertheless, yet

tamétsi: although, notwithstanding that, even if, and yet

támquam (tánquam): just as, as it were, like, as if, as though

tándem: finally, at length

tándiu: see támdiu

tángo -ere, tétigi, táctum: (3); touch, reach, seize, strike, push; undertake, comprehend, be related to

tánquam: see támquam

tantísper: meanwhile

tantópere: to such a degree, so much

tántulus -a -um: so little, so small

tántum: so much, so great; only, just, to such a degree; merely

tantúmdem (tantúndem): as much, just as much

Tántum Érgo Sacraméntum: So great a sacrament; a Benediction hymn

tantúmmodo: only, merely, alone

tantúndem: see tantúmdem

tántus -a -um: such, so much, so great, so important, of such size; tánto . . . quánto: so much . . . as

tápes -étis, tapéte -is, tapétum -i: n.; carpet, tapestry, drapery

tárditas -átis: f.; slowness, tardiness

tárdo -áre: (1); tarry, delay, loiter, be slow; hinder, impede

tárdus -a -um: slow, tardy, sluggish; tárde: slowly, tardily, late

taríncha -ae: f.; long needle, spit

Tarsénsis -is -e: of Tarsus

Társus -i: f.; Tarsus, a city in Cilicia

tártarus -i: m.; Tartarus, infernal regions, hell; pl.: tártara -órum: n.

tau: 22nd letter of the Hebrew alphabet

taúrea -ae: f.; whip made of bull hide

taúrus -i: m.; ox, bull, bullock, beef

táxa -ae: f.; fee, tax, tribute, assessment; see Appendix

taxátio -ónis: f.; taxation, assessment

táxo -áre: (1).; tax, assess, appraise

táxus -i: f.; yew tree

téchnicus -a -um: technical; téchnice: adv.

technológia -ae: f.; technology

téctum -i: n.; roof, housetop, abode, dwelling

téctus -a -um: covered

téda -ae: see taéda

tegíllum -i: n.; hood, cowl; small covering

tégmen (tégimen, tégumen) -inis: n.; shelter, covering, shield, protection

tégo -ere, téxi, téctum: (3); cover, hide, conceal, protect

tégula -ae: f.; tile, roof tile

tégulum (teguméntum) -i: n.; covering

tégumen -inis: see tégmen

tegúrium -ii: n.; canopy above an altar

Te Déum: You God; opening words of an ancient hymn of thanksgiving

Te ígitur: You therefore; opening words of the Canon of the Mass in the pre–Vatican II liturgy

teípsum: see temetípsum

téla -ae: f.; cloth, web, warp, something woven

teláre -is, telárium -ii: n.; wooden frame covered with cloth

telégraphum -i: n.; instrument for sending telegraph messages

teleológia -ae: f.; teleology

teléphonum -i: n.; telephone

téleta -ae: f.; initiation

televisíficus -a -um: broadcast by television; as a n. noun: television

televísio -ónis: f.; television

téllus -úris: f.; earth, globe, land, district, country

telonárius -ii: m.; tax collector

telónium -ii, telóneum -i: n.; tollbooth, customhouse

télum -i: n.; dart, spear, javelin

temerárius -a -um: rash, thoughtless, casual; temerárie: adv.

témere: by chance, at random, rashly

teméritas -átis: f.; rashness, chance, recklessness, accident

temetípsum (teípsum): yourself; própter temetípsum: for your own sake

témno -ere, témpsi: (3); despise, contemn, disdain, slight, scorn

temperaménter: moderately, temperately

temperaméntum -i: n.; plan and pattern of the seasons, blend, compromise; tempered mortar

temperántia -ae: f.; temperance, moderation, self-control

temperatúra -ae, **tempéries** -éi, **temperátio** -ónis: f.; proper measure or proportion, temperature, temper, refreshment, temperament, symmetry

témpero -áre: (1); be temperate, control, rule, mingle, regulate, govern, set or observe limits, learn to avoid

tempéstas -átis: f.; storm, tempest

tempestívus -a -um: at the right time, seasonable, fitting, opportune, appropriate, suitable; **tempestíve:** *adv.*

témplum -i: n.; temple, church, shrine

temporális -is -e: temporal, earthly, temporary; *see Appendix*

temporáliter: temporarily, for a time

temporáneus -a -um: timely, opportune, early

temporárius -a -um: temporary, changeable

tempt- *see also* **tent-**

témpto (ténto) -áre: (1); try, attempt, handle, touch, incite, tempt, prove

témpus -oris: n.; time, season, period; *see Appendix*

> **ad témpus:** for a while, on time
> **ómni témpore:** always
> **púncto témporis:** in an instant
> **quánto témpore:** as long as
> **quátuor témporum:** of Ember week
> **succéssu témporis:** in course of time
> **témpore súo:** in season, at the proper time
> **témpus acceptábile:** time of grace
> **témpus útile:** available time

temuléntus -a -um: drunk

tenácitas -átis: f.; tenacity, firm hold, holding fast

ténax -ácis: firm, steadfast, holding fast, tenacious, gripping

tendícula -ae: f.; snare, trap, noose

téndo -ere, teténdi, téntum (ténsum): (3); extend, stretch, bend, direct one's course of life

ténebrae -árum: f. pl.; darkness, shadows, affliction, Office of Matins and Lauds on the last three days of Holy Week

tenebrésco -ere: (3); become dark

tenebricósus (tenebrósus, tenebrárius) -a -um: dark, of darkness

ténebro -áre: (1); make dark, darken

téneo -ére -ui, téntum: (2); have, obtain, hold, keep, possess, consider

téner -era -erum: tender, soft, delicate, young

teneritúdo -inis: f.; tenderness, softness

ténor -óris: m.; tension, stretching, dominant note, sense, direction, tenor, holding fast, uninterrupted course

ténsio -ónis: f.; stretching out, extension, contraction, tension, setting up

tentaméntum -i: n.; trial, proof, test

tentátio -ónis: f.; temptation, trial, test

tentátor -óris: m.; tempter, the devil, assailant, attacker

tentátrix -ícis: f.; temptress

ténto (témpto) -áre: (1); try, prove, tempt, handle, attempt, incite, touch

tentoríolum -i: n.; small tent, canopy over the tabernacle

tentórium -ii: n.; tent, drapery

ténuis -is -e: small, weak, little, thin, slight, tender, frail, fine, shallow, plain, simple; **tenúiter:** *adv.*

ténuo -áre: (1); lessen, diminish, make thin

ténus: lengthwise, to the end, as far as, up or down to, along

tepefácio -ere -féci -fáctum: (3); make lukewarm or tepid

tepefáctus -a -um: lukewarm, tepid

tépeo -ére: (2); be tepid or lukewarm

tepésco -ere, tépui: (3); grow tepid

tépidus -a -um: lukewarm, tepid, feeble, faint; tépide: *adv.* warmly, flatly

ter: three times, thrice

tercénties: three hundred times

terebínthus -i: f.; turpentine tree

tergéminus -a -um: threefold

tergiversátio -ónis: f.; subterfuge, evasion, refusal

térgo -ere, térsi, térsum: (3), térgeo -ére: (2); wipe clean; improve, correct

térgum -i, térgus -oris: n.; back

terminátio -ónis: f.; arrangement, fixing, decision, final modulation

término -áre: (1); limit, define, end, finish, determine

terminológia -ae: f.; terminology

términus -a -um: end, goal, boundary, limit, border, terminus, quarter, term
términus a quo: end from which
términus ad quem: end toward which

térni -ae -a: three, three apiece

térnus -i: m.; group of three, list of three; *see Appendix*

téro -ere, trívi, trítum: (3); smooth, rub or wear down, afflict, bruise

térra -ae: f.; earth, ground, land, country, region

terraemótus -us: m.; earthquake

terrénus -a -um: earthly, transitory (as opposed to the eternal); terréna -órum: n. pl.; earthly things

térreo -ére -ui -itum: (2); frighten, terrify

térreus -a -um, terréster (terréstris) -tris -tre: earthly, terrestrial

terríbilis -is -e: terrible, fearful, dreadful, frightful

terribíliter: fearfully

terrífagus -a -um: dust-eating

terrífico -áre: (1); frighten, terrify, scare

terrígena -ae: c.; a mortal, earthborn creature

territoriális -is -e: territorial; territoriáliter: *adv.; see Appendix*

territórium -ii: n.; district, territory, country

térror -óris: m.; terror, fright, fear, dread, panic

terrorísmus -i: m.; terrorism

térrula -ae: f.; small piece of land

térsus -a -um: clean, neat, free from mistakes or errors

tértia -ae: f.; canonical hour of Terce

Tertiánus (Tertiárius) -a -um: of a Third Order, Tertiary

tértio (tértium): third time, for a third time

tértius -a -um: third

tertiusdécimus -a -um: thirteenth

Tertulliánus -i: m.; Tertullian, a Father of the Church

téssera -ae: f.; token, distinguishing mark, ticket, square mark or tablet

tésta -ae: f.; clay, potsherd, brick, pitcher, jug, urn

testáceus -a -um: of tile, clay or brick

testaméntum -i: n.; covenant, testament, will, written witness, Bible, Old and New Testaments

testamónium (testimónium) -ii: n., testificátio -ónis: f.; testimony, witness, evidence, proof, laws, commandments, attestation

testátor -óris: m., testátrix -ícis: f.; testator, one who makes a will

testátus -a -um: *perf. part. of* téstor

testificátio -ónis: f.; testimony, proof, evidence

testíficor (téstor, testífico) -ári: *dep.* (1); testify, bear witness, attest, charge, exhibit, bring to light

testimoniális -is -e: testimonial, serving as evidence; *see Appendix*

testimónium -ii: n.; testimony, evidence; *see Appendix*

téstis -is: m.; witness

téstor: *see* testíficor

testúdo -inis: f. tortoise

téstula -ae: f.; small potsherd

téter -tra -trum: foul, filthy, offensive, hideous

teth: ninth letter of the Hebrew alphabet

tetrárcha -ae: m.; tetrarch, governor, ruler of a fourth part

tetrávela -órum: n. pl.; four curtains formerly surrounding the altar

tétricus -a -um: harsh, severe, forbidding, gloomy

Teutónicus: *see* **Theutónicus**

téxens -éntis, **téxtor** -óris: m.; weaver

téxo -ere -ui, téxtum: (3); weave

textrínus -a -um: of weaving, weaving

téxtum -i: n.; woven goods

téxtum denticulátum: lace

téxtus -us: m.; context, text

Thábor: *indecl.;* Tabor, a mountain near Nazareth

Thaddéus -i: m.; Thaddeus, one of the apostles

thálamus -i: m.; bedroom, bridal chamber, couch, platform

thállus -i: m.; bough, stem

Thársis: *indecl.;* Tharsis, a city in Spain

thaumatúrgus -i: m.; miracle worker

theátricus -a -um: theatrical

theátrum -i: n.; theater, show, study, complete picture

Thebaéi -orum: m. pl.; Thebans, people of Thebes

théca -ae: f.; covering, case, sheath

théma -atis: n.; theme, topic

Théman: *indecl.;* Theman, a city or tribe in Edom

theológia -ae: f.; theology

theológicus (theológális) -a -um: theological

theólogus -i: m.; theologian

theophánia -ae: f.; theophany, a manifestation of God in human form

theoréma -atis: n.; theorem, proposition, formula

theoréticus -a -um: theoretical; **theorétice:** *adv.*

theória -ae: f.; theory, philosophic speculation

theosóphia -ae: f.; doctrine of theosophy, rejected by the Church

Theótocus -i: f.; God-bearing, mother of God

theotokárion -ii: n.; theotokarion; *see Appendix*

théraphim: *indecl.: n.* pl.; idols

therístrum -i: n.; veil, summer garment

thérmae -árum: f. pl.; baths, hot springs

thesaurízo -áre: (1); lay up treasure

thesaúrus -i: m.; treasure, treasury, storehouse; dictionary

Thésbites -is: m.; Thesbite, Tishbite, Elijah

thésis -is: f.; proposition, thesis

Thessalónica -ae: f.; Thessalonica, a city of Macedonia

Thessalonicénses -ium: c. pl.; Thessalonians, people of Thessalonica

théta: eighth letter of the Greek alphabet

Theúdas -ae: m.; Theudas, a Jewish imposter

theúrgus -i: m.; magician

Theutónicus (Teutónicus) -a -um: German

thólus -i: m.; rotunda, dome

Thómas (Thóma) -ae: m.; Thomas

thórax -ácis: m.; breast, chest, breastplate

thrénus -i: m.; wailing, lamentation

thrónus -i: m.; throne, canopy; an angelic order

thórus (tórus) -i: m.; bed, marriage couch

thúreus: *see* **túreus**

thuríbulum (tur-, thymiatérium) -i: n.; censer, vessel for burning incense

thúrifer: *see* **túrifer**

thuriferárius -ii: m.; thurifer, censer bearer

thurificátio -ónis: f.; incensing, offering of incense

thurífico -áre: (1); burn or offer incense

thus, thúris: n.; incense, frankincense

thyára -ae: *see* tiára

thyínus -a -um: of the citrus tree

thymiatérium -ii: n.; vessel for holding incense

thýrsus -i: m.; stem of a plant

tiára -ae: f.; papal tiara, crown, cap, tiara, turban

Tibérias -adis: f.; a city; another name for the Sea of Galilee

Tiberínus -a -um: of the Tiber

Tíberis -is: m.; Tiber River

tíbia -ae: f.; shinbone, leg, pipe, flute

tíbicen -inis: m., tibícina -ae: f.; minstrel, piper, flute player, trumpeter, entertainer

Tiburtínus -a -um: Tiburtine, of Tivoli

tígnum -i: n.; beam

tígris -is: m.; tiger

timefáctus -a -um: frightened, alarmed

timéndus -a -um: fearful, to be feared

tímeo -ére -ui: (2); fear, dread, be apprehensive

timésco -ere: (3); become afraid

tímidus -a -um: timid, fearful, afraid; tímide: *adv.*

tímor -óris: m.; fear, dread, alarm, apprehension

timorátus -a -um: fearful, devout

Timótheus -i: m.; Timothy

tinctúra -ae: f.; dye, dyeing

tínctus -a -um: dyed

tínea (tínia) -ae: f.; moth

tíngo -ere, tínxi, tínctum: (3); dye, color, moisten, wet

tínnio -íre: (4); tinkle, ring, jingle

tínnitus -us: m.; ringing, tinkling

tintinnábulum -i: n.; small handbell

tíro (týro) -ónis: c.; beginner, recruit, novice

tirocínium -ii: n.; noviceship, novitiate, apprenticeship, training, beginning, trial period

titíllo -áre: (1); tickle, titillate

títio -ónis: m.; firebrand

títubo -áre: (1); totter, waver, stagger, reel, falter, hesitate

tituláris -is -e: titular; *see Appendix*

título -áre: (1); entitle, name

títulus -i: m.; title, inscription, heading, pledge, label

Títus -i: m.; Titus

tobálea -ae: f.; altar cloth, cloth

Tobías (Tobía) -as: m.; Tobit; a book of the O.T.

tóga -ae: f.; outer garment, toga, gown, clothing

tolerábilis -is -e: light, bearable

tolerántia -ae: f.; toleration, tolerance, endurance

tólero -áre: (1); bear, endure, sustain, tolerate

tóllo -ere, sústuli, sublátum: (3); lift up, raise, elevate, hold in suspense, remove, take away, cancel, abolish, destroy

tómus -i: m.; volume, tome

tóndens -éntis: m.; shearer

tóndeo -ére, totóndi, tónsum: (2); shear, cut, shave

tonítrus -i: m., tonítruum -i: n.; thunder

tóno -áre: (1); sound, thunder, resound, roar, crash

tónsio -ónis: f.; a shearing

tonsúra -ae: f.; tonsure

tonsurátus -a -um: tonsured, shaven; *as a m. noun:* one who is tonsured

tónus -i: m.; tone, sound, accent

topárchia -ae: f.; province, district, territory

topázion -ii: m., topázius -ii, topázus -i: f.; topaz, precious stone

tórcular -áris: n.; winepress

tórculus -i: m.; a group of three notes of which the middle one is higher

torméntum -i: n.; instrument of torture, rack, engine for hurling missles

tornátilis -is -e: turned, revolving

tornatúra -ae: f.; turning

tórpeo -ére -ui: (2); be listless, sluggish, inactive, or numb

torpésco -ere, tórpui: (3); grow stiff, numb, dull, inactive, useless, or dim

tórpor -óris: m.; torpor, dullness, inactivity, sloth, stupefaction

tórqueo -ére, tórsi, tórsum: (2); twist, bend, wind; torture, torment

tórquis -is: c.; collar, necklace, wreath, ring, chain

tórrens -éntis: m.; torrent, stream, brook

tórreo -ére -ui, tóstum: (2); burn, roast, parch, dry

tórridus -a -um: hot, dry, parched

tórta -ae: f.; roll, twisted loaf

torticórdius -a -um: perverse in heart

tórtor -óris: m.; tormentor, torturer

tórtula -ae: f.; small twist or twisted loaf, small roll or cake

tortuóse: crookedly

tortuósus -a -um: winding, crooked, complex

tórulus -i: m.; red cord on a cassock

tórus -i: m.; bed, couch, marriage bed

tot: so many; tot . . . quot: as many . . . as

totális -is -e: total, entire, whole; totáliter: adv.

totalitárius -a -um: totalitarian

totálitas -átis: f.; totality, completeness

tótidem: so many, just as many, the same number

tóties: so often; tóties . . . quóties: as often as

tótus -a -um: all, whole, entire, total
    ex tóto, in tótum: wholly, entirely, completely, totally
    in tóto: on the whole, in general
    per tótum: throughout

tóxico -áre: (1); smear with poison

trábea -ae: f.; robe, official robe

trabs -is: f.; beam, beam of wood

tractábilis -is -e: manageable, pliant

tractátio -ónis: f.; treatise, treatment

tractátus -us: m.; tract, treatise, sermon, discourse, homily

trácto -áre: (1); treat, handle, haul, celebrate, drag, draw, touch, manage, discuss, conduct, transact

tráctus -a -um: flowing, fluent, continuous

tráctus -us: m.; Tract, formerly part of the Mass; tract, treatise, course, application, extension

tradítio -ónis: f.; tradition, transmission, handing over; see Appendix

traditionális -is -e: traditional

traditionalísmus -i: m.; doctrine of traditionalism, condemned by the Church

tráditor -óris: m.; traitor, betrayer

trádo (tránsdo) -ere -didi -ditum: (3); betray, hand over, yield, hand down, relate, surrender

traducianísmus -i: m.; theory of traducianism, rejected by the Church

tradúco (trans-) -ere -dúxi -dúctum: (3); lead, lead or bring across

trádux -ucis: m., tradúctio -ónis: f.; tradition, transmission, transferal

tragélaphus -i: m.; a wild animal of the goat family

tragoédia -ae: f.; tragic scene

tráha -ae: f.; vehicle without wheels, drag, sled

tráho -ere, tráxi, tráctum: (3); drag, draw, catch, pull, refer

tralátio -ónis: see transítio or translátio

trámeo: see tránsmeo

trámes -itis: m.; crossroad, road, course, path, byway

tranquíllitas -átis: f., tranquíllum -i: n.; calmness, tranquillity tranquíllo -áre: (1); pacify, make calm

tranquíllus -a -um: calm, tranquil, undisturbed, quiet, still; tranquílle: calmly, quietly; tranquíllius: rather peacefully

trans: *prep. w. acc.;* across, over

transáctio -ónis: f.; agreement, transaction, completion, compromise; *see Appendix*

transáctus -a -um: *perf. pass. part. of* tránsigo

transcendentális -is -e: transcendental

transcendéntia -ae: f.; a transcending

transcéndo -ere -scéndi -scénsum: (3); transcend

transcénsus -us: m.; ford, crossing, climbing over, surmounting, transition

transcríbo (transscríbo) -ere -scrípsi -scríptum: (3); write over, transfer, transcribe, copy, forge, alter, assign

transcríptio -ónis: f.; transcription, copy, transfer, assignment

transcúrro -ere: (3); pass through

transcúrsio -ónis: f., transcúrsus -us: m.; lapse of time; hasty treatment; passing through

tránsdo: *see* trádo

transdúco: *see* tradúco

transénna -ae: f.; altar rail

tránseo -íre -ívi (-ii) -itum: (4); pass through, go across or over to, depart

transeúnter: in passing, cursorily

tránsfero -érre -tuli -látum: irreg.; move, remove, transfer, transform, translate

transfígo -ere -fíxi -fíxum: (3); pierce through, transfix

transfigurábilis -is -e: transformable, able to be transfigured

transfigurátio -ónis: f.; transfiguration

transfigúro -áre: (1); transfigure

transfíxio -ónis: f.; act of piercing

transfluviális -is -e: coming from beyond the river

transformátio -ónis: f.; transformation, change of shape

transformatívus -a -um: transforming

transfórmo -áre: (1); change in shape, transform

transfóssus -a -um: pierced

tránsfreto -áre: (1); pass over, cross the sea

transfúndo -ere: (3); pour, pour off, transfer, transfuse

transglútio -áre: (1); to swallow

transgrédior -i -gréssus: *dep.* (3); go over, pass over, transgress

transgréssio -ónis: f.; transgression, violation

transgréssor -óris: m.; transgressor

tránsiens -eúntis: transient, transitional

tránsigo -ere -égi -áctum: (3); get along, drive through, transact, accomplish, spend time, stab, pierce

transílio -íre -ui(-ívi, -ii): (4); leap over, skip over, neglect, hasten past

transítio (translátio, tralátio) -ónis: f.; translation, transferring

transitórius -a -um: having a passageway, transitory, passing

tránsitus -us: m.; passing over, passage, transition, change

translatícius -a -um: customary, usual, hereditary

translátio (tralátio) -ónis: f.; a transporting or transferring, removal; version, translation

translátor -óris: m.; translator

translátus -a -um: *perf. pass. part. of* transféro

translégo -áre: (1); bequeath

translimitánus -a -um: from beyond the frontier

tránsmeo (trámeo) -áre: (1); go or come across, go through

transmigrátio -ónis: f.; removal, transmigration, carrying away

transmígro -áre: (1); flee, migrate, remove to another place, transplant transmíssio -ónis: f.; sending, forwarding

transmítto -ere -mísi -míssum: (3); send across, transmit, transfer

transmutátio -ónis: f.; change

transmúto -áre: (1); to change, turn

transpárens -éntis: transparent

transplánto -áre: (1); transplant, remove, move

transpóno -ere: (3); remove, transfer

transscríbo: see transcríbo

transsexuális -is -e: transsexual

transubstantiátio -onis: f.; transubstantiation; see Appendix

transúmptum -i: n.; a copy

tránsvado -áre: (1); pass by, cross over, ford

tránsveho -ere -véxi -véctum: (3); carry over, convey, transport

transvérbero -áre: (1); pierce, perforate, transfix

transvérsim: obliquely, across, crosswise, transversely

transvérto -ere -vérti -vérsum: (3); overturn, lure away, avert, change

tránsvolo -áre: (1); fly across

trecénti (tri-) -ae -a: three hundred

trédecim: thirteen

tremefácio -ere: (3); make tremble

tremefáctus -a -um: terrified

treméndus -a -um: tremendous, aweful, fearful, terrible, dreadful

trémo -ere -ui: (3); tremble, quake

trémor -óris: m.; fear, trembling, an object that causes fear

trepidátio -ónis: f.; agitation, trepidation, anxiety, disquiet, alarm

trépido -áre: (1); tremble, be agitated or busy, swarm about

tres, tres, tría: three

triángulum -i: n.; triangle

trías -ádis: f.; triad, group of three

tríbula -ae: f., tríbulum -i: n.; threshing sled or machine

tríbulans -ántis: m.; oppressor

tribulátio -ónis: f.; tribulation, affliction, trouble, distress, anguish

tríbulo -áre: (1); afflict, oppress, harass

tríbulor -ári: dep. (1); be in trouble

tríbulum -i: see tríbula

tríbulus -i: m.; a kind of thistle, thorn, or briar; caltrop

tribúna -ae: f., tribúnal (tribunále) -is: n.; tribunal, place of judgment, court of justice, judgment seat, platform, tribune, gallery

tribunális -is -e: of a tribunal; see Appendix

Tribúnal Comitátus: county court

tribúnus -i: m.; tribune, captain, commander, chieftain, appointed leader

tríbuo -ere -ui -útum: (3); give, bestow, grant

tríbus -us: m.; tribe, division of people, mass, mob, poor people

tribútum -i: n.; tribute, tax, contribution

tribútus -a -um: perf. pass. part. of tríbuo

tribútus -a -um: formed or arranged into tribes

tricamerátus -a -um: having three chambers

tricéni -ae -a: thirty each, thirty

tricénti: see trecénti

tricéreus -i: m.; a three-branched candle formerly used in Holy Week

tricésimus (trig-) -a -um: thirtieth

tricháptum -i: n.; garment woven of hair, hair shirt

triclínium -ii: n.; eating couch; parlor, dining room; stewardship

tríco -áre: (1); delay, tarry, dally

trícor -ári: dep. (1); to trifle

trídens -éntis, tridentális -is -e: having three teeth or prongs, trident, fork-shaped

Tridentínus -a -um: of Trent

triduánus -a -um: of three days

tríduo: in three days

tríduum -i: n.; space of three days; triduum, a three-day devotion

triennális (triénnis) -is -e: three years

triénnium -ii: n.; space of three years

trifórium -ii: n.; arched gallery

trígamus -a -um: thrice married

trigésimus: *see* **tricésimus**

trigínta: *indecl.;* thirty

triméstris -is -e: of three months; *as a n. noun:* trimester

tríni -ae -a: three each, thrice

trínitas -átis: f.; trinity; **Trínitas:** *see Appendix*

trínus -a -um, **tríplex** -icis: three, triune, threefold

tripartítio -ónis: f.; threefold division

trípes -edis: m.; tripod

tríplex -icis: triple, threefold

triplicábilis -is -e: threefold, triple

tríplico -áre: (1): triple

tripúdio -áre: (1); dance

tripúdium -ii: n.; joy, delight, festivities of the Middle Ages

trirégnum -i: n.; papal tiara

trirémis -is: f.; trireme, a galley with three banks of oars

Triságion (Triságium) -ii: n.; Trisagion; *see Appendix*

tríste: sadly, sorrowfully

trístega -órum: n. pl.; third story of a building

trístis -is -e: sad, sorrowful, cast down, dejected

tristítia -ae: f.; sadness, sorrow

trístor -ári: *dep.* (1); be sad

trístropha -ae: f.; three notes in the same pitch

tritíceus -a -um: of wheat, wheaten

tríticum -i: n.; wheat

trítor -óris: m.; a chafer or grinder

tritúra -ae: f.; threshing, season for threshing

tritúro -áre: (1); thresh

triumphális -is -e, **triumphatórius** -a -um: triumphant

triumpháliter: solemnly, triumphantly

triumphátor -óris: conqueror

triumphatórius: *see* **triumphális**

triúmpho -áre: (1); triumph

triúmphus -i: m.; triumph

triviális -is -e: trivial

triviáliter: in a common manner

trívium -ii: n.; crossroads, place where three roads meet, public square

tróchlea -ae: f.; pulley

tropárium -ii: n.; a book containing chants, formerly used in the liturgy

trophéum (tropaéum) -i: n.; trophy, spoils, triumph, sign of a victory

tropológice: figuratively, metaphorically

troponárius -a -um: of tropes

trópus -i: m.; trope, figure of speech, a song or manner of singing

trucído -áre: (1); slaughter, slay, massacre, cut to pieces

trúdo -ere, trúsi, trúsum: (3); push, thrust, press, shove

truélla -ae: f.; trowel

trúnco -áre: (1); mutilate, maim, cut off, mangle, shorten, deprive

trúncus -a -um: maimed, mutilated, disfigured, deprived, imperfect; *as a m. noun:* stump, trunk

trux -cis: rough, savage, grim

tu, túi, tíbi, te, te: *sing.;* you

túba -ae: f.; trumpet

túber -eris: n.; hump, bump, tumor, swelling

túber -eris: c.; a kind of apple tree

túbicen -cinis: c.; flute player

tubulátus -a -um: formed like a pipe, tubular

túeor -éri, túitus (tútus): *dep.* (2); guard, defend, protect, uphold, save; regard, look at, maintain; *see Appendix*

tugúrium -ii: n.; hut, cabin, cottage

tuítio -ónis: f.; defense, protection, care

túlo -ere, túli (tétuli): (3); bring

tum: then, thereupon, at the time; **tum . . . tum;** now . . . then, at one time . . . at another time, both . . . and, partly . . . partly

túmba -ae: f.; tomb, catafalque

tumefácio -ere -féci -fáctum: (3); puff or swell up with pride

túmeo -ére: (2); swell, be swollen or puffed up

tumetípse: you yourself

túmidus -a -um: tumid, swollen, puffed up, elated, inflated, haughty; **túmide:** pompously, bombastically

túmor -óris: m.; tumor, pride, bombast

tumulátio -ónis: f.; burial, interment, entombment

túmulo -áre: (1); bury, heap over

tumultárie (tumultuárie): suddenly, in a disorderly manner, hastily

tumúlto (tumúltor) -áre: (1); make a tumult, be in confusion, rant, storm

tumúltus -i:, **tumultus** -us: m.; tumult, noise, confusion, bustle, disturbance, uproar

túmulus -i: m.; grave, mound, hillock

tunc: then, at that time; **ex tunc:** from olden times

túndo -ere, tutúndi, túsum (túnsum): (3); beat, strike, bump, buffet

túnica -ae: f.; coat, shirt, tunic, dalmatic

tunicélla -ae: f.; a tunic worn by a subdeacon

túnsio -ónis: f.; beating, striking

túrba -ae: f.; crowd, multitude

turbátio -ónis: f.; fear, confusion

turbátus -a -um: disturbed, agitated, disordered, confused, perturbed

túrben -inis: n., **túrbo** -inis: m.; whirlwind, storm, gale, hurricane

túrbidus -a -um: confused, wild

túrbo -áre: (1); disturb, trouble, dismay, confuse, agitate, disorganize

turbuléntus -a -um: troublesome

Túrcae -árum: m. pl.; Turks

túreus (thúreus) -a -um: of frankincense

túrgeo -ére: (2); swell up, be swollen

túrgidus -a -um: turgid, swollen

turíbulum -i: *see* **thuríbulum**

túrifer (thúr-) -feri: *see* **thuriferárius**

turífico -are: (1); *see* **thurífico**

turísmus -i: m.; tourism

túrma -ae: f.; crowd, throng, band, troop, squadron

túrnus -i: m.; a turn

turpilóquium -ii: n.; obscene or immodest speech

túrpis -is -e: foul, filthy, base, shameful, unsightly

túrpiter: in an unsightly manner, dishonorably, shamefully, disgracefully

turpitúdo -inis: f.; disgrace, dishonor, obscenity, ugliness

túrpo -áre: (1); befoul, defile, make bad or ugly

turrícula -ae: f.; small tower, turret

túrris -is: f.; tower; tabernacle

túrtur -uris: m.; turtledove

tus (thus), túris: n.; incense

tússis -is: f.; cough

tutaméntum -i, **tutámen** -inis: n.; safety, defense, protection

tutéla -ae: f.; charge, care, watching, keeping, safeguard, guardianship, caring for, guardian, protector

tuteláris -is -e: pertaining to the care of

tutiorísmus -i: m.; tutiorism, a system in moral theology for solving doubts

tútor (túto) -ári: *dep.* (1); watch, guard, keep, protect, defend

tútor -óris: m.; watcher, protector, defender, helper

tútum -i: n.; safety, shelter, safe place, security

tútus -a -um: safe, secure, cautious; **tútior** -ior -ius: *comp.;* **túto:** *adv.*

túus -a -um: your

tympanístria -ae: f.; timbrel player, female drummer, musical accompaniment

týmpanum -i: n.; drum, timbrel, tambourine, hand drum

týphon -ónis: m.; violent whirlwind or storm

typhónicus -a -um: stormy, like a typhoon

týphus -i: m.; pride, vanity

Týpicum -i: n.; Typikon; see Appendix

týpicus -a -um: typical, figurative; týpice: adv.

týpicus (týpus) -i: m.; figure, type, emblem, image

typográphicus -a -um: pertaining to print or printing

týpus -i: m.; type, figure, image, character, form

tyrannicídium -ii: n.; tyrannicide, killing of a tyrannt

tyránnis -idis: f.; tyranny

tyránnus -i: m.; tyrant, ruler, the devil

Týrii -órum: m. pl.; people of Tyre

týro (tíro) -ónis: c.; beginner, recruit, novice

tyrocínium -ii: n.; apprenticeship, time of training, novitiate

Týrus (-os) -i: f. city of Tyre

U

úber -eris: fruitful, copious, abundant, plentiful, rich, abounding; **ubérior** -ior -ius: *comp.;* **ubérrimus** -a -um: *superl.;* **ubérius:** *comp. adv.*

úber -eris: n.; breast, udder

ubértas -átis: f.; fullness, fruitfulness, abundance, plenty, fertility

ubértim: abundantly, copiously

ubérto -áre: (1); make fruitful

úbi (úbinam): where, in which place, when

ubicúmque: wherever, wheresoever

ubílibet: anywhere you please, everywhere

úbinam: *see* **úbi**

ubíque: wherever, everywhere, in all places

úbivis: where you will, anywhere, everywhere

údo -ónis: f.; stocking, stocking worn by a bishop at a Pontifical Mass

údo -áre: (1); wet, moisten

údus -a -um: wet, moist, tearful

ulcerátus -a -um: covered with sores

ulcíscor -i, últus: *dep.* (3); take vengeance on, avenge, punish

úlcus -eris: n.; sore, ulcer, boil

ullátenus: in any respect whatever

úllus -a -um: any; *as a pron.:* anyone, anything

úlna -ae: f.; arm, elbow

ultérior -ior -ius: further, beyond, later, more, longer, in a higher degree; **ultérius:** *comp. adv.*

últimus -a -um: farthest, last, extreme, final, ultimate; **última** -órum: n. pl.; final events, the end; **últime**

(**últimum, ultimátim**): to the last degree, utterly, finally, at last

últio -ónis: f.; revenge, vengeance, punishment

últor -óris: m.; avenger, punisher

últra: *adv. & prep. w. acc.;* further, besides, beyond, longer, on the other side; *frequently followed by* **quam** *(than)*

últra fídem: incredible

últra módum: immoderate

ultraterréstris -a -um: beyond the earth, ultraterrestrial

últro: spontaneously, of itself, of one's own accord, voluntarily, beyond, afar, on the other side, besides, too

ultróneus -a -um: voluntary

ululátus -us: m.; wailing, shrieking, shouting, howling

úlulo -áre: (1); shout, shriek, wail

um- *see also* **hum-**

umbélla -ae: f.; canopy, sunshade, parasol, umbrella

umbilícus -i: m.; navel, navel cord

úmbra -ae: f.; shade, shadow

umbráculum -i: n.; covering for a tabernacle, shade, covert, shady place

umbráticus (umbrósus) -a -um, umbrátilis -is -e: shady, pertaining to shade, in retirement, at home, private, contemplative; **umbrósa** -órum: n. pl.; dim light, twilight

umbrátio -ónis: f.; overshadowing

úmbro -áre: (1); shade, overshadow

umbrósus: *see* **umbráticus**

umérulus -i: m.; little shoulder

úmerus (húmerus) -i: m.; shoulder, upper arm

úmidus -a -um: moist, humid

úmquam (únquam): ever, at any time

úna: together, at the same place; úna símul: at the same time

unánimis -is -e, unánimus -a -um: of one mind, heart or will, with one voice, like-minded, harmonious

unanímitas -átis: f.; unanimity, concord; unanímiter: adv.

úncia -ae: f.; inch, ounce

uncínus -i: m.; hook, barb

únctio -ónis: f.; anointing, unction

únctor -óris: m.; anointer

únctus -a -um: anointed, smeared; as a n. noun: banquet, feast, ointment

únda -ae: f.; wave, water, stream, billow, surge, storm, moisture

únde: whence, wherefore, thence, whereupon, from whom

undecéntum: ninety-nine

úndecim: eleven

undécimus -a -um: eleventh

undecúmque: from wherever

undélibet: from whatever place

undequáquam: from everywhere

undequáque: on all sides, totally, everywhere

undevigínti: nineteen

úndique: on every side, on all sides

úndo -áre: (1); surge, swell, undulate, flow, inundate, deluge

undulátus -a -um: wavy, undulated

úngo (únguo) -ere, únxi, únctum: (3); anoint, smear, oil, perfume

unguentárius -a -um: of ointments; unguentárius -ii: m.; dealer in ointments; unguentária -ae: f.; art of making ointments; unguentárium -ii: n.; money to buy ointments or perfumes

unguénto -áre: (1); anoint, perfume

unguéntum -i: n.; ointment, fragrant oil, perfume

únguis -is: m.; claw, nail

úngula -ae: f.; hoof, claw, talon, hook, torturing hook, extremity; aromatic spice

ungulátus -a -um: hoofed, clawed

únguo: see úngo

unicúltor -óris: m.; monotheist

únicus -a -um: only, sole, single, uncommon, singular, alone, lonely, special; as a f. noun: dear one or darling; únice: adv.

unicórnis -is, unicórnuus -i: m.; unicorn

unificátio -ónis: f.; unification, unity

unífico -áre: (1); unite, unify

unifínis -is -e: having one termination

unifórmis -is -e: uniform, having one form, simple; unifórmiter: in one and the same manner, uniformly

unígena -ae: m.; only-begotten

unigénitus -a -um: only-begotten, born of one parent

unilaterális -is -e: unilateral; unilateráliter: adv.

únio -ónis: f.; union

únio -íre: (4); unite, join together

Unionítae -árum: m. pl.; Unionites, Unitarians

únitas -átis: f.; unity; see Appendix

unítus -a -um: united, joined

universális -is -e: universal, of all; universáliter: adv.

universálitas -átis: f.; universality, togetherness

universitárius -a -um: of a university

univérsitas -átis: f.; completeness, wholeness, company, community, guild, society, corporation, the whole, university, large educational institution

univérsus -a -um: whole, entire, all together, general, universal, collective, all; as a n. noun: the universe, the whole world; univérsim: adv.

univirátus -a -um: married but once

unóculus -a -um: one-eyed

únquam (úmquam): ever, at any time

únus -a -um: one, only one, single
  in únum: as one, in unity, together
  úna: at one and the same time or place
  úna cum: together with
  únum post únum: one by one
  únus solúsque: the sole and only
unusquísque, unaquaéque,
  unumquídque (unumquódque): every,
  everyone
upílio -ónis: m.; shepherd
Urbaniánus -a -um: relating to Urban
urbánitas -átis: f.; city life, urbanity,
  good breeding, politeness, courtesy,
  refinement, affability
urbanizátio -ónis: f.; urbanization
urbánus -a -um: urbane, urban, of the
  city, citified
urbs, úrbis: f.; city, town
Úrbs, Úrbis: f.; the city of Rome; see
  Appendix
úrceus -i: m.; vessel, jug, pitcher,
  earthenware container
urédo -inis: f.; rust, blight on plants
úrens -éntis: burning, scorching
úrgeo -ére, úrsi: (2); press hard, force,
  drive, impel, urge, weigh down,
  burden, push; urgénter: adv.;
  urgéntius: comp. adv.
úrna -ae: f.; urn, pitcher, water jar
úrnula -ae: f.; small urn
úro -ere, ússi, ústum: (3); burn, dry up,
  parch, scorch
úrsa -ae: f.; female bear
úrsus -i: m. bear
urtíca -ae: f.; nettle
úsio -ónis: f.; use, using
usitátus -a -um: usual, customary,
  familiar; usitáte: in the usual manner
úsito -áre: (1); to use
úsitor -ári: dep. (1); use often, be in the
  habit of using
úsquam: anywhere, in or at any place
úsque: as far as, all the way, to, up to,
  constantly, continuously

úsque ad: as far as, even, until
úsque nunc: up to now
úsquedum: until
usquequáque: everywhere, utterly,
  exceedingly, altogether
úsquequo: interr. adv.; how long,
  wherefore
ústulo -áre: (1); singe, burn a little
usuális -is -e: usual, common, ordinary
usúra -ae: f.; usury, use, interest
usurárius -a -um: interest-bringing,
  useful, pertaining to interest
usurpátio -ónis: f.; using, using
  unlawfully, seizing, usurpation
usurpatórie: presumptuously
usúrpo -áre: (1); usurp, make use of,
  assert a right, take possession of, seize
  wrongfully
úsus -a -um: perf. part. of útor
úsus -us: m.; use, want, need,
  enjoyment, practice, skill,
  employment, exercise of a thing
ususfrúctus -us: m.; use and enjoyment
  of property belonging to another,
  profit, revenue, benefit
ut (úti): w. indic.: as, when; w. subj.: that,
  in order that; after verbs of fearing: lest,
  that not
  ut ínfra: as below
  ut púta: as for example
  ut quid: to what purpose, why
  ut súpra: as above
  ut únum sint: that they be one
utcúmque: howsoever, in any way
  soever, somehow
utensília -órum: n. pl.; furnishings,
  utensils, materials
úter -tra -trum: either, which, whichever
úter -tris: m.; wineskin, bottle,
  container, vessel
utercúmque: whichever of two
uterínus -a -um: of the same mother
utérlibet: either one you please

utérque, utráque, utrúmque: both, each of two

úterum -i: n., **úterus** -i: m.; womb, uterus

útilis -is -e: useful, profitable, beneficial, serviceable, advantageous; **utíliter:** *adv.*

utílitas -átis: f.; profit, benefit, advantage, utility, usefulness

útinam: would that, oh that

útique: indeed, doubtless, surely, certainly, verily, yes

útor, úti, úsus: *dep.* (3); use, make use of, employ, enjoy

útpote: inasmuch as, since, as

utrímque (utríque): on both sides, in both cases

utróque: to both, to both sides, in both directions

útrum: whether; **útrum . . . an:** whether . . . or

úva -ae: f.; grape, bunch of grapes

úvens -éntis, **úvidus** -a -um: moist, wet, damp

úvor -óris: m.; wetness, dampness

úxor -óris: f.; wife

uxorátus -a -um: having a wife, married

uxórius -a -um: pertaining to a wife

V

va: *see* vah

vacábilis -is -e: vacant, free

vácans -ántis: unoccupied, vacant

vacátio -ónis: f.; exemption or freedom from anything, suspension, period of suspended force; vacancy, vacation; vacátio légis: *see Appendix*

vácca -ae: f.; cow; vácca fósta: milch cow

vacíllo -áre: (1); doubt, totter, falter, waver

váco -áre: (1); be without, free from, have time, be free from, have time for, be empty, become vacant, be idle

vacúitas -átis: f.; vanity, emptiness

vácuo -áre: (1); make empty, empty, void

vácuus -a -um: void, empty free; worthless, useless; in vácuum: in vain

vadimónium -ii: n.; promise secured by bail

vádo -ere -vási: (3); go, walk, hasten, rush

vádo -áre: (1); wade through, ford

vádor -ári: *dep.* (1); bind over by bail

vadósus -a -um: shallow

vádum -i: n., vádus -i: m.; shallow place, ford, shoal

vae: *interj.;* woe, alas (showing pain or dread)

vaenúndo: *see* venúndo

váfer -fra -frum: sly, crafty, artful, subtle

vagína -ae: f.; sheath, vagina, scabbard, husk, hull, holder

vágio -íre: (4); wail, whimper, cry

vágo (vágor) -áre: (1); wander about, ramble, rove, prowl

vágus -a -um: wandering, harborless, unsettled, roaming; *as a noun:* one

without a domicile or quasi domicile, wanderer, vagrant, transient

vah (va, váha): *interj.;* aha, ah, oh (showing astonishment or joy)

válde: greatly, exceedingly, very, very much; válde quam: immensely

valefácio (valedíco) -ere: (3); bid farewell or goodby to, abandon

válens -éntis: strong, powerful, healthy, hearty, well

valénter: strongly, powerfully, with a strong voice

váleo -ére -ui -itum: (2); be well, healthy, worthy or able, prevail, be valid, be effective

valésco -ere -ui: (3); grow strong

valetudinárium -ii: n.; sanatorium, hospital

valetúdo -inis: f.; health, strength, state of health, condition of the body

valíditas -átis: f.; validity, strength

validátio -ónis: f.; validation; *see Appendix*

válidus -a -um: mighty, strong, powerful, influential, boisterous, efficacious; valídior -ior -ius: *comp.;* válide: *adv.; see Appendix*

válles (vállis) -is: f.; valley

vállo -áre: (1); enclose, fortify

vállum -i: n.; trench

válor -óris: m.; value, validity, worth

válva -ae: f.; folding door; *mostly pl.:* folds, valves, leaves or parts of a door, doors

vanilóquium -ii: n.; useless or idle talk, gabble, vaunting, boasting

vaníloquus (-locus) -i: m.; a vain talker, prattling person

vanitántes -ium: c. pl. ; vain people

vánitas -átis: f.; vanity, emptiness, vain things, boasting, lying, deception, worthlessness

vanitúdo -inis: f.; idle or lying talk; emptiness, vanity

vánus -a -um: vain, idle, profitless, null, empty, void; **vána** -órum: n. pl.; vain things

vápor -óris: m.; vapor, steam, exhalation, mist, warmth

vaporáliter: vaporlike

vapóro -áre: (1); emit steam or vapor, reek, fumigate, incense, perfume

vápulo -áre: (1); be flogged, lashed, afflicted, or beaten, cry out

variátio -ónis: f.; variation, difference, change

variegátus -a -um: of many colors

varíetas -átis: f.; variety

vário -áre: (1); change, alter, vary

várius -a -um: various, varied, diverse, inconsistent, unsteady, untrustworthy; **várie:** *adv.*

várus -a -um: diverse, different, deviating

vas, vádis: m.; surety, bail, security

vas, vásis; vásum -i: n.; **vásus** -i: m.; vessel, vase, dish

vása psálmi: harps

vásculum -i: n.; small vessel or vase

vastátio -ónis: f.; devastation, laying waste

vastátor -óris: m., **vastátrix** -ícis: f.; destroyer, ravager, devastator, waster

vástitas -átis: f.; waste, desolation, emptiness, empty space

vásto -áre: (1); spoil, destroy, lay waste

vástus -a -um: empty, desolate, deserted; vast, immense, rough; **váste:** *adv.*

vásum, vásus -i: *see* **vas**

vátes (vátis) -is: m.; prophet, seer

Vaticána basílica: St. Peter's church in Rome

Vaticána Cívitas: Vatican City

Vaticánus -a -um: of the Vatican; *as a n. noun:* the Vatican

vaticínium -ii: n.; prophecy, revelation

vaticíno (vaticínor) -áre: (1); prophesy, foretell

vátis -is: *see* **vátes**

vau: sixth letter of the Hebrew alphabet

-ve: *enclitic;* or

  plus . . . minúsve: more or less

  -ve . . . -ve: either . . . or

vecórdia -ae: f.; foolishness, folly

vécors -córdis: silly, foolish, mad, senseless

vectátio -ónis: f.; carrying, riding

vectígal -ális: n.; revenue, rent

vectigális -is -e: of taxes, subject to taxes, taxable, taxed

véctis -is: m.; bolt, bar, lever, doorbolt, crowbar, handspike

vécto -áre: (1); carry, convey

véctor -óris: m.; carrier, bearer, rider, conveyor, passenger, traveler, sailor

véemens: *see* **véhemens**

végeo -ére: (2), **végeto** -áre: (1); stir up, quicken, excite, move to rapid action, bring to life, nourish

vegetábilis (vegetális) -is -e: animating, growing, vegetable; *as a n. noun:* vegetable

vegetátio -ónis: f.; new life, quickening, excitment

végeto: *see* **végeo**

végetus -a -um: strong, vigorous, animated, brisk, lively, active, busy; **vegétior** -ior -ius: *comp.*

véhemens (véemens, vémens) -éntis: violent, furious, vigorous, impetuous, eager, ardent; **veheménter:** *adv.;* **veheméntius:** *comp. adv.*

vehículum -i: n.; conveyance, vehicle

vého -ere, **véxi, véctum:** (3); carry, bear, convey

véhor, véhi, véctus: *dep.* (3); ride

vel: or, or even, even actually, for instance, perhaps

vel ... vel: either ... or

seu ... vel: whether ... or

velámen -inis: n.; veil, cloak

velaméntum -i: n.; covering, veil, shelter, protection

véllo -ere, vélli (vúlsi), vúlsum: (3); pluck

véllus -eris: n.; fleece

vélo -áre: (1); cover, veil, hide, conceal, blindfold

velóciter: swiftly, speedily, quickly, rapidly

vélox -ócis: swift, rapid, quick, fleet

vélum -i: n.; veil, curtain, awning; cover for a ciborium

vélum humerále: humeral veil

vélut (velúti): as, like, even as, just as, as it were

vémens: see véhemens

véna -ae: f.; vein, inclination

venábilis -is -e: saleable

venális -is -e: for sale, to be sold

vénans -ántis: m.; hunter, fowler

venátio -ónis: f., venátus -us: m.; hunting, game, venison

venátor -óris: m.; hunter, fighter with wild animals in the arena

venátrix -ícis: f.; huntress

venátus -us: see venátio

vendítio -ónis: f.; selling, sale

vénditor -óris: m.; seller, vendor

véndo -ere -didi: (3); sell, put up for sale

venefícium -ii: n.; witchcraft, magic, sorcery

venéficus -i: m.; sorcerer, wizard, enchanter, magician

venenátus -a -um, venenósus -a -um: venemous, poisonous

venéno -áre: (1); to poison

venénum -i: n.; poison, venom

véneo -ire, vénii, vénitum: (4); go on sale, be sold

venerábilis -is -e: venerable, worthy of reverence, to be revered, reverend, a title of honor for some in the Church

venerabúndus -a -um: venerating, revering, reverential

venerándus -a -um: venerable, worthy of veneration

veneránter: reverently

venerátio -ónis: f.; veneration, honor, great respect

véneror (vénero) -ári: dep. (1); venerate, respect, worship, honor, revere; pray to, implore, beg

vénia -ae: f.; pardon, indulgence, grace, favor, forgiveness; permission

veniábilis (veniális) -is -e: pardonable, venial

veniáliter: venially

vénio -íre, véni, véntum: (4); come

vénor -ári: dep. (1); hunt, pursue, strive after, chase

vénter -tris: m.; womb, stomach, entrails, belly, bowels

ventilábrum -i: n.; fan

véntilo -áre: (1); fan, winnow, toss, scatter

véntio -ónis: f.; coming

ventíto -áre: (1); come often

ventrícola -ae: m.; glutton

ventúrus -a -um: about to come, coming

véntus -i: m.; wind

venúndo (vaen-) -áre -dedi -datum: (1); sell

venústas -átis: f.; beauty

venúste: beautifully, gracefully, charmingly

vépres -is: m.; briar, thornbush

ver, véris: n.; spring

verácitas -átis: f.; veracity, truthfulness

veráciter: truly, truthfully

vérax -ácis: true, truthful; as a c. noun: truthful speaker

verbális -is -e: verbal

vérber -eris: n.; lash, blow, stripe, lashing, scourging

verberátio -ónis: f.; chastisement, punishment, whipping

vérbero -áre: (1); beat, strike, whip

vérbi grátia (v.g.): for example

verbósus -a -um: wordy, verbose

vérbum -i: n.; word, saying, speech, message, expression, formula
ad vérbum: word for word, literally
Vérbum Incarnátum: Incarnate Word, God-Man, Word made Flesh, Jesus Christ

vére: truly, in truth, indeed, rightly

verecúndia -ae: f.; modesty, shame

veredárius -ii: m.; messenger, letter carrier

veréndus -a -um: venerable

véreor -éri: *dep.* (2); fear, reverence

vérgo -ere, vérsi: (3); be inclined, bend, incline, turn

verícola -ae: c.; truthful person

verífico -áre: (1); verify

verisímilis -is -e: probable, likely, realistic

versimíliter: in all probablility

véritas -átis: f.; truth, fidelity; accuracy, correctness

vermiculátus -a -um: inlaid, checkered, adorned with inlaid work

vermículus -i: m.; scarlet, crimson

vérmis -is: m.; worm

vernáculus -a -um: common, vernacular, native; *as a noun:* home-born slave, domestic

vernális -is -e, **vérnus** -a -um: vernal, of spring

vérnans -ántis: springlike

vérno -áre: (1); flourish

véro: in truth, in fact, really, to be sure, certainly, even, but, truly
mínime véro: by no means
nísi véro: unless indeed

vérro -ere, vérsus: *semidep.* (3); sweep

versánia -ae: f.; madness, wild rage

versánus -a -um: furious, insane

versátilis -is -e: revolving

versátus -a -um: versed

versículus -i: m.; short verse, versicle

vérsio -ónis: f.; version, translation

versipéllis -is -e: changeable, cunning

vérso -áre: (1); change, turn, treat, deliberate

vérsor -ári: *dep.* (1); dwell, remain, live, stay, occupy one's self with

vérsus -a um: *perf. pass. part. of* **vérto**

vérsus -us: m.; verse

vérsus clúsor: final verse

versútia -ae: f.; craftiness, subtlety

versútus -a -um: crafty, subtle

vértex (vórtex) -icis: m.; top, crown of the head, pate, highest point, head, peak, summit, pole, eddy, whirlpool

vertíbilis -is -e: convertible, able to be turned around or back

vérto (vórto) -ere, vérti, vérsum: (3); turn, transform, alter, convert, change; translate; rout; **verténte ánno:** at return of the year

vérum: truly, indeed; **vérum étiam:** but also

verúmtamen: but, nevertheless, notwithstanding, surely, verily, truly

vérus -a -um: true, real, actual, genuine; *as a n. noun:* truth, duty, right, honor, reality; **vére:** *adv.*

véscor, vésci: *dep.* (3); eat, use, enjoy, feed on

vésper -i(-is): m., **véspera** -ae: f.; evening star, eventide, evening; **véspere:** in the evening

Vésperae -árum: f. pl.; Vespers, Evensong

vesperális -is -e: of Vespers

vesperásco -ere: (3); become evening

vespertínus -a -um: evening, belonging to evening

véster -tra -trum: your, yours

vestiárium -ii: n.; sacristy, vestry

vestiárius -ii: m.; sacristan

vestíbulum -i: n.; court, porch, vestibule

vestígium -ii: n.; foot, footstep, footprint, the sole, track, trace

vestiméntum -i: n., véstis -is: f.; garment, vestment, robe, raiment

véstio -íre -ívi (-ii) -ítum: (4); dress, clothe, vest, decorate

véstis -is: f.; clothes, clothing, attire, dress

vestítio -ónis: f.; investiture

vestítus -us: m., véstis -is: f.; clothing, vesture, apparel, raiment, attire, vestiture

veteránus -a -um: veteran

veterásco -ere -rávi: (3); grow old, become old, decay, vanish

veternósus -a -um: dull, lethargic

vétero -áre: (1); to make old, consider old

vétitus -a -um: forbidden; *as a n. noun:* prohibition, veto; *see Appendix*

véto -áre -ui -itum: (1); forbid, prohibit, protest, oppose, veto

vétus -eris: original, old, former

vétus érror: ancient enemy, devil, former sins

vetústas -átis: f.; old age, old life, former ways, antiquity, posterity

vetústus -a -um: old, ancient; vetustíssimus -a -um: very ancient

vexátio -ónis: f.; annoyance, trial, agitation, ill-treatment, vexation

vexíllifer -eri: m.; standard-bearer

vexíllum -i: n.; standard, banner; Vexíllum: Roman cavalry standard with a cross instead of an eagle

véxo -áre: (1); oppress, afflict, vex, harass, torment, trouble, annoy

vía -ae: f.; way, path, road, highway, street; manner of life

viárius -a -um: relating to roads

viáticum -i: n.; fare, money or provision for a journey, Holy Viaticum or Eucharist for the dying

viáticus -a -um: pertaining to travel

viátor -óris: m.; traveler, wayfarer

víbro -áre: (1); brandish, shake

vicariátus -us: m., vicárium -ii: n., vicária -ae: f.; vicariate

vicárius -a -um: vicarious; *as a m. noun:* vicar; substitute, representative; *see Appendix*

vicárius episcopális: episcopal vicar

vicárius foráneus: dean; *see Appendix*

vicárius generális: vicar-general; *see Appendix*

vicárius judiciális: judicial vicar

vicárius paroeciális: parochial vicar

více (vícem): *prep. w. gen.;* on acount of, like, after the manner of, in place of, instead of; *adv.:* in turn

více-cancellárius -ii: m.; vice-chancellor

vicéni -ae -a: twenty

vicénnis: at the age of twenty

více-officiális -is: m.; vice-officialis, adjutant judicial vicar

více-párochus -i: m.; one who takes the place of the parish priest

více-postulátor -óris: m.; vice-postulator

více-réctor -óris: m.; vice-rector

vicésimus: *see* vigésimus

více-tabulárius -ii: m.; vice-archivist

více-vérsa: conversely, vice versa

vícia -ae: f.; climbing herb, leguminous plant, vetch

vícies (víciens): twenty times

vicínor -ári: (1); be neighboring to

vicínus -a -um: neighboring, nearby, close, near; vicínior -ior -ius: *comp.*

vícis: *gen., no nom.:* f.; change, alteration, alternation, return, interchange, position, place, time, duty, office, role, position, function

in vícem *or* ad vícem: for, instead of, in place of

pro hac více: for this once; *see also* ínvicem

vicíssim: in turn, by turns, in return, on the other hand, on the contrary

vicissitúdo -inis: f.; change, alternation, alteration, interchange

víctima -ae: f.; victim, sin offering, sacrifice

Víctima Paschális: Paschal Lamb

víctimo -áre: (1); offer in sacrifice

víctito -áre: (1); live upon

víctor -óris: m.; victor, conqueror, winner

victória -ae: f.; victory

víctrix -ícis: victorious, conquering

victuália -ium: n. pl.; victuals, food, sustenance, provisions

víctus -us: m.; food, support, way of living, nourishment

vícus -i: m.; town, district, lane, way, street, village, hamlet

vidélicet (viz.): namely, plainly, evidently, manifestly

víden: *short for* vidésne; do you see?

vídens -éntis: m.; seer, prophet

vídeo -ére, vídi, vísum: (2); see; review, consider, deal with

vídeor -éri, vísus: *dep.* (2); seem, appear

vídua -ae: f.; widow, unmarried woman

viduális -is -e: pertaining to a widow

vidúitas -átis: f.; widowhood

víduo -áre: (1); deprive of

víduus -a -um: separated from, bereaved of, destitute of

vígeo -ére -ui: (2); be alive, flourish, thrive; be in force, be brought to power

vigésimus -a -um: twentieth

vígil, vígilis: watchful, alert, awake, on guard; *as a m. noun:* sentinel, watchman

vigilánter: vigilantly, watchfully

vigilántia -ae: f.; vigilance, watchfulness, wakefulness

vigília -ae: f.; watch, vigil, night watch, evening before a feast

vigíliae -árum: f. pl.; Matins

vígilo -áre: (1); watch, keep watch, be on guard, be awake

vigínti: twenty

vígor -óris: m.; strength, vigor, force, activity, energy

vilésco -ere: (3); become valueless, cheap, or vile

vili-: *see also* **villi-**

vílis -is -e: cheap, vile, base, worthless, common

vílitas -átis: f.; baseness

vílla -ae: f.; villa, farm, country estate

villicátio (vili-) -ónis: f.; stewardship

víllico (víli-) -áre: (1); be a steward, manage an estate

víllicus (víli-) -i: m.; steward, overseer, manager, keeper of an estate

vímpa -ae: f.; silk veil worn by miter and crosier bearers

vináceus -a -um: pertaining to wine or the grape; *as a n. noun:* wine cup

vinárius -a -um: of wine

víncio -íre, vínxi, vínctum: (4); bind, fetter

víncla -órum: n. pl.; bonds

vínco -ere, víci, víctum: (3); conquer, overcome, prevail, excel

vínctus -i: m.; captive, prisoner

vínculo -áre: (1); bind

vínculum -i: n.; bond; chain, fetter; **in vínculis:** in prison; **vínculo matrimónii:** by the bond of marriage

vindémia -ae: f.; grape gathering, vintage wine, wine; pl.: vintage season

vindemiátor -óris: m.; grape picker

vindémio -áre: (1); gather grapes, pluck, pick

víndex -icis: c.; avenger; claimant

vindicatívus -a -um: revengeful, spiteful, vindictive, punishing; *see Appendix* víndico -áre: (1); claim, avenge

vindícta -ae: f.; revenge, vengeance

vínea -ae: f.; vineyard, vine

vínitor -óris: m.; vinedresser

vinoléntus (vinósus) -a -um: wine-drinking; drunk

vínum -i: n.; wine

vío -áre: (1); go, travel, wander

violáceus -a -um: violet

violátio -ónis: f.; violation, profanation

violátor -óris: m.; violator, profaner

violénter: violently, vehemently

violéntia -ae: f.; violence

violéntus -a -um: violent, furious, impetuous, raging

víolo -áre: (1); violate, profane, dishonor, injure

vípera -ae: f.; viper, adder, snake

vir -i: m.; man, male person, husband

virágo -inis: f.; woman, heroine

virátus -a -um: manly, valiant

viréctum (virétum) -i: n.; green place, glade, greensward

vírens -éntis: green

víreo -ére: (2); be green, blooming

víres, vírium: f. pl.; forces, powers

virésco -ere: (3); become green

virétum -i: see viréctum

vírga -ae: f.; rod, scepter, staff, shepherd's crook, wand; twig, bough; vertical tail on a note; penis

virginális -is -e, virgíneus -a -um: virginal, pure, untouched, unspotted; virgináliter: adv.

virgínitas -átis: f.; virginity

vírgo -inis: f.; virgin, maiden

vírgula -ae: f.; small rod, comma

virgúltum -i: n.; plant, shrub, copse, thicket, brushwood

víriae -árum: f. pl.; bracelets

viridárium -ii: n.; garden, park, plantation

víridis -is -e: green

vírido -áre: (1); be green

virílis -is -e: manly, male, virile

viríliter: manfully, courageously, vigorously

virítim: individually, man by man

víror -óris: m.; verdure, vigor, freshness

virtuáliter: virtually

virtuóse: virtuously

vírtus -útis: f.; virtue, power, excellence, ability, strength, host

vírus -i: m.; poison, venom; slime

vis, vis; pl. víres -ium: f.; force, might, violence, strength, physical or mental power

víscera -um: n.; pl. of víscus (víscer) -eris; bowels, innermost parts, flesh, heart, stomach, noble or ignoble parts

víscum -i: n., víscus -i: m.; birdlime, mistletoe, viscous substance

vis et métus: force and fear; vis vel métus: force or fear

visíbilis -is -e: visible, outward; visibíliter: adv.

vísio -onis: f.; vision, appearance, act of seeing, apparition; notion, idea

visitátio -ónis: f.; visitation, visit

visitátor -óris: m.; visitor; protector

vísito -áre: (1); visit, survey, go to see, send, visit with wrath, punishment, or favor

visívus -a -um: visual

víso -ere: vísi, vísum: (3); see, behold, contemplate

vísor -óris: c.; one who sees, scout

vísu: supine; to see, in the seeing

vísum -i: n.; dream, vision, appearance

vísum et approbátum: seen and approved

vísus -a -um: perf. pass. part. of vídeo

vísus -us: m.; sight

víta -ae: f.; life, eternal life, course of life, livelihood, career; biography

vitális -is -e: vital, of life, living

vitiátor -óris: m.; corrupter

vítio -áre: (1); injure, damage, mar,
spoil, hurt, corrupt; nullify

vitióse: viciously

vitiósitas -átis: f.; wickedness,
viciousness

vítis -is: f.; vine, grapevine

vítium -ii: n.; vice, sin, defect, default,
blemish, wrong

víto -áre: (1); avoid, shun, withstand

vítreus -a -um: transparent, of glass or
porcelain

vítrum -i: n.; glass

vítta -ae: f.; ribbon, band, lace, two
ribbons on a miter

vítula -ae: f.; heifer, calf

vitulámen -inis: n.; shoot, sprout

vítulor -ári: dep. (1); celebrate, keep
holiday

vítulus -i: m.; bull, bullock, calf

vituperátio -onis: f.; defamation,
slandering, defaming, censuring

vituperátor -óris: m.; blamer, censurer,
vituperator

vitúpero -áre: (1); blame, censure

vívax -ácis: vigorous, long-lived

vívidus -a -um: healthy, animated,
living; vívide: adv.

vivíficans -ántis: life-giving

vivificátio -ónis: f.; quickening, giving
of life, vivification

vivificátor -óris: m., vivificátrix -ícis: f.;
vivifier, quickener

vivífico -áre: (1); vivify, bring to life,
make alive, quicken, give life

vivíficus -a -um: making alive,
quickening, vivifying, vivific

vívo -ere, víxi, víctum: (3); live, have life,
be alive; reside

vívus -a -um: alive, living, fresh; as a
noun: living person

vix (víxdum): hardly, scarcely, with effort

vobismetípsis: dat. pl.; you yourselves

vocabulárium -ii: n.; word list,
vocabulary

vocábulum -i: n.; name, word, noun,
designation, substantive

vocális -is -e: spoken, vocal, speaking

vocátio -ónis: f.; calling, summons,
vocation

vociferátio -ónis: f.; jubilation, loud
calling, clamor, or outcry

vóco -áre: (1); call, summon, invite

vol- see also vul-

voláticus -a -um: fleeting, ephemeral

volátile -is: n.; fowl, bird

volatília -ium: n. pl.; birds, winged
creatures

volátilis -is -e: flying, winged; fleeting,
transitory

volátus -us: m.; flight

vólens -éntis: willing, voluntary, ready,
favorable

vólgo: see vúlgo

volítio -ónis: f.; volition, will

vólito -áre: (1); fly about, fly, fly to and
fro, flutter, flit, hover

vólitus -a -um: wished, willed, wanted

vólo -áre: (1); fly

vólo, vélle, vólui: irreg.; will, wish,
desire; determine, propose

vólucer (vólucris, volúcris) -cris -cre:
flying

volúcra -ae: f. worm, caterpillar

vólucris (volúcris) -is: f.; fowl, bird

volúmen -inis: n.; book, volume, tome,
roll, scroll

voluntárius -a -um: voluntary, free,
gracious, generous, willing; voluntárii
-órum: m.; volunteers; voluntárium
-ii: n.; freewill offering; voluntárie:
adv.

volúntas -átis: f.; will, wish, inclination,
desire, will and testament

volúptas -átis: f.; pleasure, delight

volutábrum -i: n.; hog pool, wallowing
place

volúto -áre: (1); roll, twist, tumble,
wallow, revolve in the mind

vólvo -ere, vólvi, volútum: (3); roll,
ponder, meditate, turn over, reflect

vólva -ae: *see* vúlva

vómer -eris: m.; plowshare

vómo -ere -ui -itum: (3); vomit

voráciter: greedily

vorágo -inis: f.; breach, chasm, abyss

vórax -ácis: gluttonous, voracious

vóro -áre: (1); eat greedily, devour

vórtex -icis: *see* vértex

vórto: *see* vérto

vos: pl.; you

vosmetípsos: *acc.* pl.; you yourselves

votívus -a -um: votive, devotional

vótum -i: n.; vow, prayer, petition;
desire, wish, recommendation, vote;
see Appendix

vóvens -éntis: c.; one who makes a vow

vóveo -ére, vóvi, vótum: (2); vow,
promise solemnly or sacredly,
consecrate, dedicate

vox, vócis: f.; voice, sound, saying,
speech, word; *see Appendix*

vóce mágna: with a loud voice

vox víva: living voice

vul- *see also* vol-

vulgáris -is -e: common, coarse, plain,
usual, ordinary

Vulgáta -ae: f.; the Vulgate or Latin text
of the Bible; *see Appendix*

vulgátus -a -um: common, usual, public

vúlgo (vólgo) -áre: (1); publish, spread,
make known

vúlgo: commonly, generally, publicly,
everywhere

vúlgus -i: n.; multitude, common
people, crowd, public

vulnerátio -ónis: f.; wound, wounding

vúlnero -áre: (1); to wound

vúlnus -eris: n.; wound, injury, blow,
disaster

vúlpes -is: f.; fox

vúltur -uris: m.; vulture

vúltus -us: m.; countenance, face

vúlva (vólva) -ae: f.; womb, covering

X

Xánthicus -i: m.; a month
  corresponding to April
Xavérius -ii: m.; Xavier
xeniólium -ii: n.; small gift
xénium -ii: n.; gift, present
xenodochíum -íi, xenodochéum -i: n.;
  guesthouse, house for travelers, inn;
  hospice, hospital

xenodóchus -i: m.; one who receives
  strangers, guestmaster
xerophágia -ae: f.; meal of dry food, dry
  fast
xýlon -i: n.; cotton tree
xýstus -i: m.; walk planted with trees

Z

Zábulon -ónis, *or indecl.:* m.; *Hebrew;*
Zabulon, Zebulun; a son of Jacob and
Leah; a tribe of Israel

zábulus -i: m.; devil

Zachaéus i: m.; Zachaeus

Zacharías -ae: m. Zechariah, a minor
prophet; a book of the O.T.

zain: seventh letter of the Hebrew
alphabet

Zálmon -ónis, *or indecl.:* n.; *Hebrew;*
Zalmon, a mountain in Palestine

Zalmúnna -ae, *or indecl.:* m.; Zalmunna,
a Moabite chieftain

zámia -ae: f.; loss, damage, injury

Zárepath: *indecl.;* Zarephath, a city in
Phoenicia

zéa -ae: f.; grain, spelt

Zeb: *indecl.:* m.; *Hebrew;* Zeeb, a
Midianite chief

Zébee: *indecl.:* m.; *Hebrew;* Zebah, a
Midianite chief

Zebedaéus -i: m.; Zebedee

zelátor -óris: m.; zealot, enthusiast

zélo (zélor) -áre: (1); be jealous of, envy;
be zealous for

zelótes -ae: m.; one who loves with zeal;
Zelótes: surname of Simon the apostle

zelótypus -a -um: jealous; *as a noun:*
jealous person

zélus -i: m., zelotýpia -ae: f.; zeal,
jealousy, emulation

Zephanías -ae: m.; Zephaniah, a minor
prophet; a book of the O.T.

Zeus -i: m.; Greek god Zeus

zetárius -ii: m.; valet, chamberlain

zimárra -ae: f.; cassock with a small cape

Zipháei -órum: m. pl.; Ziphites, people
of Ziph

zizánia -ae: f., zizánia -órum: n. pl.;
cockle, tares, a weed

zmarágdus -i: *see* smarágdina

zmégma -atis: *see* smégma

zóna -ae: f.; sash, belt, girdle

zonárius -a -um: of a belt or girdle

Appendix

The following terms and their translations and/or definitions have been gathered from a variety of sources. Most of them came from chancery offices throughout the country in answer to a request for words and phrases that people thought ought to be included in a handy reference book. Their use should be to guide the user toward a general understanding; further investigation and research may be necessary in many instances. A list of helpful books follows this *Appendix*. Although most entries have a connection with Canon Law, with either the Code of 1918 or that of 1983, many do not. If a Latin word is not found here, consult the general dictionary. The letter *c* followed by a number indicates a canon in the 1983 Code of Canon Law; the letters *cc* followed by a number indicate the individual canons in the 1990 Code of Canons of the Eastern Churches.

a

ábbas: abbot, father; the name and title of the superior of an autonomous monastery of one of the monastic orders, i.e., Benedictine, Camaldolese, Vallombrosan, Cistercian, Norbertine.

ábbas nullíus: an abbot who has actual episcopal jurisdiction over all clergy and laity in a specified territory subject directly to the abbey.

archiábbas, ábbas praéses, ábbas generális: designations for an abbot who is head of a monastic congregation.

ábbas prímas: abbot primate or head of today's Benedictine confederation.

ábbas tituláris: one who has the rank, title, and insignia of an abbot but does not govern the abbey whose name he bears.

ábbas in comméndum: a person who was allotted the usufruct of a monastic benefice and its revenue (forbidden by the Council of Trent).

ab inítio: from the beginning.

ab ípso (ípsa) convénto (-ta): by the very man (woman) summoned or cited.

abjúratio: abjuration; the process whereby apostates, heretics, and schismatics renounce their errors in order to be reconciled to the Church.

abrogátio: abrogation; the cancellation, repeal, or abolishment of an entire law by revocation of competent authority.

absolútio generális: general absolution; absolution granted to a large number of people at one time without individual confession of sin and allowed under certain conditions.

accéptio: acceptance; the act of the candidate accepting an office that has previously been proffered in an election needing no confirmation.

ácta caúsae: acts (records) of the case.

ácta procéssus: acts (records) of the process.

áctus hóminis: an act of a human being performed without deliberate reason and will, and which is amoral.

áctus humánus: a human act proceeding from deliberate reason and will, and which is subject to moral evaluation.

áctus judiciális: judicial act; an act performed by a judge in the course of a trial.

áctus jurídicus: juridic act; an act that has legal effect or recognition by the Church authority.

Ad Cathólici Sacerdótii: of the Catholic priesthood; an encyclical of Pius XI on the Catholic priesthood, 1935.

Ad Géntes: to the nations; decree of Vatican II on the Church's missionary activity, 1965.

adhortátio apostólica: *See* apostólica exhortátio.

ad límina: at the threshold; name given to the periodic visit of each diocesan bishop who is required to come on a scheduled basis to the city of Rome to venerate the tombs of the blessed apostles Peter and Paul and to visit the Roman Pontiff.

admíssio: admission; the act of the superior conferring an office on an eligible candidate who has previously been designated by postulation.

advocátus: advocate; a person in the ecclesiastical tribunal system who is appointed to safeguard the rights of a client and who assists in drafting the libéllus of a case.

aétas superadúlta: superadult age, relatively advanced age; a possible reason for a dispensation; recommended at one time for parish domestic help.

a fortióri: from the stronger (position), all the more reason for; used in drawing a conclusion from a point that is considerd more certain than another.

affínitas: affinity, relationship; a spiritual and/or blood relationship that becomes an impediment to marriage (c. 1092).

angústa lóci: narrowness or smallness of the place; possible reason for a dispensation.

animadversiónes: remarks, observations; the comments of the defender of the bond upholding the validity of a particular marriage under investigation by a Church court.

Annuario Pontificio: Pontifical Annual; the official directory of the Holy See published annually and containing lists of offices of the Holy See and the names of cardinals, bishops, prelates, and dioceses throughout the entire world.

Ánnuit coéptis: He has nodded assent to the things begun.

apostásia: apostasy; the total repudiation of the Christian faith.

apostolátus: apostolate; a general term referring to the particular way a member of the Church carries out his or her part of the Church's mission, i.e., family, teaching, lay, or priestly apostolates.

apostólica administrátio: apostolic administration; the administration of a certain portion of the people of God, not yet erected into a diocese by the Pope, and whose pastoral care is entrusted to an apostolic administrator who governs in the name of the Supreme Pontiff.

apostólica exhortátio: apostolic exhortation; the name given to a Pope's reflections on a certain topic, which do not contain dogmatic definitions or policy directives. Exhortations are not legislative.

a posterióri: from the latter; from inductive reasoning; from observed facts.

apostólica praefectúra: apostolic prefecture; a portion of the people of God cared for by an apostolic prefect appointed by the Supreme Pontiff.

apostólica signatúra: apostolic signatura; the supreme tribunal of the Church.

apostólicae constitutiónes: apostolic constitutions; documents considered of the most solemn form, issued by the Pope in his own name, which deal with doctrinal or disciplinary matters and are issued only in relation to most weighty questions. They are published as either universal or particular law.

Apostólicam Actuositátem: apostolic activity; decree of Vatican II on the apostolate of the laity, 1965.

apostólicus delegátus: apostolic delegate; a prelate sent by the Pope to countries which do not have full diplomatic relations with the Holy See and whose ordinary function is to keep the Pope informed about the condition of the Church in that territory.

apostólicus vicariátus: apostolic vicariate; a certain portion of the people of God, not yet erected into a diocese, whose pastoral care belongs to an apostolic vicar, who governs in the name of the Supreme Pontiff.

a prióri: from the former; from inductive reasoning; self-evidently

archiepíscopus: archbishop; the ordinary of an archdiocese who presides over his ecclesiastical province. Each of the other bishops in that province is a suffragan.

archiepíscopus máior: major archbishop; a metropolitan of a see, determined by the supreme authority of the Church, who presides over an entire Eastern Church súi júris and is not endowed with the patriarchal title (cc. 151).

archívum: archives; the depository where all documents pertaining to the spiritual and temporal affairs of the diocese are preserved.

arguméntum ad hóminem: an argument directed toward or based on human nature; evidence or proof based on principles admitted by human beings.

Arianísmus: Arianism; the heresy of Arius, a priest of Alexandria in the third century, who held that the Son was neither equal to the Father nor divine. It was condemned at the first ecumenical council held in Nicea in 325.

Armenian rite: See Orientáles Ecclésiae.

ascríptio ut cléricus: enrollment as a cleric (cc. 357); the process in the Eastern Churches whereby one is enrolled either in some eparchy or exarchy or religious institute or society of common life by diaconal ordination.

audítor: auditor; a person, often a judge, who gathers proofs, summons and hears witnesses, and draws up the record of a judicial case but does not actually decide it.

auxiliáris epíscopus: auxiliary bishop; a bishop appointed by the Pope who acts as an aid to the bishop of a diocese who may need help because of age, sickness, or a great amount of work. He is a titular bishop.

b

Benedíctus: blessed; the opening words of the Canticle of Zachary as found in Luke 1:68–79 and used in Morning Prayer of the Divine Office.

benefícium: benefice; a juridic entity permanently established or created by competent ecclesiastical authority consisting of a sacred office and the right to receive the revenues from the endowment attached to that office.

bishop: See epíscopus.

bónum cónjugum: the good of the spouses; as traditionally held by St. Augustine, this meant children, fidelity, and sacramentality; in more recent times these words include the partnership of life and love.

bónum ecclésiae: the good of the Church.

bónum ecclesiásticum, bóna ecclesiástica: ecclesiastical good, goods; all temporal goods that belong to the universal Church, the Apostolic See, or other juridic persons in the Church.

bónum fídei: the good of fidelity; an object of marital consent by which partners in a marriage hand over to each other the right to a sexually exclusive or faithful relationship.

bónum prólis: the good of offspring; an object of marital consent by which partners in a marriage hand over to each other the right to acts that of themselves are open to procreation of offspring.

bónum sacraménti: the good of the sacrament; an object of marital consent by which the partners in a marriage make a commitment to an indissoluble union.

brévia: briefs; documents, developed out of the notion of bulls (*see below*), to which a waxen seal (búlla) is affixed. They usually deal with minor affairs but sometimes are issued on major matters.

búllae: bulls; important papal documents that take their name from the seal of lead appended to, or impressed upon, the paper or parchment and bearing on one side the images of Saints Peter and Paul and on the other the name of the reigning Pope.

bullária: collections in chronological order of the Roman Pontiffs' bulls, constitutions, acts, briefs, and other letters that are not found in the Decretum or the collections of decretals.

Byzantine rite: *See* Orientáles Ecclésiae.

c

Cámera Apostólica: Apostolic Chamber; an office of the Roman Curia entrusted with the administration of temporal goods of the Holy See.

Cancellária Apostólica: Apostolic Chancery; an office of the Roman Curia in charge of the establishment of new dioceses and of the preparation of decretals and papal bulls.

canonicális: canonical; describes a just and reasonable cause for granting a dispensation from ecclesiastical laws.

canónica míssio: canonical mission; the conferring of an ecclesiastical office by the competent Church authority in accordance with the sacred canons.

Canon Law: See jus canónicum.

Cáput Canónum: chapter of canons; a corporate body of clerics attached by ecclesiastical authority to a church for the purpose of performing the functions of the liturgy. Specifically, a cathedral chapter is a corporate body of clerics established by the Roman Pontiff in a cathedral church for the principal purpose of assisting the bishop as his council in accordance with Canon Law and of assuming the government of the diocese when the see becomes vacant, and for the secondary purpose of promoting in the cathedral the more solemn observance of the liturgy in accordance with the sacred canons.

Cardinális: cardinal; in the Roman Catholic Church, a member of a special college the responsibility of which is to provide for the election of the Roman Pontiff in accord with the norm of special law; the cardinals also assist the Roman Pontiff collegially when they are called together to deal with questions of major importance. Likewise, they individually assist the Roman Pontiff in the daily care of the universal Church by means of the different offices they perform.

cáritas príma síbi: the first charity is to itself.

Cásti Conúbii: of chaste marriage; an encyclical of Pius XI on Christian marriage, 1930.

catechumenátus: catechumenate; a process of instruction and formation for entrance into the Church. Vatican II restored the catechumenate as part of the Rite of Christian Initiation of Adults (RCIA).

Cathedráticum: an annual contribution to the support of the diocese from all churches and benefices in the diocese.

Catholic Charities: an agency or office existing in most dioceses to aid in taking care of the temporal needs of the people.

Cathólici: Catholics; those baptized who are fully in communion with the Catholic Church on earth being joined with Christ in its visible structure by the bonds of (1) profession of faith, (2) the sacraments; and (3) ecclesiastical governance.

caúsa efficiens: effecting cause; the agent that produces an effect by its action.

caúsa excúsans: excusing cause; a cause that renders the observance of a law impossible or extremely difficult, while the person remains a subject of the law or superior.

caúsa exempláris: exemplary cause; a model or pattern in the likeness of which an effect is produced.

caúsa éximens: removing cause; a cause in virtue of which a person ceases to be a subject of the law as the cause may actually remove the person from the jurisdiction of the superior.

caúsa finális: final cause; the good in view of which an agent acts.

caúsa formális: formal cause; the intrinsic specifying principle giving a being its particular mode of being.

caúsa materiális: material cause; the matter or potential principle of a being.

célebret: he may celebrate; a document issued by a local ordinary or religious superior that testifies that a priest is in good standing; it is used as proof that a priest is allowed to celebrate Mass or other functions.

censúra: censure; a penalty that deprives a baptized person who has committed a crime and is contumacious of certain spiritual goods until he or she repents the misdeed and is absolved. There are three classes of censures: excommunication, suspension, and interdict.

Chaldean rite: *See* Orientáles Ecclésiae.

chancellárius: chancellor; the officer within a diocesan curia whose principal responsibility is the care of the archives, correspondence of the diocese, and those administrative duties entrusted by the diocesan bishop.

charismáticus: charismatic; from the Greek for gift or grace; charismatic refers to the gifts of the Holy Spirit as they are manifested in the lives of individuals and communities. These gifts take many forms, including the gifts of prayer commonly associated with Catholic charismatic renewal.

Chrismátio Sáncti Mýri: chrismation with holy myron; the sacrament of chrismation (confirmation) in the Eastern Churches.

Christifidéles: the Christian faithful; inasmuch as they have been incorporated in Christ through baptism, they have been constituted as the people of God.

Chrístus Dóminus: Christ the Lord; decree of Vatican II on the bishops' pastoral office in the Church, 1965.

circular letters: a relatively new form of pronouncement from the Roman Curia often accompanying a set of norms or laws on a given subject.

circuminséssio: the shared existence of the three Divine Persons in the same Being.

citátio: citation; a judicial summons informing the respondent of the existence of a libéllus and calling for a written response to the claim.

Coadjútor epíscopus: coadjutor bishop; an auxiliary bishop appointed by the Holy See who receives special faculties and possesses the right of succession.

Códex Canónum Ecclesiárum Orientálium: Code of Canons of the Eastern Churches; promulgated by John Paul II in 1990.

co-disciples: a term used by the United States bishops at the 1987 synod to signify the equality and close working relationship of all the members of the Church as disciples of the Lord.

cógito érgo sum: I think, therefore I am; the statement of the 17th-century philosopher Descartes, used to prove his own existence.

collaborátio: collaboration; the working together of all the baptized, clergy and laity, each contributing specific gifts.

collegiális áctus: collegial act; a decision reached by all the delegates of a college together, arrived at by an absolute majority vote.

collégium consultórum: college of consultors; six to twelve priests appointed by the bishop from among the members of the presbyterial council to provide financial advice to the bishop and to function when the see is impeded or vacant.

Collégium Episcopórum: *See* episcopále collégium.

Collégium Sácrum: college of cardinals.

commúne bónum: common good; "the sum of those conditions of social life which allow social groups and their individual members relatively thorough and ready access to their own fulfillment" [Gaúdium et Spes, n. 26].

communicátio in sácris: participation in sacred rites; sharing sacraments or other liturgical worship with those of other faith communities.

Commúnio: Communion; the sharing of the Eucharist, Holy Communion.

commúnio: communion; designates the close, spiritual bonds among the baptized who are in union with Jesus.

commúnio conjugális vítae: bond of conjugal life. *See* consórtium.

commúnio totális vítae: bond of total life. *See* consórtium.

commúnis érror: common error; an error common to the people of a place where an act of jurisdiction is being exercised in which the Church supplies the jurisdiction, thought erroneously to be possessed by the individual, as far as it is needed.

conciliáres constitutiónes: conciliar constitutions; documents addressed to the universal Church.

conciliáres declarátiones: conciliar declarations; documents that are policy statements giving the ordinary teaching of the Church.

conciliária decréta: conciliar decrees; council documents directed more specifically to a given category of the faithful or to a special form of apostolate.

conciliária núntia: conciliar messages; exhortations addressed to various categories of people at the conclusion of the final session of a council.

concílium: council; a group of advisors whose consent or advice one in authority must seek as required by general or particular law. The Latin *concílium* and the Greek *sýnodus* are interchangeable. Therefore a council or a synod in the strict sense meant a gathering together of people. Councils are legally convened assemblies of ecclesiastical dignitaries for the purpose of discussing and determining matters of an ecclesiastical nature. Councils were historically classified: *ecumenical* (whole world, universal); *plenary* (more than one jurisdiction, e.g., of a nation or country); *provincial* (local).

concordátum: concordat; an agreement between the Church and a sovereign state having the force of law regarding matters of mutual concern such as the appointment of bishops, legal actions against clerics and members of religious institutes, and other matters agreed upon in the document.

conferéntia episcopórum: *See* episcopális conferéntia.

conféssio: confession; a written or oral assertion against oneself made by a party regarding a matter under trial; this word also is used to refer to the sacrament of reconciliation.

Congregatiónes Románi: Roman congregations; permanent committees of cardinals, bishops, and others in Rome in charge of various aspects of the administration and governance of the Church.

cóngrua cóngruis referendo: by referring the proper matters to the proper people.

consanguínitas: consanguinity, blood relationship; the impediment of consanguinity is a relationship between persons based on carnal generation; it is computed in the direct and collateral lines (c. 1091).

consénsus matrimoniális: matrimonial agreement or consent; the act of the will by which a marriage is created by a man and a woman who are capable of marriage according to the formalities recognized by law.

consórtium conjugális vítae: partnership of conjugal life; this is a term used to describe marriage as an intimate partnership of life and love with the characteristics of self-revelation, understanding, and caring. *See* Gaúdium et Spes, n. 48.

consórtium totális (totíus) vítae: partnership of total life; this is a term used to describe the constitutive elements of marriage, such as maturity and balance, capacity for interpersonal and heterosexual friendship, conjugal complementarity, a sense of material responsibility, and the mental capacity to contribute as parents to the good of children.

consórtium vítae: partnership of life; it is impossible to translate the word consórtium exactly. Its literal meaning is that of a close association of persons sharing the same fortune, fate, and destiny. It means less than commúnio (the closest of intimate relationships) and yet is more than socíetas (a loose partnership). In using the word "consórtium" the law tries to indicate a middle course between the ideal of a perfect union of minds and hearts and the unsatisfactory state of mere external association. Because it indicates more a state of life than a given act, it is difficult to make it into a legal definition.

cónstat de nullitáte: it stands concerning the nullity; the nullity is in effect, is recognized.

constitútio: constitution; a Vatican II document that addresses doctrinal questions and offers doctrinal responses. The four constitutions of Vatican II are on the Church, the liturgy, revelation, and the Church in the modern world.

consuetúdo, úsus: custom, use; an unwritten law introduced by a uniform course of conduct in a community; or the repetition of an action for an uninterrupted length of time by a community that may result in the action having the force of law. It may be universal or particular.

consuetúdo amatória: courtship.

consuetúdo particuláris: particular custom. *See* lex.

consuetúdo univérsa: universal custom. *See* lex.

consuetúdo vítae: way of life, habit of life.

contestátio lítis: attesting of the litigation; action by which the terms of the controversy of a lawsuit are defined and determined by decree of the judge so that judgment can follow.

cóntra bónum cónjugum: against the good of the spouses. *See* bónum cónjugum.

cóntra bónum fídei: against the good of fidelity. *See* bónum fídei.

cóntra bónum sacraménti: against the good of the sacrament. *See* bónum sacraménti.

contradictórium: a speaking against; the opportunity granted each party to defend himself or herself against the charges and statements of the other party.

convalidátio símplex: simple convalidation. The Church uses two terms, convalidátio and sanátio in radíce, to describe the process of healing a marriage. The translation of these terms would be "simple convalidation" and "retroactive convalidation." Convalidation, or the renewal of consent for marriage, is the giving of a new act of consent to a marriage that was canonically invalid because of an impediment that has now ceased to exist or because of a defect in canonical forum. *See also* sanátio in radíce.

convéntus eparchiális: eparchial assembly; meets to assist the eparchial bishop regarding the special needs of the eparchy (cc. 235–42).

convéntus hierarchárum plúrium Ecclesiárum súi júris: assemblies of hierarchs of several Churches súi júris (cc. 322).

convéntus patriarchális: patriarchal assembly; in the Eastern Church, a consultative group of the entire Church with the patriarch presiding (cc. 140). Also known as a holy synod.

convíctus conjugális: conjugal living.

córam: before, in the presence of; this word designates the judge before whom a case is tried; tribunal and rotal decisions are cited by indicating the name of the judge and the date or protocol number of the case.

Córpus Júris Canónici: Body of Canon Law: a 1500-document collection containing the Decretum of Gratian as well as the Decretales of Gregory IX, Boniface VIII, Clement V, and John XXII and those collected by John Capuis, the collection's editor.

crímen, delíctum: crime, delict: an external and morally imputable violation of law to which a sanction, at least indeterminate, has been attached.

cúius régio, éius relígio: whose rule, his religion; a maxim used to determine the official religion of various parts of Germany at the time of the Protestant revolution.

cúra animárum: the care of souls; the pastoral duty for the fulfillment of which the exercise of priestly orders is required.

curátor: guardian; a person either appointed by or accepted by an ecclesiastical court to safeguard the rights of another person and to represent that person at a trial in those instances where the person is either of diminished mental capacity or is a minor.

cúria: curia or court; a group of administrative officials who assist in carrying out the duties and responsibilities of an office and who act in the authority of the one appointing them.

diocesan curia: appointed by the bishop and usually made up of the vicar general, chancellor, ecclesiastical judges, etc.

Roman Curia: the entire group of organized bodies that assist the Pope in the government of the Church. In this are included the congregations, the tribunals, and the curial offices.

curial offices: See Cámera Apostólica, Cancellária Apostólica, and Datária Apostólica.

d

Datária Apostólica: an office of the Roman Curia from which certain types of dispensations and appointments are issued.

de actióne ad dámna reparánda: concerning an action for restoring damages

decísio: decision; an administrative act or a judicial act resolving a particular controversy or dispute.

declamátio: declaration.

simple declaration: a statement that is not a new law, and must be interpreted in the light of existing legislation.

authentic declaration: an declaration which is retroactive and does not require further promulgation.

extensive declaration: a declaration which modifies the law, must be promulgated according to norms of the law, and is not retroactive.

declarátio: declaration; a statement given by a party that is in no way self-accusatory; it is opposed to a confession.

de condígno: from worthiness.

de cóngruo: from fitness or suitability.

decretália (epístola decretális, líttera decretális): decretal; a letter containing a papal ruling, more specifically one relating to matters of canonical discipline, and most precisely a papal rescript in response to an appeal.

decretalísta -ae: m., decretalist; a canonist in the history of Canon Law whose main object of study was papal decretals, papal replies or mandates of a canonical nature.

decretísta -ae: m., decretist; a canonist whose primary object of study was the legal tradition of the Church as contained in the Decretum of Gratian.

decrétum: decree; a term that can include laws, precepts, and judicial decisions.

In a broad sense it is an ordinance issued by public authority, bearing a relation to the public good by one who has legislative, administrative, or judicial power.

In a strict sense it is an ordinance by one having the power of jurisdiction and acting in an administrative way to promote compliance with a law.

deféctus consénsus: defect of consent; a deficiency in the operation of the mind in formulating an act of consent; in marriage this occurs if one or both of the parties to a marriage did not mutually give and receive the essential rights and obligations of marriage.

deféctus discretiónis judícii: lack of due discretion; a defect in the discretion of judgment about the essential rights and duties that must be mutually given and accepted in marriage.

deféctus fórmae: defect of form; lack of the proper canonical form required by the law of the Church. *See* fórum canónicum.

defénsor vínculi: defender of the bond; a tribunal officer who is appointed by the bishop and whose primary duty is to uphold the existence, the continuance, and the validity of the marriage bond.

de Fíde definíta: concerning the defined faith; a doctrine that has been defined by the Church and must be believed.

de Fíde ex júgi et ordinário magistério: concerning faith from the continual and ordinary magisterium; a doctrine that belongs to the Catholic faith because it has always been taught by the magisterium of the Church.

definiénda: matters that must be defined or clarified.

degradátio: degradation; a punitive penalty inflicted on clerics that includes deposition, perpetual privation of ecclesiastical garb, and reduction to the lay state for crimes to which the law attaches such a penalty.

Déi Vérbum: the word of God; dogmatic constitution of Vatican II on divine revelation, 1965.

de júre: concerning the law, according to the law, by law.

delegáta jurisdíctio: delegated jurisdiction; the power of governance granted to a person not by means of an office but rather granted by a person. *See also* ordinária jurisdíctio.

delegátio: delegation; the act of empowering someone to act for one in the exercise of one's office. There are two kinds: general delegation, granted for any number of cases of the same kind special delegation, given for a particular act.

delegátus: delegate; one who receives a commission to act from someone who is empowered to authorize the action.

de mínimis: concerning the smallest or least.

de queréla nullitátis: concerning a complaint (action) of nullity.

de recúrsu: concerning an appeal or recourse.

derogátio: derogation; the partial revocation of an existing law by competent authority.

designated receiver: the person assigned by a judge to obtain the testimony or affidavit of a person who refused to appear before a judge or instructor.

diáspora: dispersion; the faithful dispersed throughout the world.

Dignitátis Humánae: of human dignity; the declaration of Vatican II on religious freedom, 1965.

dioecesána cúria: diocesan curia; the personnel and offices of a diocese by which a bishop conducts the business of the diocese, including, for example, the vicar-general, chancellor, judicial vicar (officiális), and consultors.

dioecesáni consultóres: diocesan consultors; priests who are appointed by the bishop of a diocese to provide counsel to the bishop as called for in the Code of Canon Law; consultors may also oversee the diocese when there is no bishop.

dioecesánus administrátor: diocesan administrator; a cleric who is appointed to govern a diocese during interim periods when the see is vacant, without a bishop.

dioecesánus epíscopus: diocesan bishop; that bishop to whom the care of a diocese has been entrusted; all others are called titular bishops.

dioecesánus sýnodus: diocesan synod; a consultative body called by the bishop to consider matters for the welfare and pastoral ministry of the diocese.

dioecésis: diocese; a geographical portion of the people of God, entrusted for pastoral care to a bishop with the cooperation of the presbyterate and thus constituting a particular Church. See territoriális praelatúra, territoriális abbátia, apostólicus vicariátus, apostólica praefectúra, apostólica administrátio.

directória: directories; guidelines for the application of accepted principles and whose content includes the ways both of carrying out the law and of pointing out its urgency.

discrétio judícii: See deféctus discretiónis judícii.

dispáritas cúltus: disparity of cult; a marriage impediment that exists between a baptized Catholic and a nonbaptized person (c. 1086).

dispensátio: dispensation; a relaxation of the law in a particular case by the legislator, a successor or superior, or any person to whom one of the above may have given the faculty to dispense.

distinctiónes decréti: differences of the decree; short systematic treatises on the canons and the maxims of Gratian.

Divína Eucharístia: Divine Eucharist; Blessed Sacrament, Holy Communion in the Eastern Churches (cc. 708–14).

Divína Litúrgia: Divine Liturgy; Holy Sacrifice of the Mass, the celebration of the Eucharist in the Eastern Churches (cc. 698–717).

Divíni Redemptóris: of the divine Redeemer; an encyclical of Pius XI on atheistic communism, 1937.

Divíno Afflánte Spíritu: with the Holy Spirit teaching; an encyclical of Pius XII on biblical studies, 1953, on the 50th anniversary of Providentíssimus Déus.

Doctóres Ecclésiae: Doctors of the Church; the conditions required to constitute a Doctor of the Church are: orthodoxy of teaching, eminent learning, a high degree of sanctity, and explicit declaration by the Church.

domicílium: domicile; legal status acquired in a parish and a diocese by residence and/or the intention of living in a particular place.

dominatíva potéstas: dominative power; power that flows from a free agreement of subjects to obey their superiors.

dormítio: dormition; the name given in the Eastern Churches to the Assumption of the Blessed Virgin into heaven.

doxology: a hymn of praise to God.

dúbium fácti: doubt of fact; exists when there is insufficient information to know the true state of some facts.

dúbium júris: doubt of law; exists when the text of a law is so obscure that its meaning on some substantial point cannot be determined.

e

Eastern Churches: *See* Orientáles Ecclésiae.

Écce sacérdos mágnus: behold, the great priest; entrance hymn for a ceremony or rite led by a bishop.

ecclésia archiepiscopális máior: major archiepiscopal Church; a Church presided over by a major archbishop (cc. 151–54).

ecclésia díscens: the Church learning.

ecclésia dócens: the teaching Church.

ecclésia metropolitána súi júris: a metropolitan Church súi júris; a Church that is presided over by a metropolitan of a determined see who is appointed by the Pope (cc. 155).

ecclésia patriarchális: patriarchal Church; a Church presided over by a patriarch (cc. 55–150). *See* patriárcha.

ecclésia reformáta, ecclésia sémper reformánda: a reformed Church, a Church always in need of reform.

ecclésia rituális: *See* rituális.

ecclésia súi júris: Church of its own rite; this term is in use in the new Code of Canons of the Eastern Churches; it is used in preference to the term Eastern rite (cc. 27, 174).

ecclésia súpplet (súpplex): the Church supplies. *See* supplied jurisdiction.

ecclesiástica bóna: ecclesiastical goods; all temporal goods that belong to the universal Church, the Apostolic See, or other public juridic persons within the Church.

ecclesiásticae regiónes: ecclesiastical regions; groupings of provinces within a nation at an intermediate level between the national and provincial levels.

ecclesiásticum offícium (múnus): ecclesiastical office; any function constituted in a stable manner by divine or ecclesiastical law to be exercised for a spiritual purpose.

ecumenical (oecuménicus): the whole or inhabited world; in modern times it refers to the effort to restore unity in the whole of Christianity; sometimes used as a synonym for interdenominational or interreligious.

ecumenical council (oecuménicum concílium): a meeting of the bishops and major prelates of the whole Church, convoked by the Pope, to treat of matters concerning the universal Church under the presidency of the Pope or his legate.

encýclica epístola: encyclical letter; a formal pastoral letter written by the Pope for the entire Church and not used for dogmatic definitions, but rather to give counsel or to shed greater light on points of doctrine that must be made more precise or that must be taught in view of specific circumstances in various countries.

epárchia: eparchy; in the Eastern Churches, a portion of the people of God that is entrusted for pastoral care to a bishop (cc. 177). This word is synonymous with "diocese".

epikeía: a Greek term that means "reasonableness, fairness, or equity" and is used to reflect a benign interpretation of the law whereby one looks to the mind of the legislator and concludes that a positive law should not bind in a certain circumstance.

episcopále collégium: episcopal college; all the bishops of the world, of whom the Supreme Pontiff is the head.

episcopális conferéntia: episcopal conference; a permanent institution consisting of the bishops of a given country or territory organized for the welfare and pastoral care of the faithful of that place.

episcopális vicárius: episcopal vicar; a cleric, bishop or priest, who exercises responsibility and authority over a determined group or certain class of affairs within a diocese.

epíscopus: bishop; a successor of the apostles and appointed by the Pope as the supreme ecclesiastical ruler of a diocese.

epíscopus auxiliáris: *See* auxiliáris epíscopus.

epíscopus diocesánus: *See* diocesánus epíscopus.

epíscopus suffragáneus: *See* suffragáneus epíscopus.

epíscopus tituláris: *See* tituláris epíscopus.

equity (aéquitas): prudent moderation of the written law against the right of the words of the law.

érror commúnis: *See* commúnis érror.

euchológion: euchologion; a book containing the texts of the liturgies and prayers required for the administration of the sacraments in the Eastern Churches.

evangelizátio: evangelization; the proclamation and spreading of the good news of the gospel of salvation through Jesus Christ in both words and deeds.

exarchía: exarchy; a portion of the people of God in the Eastern Church that, because of special circumstances, is not erected as an eparchy, and that is established within territorial or other kinds of limits and is committed to an exarch (cc. 311–321).

exárchus: exarch; in the Eastern Church, a bishop who governs an exarchy in his own name or in the name of the one who appointed him. *See* exarchía.

excardinátio: excardination; a process whereby a cleric leaves his affiliation in one diocese to be affiliated with another diocese or to join an institute of consecrated life. *See also* incardinátio.

ex Cáthedra: from the throne; the term used to describe a solemn and binding definition made by the Pope in revealed matters concerning faith and morals.

exclaustrátio: exclaustration; the permission issued by competent authority for a member of a religious institute to remain outside the cloister or the religious institute for a definite or indefinite period of time.

excommunicátio: excommunication; a censure by which an individual Catholic is excluded from communion with the faithful within the limits determined by the law. In the Code for the Eastern Churches, it may be major or minor according to the canons (cc. 1431, 1434).

excusing cause: *See* caúsa excúsans.

exempting cause: *See* caúsa éximens.

ex íntegro: in entirety; areas or institutes of the law that have been wholly or entirely recognized.

ex níhilo, níhil fit: from nothing, nothing is made.

ex offício: from the office; refers to a right that arises by reason of the office and not through personal delegation.

ex ópere operántis: on the basis of the one acting; the subjective dispositions for receiving the sacraments.

ex ópere operáto: on the basis of the action performed; the objective efficacy and fruitfulness of the sacraments.

expeditíssime: most expeditiously; judicial decisions made without delay and with no room for appeal.

exsecútor: executor; one whose function is to carry out an administrative act.

necessary executor, whose function is simply to carry out the directive of competent authority.

voluntary executor, who is given discretion on whether or not an administrative act should be administered.

external forum: *See* fórum.

éxtra ecclésiam, núlla sálus: outside the Church there is no salvation; a dogmatic axiom, first formulated by Origin in the third century, that holds that the existence of, and either explicit or implicit membership in, the Catholic Church are necessary for salvation.

f

facúltas cognoscitíva: cognitive faculty; a person's ability or power to perceive and know.

facúltas crítica: judging faculty; a person's ability to make judgments.

facultátes: faculties; grants of jurisdiction or authorization made by Church law or by a competent superior to individuals to perform

ministerial acts such as administering the sacraments, preaching, and granting dispensations.

fatália légis: the time limit of the law; legal deadline.

Fathers of the Church (Pátres Ecclésiae): those distinguished by four marks: antiquity, sanctity of life, orthodox doctrine, and approbation of the Church, either explicit or by custom.

favórem (favóre) fídei, in: in favor of the faith. See privilégium.

feréndae senténtiae: a sentence to be imposed; the imposition of a penalty by the order of the court or by the action of a legitimate superior. *See also* látae senténtiae.

Fidéles: the faithful; a term referring to all the baptized disciples of Jesus. It is equivalent to the people of God, the Mystical Body of Christ, or the Church.

Fídes quaérens intelléctum: faith seeking understanding.

filiátio: filiation; the relationship between Christ as Son and Second Person of the Blessed Trinity and God the Father the First Person of the Trinity.

Filmóteca Vaticána: Vatican Film Agency; established by the Holy See to coordinate information on film and television programs.

filióque: and from the Son; the clause in the Nicene Creed that affirms the double procession of the Holy Spirit "from the Father and the Son."

finance council: a body of clerical and lay experts in finance and civil law, appointed by the bishop for at least a five-year term, to provide financial planning and guidance to the diocese.

fínis cúius: of what end or purpose, of whose end or purpose.

fínis operántis: the purpose of the one working.

fínis óperis: the purpose of the work itself.

fínis quo: the purpose or end by which.

flagránte delícto: while the crime is blazing; signifies that someone is

caught in the very act of committing the crime.

flectámus génua: let us bend the knees, let us kneel.

fórma: form
(1) the manner or way in which an act is administered according to the law.
(2) the determining or specifying part of a sacrament. *See also* matéria.

fórma substantiális: substantial form; the determining or specifying element that actuates prime matter to constitute a particular kind of being. *See* matéria príma.

fórum: forum; a Latin term for a marketplace or place of commerce that is applied in the Church to that sphere in which jurisdiction or authority is exercised.

internal forum, personal and private; the forum of conscience; looks to the good of the individual.

external forum, public and juridical; looks to the private good or the good of the faithful.

fórum canónicum: canonical forum; a requirement, under pain of invalidity of the marriage, that a Catholic enter marriage in the presence of a delegated representative of the Catholic Church and two witnesses unless competent Church authority has previously dispensed from this requirement.

fraud (dólus): deceit or action deliberately perpetrated by another party to cause an action.

free conferral: the free granting of an office by the ecclesiastical superior, without the intervention of any preliminary action by a privileged person.

g

Gaúdium et Spes: joy and hope; the constitution of Vatican II on the Church in the modern world, 1965.

generália administratíva decréta: general executory decrees; not technically laws, but decrees that presuppose laws and that need to be applied and interpreted in practice.

generália decréta: general decrees; decrees by which common prescriptions are issued by a competent legislator for a community capable of receiving a law. They are laws properly speaking and are governed by the prescriptions of the canons on laws.

glóssa: gloss; a marginal or interlinear annotation of a word, phrase, or passage in the Decretum.

good faith (bóna fíde): a prudent judgment by which one holds that one's actions are proper and right.

Gravíssimum Educatiónis: seriousness of education; a declaration of Vatican II on Christian education, 1965.

h

hábeas córpus: you may have the body; a legal writ, issued to bring a party to court or before a judge, that releases a party from unlawful restraint and protects against illegal imprisonment.

habémus Pápam: we have a Pope; the announcement at the time of the election of a Pope.

haéresis: heresy; the obstinate postbaptismal denial of some truth that must be believed with divine and catholic faith, or likewise an obstinate doubt concerning the same.

Hagía Sophía: Holy Wisdom; the Church of Holy Wisdom in Constantinople, built under the emperor Justinian in 532.

hagiographía: hagiography; the lives of the saints.

Hierárcha: hierarch; the Roman Pontiff, a patriarch, a major archbishop, a metropolitan who presides over a Church súi júris, and an eparchial bishop (cc. 984).

Hierárcha lóci: hierarch of a place; the Roman Pontiff, an eparchial bishop, an exarch, and an apostolic administrator (cc. 984).

Holy See (Sáncta Sédes): the Roman Pontiff and the offices that make up the Roman Curia, by which authority is exercised in the name of the Pope.

horológion: horologion; a book for use in the Eastern Churches containing prayers and hymns for the daily hours.

Humánae Vítae: of human life; an encyclical of Paul VI on the regulation of birth, 1968.

hypostática únio: hypostatic union; name used to indicate that the two natures of Christ—both God and man—are united to form the one Person who is Jesus Christ.

i

ICEL: International Commission on English in the liturgy, established in 1963.

ignorántia: ignorance; a lack of due knowledge; the absence of data in the process of knowing, to the point that no judgment can be reached.

illícitum: illicit; an unlawful or illegal action by someone.

impediméntum: impediment; a condition or a fact considered by the law as an obstacle to certain actions, such as an impediment to a marriage.

impédiens: impeding; makes an action illegal.

dírimens: diriment; makes an action invalid as well as illegal.

imperáta: ordered; prayers added by the bishop to the orations at Mass.

imprimátur: it may be printed; permission from competent ecclesiastical authority for publication.

incapácitans lex: *See* inválidans lex.

incapácitas psýchica: psychological incapacity.

incardinátio: incardination; the affiliation of a cleric to a diocese for ministry in that diocese. *See also* excardinátio.

íncola: inhabitant; a resident who possesses a domicile.

incompetent: *See* non súi cómpos.

indevolutívo: indevolutively; the effects of the decree are not suspended or transferred during recourse.

individuále decrétum: individual decree; an administrative act issued by a competent executive authority in which a decision is given or a provision is made in a particular case in accord with the norms of law.

indulgéntia: indulgence: a remission before God of the temporal punishment for sin, the guilt of which is already forgiven, which remission a properly disposed member of the Christian faithful obtains under certain and definite conditions.

indúltum: indult; a concession, such as a dispensation, permission, faculty or privilege, granted by a lawful superior to do something not permitted by the common law of the Church.

indúltum discedéndi: indult of departure; for a member of a religious institute, the cessation of the rights and obligations that arose from the contract of profession in that institute. Such a person is either a lay person or a cleric, depending upon whether sacred orders were received.

indúltum saecularizatiónis: indult of secularization: the name formerly used for the definitive departure of a member from a religious institute.

in fácto ésse: being, to be in actuality; a scholastic expression indicating existence, opposite of in fíeri ésse. *See also* matrimónium in fácto ésse.

ínfans: infant; in the canonical sense a minor who has not completed the seventh year.

in favórem (favóre) fídei: in favor of the faith. See privilégium.

in fíeri ésse: to be in becoming; a scholastic expression designating the passage from potency to act. *See also* matrimónium in fíeri.

in fórma commissória: in commissorial form; the form by which a rescript is granted to a petitioner through an intermediary or executor.

in fórma commissória necessária: in necessary commissorial form; indicates that the executor of a rescript has no choice but to execute the rescript according to the terms contained in it.

in fórma commissória voluntária: in voluntary commissorial form; indicates that the execution of a rescript is left to the discretionary power of the executor.

in fórma gratiósa: in favored form; the form by which a rescript is granted directly to the petitioner.

in fórma paúperum: in the form of poverty; granted without the required payment of a stipend or táxa.

in glóbo: in a ball or lump; indicates something done together or as a group rather than individually.

inhabilitántes léges: inhabilitating laws; invalidating laws that touch the persons so that, regardless of territory, those who act contrary to the laws do so invalidly.

in hoc sígno vínces: in this sign you will conquer; said to have been seen in the sky by the emperor Constantine before his victory over Maxentius at the Mulvian bridge in 312.

in júre: in law.

in necessáriis únitas, in dúbiis libértas, in ómnibus cáritas: in essentials unity, in doubtful matters freedom, in all things charity.

In paradísum: into paradise; the first words of a hymn sung at the conclusion of a funeral service as the body is being led from the church.

in pártibus infidélium: in the lands of unbelievers; in mission territories.

in péctore: in the heart; denoting that the Pope has named someone to an office or honor but has not yet made the name public; the name is known only to the Holy Father.

in re: in fact.

in se: in itself.

in sólidum: jointly, as a body; two or more persons delegated to act equally, but the delegation can be fulfilled by any one of them, in such a way however, that if one fails or refuses or is unable to act, the others continue to be obligated.

instántia príma, secúnda, tértia: in the first, second, third instance; these are three levels of adjudicating procedure according to Church law. The first instance trial is conducted at the diocesan level, the second instance at a court of appeal, and the third instance in marriage cases at the Roman Rota.

instrúctio: instruction; calls attention to the specific laws that it is intended to clarify and explain; textual conflicts between the law and any instructions should be resolved in favor of the law, and if the two are irreconcilable, the instruction loses its force.

instrúctor: instructor; a person, often a judge, designated to gather proofs and present them to a judge in an ecclesiastical trial. *See* auditor.

instruméntum labóris: instrument of work; a working paper or outline in preparation for a discussion on a specific topic.

in témpore non suspécto: at a time not suspected.

interdíctum: interdict; a penalty applied to persons by which a member of the Church is forbidden to take part in certain liturgical services and to administer or to receive certain sacraments. A local interdict is a penalty forbidding certain liturgical services or the celebration or reception of certain sacraments in certain places.

Ínter Mirífica: among wonderful things; a decree of Vatican II on the instruments of social communication, 1963.

internal forum: See fórum.

interpretátio: interpretation; the meaning of law, taking into account the elasticity of words in text and context.
Broad interpretation represents the maximum that a term can honestly carry.
Strict interpretation represents the minimum that a term must honestly include.

in túto collocáre: to arrange in a safe place.

inválidans lex: invalidating law; one that pertains directly to the act itself, no matter who performs the action, so that the law denies any juridic effect to the action. Incapácitans lex is incapacitating law; one that pertains to the person who performs the action and denies him/her or her the capacity to act in a way that produces juridic effect.

investitúra: investiture; the act of the superior granting the office to a person previously designated either by presentation or nomination.

in vigilándo efficácius: in being on guard more effectively.

irreguláritas: irregularity; an impediment to the reception or the exercise of sacred orders.

írritans lex: nullifying law; a type of invalidating law that touches the action within a territory so that anybody who acts contrary to the law in that territory does so invalidly.

J

júdex praéses: presiding judge; a judge is a person with a canonical degree who is appointed by the diocesan bishop to decide cases brought before an ecclesiastical court.

judiciális conféssio: judicial confession; a written or oral assertion against oneself made by a party regarding the matter under trial and made before a competent judge, whether spontaneously or upon interrogation by the judge.

judiciális vicárius: judicial vicar; also called an officiális; a priest, holding an advanced degree in Canon Law, whom the bishop is required to appoint in each diocese and who has the ordinary power to judge ecclesiastical cases submitted to the diocese.

júre divíno: by divine law; by a law that does not admit of dispensation or change.

jurídica persóna: See persóna jurídica.

jurisdíctio: jurisdiction; the power, right, or authority to govern the faithful.
ordinary: jurisdiction that the law attaches to an office
delegated: jurisdiction that is granted to a person by another person.

jurisprudéntia: jurisprudence; the procedure of judges and tribunals, that is, the form or mode of proceeding in tribunals for dealing with various cases and other matters. It also is understood to describe canonical jurisprudence, that is, the science and art of utilizing, interpreting, and supplying the codified law by rescript and by judicial opinion.

jus ad rem: right to the thing; the right to obtain something.

jus canónicum: Canon Law; the norms governing the practice of Catholics throughout the Church; also called universal Church law.

jus commúne: common law; all laws and legitimate customs of the universal Church as well as of the Eastern Churches.

jus defensiónis: right of defense; the right to defend oneself before court of law.

jus in córpus (córpore): right toward or in the body; in old marriage law it meant the right over the body for acts of sexual intercourse.

jus in re: a right itself.

jus particuláre: particular law; all laws, legitimate customs, statues, and other norms of law not common to the universal Church nor to all the Eastern Churches. See lex.

jústa de caúsa: concerning a just cause, for just cause.

justítia: justice; a cardinal virtue whereby one gives to others that which is due to them as a matter of right.

jus vígens: living law; that law which is actually in effect and operating in the Church at that time.

1

Labórem Exércens: performing work; an encyclical of John Paul II on human work, 1981.

lacúna légis: gap of the law; a term in Canon Law that acknowledges that there is a gap, hiatus, or place where something is missing in a law so that an interpreter of the law must decide a case by other principles.

laicáles (láici): laity; a name for the Christian faithful who are distinguished from the clérici, clerics, that is, sacred ministers.

laicisátio: laicization; the reduction of an ecclesiastical person or thing to a lay status.

látae senténtiae: a sentence already passed; a penalty inflicted by the law itself immediately upon commission of the offense; automatic imposition of the penalty. See also feréndae senténtiae.

legális personálitas: legal personality; the ability to demonstrate self-determination and the right to possess.

legátus a látere: legate from the side; a confidential representative of the Pope sent on a mission of particular importance and possessing special powers.

lex: law; an ordinance of reason that is promulgated by the lawgiver for the sake of the common good.

Ecclesiastical law is a norm regulating the activity of Christians, instituted permanently by legitimate ecclesiastical authority, for the common good of the ecclesial society.

Universal laws are those which have been enacted by those who have legislative power for the entire Church and are intended primarily for the common good of the universal community.

Particular laws are those enacted by those who have legislative power over a particular territory and intend the common good of that particular group.

lex orándi, lex credéndi: the law of praying (is) the law of believing; prayers express beliefs.

lex vígens: *See* jus vígens.

libéllus: petition; the formal document that introduces a case into court; also know as libéllus lítis introductórius or bill of complaint.

Líber Usuális: the ordinary book; a book containing the Gregorian chant musical notation and text for the Divine Office and liturgy.

lícita áctio: licit action; a lawful action, or an action performed according to the requirement of the law.

ligámen: tie, bond; an impediment based on a prior bond of marriage (c. 1085).

lineaménta outline: a term used by the Holy See for a preliminary document outlining topics to be treated at a meeting.

lítes finítae: allegations ended, controversy terminated.

lítis contestátio: *See* contestátio lítis

lítterae dimissoriáles: dimissorial letters; written permission and authorization granted by an ecclesiastical superior to his own subject to receive holy orders outside that superior's jurisdiction.

lítterae testimoniáles: testimonial letters; written affidavits concerning persons or situations.

litúrgia: liturgy; the exercise of the priestly office of Jesus Christ by which the Church fulfills the office of sanctifying through sensible signs in the public worship of God.

Lúmen Géntium: light of the nations; the constitution of Vatican II on the Church, 1964.

m

magistérium: magisterium; the teaching authority or the teaching body of the Church.

Magníficat: it magnifies or praises; the opening words of the Song of Mary (Luke 1:46–55) used at Vespers.

maióra vidébis: you will see greater things.

máneat úbi est: let it remain where it is.

Maronite rite: *See* Orientáles Ecclésiae.

Máter et Magístra: mother and teacher; an encyclical of John XXIII on Christianity and social progress, 1961.

matéria: matter; the undetermined part of a sacrament that needs to be clarified by words. *See also* fórma.

matéria príma: prime matter; pure potency as a basic constitutive element of material beings, which is actuated by a substantial form. *See also* fórma substantiális.

Matrimónia Mixta: mixed marriages; an apostolic letter of Paul VI regarding mixed marriages, 1970.

matrimónium in fácto ésse: marriage existing in actuality; a true and unique conjugal union.

matrimónium in fíeri: marriage happening or taking place; the actual exchange of marital consent.

matrimónium míxtum: mixed marriage; a marriage between a Catholic and a baptized person of another faith.

matúritas judícii: maturity of judgement; refers to the ability to make a binding commitment to something as serious as the marriage contract; often translated "due discretion."

medicinális poéna: medicinal penalty; a censure whose goal is the reform of the delinquent by some kind of privation inflicted in response to an action that was culpable.

Melkite rite: *See* Orientáles Ecclésiae.

Metropólita Ecclésiae Patriarchális: metropolitan of a patriarchal Church; one who presides over a certain province inside the territorial boundaries of the patriarchal Church (cc. 133).

Metropolitánus, metropólita: metropolitan; in the Latin Church, an archbishop who, presiding over an ecclesiastical see that has been designated or approved by the Pope as the head of a province, exercises some degree of actual jurisdiction over the suffragan bishops of that province. In the Eastern Churches, there are four types:.

(1) independent: equivalent to the Latin metropolitan.

(2) quasi-independent: not subject directly to the Pope or even to a patriarch but to a major archbishop or some other prelate inferior to a patriarch.

(3) dependent: having real suffragans but no de facto jurisdiction over them since he and they are both directly subject to a patriarch.

(4) honorary: presiding over only a fictional province and remaining subject to a prelate inferior to the Pope.

métus et vis: fear and force.

mínor: minor; a person, in the canonical sense, who has not completed the 18th year of age.

mínus hábens: having less.

Míssa Latína: Latin Mass; also known as the Paul VI Mass. In 1963 the Constitution on the Sacred liturgy of Vatican II permitted the use of vernacular languages for Mass, and in 1970 a New Order of the Mass, which included some internal changes, was published in the Roman Missal at the direction of Paul VI. This is the text from which all translations into the vernacular are to be made. This New Order of the Mass replaced the Tridentine Mass, and may be celebrated in either Latin or the vernacular.

Míssa pro pópulo: Mass for the people; the bishop and pastors must offer Mass for the people on all Sundays and holy days.

Míssa Tridentína: Tridentine Mass; the Order of the Mass, authorized by the Council of Trent in the 16th century, is always celebrated in Latin and follows the pre–Vatican II formula.

míssio: mission; the task entrusted to the Church by Jesus to proclaim the gospel to the world and make disciples of all people; the word mission is often used to indicate a parish that has no resident priest but is regularly served by a priest from a neighboring parish; in the plural the word missions often refers to the activity involved in spreading the faith in foreign and/or non-Christian areas.

míssio canónica: *See* canónica míssio.

míssus speciális: special envoy; someone sent to fulfill a specific mission.

Moderátor Cúriae: moderator of the curia; a priest appointed by the diocesan bishop and whose primary concerns are coordinating administrative matters and the supervision of those working in the curia.

Monastérium Stauropegíacum: stauropegial monastery; an Eastern Church monastery erected by a patriarch (cc. 434).

Monophysítae: one nature; an early heresy that held that there is only one nature in Christ and that His humanity was absorbed by His divinity.

morális impossibílitas: moral impossibility; a legal condition arising when the observance of a law is rendered very difficult by reason of grave fear, serious harm, or extrinsic inconvenience connected with the fulfillment of the law in question.

motívum: motive; in Canon Law, a cause that is sufficient to request and grant a dispensation.

mótu próprio: by one's own initiative; a papal decree or legislative document issued by the Sovereign Pontiff at his own initiative rather than in response to a request.

Mýron: holy myron; a mixture of olive oil and other plants and aromatics, blessed only by a bishop, and used in chrismation (confirmation) and in the administration of some of the sacraments in the Eastern Churches (cc. 693).

Mýstici Córporis: of the Mystical Body; an encyclical of Pius XII on the Mystical Body of Christ, 1943.

n

NCCB: National Conference of Catholic Bishops; a permanent ecclesiastical entity, composed of all the Catholic bishops of the United States of America, that deals primarily with matters connected with the internal life of the Church and functions with juridical authority. *See also* USCC.

necéssitas pastorális: *See* pastorális necéssitas.

némo dat quod non hábet: no one gives what he does not have.

némo júdex in súa caúsa: no one is a judge in his own case.

néqueant: let them not be able.

Nestorianísmus: the fifth-century heresy of Nestorius, a bishop of Constantinople, that held that there were two persons in Christ.

níhil innovétur: let nothing new be introduced, let nothing be altered

níhil óbstat: nothing stands in the way; the statement of the censor of books that nothing contrary to faith or morals that might prevent publication is found in the book. *See also* imprimátur.

nómen est ómen: the name is an omen.

nominátio: nomination; the designation of a person made by virtue of some privilege other than the strict right of patronage.

nomocánon: nomocanon; a compendium of civil and ecclesiastical law created before the sixth century by

Roman emperors who wished to act as legislator and judge in certain Church matters.

non cónstat de nullitáte: it does not stand concerning the nullity; the nullity is not in effect, is not recognized. This is the conclusion of the judge in marriage cases when the doubt has not been proved.

non suí cómpos: not of sound mind, incompetent; one who is not legally in control of oneself nor responsible for one's actions, and who does not possess the ability or capacity to posit a juridical act.

nórma: norm, ordinance; a rule or regulation to be applied in a specific situation; sometimes used as another name for a law.

Nóstra Aétate: in our age; a declaration of Vatican II on the relationship of the Church to non-Christian religions, 1965.

notárius: notary; one who works within a diocesan curia to authenticate documents by his or her signature.

notificátio: notification; a clarification of an existing law; similar to a declaration.

nóvus órdo seclórum (saeculórum): a new order of the ages.

Nunc dimíttis: now you dismiss; the opening words of the Song of Simeon (Luke 2:29–32), sung at night prayer in the Divine Office.

Núncio Apostolic: Núntius Apostólicus; an ambassador of the Holy See to a foreign power; permanent diplomatic representative of the Pope.

nunc pro tunc: now for then; something done or given now with a future result in view.

O

oath (juraméntum, jusjurándum): the invocation of the divine name in witness of the truth that one is stating.

obréptio: statement of falsehood; reason for which an administrative act may be declared null and void.

obrogátio: obrogation; the change of an existing law by the creation of a second law that is contradictory to the meaning of the existing law.

obséquium: compliance; ready and respectful allegiance; loyal and obedient assent; submission.

obséquium religiósum: religious submission; the submission due the ordinary teachings of the magisterium of the Church.

observántia affirmatíva: the repetition of like acts.

observántia negatíva: the uniform omission of acts.

officiália respónsa: official responses; a type of curial pronouncement that consists of answers to questions issued by a particular congregation.

officiális: official, judicial vicar; the head judge of an ecclesiastical tribunal. See also judiciális vicárius.

offícium ecclesiásticum: ecclesiastical office; a function lawfully exercised for a spiritual purpose established either by divine or Church law and entailing some participation in the power of orders or of jurisdiction.

ólea sáncta: holy oils; oils blessed by the bishop on Holy Thursday and used in consecrations and some sacraments.

ómne inítium difficile: every beginning is difficult.

ómnia paráta sunt: all things are prepared; a possible reason for a dispensation.

Optátam Totíus: desired entirely; the decree of Vatican II on priestly formation, 1965.

óra et labóra: pray and work; motto of St. Benedict.

oratórium: oratory; a place designed, by permission of the ordinary, for divine worship for the benefit of some community or assembly of the faithful who gather there.

ordinária jurisdíctio: ordinary jurisdiction; the power of governance that is connected with some office by the law itself. *See also* delegáta jurisdíctio.

Ordinárius: ordinary: one who has ordinary jurisdiction. A list includes the Roman Pontiff, residential bishops, abbots and prelates nullius, vicars and prefects apostolic, those who temporarily fill the office vacated by one of the above, vicars-general, and major superiors in exempt clerical institutes of consecrated life. Local ordinary: technically applies to all of the above except major superiors, but is more often applied to the bishop of a diocese.

Ordinárius castrénsis: bishop for the military.

órdines: rules of order; the norms or rules of order to be followed in an assembly or gathering of people or celebration.

órdo: rank; Órdo Sáncta: the holy order; the sacrament by which priesthood is conferred; this sacrament is often referred to in the plural, holy orders; the word "order" is also used to refer to some communities of religious men and women; órdo: directive; a guide for celebrating Mass and the liturgy of the hours for each day of the year.

Orientáles Ecclésiae: Eastern Churches; Churches, some in full communion with the Supreme Pontiff in Rome, and some not, that observe a variety of rites in the liturgical, theological, spiritual, and disciplinary patrimony of the individual Churches, and that take their origin from Alexandria, Antioch, Armenia, Chaldea, and Constantinople (Byzantium). In the United States the following rites are found: Armenian, Chaldean, Maronite, and Byzantine (Melkite, Romanian, Ruthenian, and Ukrainian).

Orientálium Dígnitas: the dignity of the Eastern (Churches); an apostolic letter of Leo XIII on the Eastern Catholic Churches, 1894.

Orientálium Ecclesiárum: of the Eastern rite Churches; a decree of Vatican II on Eastern rite Catholic Churches, 1964.

Orthodox Churches, Orthodox Christians: Eastern Churches and Christians of any of the various rites who do not recognize the jurisdiction of the Pope in Rome.

P

Pácem in Térris: peace on earth; an encyclical of John XXIII on universal peace, 1963.

pállium: pallium; a circular band of white woolen cloth with two hanging strips, worn by an archbishop over his shoulders on top of the vestments at Mass and in other solemn liturgical celebrations as a symbol of his authority as metropolitan in communion with the Church of Rome.

papális legátus: papal legate; an envoy of the Supreme Pontiff who exercises whatever power is accorded to him/her by the Pope.

paróchia: parish; a definite community of Christian faithful established on a stable basis within a particular Church whose pastoral care is entrusted to a pastor under the authority of the diocesan bishop.

parochiális administrátor: parochial administrator; a priest, appointed by the bishop, who substitutes for the pastor when a parish becomes vacant or when the pastor is prevented from exercising his pastoral office (c. 1539). *See also* pastoral administrator.

parochiális vicárius: parochial vicar; a priest who is assigned by competent authority as an assistant or associate to the pastor (c. 545); formerly know as curate, assistant, or associate.

pars actóris (actrícis): party of the doer; the initiating party or the plaintiff or petitioner in an ecclesiastical court case.

pars convénta: party summoned; the respondent or defendant in an ecclesiastical court case.

párvulum pro níhilo: little for nothing.

pástor: pastor; the proper shepherd of a parish entrusted to him/her under the authority of the diocesan bishop in whose ministry of Christ he has been called to share.

pastoral administrator: a term not in the Code but currently in use to indicate a deacon or someone not a priest who is entrusted with pastoral care because of the shortage of ordained priests (c. 517.2).

pastorále concílium: pastoral council; a recommended but discretionary body which a diocesan bishop may implement in his diocese to discuss pastoral matters and to formulate practical suggestions to implement pastoral activities; may be either parish or diocesan.

pastorális necéssitas: pastoral necessity; the application of the law to meet the pastoral needs of the people and the requirements of the Church.

Pastóres Dábo Vóbis: I will give you shepherds; pastoral exhortation of John Paul II, 1992.

patriárcha: patriarch.

in the Eastern Church, a bishop who has jurisdiction over all the bishops, including metropolitans, and over the clergy and people of a territory or a special rite. He is a bishop with supra-episcopal jurisdiction (cc. 56)

in the Latin Church, a bishop who enjoys no special jurisdiction, as his title is one that carries with it only a prerogative of honor and the right of precedence over Primates.

Pax Romana: Roman peace; international movement of Catholic students founded in Switzerland in 1921.

pax técum, pax vobíscum: peace to you (sing. and pl.).

per módum áctus: by means of an act; a juridic act placed in a particular situation with its juridic effects limited to that situation.

peregrínus: wanderer; a traveler, a person at the time outside his or her domicile or quasi domicile.

Perféctae Caritátis: of perfect charity; the decree of Vatican II on religious life, 1965.

perículum matrimónii: danger of a civil marriage being contracted; a possible reason for a dispensation.

perítus, períta: expert; a specialist who is skilled and experienced in a profession or science and who is able to provide advice and help; períti: m. pl.; used for mixed groups of both sexes.

persóna jurídica: juridic person, also known as a moral person; a legal person in the Church who is the subject of obligations and rights, as, for example, physical persons, institutions, or other entities recognized by law.

persóna phýsica: physical person; a person who is alive.

personále privilégium: personal privilege; a nontransferable privilege granted to a person that ceases at the death of the individual.

plácet: it pleases; the vote is yes.

plácet júxta módum: it pleases according to the manner; the vote is yes according to the amendments made.

plácet non (non plácet): it does not please; the vote is no.

plácitum: agreeable, agreed upon, approved.

plenárium concílium: plenary council; a gathering of bishops belonging to the same conference (usually of one country or nation) and convoked with the approval of the Holy See.

poéna: penalty; the deprivation of some good by competent Church authority for the correction of a delinquent or for the punishment of a crime.

Pónens: reporting judge; the collegiate judge who studies the case and reports on it at the meeting of the panel of judges and who commits the sentence to writing.

Populórum Progréssio: the progress of peoples; an encyclical of Paul VI on the development of peoples, 1967.

postulátio: postulation; a petition to a higher authority by an electoral body.

potéstas administrátiva: administrative power. See jurisdíctio.

potéstas delegáta: delegated power. See jurisdíctio.

praecéptum: precept; a command given by a lawful superior to an individual, to a group of persons, or to a community but having force for only a determined period of time.

praelátus: prelate; a cleric, either diocesan or a member of an institute of consecrated life, who possesses jurisdiction in the external forum; it is also an honorary title granted to certain individuals by the Holy See, but such prelates lack any jurisdiction.

prae óculis habeátur: let it be held before the eyes.

praescríptio: prescription; a method of acquiring ownership of property by possessing it for a required period of time under conditions prescribed by the law; the same term is used to describe a method of freeing oneself from an obligation.

praesentátio: presentation; the designation of a person for an ecclesiastical office, made by virtue of the right of patronage.

praesúmptio: presumption; technically the probable conjecture of an uncertain act; more commonly, a statement that the law will ordinarily act or consider an action of another in a certain legal way.

praesúmptio hóminis: presumption of the person.

praesúmptio júris: presumption of the law; also called a simple presumption; it allows proofs to the contrary.

praesúmptio júris et de júre: presumption of the law and concerning the law; it excludes all proofs to the contrary.

praesúmptio mórtis: presumption of death.

praéter jus: beyond the law; refers to a custom outside of, or beyond, or apart from, the stated law.

praéter légem: beyond the law. See praéter jus.

práxis Cúriae: the practice of the Curia; the manner of procedure followed by the Roman Curia in expediting cases.

presbyterális concílium: presbyterial council; a body of elected and appointed priests, who, functioning as a senate for a residential bishop, aid him/her in the governance of the diocese.

Presbyterórum Órdinis: of the order of priests; the decree of Vatican II on the priesthood, 1965.

Prímas: Primate; a term formerly employed to designate a bishop who enjoyed a certain degree of jurisdiction over surrounding sees. Today, "Primate" is an honorific title, conferred or confirmed by the Holy See, on a metropolitan bishop whose

see was established first in a particular region or nation.

prímus ínter páres: first among equals; one holding a position of honor among those with equal jurisdiction.

privátio: privation; the removal from an office as a penalty for an offense.

privilégium: privilege; a particular right granted, not through necessity, but by the benevolent intent of the legislator and, according to the discipline of the revised Code, through an administrative act.

privilégium canónis: privilege of the canon.

privilégium fóri: a privilege whereby formerly clergy were not permitted to be tried before a civil magistrate for crimes but had to be tried before an ecclesiastical court.

privilégium fídei, privilégium in favóre (favórem) fídei: privilege of the faith or in favor of the faith; a privilege whereby the nonsacramental bond of marriage between two individuals is dissolved by competent Church authority so that a new sacramental and indissoluble bond of marriage may be permitted.

privilégium júris: privilege of the law; a favor granted to certain persons, whether physical or juridical, by means of a special act of a legislator or executive authority.

privilégium Paulínum: Pauline privilege; the dissolution of the nonsacramental marriage between two nonbaptized persons.

privilégium Petrínum: Petrine privilege; the dissolution of the nonsacramental marriage between a nonbaptized person and a baptized Christian.

privilégium reále: real privilege; a privilege attached to a thing or place that does not cease unless the nonexistence of the item is completed.

Procurátor: procurator, proxy; a person who by legitimate mandate performs judicial business in the name of someone else.

Promótor Justítiae: promoter of justice; an officer appointed for the diocese in contentious cases in which the public good could be at stake, and for penal cases in order to protect the common good.

promulgátio: promulgation; one of the stages in the life of a law; it is the process whereby the lawmaker communicates the law to those for whom the law was given.

Pro-Núntius : pro-núncius; one acting in place of the nuncio.

Protonotárius (less correctly, Prothonotárius): protonotary or notary of the first class; those who are given this title are prelates who enjoy certain honors and privileges; there are four types, some of which confer only these honors and privileges, while others entail also duties and responsibilities.

protoprésbyter: protopresbyter; a presbyter who is placed over a district consisting of several parishes (cc. 276).

protosyncéllus: protosyncellus; a presbyter appointed in each eparchy and given ordinary vicarious power according to law to assist the eparchial bishop (cc. 245–251). The juridic counterpart in the Latin Code is the vicar-general. If necessary, more such can be appointed and are known as syncélli (cc. 245–51).

Próvida Máter: prudent mother; an instruction of the Holy See regarding marriage cases, 1936.

Providentíssimus Déus: the most provident God; an encyclical of Leo XIII on the study of Holy Scripture, 1893.

província: province; a division of the Church, comprising an archdiocese (metropolitan) and one or more dioceses (suffragan sees). The term also is used in some religious communities to identify divisions, commonly but not always territorial, under the jurisdiction or authority of a minister provincial.

provinciále concílium: provincial council; a gathering of bishops within a territorial province. The term "plenary council" is used to describe gatherings involving several provinces.

provísio: provision; a particular administrative act that calls for adjustment or regularization in order to remedy a particular situation.

(doctrína) próxima Fídei: a doctrine nearest to the faith; a doctrine that in the judgment of theologians probably could be defined but has not been.

pública ecclesiástica documénta: public ecclesiastical documents; those which official persons have drawn up in the exercise of their functions in the Church, after having observed the formalities prescribed by law.

públicae honestátis, impediméntum: impediment of public propriety; an impediment that forbids under pain of invalidity a marriage between a man and the blood relatives of a woman (and vice versa); arises from an invalid marriage after common life has been established, or from notorious and public concubinage (c. 1093).

q

Quadragésimo Ánno: in the 40th year; an encyclical of Pius XI (on the 40th anniversary of Rérum Novárum) on improving the social and economic order.

quási-domicílium: quasi domicile; a place of temporary residence.

r

ratióne súi: by reason of one's own.

rátum: ratified; a marriage for which a man and woman have given their expressed consent to each other.

rátum et consummátum: ratified and consummated; a marriage in which the expressed consent has been completed by intercourse in a human manner.

rátum et non consummátum: a ratified but not consummated union.

reátus cúlpae: guilt of sin.

reátus poénae: necessity of undergoing punishment for sin.

records (Líbri, Tábulae, Ácta): Books, Tablets, Acts; parish books in which the events of a person's baptism, confirmation, marriage, ordination, and death are recorded.

recúrsus: recourse; a demand for a review of a decree, precept, or other non-judicial decision.

Redémptor Hóminis: the Redeemer of mankind; an encyclical of John Paul II on the dignity of the human race, 1979.

Redemptóris Máter: mother of the Redeemer; an encyclical of John Paul II on Mary and her life in the Church, 1987.

relátor: *See* Pónens.

religiósae communitátes: religious communities; common designation for those faithful with public perpetual vows of poverty, chastity, and obedience as members of a religious order or community; members are often simply called "religious" and their way of life the "religious life."

renuntiátio: renunciation; an action in an ecclesiastical trial whereby the petitioner declares that he or she wishes to terminate the process prior to a sentence.

reponátur: let it be kept or preserved.

Rérum Novárum: of new things; an encyclical of Leo XIII on the reconstruction of the social order, 1891.

rescríptum: rescript; a written reply from the Holy See or from some other ordinary, granting a dispensation or favor, or giving information or a decision.

res et sacraméntum: matter and sacrament; the reality (res) immediately produced by a sacrament (sacraméntum), which points to and causes a further effect.

resident (íncola): a person who has a domicile in a place; temporary resident (ádvena): a person who has a quasi domicile.

res íntegra: a matter still whole; a matter not yet before the court or not yet brought to the judicial forum.

res judicáta: the judged matter; a case irrevocably adjudged so that it cannot be opened again by any court in ordinary procedure.

res tántum: the ultimate effect of the sacrament, which is grace. *See also* res et sacraméntum.

restitútio in íntegrum: restitution in entirety; reinstatement in one's former position; all things are restored to the way they were before the sentence was pronounced.

re túrpe: by a shameful thing.

revocátio: revocation; an act by which prior laws are abolished by the promulgation of new laws.

rituális, rítus: ritual, rìte

In a broad sense, ritual and rite denote the entire system of theology, spirituality, government, history, culture, law, disciplinary patrimony, liturgy, and Church life of a particular Church (for example, the Ruthenian rite, the Byzantine rite, the Greek rite, the Latin rite), or of a group of Churches (for example, the Latin rite Churches and the Eastern rite Churches).

In a narrow sense, ritual and rite refer to the ceremonies used in public worship.

Róma aetérna, ecclésia sempitérna: Rome is forever, the Church is forever and ever.

Róma locúta, caúsa finíta: Rome has spoken, the case is closed.

Romána Cúria: Roman Curia; the complex of departments and institutes that assist the Pope in the exercise of his supreme pastoral function for the good and the service of the universal Church and of the particular Churches.

Romána Róta (Roman Rota): the Roman wheel; the title of this tribunal since 1350; the court of first instance or final appeal in the Church, depending upon history and origin of the case; the title arose either because the judges originally sat in a circle or because there was a circle on the chamber floor at Avignon, where the title was first used, or because cases under consideration were moved from judge to judge on a bookstand on wheels.

Romanian rite: *See* Orientáles Ecclésiae.

Ruthenian rite: *See* Orientáles Ecclésiae.

S

Sacerdotális Caelibátus: priestly celibacy; an encyclical of Paul VI on priestly celibacy, 1967.

Sácrae Órdines: sacred orders; the sacrament of ordination conferred on deacons, priests, and bishops. Those who are ordained are sometimes said to be "in sacred orders."

Sacraménta própter hómines: the sacraments on account of people; since the sacraments were instituted for the benefit of people, sacramental legislation is to be interpreted with that principle in mind.

sacraméntum tántum: the sign or rite of the sacrament considered in itself. *See also* res et sacraméntum.

Sácra Poenitentiária: Sacred
Penitentiary; the tribunal of the
Roman Curia having jurisdiction over
affairs that concern the internal
forum, both sacramental and
nonsacramental.

Sacrosánctum Concílium: the sacred
council; the constitution of Vatican II
on the liturgy, 1963.

sácrum óleum: sacred oil: oil, pressed
from olives or from other plants, that
has been recently consecrated or
blessed by the bishop. See also ólea
sáncta.

sálus animárum: the salvation of souls.

sanátio in radíce: healing at the root; a
judicial procedure by which an invalid
marriage is given legal and retroactive
recognition by the Catholic Church.

schísma: schism; the refusal of
submission to the Roman Pontiff or of
communion with the members of the
Church subject to him/her.

séde impedíta: the seat being impeded.
See see.

séde vacánte: the seat being vacant. See
see.

sedia gestatoria: Italian; portable chair
in which the Pope is carried in
procession.

see: from the Latin word sédes, seat; a
diocese or archdiocese.

impeded see: a see in which by reasons
of captivity, banishment, exile, or
incapacity, the diocesan bishop is
wholly prevented from fulfilling his
pastoral function and cannot
communicate with his people.

vacant see: a see in which the diocesan
bishop has died, resigned, been
transferred, or been removed from
office.

sénsus Fídei: sense or understanding of
the faith.

sénsus Fidélium: sense or
understanding on the part of the
faithful.

senténtia: sentence; a legitimate and
definitive pronouncement by which a
judge settles a question or a case that
was proposed by litigants and tried
judicially.

sententíae prolátae: sentences
pronounced, opinions set forth.

servátis servándis: with the things
preserved that must be preserved.

Signatúra: the supreme tribunal of the
Church.

simónia: simony; the deliberate buying
or selling of a spiritual reality, or a
temporal thing (a benefice) joined to a
spiritual reality or power, for a
temporal price.

sóla Fídes: faith alone.

sóla Scriptúra: Scripture alone.

spécies fácti: appearance of the fact; the
first part of a judicial sentence, it lists
the particulars of the case being tried
before the court.

spirátio: spiration; the manner in which
the Holy Spirit proceeds from the
Father and Son; this is the act of love
between Father and Son.

Spléndor Veritátis: the splendor of
truth; an encyclical of John Paul II on
Christian morality.

Státus Animárum: the state of souls;
annual reports from pastors to
bishops, and from bishops to Rome,
that must be sent with statistics about
parishes and dioceses.

statúta: statutes; ordinances established
in aggregates of persons or of things to
define the constitution, government,
and operation of the aggregate.

statútum: statute; a particular species of
ordinance that is an authoritative rule,
or a public injunction, imposing the
obligation of obedience on the

members of the community to which it is directed.

stípite démpto: when the stem has been removed; when the lines or degrees of consanguinity are being determined, the common root parent is not included in the numbering.

stýlus Cúriae: the style of the Curia. See práxis Cúriae.

subrogátio: subrogation; the change of an existing law by a second law that adds to or substitutes for the existing law.

suffragáneus epíscopus: suffragan bishop; a diocesan bishop who is subject to an archbishop as the metropolitan of the province.

súi júris: of its own right; having an acknowledged autonomy with regard to government and discipline. See also ecclésia súi júris.

súmma: complete treatment; a composition that presents a concise, ordered rendering of, and commentary upon, the principal contents of the Decretum.

Súmmi Pontificátus: of the supreme pontificate; an encyclical of Pius XII on the unity of human society, 1939.

súper ráto: on a ratified (but nonconsummated marriage); an abbreviated reference to the process of dispensing from a marriage that was never sexually consummated.

supplied jurisdiction (ecclésia súpplet): the Church supplies jurisdiction both for the external and internal forums in cases of common error or in a case of

positive and probable doubt of law or fact.

suspénsio: suspension, interruption; the temporary interruption of a particular negotiation.

suspénsio a divínis: a censure by which a cleric is forbidden to perform any act of the powers of orders.

suspénsio a jurisdictióne: a censure that forbids every act of jurisdiction in the Church.

synáxis: an assembly, a committee, a group gathered for a specific purpose, monastic chapter; Synáxes:d monastic chapters.

syncéllus: See protosyncéllus.

sýnodus: synod; a Greek term referring to any type of gathering or meeting; in Church usage after Vatican II, it refers primarily to the meeting of bishops representing each country of the world every three years to discuss with the Pope issues of concern to the whole Church. See also concílium.

Sýnodus Episcopórum: Synod of Bishops; a permanently constituted body of bishops, selected from around the world, charged with advising the Pope on matters of importance to the whole Church.

Sýnodus Episcopórum Ecclésiae Patriarchális: Synod of Bishops of the Patriarchal Church.

sýnodus pérmanens: permanent synod; the permanent synod is composed of the patriarch and four bishops designated for a five-year term (cc. 115).

t

táxa: tax; a fee or stipend for handling judicial cases.

temporália: temporal affairs; secular life and activity.

temporália bóna: temporal goods; all those nonspiritual things that possess an economic value, such as real property, rights, and assets.

temporális órdo: temporal order; the way society is structured and governed.

témpus suspéctum: critical time; the time after which a person learns of the possibility of introducing a cause or begins to consider such an action.

témpus útile (díes útiles): available time (days).

térnus: list of three names; a list of names of possible candidates to be appointed to an office or rank.

territoriális abbátia: territorial abbacy; a certain portion of the people of God, normally a territorial portion, that is established under the pastoral care of an abbot.

territoriális praelatúra: territorial prelature; a certain portion of the people of God that is established within certain territorial boundaries and whose care is entrusted to the pastoral care of a prelate.

testimoniáles: testimonials; written evidence indicating that an individual is qualified and has official permission to be admitted to a higher position.

testimónium: testimony; a deposition given under oath by a witness to a judge or auditor and recorded by an ecclesiastical notary.

theotokárion: theotokarion; a book used in the Eastern Churches containing praises honoring the Mother of God.

tituláris epíscopus: titular bishop; a title given to a bishop who has no territorial or residential diocese of his own; such titles often come from the names of dioceses and/or towns that no longer exist.

titular see: a diocese that now exists in name only; it is the name of a suppressed diocese given to a bishop without a territorial or residential diocese of his own.

tort: a wrongful act, injury, or damage (not involving a breach of contract) for which a civil action can be brought.

tradítio: tradition; the ancient testimony concerning doctrine or Christian institutions, which in the early Church was transmitted from one generation to another by word of mouth.

transáctio: settlement; an agreement by which a controversial matter is settled without a formal trial.

transubstantiátio: transubstantiation; the change of the whole substance of the bread and wine into the whole substance of the Body and Blood of Christ.

Tribunális Romána: Roman Tribunal; court of law of the Roman Curia with three divisions. See Sácra Poenitentiária, Romána Róta, and Signatúra.

Tridentine Mass: *See* Míssa Tridentína.

Trínitas: Trinity; the unity of the three Divine Persons in the one God.

Triságion: Trisagion; the thrice-holy hymn sung at Divine liturgy.

tuéri vínculum: to protect the bond.

Týpicum: Typikon; in the Eastern Churches a book of liturgical and ritualistic rubrics, and monastic rules, directives, and statutes (cc. 421).

U

Ukrainian rite: *See* Orientáles Ecclésiae.

Uniat: one of the Eastern Churches that have returned to communion with the Supreme Pontiff in Rome but retain their own rites.

Unitátis Redintegrátio: restoration of unity; the decree of Vatican II on ecumenism, 1964.

úrbi et órbi: to the city (Rome) and the world.

USCC: United States Catholic Conference; a civil entity under the sponsorship of the NCCB, composed of bishops and laity and providing an organizational structure and the resources needed to insure coordination, cooperation, and assistance in the educational and social concerns of the Catholic Church at national, state, and diocesan levels. *See also* NCCB.

V

vacátio légis: exemption of the law; the period of time between promulgation and enforcement.

vágus: transient; one who has neither a domicile nor a quasi domicile anywhere.

validátio: validation. See convalidátio símplex.

válidus áctus: valid act; an action performed in compliance with the requirements of the law and having juridical value. Inválidus áctus: invalid act; noncompliance with a requirement that is necessary for validity.

vétitum: prohibition, forbidden; a prohibition that does not have an invalidating effect.

vicariátus foráneus: vicariate forane (outside); a deanery or section or division of a diocese.

vicárius foráneus: vicar forane (outside); also known as a dean or archpriest; a priest who is placed over a vicariate forane or deanery.

vicárius generális: vicar-general; a bishop or priest appointed by a residential bishop to assist him/her as a deputy in the administration of a diocese.

vicárius pro religiósis: vicar for religious.

vicárius pro sacerdótibus: vicar for priests.

vindictíva poéna: vindictive penalty; a censure the goal of which is to punish an individual by some kind of privation inflicted in response to an action that was culpable.

vótum: recommendation; formal evaluation of a superior, council, or tribunal sent to a higher authority and addressing the merits of a petition.

vox: voice; an individual's ability to make known legally one's thoughts and will on a particular matter.

deliberative voice: the right to determine a particular position.

consultative voice: the right to be heard on a particular subject.

Vulgáta: the Vulgate; text of the Bible translated from Hebrew and Greek into Latin by St. Jerome in the later part of the fourth century. Clementína Vulgáta: Clementine Vulgate; the Latin text of St. Jerome in an emended edition issued under the auspices of Pope Clement VIII in 1593 and proclaimed as the authentic and official Latin text of the Bible.

Nóva Vulgáta: the new Vulgate; a revision of the Latin text of the Vulgate, commissioned in 1907 by Pius X, encouraged by Paul VI in 1965, and completed and approved as the official Latin text of the Bible by John Paul II in 1979.

Bibliography

Annuario Pontificio: Vatican City: Libreria Editrice Vaticana, 1992.

Attwater, D. *A Catholic Dictionary.* New York: Macmillan, 1949.

Blaise, A. *Dictionnaire latin-francais des auteurs du Moyen-Âge,* Corpus Christian-orum. Turnhout, Belgium: Brepols, 1975.

Burke, Raymond, Ronald W. Gainer, and Michael J. Gorman. *Vocabularium Canonicum Latino-Anglicum.* Ad usum privatum. Rome, 1986.

Code of Canon Law. Latin-English Edition. Washington, D.C.: Canon Law Society of America, 1983.

Code of Canon Law of the Eastern Churches. Latin-English Edition. Washington, D.C.: Canon Law Society of America, 1990.

Collins, J. F. *A Primer of Ecclesiastical Latin.* Washington, D.C.: Catholic University of America Press, 1985.

Deferrari, R. J. *A Latin-English Dictionary of St. Thomas Aquinas.* Boston: Daughters of St. Paul, 1960.

Denzinger, H. J., and A. Schönmetzer. *Enchiridion Symbolorum Definitionum et Declarationum de Rebus Fidei et Morum.* 36th ed. Barcelona: Herder, 1973.

Diamond, Wilfred. *Dictionary of Liturgical Latin.* Milwaukee: Bruce, 1961.

Fink, P., S. J. *The New Dictionary of Sacramental Worship.* Collegeville, Minn.: Liturgical Press, 1990.

Harden, J. M. *Dictionary of the Vulgate New Testament.* New York: Macmillan, 1921.

Hardon, John A., S. J. *Modern Catholic Dictionary.* New York: Doubleday, 1980.

Hartman, Louis F., C.Ss.R. *Encyclopedic Dictionary of the Bible.* New York: McGraw-Hill, 1963.

Hoffman, A. *Liturgical Dictionary.* Collegeville, Minn.: Liturgical Press, 1928. This work is especially useful for finding the names of saints, people, dioceses and other places, and hymns.

Komonchak, J. A., M. Collins, and D. A. Lane. *The New Dictionary of Theology.* Wilmington, Del.: Michael Glazier, 1987.

Konus, William J. *Dictionary of the New Latin Psalter.* Westminster, Md.: Newman Press, 1959.

Lang, P. J. *Dictionary of the Liturgy.* New York: Catholic Book Publishing, 1989.

Lauer, A. *Index Verborum Codicis Iuris Canonici.* Vatican City: Typis Polyglottis Vaticanis, 1941.

Lee, F. G. *A Glossary of Liturgical and Ecclesiastical Terms.* London: Quaritch, 1877.

Lewis, Charlton T., and Charles Short. *Harper's Latin Dictionary.* New York: American Book Company, 1907. Founded on the translation of *Freund's Latin-German Lexicon,* edited by E. A. Andrews.

Lorsing, T. N. *Stylebook on Religion.* Washington, D.C.: Catholic News Service, 1990.

McKenzie, J. L., S. J. *Dictionary of the Bible.* Milwaukee: Bruce, 1965.

Nevins, A. J., M. M. *The Maryknoll Catholic Dictionary.* New York: Grosset & Dunlop, 1965.

O'Brien, Thomas C. "A Lexicon of Terms in the *Missale Romanum.*" Washington, D.C.: International Commission on English in the Liturgy.

O'Collins, G., S. J., and E. G. Farrugia, S. J., *A Concise Dictionary of Theology.* New York: Paulist Press, 1991.

Ochoa, Xaverius. *Index Verborum ac Locutionum Codicis Iuris Canonici,* Vatican City: Libreria Editrice Lateranense, 1984.

_____. *Index Verborum cum Documentis Concilii Vaticani Secundi.* Rome: Commentarium pro Religiosis, 1967.

Oxford Latin Dictionary. Oxford: Clarendon Press, 1968.

Podhradsky, G. *New Dictionary of the Liturgy.* Staten Island: Alba House, 1966.

Scanlon, C. C., and C. L. Scanlon. *Latin Grammar: Grammar, Vocabularies, and Exercises in Preparation for the Reading of the Missal and Breviary.* Rockford, Ill.: Tan Books and Publishers, 1982.

Schnitker, T. A., and W. A. Slaby. *Concordantia Verbalia Missalis Romani,* Münster: Aschendorf, 1983.